Jörg Böttcher (Ed.)

Green Banking

Green Banking

Realizing Renewable Energy Projects

Edited by
Jörg Böttcher

DE GRUYTER
OLDENBOURG

ISBN 978-3-11-060462-7
e-ISBN (PDF) 978-3-11-060788-8
e-ISBN (EPUB) 978-3-11-060569-3

Library of Congress Control Number: 2020933706

Bibliographic information published by the Deutsche Nationalbibliothek
The Deutsche Nationalbibliothek lists this publication in the Deutsche Nationalbibliografie; detailed bibliographic data are available on the Internet at http://dnb.dnb.de.

Cover image: LeoPatrizi/E+/gettyimages.com
Typesetting: Integra Software Services Pvt. Ltd.
Printing and binding: CPI books GmbH, Leck

www.degruyter.com

Foreword

E pluribus unum, one of many, was considered a de facto motto of the United States until 1956. It can also serve as a guiding principle for the structuring of this book, which combines legal, technical and economic aspects in different renewable energy classes.

The energy transition is one of the greatest challenges facing society today. Worldwide, policymakers build the economic and energy policies, ensuring an energy supply that is reliable, climate-friendly and affordable.

From what we see, worldwide primary energy consumption is expected to continue to rise, much improving the quality of life for many people. However, the actual challenge is that the share of fossil fuels in total energy consumption is still at 81%. Solar and wind power afford very great potential, but they currently meet less than 2% of the energy demand. Hence, the status quo stands in strong contrast to the demands and commitments of international climate protection, and there is a need to make much more progress at all levels, including a change in national and international politics.

In this book, we will show how we can support the further deployment of renewable energies worldwide. "Green Banking" is the first guide encompassing all of the disciplines necessary to realize renewable energy projects. This book focuses on cost-competitive and mature technologies, and on the processes enabling one to develop, finance and execute such utility-scale projects.

It starts with aspects relevant for every form of renewable energy and covers essential legal, technical, social and economic themes, such as the role of renewables amid a changing energy world, the importance of the regulatory regime, its social acceptance and bankability criteria, to name only a few. The specific asset sections describe project financing vehicles for a range of renewable energy technologies, including solar photovoltaic power plants, onshore wind farms and offshore wind farms.

This book offers readers a unique perspective on how renewable energy projects are realized and is a go-to reference manual for understanding how the different project stakeholders act. All articles are provided by authors with ample experience in the renewable energy industry.

We are amid a deep-reaching restructuring of our energy system. It is essential to increase the share of renewables in gross final energy consumption. It is critical to immediately begin a massive reduction in CO_2 and other greenhouse gas emissions. These are enormous tasks, which we can master better and more effectively by using innovations. In addition, communication and cooperation are key to understanding and implementing feasible energy projects worldwide.

The avoidance of the effects of climate change requires immediate and bold actions. The young protesters of "Fridays for Future" rightfully demand that these solutions be used to achieve an open and sustainable society. We only have one shot

https://doi.org/10.1515/9783110607888-202

at this. There is no room for half measures. The authors present their own opinions, which do not necessarily reflect those of their employers.

Dr. Jörg Böttcher
Kiel, November 2019

List of Figures

General Section

https://doi.org/10.1515/9783110607888-203

Offshore Wind Energy

Onshore Wind Energy

Solar Energy: Photovoltaics

Solar Energy: Concentrated Solar Power

List of Tables

General Section

https://doi.org/10.1515/9783110607888-204

Offshore Wind Energy

Onshore Wind Energy

Solar Energy: Photovoltaics

Solar Energy: Concentrated Solar Power

Contents

General Section

Offshore Wind Energy

Onshore Wind Energy

Solar Energy: Photovoltaics

General Section

1 Renewable Energy, Climate Change, and Sustainability

Ulf Moslener, Menglu Zhuang

1.1 Challenges Related to Climate Change and Sustainability

Climate change is often described as one of the biggest risks facing humanity in the coming decades. As such it is part of the challenges the global society is facing with regard to long-term-sustainability. Both, climate change and sustainability have been raising on the policy agenda and are a driving force for a lot of policies and regulatory interventions. The driver of man-made climate change is known to be the emission of greenhouse gases into the atmosphere. A substantial part of those emissions is caused by energy conversion, mostly from burning fossil fuels – often for electricity generation. As a consequence, policies in order to mitigate climate change – in other words: policies aimed at reducing the emissions of greenhouse gases – are first and foremost targeting the actual emissions, or the activities and sectors which directly generate GHG emissions.

Since the energy and electricity sectors are particularly emission-intense, a significant part of the regulation related to the energy and the power sector is climate-related regulation. In fact, there are considerable overlaps between energy market regulation and climate-related policies. This overview focuses on climate and related renewable energy support rather than energy market regulation.

Therefore, climate change is the reason for a plethora of regulatory instruments aimed at reducing carbon emission by supporting renewable energy. However, increasingly climate change is also one reason for a broader perspective that puts financing in a more direct relation to climate change: Firstly, activities or assets that are financed are increasingly screened and evaluated along the question to what extend they contribute to climate change or to what extent they are consistent with a so-called two-degree target. Secondly, activities or assets that receive funds are increasingly analyzed with respect to the question how their value may be affected by climate impacts or ambitious climate policies.

Indeed, what we observe is a sustainability view increasingly being part of the overall perspective of economic actors, including (civil) society, policymakers, corporations as well as investors and the financial industry. Aspiration to move the world towards a long-term sustainable (including climate resilient, low carbon) future is a global trend. **It is one purpose of this section to put the act of "financing**

Ulf Moslener, Menglu Zhuang, Frankfurt School – UNEP Collaborating Centre for Climate & Sustainable Energy Finance

https://doi.org/10.1515/9783110607888-001

the energy transition" in context with this global trend towards a sustainable economic system.

Therefore, the section is structured as follows: Section 1.2 provides an overview on climate policy trends and instruments and how this influences the financing of electricity based on renewables. It touches upon the international policy level for contextual reasons and looks in more detail at the landscape of national-level legislation as this is more directly relevant for the attractiveness of an individual project. That section also examines how some of those instruments – including investment support instruments – may have shaped the banks' general view towards such projects. Section 1.3 is then focusing on the financial system. Despite the focus on the financial system, this section will broaden the view beyond reducing carbon emissions. As outlined above it will reflect **the trend towards integrating a sustainability view into investment and financing decisions**. This includes a perspective on climate related risks, broader considerations of risks related to social or governance issues but will also reflect about the consistency of investment decisions with the structural change as it is widely expected (and envisaged by regulator and societies). A number of initiatives at the international level, such as the G20 Task Force on Climate-related Financial Disclosure (TCFD), or driven by the financial centres are illustrating and accompanying this trend. Section 1.4 will conclude by combining the two trends and providing an outlook on some of the questions which remain open – such as **how future regulation of the financial system may be influenced by sustainability considerations**. Banks will need to navigate within this evolving landscape where new business opportunities will arise, and other business models will disappear. There is change ahead.

1.2 Climate Policy and Renewable Energy

In the past, in most cases the increased use of renewable energy-based power production has mainly been motivated by climate related concerns rather than cost-advantages. Climate policy processes can be observed at all political levels, the global (UN) level, the regional, the national and sub-national levels. Typically, UN-level activities will less directly have an impact on the attractiveness of individual projects but will be one of several drivers of regional or national-level policies.

In this section we will therefore only briefly introduce the UN Climate Process and then provide a general overview on policy instruments at the national and regional level. In parallel we discuss the impact of the different instruments at the project level. We finally consider how this may have shaped the financing banks over time.

1.2.1 The UN Climate Policy Process

The international community established a consensus that climate change would pose a serious threat to mankind already in 1992 at the Rio Summit where the UN-Framework Convention of Climate Change (UNFCCC) was signed by 154 states and entered into force two years later. Since then it is legally binding for major emitters including, e.g., the countries of the European Union, China and the United States. The Convention essentially recognized the need to act, and it introduced the principle of "common but differentiated responsibilities" of industrialized and developing countries.

As common in case of international conventions, further, more concrete action is taken through protocols to the convention. Within the frame of the Kyoto Protocol to the Climate Convention, a large group of countries formulated quantitative emission targets for the industrialized (so-called Annex-I) countries. Despite being signed by many countries in 1997 – including the United States – at the Climate Summit in Kyoto it was not ratified by all of them and entered into force only in 2006 – e.g., including the European Union and China, but without the United States.

In addition to quantitative targets, the Kyoto Protocol also contains elements to implement those targets flexibly – making use of some economic principles that would allow including countries without quantitative targets in the search of the least cost abatement options. In that sense the Kyoto Protocol allowed for so-called "emissions trading" between industrialized countries. It also allowed for the "clean development mechanism" (CDM) which would allow to establish project-based baselines in order to identify emission reductions in developing countries which do not have a quantitative target. These "certified emission reductions," generated through project investments, could then be used by industrialized countries to meet their own targets. They would therefore carry a value and were supposed to generate cash flows for clean projects in developing countries. The lack of the ability of the international community to establish an emission constraint that would lead to a scarcity and relevant CDM price levels and widespread abuse of the CDM provided a fast end to a market phase where this UN-level regulation actually started to have direct impacts at the individual project level.

A number of years later in 2010 industrialized countries committed to "jointly mobilize" one hundred billion US dollars annually from 2020 on for mitigation and adaptation investment, coming from a "variety or sources" including public and private. The UN Climate process then established the so-called *Green Climate Fund (GCF)* as a new financial mechanism under the Climate Convention, which would have a dedicated window – the private sector facility – to also finance projects brought forward by commercial finance institutions if they are accredited to the GCF. However, the majority of projects receiving financing from the GCF remained co-financed by public institutions.

In 2015 the international community established the *Paris Agreement*. This agreement (although formally a protocol to the convention) had the goal of creating a new long-term perspective and at the same time include all countries around the globe to assume an explicit role in mitigating climate change. The most relevant provision of the Paris Agreement with respect to the long-term perspective is the (agreed and ambitious) goal to achieve zero-net greenhouse-gas emissions by the second half of the century.

The most relevant provision with respect to national-level policies is the mechanism that all parties to the convention are supposed to provide *Nationally Determined Contributions (NDCs)*. In those NDCs the countries are expected to formulate their actions and ambitions, potentially including national policies but also potentially explicitly including areas where they would be able to implement more ambitious measures if international public financial support is available. Under the provisions of the Paris Agreement the countries are expected to revise their NDC every five years and it is expected that the degree of ambition of those NDCs is increasing over time. Those NDCs provide a relevant and periodically updated source of information about the strategies of the individual countries – potentially including relevant information about support policies relevant for renewables' investment.

The Paris Agreement also contains provisions to use instruments similar to the international emissions trading and the CDM under the Kyoto Protocol (Article 6, Paris Agreement). A detailed rulebook – the so-called "Article-6-Rulebook" will be necessary and will be developed and negotiated over time.

1.2.2 A Variety of Climate Policy Instruments at the Regional and National Levels

Instead of looking at different countries and their respective policy portfolios related to supporting renewables, we rather provide an overview of all the different policy instruments which are typically used at the national level. If those instruments and their impact at the renewables project (or investment) level are understood, then this provides a flexible tool to analyze and understand the concrete situation in a given country where a subset of the policy instruments is in place.

Policies supporting renewables investment may be classified in different ways. For the purpose of providing an overview, we start by the oldest class of environmental policy instruments, the so-called "command-and-control" regulation, where legal rules directly impose technology (or emission) standards at the source or company level. We continue by considering instruments which directly address the carbon externality by putting a price on carbon (a carbon tax and carbon emission permit trading schemes). Then we discuss instruments which act through specifying a price differential between electricity produced based on renewables and "non-renewables-based" electricity. Examples are feed-in tariffs, auctioned PPAs and tenders or green quota schemes. Finally, there are instruments providing support through making the investment itself more attractive. Prominent examples for this are investment tax credit (or production tax credit) schemes or general investment subsidies targeted at renewables investment, e.g., through grants, concessional loans or risk-taking instruments.

Figure 1.1 illustrates the widespread use of the instruments throughout the world. Among the 54 – sometimes sub-national – carbon pricing schemes in place in 2018, there are 27 emissions trading schemes and 27 carbon tax approaches. In total they are part of the policy mix in 44 countries. Renewables feed-in tariffs remain a major policy globally with 84 countries having them in place one way or the other. A strongly rising trend can be seen the area of renewable power auctions. Those have been used in 48 countries in 2018, which is a jump up from 29 countries in the year before. Tradable renewable energy certificates are less extensively used in about 30 countries, while a larger number (43) includes support of renewable through tax credits – either based on investment or actual production of renewables-based electricity. The most widespread instrument is the broader field of public investment support, including loans, grants, etc., which are available in some form in over a hundred countries. At the same time the figure also indicates that typically a number of policy approaches are in place in a given country.

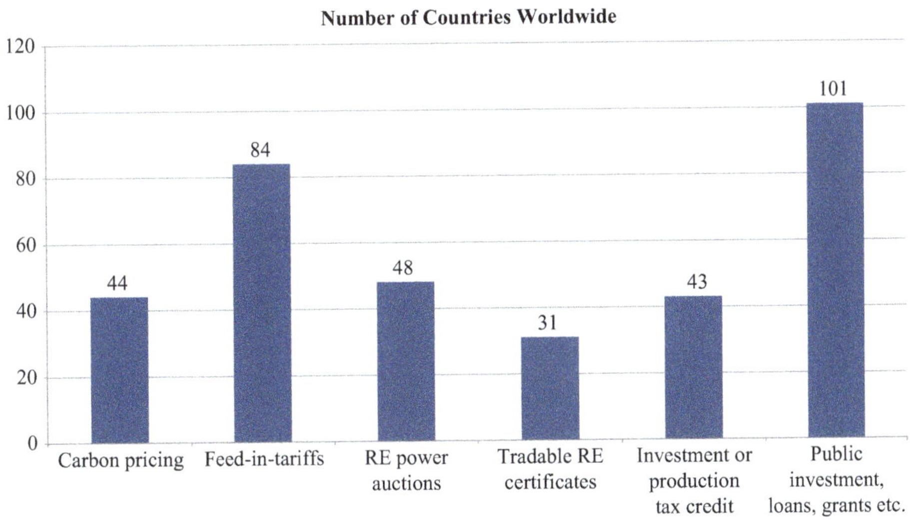

Figure 1.1: Number of countries where the respective RE support instruments are part of the policy mix (Source: Own representation based on REN21 (2019)).

Standards and Command & Control Instruments

Regarding environmental regulation, command & control regulation has been the classical instrument to intervene. It is implemented through a law that may directly impose a standard, such as an absolute emission volume, or a relative emission volume based on production output. In other cases, it just prescribes the technologies that may be used or it simply forbids (dirty) technologies which are not to be used. Such standards can be implemented motivated by various policy goals, so that environmental (or climate) policy related goals are only one example. In most cases of climate-policy motivated standards, the regulation is targeted rather at putting conditions and restrictions on the use of emission-intense technologies. In other words, the regulation is relevant at the level of the project design. Such standards typically provide restrictions on the non-renewables projects rather than the renewables-based projects. In those cases, they are not directly relevant for the individual project planning and financing.

Such standards are not considered as market-based instruments for climate policy, and therefore they are often criticized to directly regulate behavior rather than leaving considerable flexibility to the markets to identify cost-minimizing solutions. This is different in case of market-based instruments for climate policy, such as emission taxes or carbon permit trading schemes.

Carbon Permit Trading and Emission Taxes

Carbon permit trading schemes and carbon emission taxes essentially put a price on emissions. They do not care how certain emission reductions are achieved in detail but rather want to ensure that there is an economic incentive for market actors to avoid carbon emissions. Therefore, at the project level carbon pricing policies are directly relevant to projects using emission intensive technologies, such as fossil fuel-based electricity or heat production. Their goal is to internalize the so-called carbon externality, in other words to make sure that project planning is taking into account the negative effects of carbon emissions, because carbon emissions also generate costs at the project level. This way, a carbon price contributes to establishing a so-called level playing field between fossil-fuel-based and renewables-based electricity production such as wind or photovoltaic. Note, that there are also renewables-based power production technologies which produce carbon emissions at the project level. Biomass is the most prominent example. If we assume that biomass which is burnt for electricity (or heat) production is re-grown at the same rate at which it is used, then the net carbon emission of that process are zero. This could – from a climate perspective – justify an exemption of biomass-based electricity production from carbon taxes or carbon trading schemes.

How do the two most relevant carbon pricing policies work in more detail? A carbon tax may simply be implemented through (i) setting a carbon tax rate and (ii) requiring the firms to report on their emissions and then collect the tax on that base. Before emitting carbon dioxide, the firms will consider the tax rate and evaluate if it is more attractive to pay the tax or to avoid the emission. The higher the tax rate the more effort firms will put into emission abatement. Abatement could in principle happen through (i) reducing production, (ii) applying technologies with higher efficiency, or (iii) through applying some end-of-pipe carbon abatement technology (e.g., carbon capture, storage and use).

An emissions trading scheme works slightly different: At first, the government needs to set an overall emissions target. Then this target volume needs to be created as a tradable security (e.g., an "emission allowance" for one ton of carbon dioxide). These newly created securities need to be put on the market – e.g., through some distribution rule or simply through an auction. Then all emitting firms are required to possess the equivalent of what they have emitted in the form of those securities (tradable emission permits). As opposed to the carbon tax (where the carbon price is set and the emission volume results) the starting point is to set the target emission volume and in the following a resulting market price for emissions will be observed. The tighter the emission target set by the government, the higher the resulting price for the carbon emission permits will be, and the higher the ambitions to avoid carbon emissions by the firms. Similar to a carbon tax, the firm can reduce by (i) reducing output, (ii) using a more or less carbon intense production method, or (iii) using an end-of-pipe technology (such as carbon capture) to adjust to a rising price. This also means, that the reaction of firms to a rising carbon price is strongly determined by the available technologies.

While carbon taxes and tradable permits as described above do not directly show up in cash-flow considerations of a typical renewables' project, there are carbon price-based instruments which do. These mechanisms or policies are often called "project-based-mechanisms." The historically most relevant example is the Clean Development Mechanism (CDM) which is working on a global scale between developing and developed countries. The general approach of project-based-mechanisms is to first establish a project-level business-as-usual emission baseline. Then the actual carbon emissions under the project using the clean (or renewable) technology are determined. The emission difference between those two scenarios is then considered the carbon abatement. Once that "carbon abatement" is quantified, it can also form the base of, e.g., receiving financial support per tonne of carbon abatement or securitizing the emission abatement and trade it on an international market, e.g., as Certified Emission Reductions (CERs).

In such cases of project-based mechanisms, the (hypothetically) avoided emissions vis-à-vis the project baseline may indeed appear as revenues in the project cash-flow analysis. In the case of a project that expects to generate a certain volume of CERs per year, this enters the planning process and makes the renewables project more attractive. As the CDM has suffered from the inability of the international community to agree on emission scarcity, the use of CDM has essentially stopped. However, as discussed above in the context of the UN climate process and the related "Article 6" of the Paris Agreement the processes and lessons learned from the CDM are likely to lead to a new form or international emissions trading.

Feed-In Tariffs, Cuctioned PPAs and Green Quota Schemes

There are a number of climate-motivated policies which specifically target renewables themselves and their attractiveness at the investment level. These instruments can either provide support through the revenue side of the project or through the costs side at the project level. This section will introduce the revenue-support instruments, while the following one will explain support instruments through reducing financing costs.

Revenue support instruments mostly act through securing the price at which the electricity produced based on renewables can be sold. That support has two dimensions: one is the level of the price and another one is the volatility or predictability of the price. We discuss the three most common schemes: feed-in tariffs (FiTs), auctioned power purchase agreements (PPAs) and so-called green quota schemes (or tradable renewable energy certificates – RECs).

For quite some time FiTs have been the most successful policy from the perspective of incentivizing investment in renewable electricity.[1] They act very simply: First, the government sets a (typically technology-specific) price at which the electricity produced from renewables has to be bought by the grid operator. As a consequence, the project developer of a wind or photovoltaic power project is only left with the uncertainty about the resource provision (i.e., wind or sun availability), not with a potentially low and certainly more volatile electricity spot market price or a benevolent grid operator buying the electricity. This emphasizes the relevance of wind and sun availability at the level of the feasibility study, but on the whole strongly increases the predictability of the project revenues. If this is combined with an optimized (or tailored) financing structure the project can – also from a debt (or bank) perspective – produce the debt service with a fairly transparent and plannable buffer (debt service coverage ratio or DSCR).

This predictability in combination with an initially high level of the feed-in tariff created the strong investment incentive in the past, while some also argued that the support comes at high overall costs to whoever will need to pay the renewable-power-producer. In most cases this is either the government (i.e., taxpayer) or the common electricity consumer (through a premium included in the final electricity consumption price).

As discussions were criticizing that FiT levels are too high and politically difficult to lower together with falling costs, a more market-oriented approach took ground: reverse auctions. Renewable power auctions introduce a competitive market element into the support of renewables. The general idea is, that the government announces a

1 For a general overview, see Goldner/Torwegge in section 5.

certain additional capacity of (typically technology specific) renewable electricity to be installed. Developers will then plan a project including all the costs and potential revenues and finally submit a bid indicating at which guaranteed price per kWh electricity they would implement the proposed project. Governments will then turn to some previously announced selection mechanism and select a number of the proposed projects – mainly based on the price, starting to award the building concessions with the lowest offer fulfilling all other additional requirements.

As opposed to the feed-in tariff, in the case of auctions it is unclear to the end if the project will be realized. In fact, as the financing costs are a major driver for the costs of producing electricity based on wind or sunlight, the interest rate offered by the bank is a major cost driver, and thereby a major driver of the price that the project developer will be able to offer in such an auction. In other words, the higher the interest rate offered by the bank, the higher the price that will enter the auction (or the lower the expected equity dividends in the first years) and the lower the chance that the project will materialize at all. Experience with renewable power auctions show that the resulting prices indeed do fall considerably, and in many cases – also in industrialized countries such as the UK – we observe prices below the typical costs (LCOE) of providing power based on coal.

Another less widely used support scheme for renewable energy investment are so-called tradable green quotas, sometimes also tradable renewable energy certificates. The idea of that support instrument is similar to the idea of a carbon price through an emissions trading scheme. The difference is, that the price is not put on carbon but on the abstract "greenness" of the electricity production. Therefore the government would first need to define which technologies to produce electricity will be considered "green." Instead of formulating a carbon emissions target, the government would now formulate a target of "greenness," typically a "green quota." The scheme would now implement the target in the following way: (i) Electricity producers are required to hand over renewable energy certificates corresponding to the green quota of their electricity production. (If the government has announced a 10% green quota, and the electricity production amounts to 200 GWh, then the producer has to provide renewable energy certificates for 20 GWh to the regulator.) (ii) Those permits are generated through the electricity production process and they are tradable (separate from the electricity). As a consequence, the 100% renewables producer (e.g., the owner of a wind farm) will generate not only electricity, but also permits – which carry a value. He or she will then be able to sell the electricity as well as the unused permits to some other electricity producer who does not produce green electricity himself but needs to comply with the quota regulation by just buying the required renewable energy certificates from the market (or the actual producers of "green electricity.") This way, the certificates will have a value or price, thereby making the renewables based project financially more attractive.

Investment Support Instruments

Instead of increasing the revenues from producing renewables-based electricity, another approach is to reduce the cost side of renewables. Since the costs are strongly driven by capital costs, the approach is to directly lower the financing cost. Investment support may come in different forms. The simplest form is to provide grants to a project, which directly lowers the volume of funds that need to be raised as debt or equity. Grants are particularly attractive to support project phases when no revenues are expected or the risk is high – such as the starting phase or the project feasibility study, when it is not even clear if the project will materialize at all.

In terms of financial volume, the most common form of investment support is the so-called concessional loan. That is essentially a loan that is offered at more attractive conditions than a comparable commercial loan.

The main three criteria along which an concessional loan could be more attractive are (i) interest rate below the market, (ii) longer tenor (or more interest free years) than would be available commercially or (iii) subordination relative to other (e.g., commercial) loans, which would mean that in case of difficulties to pay back the loan, other lenders would be preferred. The most common support element is the subsidized interest rate. An interest rate lower than the market affects a project in two related ways: firstly, it directly lowers the financing costs through the lower interest. Secondly, in the context of different loans to one project, the change of one loan towards a lower interest rate will lead to a situation where the cash-flow that is available to pay debt service including interest will stay the same, but the debt service is reduced. As a consequence the buffer between cash flow available for debt service and the debt service itself rises (rising debt-service coverage ratio – DSCR).[2] Consequently other lenders may feel safer. Indeed, in case of the involvement of government-owned (public) finance institutions they may feel safer anyway – but for reasons related to reduced political risk rather than cash flow effects.

Concessional loans as an investment instrument are very common across national and international public finance institution around the world. There are two main ways how they are delivered: the first is as straight direct loans, e.g., to projects or to companies. The second one is through so-called on-lending by commercial institutions. In this case the actual loan to the final customer is extended through a commercial bank. Typically it is the bank that is already in a business relationship with the borrower (the recipient of the concessional loan). The commercial bank extends the loan – typically at standardized conditions, sometimes depending on the ambition of the project (e.g., the energy efficiency, or the particular renewable energy technology that will be employed in the project). The commercial institution then gets this loan refinanced by the (public finance) institution that is running the concessional lending program. As opposed to the case of directly providing concessional

2 See Böttcher in Section 6.

loans to the project that is supposed to benefit, the case of on-lending involves the commercial players – which typically get a fee in turn.

The involvement of another intermediary requires to determine some operational aspects of running the program. Particularly, the program design needs to fix the risk sharing between the two banks and the interest rate of the final loan (and the refinancing conditions). In most cases the risk of the final loan to the end-customer is taken by the commercial bank, as it is already in a commercial relationship with that customer and is therefore in a better position to determine the related risk. Interest rates of the final loan are typically fix and determined by the program.

A particular grant program, or a concessional loan program, is therefore characterized by a number of parameters. This starts with selection criteria or a list of activities that are targeted by that support program. Then the volume of support needs to be determined, i.e., how the grant or the loan volume is determined. Finally, particularly in the case of a loan, there are a number of technical implementation details that would need specification – such as the risk distribution, interest rate, tenor, potential interest free years, etc.

An approach that is becoming increasingly relevant is to provide public support not just in the form of monetary value (such as grants) but to add a component of risk taking. The simplest instrument in the context of direct investment support is to provide a guarantee. In addition to specifying target projects, etc., a guarantee faces the challenge that the corresponding contract needs to exactly determine the risks that will be covered by that guarantee. Often that will be limited to particular risks, such as political risk. It needs to be specified what exactly triggers the guarantee. Well-known and widely used examples are the so-called export credit guarantees. These are essentially a policy instrument used by many countries to cover the risk of exporters in order to enable export deals and thereby facilitate exports. As this policy instrument systematically runs the risk to carry elements of export subsidies, there is a set of rules governing the use and design of instruments of such export credit agencies. This is the so-called OECD Consensus. This is a detailed set of rules to avoid excessive export support to avoid detrimental "support competition" (the so called "race to the bottom"). The details are changing frequently and larger financing institutions involved in export financing will typically have dedicated experts to be consulted in this respect. Another well-known guarantee instrument in the context of larger scale international projects is the World Bank political risk guarantees. Those guarantees are used to address political risk and require an agreement between the host country government and the World Bank in the background in order to reduce the moral hazard effect of shifting costs and risks to the international community.

There is one other prominent policy approach to support renewable energy somewhat through making the investment case more attractive via tax credits: Investment or production tax credit support schemes. As opposed to directly providing a grant subsidy, those schemes provide tax advantages on the base of either the investment volume in a given technology (for example the investment tax credit for solar PV in the United States) or on the base of the actual electricity that has been produced based on renewables (for example the production tax credit for wind facilities in the United States). As this support policy acts through the normal income tax system of a country, the attractiveness of the support depends on the overall tax situation of the investor or electricity producer.

Recently, discussions emerged about the role of the financial sector in scaling up renewables' investment. The reaction of the banks themselves to regulation as well as some approaches to introduce aspects of green finance and green banking into financial market regulation will, however be the subject of the following subsection and section.

1.2.3 How This Trend Shapes the Banks' Behavior

Banks make lending decisions primarily based on the profitability and cash flow analysis of a firm or a project. The nature of a debt contract means that there is a fixed obligation from the borrower to repay the principal and interests of the loan. However, there is no additional profit for the lenders if the project has achieved more financial success than expected. Therefore, risk-averse banks sometimes prefer to limit lending to certain sector and projects with high investment risks instead of offering the loans at higher interest rates as would be expected in a perfect financial market (Wiser & Pickle 1998). This gives rise to the so-called credit rationing problem. In this subsection, we will discuss how renewable energy policies shape the banks' behavior by improving the risk-return profile of the renewable energy projects.

Renewable energy projects need to meet certain conditions to be attractive for banks to finance. Simply speaking, the supported renewable energy project should generate enough cash flow to repay the debt obligation. In addition, the renewable energy project should have a more attractive overall risk-return profile than a competing project. Renewable energy financing in reality is faced with many market barriers. Renewable energy projects are characterized by high capital intensity, a long payback period and high reliance on external financing. The financing needs of these projects require long-term loans rather than short-term loans. However, the long-term debt markets are relatively illiquid, which is one reason why the willingness of banks to provide long-term loans is low. Difficult access to credit, lack of financial institutions capable of lending and inappropriate financial instruments are identified as some of the key barriers to renewable energy growth (Painuly 2001).

As discussed in *Subsection 1.2.2* above, policy instruments have positively shaped the attractiveness of the individual renewable energy project. One group of policies such as FiT enhances the risk-return profile of renewable energy projects relative to others. Another group of policies puts a price on the polluting projects to address the externality problem, e.g., policies such as carbon tax or emissions trading system set a price on the externalities produced by the polluting firms. Policies that target the risk-return profile of renewable energy projects are most frequently observed around the world.

Renewable energy supporting policies that improve the risk-return profile of renewable energy projects do so by increasing the revenues or reducing the costs of the projects (certain projects sometimes benefit from both). As a result, the increased remaining cash flow transforms the project into a less risky one for the banks to lend to. Haas & Kempa (2018) show that over time credit rationing tends to disappear as investment risks decrease. Moreover, the policy support provides banks with an incentive to accumulate know-how in credit assessment and risk management of complicated renewable energy projects as they increasingly perceive renewables as a business opportunity.

Supported by the policies, renewable energy investments have been growing over the past decade. Due to the lack of a global carbon price, public finance channeled through supporting policies has been playing a key role in unlocking private capital to flow into renewable energy investments. Private financing capital provided more than 90% of the renewable energy investments in 2016, in which conventional debt and equity instruments are most prominent (IRENA/CPI 2018). As an important financial intermediary, banks lending to renewables is an important part of the story of increasing renewable energy investment volume. Figure 1.2 shows the financing volume of renewable energy projects from 2014 to 2017 by financing types. On balance sheet financing from utilities and energy companies amounted to $121.5 billion while the volume of project finance reached $91.2 billion in 2017. This is a significant increase compared to more than a decade ago when the balance sheet and project finance volumes were only $28.1 billion and $5.2 billion respectively in 2004 (Frankfurt School – UNEP Centre/BNEF 2018).[3]

Though supporting policies can increase the attractiveness of renewable energy projects for financiers, retroactive policy changes can create a source of uncertainty. Policies which may not be in place anymore when the project starts and policies that fail to guarantee stable long-term revenues will increase the financing costs of the renewable energy projects (Wiser & Pickle 1998). Banks that have experienced retrospective policy changes, e.g., regarding a FiT, are likely to be more cautious about lending to renewables in the future and price the risks into their lending interest rates. In some cases, banks may even stop lending to renewable

3 Project finance refers to debt and equity provided directly to the projects, and not to the company. Balance sheet refers to internal company balance sheet financing from debt or equity. A bond is issued by a bank or company, the proceeds of which go into the projects.

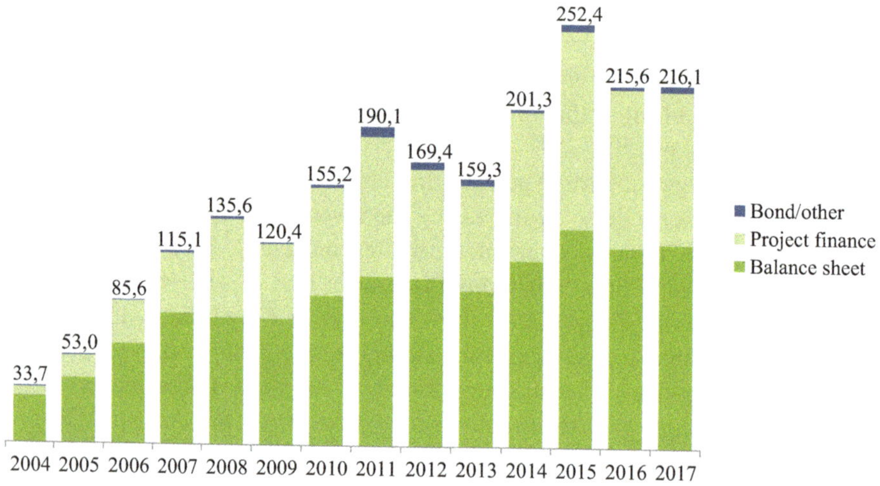

Figure 1.2: Financing of renewable energy by type, 2004–2017 ($ billon), Source: Frankfurt School – UNEP Centre/BNEF (2018).

energy power generation projects. Spain implemented a retrospective changes to its FiT, which cut the revenue support to renewables by about 25% during 2010–2013 (May & Olga 2018).[4] As a consequence, after 2012, the investment volumes in renewables experienced a stand-still given the uncertainty involved in investing in renewables in Spain.

Not all banks adjust their behavior exclusively based on the commercial attractiveness of the projects, bank behavior may also be influenced by institutional and political factors, depending on the specific market an political environment. The discussion of this issue across and particularly beyond the OECD countries is out of the scope of this section, but we will provide an informative and relevant example: China issued the Green Credit Policy in 2007 to direct financial resources of banks towards environmental purposes. The financial sector policy guides banks to implement differentiating credit policies towards environmental and pollution projects. Banks are guided to restrict lending to high polluting firms and projects and extend priority lending to green projects including renewables energies (Wang, Yang, Reisner, & Liu 2019). “Guiding banks” is not equally common or simple in all jurisdictional contexts, but for the case of China it is established that the behavior of Chinese banks is clearly affected by political direction in addition to financial considerations (Wu 2018).

4 See also Section 5.4.1.

1.3 A Future-Proof Financial System: Sustainable Finance

Green finance is often understood to be collection of financing measures which can be seen as a subset of sustainable finance. The capital flow of green finance is used to finance climate mitigation and adaptation measures, in order to facilitate the transformation to a low-carbon economy. Under the goals set by United Nation Sustainable Development Goals (SDGs) and the Paris Agreement, financing sustainable growth is identified as a major challenge that needs to be addressed with collective efforts. The Paris Agreement asks for "[m]aking finance flows consistent with a pathway towards low greenhouse gas emissions and a climate-resilient development." (Article 2.1c) Sustainable finance includes financing green technologies and projects, but also financing of other sustainability measures, and potentially moving towards asking for every investment, if it can be considered consistent with a long-term sustainable path. To provide the readers with a perspective on green finance framed in the increasingly important sustainable finance discussion, this section looks at sustainable financial system, regulatory developments for sustainable finance and the changes ahead for banks.

1.3.1 Sustainability and the Financial System

Sustainability is drawing more and more attention in the policy discussions around the world. According to the Cambridge Dictionary, sustainability refers to "the quality of causing little or no damage to the environment and therefore able to continue for a long time." In the business context, sustainable businesses consider the impact of their products or services on environment, social and governance issues besides economic returns. In the financial context, sustainable finance refers to the provision of finance taking environmental, social and governance and other sustainability-related issues into consideration (European Commission 2019). In particular, a sustainable financial system is a system that integrates sustainability considerations, taking into account all the externalities that shift market outcomes away from what can be considered a sustainable outcome (UNEP/World Bank 2017).

The economic role of a financial system is the allocation of resources efficiently to maximize societal welfare. A bank is a financial intermediary in the financial system that channels funds from savers to spenders. A perfect financial market should correctly price all assets. Riskyness and promised interest are supposed to signal to the investor where to put his money such that it is put to most productive use (from the perspective of the society). However, existing real-world financial markets in most countries cannot reflect the true value of the sustainable assets due to externalities and other market imperfections. For example, under mispricing caused by market imperfection to internalise environmental externality, banks are not able to carry out its function optimally after receiving distorted price signals. In this situation, sub-optimal projects that cause harm to the environment and society may receive financing, potentially threatening long-term human development.

Amongst sustainability issues, the climate change-induced risks are the first and most widely discussed risks, where some even argue that they could become a systemic risk for the financial sector. Climate-related risks include physical risks and transition risks in general. Physical risks come from physical damages caused by climate change, which can have direct and indirect financial implications for organizations. Transition risks refer to policy, technology and market changes that are put in place to meet the requirements of transitioning to a low-carbon economy (TCFD 2017).

Phases of structural change such as the path towards long-term sustainability are characterized by strong and sometimes fast changes of assets in the real economy over time. The majority of the sectors are under the pressure to transform towards being clean or green. The transformation will affect banks because the underlying assets of banks' loan portfolios are in the real sector. For instance, Germany plans to exit out of coal by 2038. Under this scenario, coal-fired power plants will be shut down. Banks that have coal power generation assets in their portfolio are exposed to climate policy induced risks. In this situation, banks need to re-evaluate the risks attached to the loans to coal power generation borrowers and adjust future lending strategies to account for the sectorial risk in coal.

If the financial system substantially delays its adaptation or transition to this new perspective including changes in risks and opportunities, then transition and physical risks of climate change may hit the financial sector forcing institutions to act fast in an almost disruptive way potentially causing stability risks (sometimes called a "hard landing"). Being aware of the potential risks, the central banks are increasing paying attention to the impact of climate change on monetary regimes and the possibility of climate change induced financial risks. In his well known speech "Breaking the tragedy of the horizon" Mr. Mark Carney, Governor of Bank of England and Chairman of the Financial Stability Board, pointed out the short-term horizon of business cycles, political cycle and authorities like central banks and asked for this to be changed (Carney, 2015). The financial policy implication is that the financial market need better information to adjust efficiently, thus the disclosure requirements are discussed which also affect banks. This situation is essentially driving the regulatory developments in sustainable finance discussed in the following Subsection 1.3.2.

1.3.2 Regulatory initiatives for sustainable finance

Market imperfections provide justification for policy interventions. Information asymmetry is a market imperfection that hinders the development of sustainable finance. In an information asymmetry problem, one party has superior information compared to another party. The market cannot correctly price the sustainability-related risks in the assets with incomplete information. For example, companies are in a better position to know the effects of their production on the environment, however this information is usually not known by the public. Investors need better information to form a view on the risk-return profile of the green projects or assets compared to, e.g., a project that is environmentally harmful or is associated with other negative externalities. Better information would put the investor in a position to better assess the material ESG risks in his portfolio. To correct the information asymmetry in the financial market, regulatory efforts are discussed to improve transparency and data availability.

Many regulatory initiatives are advancing disclosure requirements to provide better information for the financial market. Among others, the Group of 20 (G20) requested the Financial Stability Board to establish the Task Force on Climate-related Financial Disclosures (TCFD) to consider climate-related financial sector implications. According to the TCFD recommendations, the disclosure efforts of the organization, including both financial and non-financial institutions can be structured around four aspects: governance, strategy, risk management and metrics & targets. The recommendations suggest a first of its kind reporting framework for integrating climate-related considerations throughout the organization.

Regulatory work that aims to provide information for the financial market is ongoing at the European level. In early 2018, the European Commission issued an action plan on financing sustainable growth, which set out a roadmap for legislative and non-legislative actions. Under the action plan, the first three legislative proposals include creating a unified classification system for economic activities – the EU taxonomy, disclosure requirements on ESG related risks and establishment of new climate benchmarks. The EU taxonomy serves to provide a common language on discerning which activities are environmentally sustainable (TEG 2019). The taxonomy addresses the problem of divergent classifications appearing in the field that may confuse the investors and the problem of green washing. The proposed new disclosure requirements aim to facilitate the integration of sustainability-related risk assessments in the financial sector, which various market players such as asset managers, institutional investors or pension funds are then obliged to disclose. Figure 1.3 shows the broad relevance which the different fields in the EU Action Plan may have for the different players in the financial market.

Faced with the regulatory changes in the financial market and the urgency to identify the most relevant sustainability-related risks, banks need a method to assess the risks and opportunities in their loan portfolios. Potential financial distress of businesses that are not favored under the structural change are likely to materialize as default risks for banks' loan portfolios. Scenario analysis is one method recommended by the TCFD taskforce for financial and non-financial

EU Action Plan on Financing Sustainable Growth		
Reorienting capital flows towards a more sustainable economy	Mainstreaming sustainability into risk management	Fostering transparency and longtermism

Implementation of recommendations through legislative package

Affected Market Players	Relevant Action Fields
Companies Projects	EU Sustainable Taxonomy Investment in Sustainable Projects Foster Sustainable Corporate Governance
Banks	EU Sustainable Taxonomy Sustainability in prudential requirements
Institutional Investors Asset Managers Insurance Companies	Sustainability in Disclosure & Accounting Institutional investors duties Foster Sustainable Corporate Governance
Service Providers e.g. ESG Data Providers	ESG in Ratings and Market Research Sustainability Benchmarks
Investment Advisors	Create Standards and Labels Sustainability Benchmarks Incorporate Sustainability in Investment Advice
Retail Investors	Create Standards and Labels

Figure 1.3: EU Action plan and affected parties in the financial market (Source: Author's presentation based on the European Commission (2018)).

institutions to develop strategic plans that are more flexible or robust to be applied to a range of plausible future states (TCFD 2017). The information generated from scenario analysis can be used for the disclosure of climate-related risks of banks for compliance purposes. It will also help banks to develop a profound understanding of sustainability-related risks and opportunities in their operations, which will help them to deal with climate change challenges in the future.

1.4 Change Ahead

Sustainability is a key factor that is driving changes in the policy regime and in the financial market. The financial industry senses the market and policy changes that are challenging their business models and many potential early movers are paying close attention to the latest developments. This is evident in financial institutions' efforts to invest in Research & Development (R&D) into digitalization and participation in initiatives that push forward the integration of climate-related risks assessment within organizations.

The financial market is changing as more and more investments taking sustainability into consideration are being observed. Risk identification and screening of environmental, corporate and governance issues are employed by professional investment institutions for generating better returns. Investors are increasingly demanding financial products that achieve financial returns and are aligned with their personal values in sustainability at the same time. The expectation is not unrealistic. A literature review of more than 2,000 studies on the relationship between ESG criteria and investment performance shows that ESG investing is in the position to compete with traditional investing strategies; about 90% of the studies show a non-negative relationship and the majority of these reported positive relationships (Friede, Busch, & Bassen 2015).

Changes are ahead for the banking industry. The new dynamic has implications on the business model, organizational structure and compliance capacity of the banks. The nature of the game for financial institutions is changing. Sustainability factors in financial decisions are becoming a key part of the strategic and risk management function of the organization. The need for the analysis of climate-related risks in portfolios and disclosure requirements increases, and bank customers increasingly ask for that. What green finance means for the financial institutions is no longer only investment opportunities, but also a risk measure that protects the portfolios from climate-related risks in the midst of a process of substantial structural change.

References

Carney, Mark. 2015. "Breaking the Tragedy of the Horizon: Climate Change and Financial Stability." Speech given at Lloyd's of London, Bank of England.

European Commission. 2018. *Action Plan: Financing Sustainable Growth.*

European Commission. 2019. *Nachhaltige Finanzierung.*

Frankfurt School – UNEP Centre/BNEF. 2018. *Global Trends in Renewable Energy* Investment *2018. Bloomberg New Energy Finance*. Frankfurt am Main. https://doi.org/10.3928/00220124-20081201-03.

Friede, Gunnar, Timo Busch, and Alexander Bassen. 2015. "ESG and Financial Performance: Aggregated Evidence from more than 2000 Empirical Studies." *Journal of Sustainable Finance and Investment* 5, no. 4: 210–33. https://doi.org/10.1080/20430795.2015.1118917.

Haas, Christian, and Karol Kempa. 2018. "Clean Energy Investment and Credit Rationing." In *6th International Symposium on Environment & Energy Issues*, 1–42. Paris.

IRENA / CPI. 2018. *Global Landscape of Renewable Energy Finance 2018. International Renewable Energy Agency.*

May, Nils, and Olga Chiappinelli. 2018. "Too Good to Be True? How Time-Inconsistent Renewable Energy Policies Can Deter Investments." *DIW Berlin Discussion Paper* 1726. https://doi.org/10.2139/ssrn.3146774.

Painuly, J. P. 2001. "Barriers to Renewable Energy Penetration: A Framework for Analysis." *Renewable Energy* 24, no. 1: 73–89. https://doi.org/10.1016/S0960-1481(00)00186-5.

REN21. 2019. *Global Status Report 2019*. https://www.ren21.net/gsr-2019/chapters/chapter_02/chapter_02/.

TCFD. 2017. *Recommendations of the Task Force on Climate-Related Financial Disclosures*. https://www.fsb-tcfd.org/publications/final-recommendations-report/.

TEG. 2019. *Taxonomy Technical Report.*

UNEP / World Bank. 2017. *Roadmap for a Sustainable Financial System.*

Wang, Feng, Siyue Yang, Ann Reisner, and Na Liu. 2019. "Does Green Credit Policy Work in China? The Correlation between Green Credit and Corporate Environmental Information Disclosure Quality." *Sustainability (Switzerland)* 11, no. 3. https://doi.org/10.3390/su11030733.

Wiser, Ryan H., and Steven J. Pickle. 1998. "Financing Investments in Renewable Energy: The Impacts of Policy Design." *Renewable & Sustainable Energy Reviews* 2, no. 4: 361–86. https://doi.org/10.1016/S1364-0321(98)00007-0.

Wu, Guiying Laura. 2018. "Capital Misallocation in China: Financial Frictions or Policy Distortions?" *Journal of Development Economics* 130: 203–23. https://doi.org/10.1016/j.jdeveco.2017.10.014.

2 Electricity Supply Systems: The Current and Future Role of Renewable Sources of Energy

Jerrit Hilgedieck, Jelto Lange, Martin Kaltschmitt

2.1 Introduction

The global primary energy consumption amounted to 565 EJ (157 PWh) in 2017 [1]. This demand will most likely grow significantly in the next decades; until 2040 a growth of 200 EJ/a (56 PWh/a) is expected, resulting in a total energy consumption of roughly 770 EJ/a (213 PWh/a) [2]. About 86% of this energy demand is met by the use of fossil fuels; roughly 94% of these fuels are coal, natural gas and crude oil. The energy-related use of the latter leads to a release of additional carbon dioxide effecting global climate [2]. According to current knowledge, the combustion of such fossil fuels constitutes the main contribution to manmade greenhouse gas (GHG) emissions and thus the anthropogenic greenhouse effect. Already today, the impacts of climate change are becoming more and more visible. Nearly every year new temperature records are measured and 10 of the warmest 15 years since the beginning of climate recording lie within the 21st century [3]. Figure 2.1 exemplary shows the average summer temperatures in central Switzerland throughout the last roughly 150 years. Consequently, extreme natural events (e.g., droughts, floods) are occurring more often, which might be increasingly threatening for human civilization.

To bring these opposing tendencies (a rising global primary energy demand and the necessity to reduce GHG emissions to stabilize global climate) into accordance, the global energy supply has to become less dependent on fossil carbon-based energy carriers; i.e., from a fossil carbon perspective the energy supply has to be "decarbonized." The only way to reduce the anthropogenic climate-impacting emissions in a sustainable manner, without producing nuclear waste, lies in an increased use of renewable energies. If electrical or thermal energy is supplied through the use of renewable energies, greenhouse gas emissions can be directly avoided e.g., compared to a coal- or oil-fired power plant; merely during construction and decommissioning of the specific power stations, greenhouse gases are emitted as long the decarbonization (concerning carbon of fossil origin) of our energy system is not yet fully completed. Anyhow, these construction- and decommissioning-related GHG emissions are typically one or two orders of magnitude below those from exclusively fossil fuel-based power plants [5]. Thus, the fundamental option to achieve a (nearly) climate-neutral energy supply does indeed exist.

The easily, efficiently and almost arbitrarily realizable transformation of electrical energy into any other form of energy allows it to be used simultaneously in various other energy sectors (e.g., heating sector, mobility sector), so that even in these

https://doi.org/10.1515/9783110607888-002

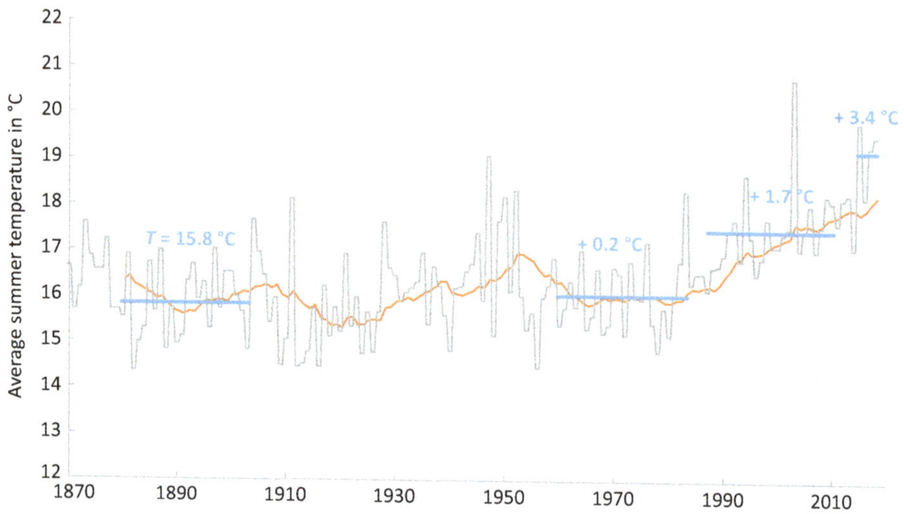

Figure 2.1: Average summer temperatures in Switzerland between 1870 and 2018 [4].

areas of energy supply fossil carbon-based energy carriers can be replaced, and the related greenhouse gas emissions can be avoided.

Besides the transformation of the energy provision system within different energy sectors (i.e., reduction of conventional fossil-based power production and increase of power production based on renewable energies) internal restructurings within each energy demand sector are also necessary. For example, the electrical energy system has to be modified and developed to sustain a secure system operation even with much higher shares of power generation from for instance wind power and solar radiation – and thus fluctuation sources of energy. Until now the supply's task within the electricity sector has been to meet consumer's demand for electrical energy by staring up or shutting down (large) power stations centrally operated by the local utility. Due to the fact that some renewable energies (e.g., wind energy, solar radiation) are characterized naturally by strong fluctuations, the supply side has to be increasingly adapted, so that even with a partly stochastically fluctuating energy provision from renewable sources of energy, a stable and secure operation of the electrical supply system can be achieved. To meet this goal in a cost-efficient manner, also the demand side has to take an increasingly active part within the overall electricity supply system. Accordingly, this holds true for the other sectors of the energy industry. Therefore, to achieve a reduction of the use of fossil fuels, which is necessary for climate protection, within energy supply systems, in the upcoming decades a fast and significant transformation of local/regional/national and global energy systems is needed.

Against this background, it is the aim of the following explanations to discuss and analyse the looming development trends of electricity supply systems under the specific consideration of energy supply systems with a high share of renewable energies – including the resulting necessities of modified configurations concerning the whole energy supply structures. For that, it will be described, which driving forces determine future energy demand in general and the demand for electricity in particular. Afterwards the current situation of selected energy supply options based on renewable energies are described. Subsequently, it will be analyzed, how electricity supply systems might (or should) develop in the upcoming years and which conclusions are to be drawn from that.

2.2 Global Trends and Key Drivers

The further development of the energy demand and thus of the global energy supply system are fundamentally influenced or determined by only a few key drivers. Some of these globally emerging trends are also referred to as global megatrends because of their significant and profound implications for worldwide development; they are described hereinafter.

2.2.1 Growing Energy Demand

Certain trends inevitably lead to an increase in global energy demand. The following four developments are discussed exemplarily below:
- World population
- Prosperity
- Mobility
- ICT products

World Population

The current world population of around 7.5 billion people demands on average around 76 GJ/a or 21.2 MWh/a of primary energy per person [6, 7]. By the end of this century, about 10 to 11 billion people will populate our planet (Figure 2.2) [6]. Because of the still increasing life expectancy, despite potentially further declining birth rates, there will be a significant increase in the world population in the decades to come.

Especially in highly populated countries such as China or India, the strongly increasing life expectancy in recent decades is particularly apparent. As an example, Figure 2.3 shows the average life expectancy in China, India and the USA. Accordingly, the expected average life span in the two emerging countries (China, India) – despite brief drops due to wars, etc. – is gradually approaching that of a

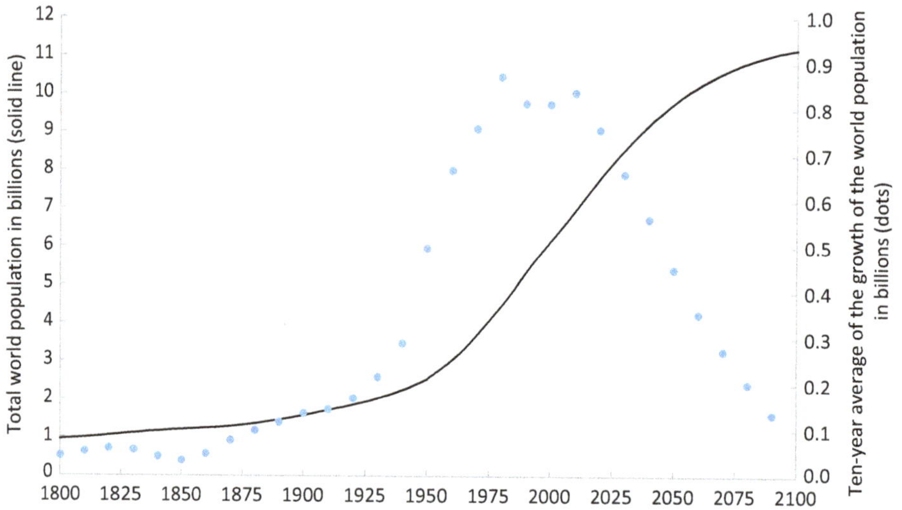

Figure 2.2: Development of the world population (solid line: left axis; points: right axis) [6].

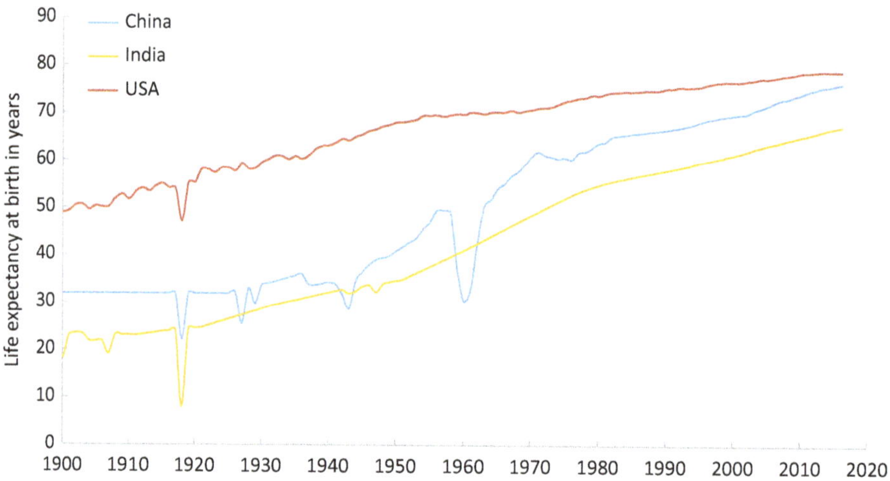

Figure 2.3: Life expectancy in selected countries [8].

developed industrialized country such as the USA. Under the (realistic) assumption, that the global energy demand (without consideration of the individual energy demand) is at least proportional to the population, this alone will inevitably lead to a (strongly) increasing energy demand in the future.

Prosperity

In addition to population growth, the average prosperity of ever-larger parts of the overall society is increasing globally. In recent decades, there has been a clear trend towards significantly higher incomes of larger population groups in increasingly more countries with a former low-income level; that means the middle class is growing very fast worldwide. Figure 2.4 shows an example of the average per capita income of the countries China, India and the USA as well as the GDP of these nations. Clearly visible is the strong growth in China and India in the 1990s. In addition, a time lag between China and India as well as an even more significant time lag between China and the US in per capita income is recognizable.

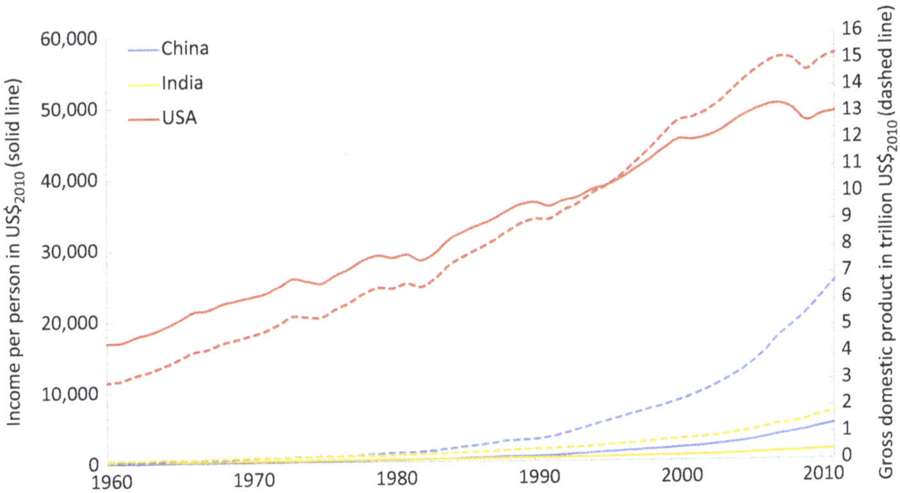

Figure 2.4: Income per person and gross domestic product (GDP; solid line: left axis; dashed line; right axis) [6, 9].

Overall, both the average life expectancy (Figure 2.3) and the average income (Figure 2.4) of both countries show a similar but delayed development. Moreover, there are strong indications that such effects, which are visible in China today, will also occur in India and other Asian, South American and African countries in the years to come.

Generally, growing prosperity leads to rising energy demand. With growing incomes and the associated additional financial opportunities, more (new) needs are emerging to be fulfilled, typically associated with (increasing) energy consumption (including mobility, air conditioning, communication, consumption of high-quality (energy-intensive) food and consumer goods). Figure 2.5 therefore shows the energy consumption per capita of different countries above the median income of selected

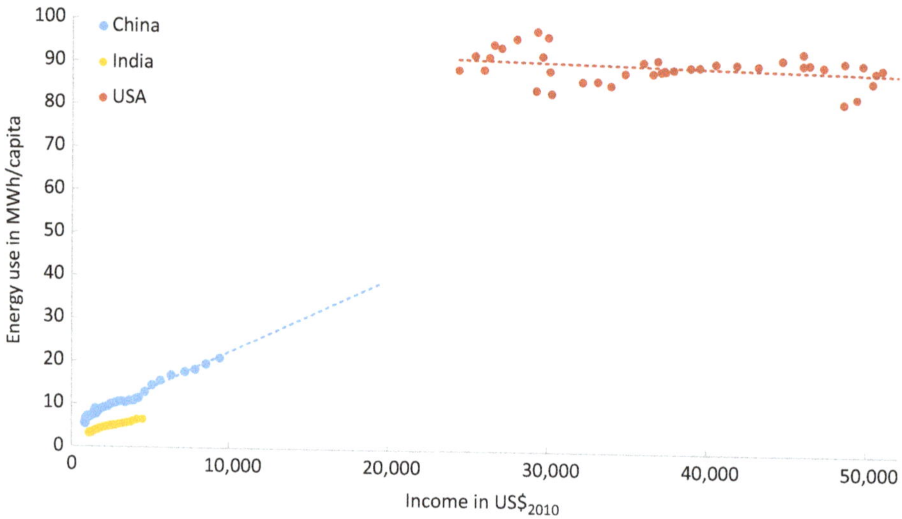

Figure 2.5: Energy consumption per capita of different countries above the median income (1970 to 2010) [8].

countries. It becomes clear that energy use correlates directly with income (especially China and India); similar tendencies are also visible in other developing and emerging countries. By contrast, energy consumption in the OECD countries – illustrated exemplarily for the USA in Figure 2.5 – is nearly independent of income. The average income in these countries is typically so high that energy costs do not dominate the expenses, so that market dependent influences have a much more significant impact, especially since industrial production typically dominates energy consumption in OECD countries. In addition, energy consumption in OECD countries has been mostly constant or even slightly declining in recent years as a result of governmental efforts.

In the medium to longer term, it is likely that the rise in energy demand due to increasing prosperity in many developing and emerging countries will approach the level of the OECD countries. Even if in the industrialized countries (OECD countries) – and also in many developing and emerging countries – further energy efficiency efforts should be more successful in the future than in the past, this development will most likely lead to a significant increase in global energy demand in the future.

Mobility

Increasing population and prosperity will inevitably lead to an increased demand for mobility services.

- Road traffic is growing globally. If around 40 million passenger cars were sold worldwide before the turn of the century, in 2017 this number was almost twice as high at around 79 million sold cars [10]. At the same time, the road network is getting better and better all over the world. Also due to these developments, the total annual mileage of the vehicles increases considerably. As a result, the efficiency gains achieved in the global fleet of vehicles have been more than compensated in recent years by an expansion in fleet size and specific mileage. In the coming years, a further increase in the vehicle fleet and thus the corresponding mileage is expected (Figure 2.6).

- In air traffic, around 4 billion passengers were counted in 2017. Current forecasts assume that the number of air passengers will almost double to 7.8 billion by 2036 [11]. Simultaneously, the average journey length also increases. In 2017, around 7 trillion passenger kilometers were recorded and by the year 2040 the number is expected to increase to about 20 trillion person kilometers (increase of average travel length by a factor of 1.5). The fastest growing market and thus the most dynamic growth is due to the rapidly rising population and increasing prosperity in Asia. Inner-Asian air traffic is expected to increase by a factor of 8 by 2042 [12]. As a result, global aviation will continue to increase significantly in the coming years (Figure 2.6).
- There is a similar trend in international shipping. In 2016, 10.3 Gt/a of freight were transported, which means an increase by factor of 4 in comparison to 1970 [13]. As a result of globalization, there has been an increased global division of labor worldwide in recent decades; this resulted in an excessive increase in international trade, which is heavily carried out by ships. There are many indications that this trend will continue in the years to come (Figure 2.6).

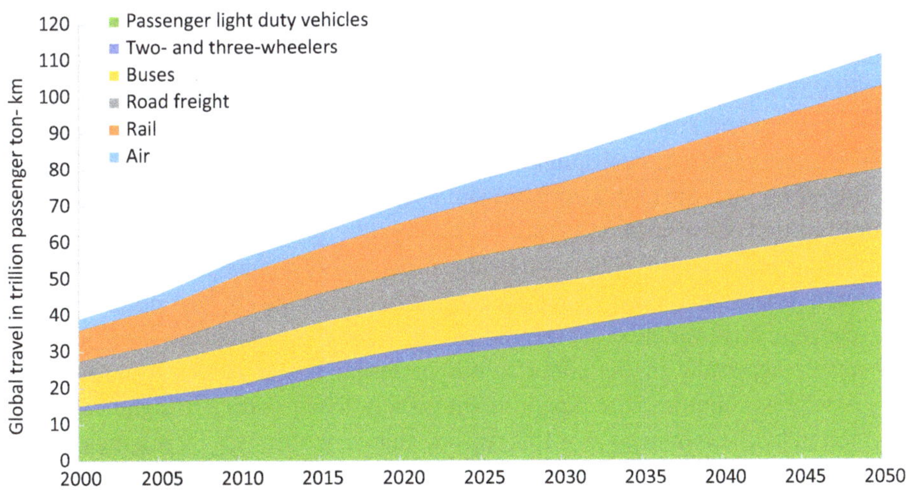

Figure 2.6: Development of the global passenger ton-kilometer performance [14].

In total, in the future disproportionately more people and goods will be transported over ever longer distances. Despite increasing transport efficiencies, this will inevitably lead to a noticeable increase in energy demand in the coming years.

ICT Products

Modern information and communication technology (ICT) has significantly changed the lives of people globally in recent years. The fundamental need for communication and the potential increase in wealth has led to a strong increase in demand for individual information technology; for years, the sales of smartphones, tablets and other such devices have been growing rapidly on a global scale. Currently about 1.45 billion devices are sold per year and by 2022 an additional 200 million devices will be sold annually. Furthermore, televisions and other multimedia devices (i.e., game consoles) add up to this [15].

Not only the direct production and use of these devices leads to a corresponding energy demand; the data centres and servers (including cloud operation) also require energy. For example, the global power consumption of data centres in 2015 sums up to around 416 TWh. Forecasts expect that this power consumption will be tripled within the next 10 years [16]. This also applies, for example, to the field of cryptocurrencies; an estimated 180 TWh of electrical energy is required to mine new Bitcoins in 2018 (this equals to Argentina's total electricity consumption) [17].

2.2.2 Environmentally Friendly Energy Supply

In many cases, the strong economic growth, coupled with the sharp rise in energy consumption in recent years and the increase in population have led to massive consequences within the natural environment – and thus in soil, water and air. In addition, anthropogenic environmental catastrophes cross national borders (e.g., the Chernobyl and Fukushima Daiichi nuclear disasters, the Deepwater Horizon explosion and the resulting oil spill in the Gulf of Mexico).

Based on this, the global environmental discussion in recent years has focused mainly on the following two topics:

- Local environmental effects. An increasingly mobile society producing more and more goods and services and increasingly concentrates in metropolitan areas, causes a huge variety of local direct or indirect energy-related environmental impacts. Especially in the conurbations or megacities of many developing and emerging countries, the health of the locally living people is significantly affected by these impacts. For this reason, many countries are increasingly implementing regulatory steps to reduce the impact of energy related environmental effects on the local environment to improve quality of life of their inhabitants.

- Global environmental effects. As a result of the Kyoto process, the need for the reduction of global greenhouse gas emissions has been recognized by more and more people and governments; i.e., 90% of the warmest years since the start of temperature records in 1880 occurred within the past decade [18]. The consequences of this globally visible development have been a multitude of multilateral agreements aiming to reduce GHG emissions in the coming years. Even though global climate gas emissions continue to increase significantly worldwide, such agreements – even if certain states have temporarily stepped out of these agreements for primarily domestic political reasons – support a rethinking process within the global energy industry.

In addition to the growing awareness related to environmental aspects, due to significant impacts on the environment in recent years (e.g., extinction of more and more species) there is also an increasing sensitivity for a (more) "sustainable development" globally. In particular, the UN have – based on the work of the Brundtland Commission – in recent decades – within its capabilities – set the course for an increasing implementation of sustainability criteria within the global and some national political frameworks. Even though many governments have implemented the relevant sustainability requirements only to a limited extent (or not at all) and only a few (globally operating) companies implement these goals in their day-to-day activities, this global framework is leading to a process of rethinking in the medium to longer term increasingly sustainable economies.

Overall, sustainable environmental management becomes increasingly important for a large number of people worldwide. For this reason, considerable R&D funds are being spent in many countries in order to develop appropriate alternatives to the "traditional" energy sources as coal, oil and gas; usually these R&D efforts are based on the reduction of local and global environmental effects.

2.2.3 Expansion of Renewable Energies

The search for and development of new energy technologies for cost-effective and environmentally and/or climate compatible coverage of the rising energy demand is a central concern of public welfare in many countries since decades. In order to reduce local and global environmental effects, "new" technological solutions for energy provision must always take into account such requirements. In this field of research, in recent decades, technological development has focused primarily on the more efficient use of wind and solar power, as these options can certainly meet the named criteria and, secondly, contribute to the decentralized, rural electricity supply, which does only exist rudimentary (or not at all) in many developing and emerging countries. In addition, significant technological progress has been made for these two energy technologies over recent years, while the specific investment was significantly reduced. At the same time, other "traditional" energy technologies have also been optimized (e.g., increasing efficiency in conventional power plants). Thus, it can be assumed for the coming years, that – as a result of the global R&D efforts – further progress will be achieved [19].

These technological trends towards more efficient and less expensive technologies for energy supply from renewable energy sources have contributed significantly to an unexpected expansion of renewable energies on a global scale; and this development will continue in the years to come due to the reasons outlined above.

2.3 Global Energy Supply and Renewable Energies

The energy system existing today has grown historically over decades. Figure 2.7 exemplary shows the development of energy use in the USA within the last 200 years. Accordingly, from 1875 onward, coal and, from around 1960, crude oil played a dominant role for covering the given energy demand. In the context of Figure 2.4, it is also clear that the considerable overall economic growth achieved during the period shown in this graphic has led to a significant increase in energy demand, especially for fossil fuels. These energy options were the most promising options from a cost and resource perspective at the time when they entered the energy market. Once an energy source option has been implemented within the market, it is typically used over a longer period to fully pay for the investments once made. Thus, the heavily

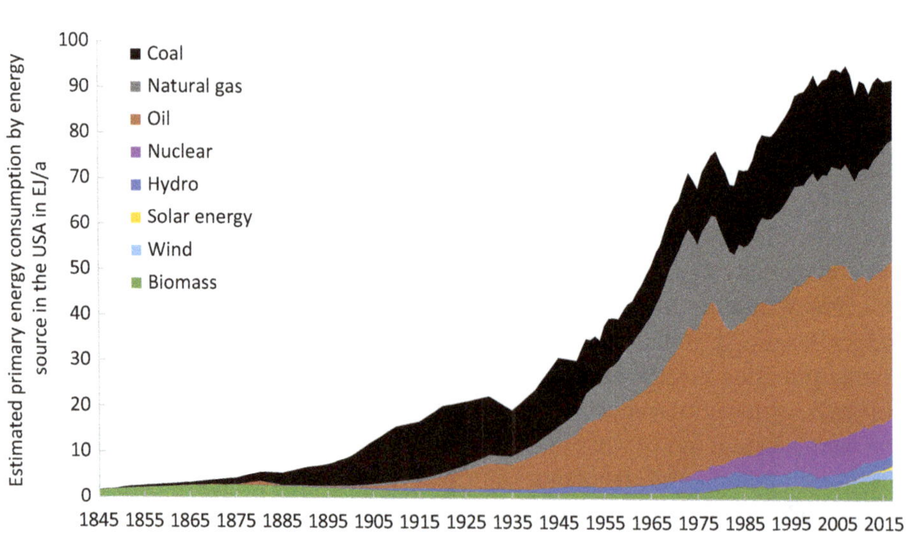

Figure 2.7: Development of energy use by source in the USA [20, 21].

fossil fuel based energy supply is a direct result of this historically evolved and developed energy supply structure and the respective national conditions that determined it. However, countries, which are at an earlier stage of development of energy supply structures compared to the US energy system, will base their decisions for a growing energy system – assuming rational decision-making – on the most promising options available today, because they do not have to take already established structures and sunk investments into account.

Since almost all of the OECD countries have developed in a way comparable to the USA, there is a clear dominance of fossil fuels in terms of total energy supply. Thus in 2017, fossil fuels accounted for more than 80% of the world's primary energy supply; coal, crude oil and natural gas are currently the most commonly used energy carrier worldwide. Renewable energies play a minor role with a total of about 14% [22].

In the electricity sector, there is a slightly different distribution. Due to the historical development, fossil fuels also dominate the electricity provision (Figure 2.8). The main sources of energy – coal and natural gas – still show a growing tendency. However, the highest growth rates are in the field of renewable energies, so that they already contribute significantly to the global electricity supply.

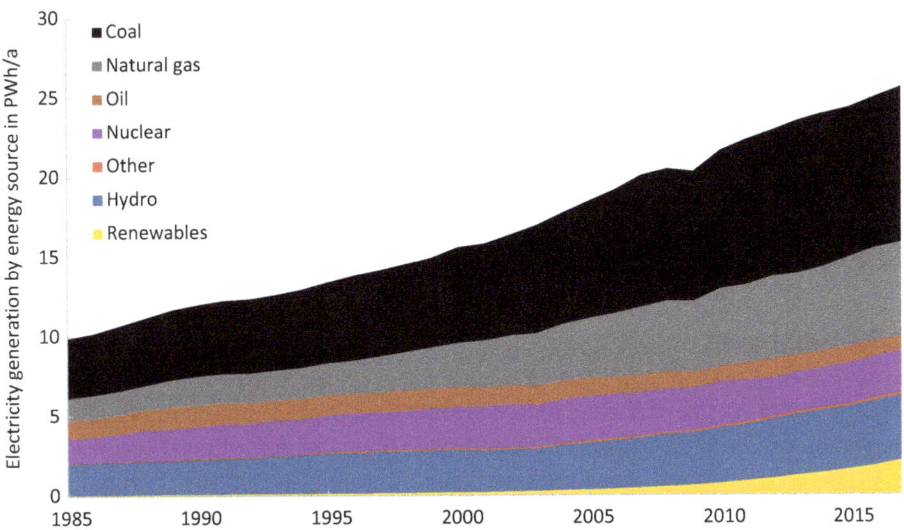

Figure 2.8: Evolution of global electricity generation [23].

Despite the continued dominance of fossil energy sources, renewable energies (including hydropower) already cover almost a quarter of global electricity production (Figure 2.9). And, in addition, this share has increased significantly in recent years, due to the fact that in the near past more and more global investment has

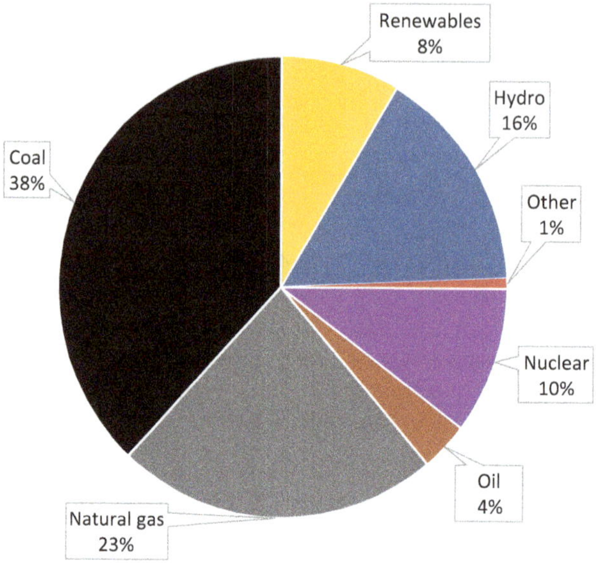

Figure 2.9: World electricity production form all energy sources in 2017 [23].

been made in developing such facilities; i.e., more than 67% of the world's installed power generation capacity in 2017 have been energy installations using renewable sources of energy as a primary energy source [24].

The trends described above have led to a significant increase in the use of renewable energies globally in recent years. Therefore, based on the current status of the global energy system, these previous developments are discussed below with a distinct focus on electricity generation.

2.3.1 Hydropower

The potential energy of a watercourse flowing, e.g., from a mountain range into the lowlands can be used to generate electricity. Typically, an artificial height drop is provided, at which the water is passed over a turbine, so that the potential energy of the water can be converted into mechanical energy, which can then be further transformed into electrical energy by an electric generator.

In 2017, around 1,154 GW of capacity were installed worldwide in hydropower plants. In total, around 4,185 TWh of electricity was generated. In 2017, approx. 23.4 GW of new capacity was added. Broken down by country, most of the power was installed in China and also most of the electricity from hydroelectric power is generated there (Figure 2.10) [25, 26].

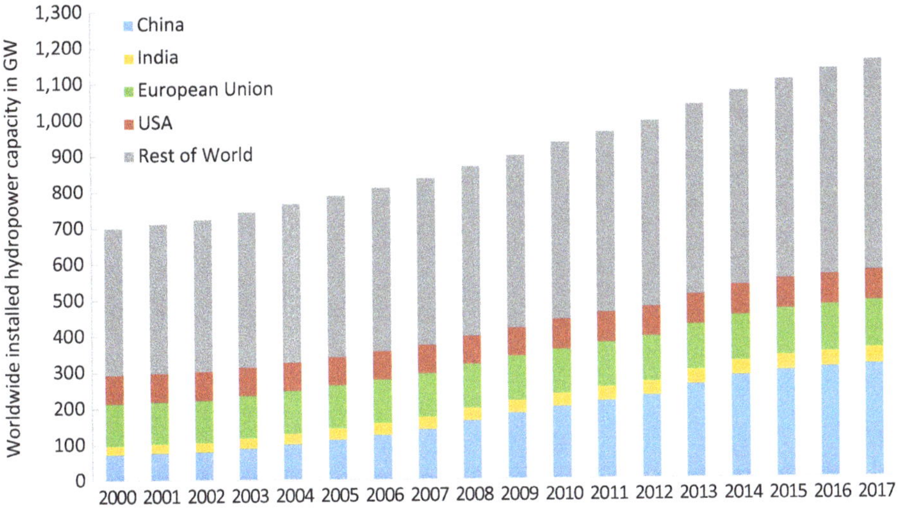

Figure 2.10: Globally installed hydropower capacity [25].

2.3.2 Photovoltaics

Due to the photovoltaic effect, there is a charge separation (that means a generation of free electrons) as a result of the solar radiation impinging on a correspondingly assembled semiconductor. Since the recombination of the separated charges is prevented by an internal electric field implemented within the photovoltaic cell material, direct current can be generated depending on the solar radiation impacting the cell surface. This direct current can be transformed via an inverter into alternate current. Since photovoltaic power generation depends directly on the available solar radiation, this is a supply-dependent power generation technology.

Photovoltaic power generation has taken an increasingly important role in global power generation systems since the end of the 2000s. At the end of 2017, around 400 GW of power had been installed worldwide (Figure 2.11); this corresponds to an increase of 99 GW or an increase in installed capacity of around one third in 2017 alone. For several years now, photovoltaics has been the world's fastest growing technology for generating electricity from renewable energies [26, 27].

The largest market for photovoltaics has been China in recent years. In 2017, 53 GW were installed there, which is more than half of the total worldwide new installations. Additionally, 10.6 GW are newly installed 2017 in the USA (54 GW in total), 9.6 GW in India (19 GW in total) and 1.7 GW in Germany (42 GW in total) [28].

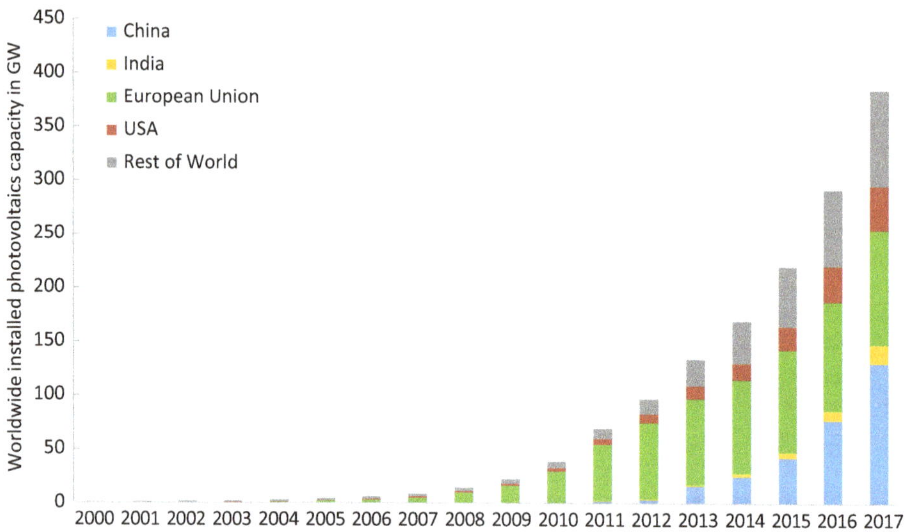

Figure 2.11: Worldwide installed photovoltaic capacity [25].

The regional distribution shows that the rapid growth of the few previously relevant markets in Asia (China, Japan, India, Thailand, South Korea) now results in a total capacity of 150 GW of photovoltaic power. Europe follows with around half of this capacity. Far less significant – despite potentially high solar yields – are Australia, the Middle East and Africa [26].

2.3.3 Wind Energy

The energy of flowing air masses and thus of wind primarily caused by regionally different solar radiation and the resulting differences in air pressure can move a suitable rotor; i.e., mechanical energy at the rotor axis can be provided. The power of this mechanical energy depends on the third power of the strongly varying wind energy – and thus the primary energy supply. An electric generator can convert the kinetic energy of the rotor axis into electrical energy.

At the end of 2017, wind turbines with an electrical output of 539 GW were installed worldwide, providing around 1,060 TWh of electrical energy (Figure 2.12). Most of the wind power plants are installed onshore; only 4% of the global wind park is installed at sea (offshore). In 2017, 52 GW of capacity was newly build worldwide. In Asia, the world's highest expansion of installed wind turbines with more than 24 GW has been realized; 20 GW were installed in China and around 4 GW in India. In particular, the less developed markets in Asia are rapidly gaining importance. In North America, 7.8 GW were installed in 2017 (of which 7.0 GW have been built in the USA) [29, 30].

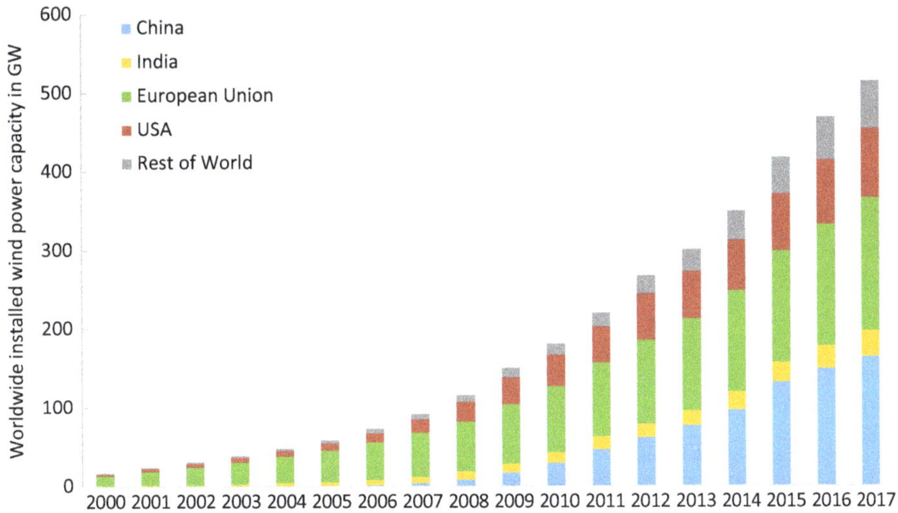

Figure 2.12: Worldwide installed wind power capacity [25].

2.3.4 Biomass

Biomass is used worldwide – beside the provision of heat and biofuel – also for electricity generation. A distinction can be made between generating electricity from solid biofuels and from biogas.

- Solid biofuels are – similar to fossil fuels – typically combusted most often within a classical grate fired system. With the produced heat, a steam process (Rankine cycle) – partly in CHP (combined heat and power) – is operated so that heat can be provided for the local consumer in addition to electrical energy, which is typically fed into the local electricity grid. At the end of 2017, around 112 GW of power plants using solid biofuels were installed, generating a total of 555 TWh of electricity. The largest existing capacities are located in the USA (17 GW) [31]. Typically, the use of solid biofuels (such as residues from the wood processing industry) also includes the use of solid organic waste fractions. For this biogenic fuel, about 2,450 plants with a capacity of around 18 GW for generating electricity are in operation worldwide. In 2017, about 330 million tons of organic waste were thermally utilized; i.e., between 82 and 110 TWh of electricity were generated [26, 32].
- Certain organic substances can be biochemically degraded in an aqueous environment with exclusion of oxygen. Within this process a so-called biogas is released, which can be used in gas engines for electricity production or for the combined generation of electricity and heat (CHP). Such processes can take place in a reactor or a landfill. For 2017, it can be assumed that the installed capacity for biogas lies between 19 to 23 GW. With this capacity, a potentially power generation of globally 114 to 137 TWh is possible. Most plants are located in Europe and the USA.

2.3.5 Geothermal Power

Under certain conditions, geothermal heat can be converted into electricity with a steam power process. Basic requirement for this is a corresponding temperature level of the accessible geothermal energy. However, due to the globally limited geothermal high-enthalpy resources, at the end of 2017 only about 13 GW of electrical power had been installed in geothermal power plants, providing about 73 TWh of electricity (Figure 2.13). The currently largest capacities are installed within the USA (3.6 GW), in the Philippines (1.9 GW) and in Indonesia (1.4 GW) [25, 26].

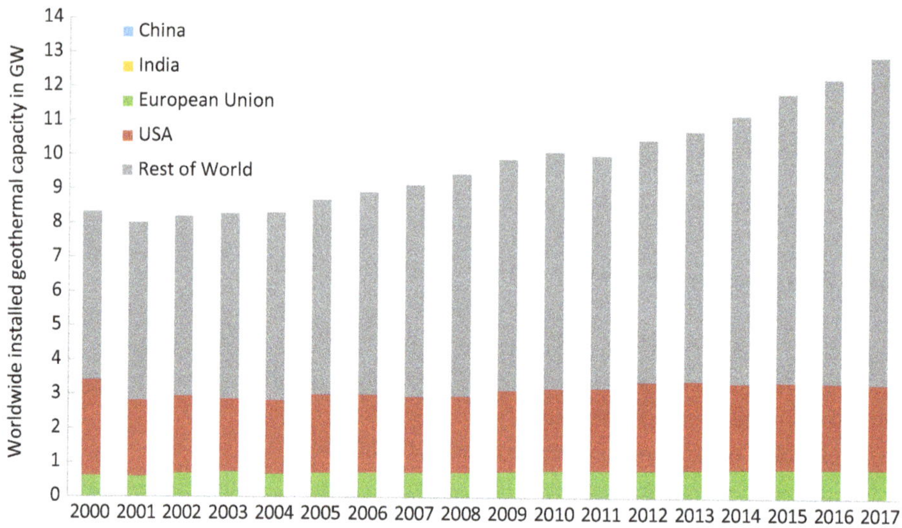

Figure 2.13: Worldwide installed geothermal capacity 2017 [25].

2.3.6 Concentrated Solar Power

The incident direct sunlight can be focused by mirror on a point or a line. This concentrated solar energy can then be further converted into thermal energy within a suitable receiver. The provided high-temperature heat can subsequently be transported by a suitable heat transfer medium directly or indirectly to a conventional steam power process (Rankine process), providing electrical energy.

In 2017, concentrated solar power plants with a total electrical output of around 5.1 GW were installed; the additional capacity realized in 2017 was only 0.1 GW (Figure 2.14). The potential electricity generation is 10 to 13 TWh [33].

At present, the world's largest capacities for concentrated solar power plants are in Spain with 2.3 GW. In the USA, 1.8 GW of capacities are under operation. In addition to these two established markets, in the past few years, countries such as South

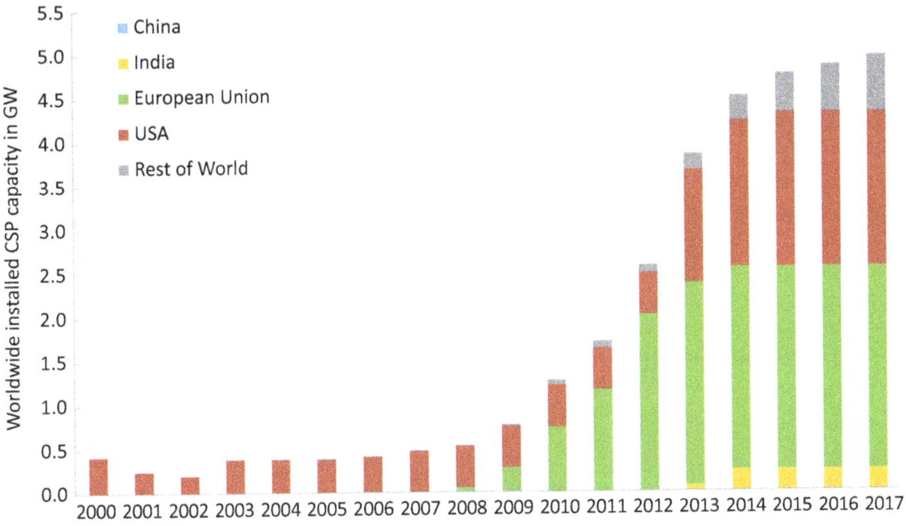

Figure 2.14: Worldwide installed CSP capacity 2017 [25].

Africa (100 MW) and Oman (9 MW) entered the markets for concentrated solar power plants [26].

2.4 Developing Trends and Needs within the Electricity System

Section 2.2 shows clearly, that the overall energy demand will increase significantly in the coming years and decades; this development seems nearly unstoppable, if no global chaotic developments (e.g., world wars) are assumed. In addition, electrical energy is becoming relatively more and more important in nearly all energy systems, as electricity can be efficiently converted into all other energy forms with existing technologies. Additionally, in many developing and emerging countries, rural development is tantamount to electrification.

Parallel to these developments, the power supply system is undergoing profound change (Section 2.3); renewable energies are becoming more and more important. As a consequence of this ongoing development, renewable power supply system's become increasingly system defining in more and more local, regional and national energy systems.

Against this background, a possible (probable) further use of the renewable energy supply for electricity generation on a global level is discussed below. The developments emerging here will then be analyzed against the background of expected developments in the area of total electricity generation; while amongst other things it is clear that in the coming years wind and solar power will cover increasingly larger shares of the world's rapidly rising electricity demand. The generation characteristics of these two electricity generation options is strongly affected by the partly stochastic and often strongly fluctuating primary energy supply of wind and solar radiation. Since the existing power supply systems are not (yet) designed for high shares of such a generation characteristic, it is discussed which technical, systemic and organizational activities need to be implemented within the global electricity markets in the years to come, so that they show no expected disadvantages for the consumer.

2.4.1 Renewable Energies

The described megatrends (Section 2.2) will significantly influence the advancement of using renewable energies in the coming decades. Additionally, most likely there will be further technological development. Consecutively, it will be discussed, which factors will dominate the development of the most important renewable energy options and how a possible advancement might look like in the following years.

Hydropower

From a technological perspective, there have not been any significant advancements of hydropower in the past decades. Independent of the ongoing improvement processes taking place also for other power production technologies (e.g., better materials, improved design tools), it is not foreseeable that there will be any major improvements in the future; the overall efficiency is already quite high (80 to 90%) and the technological lifespan is rather long (up to 100 years).

Only the strong dependency on suitable locations and the often very high specific investments – which are not expected to decline significantly despite the market expansion visible in recent years – are disadvantageous.

Globally, the investment volume for hydropower projects amounted to roughly US$ 48 billion in 2017. Many partly large projects are being developed. Especially in China, there has been an increase of up to 9 GW/a in recent years [34]. Additionally, new capacities have been built particularly in India (1.9 GW) and in Angola (1 GW) in 2017; in South America Brazil showed the largest increase with an additional capacity of 3.3 GW [34, 35].

Despite growing challenges in the development of new sites, there are still large untapped hydropower potentials globally. Thereby, sites particularly suited for large hydropower facilities are often quite remote with bad infrastructural connection and / or limited demand capacities as a result of primarily politics-related unrealized grid connections in Africa, South America and parts of Asia.

Additionally, the exploitation of such locations is often very cost-intensive. Therefore, the focus increasingly lies on developing small hydropower facilities, also partly due to otherwise restricted resources in many regions. Thus, in the coming years it seems highly probable that hydropower use will expand primarily in the field of small hydropower systems. Due to the fact that even for small hydropower facilities the availability of suitable locations will further decline (on the basis of increased development in these regions) the overall speed of expansion will most likely decrease in the next decades.

Nevertheless, due to (large) hydropower plants that are currently being constructed, hydro-based electricity generation will increase in the following years. By 2022 the installed capacity might potentially grow to around 1,400 GW (Figure 2.15) producing roughly 4,600 TWh/a of electricity. This expansion will mainly happen in Asia, Africa and South America. By the year 2030, hydropower will potentially have a global capacity of 1,500 to 1,600 GW with an electricity production of roughly 5,000 TWh/a [26]. After that, there might be a global hydropower capacity of 2,200 GW installed till 2050, which will supply around 7,300 TWh/a.

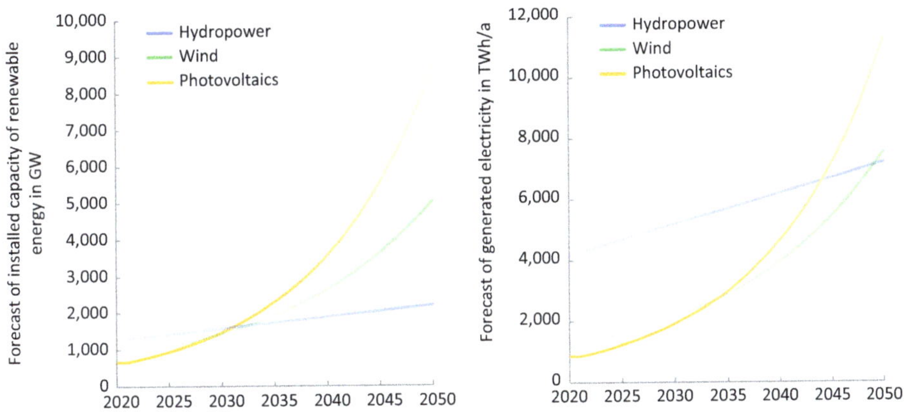

Figure 2.15: Forecast of installed capacity (left) and the generated electricity (right) of renewable energy [26].

Photovoltaics

The past decade was characterized by an unexpected technological and economic advancement of photovoltaics, concerning solar cells or rather the module as well as other system components. Today one can buy photovoltaic systems, which are durable, robust, adapted to the overall system and show rather high efficiencies. Despite these already substantial improvements, the coming years will probably still be characterized by increasing efficiencies (of photovoltaic modules and other system components) as well as a better system integration. This development was and will further be accompanied by a decline of costs/prices. This will further reduce specific investments in the future and will thus further enable the development of photovoltaic systems through lowering electricity generation costs; the most recent tender proposals in the Middle East showed electricity generation costs below 0.02 US$/kWh. To sum up, there are many indications that the upcoming years will show an ongoing decline in specific investment and an ongoing rise in overall system efficiencies [28].

In the last years, there has been a significant global expansion of photovoltaic power production; this holds true for developing, emerging and industrialized nations as well as small decentralized (rooftop) power stations and large PV power plants with multiple MW of capacity. Thereby, development potentials are nearly unlimited from a technological perspective. Rooftop areas on residential and industrial buildings, which are close to the actual demand, are abundant (and nearly untapped) and even areas for large photovoltaic power stations are available; from today's view point there are no area-related limitations foreseeable in the coming years. Considering the known development goals for the currently main active markets till 2022 and adding the remaining nations (with the average growth rate from the past years), a globally installed photovoltaic capacity of at least 835 GW (Figure 2.15) can be assumed; the electricity production would then amount to 900 till 1,300 TWh/a. With an accelerated forward projection of this expansion, until 2030 there could potentially be roughly 1,600 GW of photovoltaic capacity installed with an electricity production between 1,700 and 2,500 TWh/a. By the year 2050, there might be over 8,000 GW under operation, which could provide 8,500 to 12,500 TWh of energy each year. From today's perspective, photovoltaics will experience a huge expansion and will become one of the most important power generation technologies based on renewable energies in the years to come [26].

Wind Energy

Wind energy has also been characterized by technological improvements in the last years. Thereby, one has to differentiate between the onshore and the offshore market.

- Following a significant increase in size of onshore wind power stations primarily in the 1990s and early 2000s, the installed plant capacity is stagnating at around 3 to 5 MW for the last decade. Most recent technological advancements have been realized in plant reliability, successively increasing tower height and increasing efficiencies. This development will continue – also concerning continuously but slowly increasing installed wind mill capacities and improving adaptation to light wind locations.
- Offshore wind power showed a significant technological development in the past decade; today offshore wind park construction and operation is highly calculable even under challenging conditions at sea. Developments trends clearly

show growing installed wind mill capacities (10 MW and larger), which will be installed on ever growing foundations; the monopile is the most widely used type of foundation offshore so far and most likely also in the years to come.

Due to energy-political implementations (e.g., feed-in tariffs, calls for tender) and increasing competition, specific investments of wind power plants dropped in the past years; simultaneously plant technology has been successively improved. This development, which has been most significant for offshore wind exploitation, will most likely continue in the following years. Based on this ongoing cost reduction, power generation from offshore wind parks with a good connection to the coast and high average wind speeds can partly compete with the power production cost of onshore wind parks. Especially through new wind mill technology and intelligent maintenance schemes (e.g., predictive maintenance), downtime could be minimized and thus the plant availability be optimized. A dampening effect on onshore wind expansion might be the fact that for some countries most attractive sites are already developed. This results in additional pressure to advance in offshore wind technology in these countries. Nevertheless, there are many countries with huge untapped onshore wind potentials with partly very high average wind speeds, which might be developed in the coming years; therefore, globally there are no real restrictions to wind power potential.

Adding up national goals for on- and offshore wind power expansion, about 50 to 60 GW of additional capacity will be installed in the coming years. The most significant expansion will happen in Asia, followed by Europe and North America. By 2022, there could potentially be wind power plants in operation with a total installed capacity of 370 GW in Asia, 250 GW in Europe and up to 160 GW in North America. This corresponds to a global installed capacity of about 840 GW (Figure 2.15), which would allow for an electricity production of around 1,700 TWh/a. Only roughly 50 GW of this will be installed offshore, so that only 120 TWh/a of electricity can be supplied by offshore wind parks. Assuming a continuously progressive expansion, one can expect a global installed capacity of 1,400 GW with an electricity production of 3,000 TWh/a by the year 2030. Until 2050 – implying an ongoing stable expansion – there might be roughly 5,000 GW of wind power installed. These wind parks can potentially supply around 10,000 TWh/a of electricity. Therefore, in the long run wind power and photovoltaics will most likely show the largest market shares of renewable energies [26].

Biomass

Modern biomass utilization has increased globally for heat production as well as for electricity generation in the last decades, due to increasingly improved conversion technologies. This holds true mainly for the use of organic residues, by-products and waste. The use of energy crops plays – apart from very few exceptions due to national legislation – no significant role globally. Those biogenic material flows can either be utilized thermally (i.e., thermochemical conversion) or be transformed to biogas (i.e., biochemical conversion); for the former option, one typically uses dry organic material streams and for the latter one uses organic material with water contents significantly above 50%.

- The combustion of solid, dry biomass (including organic waste) with subsequent electricity generation based on a conventional steam power process is state-of-the-art. Due to parallels to coal and non-biogenic waste combustion and the looming development tendencies in these fields, no significant advancements in biomass combustion technology are expected in the coming years. Independent of that, conversion plants will be further optimized, with increased life spans and increasingly smaller electrical capacities, but still relatively high electrical efficiencies. Biomass gasification will most likely – despite theoretical advantages – not see a global breakthrough in the coming 10 to 15 years.
- Anaerobic fermentation has seen a much stronger technological development in the past years compared to combustion technology. Today there are process facilities for nearly every organic material stream, even though many of those solutions still have clear potential for technological improvements. This holds true for biogas generation as well as for the efficient use of fermentation residues (i.e., digested slurry). Therefore, it can be expected, that this technology will experience increased used, especially for organic residential waste and undergo various technological improvements to higher efficiencies, a more stable operation and a better integration with up- and downstream process steps (e.g., with composting of the fermentation residues for a more efficient use) in the following years.

Primarily due to economic reasons, biomass utilization will be restricted to organic wastes, by-products and residues, which occur during agricultural or forestry based primary production or due to industrial processing and end use. Typical material streams used as a solid biofuel are bagasse, bark and scrap wood and characteristic substances with a higher water content are manure, organically contaminated washing water, slop and whey as well as food residues from industrial kitchens; the latter are predestinated to be used as a biogas substrate. The volume of such material streams directly depends on primary production, which itself is defined by population growth and its specific food consumption. A growing global population with increasing overall wealth leads to an increase of such material streams. Thus, biomass will increasingly be used in the coming years. This use will nevertheless be restricted to the discussed material streams.

With a continuing increase of the globally installed capacity of biomass fired power plants until 2022 about 112 GW of installed capacity might be available worldwide. This leads to an electricity supply from solid biomass of about 360 TWh and of biogenic solid waste streams of about 100 TWh. Till 2030 this installed capacity could rise to 130 GW with a potential energy supply of about 450 TWh from solid biomass and 150 TWh from organic waste streams. Until the year 2050 global installed capacity could amount to about 190 GW (850 to 950 TWh/a).

Assuming a moderate growth power generation from biogas is expected to reach an installed capacity of 25 GW by 2022. These power plants could generate up to 162 TWh of electricity per year. Until 2030 there might be 30 GW of installed capacity producing 230 TWh/a of electricity [26]. In the year 2050 this value could additionally increase up to 40 GW (about 300 TWh/a).

Overall Electricity Supply

Even though renewable energies are currently experiencing an unexpected fast expansion (section 2.3), they will only make up a (small, but gradually increasing) part of global electricity supply in the coming years. Even in the future, fossil and nuclear energy sources will contribute (slowly declining) to cover the global electricity demand. Therefore, Figure 2.16 shows – originating from the historical development – a projection of the evolution of the global power supply system.

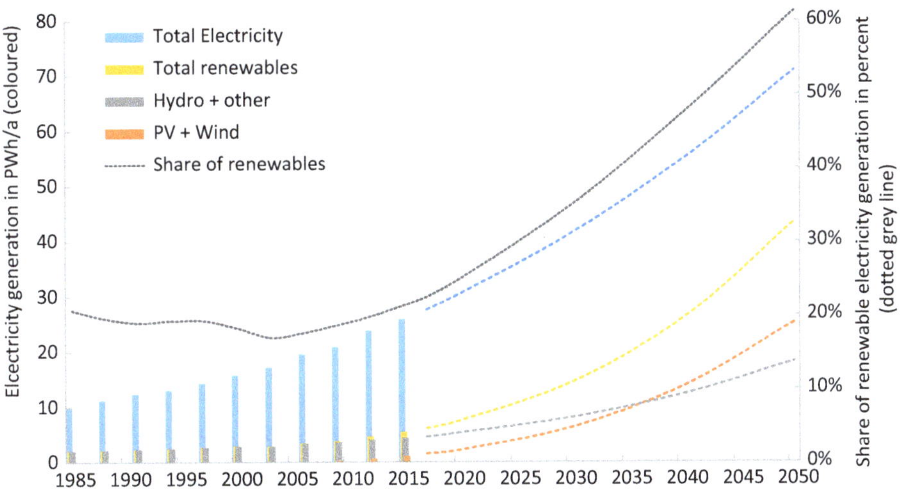

Figure 2.16: Forecast of global electricity generation (colored: left axis; dotted gray line: right axis) [23].

Irrespective of whether the actual development will proceed approximately like Figure 2.16 or whether the electricity demand will rise even more intensely – or less, due to possible global crisis – the diagram especially shows the following aspects.

- Coal (hard coal and lignite) as well as natural gas will contribute considerably to global electricity production. Many power plants using these fossil primary energy sources have already been built and fossil fuels are abundant and inexpensive in some regions. Additionally, these power plants can typically be operated demand-orientated.

- The use of nuclear power has been constant (or even declining) over the last decade. Due to high specific investments and still unsolved disposal issues concerning the radioactive nuclear waste, a significant expansion of nuclear power plants is not expected in the coming years. The strong price decline of renewable energies in recent years supports this development significantly.
- Electricity generation from hydropower has strongly expanded during the last two decades. The biggest driver of these tendencies was and still is China. Currently, multiple large hydropower plants are being planned or are already under construction. Therefore, hydropower will continue to grow in the years to come. Nevertheless, this option will lose shares related to the overall electricity production due to increasing shortage of cost-effective exploitable sites.
- The use of wind power and especially solar radiation showed an intense expansion-dynamic during recent years, although still on a low level. Due to the abundant and nearly untapped potential, the price drop in recent years, the possibility of a modular expansion and the good possibilities for integration into local and decentralized energy systems, this development will most likely continue for wind power as well as photovoltaics and will even accelerate. If this highly probable tendency will take effect, even further cost reductions are to be expected – an over proportional growth of wind and photovoltaic power provision on a global scale is therefore most likely. Support for this development also comes from the worldwide urged advancements in battery technology, which, especially for more rural, decentralized implementations in combination with photovoltaic systems, contribute to a cost-effective overall solution. Nevertheless, the largest expansion of wind and solar power can be expected as part of the grid-connected electricity supply.
- All other power production options from fossil or renewable energies will most likely not contribute significantly to electricity production in the coming decades; nevertheless, some local variations and deviations from this global tendency are possible (e.g., geothermal energy in Iceland).

All in all, this means that electricity supply systems will increasingly include higher shares of fluctuating power production from wind and solar radiation. Additionally, photovoltaic systems (and partly wind power plants) are often installed in quite small units/systems; that means that the power supply will be realized by a strongly increasing number of (very) small generating units in more and more decentralized production structures.

2.4.2 Challenges

Against the background of these expansion tendencies on the production side, currently existing electricity supply systems and structures have to be evolved and advanced technologically and systemically. Existing structures – including the current regulatory framework – will only quite limitedly be able to guarantee a secure energy supply – which is state-of-the-art in OECDnations and necessary for an interruption-free industrial production – with higher shares of fluctuating wind and solar power production. Therefore, the whole power supply system has to be technologically improved to cope with an increasing share of fluctuating energy sources. This goal can be reached through various options.

- An increased flexibility of power plants and thus the electricity production.
- An improved spatial and temporal compensation of fluctuations (i.e., strong grids, large scale storage systems).
- An increased flexibility of demand and therefore the consumers of the electrical energy.
- A coupling between the power production system and other energy systems (i.e., sector-coupling; e.g., heat supply).

Following, different activities, which affect different areas of the power supply system, will be further discussed.

Increased flexibility of electricity production

To securely and adequately supply a given demand even with a strongly fluctuating primary energy availability from wind or solar radiation, more flexible production structures are urgently needed. This flexibility should be as independent of the given primary energy as possible. This is only partly possible solely from solar radiation and wind, considering the limitedly controllable production of wind power plants and photovoltaic systems due to their dependency on the wind and solar energy supply. Therefore, these options for electricity production increasingly call for power plants and other measures to flexibly meet the residual load in a secure manner.

- **Power reduction or shutdown.** Power production from wind power plants and photovoltaic systems can be reduced or turned off quite easily. For instance, wind power plants can rotate their rotor blades and therefore their rotor away from the wind direction and thus reduce their power supply significantly in a matter of seconds. Nevertheless, this power reduction results in a loss of potentially (inexpensively) available electricity. This may result in economic drawbacks.
- **Forecast quality.** A high calculability of power production from renewable energies improves the possibility to securely meet a given demand. However,

forecasts for wind and solar power production currently often show considerable mistakes especially for longer prognosis periods. An improved forecast quality therefore can contribute to securely integrate higher shares of fluctuating power production from renewable energies into electricity supply systems.
- **Increased flexibility of further electricity production.** Another option is to increase the flexibility of power plants, which have to meet the demand, that cannot be fulfilled by the power production from wind and photovoltaics (i.e., the residual load). Especially for thermal power plants (e.g., biomass and biogas based power production, whose primary energy is storable) and/or (storage) hydropower plants this most likely results in the demand for even higher load gradients with potentially fewer full load hours [36]. For that, the existing plants have to be upgraded and/or new and improved plants have to be installed.
- **Regulatory framework.** An adapted regulatory framework has to assure, that this kind of production structures emerge from the currently existing supply structures.

Compensation of fluctuation

Non-controllable fluctuation, for instance from wind or solar power, can be homogenized in a spatial and temporal manner in regard to a given demand. This will be discussed below.

Renewable energies are unevenly distributed geographically. For instance, solar radiation is generally higher the closer a region is to the equator. Analogously there are regions with clearly above average mean wind speeds (e.g., coastal areas). For example, in Northern Germany there are many wind power plants installed due to high average wind speeds close to the coast, and in the Southern part of Germany an over-proportional amount of photovoltaic systems are installed due to the higher solar radiation [37]. If high wind speeds occur, the existing wind power plants feed large amounts of electricity into the grid, which may exceed the local demand. These energy quantities have to be transported by the local, regional and national grid to the existing demand centres. If this is not possible, due to missing power lines and/or limited transport capacities, power production from wind mills has to be partly shut down, leading to a loss of available (cheap) renewable energy [38]. One option to minimize these transport capacity-related and economically not necessarily reasonable shutdowns, lies in the expansion of existing grid structures. Through an improvement / extension of existing transport capacities or installation of additional power lines, transport capacities can be increased, to enable the energy transport from a locally high-energy supply to regions, with a simultaneously existing high demand. This holds locally, regionally, nationally and probably also internationally.

Besides transport grid capacities, due to increasing shares of fluctuating renewable energies – and especially decentralized photovoltaic power production – also the local distribution grids have to be adapted. Due to the fact, that for instance photovoltaic systems are often installed locally (e.g., on rooftops), existing low voltage grids have to increasingly function as energy collectors to take up photovoltaic electricity and transport it into the next higher grid level. If the installed capacity exceeds the designed maximum power of local grid structures, an extension of these distribution grids might also be necessary.

In addition to such a regional compensation, energy storage can compensate fluctuation over time. Such a storage can guarantee the availability of electricity, even when the supply of renewable energies is strongly restricted (e.g., situations with lack of wind and solar radiation). Therefore, below some energy storage concepts are discussed.

- **Pumped-storage power plants.** One energy storage option, which is already quite prevalent today, are pumped-storage power plants. Through the shifting of water between a geodetically high and a geodetically low water reservoir with the help of pumps and turbines, these plants are (market-oriented) able to store or supply electrical energy. Storage efficiencies of around 80% are possible (power to power) [39]. These plants can be operated highly dynamic. Low start-up and shut-down times allow to react very flexibly to fluctuations of demand and / or production. However, the potential to install such systems depends strongly on local circumstances (i.e., size of reservoir, usable height difference). In some regions (e.g., Norway, Switzerland) there are good opportunities but in other areas (e.g., the Netherlands) opportunities are rather limited (or not given at all). These regional differences based on geographical circumstances again require good grid interconnections and transport capacities.
- **Compressed air power station.** Energy can also be stored in compressed air power stations. Here, air is compressed to a high pressure and stored, e.g., in salt caverns. This air can be relaxed through a turbine, if electricity demand exceeds renewable power generation again. Storage efficiencies can amount to about 60%. Geographical circumstances (like underground caverns) are also important for such a storage option. Because these conditions are not given everywhere, this type of energy storage also needs sufficient grid capacities.
- **Electrochemical battery storage.** Especially on the small scale, electrochemical batteries are an additional possibility. Here, energy is stored as chemical energy through the change of electrical charge. Losses are often (relatively) small and even the storage of larger amounts of energy is possible by scaling multiple batteries [40]. Such battery storage systems are currently evolving quite rapidly – from a technological (i.a., higher efficiencies, higher storage density) and an economic (i.e., significant cost reduction in the last years) perspective. Therefore, already today e.g., in Germany every second photovoltaic system below 30 kW is installed in combination with a battery storage [41]. The major advantages of such systems

are the easily realizable scalability and – in contrast to the already mentioned options – the high independency of the specific location (a battery can basically be installed everywhere). Therefore, these systems do not necessarily need the same grid extension / improvement as the first two options.

Increasing flexibility of demand

Much like the production of electricity, the demand for power can be realized in a more flexible way. The goal is to adapt the instantaneous demand as far as possible to the naturally given simultaneous supply of fluctuating renewable energies. Consumers therefore would be able to participate more actively within the electricity supply system.

Intelligently shutting-down or starting-up electrical loads can influence the demand for electrical energy. For instance, flexible industrial plants could be started-up every time, when there is a high availability from renewable energies (and thus quite inexpensive power) and be shut down, when prices are high due to low availability of renewable energies. High potentials are given in industrial processes, e.g., in time-flexible processes of the metal processing industry. Additionally, electrical systems, that do not have to be operated continuously (e.g., cooling aggregates in large cold storages, heat pumps during the transition period, water pumps in mining industry) and have some sort of storage effect / flexibility can be operated more beneficially for the system. Such potentials can be developed quite easily (e.g., through an adequate tariff system) [42].

To realize some demand side flexibility, intelligent control concepts will become more and more important. Information and communication technology, which has been steadily improved during recent years, enables solutions for large industrial consumers. Additionally, small and private consumers can be integrated into such innovative power supply systems in a cost-effective manner.

Sector coupling

So far, the different parts of the overall energy system (e.g., electricity supply, heat supply, mobility) have been treated mostly separately. Additionally, some energy provision systems, which do not originally rely on electrical energy, are often much more flexible than electricity-based systems. For instance, the heat capacity of highly insulated buildings enables some kind of flexibility for heat production (e.g., through heat pumps) even with low outdoor temperatures. Therefore, the basic idea of the so-called sector coupling is to meet the energy demand in one sector through another sector by simultaneously offering system services to the other sector, by increasing the inter connectivity of both energy sectors using available flexibilities. A typical example of such sector coupling is the system-beneficial operation of heat pumps. Due to the storage effect of buildings, heat pumps can partly obtain electricity in times, when there might be an energy surplus from renewable energies, which otherwise would have to be shut down. Thus below, some concepts of sector coupling are discussed.

- **Power-to-heat.** The transformation of electrical to thermal energy is called power-to-heat. Essentially, there are two different supply concepts. Either, the heat demand is completely covered through the utilization of electricity (e.g., heat pump), or electrical energy is used situationally (for instance, if there is a surplus of energy from renewable sources) in a hybrid heating system (i.e., there are at least two energy carriers at use – like gas and electricity – and the electrical energy only serves as some kind of fuel saver). Heat supply by the use of heat pumps is a very efficient way of sector coupling, especially for new buildings with large surface heating systems (and therefore a low upper temperature level) and often very high storage effects of the respective heating system. Concerning the overall electricity supply system, heat pumps primarily lead to an increase of power and energy demand during wintertime, which anyhow shows a higher demand. With an increasing use of heat pumps, they have to be operated in a more system beneficial way based on intelligent controlling algorithms. In contrast, direct electrical heating describes the dissipative transformation of electricity into thermal energy. The overall energy efficiency of such systems is much lower in comparison to heat pumps, because at most, only the electrical energy that is given into such a power-to-heat system can be used thermally. Nevertheless, this option is a highly flexible measure to situationally take up surpluses, which otherwise would have been shut down. Such systems can stabilize the electricity supply system in the event of a possible overproduction of power from wind and solar radiation or a sudden failure of some large consumer. To significantly impact the electricity system, one has either to install large electric heaters in district heating systems or to connect a multitude of small decentralized installations to a cluster and control them by the use of intelligent algorithms.
- **E-mobility**. Electricity can be used to directly power the engine of vehicles. For rail-based transport, this is state-of-the-art. An additional future market is the electricity-based individual mobility. Here a vehicle is powered by an electric engine fed by a battery. Therefore, a reliable battery technology is needed. Additionally, an exhaustive development of loading infrastructure is necessary. If such electric vehicles are operated intelligently and beneficially for the overall system, they can provide system services within the electricity system. Another benefit is the locally nearly emission-free operation with strongly reduced noise emissions in comparison to conventional vehicles.
- **Power-to-gas.** A further possibility to couple multiple subsystems constitutes the power-to-gas technology. Electricity is used to split water by electrolysis into hydrogen and oxygen. The hydrogen can either be used directly (instantaneously or after storage) in other applications (e.g., fuel cell vehicle), or alternatively and additionally it is also possible to produce synthetic methane by adding carbon

dioxide to the hydrogen in further processing steps. For the direct use of hydrogen so far no infrastructure and end-use technologies are available; storage and distribution of hydrogen as well as the development of the respective end-use technologies is typically quite cost intensive. Methane – as the second option – is, as the main component of natural gas, a very flexibly usable energy carrier, which can be used in various energy sectors and be integrated in the often already existing natural gas infrastructure. The latter typically contains large gas storage systems allowing to store the transformed electricity in large amounts. Subsequently, the gas can be integrated in all markets, which today run on natural gas. A downside of such concepts are the so far rather low transformational efficiencies and the high costs for the provision of this synthetic methane.

- **Power-to-liquid.** Another similar concept is the power-to-liquid technology. Hydrogen gained by electrolysis, is – under the addition of carbon dioxide – transformed to a liquid energy carrier, which fulfils all specifications of currently used fuels. Therefore, one can rely on the existing petroleum infrastructure. This holds also for the storage of such energy carriers. These fuels can easily be utilized in existing drive technology (e.g., aviation, shipping). In comparison to power-to-gas, due to additional process steps, power-to-liquid is characterized by even lower efficiencies. However, power-to-liquid allows to continue to use the existing vehicle fleet.

Thereby, the described measures can contribute to further integrate electricity in other sectors and simultaneously generate benefits in the electricity system itself. To use these synergies beneficially for both coupled energy sectors, intelligent concepts are needed, which realize this cost-efficiently and securely. Another important condition are regulatory frameworks to support such approaches.

2.5 Conclusion

Power supply systems have been, are, and will be subject to a permanent process of adaptation and change. This change has been characterized in recent decades by a strong expansion of installed capacities, first by the construction of “classical” power plants based on coal and natural gas and only in recent years increasingly by conversion plants using renewable sources of energy – and here in addition to the traditional hydropower mainly wind power and photovoltaics. In the coming years, an increasing expansion of the use of the latter two options is expected, since they are relatively inexpensive and can be installed modular. Thus – if the developments emerging today prove to continue in the years to come – a fluctuating power generation characteristic will determine power supply systems and dominate them in the longer term.

Such a development can only be successful, if it goes hand in hand with a corresponding energy system transformation or a paradigm shift within the power supply sector. In the past, the electricity supply approximately followed a simple distribution; large-scale power plants have generated electricity, which has then been distributed via distribution networks to end customers (Figure 2.17). As a result of the described developments, this structure will (or has to) change considerably in the coming years and decades.

In the context of this system change, activities – if consistent supply security has to be ensured – must be taken to develop the supply system for the future:

- on the power generation side
- in the transmission of electricity and its determining system components (e.g., network coverage, storage)
- on the demand side
- at the coupling to other (partial) energy systems

There are quite various activities, possibilities, approaches, concepts and even only first considerations, which can cover the resulting needs due to the transformation process with higher shares of electricity from fluctuating renewable sources of energy to provide a stable electricity system with a high level of security of supply. The presented approaches must be further developed in the interplay between each other in the future and implemented successively into the market, since it is not expected that the upcoming challenge of a secure electricity supply under the mentioned conditions and developments will be achievable only with one activity / only one single measure. This includes technical aspects (corresponding technical developments) and, above all, organizational changes as well as modifications in the market design and in the statutory energy regulatory framework.

Figure 2.17 illustrates these transformation processes. The historical top-down structure of the electricity supply will increasingly develop into a more integrated structure. The industry and private end consumers are more and more interacting with the distribution structures and the conventional power plants are being successively reduced. Such a transformation may also contribute to the decrease of global fossil fuels usage.

These challenges are manageable. In addition, many different solutions are currently being tested and developed. In order to achieve a market implementation – with all its consequences – it requires a further paradigm shift in the energy and electricity industries. Therefore, Table 2.1 shows a compilation of the previous paradigm with regard to power generation with a focus on renewable energies and the emerging – and necessary – future developments. Accordingly, the way of thinking must change from a rather singular consideration of power generation technology based on renewable energies and their optimization to an overall system view. The limit of system optimization must be gradually extended to the power system and, in a further step, to the energy system as a whole. If this perspective sets in in the short to medium term – and a practical alternative to this is not recognizable – solutions for the challenges discussed will be found as part of this paradigm shift.

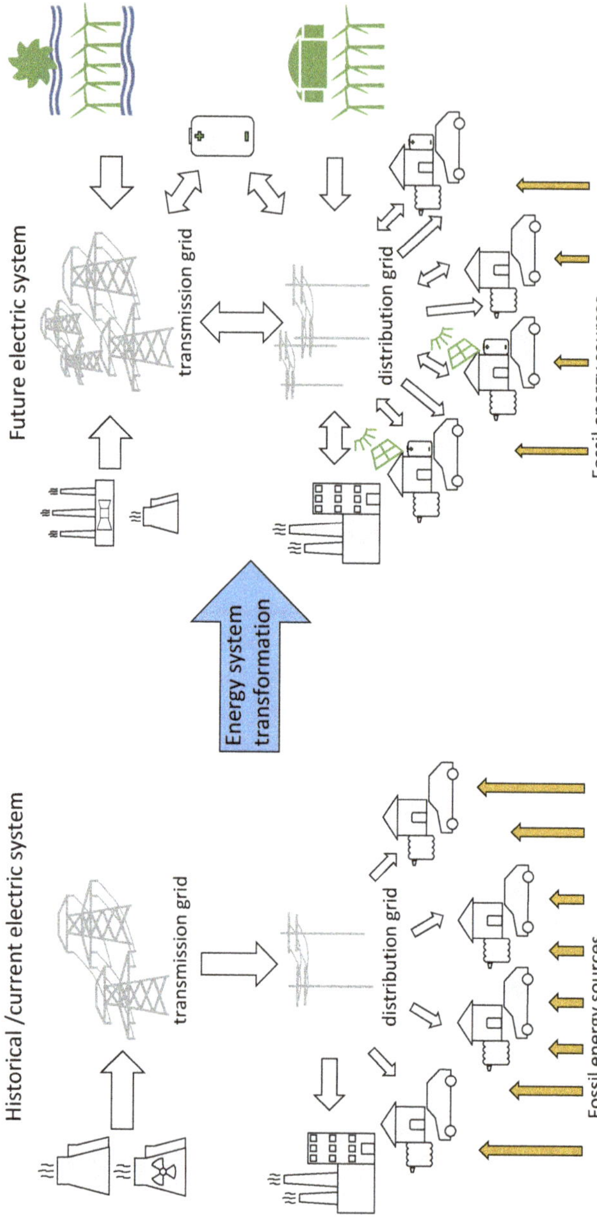

Figure 2.17: Energy system transformation (gray arrows: flow of electricity; brown arrows: flow of fossil fuels), own representation.

Table 2.1: Necessary paradigm shift in the electricity supply (own representation).

Historical	Future
Electricity generation based on fossil fuels with minor integration of electricity from renewable energies.	Transformation of the electricity system to take account of an energy system based on renewable energies.
Adjusting the conventional electricity generation to the simultaneously given demand for electrical energy (load following operation).	Flexibilization of electricity demand and integration of further flexibility measures to respond to increasingly fluctuating power generation.
Primary technical development of renewable energies.	Primary development of energy conversion technologies and system concepts that contribute to safe electricity supply and enable the handling of strongly fluctuating power generation.
Cost reduction (specific investments, operating costs) of renewable energy facilities.	Cost reduction of renewable energy facilities as well as of system concepts that are becoming increasingly important for dealing with fluctuating generation.
Mostly independent view of the electricity, heating and crude oil market and their independent optimal development.	Integrative optimization of all (sub-) energy markets in the entire energy system, taking advantage of possible cross-sector synergy effects.

References

[1] BP p.l.c. 2018a. *BP Statistical Review of World Energy 2018.* London.

[2] BP p.l.c. 2018b. *BP Energy Outlook.* 2018 edition. London.

[3] Umweltbundesamt. 2018. *Trends der Lufttemperatur.* https://www.umweltbundesamt.de/daten/klima/trends-der-lufttemperatur.

[4] Bundesamt für Meteorologie und Klimatologie MeteoSchweiz. n.d. Messdaten der Wetterstation Basel. https://www.meteoswiss.admin.ch/home.html?tab=overview.

[5] Heinz, Andreas, Martin Kaltschmitt, and Hermann Hofbauer. 2005. "Anwendung energetischer und nicht-energetischer Ressourcen in Energiesystemen: Vergleichende Bewertung." *Umweltwissenschaften und Schadstoff-Forschung* 17, no. 3 (May): 146–50.

[6] United Nations DESA/Population Division. 2017. *World Population Prospects 2017.* https://population.un.org/wpp/Download/Standard/Population/.

[7] Bundesministerium für Wirtschaft und Energie. 2018. *Primärenergieverbrauch nach Ländern und Regionen.* https://www.bmwi.de/Redaktion/DE/Binaer/Energiedaten/Internationaler-Energiemarkt/energiedaten-int-energiemarkt-01-xls.xlsx?__blob=publicationFile&v=19.

[8] Gapminder Foundation. n.d. Based on free material from GAPMINDER.ORG, CC-BY LICENSE. www.gapminder.org.

[9] The World Bank. n.d. World Bank national accounts data, and OECD National Accounts data files. data.worldbank.org.

[10] Scotiabank Economics. 2018. Global Auto Report.

[11] International Air Transport Association (IATA). 2017. "2036 Forecast Reveals Air Passengers Will Nearly Double to 7.8 Billion." https://www.iata.org/pressroom/pr/Pages/2017-10-24-01.aspx.

[12] ICOA. 2016. *ICAO Long-Term Traffic Forecasts: Passenger and Cargo*. https://www.icao.int/Meetings/aviationdataseminar/Documents/ICAO-Long-Term-Traffic-Forecasts-July-2016.pdf.
[13] United Nations Conference on Trade and Development. 2017. *Review of Maritime Transport 2017*. United Nations, New York and Geneva.
[14] International Energy Agency (IEA). 2012. *Global Transport Outlook to 2050: Targets and Scenarios for a Low-Carbon Transport Sector*.
[15] International Data Corporation. 2018. "With Expectations of a Positive Second Half of 2018 and Beyond, Smartphone Volumes Poised to Return to Growth, According to IDC." https://www.idc.com/getdoc.jsp?containerId=prUS44240118.
[16] DEIF A/S. n.d. Notstrom. Anwendungsleitfaden für Rechenzentren. Skive.
[17] Frankfurter Allgemeine Zeitung. 2018. "Kryptoanlagen: Die Stromjagd der Bitcoin-Branche." http://www.faz.net/aktuell/finanzen/finanzmarkt/bitcoin-produktion-verbraucht-mehr-strom-als-haushalte-15518138.html.
[18] National Centers for Environmental Information. 2017. *Global Climate Report – Annual 2017*. Section: Ten Warmest Years (1880–2017). https://www.ncdc.noaa.gov/sotc/global/201713.
[19] Christoph Kost, Shivenes Shammugam, and Verena Jülch et al. 2018. *Stromgestehungskosten Erneuerbare Energien*. Freiburg.
[20] U.S. Energy Information Administration. 2018. "Appendix D: Estimated Primary Energy Consumption in the United States, Selected Years, 1635–1945." *Monthly Energy Review* (September). https://www.eia.gov/totalenergy/data/monthly/pdf/sec13_21.pdf.
[21] U.S. Energy Information Administration. n.d. "Primary Energy Consumption by Source." https://www.eia.gov/totalenergy/data/browser/index.php?tbl=T01.03#?f=A&start=1949&end=2017&charted=1-2-3-5-12-11.
[22] Bundeszentrale für politische Bildung. 2019. "Zahlen und Fakten: Globalisierung. Primärenergie-Versorgung." http://www.bpb.de/nachschlagen/zahlen-und-fakten/globalisierung/52741/primaerenergie-versorgung.
[23] BP p.l.c. 2019. "Statistical Review of World Energy. All data, 1965–2017." https://www.bp.com/en/global/corporate/energy-economics/statistical-review-of-world-energy/downloads.html.
[24] Frankfurt School – UNEP Centre. 2018. *Global Trends in Renewable Energy Investment 2018*. Frankfurt am Main.
[25] International Renewable Energy Agency. n.d. "Renewable Electricity Capacity and Generation Statistics." http://resourceirena.irena.org/gateway/dashboard/?topic=4&subTopic=54.
[26] Janet Witt, Annika Magdowski, Sebastian Janczik, and Martin Kaltschmitt. 2017. "Erneuerbare Energien Weltweit: Globaler Stand 2017." *BWK* 70, nos. 7–8: 15–35.
[27] Fraunhofer Insitute for Solar Energy Systems ISE. 2018. *Photovoltaics Report*. Freiburg.
[28] SolarPower Europe. 2018. *Global Market Outlook for Solar Power / 2018–2022*. Brussels.
[29] Global Wind Energy Council. 2018. *Global Wind Report: Annual Market Update 2017*. Brussels.
[30] International Renewable Energy Agency. 2018. *Renewable Capacity Statistics 2018*. Abu Dhabi.
[31] Renewable Energy Policy Network. 2018. *Renewables 2018: Global Status Report*. Paris.
[32] ecoprog GmbH. 2017. *Waste to Energy 2017/2018: Technologies, Plants, Projects, Players and Backgrounds of the Global Thermal Waste Treatment Business*. Cologne.
[33] HELIOSCSP. 2018. "Concentrated Solar Power Installed Capacity Increased to 5133 MW by the End of 2017." http://helioscsp.com/concentrated-solar-power-installed-capacity-increased-to-5133-mw-by-the-end-of-2017/.
[34] International Hydropower Association. 2018. *Hydropower Status Report 2018: Sector Trends and Insights*. London.
[35] International Hydropower Association. 2017. *Hydropower Status Report 2017: Sector Trends and Insights*. London.

[36] Enervis energy advisors GmbH. 2014. *Der "ideale Kraftwerkspark" der Zukunft: Flexibel, klimafreundlich, kosteneffizient – Maßstab für einen optimierten Entwicklungspfad der Energieversorgung bis 2040.*

[37] Bundesverband WindEnergie. n.d. "Zahlen und Fakten: Statistische Kennziffern zur Erfolgsgeschichte Windenerge." https://www.wind-energie.de/themen/zahlen-und-fakten/.

[38] Energy Brainpool. 2016. *Kurzanalyse zur Stromerzeugung bei netzbedingter Abregelung Erneuerbarer Energien*. Berlin.

[39] Jürgen Giesecke, Stephan Heimerl, and Emil Mosonyi. 2014. *Wasserkraftanlagen: Planung, Bau und Betrieb*. Berlin and Heidelberg: Springer-Verlag.

[40] Peter Kurzweil, and Otto K. Dietlmeier. 2015. *Elektrochemische Speicher: Superkondensatoren, Batterien, Elektrolyse-Wasserstoff, Rechtliche Grundlagen*. Wiesbaden: Springer Fachmedien.

[41] Agentur für Erneuerbare Energien. 2017. "Anteil neuer PV-Anlagen unter 30 kW mit Batteriespeichern." https://www.foederal-erneuerbar.de/landesinfo/bundesland/D/kategorie/solar/auswahl/861-anteil_neuer_pv-anla/#goto_861.

[42] Deutsche Energie-Agentur GmbH (dena). 2016. *Roadmap Demand Side Management: Industrielles Lastmanagement für ein zukunftsfähiges Energiesystem, Schlussfolgerungen aus dem Pilotprojekt DSM Bayern*. Berlin.

3 Social Acceptance of Renewable Energy Technologies

Dr. Robert Sposato, Prof. Dr. Nina Hampl

3.1 Social Acceptance of Renewable Energy Technologies: An Introduction

Against the backdrop of worrying climate change predictions, the past decades have generated increasing interest in renewable energy technologies (RET) such as wind power and photovoltaics. While technological developments of RET have advanced largely unhindered, the surge in actual deployment of these technologies has triggered various social issues, which are typically discussed under the term *social acceptance of RET*. This research stream has produced evidence of numerous instances where this complex of socially anchored determinants and processes has been ignored, leading to severely delayed or even failed projects (Aitken 2010; Jobert, Laborgne, & Mimler 2007). It is now commonly accepted that social acceptance is just as important as issues that might concern the technological or legislative aspects surrounding RET, as it is described as "one of the most policy-relevant social science concepts in the field of energy technologies" (Upham, Oltra, & Boso 2015, 101).

It is safe to assume that scholarly work applicable to acceptance (or lack thereof) of large energy infrastructure has a far longer history than scholarship specific to the issue of social acceptance of RET. This finding is owed to and expressed by the wealth of perspectives and theories applicable to this research domain (Upham et al. 2015). Scholarly work on social acceptance of RET first started to gather momentum in the early eighties and has now developed into a dedicated research stream with significant scholarly contributions over the past decades (Bosley & Bosley 1988; Carlman 1982, 1984; Gaede & Rowlands 2018; Thayer 1988; Wolsink 1987; Wüstenhagen, Wolsink, & Bürer 2007). With the accelerated growth of this research stream though it is maybe not overly surprising to find that various critical remarks of lacking conceptual frameworks and poor methodology have been raised (e.g., Devine-Wright 2005).

In the same vein it is important to note that, while we broadly speak of social acceptance of RET, an overproportioned amount of publications in this research domain focuses on wind power, as it has been described as the "learning laboratory" for social acceptance research (Warren, Cowell, Ellis, Strachan, & Szarka 2012). Some authors have suggested that this is due to the perception that wind power is more controversial than other RET and has thus attracted more scholarly attention (Aitken 2009, 2010; Devine-Wright 2007). Further, it is plausible, that a focus on wind power has come with the accelerated diffusion of wind power framed by some authors as a "renewable energy gold rush" (Pasqualetti 2004; Warren, Lumsden, O'Dowd, & Birnie 2005). However, work on other utility-scale RET and associated

https://doi.org/10.1515/9783110607888-003

infrastructure, such as high-voltage power lines, certainly has not been absent in literature (Batel 2018; Batel & Devine-Wright 2017; Batel, Devine-Wright, & Tangeland 2013; Brewer, Ames, Solan, Lee, & Carlisle 2015; Devine-Wright & Batel 2013; Friedl & Reichl 2016; Michel, Buchecker, & Backhaus 2015; Sovacool & Lakshmi Ratan 2012).

The following paragraphs will offer an introduction to the wider social acceptance literature starting with a short overview on theoretical considerations with respect to social acceptance of RET, followed by a particular emphasis on contextual, personal and social-psychological factors that have been highlighted as influential in determining community acceptance of RET.

3.2 From Non-Technical Factors to Social Acceptance, Acceptability, and Support: Conceptual and Historic Developments

As alluded to in the introduction, much of the early development and deployment of RET has foregone the issue of social acceptance and so research in this domain has to a great extent been catching up with already accomplished facts, rather than assuming an accompanying role. Ignorance of social acceptance aspects in RET developments is probably best expressed through their denomination as "non-technical" factors in early work by Carlman (1982). Following this early work (Carlman 1982, 1984) other researchers increasingly dedicated scholarly attention to this topic (Bosley & Bosley 1988; Thayer 1988; Wolsink 1987), but only a few years into the turn of the century Wüstenhagen, Wolsink and Bürer's (2007) widely cited paper on social acceptance of renewable energy innovation created somewhat of a self-conception as an original field of study.

In their paper Wüstenhagen et al. (2007) propose a theoretical model, which distinguishes three major aspects of acceptance of RET (see Figure 3.1): (1) *Socio-political acceptance* which generally describes an un-/favorable policy landscape and the nature of public support for RET, the latter of which is generally found to be high (Eurobarometer 2014). (2) *Market acceptance* defined as the extent to which a RET is adopted by the market, including consumers, investors and firms. (3) *Community acceptance*, which is concerned with what is most commonly understood as acceptance, that is, the actual favorability of individuals towards a concrete RET project in a community.

Wüstenhagen et al.'s (2007) framework has been further refined by Sovacool and Lakshmi Ratan (2012). The authors propose a conceptual framework in which they operationalize the three dimensions of social acceptance through nine criteria (see Figure 3.2): (1) strong institutional capacity, (2) political commitment and (3) favorable legal and regulatory frameworks are described as sociopolitical factors; (4) competitive installation and/or production costs, (5) mechanisms for information and feedback and (6) access to financing as market factors and finally (7) prolific community and/or individual ownership and use, (8) participatory project siting, and (9)

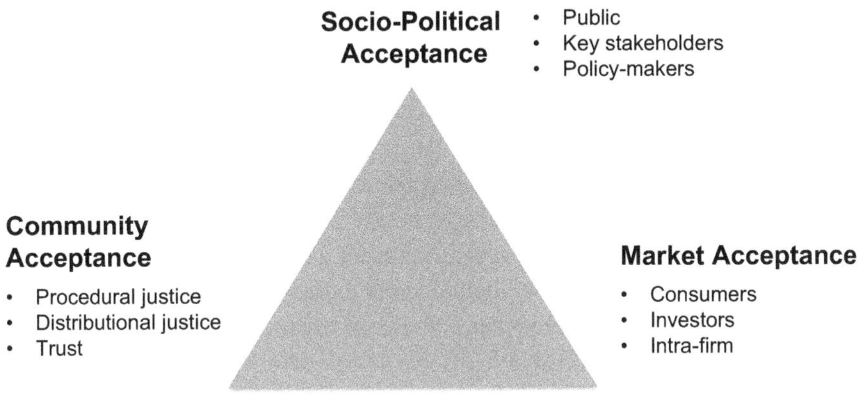

Figure 3.1: The triangle of social acceptance of renewable energy innovation (Wüstenhagen et al. 2007, 2684).

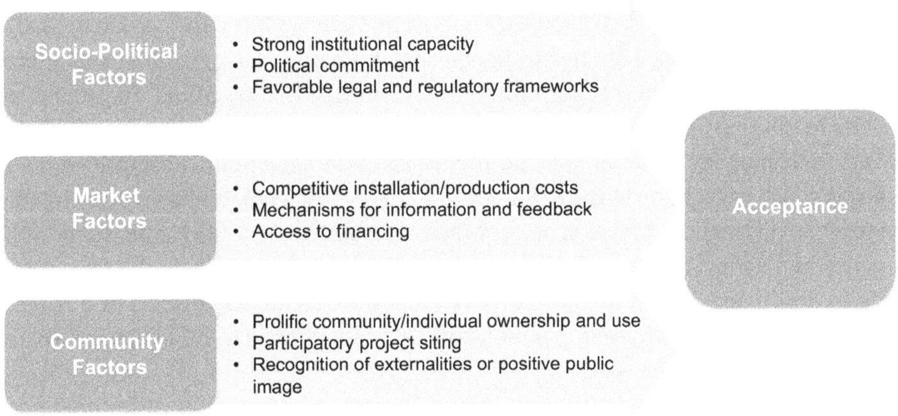

Figure 3.2: Dimensions and conditions of sociopolitical, community, and market acceptance (Sovacool & Lakshmi Ratan, 2012, 5271).

recognition of externalities or positive public image as community factors. In line with the interlinked nature of the social acceptance dimensions as defined in Wüstenhagen et al.'s (2007) framework, the authors argue that countries in which a sufficiently strong combination of these criteria exists "will see market acceptance grow and diffusion occur" (Sovacool & Lakshmi Ratan 2012).

It is often observed in practice that high sociopolitical acceptance is contrasted by relatively low acceptance at the community level – often discussed as the so-called *social gap* (Bell, Gray, & Haggett 2005; Bell, Gray, Haggett, & Swaffield 2013; Braunholtz 2003; Strachan & Lal 2004; Warren et al. 2005). The community acceptance level mostly concerns individuals that live in the vicinity of planned or already built RET projects, and thus, these are the people directly affected – positively or negatively – by a RET installation. In contrast, the overall, mostly positive, public perceptions of RET as part of the sociopolitical dimension constitute the most abstract level of the social acceptance framework.

To explain this apparent discrepancy between these two dimensions of social acceptance, previous research has discussed the *N*ot *I*n *M*y *B*ack*Y*ard syndrome. In simple terms it proposes that while people do favor RET, they do not want them near them. The NIMBY concept, however, has been extensively criticized and it is commonly accepted now that it is of limited value to the social acceptance research agenda. The most obvious challenge has come from studies that show the exact opposite effect, labelled PIMBY (*P*lease *I*n *M*y *B*ack*Y*ard) syndrome (Braunholtz 2003; Burningham 2000; Langer, Decker, Roosen, & Menrad 2018; Rand & Hoen 2017; Van der Horst 2007; Van der Loo 2001; Warren et al. 2005; Wolsink 2006, 2007b).

Apart from this empirical uncertainty, the NIMBY diction has been criticized for denigrating any opposition to the siting of a particular RET by framing it as a deviation from the norm borne out of a purely selfish motivation by certain individuals and institutions (Aitken 2010; Burningham 2000; Van der Horst 2007; Wolsink 2006, 2007b). This ties in nicely with a second line of critical considerations in social acceptance literature that concerns the terminus "acceptance" itself. In discussing the social acceptance concept, a critical discussion of the word "acceptance" and the specific theoretical and sociopolitical implications it carries must be acknowledged (Batel et al. 2013; Dreyer & Walker 2013). In this respect a distinction between *acceptance* and *support* for RET and their non-agency and agency character respectively is useful in showing how the former implies a "normative top-down perspective" and a focus on acceptance in a NIMBY syndrome tradition, where opposition to RET is something to be overcome (Batel et al. 2013; Rand & Hoen 2017).

Other scholars have distinguished *acceptance/acceptability* as attitudinal concepts from *support* as a behavioral construct (Dreyer, Polis, & Jenkins 2017; Dreyer & Walker 2013) and point to another important facet of social acceptance: the dynamic nature of acceptance, especially when considered over time (Dreyer et al. 2017). A series of studies has shown that acceptance usually follows a U-shaped curve over the lifetime of a RET project, from higher acceptance in the pre-project phase, to relatively low acceptance during the planning and siting of a RET project, to again higher acceptance as a RET project is finished and in operation (Devine-Wright 2005; Nadaï & Labussière 2009; Van der Horst 2007; Warren et al. 2005; Wolsink 2007b), as shown in Figure 3.3.

Given the importance that the community acceptance dimension of social acceptance has for the actual realization of RET projects, the remainder of this section will particularly focus on issues related to and factors determining community acceptance of RET. We choose this focus, explicitly acknowledging three caveats: (1) interlinkages to the other two dimensions of social acceptance exist, an issue

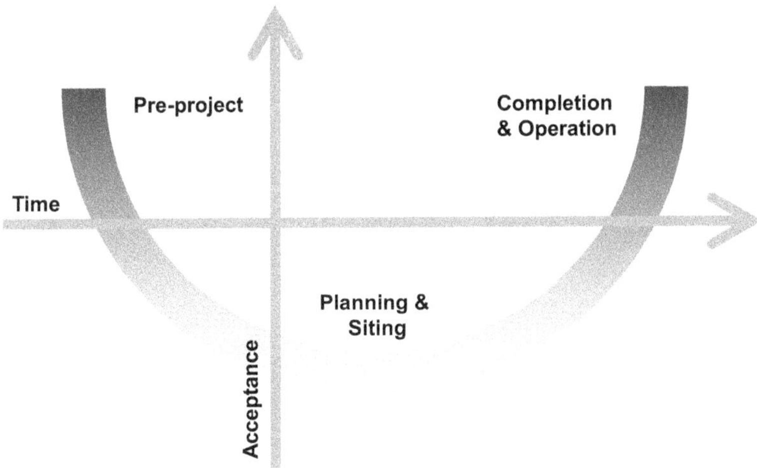

Figure 3.3: U-shaped temporal development of social acceptance (own representation).

that will become more than apparent to the reader in the following paragraphs, (2) the selection of factors and processes outlined below represent an overview and do not exhaustively explain community acceptance and even less so social acceptance, (3) we make no judgment of whether social acceptance is a preferable outcome or not.

Reviewing literature on community acceptance shows that most of the work in this field focuses on factors that determine community acceptance of RET. Scholars have proposed different frameworks that seek to categorize these factors in various subgroups. Roddis, Carver, Dallimer, Norman and Ziv (2018), for instance, propose a framework for acceptance variables at the community acceptance level that distinguishes between two groups of factors – (1) material arguments and (2) attitudinal/social influences – which are further subdivided into four categories and corresponding variables respectively, as displayed in Figure 3.4.

They analyse these variables in terms of their predictive quality with regards to planning outcomes and find that variables from all but one subcategory, namely "political," show some form of significant contribution for both onshore wind and solar farm applications.

A more comprehensive framework for community acceptance, putting more emphasis on attitudinal and social factors, is provided by Devine-Wright (2007). He distinguishes between three levels of analysis, i.e., *contextual*, *personal* and *social-psychological* factors. Thus, in the following, we will discuss relevant aspects pertinent to these levels in more detail.

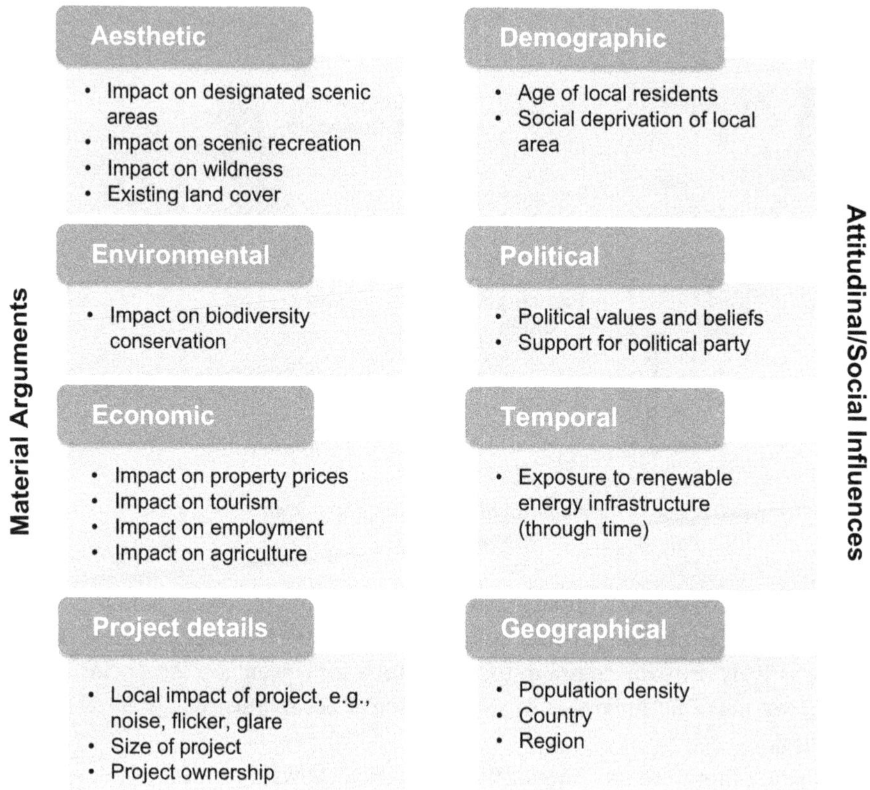

Figure 3.4: Framework of "acceptance variables" contributing to community acceptance (Roddis et al. 2018, 355).

3.3 Contextual, Personal, and Social-Psychological Factors

3.3.1 Contextual Factors

The *contextual level of analysis* is concerned with the specific characteristics of a RET project and how individuals perceive and react to those. Two central aspects at focus here are noise and visual impact (Devine-Wright 2005; Rand & Hoen 2017). Some research has highlighted noise as an important concern of residents in siting decisions (Klick & Smith 2010). The evidence basis, however, is somewhat inconclusive and it seems as though noise might not be a majorly important or particularly salient aspect (Kaldellis, Kapsali, Kaldelli, & Katsanou 2013), especially when compared to other sources of noise, such as road traffic (Pohl, Gabriel, & Hübner 2018). More detailed research suggests that attitudes built around noise could be described as a naïve a-priori concern, which subsides once infrastructure is actually built and individuals gain experience with it (Warren, Lumsden, O'Dowd, & Birnie 2005). Other studies show that annoyance with noise emissions is more strongly related to what Taylor and Klenk (2019) refer to as "psychogenic factors," such as attitudes regarding the visual impact of a wind farm, than the actual sound pressure level produced by a turbine (Krohn & Damborg 1999; Pedersen & Waye 2004; Wolsink 2007b) and a similar relationship has been confirmed for noise and the relative quality of the planning and construction process (Pohl et al. 2018).

As the visual impact certainly seems to more clearly determine acceptance of RET (Devine-Wright 2005; Roddis et al. 2018; Wolsink 2000) it is safe to assume that other large production sites mostly lacking an acoustic component, such as photovoltaic power plants, would not be treated much differently in the public eye. In terms of visual impact studies on wind farms have yielded a clear preference for smaller turbines, smaller numbers or clusters of turbines and greater distance (Betakova, Vojar, & Sklenicka 2015; Bishop & Miller 2007; Devine-Wright 2005; Lee, Wren, & Hickman 1989). Similar patterns of preference for photovoltaic installations have been reported (Naspetti, Mandolesi, & Zanoli 2016; Roddis et al. 2018). An aspect unique to wind turbines is the matter of blade movement. Bishop and Miller (2007) find that besides distance the visual effect of an offshore wind farm is most strongly determined by the movement of turbine blades. A similarly unique aspect of wind turbines are aircraft obstruction markings, which, with the exception of Xenon lights, have been shown to only produce mild annoyance (Pohl, Hübner, & Mohs 2012). Whilst the different RET do differ in certain objective visual components, a study comparing respondents' visual evaluations of wind power, photovoltaic and small-scale hydropower plants in Greece finds no real differences. It is interesting to note though that the only tentative differences seem to be a relatively lower evaluation for the potential of aesthetic disturbance from hydropower and a relatively lower evaluation for the potential of increased attractiveness from photovoltaic installations (Kaldellis, Kapsali, Kaldelli, & Katsanou 2013). As the latter finding suggests, other studies have shown that visual impact is not necessarily evaluated negatively. A study investigating the psycho-physiological impact of wind turbines found that they do not differ in terms of emotional arousal from other energy-production facilities and that they are actually rated as more pleasant, equal to churches (Maehr, Watts, Hanratty, & Talmi 2015). Similarly a substantial majority of 93% of residents near a Greek wind park thought positively of the existence of that wind park and 58% confirmed that it positively influenced the landscape (Tsoutsos, Tsouchlaraki, Tsiropoulos, & Kaldellis 2009).

It is thus clear that a negative visual impact is not a given. Again, as has been found for noise, researchers showed, that despite widespread expectancies of visual intrusion before wind farm projects are realized, significantly less think so once wind farms are built (Kontogianni, Tourkolias, Skourtos, & Damigos 2014; Warren et al. 2005). In fact, nearly two thirds of respondents at a surveyed wind farm site in southwest Ireland, for example, rated the visual impact of the local wind farm as positive. A finding that was most true, in a PIMBY sense, for those living closest to the wind farms (Warren et al. 2005). Further evidence comes from studies showing how prior experience with wind turbines positively influences how they are perceived (Hampl et al. 2019; Ladenburg 2009) and how community co-ownership positively affects noise and visual impact evaluations and overall acceptance (Musall & Kuik 2011). This type of findings for noise and visual impact again hints at the changeable nature of social acceptance, as described above with respect to the U-shaped curve of social acceptance over the project lifespan.

Wolsink (2007b), however, cautions that a return to initial levels of social acceptance according to this U-shaped curve is not necessarily an automatism and that it hinges on good practice on the developers' side and good relations with the local community. This relates to yet another set of important contextual aspects which concerns the construction and management of a structure. Various authors have stated that lacking acceptance is often a function of badly entertained interactions, lacking consultation and engagement between developers, other central actors and the affected community during the decision-making, planning and construction process (Aitken 2009; Breukers & Wolsink 2007; D'Souza & Yiridoe 2014; Krohn & Damborg 1999; Wüstenhagen et al. 2007).

Community involvement and public participation can be highlighted as contextual factors that substantially contribute to social acceptance (Aitken 2009; Breukers & Wolsink 2007; D'Souza & Yiridoe 2014; Friedl & Reichl 2016; Krohn & Damborg 1999; Rand & Hoen 2017; C. Walker & Baxter 2017; Wüstenhagen et al. 2007). In this respect, issues around fairness and justice are highlighted as majorly important aspects. Commonly two types of justice are distinguished: *distributive* and *procedural justice*. The former describing how costs and benefits of a RET project are distributed, the latter referring to a fair decision-making process that ideally has given the involved stakeholders an adequate voice (Gross 2007; Tyler 2000). Both forms of justice are significantly associated with social acceptance of RET (Baxter, Morzaria, & Hirsch 2013; Devine-Wright 2012; Gross 2007; Hall, Ashworth, & Devine-Wright 2013; Simpson & Clifton 2016; Sinclair & Löfstedt 2001; Tyler 2000; C. Walker & Baxter 2017; Wolsink 2007a; Zoellner, Schweizer-Ries, & Wemheuer 2008). More recently the aspect of *recognition justice* (Fraser 1997; Schlosberg 2007) has been added to a "triumvirate of tenets" forming the concept of *energy justice* (Jenkins, McCauley, Heffron, Stephan, & Rehner 2016; McCauley, Heffron, Stephan, & Jenkins 2008), as illustrated in Figure 3.5.

Recognition justice specifically focuses on fair representation, conscious of the fact that a formalized participation is by default less accessible to certain actors (Schlosberg 2007). Following McCauley et al.'s (2008, 109) description of how lacking recognition justice is expressed through "misrecognising – a distortion of people's views that may appear demeaning or contemptible" it becomes evident how this

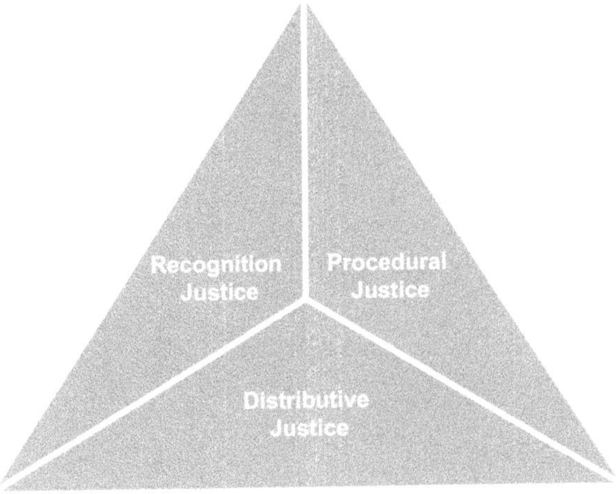

Figure 3.5: Three tenets of energy justice (own representation).

discussion resonates with, and underlines the importance of, the above-mentioned criticism of the NIMBY concept as a form of denigration of unwanted opposition.

Gross (2007) further distinguishes between outcome favorability and outcome fairness as components of distributive justice and presents evidence that acceptance of a proposed wind farm after a community consultation process is directly related to all these forms of justice. More importantly though, she finds that different groups within a community are not equally sensitive to the various aspects of justice (Gross 2007). Jenkins et al. (2016) offer a conceptual review of the energy justice research agenda and a systematization of the various energy justice aspects. They distinguish: (1) *the distribution of ills* and *benefits* as constituting components of distributive justice, (2) *injustice as non-recognition* and *injustice as misrecognition and disrespect* as facets of recognition justice, and finally, (3) *mobilizing local knowledge, disclosing information* and *representation in institutions* as important aspects of procedural justice. The breadth of aspects considered illustrates how the concept of energy justice is described now as both an analytical tool for researchers (Jenkins et al. 2016; Sovacool & Dworkin 2015) but equally a decision-making tool for planners and consumers (Sovacool & Dworkin 2015).

These aspects of justice are evidently tightly interwoven with the issue of dis-/trust, which can be highlighted as a further central aspect with regards to social acceptance of publics affected by RET siting (Barry, Ellis, & Robinson 2008; Devine-Wright 2012; Friedl & Reichl 2016; Huijts, Midden, & Meijnders 2007; Huijts, Molin, & Steg 2012; Perlaviciute & Steg 2014; Sinclair & Löfstedt 2001; Tyler 2000; G. Walker, Devine-Wright, Hunter, High, & Evans 2010; Wüstenhagen et al. 2007). Trust is in fact described as a "main key to success" (Jobert et al. 2007) as it is understood as a precondition to meaningful communication with affected audiences (Wolsink 1989) and essential for a positive contribution of procedural and distributive justice to social acceptance (Kollmann & Reichl 2015). Dwyer and Bidwell (2019) describe the *chain of trust* (see Figure 3.6) demonstrating how process leaders first build public trust in themselves, then in the process and ultimately in the outcome, which then translates into acceptance of it.

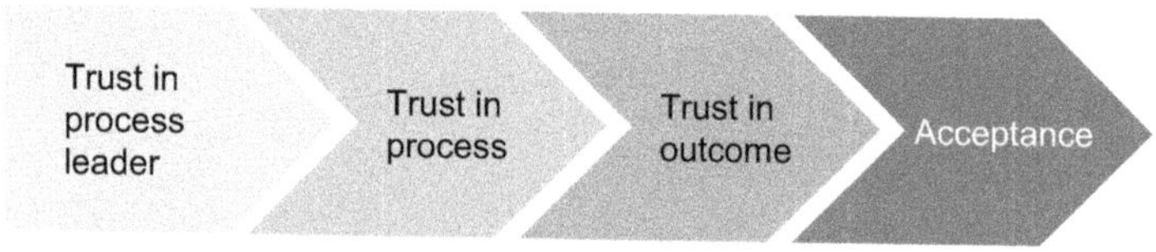

Figure 3.6: Chain of trust (Dwyer & Bidwell 2019, 168).

The issue of trust seems to be particularly salient for the increasingly popular option of co-ownership for local renewable energy projects (Goedkoop & Devine-Wright 2016). Co-ownership has been linked to more positive attitudes towards wind farms and greater acceptance regarding future developments (Enevoldsen & Sovacool 2016; Musall & Kuik 2011; Toke, Breukers, & Wolsink 2008; Warren & McFadyen 2010).

The final set of contextual factors is essentially determined by an interplay of the characteristics of a landscape and the inhabitants that make it their home. Central to this scholarly approach is the concept of *place* applied in disciplines such as environmental psychology, sociology and architecture and conceptualized as a location that holds meaning for people (Cresswell 2004). A central aspect of the construct of place then is *place attachment* described as "positively experienced bonds, sometimes occurring without awareness, that are developed over time from the behavioral, affective, and cognitive ties between individuals and/or groups and their sociophysical environment." (Brown & Perkins 1992, 284). Closely related to place attachment is the issue of *place identity*, which is understood as a set of cognitions, such as memories, ideas and preferences, with respect to a physical environment, that contributes towards an individual's sense of self (Proshansky, Fabian, & Kaminoff 1983). When a place is exposed to some form of (proposed) change, then people attached to this place can perceive this as a *disruption* or *threat* to their identity, which will trigger so-called place-protective actions aimed at preserving the affected environment in its original state. Threats or disruptions can follow as a consequence of natural disasters, changes in the neighbourhood, crime, but equally by developments, such as the building of a RET (Brown & Perkins 1992; Devine-Wright 2009).

Applying these concepts to social acceptance research, Devine-Wright (2009) reframes NIMBYism as place-protective action, which arises when existing place attachments are in danger of being disrupted or when processes associated with the specific place identity are threatened by a specific RET project. This conception of local opposition or lacking acceptance thus focuses scholarly interest on how residents feel and think about a specific place and whether a specific RET fits this subjective understanding and image of the landscape. The reaction which follows then is a product of strength of place attachment by perceived in-/congruity of the proposed RET project and the character of a place, as illustrated in Figure 3.7.

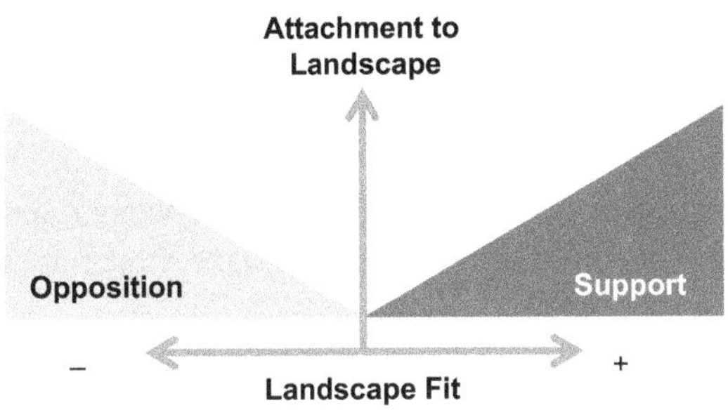

Figure 3.7: Opposition and support as a function of attachment to landscape and landscape fit (own representation).

A variety of studies has shown how people-place bonds explain acceptance of RET and associated infrastructure (Devine-Wright 2011b, 2011a, 2012; Devine-Wright & Batel 2017; Hall et al. 2013; McLachlan 2009; Michel et al. 2015; Süsser, Döring, & Ratter 2017; Van Veelen & Haggett 2017; Vorkinn & Riese 2001). Studies in this line of research have shown that if a RET is perceived as an industrialization of a predominantly natural landscape, then people who feel attached to this place will be more likely to object (Batel et al. 2015; Devine-Wright & Howes 2010; McLachlan 2009; Strazzera, Mura, & Contu 2012). It follows however, that if a RET is perceived as to conform with a particular landscape, or even promote it, the RET will generally be evaluated more positively (Carlisle, Kane, Solan, & Joe 2014; Michel et al. 2015) and people with stronger bonds to the landscape in question will be even more likely to support it (Devine-Wright 2011b, 2011a).

Authors have further suggested that different forms or levels of place attachment exist (Devine-Wright, Price, & Leviston 2015) and that these need to be distinguished with respect to their impact on acceptance of RET (Devine-Wright & Batel 2017; van Veelen & Haggett 2017). Van Veelen and Hagget (2017) in studying two community renewable energy projects in the Scottish Highlands are able to show that one form of place attachment is an important motivator to develop these projects, but yet another form serves as grounds for opposition. In their study using a series of interviews they are able to show that place attachment informs opinions in two ways: building impetus to develop on the one hand and motivating opposition on the other, a finding which the authors trace back to individually varying strengths of physical as opposed to social attachment.

Physical and social attachment have been introduced as two constituting dimensions of place attachment (e.g., Devine-Wright & Clayton 2010; Hidalgo & Hernández 2001). Place attachment is thus composed by a physical dimension which can include both a functional attachment – relying on a land for the resources it provides for example – but equally an emotional attachment – qualities of the landscape that are of symbolic quality or essential to one's identity (Williams & Vaske 2003). The substrate of the social dimension of place attachment is based on current and past social ties and other forms of personal connections and can be experienced at an individual level but equally as part of the community (Hidalgo & Hernández 2001; G. Walker & Devine-Wright 2008). Building on this two-dimensional structure of place attachment van Veelen and Haggett (2017, 544) further elaborate on the distinct effect of place attachment stating that:

> Acceptance of the projects was related to their perceived "fit" within both the physical and social dimension of the place. The, perceived, dichotomy between landscape preservation and supporting local communities arose regularly in interviews, with most participants prioritizing one over the other. This affected the symbolic meanings they attached to the proposed development. For some, a community-owned project was viewed through a lens of possibility, of social and economic recovery. For others, it was an industrial element, another reminder of unwanted human presence in an otherwise "untouched" landscape. Even for some proponents, the development of a community energy scheme is not something that is necessarily wanted, but rather something that is needed for the community's sake: a means to achieve other ends.

Recently scholars have questioned whether the narrow focus on local place attachments in studies on social acceptance is an oversimplification at the expense of similarly important attachments at the national and global level (Devine-Wright & Batel 2017). While early references of this line of reasoning exist (Feitelson 1991) it only picked up momentum in recent years and has been discussed in scholarly work building on the supposedly inherent discrepancy between immediate and local costs of mitigation strategies and the global benefits they promise. It has therefore been applied in the wider climate change perception literature (Devine-Wright 2013; Devine-Wright et al. 2015). Devine-Wright and Batel (2017) for example find that people with stronger global attachment are more likely to support decentralized energy and that those with a relatively stronger local attachment are more likely to oppose a nearby power line. These varying levels of place attachment have also been linked to ideological components showing that the latter are in fact to some extent expressed through the former. This means that the finding of increasing scepticism with respect to climate change, as place attachment becomes increasingly local, is in fact explained by ideological components mediating this relationship (Devine-Wright et al. 2015). This resonates with the idea of cultural cognition, which we introduce in Section 3.3.3, and which in essence proposes that certain aspects of our cognition, in this case the perceptions of a place, are aligned with our ideological convictions. This same process has also been investigated in a study examining the acceptance of high-voltage power lines in the UK and Norway and it shows how individual portrayals of a landscape can be ideologically constructed and strategically used, allowing the individual to legitimize his or her oppositional views (Batel et al. 2015).

3.3.2 Personal Factors

The personal level of analysis is concerned with factors directly related to the person. Devine-Wright (2007) initially highlights variables such as age, gender and social class as the primary focus of studies at this level but later (Devine-Wright 2012; Devine-Wright & Batel 2017) adds factors previously described as social-psychological such as environmental beliefs, values and attitudes. Research on the effect of the former socio-demographic category has not produced an overly coherent set of findings. This is certainly to some extent owed to the specificity of the RET and the form of acceptance (e.g., community vs. market acceptance) being studied. Tendentially, older respondents are less positive towards RETs, such as wind (Ek 2005; Pohl et al. 2012; Yuan, Zuo, & Huisingh 2015) or biogas and solar energy (Liu, Wang, & Mol 2013) but higher acceptance among older consumers of RET has also been reported (Sardianou & Genoudi 2013). A similar picture can be painted for the effects of gender, with some studies indicating lower levels of support for wind power among women (Klick & Smith 2010) and other studies finding no gender-difference for acceptance of wind power (Ek 2005; Pohl et al. 2012) and other forms of RET (Liu et al. 2013), or even higher levels among women (Devine-Wright 2007). Similarly, research investigating the effects of income and education as indicators of social class do not produce consistent results. Higher income has been found to be associated with higher acceptance of RET deployment (Liu et al. 2013) and support for electricity production from RET (Diaz-Rainey & Ashton 2011; Ek & Söderholm 2008; MacPherson & Lange 2013; Tabi, Hille, & Wüstenhagen 2014). However, contrasting findings, such as an association of higher income with a less positive evaluation of wind power (Ek 2005), are reported here too. For education a positive and significant association with support for electricity production from RET has been reported (Ek & Söderholm 2008; MacPherson & Lange 2013; Tabi et al. 2014).

3.3.3 Social-Psychological Factors

The *social-psychological level* of analysis considers variables on an individual level that influence attitudes and behaviors with respect to RET. In line with the discussion mentioned above Huijts, Moling and Steg (2012) propose that acceptability is in fact expressed through *attitudes* towards a new technology and possible behaviors in response to this technology, that is, acceptance. This means that attitudes are understood as a precursor to acceptance. Attitudes are typically conceptualized as specific to an attitude object (e.g., a wind farm) and informed by higher-order constructs, such as *values*, *beliefs* or *ideology* (cf. Banaji & Heiphetz 2015; Herek 1987; Katz 1960). Numerous studies have shown how attitudes are significantly associated with acceptance of RET (e.g., Jones & Eiser 2009; Walter 2014) but there is a persistent ambiguousness in how attitudes are conceptualized in social acceptance literature ranging from *synonymous to acceptance* to *precursory determinant of acceptance* as is expressed through varying measurements from a general national level to a local level, focusing on a particular project (cf. Devine-Wright 2007).

It is not only for this confusion of levels of analysis that an investigation of the above-mentioned higher-order constructs promises to be more useful. A prominent operationalization of this idea of higher-order values informing lower-order attitudes is Stern's (2000) Value Belief Norm Theory, which proposes that environmental concern is most strongly determined by egoistic, altruistic and biospheric values, which then in turn influences personal *norms* and environmentally significant behavior ultimately. In this respect particular environmental values or beliefs (Dietz, Fitzgerald, & Shwom 2005; Stern, Dietz, & Guagnano 1995) or the concept of environmentalism more generally have been applied to social acceptance research and it has been shown that in many instances acceptance of RET is predicted by certain values a person subscribes to (Bidwell 2013; Greenberg 2009; Smith & Klick 2007). In line with these findings greater environmental concern has been linked to greater support for and interest in RET (Ek 2005; Hobman & Ashworth 2013; Koirala et al. 2018; Zhai & Williams 2012).

Research has shown, however, that the connection of environmental concern – and very likely other value- and belief-related constructs – and social acceptance, is less straightforward than one would assume from similar research applying this concept. In fact, it seems that value-related constructs possess a somewhat paradox quality. At the core of this is the putative incongruity of addressing a global environmental problem, i.e., climate change, while at the same time saving local environments from the expected negative impacts of RET projects. This discrepancy has led to situations where environmentally concerned individuals for example find themselves on opposing sides, a situation that has been very accurately described as a "green on green" conflict (Pasqualetti 2011; Warren et al. 2005).

Further adding to this paradox quality of value associations with acceptance of RET authors have suggested that support and acceptance for RET is not yet linked to particular political beliefs or ideology (Carlisle, Kane, Solan, Bowman, & Joe 2015; Karlstrøm & Ryghaug 2014; Klick & Smith 2010). This assumption contrasts some of the existing work on RET but certainly regarding attitudes and support for various other forms of energy, or the climate change debate in more general, where political camps and separable ideologies partly assume extremely polarized positions (Carlisle et al. 2014; Kahan 2013; Kahan, Braman, Slovic, Gastil, & Cohen 2007; Michaud, Carlisle, & Smith 2008).

Much of this type of evidence comes from scholarly work on risk perception, a research domain that has recently been proposed to have kicked off the "real start of research on social acceptance of energy" (Wolsink 2018, 288). This dedicated research stream appears to have been widely neglected in scholarship on social acceptance, although a recent bibliometric analysis of the social acceptance literature by Gaede and Rowlands (2018) proposes that eventually one subgroup of seven larger future research fronts they find is and will increasingly look at individual-level psychological determinants of technological risk perception. To risk scholars this will come as no surprise, since a wealth of scientific evidence applicable to social acceptance of RET has been generated on closely related topics such as, emerging technologies, climate change and related environmental issues (Renn 1998; Slovic, Flynn, & Layman 1991).

One of the most central theories in the wider risk perception literature, Cultural Theory of Risk (Douglas & Wildavsky 1983), connects with the aforementioned discussion of higher-order constructs that influence acceptance. Cultural Theory of Risk builds on two main premises. First, individuals prefer certain forms of societal organization and this determines so-called cultural biases or cultural world views. Second, these preferences can be located in a two-dimensional space described by a group and a grid dimension, and the extreme reference points of this space are defined as four distinct cultural world views: Hierarchism, Egalitarianism, Individualism and Fatalism (Douglas & Wildavsky 1983; Kahan, Jenkins-Smith, & Braman 2011).[1] Work on Cultural Theory of Risk has looked at how these specific cultural world views relate to perceptions of certain risks and generally find that "however conceptualized – whether as political world view or cultural biases – world views best account for patterns of risk perceptions" (Wildavsky & Dake 1990, 56) outperforming other predictors among which, knowledge, personality traits and socio-demographic characteristics. In this context "patterns of risk" underlines how perceptions of risks emerge from an interaction of cultural world views an individual subscribes to and the hazard he/she is confronted with.

In applying and advancing this theory in a psychometric research tradition, scholars have proposed that cultural biases are maintained through a specific form of information processing, labeled cultural cognition. This biased form of cognition is described as functional "in forming and maintaining beliefs that signify" individuals' "loyalty to important affinity groups" (Kahan 2013, 407). The cultural cognition

1 In work on *Cultural Cognition* by Kahan and colleagues (Kahan, 2013; Kahan, Braman, Gastil, Slovic, & Mertz, 2007) building on this theory the mentioned typologies were no longer used to describe the respective quadrant of the grid-group space but were partly adapted (omitting fatalism) as extreme points of the same two-dimensional space, juxtaposing hierarchy and equality and individualism and communitarianism respectively.

approach thus posits that information processing is strongly influenced by our wish to maintain and promote our standing in the social group we adhere to. Research in this line has shown that cultural world views are predictive of people's engagement with a variety of issues ranging from national security and gun ownership to public health and climate change (Kahan, Braman, Slovic et al. 2007). Further evidence shows how individuals' perceptions and opinions concerning climate change (Corner, Whitmarsh, & Xenias 2012; Kahan 2013; Kahan et al. 2012) and even climate change mitigation policies (Hart & Nisbet 2012) are brought to align with their cultural world views and ideological commitments. For social acceptance of RET only a few studies have been able to show how cultural world views or similar ideological constructs are linked to social acceptance of RET. A study that has looked at how hierarchical and individualist world views predict support for the deployment of and support for government-funded research on low carbon technologies found a significant, albeit small, negative correlation of both cultural world views with support for government-funded research but none with support for the deployment of RET (Cherry, García, Kallbekken, & Torvanger 2014). Sposato and Hampl (2018) show how communitarian/egalitarian world views predict acceptance of wind turbines and photovoltaic power plants in local communities and another study finds that egalitarians and individualists are most diametrically opposed with respect to their views on the need for RET and how to expand capacities (West, Bailey, & Winter 2010).

Summarizing the above, social-psychological factors must be regarded as equally important determinants of social acceptance, and more specifically community acceptance of RET, besides contextual and personal attributes. Studies comparing the effect of personal (e.g., gender, age, income) and social-psychological (e.g., beliefs, motives, world views) factors on social acceptance even show that the latter have more explanatory power than socio-demographic characteristics (Sposato & Hampl 2018). This is not surprising, as already stated above, such higher-order social-psychological constructs directly inform attitudes towards RET and eventually social acceptance of these technologies. Figure 3.8 summarizes the three groups of factors (levels of analysis) that influence community acceptance.

3.4 Conclusions

This section sought to provide an overview on the concept and determinants of social acceptance of RET with a specific emphasis on community acceptance of such installations. Even though, the three dimensions of the social acceptance concept as introduced by Wüstenhagen et al. (2007) – sociopolitical, market and community acceptance – are all interrelated, community acceptance is most pertinent to the actual deployment of RET and most often referred to when talking about social acceptance issues. Factors that impact community acceptance of RET can either be

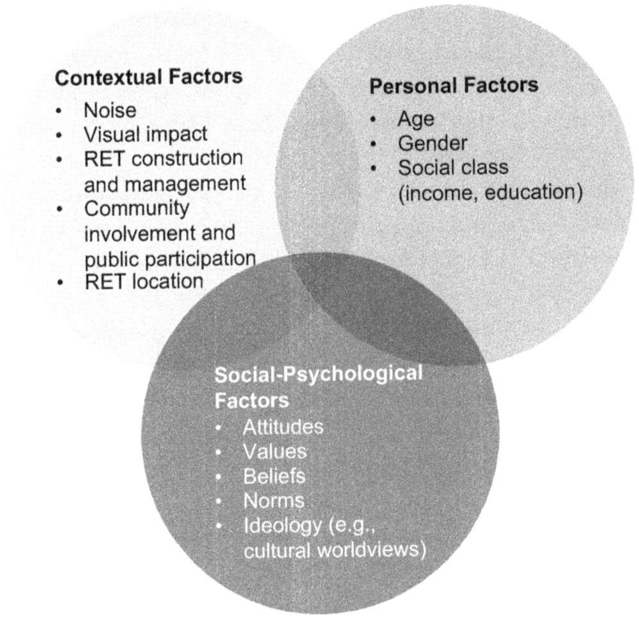

Figure 3.8: Three groups of factors that influence community acceptance (own representation).

attributed to the context (e.g., a specific RET project, location) or the individual (e.g., personal and social-psychological characteristics). The section discussed scholarly work in this research domain and provided insights that help to better understand issues related to social acceptance but has equally shown that to some extent literature lacks a theoretical foundation and construct clarity. Specifically the latter issue makes it hard to sometimes draw overall conclusions from existing research due to contradictory findings.

However, with a further increase in RET deployment social acceptance issues are expected to gain even more in importance in the future, and thus so will research in this field. This is especially the case for decentralized, large-scale RET such as wind farms and ground-mounted photovoltaic installations, which are publicly contested due to their high visual impact on the landscape. Yet these are also the technologies that public authorities of various countries in the European Union and beyond prioritize in their efforts to decarbonize the electricity sector. Austria, for instance, set the objective as part of its Climate and Energy Strategy released in June 2018 to cover 100% of the total national electricity consumption (national balance) from renewable energy sources by 2030 (BMNT/BMVIT 2018). The total share of electricity production from renewables in Austria is currently at 76% (Oesterreichs Energie 2019). It is expected, that besides hydro, substantial contributions to achieving the 100% target will have to come from wind power and photovoltaic installations. Taking the Austrian case as a reference, it is thus clear that many more planning and siting decisions for RET infrastructure will have to take place, also in regions that are characterized by the scenic beauty of their landscapes and which are important tourist destinations with high contribution to economic value creation in Austria.

Successfully dealing with social acceptance issues in RET planning and siting processes does not only increase the probability of project realization but also decreases total project costs. Best practices that have emerged mainly focus on having local citizens participate in the planning and siting processes, or even in financing the RET installations (community financing) (Goedkoop & Devine-Wright 2016; Hyland & Bertsch 2018). As already mentioned above, specifically co-ownership has been found to increase social acceptance of RET installations (Enevoldsen & Sovacool 2016; Musall & Kuik 2011; Toke et al. 2008; Warren & McFadyen 2010). One reason might be that with co-owning a RET installation local citizens not only need to carry the burden related to the construction and operation of the RET installation but can also generate financial benefits, e.g., in form of annual rates of return. Engaging citizens in the process of decarbonizing the energy system is also encouraged on a European level and one of the cornerstones of the EU Clean Energy Package, which, for instance, fosters the formation of local energy communities (European Commission 2018).

The insights provided here may help project developers and other stakeholders involved in a RET project to reflect on the different facets of social acceptance and to setup planning and siting processes that properly account for and deal with acceptance issues, for instance by including public consultation, community benefit schemes and co-ownership models. Knowledge on typical socio-psychological profiles of local supporters and opponents of RET installations and on how individuals perceive different contextual factors further might help to develop communication strategies related to planned RET projects and give guidance on what aspects of such projects should be highlighted in information campaigns.

References

Aitken, Mhairi. 2009. “Wind Power Planning Controversies and the Construction of ‘Expert’ and ‘Lay’ Knowledges.” *Science as Culture* 18, no. 1: 47–64.

Aitken, Mhairi. 2010. “Why we still don’t understand the social aspects of wind power: A critique of key assumptions within the literature.” *Energy Policy* 38, no. 4: 1834–41. https://doi.org/10.1016/j.enpol.2009.11.060.

Banaji, Mahzarin R., and Larisa Heiphetz. 2015. “Attitudes.” In *Handbook of Social Psychology*. Hoboken, NJ: John Wiley & Sons, Inc. https://doi.org/10.1002/9780470561119.socpsy001010.

Barry, John, Geraint Ellis, and Clive Robinson. 2008. "Cool Rationalities and Hot Air: A Rhetorical Approach to Understanding Debates on Renewable Energy." *Global Environmental Politics* 8, no. 2: 67–98. https://doi.org/10.1162/glep.2008.8.2.67.

Batel, Susana. 2018. "A critical discussion of research on the social acceptance of renewable energy generation and associated infrastructures and an agenda for the future." *Journal of Environmental Policy and Planning* 20, no. 3: 356–69. https://doi.org/10.1080/1523908X.2017.1417120.

Batel, Susana, and Patrick Devine-Wright. 2017. "Energy Colonialism and the Role of the Global in Local Responses to New Energy Infrastructures in the UK: A Critical and Exploratory Empirical Analysis." *Antipode* 49, no. 1: 3–22. https://doi.org/10.1111/anti.12261.

Batel, Susana, Patrick Devine-Wright, and Torvald Tangeland. 2013. "Social acceptance of low carbon energy and associated infrastructures: A critical discussion." *Energy Policy* 58: 1–5. https://doi.org/10.1016/j.enpol.2013.03.018.

Batel, Susana, Patrick Devine-Wright, Line Wold, Helene Egeland, Gerd Jacobsen, and Oystein Aas. 2015. "The role of (de-)essentialisation within siting conflicts: An interdisciplinary approach." *Journal of Environmental Psychology* 44: 149–59. https://doi.org/10.1016/J.JENVP.2015.10.004.

Baxter, Jamie, Rakhee Morzaria, and Rachel Hirsch. 2013. "A case-control study of support/opposition to wind turbines: Perceptions of health risk, economic benefits, and community conflict." *Energy Policy* 61: 931–43. https://doi.org/10.1016/J.ENPOL.2013.06.050.

Bell, Derek, Tim Gray, and Claire Haggett. 2005. "The 'Social Gap' in Wind Farm Siting Decisions: Explanations and Policy Responses." *Environmental Politics* 14, no. 4: 460–77. https://doi.org/10.1080/09644010500175833.

Bell, Derek, Tim Gray, Claire Haggett, and Joanne Swaffield. 2013. "Re-visiting the 'social gap': Public opinion and relations of power in the local politics of wind energy." *Environmental Politics* 22, no. 1: 115–35. https://doi.org/10.1080/09644016.2013.755793.

Betakova, Vendula, Jiri Vojar, and Petr Sklenicka. 2015. "Wind turbines location: How many and how far?" *Applied Energy* 151: 23–31. https://doi.org/10.1016/J.APENERGY.2015.04.060.

Bidwell, David 2013. "The role of values in public beliefs and attitudes towards commercial wind energy." *Energy Policy* 58: 189–99. https://doi.org/10.1016/J.ENPOL.2013.03.010.

Bishop, Ian D., and David R. Miller. 2007. "Visual assessment of off-shore wind turbines: The influence of distance, contrast, movement and social variables." *Renewable Energy* 32, no. 5: 814–31. https://doi.org/10.1016/J.RENENE.2006.03.009.

BMNT/BMVIT 2018. "Mission 2030: Austrian Climate and Energy Strategy." https://mission2030.info/wp-content/uploads/2018/10/Klima-Energiestrategie_en.pdf.

Bosley, P., and K. Bosley. 1988. "Public acceptability of California's wind energy developments: Three studies." *Wind Engineering* 12, no. 5: 311–18.

Braunholtz, Simon. (2003). *Public attitudes to windfarms: A survey of local residents in Scotland*. Edinburgh.

Breukers, Sylvia, and Maarten Wolsink. 2007. "Wind power implementation in changing institutional landscapes: An international comparison." *Energy Policy* 35, no. 5: 2737–50. https://doi.org/10.1016/j.enpol.2006.12.004.

Brewer, Justin, Daniel P. Ames, David Solan, Randy Lee, and Juliet Carlisle. 2015. "Using GIS analytics and social preference data to evaluate utility-scale solar power site suitability." *Renewable Energy* 81: 825–36. https://doi.org/10.1016/j.renene.2015.04.017.

Brown, Barbara B., and Douglas D. Perkins. 1992. "Disruptions in Place Attachment." In *Place Attachment*. Edited by Irwin Altman and Setha Low, 279–304. Boston, MA: Springer US. https://doi.org/10.1007/978-1-4684-8753-4_13.

Burningham, Kate. 2000. "Using the Language of NIMBY: A topic for research, not an activity for researchers." *Local Environment* 5, no. 1: 55–67. https://doi.org/10.1080/135498300113264.

Carlisle, Juliet. E., Stephanie L. Kane, David Solan, Madelaine Bowman, and Jeffrey C. Joe. 2015. "Public attitudes regarding large-scale solar energy development in the U.S." *Renewable and Sustainable Energy Reviews* 48: 835–47. https://doi.org/10.1016/J.RSER.2015.04.047.

Carlisle, Juliet E., Stephanie L. Kane, David Solan, and Jeffrey C. Joe. 2014. "Support for solar energy: Examining sense of place and utility-scale development in California." *Energy Research & Social Science* 3: 124–30. https://doi.org/10.1016/J.ERSS.2014.07.006.

Carlman, I. 1982. "Wind Energy Potential in Sweden: The Importance of Non-Technical Factors." In *4th International Symposium on Wind Energy Systems*, 335–48. Hamburg.

Carlman, I. 1984. "The views of politicians and decision-makers on planning for the use of wind power in Sweden." In *European Wind Energy Conference*, 22–36.

Cherry, Todd L., Jorge H. García, Steffen Kallbekken, and Asbjørn Torvanger. 2014. "The development and deployment of low-carbon energy technologies: The role of economic interests and cultural worldviews on public support." *Energy Policy* 68: 562–66. https://doi.org/10.1016/j.enpol.2014.01.018.

Corner, Adam, Lorraine Whitmarsh, and Dimitrios Xenias. 2012. "Uncertainty, scepticism and attitudes towards climate change: Biased assimilation and attitude polarisation." *Climatic Change* 114, nos. 3–4: 463–78. https://doi.org/10.1007/s10584-012-0424-6.

Cresswell, Tim. 2004. *Place: A Short Introduction*. Blackwell Pub. https://www.wiley.com/en-ru/Place%3A+A+Short+Introduction-p-9781118725443.

D'Souza, Clare, and Emmanuel K. Yiridoe. 2014. "Social acceptance of wind energy development and planning in rural communities of Australia: A consumer analysis." *Energy Policy* 74, no. C: 262–70. https://doi.org/10.1016/j.enpol.2014.08.035.

Devine-Wright, Patrick. 2005. "Beyond NIMBYism: Towards an integrated framework for understanding public perceptions of wind energy." *Wind Energy* 8, no. 2: 125–39. https://doi.org/10.1002/we.124.

Devine-Wright, Patrick. 2007. *Reconsidering public attitudes and public acceptance of renewable energy technologies: A critical review* (No. 1.4). *Beyond Nimbyism: A multidisciplinary investigation of public engagement with renewable energy technologies* (Vol. 1.4). Manchester. http://geography.exeter.ac.uk/beyond_nimbyism/deliverables/bn_wp1_4.pdf.

Devine-Wright, Patrick. 2009. "Rethinking NIMBYism: The role of place attachment and place identity in explaining place-protective action." *Journal of Community {&} Applied Social Psychology* 19, no. 6: 426–41. https://doi.org/10.1002/casp.1004.

Devine-Wright, Patrick. 2011a. "Enhancing local distinctiveness fosters public acceptance of tidal energy: A UK case study." *Energy Policy* 39, no. 1: 83–93. https://doi.org/10.1016/J.ENPOL.2010.09.012.

Devine-Wright, Patrick. 2011b. "Place attachment and public acceptance of renewable energy: A tidal energy case study." *Journal of Environmental Psychology* 31, no. 4: 336–43. https://doi.org/10.1016/j.jenvp.2011.07.001.

Devine-Wright, Patrick. 2012. "Explaining 'NIMBY' Objections to a Power Line: The Role of Personal, Place Attachment and Project-Related Factors." *Environment and Behavior* 45, no. 6: 761–81. https://doi.org/10.1177/0013916512440435.

Devine-Wright, Patrick. 2013. "Think global, act local? The relevance of place attachments and place identities in a climate changed world." *Global Environmental Change-Human and Policy Dimensions* 23, no. 1: 61–69. https://doi.org/DOI 10.1016/j.gloenvcha.2012.08.003.

Devine-Wright, Patrick, and Susana Batel. 2013. "Explaining public preferences for high voltage pylon designs: An empirical study of perceived fit in a rural landscape." *Land Use Policy* 31: 640–49. https://doi.org/10.1016/J.LANDUSEPOL.2012.09.011.

Devine-Wright, Patrick, and Susana Batel. 2017. "My neighbourhood, my country or my planet? The influence of multiple place attachments and climate change concern on social acceptance of energy infrastructure." *Global Environmental Change* 47: 110–20. https://doi.org/10.1016/J.GLOENVCHA.2017.08.003.

Devine-Wright, Patrick, and Susan Clayton. 2010. "Introduction to the special issue: Place, identity and environmental behaviour." *Journal of Environmental Psychology* 30, no. 3 (September): 267–70. https://doi.org/10.1016/S0272-4944(10)00078-2.

Devine-Wright, Patrick, and Yuko Howes. 2010. "Disruption to place attachment and the protection of restorative environments: A wind energy case study." *Journal of Environmental Psychology* 30, no. 3: 271–80. https://doi.org/10.1016/j.jenvp.2010.01.008.

Devine-Wright, Patrick, Jennifer Price, and Zoe Leviston. 2015. "My country or my planet? Exploring the influence of multiple place attachments and ideological beliefs upon climate change attitudes and opinions." *Global Environmental Change* 30: 68–79. https://doi.org/10.1016/j.gloenvcha.2014.10.012.

Diaz-Rainey, Ivan, and John K. Ashton. 2011. "Profiling potential green electricity tariff adopters: green consumerism as an environmental policy tool?" *Business Strategy and the Environment* 20 no. 7: 456–70. https://doi.org/10.1002/bse.699.

Dietz, Thomas, Amy Fitzgerald, and Rachael Shwom. 2005. "Environmental values." *Annual Review of Environment and Resources* 30: 335–72. https://doi.org/10.1146/annurev.energy.30.050504.144444.

Douglas, Mary, and Aaron Wildavsky. 1983. *Risk and culture: An essay on the selection of technological and environmental dangers*. London, England: University of California Press.

Dreyer, Stacia J., Hilary Jacqueline Polis, and Lekelia Danielle Jenkins. 2017. "Changing Tides: Acceptability, support, and perceptions of tidal energy in the United States." *Energy Research & Social Science* 29: 72–83. https://doi.org/10.1016/J.ERSS.2017.04.013.

Dreyer, Stacia J., and Iain Walker. 2013. "Acceptance and Support of the Australian Carbon Policy." *Social Justice Research* 26, no. 3: 343–62. https://doi.org/10.1007/s11211-013-0191-1.

Dwyer, Joseph, and David Bidwell. 2019. "Chains of trust: Energy justice, public engagement, and the first offshore wind farm in the United States." *Energy Research & Social Science* 47: 166–76. https://doi.org/10.1016/J.ERSS.2018.08.019.

Ek, Kristina. 2005. "Public and private attitudes towards 'green' electricity: the case of Swedish wind power." *Energy Policy* 33: 1677–89. https://doi.org/10.1016/j.enpol.2004.02.005.

Ek, Kristina, and Patrik Söderholm. 2008. "Norms and economic motivation in the Swedish green electricity market." *Ecological Economics* 68, no. 1: 169–82. https://doi.org/10.1016/j.ecolecon.2008.02.013.

Enevoldsen, Peter, and Benjamin K. Sovacool. 2016. "Examining the social acceptance of wind energy: Practical guidelines for onshore wind project development in France." *Renewable and Sustainable Energy Reviews* 53: 178–84. https://doi.org/10.1016/j.rser.2015.08.041.

Eurobarometer. 2014. *Climate change – Special Eurobarometer 409. European Commission.* https://doi.org/10.1503/cmaj.109-2001.

European Commission. 2018. "Commission welcomes political agreement on conclusion of the Clean Energy for All Europeans package." http://europa.eu/rapid/press-release_IP-18-6870_en.htm.

Feitelson, Eran. 1991. "Sharing the globe: The role of attachment to place." *Global Environmental Change* 1, no. 5: 396–406. https://doi.org/10.1016/0959-3780(91)90005-E.

Fraser, Nancy. 1997. *Justice Interruptus: Critical Reflections on the "Postsocialist" Condition.* New York: Routledge. https://doi.org/10.4324/9781315822174.

Friedl, Christina, and Johannes Reichl. 2016. "Realizing energy infrastructure projects: A qualitative empirical analysis of local practices to address social acceptance." *Energy Policy* 89: 184–93. https://doi.org/10.1016/J.ENPOL.2015.11.027.

Gaede, James, and Ian H. Rowlands. 2018. "Visualizing social acceptance research: A bibliometric review of the social acceptance literature for energy technology and fuels." *Energy Research & Social Science* 40: 142–58. https://doi.org/10.1016/J.ERSS.2017.12.006.

Goedkoop, Fleur, and Patrick Devine-Wright. 2016. "Partnership or placation? The role of trust and justice in the shared ownership of renewable energy projects." *Energy Research & Social Science* 17: 135–46. https://doi.org/10.1016/J.ERSS.2016.04.021.

Greenberg, Michael. 2009. "Energy sources, public policy, and public preferences: Analysis of US national and site-specific data." *Energy Policy* 37, no. 8: 3242–49. https://doi.org/10.1016/j.enpol.2009.04.020.

Gross, Catherine. 2007. "Community perspectives of wind energy in Australia: The application of a justice and community fairness framework to increase social acceptance." *Energy Policy* 35, no. 5: 2727–36. https://doi.org/10.1016/j.enpol.2006.12.013.

Hall, Nina, Peta Ashworth, and Patrick Devine-Wright. 2013. "Societal acceptance of wind farms: Analysis of four common themes across Australian case studies." *Energy Policy* 58: 200–208. https://doi.org/10.1016/j.enpol.2013.03.009.

Hampl, Nina, Werner Hoffmann, Robert Sposato, Gerhard Marterbauer, Armin Nowshad, Gudrun Senk, and Astrid Salmhofer. 2019. *Erneuerbare Energien in Österreich: Der jährliche Stimmungsbarometer der österreichischen Bevölkerung zu erneuerbaren Energien*. https://deloi.tt/2UJj4np.

Hart, P. Sol, and Eric C. Nisbet. 2012. "Boomerang Effects in Science Communication: How Motivated Reasoning and Identity Cues Amplify Opinion Polarization about Climate Mitigation Policies." *Communication Research* 39, no. 6: 701–23. https://doi.org/10.1177/0093650211416646.

Herek, Gregory M. 1987. "Can Functions Be Measured? A New Perspective on the Functional Approach to Attitudes." *Social Psychology Quarterly* 50, no. 4: 285. https://doi.org/10.2307/2786814.

Hidalgo, M. Carmen, and Bernardo Hernández. 2001. "Place Attachment: Conceptual and Empirical Questions." *Journal of Environmental Psychology* 21, no. 3: 273–81. https://doi.org/10.1006/jevp.2001.0221.

Hobman, Elizabeth V., and Peta Ashworth. 2013. "Public support for energy sources and related technologies: The impact of simple information provision." *Energy Policy* 63: 862–69. https://doi.org/10.1016/J.ENPOL.2013.09.011.

Huijts, Nicole M. A., Cees J. H. Midden, and Anneloes Meijnders. 2007. "Social acceptance of carbon dioxide storage." *Energy Policy* 35, no. 5: 2780–89. https://doi.org/10.1016/J.ENPOL.2006.12.007.

Huijts, Nicole M. A., Eric J. E. Molin, and Linda Steg. 2012. "Psychological factors influencing sustainable energy technology acceptance: A review-based comprehensive framework." *Renewable and Sustainable Energy Reviews* 16, no. 1: 525–31. https://doi.org/10.1016/J.RSER.2011.08.018.

Hyland, Marie, and Valentin Bertsch. 2018. "The role of community involvement mechanisms in reducing resistance to energy infrastructure development." *Ecological Economics* 146: 447–74.

Jenkins, Kirsten, Darren McCauley, Raphael Heffron, Hannes Stephan, and Robert Rehner. 2016. "Energy justice: A conceptual review." *Energy Research & Social Science* 11: 174–82. https://doi.org/10.1016/J.ERSS.2015.10.004.

Jobert, Arthur, Pia Laborgne, and Solveig Mimler. 2007. "Local acceptance of wind energy: Factors of success identified in French and German case studies." *Energy Policy* 35, no. 5: 2751–60. https://doi.org/10.1016/j.enpol.2006.12.005.

Jones, Christopher R., and J. Richard Eiser. 2009. "Identifying predictors of attitudes towards local onshore wind development with reference to an English case study." *Energy Policy* 37, no. 11: 4604–14. https://doi.org/10.1016/J.ENPOL.2009.06.015.

Kahan, Dan M. 2013. "Ideology, motivated reasoning, and cognitive reflection." *Judgment and Decision Making* 8, no. 4: 407–24.

Kahan, Dan M., Donald Braman, John Gastil, Paul Slovic, and C. K. Mertz. 2007. "Culture and identity-protective cognition: Explaining the white-male effect in risk perception." *Journal of Empirical Legal Studies* 5, no. 3: 465–505. https://doi.org/10.1111/j.1740-1461.2007.00097.x.

Kahan, Dan M., Donald Braman, Paul Slovic, John Gastil, and Geoffrey Cohen. 2007. *The Second National Risk and Culture Study: Making Sense of – and Making Progress In – The American Culture War of Fact* (GWU Legal Studies Research Paper No. 370; Yale Law School, Public Law Working Paper No. 154; GWU Law School Public Law Research Paper No. 370; Harvard Law School Program on Risk Regulation Research Paper No. 08–26 No. 370). https://doi.org/10.2139/ssrn.1017189.

Kahan, Dan M., Hank Jenkins-Smith, and Donald Braman. 2011. "Cultural cognition of scientific consensus." *Journal of Risk Research* 14, no. 2: 147–74. https://doi.org/10.1080/13669877.2010.511246.

Kahan, Dan M., Ellen Peters, Maggie Wittlin, Paul Slovic, Lisa Larrimore Ouellette, Donald Braman, and Gregory Mandel. 2012. "The polarizing impact of science literacy and numeracy on perceived climate change risks." *Nature Climate Change* 2, no. 10: 732–35. https://doi.org/10.1038/Nclimate1547.

Kaldellis, John, Marina Kapsali, E. Kaldelli, and E. Katsanou. 2013. "Comparing recent views of public attitude on wind energy, photovoltaic and small hydro applications." *Renewable Energy* 52: 197–208. https://doi.org/10.1016/j.renene.2012.10.045.

Karlstrøm, Henrik, and Marianne Ryghaug. 2014. "Public attitudes towards renewable energy technologies in Norway: The role of party preferences." *Energy Policy* 67: 656–63. https://doi.org/10.1016/J.ENPOL.2013.11.049.

Katz, Daniel. 1960. "The Functional Approach to the Study of Attitudes." *Public Opinion Quarterly* 24, no. 2, Special Issue: Attitude Change: 163. https://doi.org/10.1086/266945.

Klick, Holly, and Eric Smith. 2010. "Public understanding of and support for wind power in the United States." *Renewable Energy* 35, no. 7: 1585–91. https://doi.org/10.1016/j.renene.2009.11.028.

Koirala, Binod Prasad, Yashar Araghi, Maarten Kroesen, Amineh Ghorbani, Rudi A. Hakvoort, and Paulien M. Herder. 2018. "Trust, awareness, and independence: Insights from a socio-psychological factor analysis of citizen knowledge and participation in community energy systems." *Energy Research & Social Science* 38: 33–40. https://doi.org/10.1016/J.ERSS.2018.01.009.

Kollmann, Andrea, and Johannes Reichl. 2015. "How Trust in Governments Influences the Acceptance of Environmental Taxes." In *Political Economy and Instruments of Environmental Politics*, 53–70. Cambridge, MA: The MIT Press. https://doi.org/10.7551/mitpress/9780262029247.003.0004.

Kontogianni, Areti, C. Tourkolias, Michalis Skourtos, and Dimitris Damigos. 2014. "Planning globally, protesting locally: Patterns in community perceptions towards the installation of wind farms." *Renewable Energy* 66: 170–77. https://doi.org/10.1016/J.RENENE.2013.11.074.

Krohn, Søren, and Steffen Damborg. 1999. "On public attitudes towards wind power." *Renewable Energy* 16, nos. 1–4: 954–60. https://doi.org/10.1016/S0960-1481(98)00339-5.

Ladenburg, Jacob. 2009. "Visual impact assessment of offshore wind farms and prior experience." *Applied Energy* 86, no. 3: 380–87. https://doi.org/10.1016/J.APENERGY.2008.05.005.
Langer, Katharina, Thomas Decker, Jutta Roosen, and Klaus Menrad. 2018. "Factors influencing citizens' acceptance and non-acceptance of wind energy in Germany." *Journal of Cleaner Production* 175: 133–44. https://doi.org/10.1016/J.JCLEPRO.2017.11.221.
Lee, T. R., B. A. Wren, and M. E. Hickman. 1989. "Public responses to the siting and operation of wind turbines." *Wind Engineering* 13, no. 4: 188–95. http://www.scopus.com/inward/record.url?eid=2-s2.0-0024931983&partnerID=40&md5=c065955f15f6c0755124cf08e0396664.
Liu, Wenling, Can Wang, and Arthur P. J. Mol. 2013. "Rural public acceptance of renewable energy deployment: The case of Shandong in China." *Applied Energy* 102: 1187–96. https://doi.org/10.1016/j.apenergy.2012.06.057.
MacPherson, Ronnie, and Ian Lange. 2013. "Determinants of green electricity tariff uptake in the UK." *Energy Policy* 62: 920–33. https://doi.org/10.1016/j.enpol.2013.07.089.
Maehr, Anna M., Greg R. Watts, Jennifer Hanratty, and Deborah Talmi. 2015. "Emotional response to images of wind turbines: A psychophysiological study of their visual impact on the landscape." *Landscape and Urban Planning* 142: 71–79. https://doi.org/10.1016/J.LANDURBPLAN.2015.05.011.
McCauley, Darren A., Raphael J. Heffron, Hannes Stephan, and Kirsten Jenkins. 2008. *International energy law review. International Energy Law Review*, vol. 32. Sweet & Maxwell. https://dspace.stir.ac.uk/handle/1893/18349#.XJfPPhNKgWo.
McLachlan, Carly. 2009. "'You don't do a chemistry experiment in your best china': Symbolic interpretations of place and technology in a wave energy case." *Energy Policy* 37, no. 12: 5342–50. https://doi.org/10.1016/J.ENPOL.2009.07.057.
Michaud, Kristy, Juliet E. Carlisle, and Eric Smith. 2008. "Nimbyism vs. environmentalism in attitudes toward energy development." *Environmental Politics* 17, no. 1: 20–39. https://doi.org/10.1080/09644010701811459.
Michel, Annina Helena, Matthias Buchecker, and Norman Backhaus. 2015. "Renewable Energy, Authenticity, and Tourism: Social Acceptance of Photovoltaic Installations in a Swiss Alpine Region." *Mountain Research and Development* 35, no. 2: 161–70. https://doi.org/10.1659/MRD-JOURNAL-D-14-00111.1.
Musall, Fabian David, and Onno Kuik. 2011. "Local acceptance of renewable energy: A case study from southeast Germany." *Energy Policy* 39, no. 6: 3252–60. https://doi.org/10.1016/J.ENPOL.2011.03.017.
Nadaï, Alain, and Olivier Labussière. 2009. "Wind power planning in France (Aveyron), from state regulation to local planning." *Land Use Policy*. https://doi.org/10.1016/j.landusepol.2008.10.018.
Naspetti, Simona, Serena Mandolesi, and Raffaele Zanoli. 2016. "Using visual Q sorting to determine the impact of photovoltaic applications on the landscape." *Land Use Policy* 57: 564–73. https://doi.org/10.1016/J.LANDUSEPOL.2016.06.021.
Oesterreichs Energie 2019. "Energie- und Stromerzeugungsmix Österreich." https://oesterreichsenergie.at/stromerzeugung-231.html.
Pasqualetti, Martin J. 2004. "Wind Power: Obstacles and Opportunities." *Environment: Science and Policy for Sustainable Development* 46, no. 7: 22–38. https://doi.org/10.1080/00139150409604395.
Pasqualetti, Martin J. 2011. "Social Barriers To Renewable Energy Landscapes." *Geographical Review* 101, no. 2: 201–23. https://doi.org/10.1111/j.1931-0846.2011.00087.
Perlaviciute, Goda, and Linda Steg. 2014. "Contextual and psychological factors shaping evaluations and acceptability of energy alternatives: Integrated review and research agenda."

Renewable and Sustainable Energy Reviews 35: 361–81. https://doi.org/10.1016/J.RSER.2014.04.003.

Pedersen, E., & Persson Waye, K. (2004). Perception and annoyance due to wind turbine noise—a dose–response relationship. *The Journal of the Acoustical Society of America, 116*(6), 3460–3470.

Pohl, Johannes, Joachim Gabriel, and Gundula Hübner. 2018. "Understanding stress effects of wind turbine noise: The integrated approach." *Energy Policy* 112: 119–28. https://doi.org/10.1016/J.ENPOL.2017.10.007.

Pohl, Johannes, Gundula Hübner, and Anja Mohs. 2012. "Acceptance and stress effects of aircraft obstruction markings of wind turbines." *Energy Policy* 50: 592–600. https://doi.org/10.1016/j.enpol.2012.07.062.

Proshansky, Harold M., Abbe K. Fabian, and Robert Kaminoff. 1983. "Place-identity: Physical world socialization of the self." *Journal of Environmental Psychology* 3, no. 1: 57–83. https://doi.org/10.1016/S0272-4944(83)80021-8.

Rand, Joseph, and Ben Hoen. 2017. "Thirty years of North American wind energy acceptance research: What have we learned?" *Energy Research & Social Science* 29: 135–48. https://doi.org/10.1016/J.ERSS.2017.05.019.

Renn, Ortwin. 1998. "Three decades of risk research: accomplishments and new challenges." *Journal of Risk Research* 1, no. 1: 49–71. https://doi.org/10.1080/136698798377321.

Roddis, Philippa, Stephen Carver, Martin Dallimer, Paul Norman, and Guy Ziv. 2018. "The role of community acceptance in planning outcomes for onshore wind and solar farms: An energy justice analysis." *Applied Energy* 226. https://doi.org/10.1016/j.apenergy.2018.05.087.

Sardianou, Eleni, and P. Genoudi. 2013. "Which factors affect the willingness of consumers to adopt renewable energies?" *Renewable Energy* 57: 1–4. https://doi.org/10.1016/j.renene.2013.01.031.

Schlosberg, David. 2007. *Defining Environmental Justice: Theories, Movements, and Nature. Defining Environmental Justice: Theories, Movements, and Nature.* https://doi.org/10.1093/acprof:oso/9780199286294.001.0001.

Simpson, Genevieve, and Julian Clifton. 2016. "Subsidies for residential solar photovoltaic energy systems in Western Australia: Distributional, procedural and outcome justice." *Renewable and Sustainable Energy Reviews* 65: 262–73. https://doi.org/10.1016/J.RSER.2016.06.060.

Sinclair, Philip, and Ragnar Löfstedt. 2001. "The influence of trust in a biomass plant application: the case study of Sutton, UK." *Biomass and Bioenergy* 21, no. 3: 177–84. https://doi.org/10.1016/S0961-9534(01)00020-4.

Slovic, Paul, James H. Flynn, and Mark Layman. 1991. "Perceived risk, trust, and the politics of nuclear waste." *Science*. https://doi.org/10.1126/science.254.5038.1603.

Smith, Eric, and Holly Klick. 2007. "Explaining NIMBY opposition to wind power." In *American Political Science Association Annual Meeting*.

Sovacool, Benjamin K., and Michael H. Dworkin. 2015. "Energy justice: Conceptual insights and practical applications." *Applied Energy* 142: 435–44. https://doi.org/10.1016/J.APENERGY.2015.01.002.

Sovacool, Benjamin K., and Pushkala Lakshmi Ratan. 2012. "Conceptualizing the acceptance of wind and solar electricity." *Renewable and Sustainable Energy Reviews*. https://doi.org/10.1016/j.rser.2012.04.048.

Sposato, Robert Gennaro, and Nina Hampl. 2018. "Worldviews as predictors of wind and solar energy support in Austria: Bridging social acceptance and risk perception research." *Energy Research & Social Science* 42: 237–46. https://doi.org/10.1016/J.ERSS.2018.03.012.

Stern, Paul C. 2000. "Toward a coherent theory of environmentally significant behavior." *Journal of Social Issues* 56, no. 3: 407–24. https://doi.org/10.1111/0022-4537.00175.

Stern, Paul C., Thomas Dietz, and Gregory A. Guagnano. 1995. "The new ecological paradigm in social-psychological context." *Environment and Behavior* 27, 6: 723–43. https://doi.org/10.1177/0013916595276001.

Strachan, Peter A., and David Lal. 2004. "Wind energy policy, planning and management practice in the UK: Hot air or a gathering storm?" *Regional Studies* 38, no. 5: 551–71. https://doi.org/10.1080/0143116042000229311.

Strazzera, Elisabetta, Marina Mura, and Davide Contu. 2012. "Combining choice experiments with psychometric scales to assess the social acceptability of wind energy projects: A latent class approach." *Energy Policy* 48: 334–47. https://doi.org/10.1016/J.ENPOL.2012.05.037.

Süsser, Diana, Martin Döring, and Beate M. W. Ratter. 2017. "Harvesting energy: Place and local entrepreneurship in community-based renewable energy transition." *Energy Policy* 101: 332–41. https://doi.org/10.1016/J.ENPOL.2016.10.018.

Tabi, Andrea, Stefanie Hille, and Rolf Wüstenhagen. 2014. "What makes people seal the green power deal?: Customer segmentation based on choice experiment in Germany." *Ecological Economics* 107: 206–15. https://doi.org/10.1016/j.ecolecon.2014.09.004.

Taylor, Jennifer, and Nicole Klenk. 2019. "The politics of evidence: Conflicting social commitments and environmental priorities in the debate over wind energy and public health." *Energy Research & Social Science* 47: 102–12. https://doi.org/10.1016/J.ERSS.2018.09.001.

Thayer, Robert L. 1988. "The aesthetics of wind energy in the United States: Case studies in public perception." In *European Community wind energy conference*, 470–76. Luxembourg: Commission of the European Communities.

Toke, David, Sylvia Breukers, and Maarten Wolsink. 2008. "Wind power deployment outcomes: How can we account for the differences?" *Renewable and Sustainable Energy Reviews* 12, no. 4: 1129–47. https://doi.org/10.1016/j.rser.2006.10.021.

Tsoutsos, Theocharis, Androniki Tsouchlaraki, Manolis Tsiropoulos, and John Kaldellis. 2009. "Visual Impact Evaluation Methods of Wind Parks: Application for a Greek Island." *Wind Engineering* 33, no. 1: 83–91. https://doi.org/10.1260/0309-524X.33.1.83.

Tyler, Tom R. 2000. "Social Justice: Outcome and Procedure." *International Journal of Psychology* 35, no. 2: 117–25. https://doi.org/10.1080/002075900399411.

Upham, Paul, Christian Oltra, and Àlex Boso. 2015. "Towards a cross-paradigmatic framework of the social acceptance of energy systems." *Energy Research & Social Science* 8: 100–12. https://doi.org/10.1016/J.ERSS.2015.05.003.

Van der Horst, Dan. 2007. "NIMBY or not? Exploring the relevance of location and the politics of voiced opinions in renewable energy siting controversies." *Energy Policy* 35, no. 5: 2705–14. https://doi.org/10.1016/j.enpol.2006.12.012.

Van der Loo, F. A. 2001. *Mediating windpower in the Netherlands: The Task Force windpower implementation*. Utrecht: NOVEM.

Van Veelen, Bregje, and Claire Haggett. 2017. "Uncommon Ground: The Role of Different Place Attachments in Explaining Community Renewable Energy Projects." *Sociologia Ruralis* 57: 533–54. https://doi.org/10.1111/soru.12128.

Vorkinn, Marit, and Hanne Riese. 2001. "Environmental Concern in a Local Context." *Environment and Behavior* 33, no. 2: 249–63. https://doi.org/10.1177/00139160121972972.

Walker, Chad, and Jamie Baxter. 2017. "Procedural justice in Canadian wind energy development: A comparison of community-based and technocratic siting processes." *Energy Research & Social Science* 29: 160–69. https://doi.org/10.1016/J.ERSS.2017.05.016.

Walker, Gordon, and Patrick Devine-Wright. 2008. "Community renewable energy: What should it mean?" *Energy Policy* 36, no. 2: 497–500. https://doi.org/10.1016/J.ENPOL.2007.10.019.

Walker, Gordon, Patrick Devine-Wright, Sue Hunter, Helen High, and Bob Evans. 2010. "Trust and community: Exploring the meanings, contexts and dynamics of community renewable energy." *Energy Policy* 38, no. 6: 2655–63. https://doi.org/10.1016/j.enpol.2009.05.055.

Walter, Götz. 2014. "Determining the local acceptance of wind energy projects in Switzerland: The importance of general attitudes and project characteristics." *Energy Research & Social Science* 4: 78–88. https://doi.org/10.1016/J.ERSS.2014.09.003.

Warren, Charles R., Richard Cowell, Geraint Ellis, Peter A. Strachan, and Joseph Szarka. 2012. "Wind Power: Towards a Sustainable Energy Future?" In *Learning from Wind Power*, 1–14. London: Palgrave Macmillan UK. https://doi.org/10.1057/9781137265272_1.

Warren, Charles R., Carolyn Lumsden, Simone O'Dowd, and Richard V. Birnie. 2005. "'Green On Green': Public perceptions of wind power in Scotland and Ireland." *Journal of Environmental Planning and Management* 48, no. 6: 853–75. https://doi.org/10.1080/09640560500294376.

Warren, Charles R., and Malcolm McFadyen. 2010. "Does community ownership affect public attitudes to wind energy? A case study from south-west Scotland." *Land Use Policy* 27, no. 2: 204–13. https://doi.org/10.1016/j.landusepol.2008.12.010.

West, Jodie, Ian Bailey, and Michael Winter. 2010. "Renewable energy policy and public perceptions of renewable energy: A cultural theory approach." *Energy Policy* 38, no. 10: 5739–48. https://doi.org/10.1016/j.enpol.2010.05.024.

Wildavsky, Aaron, and Karl Dake. 1990. "Theories of Risk Perception: Who Fears What and Why?" *Daedalus* 119: 41–60. https://www.amacad.org/publication/theories-risk-perception-who-fears-what-and-why.

Williams, Daniel R., and Jerry J. Vaske. 2003. "The Measurement of Place Attachment: Validity and Generalizability of a Psychometric Approach." *Forest Science* 49, no. 6: 830–40. https://doi.org/10.1093/forestscience/49.6.830.

Wolsink, Maarten. 1987. "Wind power for the electricity supply of houses." *The Netherlands Journal of Housing and Environmental Research* 2, no. 3: 195–214. https://doi.org/10.1007/BF02497872.

Wolsink, Maarten. 1989. "Attitudes and expectancies about wind turbines and wind farms." *Wind Engineering* 13, no. 4: 196–206. http://www.scopus.com/inward/record.url?eid=2-s2.0-0024889970&partnerID=40&md5=122a932e213e9134d45d2ec7a28c47e7.

Wolsink, Maarten. 2000. "Wind power and the NIMBY-myth: Institutional capacity and the limited significance of public support." *Renewable Energy* 21, no. 1: 49–64. https://doi.org/10.1016/S0960-1481(99)00130-5.

Wolsink, Maarten. 2006. "Invalid theory impedes our understanding: a critique on the persistence of the language of NIMBY." *Transactions of the Institute of British Geographers* 31, no. 1: 85–91.

Wolsink, Maarten. 2007a. "Planning of renewables schemes: Deliberative and fair decision-making on landscape issues instead of reproachful accusations of non-cooperation." *Energy Policy* 35, no. 5: 2692–2704. https://doi.org/10.1016/j.enpol.2006.12.002.

Wolsink, Maarten. 2007b. "Wind power implementation: The nature of public attitudes; Equity and fairness instead of 'backyard motives.'" *Renewable and Sustainable Energy Reviews* 11, no. 6: 1188–1207. https://doi.org/10.1016/j.rser.2005.10.005.

Wolsink, Maarten. 2018. "Social acceptance revisited: gaps, questionable trends, and an auspicious perspective." *Energy Research & Social Science* 46: 287–95. https://doi.org/10.1016/J.ERSS.2018.07.034.

Wüstenhagen, Rolf, Maarten Wolsink, and Mary Jean Bürer. 2007. "Social acceptance of renewable energy innovation: An introduction to the concept." *Energy Policy* 35, no. 5: 2683–91. https://doi.org/10.1016/j.enpol.2006.12.001.

Yuan, Xueliang, Jian Zuo, and Donald Huisingh. 2015. "Social acceptance of wind power: A case study of Shandong Province, China." *Journal of Cleaner Production* 92: 168–78. https://doi.org/10.1016/j.jclepro.2014.12.097.

Zhai, Pei, and Eric D. Williams. 2012. "Analyzing consumer acceptance of photovoltaics (PV) using fuzzy logic model." *Renewable Energy* 41: 350–57. https://doi.org/10.1016/J.RENENE.2011.11.041.

Zoellner, Jan, Petra Schweizer-Ries, and Christin Wemheuer. 2008. "Public acceptance of renewable energies: Results from case studies in Germany." *Energy Policy* 36, no. 11: 4136–41. https://doi.org/10.1016/j.enpol.2008.06.026.

4 Capacity Building in Renewable Energy and Energy Efficiency Finance

Alexander Boensch, Volker Jaensch

4.1 Introduction: What Is Capacity Building and Why Is It needed?

The United Nations Framework Convention on Climate Change (hereinafter referred to as UNFCCC, or the "Convention"), that was adopted on May 9, 1992, signed in the same year by 154 countries and finally entered into force on March 21, 1994, has the ultimate objective of stabilizing "greenhouse gas concentrations in the atmosphere at a level that would prevent dangerous anthropogenic interference with the climate system," to ensure that food production is not threatened and to enable economic development to proceed in a *sustainable manner.*"[1] Article 3 of this Convention guides the undersigned Parties to "protect the climate system for the benefit of present and future generations of humankind," whereby "the developed country Parties should take the lead in combating climate change and the adverse effects thereof" and "the specific needs and special circumstances of developing country Parties [especially vulnerable, through climate change adversely-effected, and abnormally-burdened ones] . . . should be given full consideration."[2]

It is argued by UNFCCC that the establishment of sustainable, climate-friendly development pathways in developed and developing countries will depend on the adoption of a range of approaches, first and foremost the following[3]:

- **Adaptation and mitigation actions** have to be identified, planned and implemented,
- **Technology development, dissemination and deployment** is to be facilitated,
- **Access to climate finance** must be procured,
- Related aspects of **education, training and public awareness** are to be developed, and
- Information communication is to be ensured

As not all developing countries have sufficient capacities to deal with the challenges brought by climate change, the importance of building the capacity of these countries

1 See United Nations (1992), Article 2, p. 9.

2 See ibid., Article 3.

3 See "Building capacity in the UNFCCC process," https://unfccc.int/topics/capacity-building/the-big-picture/capacity-in-the-unfccc-process.

Alexander Boensch, Volker Jaensch, RENAC's Green Banking Team, Renewables Academy (RENAC) AG, Berlin

https://doi.org/10.1515/9783110607888-004

to effectively address climate change has long been recognized by the negotiating Parties, through the Convention (1992), its Kyoto Protocol (1997) and most recently the Paris Agreement (2015). Article 11 of the Paris Agreement defines capacity-building related goals, guiding principles and procedural obligations for all Parties. It calls on developed country Parties to enhance support to capacity-building in developing countries, and on developing country Parties to regularly communicate progress on implementing capacity-building plans, policies, actions or measures. The Paris Agreement also calls for country-driven capacity-building that is based on recipient countries' needs and ownership.

But what exactly is ***Capacity Building*** and how is it applied in the context of climate change adjustment activities? *UNFCCC* defines Capacity Building as "enhancing the ability of individuals, organizations and institutions in developing countries and in countries with economies in transition to identify, plan and implement ways to mitigate and adapt to climate change."[4] More generally, the term has emerged in development theory, where Capacity Building is for example viewed as a "technology of neoliberal governance," i.e., "an apparatus of rule that requires a diverse range of new rationalities that attempt to "grow" institutional frameworks, enhance the skills of people, and transfer knowledge through the formation of new partnerships" (Phillips & Ilcan 2004, 393). That is also why some authors do not necessarily see a major difference between the concept of Capacity Building and other concepts such as institution-building, institutional strengthening or development management but point out the aspect that Capacity Building should create the strengthening of the capacity to execute a specific program *independent* of the permanence of a specific institution (Potter & Brough 2004, 337). Better than just using the expression as "an over-pompous synonym for training," one should see Capacity Building as a systemic concept that takes into account "a hierarchy of capacity needs" (ibid.) and works at multiple levels of the system.

The UNFCCC seems to have considered these arguments when designing recommendations on how to conduct Capacity Building in the context of climate change adjustment activities. It has identified three levels of interaction, at which Capacity Building activities can be carried out: (1) the ***individual level*** (by developing educational, training and awareness-raising activities), (2) the ***institutional level*** (by fostering the development of and cooperation between organizations and institutions), and (3) the ***systemic level*** (by creating enabling environments through economic and regulatory policies and accountability frameworks). The Figure 4.1 below summarizes the multilevel concept of Capacity Building and the interaction between the levels in more detail.

4 See "Capacity Building," in UNFCCC eHandbook, https://unfccc.int/resource/bigpicture/index.html#content-capacity-building.

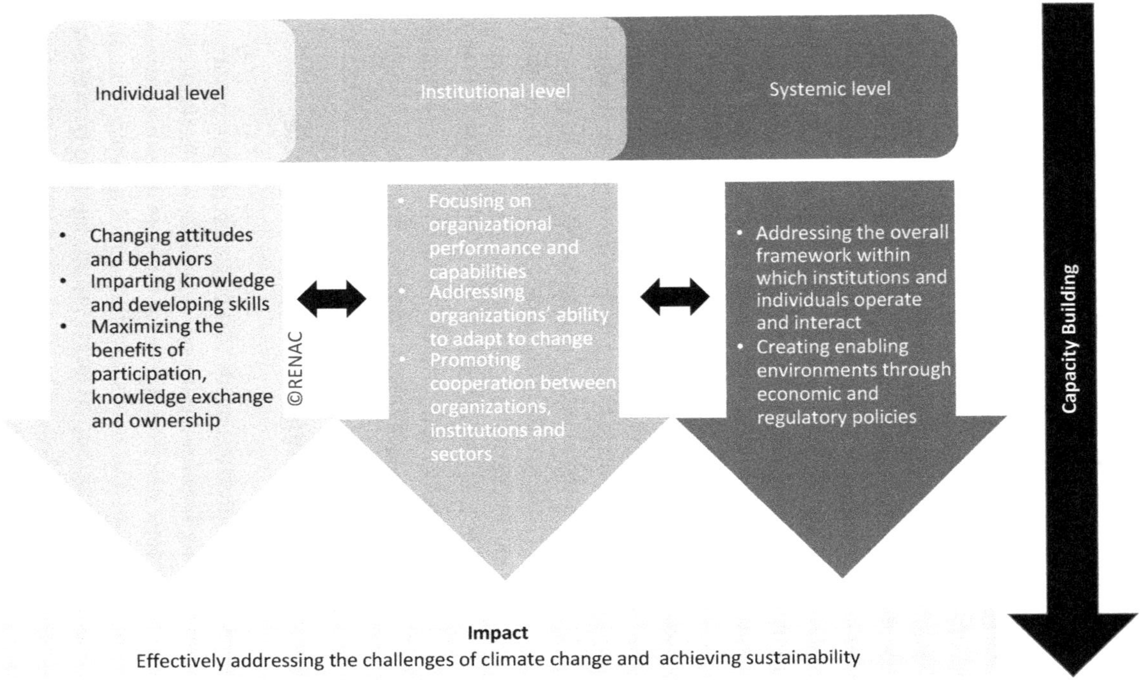

Figure 4.1: Three levels of Capacity Building activities and related interactions.[5]

5 Source: adapted from UNFCCC, https://unfccc.int/resource/bigpicture/index.html#content-capacity-building.

While the number of entities in emerging and developing countries focusing on climate change issues has substantially increased in the recent past, observers and institutions in many of these countries point to persisting capacity gaps of public and private sector staff and insufficient institutional capacities,[6] for example related to the implementation of climate change ***mitigation measures*** (such as e.g., those fostering the development of renewable energy and energy efficiency projects) and ***adaptation measures*** (such as those fostering adjustment projects that help to reduce the potential negative consequences of effects caused by climate change). In order to effectively increase the knowledge base for the subject in emerging and developing countries, suitable training programs need to be developed that also reflect individual country circumstances.

The remaining sections of this section deal with a structured discussion on training needs in the field of renewable energy (RE) and energy efficiency (EE) and will present the experiences gained during the successful implementation of the ***Green Banking Capacity Building Programme*** that has been financed by the German International Climate Initiative (IKI) supported through the German Federal Ministry for the Environment, Nature Conservation and Nuclear Safety (BMU). Under the umbrella of this project, a comprehensive training program related to RE and EE financing has been developed and is carried out in five Southeast Asian countries from October 2015 until April 2019. It is the opinion of the authors that the implemented project can serve as a case study for an overall successful Capacity Building initiative in the field of renewable energy and energy efficiency finance.

4.2 RE and EE Training Needs along the Project Life Cycle

A thorough understanding of the individual needs of a target group in a country or region, in which Capacity Building is carried out, is essential for the institutions in charge of the Capacity Building activities (the "Capacity Builders") so that they can offer suitable programs of education. The needs and the required depth of knowledge vary widely, not only from target group to target group, but also between target country markets or regions.

Any Capacity Builder that aims at implementing educational programs such as trainings on renewable energy (RE) and energy efficiency (EE) technologies must first assess the general conditions in the target country or region, such as for instance the availability of natural resources, the local electricity generation mix, the legal framework related to RE and EE and the interest and associated behavior of the public, consumers of electricity, potential investors and providers of finance and others.

6 UNFCCC, ibid.

In many cases, the potential Capacity Building assignment is assessed by taking a general ***project life cycle perspective*** into consideration.[7] The following exemplary depiction of the RE and EE project life cycle shows that technological and non-technological areas usually converge with the corresponding stakeholders involved (Figure 4.2):

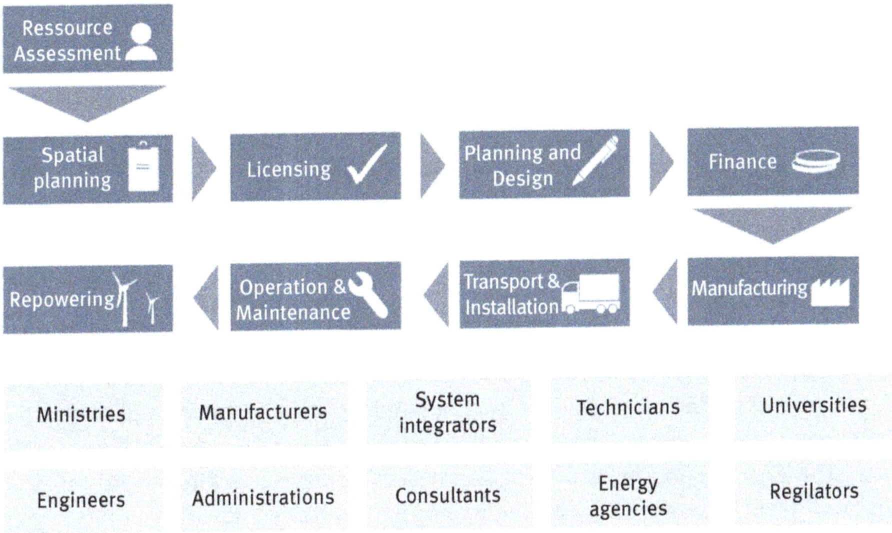

Figure 4.2: Schematic depiction of the life cycle of RE and EE projects.[8]

In order to adequately deliver the required educational contents for a Capacity Building assignment, the offered trainings must be adapted to different job profiles and other given conditions related to the target group and it must offer appropriate, relevant and variable work scopes and contents, especially in the following fields of activity:

- Technical aspects
- Economics and financing
- Project development, sizing and simulation

7 Project life cycles usually split projects into sequences from the beginning to their closure or rehabilitation. In the context of RE and EE projects, a simplistic approach can for instance define the relevant sequences in line with the project value chain as development, construction, operation and repowering phases. Figure 4.2 follows this general logic and specifies the phases further.

8 Source: Renewables Academy (RENAC), 2019.

- Legal and regulatory aspects, support schemes
- International market development
- Marketing and sales

4.3 Project Financing as a Major Educational Component in RE and EE Capacity Building

Mounting costs of conventional energy generation, increasing energy demand caused by the consumption behavior of a growing middle class and accelerated economic growth, as well as increasing greenhouse gas emissions and the burden of the cost of energy imports are typical challenges that developing and newly industrialized countries face. These challenges may call for a potential reorganization of such countries' energy supply and energy use in the areas of electricity and heat generation, cooling and mobility. In order to expand the use of RE and EE, the availability of functioning financial markets, appropriate financing options and supporting policy frameworks are necessary.

RE and EE investments are constantly growing on a worldwide scale and the improvement of financing availability as a building block for successful project development and implementation leads to more green energy projects,[9] a higher security of energy supply, more private sector development and the creation of jobs, because local professionals with the appropriate knowhow are able to profit from new business opportunities in this growing industry. At the same time, the dependency on fossil fuels and energy imports, pollution, climate-damaging emissions and subsidies can be reduced.

In many developing and newly industrialized countries, however, the lack of adequate financing options caused inter alia by underdeveloped financial market environments is still a great obstacle for opening up potentials for climate protection by means of exploiting available renewable energy and energy efficiency options. That is why a comprehensive involvement of the private finance sector and the introduction of suitable financing instruments (first and foremost the "best practice" instrument of *project finance*) via related Capacity Building became an obvious and urgent matter. However, banks in the target countries often do not yet have RE and EE financing on their agenda or do not give it sufficient priority. On the management level, RE and EE projects are often categorized as actions of Corporate Social Responsibility and are not always considered as interesting business opportunities, yet. Therefore, it is argued that government-backed financial institutions and development banks should play a

9 See e.g., Frankfurt School – UNEP Centre/BNEF (2018) for ongoing coverage of worldwide statistics on RE investment and financing activity.

crucial role in implementing national policies and motivating the local financial sector to engage in green energy and energy efficiency finance.

When it comes to the actual arrangement and execution of RE and EE project financings, a high level of in-house expertise is required in financial institutions. Typically required qualifications include for example specific knowhow of cash flow-related lending principles, project contract structures, the assessment of project-related due diligence documents and financial modeling skills. Furthermore, there is often a lack of knowledge about internationally available funding programs and refinancing options for financing climate protection projects at reasonable costs, which could act as additional "project enabler" in developing and newly industrialized countries.[10] As a consequence, banks and investors in many cases tend to be reluctant due to a lack of experience and risk evaluation capacities.

Capacity Building activities in the field of RE and EE financing should help to improve the accessibility as well as the use of adequate financing options and make financial institutions become more confident with the assessment of the risks associated to lending to such projects. Furthermore, it should increase the availability and use of (private sector) financing instruments for RE, EE and climate change mitigation projects on the national and international level and show that involvement in this sector also provides profitable and sustainable business opportunities for banks. This would help to develop a willingness of financial institutions to get more deeply involved in RE and EE finance.

4.4 Experiences with the Green Banking Capacity Building Programme on Green Energy and Climate Finance in Southeast Asia

4.4.1 Introduction to the Case Study

In 2015, just at the same time when the Paris Agreement was enacted, German Capacity Building specialist Renewables Academy (RENAC) firstly developed and implemented a large-scale educational program that exclusively deals with the subject of RE and EE finance, appropriate risk evaluation and mitigation schemes and the accessibility of international climate finance options. This "Green Banking" project was chosen in the course of an ideas competition launched by and subsequently funded through the German International Climate Initiative (IKI) which is supported

10 Such providers of program funding for RE and EE financing include, among others, multi-, bilateral and regional development banks, but also international climate finance institutions, such as the Green Climate Fund, established in 2010 under the UNFCCC framework.

by the German Federal Ministry for the Environment, Nature Conservation and Nuclear Safety (BMU).

Under the framework of this project, a comprehensive training program related to RE and EE financing has been developed and is carried out in five Southeast Asian countries between October 2015 and April 2019 (Figure 4.3). Participation in "Green Banking" trainings is exclusively based on scholarships and especially targeted to participants located in the partner countries India, Indonesia, the Philippines, Thailand and Vietnam. These five countries have been selected because they happen to be the most populated destinations in the IKI target region and are jointly facing the challenge of ensuring viable energy supply to their growing populations.

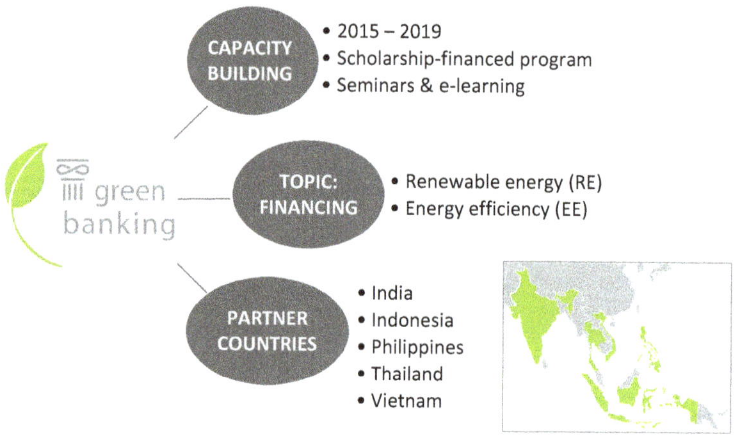

Figure 4.3: Content-related and geographical scope of the Green Banking Capacity Building Programme.[11]

The aim of the Green Banking Programme is to promote the market development of RE and EE by significantly increasing the availability of suitable financing options, mainly in the form of project-related loans and by making international climate protection funding instruments accessible to local entrepreneurs via their domestic financial institutions.

The main target group, from which delegates for the Green Banking Programme have been selected, are private and public institutions concerned with the direct or indirect financing of RE and EE or those who plan to do so in the future. These institutions include:

11 Source: Renewables Academy (RENAC), 2019.

- Development and commercial banks
- Private equity, risk capital and infrastructure funds
- Other institutional investors and subject-related intermediaries (e.g., consultants)

Further, applicants from the following associated group of institutions were eligible to apply for scholarships in the Green Banking Capacity Building Programme:
- RE and EE project developers concerned with the structuring of financings and involved in due diligence assignments
- Ministries and public institutions involved in designing political and economic structures which need information on the financing and general feasibility requirements of RE and EE projects

4.4.2 Educational Components of the Green Banking Programme

Activities conducted under the Green Banking Capacity Building Programme on Green Energy and Climate Finance have been divided into three main components:

Capacity Needs Assessments (CNAs)
The specific learning needs of the target groups in the participating countries related to RE and EE Capacity Building were initially assessed in so-called "fact-finding missions" or "Capacity Needs Assessments" (CNAs) that were carried out in each of the countries prior to any designing of educational contents. Such preparatory visits were important to adjust and tailor the planned course contents to the RE- and EE-related environment in the respective country and the requirements of the main target group of participants. Close contacts with important target group members and institutions were established and national strategies as well as planned and ongoing measures or undertakings related to the RE and EE sector of the target countries were integrated into the training contents. This also proved to be useful for initial marketing of the project and approaching prospective suitable candidates for the advanced training program.

Trainings and Seminars
Participants of Green Banking trainings and seminars gain specific know-how in RE and EE technologies, project structuring, financial modeling and financing skills, as well as knowledge about appropriate risk evaluation (due diligence) and risk mitigation measures. The development of private sector finance instruments for climate change mitigation are fostered and the readiness to leverage national credit lines with international climate change mitigation schemes increased. Further, specific knowledge about funding opportunities provided by the UNFCCC-enacted Green Climate Fund (GCF) and the available access opportunities are disseminated. The

following educational components have been developed and are delivered to the selected target group participants under the program:

- **Online Training (8 weeks):** It provides a comprehensive introduction and delivers an overview to green energy and energy efficiency finance through a 100% distance learning approach.
- **Blended Learning:** It includes the comprehensive introduction and overview to green energy and energy efficiency finance of the 8-week Online Training and extends it by one country-specific interactive training on technical and financial aspects (3-day face-to-face seminar conducted in each partner country) that builds upon the content of the previous Online Training.
- **"Green Energy Finance Specialist" (GEFS) certificate program:** This extensive 6-month training accredited by the Finance Accreditation Agency (FAA) in Kuala Lumpur provides comprehensive and in-depth knowledge on green energy, energy efficiency and climate finance topics based on eight online modules and a 3-day interactive face-to-face seminar.
  The GEFS deals with the following main contents and learning objectives[12]:
- **Introduction to green finance**. The introductory module aims at enabling learners to demonstrate principles of commonly used renewable energy technologies, to breakdown the principles of renewable energy and energy efficiency projects, to summarize the global and regional market development for renewable energy and energy efficiency investments, as well as to assess the potential of renewable energy technologies and energy efficiency sectors in their home country.
- **Political and legal market frameworks for RE and EE (country-specific)**. In the second module, students will learn how to categorize different policy measures for renewable energy and energy efficiency, discuss the pros and cons of different policy measures and propose suitable policy measures, and assess the political and market framework regarding renewable energy and energy efficiency deployment in their country.
- **Financing EE and RE projects**. After completing modules three and four, students will be able to demonstrate two different approaches how companies can achieve energy savings, explain the special features of energy efficiency finance and ESCO models and appraise an energy efficiency project in detail, also under the use of the ESCO model. In relation to RE projects, participants will learn how to perform a risk assessment for such projects, develop a term sheet for a sample case, and learn how to amend bank-internal procedures for credit evaluation in a way that they are suitable for assessing RE project loans.
- **Project contracts and financial modeling**. The fifth module enables learners to utilize a provided financial model (the RE Project Evaluator) for the assessment of a project's financial attractiveness, debt servicing capacity as well as pricing in the

12 See also Figure 4.4 for a detailed outline of the individual topics delivered in each module.

context of an acquisition or disposal. Further, the participants learn to choose and analyse different types of contracts required in renewable energy project finance.
- **Special issues in project evaluation (insurance, ESIA, O&M strategies).** Students of the sixth module explore, how to assess the impact of insurance and O&M programs on the risks and structuring of RE projects, utilize adequate insurance and O&M programs to reduce the risks for the involved stakeholders and the learn about the importance of fulfilling the equator principles in their environmental and social impact assessment.
- **International climate finance.** Taking part in the seventh module will enable learners to assess the current climate finance landscape including its current institutions, sources of finance and mechanisms, organize procedures to receive funding from domestic or international climate finance sources, and to carry out a study to identify the most suitable climate finance option for their organization.
- **RE projects in the portfolio context.** The final online module deals with how to assess and structure RE investments in a project portfolio context.
- **Train-the-Trainer seminars:** This seminar features a didactics training for professionals with experience in green energy finance that are willing to contribute as local trainers to the GEFS certificate program seminars in the partner countries.

Networking Events

In order to complement the educational component (trainings and seminars) with the practical exchange of project financing and market experience among participants from the partner countries and with German experts from the banking, investment and RE and EE market sectors, the Green Banking Programme additionally offers the following two networking event formats:
- **Delegation Tour with Business-to-Business (B2B) meetings:** This Delegation Tour to Germany enables senior professionals from the partner countries to engage in networking activities with RE and EE financing experts in Germany and to have B2B meetings with financial institutions.
- **Alumni conferences:** 1-day conferences are carried out in each of the partner countries at the end of the program to allow former Green Banking participants to network with fellow participants and Green Banking alumni in the context of a structured event. Alumni conferences feature speaker presentations, panel discussions, case studies and ideas/experience exchange.

4.5 Practical Experience with the Programme in Southeast Asia

Lessons Learned from the Capacity Needs Assessments

Already during the CNA trips to India, Thailand, the Philippines, Indonesia and Vietnam, financial sector institutions in the target countries showed vital interest in

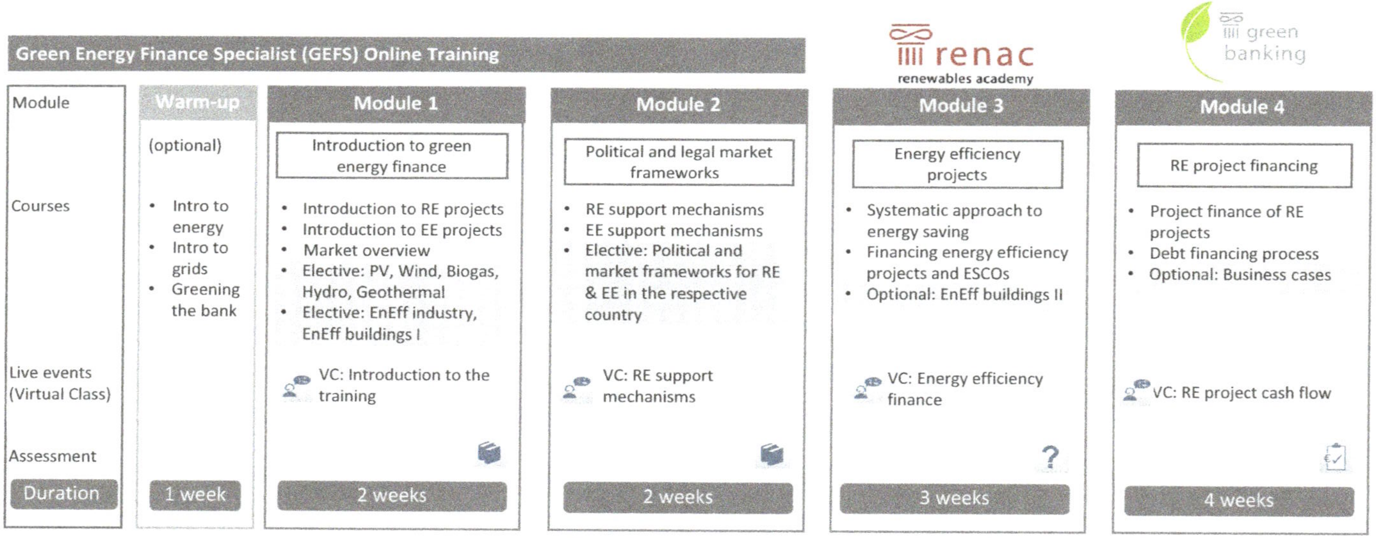

Figure 4.4: Time schedule and course modules of the Green Energy Finance Specialist (GEFS) Training.[13]

13 Source: Renewables Academy (RENAC), 2019.

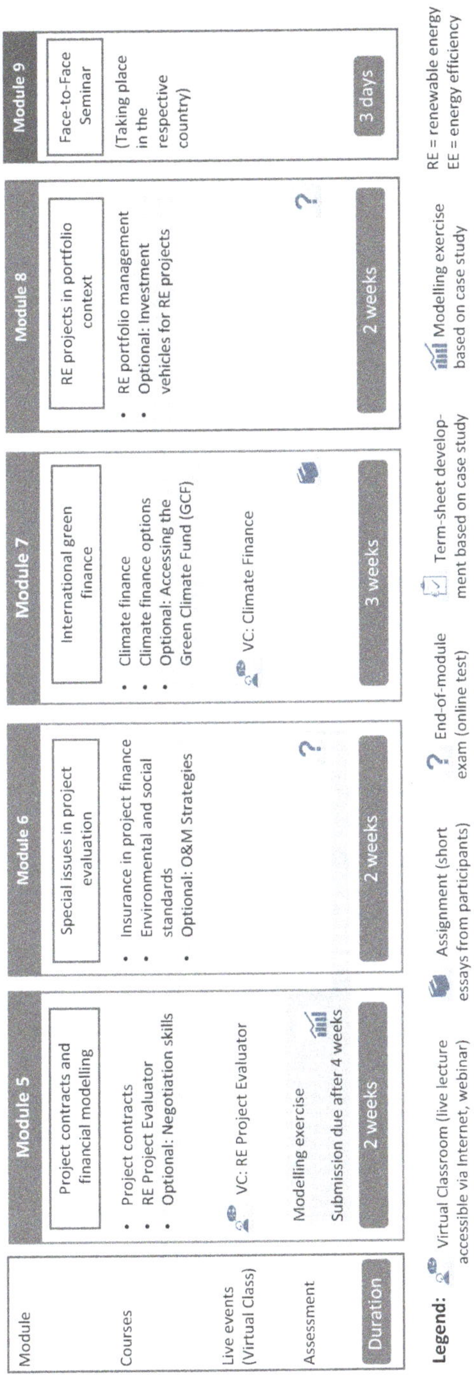

Figure 4.4 (continued)

the Green Banking Capacity Building Programme. The different trainings were developed by the Capacity Builder according to the derived results of the fact-finding missions. The following lessons could be learned in that phase of the project:

- Through the CNA, the Capacity Builder identified the different focus areas for suitable and promising RE and EE applications in each partner country. These findings formed the basis for the development of the country-specific training designs and conducting of the face-to-face seminars.
- It became clear that, due to the different assessment perspectives in RE and EE finance (mainly project vs. corporate finance-based approach), these topics had to be treated separately within the training formats, because working professionals involved in one of the topics were typically not directly involved in the other one and vice versa.
- In terms of desired training contents, the CNA-results pointed out that the interviewed stakeholders and institutions in all partner countries mainly indicated potential learning interest in the area of feasibility assessment of RE and EE projects. Other popular topics named were (1) project life cycle analysis, (2) how to conduct project-specific due diligence? (3) suitable financing instruments and (4) assessment of regulatory frameworks in terms of their bankability.
- Representatives of the financial sector in all partner countries explicitly expressed their wishes to include learning components into the training about how to access international climate finance schemes, specifically the GCF.

4.6 Lessons Learned from Conducted Training and Seminars, as well as Network Events

As per the beginning of 2019, more than 600 industry professionals have been trained in Green Banking Programme activities in Southeast Asia. Figure 4.5 presents an overview of some of the financial institutions that, among institutions from other industries and the public sector, recommended the program to their employees and also sent participants:

It is interesting to note that the majority of financial institutions that sent participants in the Green Banking Capacity Building Programme had previously already been active in the field of RE and EE financing. Financial institutions without existing green energy lending exposure were also more reluctant to send participants in the program. Therefore, a matter of improvement in future Capacity Building programs of that kind should be to develop a more direct access to financial institutions without RE and EE lending track record and find ways to motivate such institutions to participate in the program by actively marketing the commercial benefits of RE and EE lending activity to them.

During the implementation of the different educational formats it became apparent that the financial sector institutions preferred accredited trainings and seminars with

Country	Institutions
Indonesia	• ExIm Bank ID • Bank BRI • IFC • Bank Central Asia (BCA) • Bank Mandiri
India	• ExIm Bank IN • Axis Bank • Yes Bank • RBL Bank • State Bank of India • NABARD (National Bank for Agriculture & Rural Development)
Philippines	• Banco de Oro • Land Bank of the Philippines • Bank of the Philippine Islands • Development Bank of the Philippines • IFC
Thailand	• Bank of Ayudhya PCL. • BNP Paribas • Kasikornbank • Siam Commercial Bank
Vietnam	• Vietnam Development Bank • State Bank of Vietnam • Asian Development Bank • Saigon-Hanoi JSC Bank (SHB) • Ho Chi Minh City Development Joint Stock Commercial Bank • SaiGon Thuong Tin Bank (Sacombank)

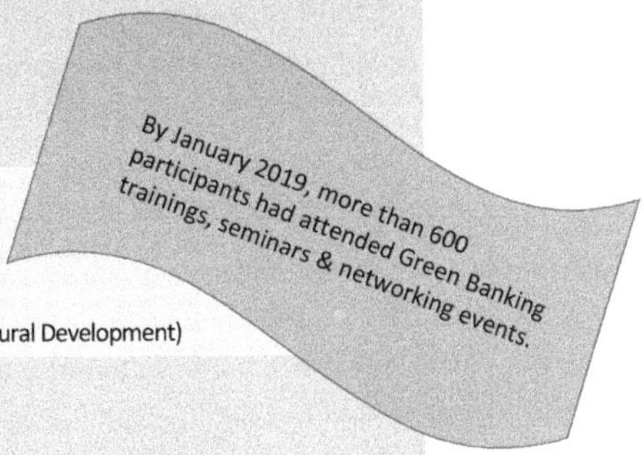

Figure 4.5: Overview of institutions that sent participants in the Green Banking Capacity Building Programme.[14]

graded certificates, even if the required personal work load for the participating delegates was much higher compared to the other (non-accredited) training formats. This conclusion can be drawn when we analyse the development of the application figures for the (non-accredited) Blended Learning training as compared to the applications for the training leading to the (accredited) GEFS certificate (see Figure 4.6). In 2017, when both training components were offered in parallel, the number of applications received was considerably higher for the GEFS certificate than for the Blended Learning training. Due to the positive response related to the 2017 GEFS training, applications even increased by 50% for the second intake of the Green Energy Finance Specialist in 2018.

The Green Banking Capacity Building Programme also received continuous interest for seats offered for the three available Delegation Tours with B2B meetings and the two Train-the-Trainer seminars, as shown in Figure 4.7.

Both the network and educational components of the program target more senior staff in the partner country institutions and have been conducted in Germany. Senior representatives that primarily came from the financial services sector in all five partner countries valued the opportunity to network with peers from the financial services and RE industry in Germany during the Delegation Tour, while delegates from a

14 Source: Renewables Academy (RENAC), 2019.

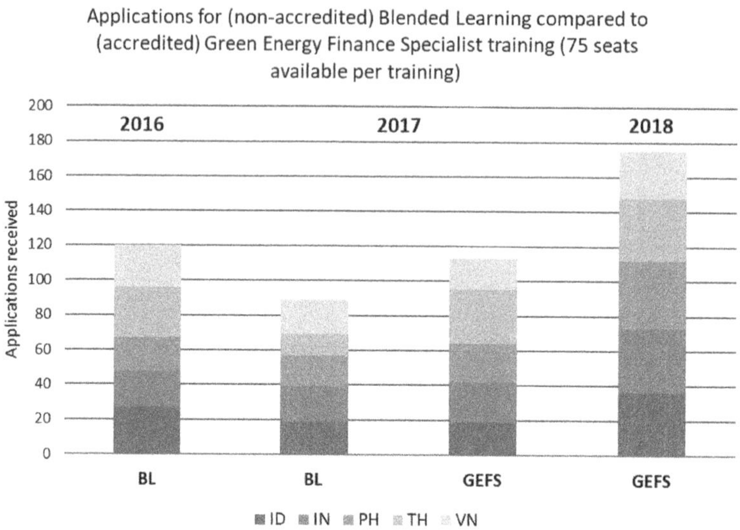

Figure 4.6: Number of received applications for Blended Learning versus GEFS training (own representation).

more mixed RE and EE sector and educational audience appreciated the chance to develop or build up own training skills in the Train-the-Trainer seminars.

All trainings and seminar activities conducted online and face-to-face are evaluated using structured feedback questionnaires in order to receive a balanced and anonymous feedback of the participants and to estimate the Capacity Building impact of the Green Banking Programme.

The feedback given to the program was positive throughout all educational and networking activities conducted between early 2016 and the end of 2018 and several involved stakeholders from the financial sector in the partner countries expressed the need for a continuation of the Green Banking Capacity Building activities to further support expansion of the RE and EE financing markets and general sustainable development in their countries.

As a consequence, the Capacity Builder decided to continue to offer the accredited GEFS certificate program in Southeast Asia even after the public funding through the German International Climate Initiative (IKI) expires in Q2/2019 (albeit on a commercial basis).

4.7 Future Development of the Green Banking Programme

After the successful implementation of the Green Banking Programme in Southeast Asia, the Capacity Builder was given the opportunity by the German International

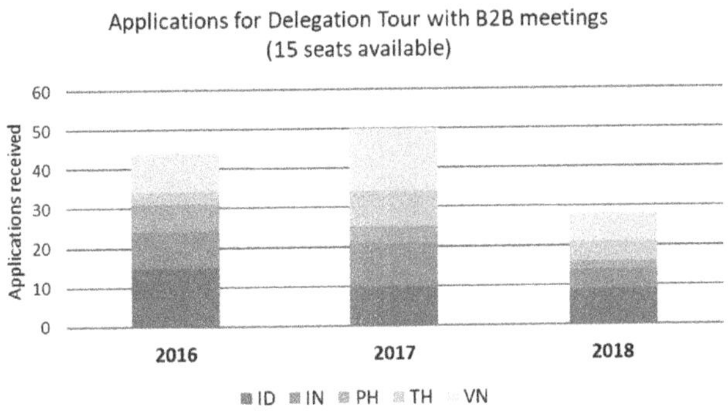

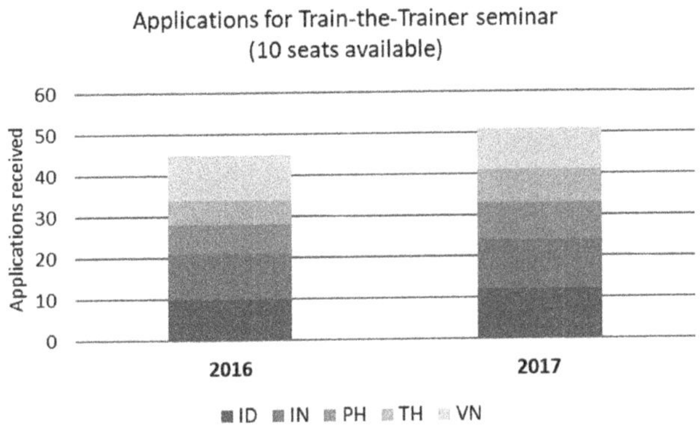

Figure 4.7: Number of received applications for Delegation Tours and Train-the-Trainer seminars (own representation).

Climate Initiative (IKI) to expand the program to selected countries in Latin America. This again scholarship-based, publicly-funded program extension is being implemented from late 2018 until mid-2022 and encompasses the partner countries Peru, Colombia, Honduras, El Salvador, Guatemala, Costa Rica, Nicaragua and Panama. For the implementation of the program, the Capacity Builder teamed up with the newly founded ***IFC – Green Banking Academy (IFC–GBAC) of the International Finance Corporation*** (which is a member of the World Bank Group). All new Green Banking educational and networking activities in the Latin American partner countries will be offered under the umbrella of IFC–GBAC. The involvement of IFC will guarantee an excellent access to the financial sector in the Latin American partner countries.

The main objective of the cooperation between the Capacity Builder and IFC is to support the green transformation of the financial services sector in Latin America towards a greener business model that mitigates challenges from climate change and that fosters green business opportunities. A major IFC study, conducted in 2017 among 25% of all Latin American commercial banks, revealed that insufficient knowledge about climate-related challenges and opportunities is considered to be the main barrier for Latin American banks to become "greener" (IFC 2017) providing in fact the rationale to conduct RE and EE Capacity Building activities also in this region of the world. The IFC GBAC – RENAC alliance is centered around providing educational components to train bankers in the economic and financial aspects of RE and EE projects and to connect them via networking events.

In parallel to the activities in Latin America, RENAC also started another Green Banking Capacity Building Programme which focuses on the MENA region specifically on Egypt, Jordan, Tunisia and Morocco. The Programme is part of the DIAPOL-CE – Policy dialogue and knowledge management on low emissions development strategies in the MENA region project. DIAPOL-CE is funded by the German International Climate Initiative (IKI) and implemented by the German Corporation for International Cooperation (GIZ).

Having initially started in Southeast Asia, the success and fast extension of the Green Banking Capacity Building Programme demonstrates that there is a strong demand for RE and EE Capacity Building in the financial sector on a global scale. The Green Banking Programme is one instrument to meet this unmet demand. The mainly publicly-funded program is now moving forward into different parts of the world.

References

Frankfurt School – UNEP Centre/BNEF. 2018. "Global Trends in Renewable Energy Investment 2017." Published by Frankfurt School FS-UNEP Collaborating Centre & BNEF Bloomberg New Energy Finance. Main authors: Angus McCrone, Ulf Moslener, Francoise d'Estais, and Christine Grüning. http://www.fs-unep-centre.org.

International Finance Corporation (IFC). 2017. "Green Finance Latin America 2017 Report: What is the Latin American banking sector doing to mitigate climate change?" https://www.ifc.org/wps/wcm/connect/baf83cc2-21c0-47c8-a4a8-d062e7e8e896/Green+Finance+Report+2017+Nov28.pdf?MOD=AJPERES.

Phillips, Lynne, and Suzan Ilcan. 2004. "Capacity-Building: The Neoliberal Governance of Development." *Canadian Journal of Development Studies* (January 2004): 393–409

Potter, Christopher, and Richard Brough. 2004. "Systemic capacity building: a hierarchy of needs." *Health Policy and Planning* 19, no. 5: 336–45.

UNFCCC eHandbook. https://unfccc.int/.

United Nations. 1992. "United Nations Framework Convention on Climate Change." https://unfccc.int/resource/docs/convkp/conveng.pdf.

5 The Legal Framework of Promoting Renewable Energies: A Cross-National Study

Christoph Torwegge, Thies Goldner

5.1 Introduction

5.1.1 Short Overview of the Historical Background of the Development of Promotion Systems for Renewable Energy

In the past 50 years, several sociopolitical factors played a role in the prosperous development of renewable energies ("**RE**"). A first expression of a rising environmental awareness serving as an initial spark for the concept of RE was the report from the Club of Rome named "*Limits of Growth*," released in 1972, which suggested an end of commodities, especially fossil fuels, if economic growth continued at the same rate. The desire for a sustainable energy source intensified with the first (1973–1974) and second (1979–1980) oil crises. The artificial shortage of oil supply by the Organization of Arab Petroleum Exporting Countries ("**OAPEC**") in the first oil crisis and the uncertainty about a decline in production due to the Islamic Revolution in Iran, as well as the first gulf war in the second oil crisis, led to a significant increase in oil prices and demonstrated the dependence on fossil fuels to the industrial nations.[1] Additionally, the Global 2000 Report from 1980, prepared over a three year period by the U.S. President's Council on Environmental Quality ("**CEQ**") in cooperation with the U.S. Department of State and other federal agencies, warned of serious consequences for humanity if changes were not made in environmental policies around the globe. The report specifically stated:

> Atmospheric concentrations of carbon dioxide and ozone-depleting chemicals are expected to increase at rates that could alter the world´s climate and upper atmosphere significantly by 2050. Acid rain from increased combustion of fossil fuels (especially coal) threatens damage to lakes, soils, and crops.[2]

1 Agentur für Erneuerbare Energien e.V., in Renews Spezial 41: 20 Jahre Förderung von Strom aus Erneuerbaren Energien in Deutschland - eine Erfolgsgeschichte, 2010, p. 7, https://www.unendlich-viel-energie.de/media/file/171.41_Renews_Spezial_20_Jahre_EE-Strom-Foerderung.pdf.

2 Gerald O. Barney, The Global 2000 to the President: Entering the 21th Century, 1980, p. 3, https://www.cartercenter.org/resources/pdfs/pdf-archive/global2000reporttothepresident--enteringthe21stcentury-01011991.pdf.

https://doi.org/10.1515/9783110607888-005

To counteract these developments and to secure electricity supply, many national governments engaged in nuclear energy. However, with the meltdown of the nuclear reactor in Chernobyl in 1986, the anti-nuclear movement of the 1980s gained considerable importance and together with other environmental movements pushed governments to the development of more secure and sustainable solutions. A first outcome of this was the so-called "Brundtland Report," written by the World Commission on Environment and Development ("**WCED**") and published by the United Nations in 1987, which defines and describes sustainable developments and became one of the most frequently quoted works of environmental and development literature. This report was accompanied by further scientific essays and debates on sustainability and anthropogenic climate change,[3] leading to a broad public discussion about the heating of the earth's atmosphere, the melting of glaciers and the expected rise in sea levels.[4]

Climate change primarily appeared on the international political agenda in 1992 with the United Nations Conference on Environment and Development in Rio de Janeiro ("**UNCED**"; also known as the Rio Conference), where environmental issues were discussed on a broad level. The Rio Conference is considered a milestone for the integration of environmental and development efforts. The same holds true for the Kyoto Protocol from 1997. This agreement by the UN, which entered into force on February 16, 2005, set internationally binding target values for greenhouse gas emissions in industrialized countries for the first time. In essence, participating industrialized countries committed themselves to reducing their annual greenhouse gas emissions within the so-called first commitment period (2008–2012) by an average of 5.2% compared to 1990 levels.

The rising awareness of the environmental impact of climate change and the desire for a sustainable solution led to first legislative acts. In Directive 96/92/EC, for example, the EU gave Member States the option of prioritising renewable energy sources and thus made a first – still timid – attempt at subsidized expansion of RE by focussing on the electricity sector. By implementing this directive into national law, many countries such as **Austria,**[5] **Germany,**[6] **Spain**[7] and **France**[8] decided to use the

3 For instance, the statement of the German Meteorological Society together with the German Physical Society in 1986, in which a warning was given of the feared consequences of anthropogenic climate change.

4 Agentur für Erneuerbare Energien e.V., in Renews Spezial 41: 20 Jahre Förderung von Strom aus Erneuerbaren Energien in Deutschland - eine Erfolgsgeschichte, 2010, p. 8.

5 Elektrizitätswirtschafts- und -organisationsgesetz ("ElWOG"), entry into force in 1998.

6 Erneuerbare-Energien-Gesetz ("EEG 2000"), entry into force in 2000.

7 Real Decredo 1955/2000, entry into force in 2001.

8 Loi n°2000–108 du 10 février 2000 relative à la modernisation et au développement du service public de l'électricité, entry into force in 2000.

option and to grant electricity produced by RE plants a priority in regard to the connection to the grid, grid access and/or grid expansion. Apart from these priority regulations, early investments in the sector were largely driven by accompanying support schemes such as quotas, feed-in tariffs and premiums.[9] The establishment of support regimes continued steadily and led to a total of 187 countries worldwide having a state support scheme for renewables by 2017.[10] In addition, a total of 87 countries now have economy-wide targets for the renewable energy share of primary or final energy consumption.[11]

However, the administratively set pricing and promoting policies needed continuous adaption to changing market conditions[12] and regular tariff-level adjustment is one example of measures needed to reflect the falling cost of technology.[13] In this context, auctions are being increasingly adopted by national legislators, moving RE towards a higher cost-competitiveness in comparison to fossil fuels. These developments resulted in electricity prices from solar PV in 2016 being almost a fifth of what they were in 2010. Prices for onshore wind were almost halved in that period.[14]

5.1.2 Other Sectors (than Electricity) in which RE Are Promoted

In general, the energy industry is divided into three sectors: power (or electricity), heat (including cooling) and transport. Although power generally gets most of the governmental attention, it is the smallest of the three sectors in terms of its share of the total global energy consumption, which amounts to 20% and is followed by transport with 32% and heat with 48%.[15] The latter industry includes – among other things – production of steam for industrial processes, heating for buildings and water, for cooking, and for agricultural uses (e.g., drying). Energy consumption for cooling is used for purposes such as space cooling and refrigeration.[16] The second-largest sector is transport, which involves the movement of passengers and freight by various means, and may be divided into several sub-sectors, including road

---

9 For an overview of the range of different national promotion systems see chapter 5.3.2.

10 REN21, Renewables 2018: Global Status Report, 2018, p. 51, https://www.ren21.net/wp-content/uploads/2019/05/GSR2018_Full-Report_English.pdf.

11 REN21, Renewables 2018: Global Status Report, 2018, p. 49.

12 For particularly impressive examples of undesirable developments due to misguided state subsidy systems, see Chapter 5.4.

13 See chapter 5.2.

14 IRENA, IEA and REN21, Renewable Energy Policies in a Time of Transition, 2018, p. 14, http://www.irena.org/-/media/Files/IRENA/Agency/Publication/2018/Apr/IRENA_IEA_REN21_Policies_2018.pdf.

15 REN21, Renewables 2018: Global Status Report, 2018, p. 32.

16 IRENA, IEA and REN21, Renewable Energy Policies in a Time of Transition, 2018, p. 24.

transport, aviation, shipping and rail. The energy needs in the transport sector are complex due to the various transport modes, vehicle types, energy carriers and fuels, as well as related transport and distribution infrastructure.[17] Similar to the power sector, transport and heat are also subject to governmental regulation. However, despite the share of the total global energy consumption, national legislators focus less on these two sectors: While 128 countries have regulatory incentives with regard to RE for the power sector, this holds true for only 70 nations concerning the transport sector and even less (24) for the heat sector.[18]

In the **heat sector,** building energy codes are one of the most common policy tools used to promote renewable energy and energy efficiency, in which measures are routinely aimed at both increasing renewable energy supply and reducing energy demand. Policies can range from requiring the use of specific technologies – i.e., solar water heaters or energy-efficient cooling appliances – to setting targets for the share of energy or electricity needs that must be met through renewable sources or can be framed in terms of setting performance standards for either maximum energy use or greenhouse gas creation. One example of a national RE policy is **India**. The Indian Ministry of Power updated the country's Energy Conservation Building Code to establish new energy efficiency standards and a range of mandates for the share of hot water demand met by solar power in 2017. The code promotes efficient lighting, passive energy building design and renewable energy technologies and applies to buildings with a peak load of 100 kilowatts (kW) and above.[19]

The **transport sector** is mainly concerned with substituting fossil fuels with renewable fuels (i.e., biofuel or hydrogen) and encouraging a move to electric mobility as transport accounts for more than half of global oil demand. Promotion policies focus primarily on road transport, especially at a national level. Other sub-sectors such as aviation, rail and shipping have drawn comparably less attention despite having a greater share of total energy consumption.[20] Biofuel blend mandates therefore remain one of the most widely adopted mechanisms for increasing renewable fuel use in the road transport sector. These mandates are prevalent across all geographic regions and countries at all economic development levels. As in past years, in 2017 many national and sub-national governments continued to require specific shares of biodiesel or ethanol to be blended into transport fuels, with **China**, **India** and **Brazil** as popular examples of national mandates with a requirement of at least 10% biofuel.[21]

Traditionally, the three sectors (power, heat and transport) were considered separately by regulators. However, the majority of experts and most of the governments

17 IRENA, IEA and REN21, Renewable Energy Policies in a Time of Transition, 2018, p. 38.
18 REN21, Renewables 2018: Global Status Report, 2018, p. 51.
19 REN21, Renewables 2018: Global Status Report, 2018, p. 52.
20 REN21, Renewables 2018: Global Status Report, 2018, p. 56.
21 REN21, Renewables 2018: Global Status Report, 2018, p. 56.

have come to the conclusion that the lasting success of renewables would be inconceivable without **sector coupling** or **integrated energy**, as it is also called. In general, this means interconnecting the respective sectors. The need for sector coupling arises from the fact that wind and solar energy, the most important renewable energy sources, are much better suited for electricity generation than for the production of fuels and heat. In countries such as Germany, the potential of other renewable energy sources like bioenergy, geothermal energy and solar thermal energy is also limited, so that for this reason too, the majority of energy must be produced by wind power and photovoltaic systems. Key elements of integrated energy are therefore technologies that transfer electricity to other forms of energy such as fuel or heat – the so-called Power-to-X technologies. In addition to interlinking the sectors, the technologies can also compensate for fluctuations, for example, in the generation of electricity from wind energy, by ensuring that re-conversion into electricity is made possible. One popular example is Power-to-Gas. It is a chemical process in which a fuel gas is produced from water by means of water electrolysis using (RE-)electricity. This fuel gas can be stored and used later for various purposes. Among other things, it can be utilized in the form of power-to-fuel in transportation, used as a chemical raw material (usually referred to as power-to-chemicals) or temporarily stored in the gas infrastructure for subsequent power generation in gas power plants.

In another step towards the widespread use of RE, the heat and transport sectors are beginning to transfer their energy demand to electricity, with electric cars as a popular example. The electrification of transport is being promoted in many countries by setting a date by which diesel and petrol cars are to be banned (this may mean a ban on the registration of new cars or the sale of cars, or it may mean introducing a requirement of emission-free cars) for the further promotion of electrification in road transport: i.e., **Norway** (2025), **Netherlands** (2030), **Slovenia** (after 2030), **Scotland** (2032), **United Kingdom** (2040) and **France** (2040).[22] Similarly, China is encouraging the electrification of residential heating, manufacturing and transport in regions that have high concentrations of renewable power in order to promote wind power and other RE sources, as well as to combat air pollution. At the same time, a number of US states are examining options to electrify the transport, industrial, residential and commercial end-use sectors to increase the overall renewable energy share.[23]

Together, the expansion of RE in terms of electricity production, the electrification trend in the remaining sectors and efforts for sector coupling point to renewables as the key energy source of the future.

22 REN21, Renewables 2018: Global Status Report, 2018, p. 58.
23 REN21, Renewables 2018: Global Status Report, 2018, p. 32.

5.2 Is Governmental Promotion of RE (Still) a Prerequisite for an Investment in RE Projects?

5.2.1 Overview of the Development of Electricity Prices and Generation Costs

Excluding state support schemes, the electricity price is the main source of revenue for all types of electricity producers. In this context, the **consumer price** is not always relevant, as it may contain taxes, levies or charges that do not pass to the producer but are collected by the state. Additionally, the consumers are usually paying further grid fees. These charges can make up a significant amount of the consumer price, such as in **Germany**, where they add up to 78.5% of the consumer price for electricity. Only the remaining 21.5% go to the producers.[24] This is the reason why in many countries **producer prices** (meaning the share of consumer prices that go to the producer) have developed differently from consumer prices in the past. Accordingly, consumer prices in Germany have increased steadily from 2008 to 2017 and have risen by about 25% in the case of consumption between 2,500 and 5,000 kWh per year. This reflects a similar development to that seen in the rest of the 28 EU countries, where overall consumer prices rose by almost 29% between 2008 and 2017.[25] However, in the same period the corresponding producer prices, which include the generation or purchasing costs as well as sales cost and a profit margin, decreased by nearly 12% in Germany,[26] 24% in Belgium, 51% in Denmark and 14% in Italy.[27]

Similar trends in respect of producer prices can also be seen at electricity exchanges, where an increasing proportion of producers sell their energy directly at market conditions, instead of selling it individually to a power purchaser (i.e., electricity suppliers). Taking the spot market (meaning the short-term/Interday trading of electricity) EPEX in Paris as an example, a decline in prices by over 43% can be observed from 2011 to 2016.[28] Similarly, the prices at the EEX Leipzig for long-term trading (meaning contracts with a settlement date of one year or longer in the future) also declined from 2011 to 2016 by over 47%.[29] Even though these are only individual examples and a significant part of the electricity produced is still traded OTC (with the result that no reliable statistics on price developments are available

24 Bundesnetzagentur, https://www.bundesnetzagentur.de/SharedDocs/FAQs/DE/Sachgebiete/Energie/Verbraucher/PreiseUndRechnungen/WieSetztSichDerStrompreisZusammen.html.

25 Eurostat, https://ec.europa.eu/eurostat/web/energy/data/main-tables.

26 Bundesnetzagentur/Bundeskartellamt, Monitoringbericht, 2017, p. 235, https://www.bundesnetzagentur.de/SharedDocs/Mediathek/Monitoringberichte/Monitoringbericht2017.pdf?__blob=publicationFile&v=4.

27 Eurostat, https://ec.europa.eu/eurostat/web/energy/data/database.

28 Bundesnetzagentur/Bundeskartellamt, Monitoringbericht, 2017, p. 192.

29 Bundesnetzagentur/Bundeskartellamt, Monitoringbericht, 2017, p. 199.

here), a clear trend can still be seen, which shows a steady decline in producer prices for electricity and a steady increase in consumer prices.

A key factor behind the declining producer prices is the falling generation costs for electricity, attributable to the steadily increasing efficiency of the various power generation sectors. A useful tool for comparing the unit costs of different technologies over their operating life are the so-called Levelised Costs of Electricity (**"LCOE"**), which are defined as the costs required to convert non-electric-energy into electricity. They represent the per-megawatt-hour cost (in discounted real dollars) of building and operating a generating plant over an assumed financial life and duty cycle. Essential inputs to calculating LCOE include capital costs, fuel costs, fixed and variable operations and maintenance costs, financing costs, and an assumed utilization rate for each plant type.[30]

The development of the global weighted-average LCOE of RE from 2010 to 2017 is characterized by a broad decline in nearly every technology sector, led by a cost drop from 0.36 USD/kWh to 0.10 USD/kWh (nearly 73%) in case of solar photovoltaic. The costs for electricity generated by concentrated solar power declined by 33% (from 0.33 USD/kWh to 0.22 USD/kWh) at the same time. Wind energy experienced a similar, though lower, decline, with prices for offshore wind power falling at a rate of nearly 18% (from 0.17 USD/kWh to 0.14 USD/kWh) and for onshore wind power at a rate of 25% (from 0.08 USD/kWh to 0.06). While the corresponding cost for electricity from biomass plants nearly stayed the same in this period, only geothermal and hydropower became more costly with rates increasing by 40% and 25% respectively. However, compared to the LCOE of fossil fuels, which range, from approximately, 0.05 USD/kWh to 0.18 USD/kWh, both technologies are still amongst the cheapest ways to produce electricity, with average LCOE of 0.07 USD/kWh for geothermal power and 0.05 USD/kWh for hydropower. The aforementioned developments led to a higher cost competitiveness of RE generation plants. With the exception of concentrating solar power, every RE technology is on average within the cost range of fossil fuels.[31]

The main drivers behind cost reduction in the RE sector are increasing economies of scale in manufacturing, vertical integration and consolidation among manufacturers as well as improvements in manufacturing processes that reduce material and labor needs, while optimising the utilization of capital. Additionally, technology improvements are raising capacity factors and/or reducing installed costs. The use of real-time data allows an improved predictive maintenance, reducing operating and maintenance costs as well as generation loss due to planned and

---

30 U.S. Energy Information Administration, Levelized Cost and Levelized Avoided Cost of New Generation Resources in the Annual Energy Outlook, 2018, p.1, https://www.eia.gov/outlooks/archive/aeo18/pdf/electricity_generation.pdf.

31 IRENA, Renewable Power Generation Costs in 2017, 2018, p. 17, https://www.irena.org/-/media/Files/IRENA/Agency/Publication/2018/Jan/IRENA_2017_Power_Costs_2018.pdf.

unplanned outages. Finally, the falling or low cost of capital, driven by supportive policy frameworks, contributes significantly to this development.[32]

5.2.2 The Route to "Grid Parity" and Future Prospects

The on-going progress in reducing costs when producing electricity from RE sources leads towards a situation that is called "grid parity." This concept can be defined in two different ways, depending on the perspective taken: From a private consumer point of view, grid parity commonly means that the costs per megawatt-hour of self-produced electricity from renewable sources (i.e., from solar panels on a rooftop) are equal to the costs per megawatt-hour for electricity purchased from a commercial electricity supplier. Taking the perspective of a commercial electricity supplier, grid parity, by contrast, essentially means that the costs of purchasing electricity from renewable sources are equal to the costs of purchasing electricity from conventional sources (i.e., at a spot market exchange). As the price for electricity purchased by a consumer generally contains a considerable amount of taxes and levies,[33] grid parity, from this point of view, is more easily achieved than the pendant from a supplier's perspective. Grid parity in the latter sense ultimately means that the LCOE from renewable sources are equal to or lower than those of conventional sources. Since a large part of the RE technologies can already compete – on average – with fossil fuels (see preceding section), grid parity is no longer wishful thinking but is gradually becoming a reality.

Additionally, studies suggest that LCOE for renewables are expected to further decline in the future, while LCOE for conventional production is likely to increase. For instance, a study from the Fraunhofer Institute for Solar Energy Systems ISE estimates lower costs for small and large photovoltaic systems as well as wind onshore plants (all together in a range of 2.1€ct/kWh and 7.1€ct/kWh) by 2035 in comparison to hard coal and gas turbines, with prices ranging from 7.2€ct/kWh to over 24.0€ct/kWh in Germany. Similarly, wind offshore plants will also be able to reduce costs and prices will therefore range from 5.8€ct/kWh to 10.1€ct/kWh. Only brown coal will stay comparatively cost competitive with LCOE between 5.2€ct/kWh and 9.7€ct/kWh in 2035.[34] This ongoing process towards complete grid parity has led legislators to update their policies, which take into account the increasing marketability of RE. One way to do this is by introducing a tendering system to determine

32 IRENA, Renewable Power Generation Costs in 2017, 2018, p. 33.

33 See preceding chapter.

34 Fraunhofer Institute for Solar Energy Systems ISE, Levelized Cost of Electricity Renewable Energy Technologies, 2018, p. 22, https://www.ise.fraunhofer.de/content/dam/ise/en/documents/publications/studies/EN2018_Fraunhofer-ISE_LCOE_Renewable_Energy_Technologies.pdf.

the amount of governmental remuneration, so that only the most cost-effective plant operators receive the bid. As of 2017, 84 countries, and thus 11 more than in the previous year, adopted a form of tendering system in their policy, partially by replacing foundational elements of numerous renewable energy support programs like fixed feed-in tariffs.[35]

Germany, for example, introduced a tendering system in the revised version of its RE legislation ("Erneuerbare Energien Gesetz") in 2017. Biogas, wind and solar plants permitted by the competent state authorities after January 1, 2017 (subject to transitional regulations for plants commissioned before January 1, 2019) are generally obliged to take part in a tender in order to receive state funding. Only small plants are still eligible for the fixed feed-in tariffs. In the tenders, which are divided according to the type of generation, the cheapest bidders (in terms of costs per kWh) in each case are awarded a bid until the fixed tender volume has been reached. This way, only operators providing the highest cost-competitiveness are rewarded, taking the RE industry in Germany on a faster route to grid parity.

The steady increase in cost competitiveness is gradually eliminating the requirement for financial support for electricity from renewable sources. Moreover, the need for the physical priority of renewable electricity over conventional electricity (i.e., in terms of a prioritized dispatch and distribution of renewable energy by the grid operator) is also increasingly being removed. This is a result of many network operators implementing the merit order principle. Merit order is defined as the sequence in which the power plants producing electricity are used on an electricity exchange in order to guarantee an economically optimal supply of electricity. The merit order is based on the lowest marginal costs, i.e., the costs incurred by a power plant for the last megawatt-hour produced. It is therefore independent from the fixed costs of a power generation technology (and is not equal to the LCOE of a technology). The power plants, which produce electricity at a very low cost on an on-going basis, are the first to be connected for feed-in in accordance with the merit order. Thereafter, power plants with higher marginal costs will be added until the demand is met. Since a large part of renewables already have very low or no ongoing costs, they already have a "natural" priority without the need for legislative intervention.

In summary, the route to grid parity is already being taken by a considerable number of RE technologies. Future prospects indicate that ever larger parts of renewables will achieve this goal. Some policymakers are taking this development into account by reducing legislative interventions in favor of renewables.

35 REN21, Renewables 2018: Global Status Report, 2018, p. 19 et. seq.

5.2.3 Secondary Sources of Revenue in RE Projects

Despite income from the sale of electricity and corresponding governmental subsidies, RE plants have the opportunity to access secondary sources of revenue. For example, hydropower can generate significant revenue in some markets by providing **ancillary grid services**. These services refer to functions that help grid operators maintain a reliable electricity system. They, for instance, (i) maintain the proper flow and direction of electricity, (ii) address imbalances between supply and demand by storing electricity in times of high grid capacities and providing it in times of low grid capacities, and (iii) help the system recover after a power system event. In power grids with significant variable RE penetration, additional ancillary services are often required to manage increased variability and uncertainty. However, not every RE plant qualifies for providing ancillary services, since some (older) systems are not able to store or provide electricity on short-term demand. Nevertheless, improved technology for solar and wind technologies is making these more grid friendly. For example, wind turbines can earn money in times of low wind by keeping the blades running and providing so-called reactive power, meaning the capability to withdraw power from the grid in times of too high voltages. Additionally, hybrid power plants (with combined producing and storage units) plus the creation of "virtual" power plants that mix generating technologies, can all transform the nature of variable renewable technologies into more stable and predictable generators.[36] Moreover, with storage units, the electricity produced can be stored at times of low exchange prices (in some cases negative prices already occur on the exchanges at peak times) to sell it at a later point in time at higher prices. In this way, the electricity produced can be sold more efficiently, which provides for more revenue at constant electricity output.

Another way for wind farms to gain additional revenues is through **repowering**. When a turbine has reached the end of its operating period, it usually is time for dismantling. However, if the turbine and its components are still in a satisfactory condition, it could be sold on the second hand market. The residual value is then treated as a disposable income during the final year of the operation period. Residual value is common for turbines that have been situated onshore, where companies buy the old turbines and put them up in new environments. For offshore turbines, this is only partially true due to less standardized structures and processes in the industry. Additionally, most offshore turbines have endured rougher climates, which affect the technical status of the turbines negatively.[37]

---

36 IRENA, Renewable Power Generation Costs in 2017, 2018, p. 29.

37 Broliden/Regnér, On Asset Life Cycle Management for Offshore Wind Turbines, 2015, p. 41, https://www.diva-portal.org/smash/get/diva2:841750/FULLTEXT01.pdf.

5.3 International and National Concepts of Promotion of RE

The promotion of energy generated from sustainable energy sources remains a high priority issue for policymakers worldwide, while targets are still deemed to be one of the most important measures to demonstrate their commitment to RE deployment.[38] 2017 was another record year[39] for the RE sector: As of year-end 2017, targets for the renewable share of final energy (the form of energy that is available to end-consumers following the conversion or transformation of primary energy sources) were in place in 87 countries, while sector-specific targets for renewable power were in place in 146 countries, for renewable heating and cooling in 48 countries, and for renewable transport in 42 countries.[40]

5.3.1 International Regulations for the Funding of RE, Particularly in the EU

Setting up international regulations is a rather complex process, as international regulations are commonly based on international treaties, i.e., agreements under international law. They are concluded by sovereign states and international organizations who are the subjects of international law. One example of such an international treaty is the 2016 Paris Climate Agreement which aims to reduce global warming. The complexity of agreeing on standards internationally lies, amongst other factors, in the sovereignty of individual states and the political liability of their leaders in policy areas which may have an impact on national economic developments. These factors commonly limit the area of overlapping interests in international negotiations. Against this background, supranational entities such as the EU play a special role because the member states have delegated parts of their sovereignty to the supranational entity. The EU has the power to create binding supranational law for its Member States in the form of EU directives. Energy policy forms part of the EU policy areas and the promotion of renewables is a key element of the EU energy policy, as explicitly acknowledged in Article 194 of the Treaty on the Functioning of the European Union ("**TFEU**"). The EU has already made extensive use of its legislative competence in the RE sector.

38 REN21, Renewables 2018: Global Status Report, 2018, p. 20.
39 REN21, Renewables 2018: Global Status Report, 2018, p. 17.
40 REN21, Renewables 2018: Global Status Report, 2018, p. 20.

1. Promotion of Renewable Energy within the EU

a) Directive 2009/28/EC of April 23, 2009 on the promotion of the use of energy from renewable sources – Status quo

The Directive 2009/28/EC[41] dated April 23, 2009 on the promotion of the use of energy from renewable sources (the "**2009 Directive**") constitutes the current legal framework for the promotion of RE on EU level.

The overall EU target for using RE is 20% by the year 2020. Furthermore, the 2009 Directive lays down binding national targets for the share of energy from renewable sources in gross final consumption for each Member State, taking into account the differences between their starting points and potentials, so that RE objectives in each country range from a minimum of 10% in Malta to 49% of total energy use in Sweden. The countries are, of course, free to exceed these targets. Among the 28 Member States, 11 have already overshot the level required to meet their mandatory targets: Bulgaria, Croatia, the Czech Republic, Denmark, Estonia, Finland, Hungary, Italy, Lithuania, Romania, and Sweden.[42]

While the targets are binding for each country, Member States are free to decide how they wish to achieve the goals set out in the 2009 Directive. They can act alone using a range of support schemes at a national level (national support schemes) or cooperate with other Member States or even third countries outside the EU (cooperation mechanisms).

According to the definition in Article 2 of the 2009 Directive, "support scheme" means any instrument, scheme or mechanism applied by a Member State or a group of Member States that promotes the use of energy from renewable sources by reducing the cost of that energy or increasing the price at which it can be sold or increasing the volume of such energy purchased (e.g., by means of a renewable energy obligation). This includes investment aids, tax exemptions or reductions, tax refunds, renewable energy obligation support schemes (including those using green certificates) and direct price support schemes including feed-in tariffs and premium payments. In this way, Article 2 of the 2009 Directive lists various options for promoting RE without defining the path to follow. Recitals 19 and 25 also make it clear that the choice between the respective promotional instruments is subject to the discretion of the Member States.

Member States may also cooperate with other countries within or outside the EU, in order to accomplish predefined goals. Cooperation mechanisms can take the form of

---

41 Directive 2009/28/EC of April 23, 2009 on the promotion of the use of energy from renewable sources and amending and subsequently repealing Directives 2001/77/EC and 2003/30/EC, OJ 2009 L 140/16.

42 ICIS Editorial: EU remains on course for 2020 RES target, though some member states see worsening perfomance, 2 February 2018, https://www.icis.com/explore/resources/news/2018/02/02/10189620/eu-remains-on-course-for-2020-res-target-though-some-member-states-see-worsening-performance/ (last date of access 21 April 2020).

statistical transfers of RE (i.e., a certain amount of RE is deducted from one country's progress towards its national overall target and added to another's without actual energy changes), joint RE projects or joint RE support schemes. These measures have an impact on target calculation and target compliance and, thus, enable Member States to achieve their national overall targets on the best cost-benefit basis. In addition, Member States may agree on other forms of cooperation, such as exchanges of information and best practices.

Article 22 of the 2009 Directive imposes an obligation on the Member States to submit a report to the European Commission on achievements made in promoting and using energy from renewable sources every two years. According to the progress report[43] of the European Commission (based on the reports submitted by Member States), Europe is on track to reach its 2020 climate and energy targets. Nevertheless, some countries, such as Ireland[44] and Germany,[45] are expected to miss predefined targets for the year 2020.

The 2009 Directive will remain in force until 2020. The 2009 Directive has been recently updated for the period after 2020 within the framework of the "Clean Energy for all Europeans package"[46] launched by the European Commission on November 30, 2016.[47]

b) EU state aid law as a limit for the legislative competence of the EU in the energy sector

The legislative competence of the EU is limited insofar as certain policy areas are generally not covered by its legislative competence. Furthermore, within its legislative competence equal or higher ranking goals have to be considered which have the effect of legal barriers for a regulation. According to the 2009 Directive, the EU Member States are free to decide on how they want to reach their 2020 RE target

---

43 European Commission: Europe's energy transition is well underway, Press Release, 1 February 2017, http://europa.eu/rapid/pressrelease_IP-17-161_en.htm (last date of access 21 April 2020): European Commission: Europe on track to reach its 20% target by 2020, Fact Sheet, 1 February 2017, http://europa.eu/rapid/press-release_MEMO-17-163_en.htm (last date of access 21 April 2020).

44 The Irish Times: Penalities for missing climate change goals less than claimed, Minister says, 25 May 2018, https://www.irishtimes.com/news/environment/penalties-for-missing-climate-change-goals-tobe-less-than-claimed-minister-says-1.3508293 (last date of access 21 April 2020).

45 Clean Energy Wire: Germany on track to widely miss 2020 climate targets - government, 13 June 2018, https://www.cleanenergywire.org/news/germany-track-widely-miss-2020-climate-targetgovernment (last date of access 21 April 2020).

46 Clean Energy For All Europeans package, COM(2016) 860 final.

47 European Commission: Europe leads the global clean energy transition: - Commission welcomes ambitious agreement on further renewable energy development in the EU, Press Release, 14 June 2018, https://ec.europa.eu/commission/presscorner/detail/en/STATEMENT_18_4155 (last date of access 21 April 2020).

quotas. However, the discretion of Member States to choose a support scheme is limited by EU state aid rules.

aa) Key provisions in the TFEU governing state aid issues

State aid is defined in Article 107(1) TFEU as "any aid **granted by a Member State or through State resources** in any form whatsoever which **distorts or threatens to distort competition** by **favoring certain undertakings or the production of certain goods** shall, in so far as it **affects trade** between Member States, be incompatible with the internal market."[48] In other words, state aid covers all advantages granted by national public authorities through state resources selectively to undertakings (i.e., any entity which places goods or services on the market and is engaged in economic activity) that could potentially distort competition and affect trade within the EU. Since state aids can be granted "in any form whatsoever," the given definition of state aid is very broad. As a result, state aid can take many forms, such as grants, loans or tax breaks.

Member States have an obligation to notify state aid measures to the European Commission. The latter then has to decide whether the measure in question constitutes state aid that is incompatible with the internal market. Under certain conditions, the European Commission is authorized to declare state aid as an admissible measure. The decision-making depends on individual circumstances. In case the EU Commission finds the aid to be not compatible with Article 107(3) TFEU, it may request the relevant state to abolish or adjust such aid.

bb) Brief overview over the case law on the admissibility of feed-in tariffs

The decisive factor in classifying the relevant measure as state aid is whether the aid is granted **by a Member State** or **through state resources** in any form whatsoever. This definition covers both advantages which are granted directly by the state and those granted by a public or private body designated or established by the state.[49] Against this background, the categorization of feed-in tariffs is difficult. Given the absence of explicitly defined criteria for justifying state aid measures in the TFEU or other EU legislation, the case law of the Court of Justice of the European Union ("**CJEU**," consisting of two major courts: the European Court of Justice and the General Court) should be taken into account in order to elaborate characteristics of state aids. As feed-in tariffs turned out to be very attractive in EU countries in the past,[50] the case law of the CJEU has been developed primarily around the question of

---

48 Four cumulative state aid criteria have been highlighted.

49 ECJ, Case 82/77, *Van Tiggele*, 24 January 1978, paras. 24, 25; ECJ, Case C-72/91, *Sloman Neptun*, 17 March 1993, para. 19.

50 In particular, in the time frame 2007–2012: see Fruhmann/Tuerk, Renewable Energy Support Policies in Europe, 3 November 2014, https://climatepolicyinfohub.eu/renewable-energy-support-policies-europe (last date of access 21 April 2020).

the permissibility of feed-in tariffs and, therefore, concentrated in particular on the criterion of state resources. In its fundamental decision *PreussenElektra*[51] with regard to the German support system under the former German Electricity Feed-in Act of 1991 (*Stromeinspeisegesetz*) – a predecessor of the current German Renewable Energy Sources Act (*Erneuerbare-Energien-Gesetz*), the European Court of Justice ("**ECJ**") ruled that the former German model for feed-in tariffs was in line with state aid rules. The court relied on the circumstances that the fixed remuneration originated from private electricity consumers and that it was passed on by private distribution and transmission grid operators to the RE plant operators.[52] The following rulings,[53] examining the issue in more detail, illustrate that the decision on the admissibility of fixed tariffs must be taken on a case-by-case basis. After the application of the German RE support scheme under the former German Electricity Feed-in Act of 1991 was confirmed by the ECJ, the EU Commission challenged the RE support scheme under the German Renewable Energy Sources Act 2012 (the "**EEG 2012**") in 2014. The EEG 2012 provided for a renewables surcharge (the "**EEG-Surcharge**") payable by consumers by way of which, finally, the remuneration of RE producers was refinanced. In contrast to the previous support scheme, which was the subject of the *PreussenElektra* judgment, according to the EEG 2012, the network operators, namely the transmission system operators ("TSOs"), had to collect and administer the EEG-Surcharge and pay it to RE producers. The European Commission considered that the support of RE through the EEG-Surcharge in the described manner involved state resources and was, thus, qualified as state aid.[54] On appeal by the German government against the EU Commission's decision, the General Court ("**EGC**"), which also forms part of the CJEU, shared the position of the European Commission. The EGC[55] relied in particular on the following circumstances: The financing of RE production by the EEG-Surcharge was the consequence of the German government's policy in the form of the EEG 2012, which prescribed rules for collecting and administering the EEG-Surcharge. In addition, even if the payment was not made directly from the state budget, the TSOs did not act at their own discretion but on the basis of the state's authorization to collect the EEG-Surcharge. The EEG-Surcharge was considered to be a special type of levy, which remained under the dominant influence of the state and, thus, constituted state aid. The German government tried to rely on the *PreussenElektra* ruling. According to the EGC, however, the *PreussenElektra* case was different, since the funding under the former support scheme occurred without any involvement of the state budget.

---

51 ECJ, Case C-379/98, *PreussenElektra*, 13 March 2001.

52 ECJ, Case C-379/98, *PreussenElektra*, 13 March 2001, para. 66.

53 ECJ, Case C-206/06, *Essent*, 17 July 2008; ECJ, Case C-262/12, *Vent De Colère*, 19 December 2013; EGC, Case T-47/15, Germany v. Commission, 10 May 2016.

54 Commission Decision on the Aid Scheme, C(2014) 8786 final.

55 EGC, Case T-47/15, Germany v. Commission, 10 May 2016.

The case law of the CJEU underlines that one of the most essential criteria for state aid – state resources – is to be understood in a broad sense. For the purposes of RE support through feed-in tariffs, this means that the statutory obligation of a utility company to purchase RE at a fixed price determined by the state itself does not constitute state aid. Only if a public body or a state-controlled private entity further participates in the fund management, as it happened in the discussed case of the German support scheme under the EEG 2012, are state resources deemed to be involved.[56]

cc) The 2014 Guidelines of the European Commission

In April 2014, the European Commission issued the Guidelines on state aid for environmental protection and energy 2014–2020 (the "**2014 Guidelines**"). These guidelines are soft law instruments that are recommendations only and not binding on the EU Member States. The 2014 Guidelines do not change the definition of state aid. However, they are intended to help Member States to design support systems that are compatible with EU state aid law. The observance of the 2014 Guidelines shall give Member States more certainty that planned funding measures would not be challenged by the European Commission. The 2014 Guidelines include an entire section on aid to energy from renewable sources. The European Commission demonstrates its long-term intention to phase out feed-in tariffs in the light of falling RE production costs. Consequently, the key point of these guidelines is the gradual introduction of market-based mechanisms.[57]

The 2014 Guidelines require the Member States:

- to guarantee market premiums on top of the market price from January 1, 2016 onward, whereby RE producers are obliged to sell electricity directly at the market price and subject to market conditions;
- to set out a competitive bidding process for allocating public funding on the basis of clear, transparent and non-discriminatory criteria from January 1, 2017 onward.

Specific exceptions are foreseen for small installations and demonstration projects.

The new approach towards feed-in premiums and tendering procedures enable the EU Member States to respond to market signals, increase cost-effectiveness, limit distortions, integrate electricity from renewable sources into the electricity

56 Hirner, SPRW 2014, p. 280.

57 European Commission: Energy and Environmental State Aid Guidelines, Frequently Asked Questions, 9 April 2014, http://europa.eu/rapid/press-release_MEMO-14-276_en.htm (last date of access 21 April 2020); European Commission: State aid - Commission adopts new rules on public support for environmental protection and energy, Press Release 9 April 2014, http://europa.eu/rapid/press-release_IP-14-400_en.htm (last date of access 21 April 2020).

market and to avoid producing green electricity regardless of demand. The 2014 Guidelines cover the period from July 1, 2014 to December 31, 2020 and, therefore, they do not affect payments already received by owners of existing plants. For the period after 2020, the European Commission needs to assess the situation and decide on future regulations in light of this.

c) Major changes to be expected after 2020

In 2016, the European Commission launched the "Clean Energy for all Europeans" package (the "**Winter Package**"). The Winter Package comprised eight legislative proposals, including the proposal for a Directive of the European Parliament and of the Council on the promotion of the use of energy from renewable sources for the period 2021–2030. The negotiations of the European Council and the European Parliament on the proposed changes started in February 2018. On June 14, 2018, the European legislators reached agreement on the final version of the proposal.[58] The proposal for a Directive on the promotion of the use of energy from renewable sources for the period 2021–2030[59] (the "**Post-2020 Directive**") is of particular relevance to investors working in the RE sector, as it aims to create more guarantees by establishing a robust and transparent legal framework at EU level. The Post-2020 Directive is closely linked to other parts of the Winter Package. These are the Energy Union Governance Regulation[60] and the Electricity Market Regulation,[61] to which some relevant provisions of the present 2009 Directive are transferred. In the case of the Energy Union Governance Regulation, the transferred provisions refer to the monitoring and reporting obligations towards target compliance and in the case of the Energy Market Regulation to grid-related issues.

The Post-2020 Directive sets a binding overall EU target of at least 32% final energy consumption from renewable sources by 2030, including a clause allowing that target to be revised upwards before 2023 and, in comparison to the existing 2009 Directive, no longer prescribes mandatory targets at a national level. The current binding national targets will only serve as baseline levels for the period after 2020, i.e., the involved countries are not allowed to go below the 2020 objectives. By the start of 2019, Member States are required to define and communicate their

58 European Commission: Europea lead the global clean energy transition - Commission welcomes ambitious agreement on further renewable energy development, 14 June 2018, http://europa.eu/rapid/pressrelease_STATEMENT-18-4155_en.htm (last date of access 21 April 2020).

59 Proposal for a Directive of the European Parliament and of the Council on the promotion of theuse of energy from renewable sources, 2016/0382 (COD).

60 Proposal for a Regulation of the European Parliament and of the Council on the Governance of the Energy Union, COM(2016) 759 final.

61 Proposal for a Regulation of the European Parliament and of the Council on the internal market for electricity (Recast), COM(2016) 861 final.

envisaged contributions to the achievement of the overall 2030 target as part of their Integrated National Energy and Climate Plans.

Compliance with the overall EU target will be monitored by the European Commission. In order to ensure that the overall EU target of at least 32% final energy consumption from renewable sources by 2030 is achieved, the proposed Energy Union Governance Regulation provides for appropriate instruments such as the "gap avoider" and the "gap filler." The "gap avoider" expresses the idea of early actions: The European Commission checks, whether envisaged goals by Member States are sufficient to comply with the overall target. In addition, it should provide financial incentives for ambitious national contributions. The "gap filler" refers to the improvement mechanisms to be applied as from 2024 in case of non-compliance with the overall target.

Unlike the current 2009 Directive, which lists possible support instruments for promoting RE (including fixed remuneration in the form of feed-in tariffs) and provides Member States with a broad discretionary power in designing their support systems, the new Post-2020 Directive explicitly requires Member States to choose only market-based support instruments. The market-based support instruments have to be granted either in the form of feed-in premiums (fixed or sliding) or green certificates. In a feed-in premium system, "green" power plant operators have to sell the electricity directly on the market. They receive an additional payment on top of the electricity market price, i.e., the market premium. Depending on whether the additional payment is fixed or adjusted to variable market prices, the feed-in premium is fixed or sliding (in the meaning of variable). In EU countries market premiums are preferred (e.g., in Denmark, Germany, Italy, Spain, Estonia).[62] In the case of green certificates, "green" power plant operators sell the energy through tradable certificates to the market participants with renewables quota obligation (i.e., mandatory minimum share of RE sources in the energy mix of electricity suppliers) and receive an extra revenue on top of the common market price of the energy sold. Green certificates are used, for example, in the UK and Sweden. The fixed remuneration of RE electricity producers in the form of feed-in tariffs, which are paid for each unit of generated electricity independent of the electricity market price, is, however, no longer permitted. In this way, the Post-2020 Directive takes into account recent developments in RE technologies, which have led to a reduction of RE electricity production costs. This market evolution nearly eliminates the necessity to support RE electricity producers with a fixed payment irrespective of actual electricity demand. In this respect, the Post-2020 Directive basically follows the market-oriented pathway already foreseen in the discussed 2014 Guidelines of the European Commission. Nevertheless, introducing support schemes which design

---

62 Energypedia, Feed-in Premiums, https://energypedia.info/wiki/Feed-in_Premiums_(FIP) (last date of access 21 April 2020).

rules at the level of the directive makes a significant difference between the recent and future legal framework for promoting RE. While the 2014 Guidelines build a part of the soft law (i.e., non-binding), the Post-2020 Directive has a direct binding effect for Member States, so that the given rules for designing national support schemes will be mandatory. Moreover, allocation of prescribed market-oriented support instruments needs to occur in an open, transparent, competitive, non-discriminatory and cost-effective manner. This implies the idea that RE electricity generators have to compete with each other for getting supported. The support will be granted through tendering or auctioning procedures. To ensure greater predictability and transparency for participants in auctions or tenders, Member States are obliged to define and publish transparent, non-discriminatory criteria for participating in the tendering process to define clear deadlines and rules for project implementation and also to publish information on previous tendering procedures, including project implementation rates. These measures shall contribute to ensuring project realization. With regard to the new market-oriented support designing rules, exemptions are only foreseen for small-scale installations and demonstration projects. In other words, they are not bound to participate in the auction/tender in order to obtain support and would still profit from feed-in tariffs.

Moreover, the Post-2020 Directive encourages the harmonization of national support schemes throughout the EU and provides for opening support to RE electricity suppliers from other Member States. However, such opening of RE support is subject to the discretion of Member States (indicative shares in each year: at least 5% between 2023 and 2026 and at least 10% between 2027 and 2030). Nevertheless, if necessary, the European Commission will introduce binding obligations in this regard in 2023.

The Post-2020 Directive explicitly recognizes the unpredictability and instability of renewables support policies in the past. Therefore, renewables support policies have to be predictable, stable and avoid frequent or retroactive changes. For example, in the past, feed-in tariffs have already been reduced or abolished with retroactive effect in Italy, Spain and the Czech Republic. These changes in support schemes have led to significant profitability losses for investors operating in the RE sector, who then sued the countries mentioned for compensation. To prevent such practices, the Post-2020 Directive contains guarantees of stability, long-term certainty, and predictability. Article 6 of the Post-2020 Directive prohibits Member States from revising support (level and conditions) granted to RE projects in a way that negatively impacts the rights conferred thereunder and undermines the economic viability of already supported projects (preservation of existing support). Member States are allowed to adjust the support level only in accordance with objective criteria laid down in the original design of the support scheme. In addition, the Post-2020 Directive imposes on Member States an obligation to publish and annually update a long-term schedule on the expected allocation of support for, at least, the following five years (or three years in case of budgetary planning constraints) covering the main aspects of the expected support (e.g., indicative timing, frequency of tendering, expected capacity and budget). This enables investors to better predict the success of the proposed investments. Finally, Member States need to assess the effectiveness of the RE support schemes, taking into account the effect of possible changes to the support schemes. The amendments in question, in particular the prohibition of retroactive changes, are amongst the main achievements of the Post-2020 Directive, as they contribute to enhancing investors' confidence in the regulatory framework.

The Post-2020 Directive provides for a "one-stop-shop" approach: National governments are obliged to set up or designate single administrative contact points in order to coordinate the entire permit application and granting process, upon request by the applicant. Consequently, the new legal framework is more convenient for investors as administrative procedures are simplified and summarized. The new directive aims to reduce administrative burdens as well as to decrease costs for all authorization, certification and licensing procedures, applied to plants and associated transmission and distribution networks for "green" power generation. Furthermore, the Post-2020 Directive foresees a general maximum time limit of two years for the approval procedure of RE projects. In the case of repowering existing RE plants or for installations with an electricity capacity below 150 kW, the approval procedure shall not exceed one year. However, in extraordinary circumstances, all these listed time limits could be extended for one additional year. For small-scale projects (i.e., installations with the electric capacity of equal to or less than 10.8 kW), simple notification procedures are foreseen. Member States are also free to apply simple notification procedures to projects up to 50 kW.

In relation to grid access, the present version of the 2009 Directive foresees that the grid operators have to grant priority access and "dispatch" to RE producers. In other words, the electricity produced from RE has preference over electricity from conventional energy sources. In this way, producers of RE are ensured to sell and transmit the produced electricity whenever they generate it. However, in case of congestion (i.e., oversupply) on the electricity network, grid operators are entitled to curtail the electricity from RE, provided that compensation is paid. The proposed Electricity Market Regulation, however, abolishes the priority dispatch for RE starting from 2021. Given the fact that the RE technologies are developed enough and, due to the falling costs of producing RE, European legislators consider that there is time for RE to fully join the market. As a result, non-discrimination and market-based principles would apply in relation to grid access after 2020. Grid operators will distribute and transmit the cheapest electricity (produced from renewable or non-renewable energy sources) available on the market, so that the final consumers will receive the electricity at the lowest price possible. Furthermore, according to the Energy Market Regulation, the compensation in case of curtailment/redispatch should be calculated by using the market-based approach. The removal of priority dispatch does not apply to the following exceptional cases: "grandfathering" (i.e., existing RE plants), small-scale installations and innovative installations. They will still be able to benefit from priority dispatch. Regarding these proposed changes, there are two different opinions. The first one assumes that the removal of priority dispatch would not have any negative effects for the RE sector and thus supports the planned changes. The assumption is based on the consideration of falling costs for producing RE. This would enable the RE sector to actually maintain the priority when dispatching electricity. The second one is opposed to the planned changes. It considers that, in case of congestion, the redispatch of electricity from RE sources would be cheaper than the redispatch of electricity from conventional energy sources. Against this background, there is a risk for RE plant operators to be curtailed in most cases.

The amendments outlined above indicate that investment conditions within the EU continue to improve beyond 2020. The Post-2020 Directive will enter into force on January 1, 2021 and Member States will have to transpose the recent revisions to the directive into national legislation by June 30, 2021. In 2026, the European Commission is obliged to present a legislative proposal on the regulatory framework for funding renewables already for the period after 2030.

2. Promotion of Renewable Energy on the International Level: The 2016 Paris Climate Agreement

The 2016 Paris Climate Agreement (the "**Paris Agreement**")[63] is the world's first all-encompassing agreement in the fight against climate change. It was adopted at the 21st Conference of the Parties ("**COP 21**") by the members of the United Nations Framework Convention on Climate Change ("**UNFCCC**") on December 12, 2015 and entered into force on November 4, 2016. To this date, from 197 UNFCC members 183 already ratified the Paris Agreement.[64] Among the parties are also the world's largest carbon dioxide (CO2) emitters[65] – China, the US, the EU and India. However, in June 2017, the US announced its exit from the Paris Agreement.[66] The withdrawal of the US can only be effective in November 2020, shortly before the end of Donald Trump's term in office.

The main objective of the Paris Agreement is to mitigate global warming by keeping the increase in the global average temperature to well below 2 degrees

63 See more detailed overview on the Paris Agreement at: Streck/Keenlyside/von Unger, JEEPL 2016, 3 passim.

64 United Nations, Paris Agreement - Status of Ratification, https://unfccc.int/process/the-paris-agreement/status-of-ratification (last date of access 21 April 2020).

65 Largest producers of territorial fossil fuel CO2 emissions worldwide in 2018, based on their share of global CO2 emissions, Statista 2019, https://www.statista.com/statistics/271748/the-largest-emitters-of-co2-in-the-world/ (last date of access 21 April 2020).

66 U.S. submits formal notice of withdrawal from Paris climate pact, Reuters, 4 August 2017, https://www.reuters.com/article/us-un-climate-usa-paris/u-s-submits-formal-notice-ofwithdrawal-from-paris-climate-pact-idUSKBN1AK2FM (last date of access 21 April 2020).

Celsius above pre-industrial levels and pursuing efforts to limit the temperature increase to 1.5 degrees Celsius above pre-industrial levels. In order to reduce global warming, the participating states have mitigation, adaptation and financing obligations. Mitigation obligations mean that the contracting parties have to reduce greenhouse gas (i.e., carbon dioxide) emissions. Adaptation obligations relate to the states' efforts to adapt better to the negative impacts of climate change and to improve climate resilience. Finally, the financing obligations comprise states' commitments to finance both mitigation and adaptation measures.

To achieve the overall goal, the Paris Agreement requires the parties to prepare, communicate and maintain successive nationally determined contributions ("**NDCs**"). As for national actions, the Paris Agreement is based on the principle of common but differentiated responsibilities. The idea behind this principle is that all contracting parties to the Paris Agreement, developed as well as developing countries, have the common responsibility to fight against climate change. Nevertheless, the Paris Agreement considers the diversity in potentials and resources between the contracting parties. Therefore, the responsibility of the developed countries could be greater than the responsibility of the developing countries. For example, developed countries should continue taking the lead by adopting economy-wide absolute emission reduction targets and should encourage developing countries by providing financial resources. The Paris Agreement sets the collective goal of USD 100 billion annually until 2025 (covering both mitigation and adaptation measures).[67] However, the most critical point[68] is the lack of enforcement mechanisms vis-à-vis the parties in the event of non-compliance with their respective commitments. The effective implementation and real success of the Paris Agreement crucially depend not only on national governments but also on the active involvement of the private sector. The public funding alone would not be sufficient to achieve the ambitious goals set out in the Paris Agreement. Therefore, investors play a major role in driving the cash flow for global climate actions.[69]

---

67 Paras. 54, 115 of the accompanying decision to the Paris Agreement, serving as guidance for the implementation and pre-2020 action: United Nation, Draft Decision -/CP.21, https://unfccc.int/resource/docs/2015/cop21/eng/l09.pdf (last date of access 21 April 2020).

68 The Paris Agreement is the Shove the World Needs, 14 December 2015, https://slate.com/business/2015/12/the-paris-agreement-wont-punish-countries-that-fall-short-but-its-still-the-shove-the-world-needs.html (date of last access 21 April 2020); Expect Climate Catastrophe: Paris Agreement Lacks Enforcement, 1 December 2016, https://www.forbes.com/sites/anderscorr/2016/12/01/expect-climate-catastrophe-paris-agreement-lacks-enforcement/#4fe0605b3313 (date of last access 21 April 2020).

69 UN Calls on Investors to Align Portfolios with Paris Agreement, 1 February 2018, https://unfccc.int/news/un-calls-on-investors-to-align-portfolios-with-paris-agreement (last date of access 21 April 2020).

5.3.2 Overview of the Range of Different National Promotion Systems

1. Price-Driven Support Mechanisms

a) Feed-in tariffs (FiT) and current trends

In a feed-in tariff regime, the electricity generated from renewable energies is rewarded with statutory fixed revenues which are guaranteed for a certain period of time.[70] Additional costs arise out of the difference between the level of the tariff and the market price for electricity. Such additional costs are borne either by the taxpayer or the electricity consumer.[71] The feed-in tariff decouples the revenue of renewable energy from the market price through the support of a promotion. The tariff design is often tailored to the chosen form of production of renewable energies. Most of the designs have a degressive approach in common, which means that funds for new renewable energy plants decrease each year.

This approach bears advantages for the spread of renewable energies technologies. Due to the stable and predictable revenue over a long period of time, investment security is ensured for plant operators and investors. As all renewable energy technologies are subject to promotion, whereas the plant operators do not face competition and do not have to offer their energy on competitive terms, a cross-technology expansion is promoted. In this way, all renewable energy technologies are promoted in the same way. Hence, it is possible to expand technologies that would not be economically viable without promotion. Thus, those promoted technologies can develop with the help of governmental promotion until they can operate independently of any government support. This will ensure green electricity production by exploiting all the benefits from diversification of the technologies used and decentralization of the locations.

A disadvantage of feed-in tariffs arises from the investment in all technology forms (not only the most economical) of plant operators under the promotion system. This causes a higher cost structure to develop compared to other promotion systems, for example, under a quota system. Through the stable and predictable promotion of renewable energy plants the operators act unbundled from the market and market laws. This can result in higher electricity prices for consumers and a market for renewable energies that is unbundled and unadjusted to the remaining electricity market.

Feed-in tariffs are the most common promotion system in Europe. They were used by 21 out of 28 Member States of the European Union between 2014 and 2015

70 REN21, Renewables 2011: Global Status Report, 2011, p. 56, https://www.ren21.net/wp-content/uploads/2019/05/GSR2011_Full-Report_English.pdf.

71 Support Schemes for Renewable Energy, 31 Kirschen/Strbac, Fundamentals of Power System Economics, 2nd ed., 2019, p. 120.

as a main promotion system.[72] Nevertheless, it is foreseeable that the promotion of renewable energies through statutory feed-in tariffs will gradually decline in Europe. Because of European state aid law, the European Commission is demanding that promotion systems should no longer be based on statutory feed-in tariffs but on more competitive procedures.[73] With the EEG 2017, the **German** legislator followed this demand. The law led to a paradigm shift of promotion from statutory feed-in tariffs to a tender procedure.[74] This demand also led to changes in the promotion systems in other European Member States. In **France,** the act of Energy Transition for Green Growth of August 17, 2015 provided for a replacement of the promotion system from the previously applied feed-in tariffs to a so-called compensation mechanism step-by-step. The compensation mechanism used is basically a feed-in premium allocated through a direct contract or a tender process, which depends on the technology used and the size of the plant. Small or non-marketable plants can still benefit from feed-in tariffs.

Portugal also follows this demand by stopping the promotion through feed-in tariffs for new investments and implementing a new promotion system which brings competition to the renewable energy market and drops the governmental shielding of renewable energy promoted by feed-in tariffs. Therefore, Portugal implemented an auction system and a modified Contracts for Difference (**CfD**) scheme. While these changes are intended to take the promotion of renewable energies to the next level, the market for renewable energies has come to a complete stop in other states.

Due to the consolidation of the state budget and the deficits in the electricity market, the **Spanish** government agreed with Real decreto 9/2013 on the termination of the promotion for renewable energies by feed-in tariffs and promotion in 2013. The promotion schemes have been replaced by an additional payment at relevant market prices and an investment bonus, which is intended to ensure reasonable profitability. However, it was not only feed-in tariffs that were terminated in Spain; further retroactive changes were also made to tariffs for already constructed plants, especially photovoltaic plants. Hence, investors faced huge insecurity which in the end led to a standstill of the renewable energy market between 2012 and 2017 and caused major profit losses for investors up to 50% in some cases.[75] However, in 2017 the Spanish photovoltaic market was reborn, with a newly installed capacity of 147 MW.[76] The reasons for this are diverse. After complaints by

72 CEER, Status Review of Renewable Support Schemes in Europe 2017, p. 10, https://unfccc.int/resource/docs/2015/cop21/eng/l09.pdf.

73 Boemke, NVwZ, p. 3.

74 Boemke, NVwZ 2017, p. 3 et. seq.

75 IEA, 2018 Snapshot of global photovoltaic markets, 2018, p. 7, https://iea-pvps.org/wp-content/uploads/2020/01/IEA-PVPS_-_A_Snapshot_of_Global_PV_-_1992-2017.pdf.

76 IEA, 2018 Snapshot of global photovoltaic markets, 2018, p. 3.

the European Union that Spain would not meet the set goal of a 20% quota of renewable energies in the total production until 2020, it introduced technology-neutral tenders in 2017, which provide an additional payment to each produced MW. In addition, the costs for solar panels have decreased 80% compared to 2011, making photovoltaic technology more competitive with other sources of energy.[77] As there is now almost no more governmental promotion for renewable energy in Spain, the Spanish market can be considered a test market for funds and banks for renewable energy under free market conditions.[78] Taking into account Spain's ideal conditions for the energy production of solar and wind, the above developments have led to the revival of the PV market in particular.

Similar proceedings occurred in the **Czech Republic**, where feed-in tariffs were abolished in 2013, and in **Greece**. In Greece the government introduced measures that retroactively reduced the attractiveness of investments into solar power. From January 2014, plants that operated less than 12 years have the option to sell the energy on the market at market conditions or to a set price of € 80 per MWh to the grid. Furthermore, investors in photovoltaic power plants had to grant 35% of their 2013 earnings to Hellenic Electricity Market Operator (**LAGIE**) to fill a financing gap of € 700 million. However, a revival of the market of Greece and the Czech Republic did not yet take place.[79]

Feed-in tariff cuts in **Australia** and **China are also noteworthy**. The Australian Independent Pricing and Regulatory Tribunal (**IPART**) recommended cutting the feed-in tariff for households feeding their electricity surplus out of photovoltaic into the grid from 11¢–15¢ per kWh to about 6.9¢–8.4¢ per kWh in 2018.[80] Similar developments occurred in China, where feed-in tariffs for grid connection were cut for photovoltaic plants and distributed photovoltaic plants mainly for own use with excess output fed into the grid inaugurated after January 1, 2018. An exception was made for the photovoltaic plants installed to fight poverty on village-level. Feed-in tariff rates for distributed photovoltaic plants smaller than 0.5 MW therefore remain unchanged.[81] In China,

77 The Spanish PV market has entered into a new phase, PV Europe 6 April 2018, https://www.pveurope.eu/News/Markets-Money/The-Spanish-PV-market-has-entered-into-anew-phase (last date of access 21 April 2020).

78 Run auf spanische Wind- und Solarparks, Wirtschaftswoche, 15 June 2017, https://www.wiwo.de/unternehmen/energie/erneuerbare-energien-run-auf-spanische-wind-und-solarparks/19933076.html. (last date of access 21 April 2020).

79 IEA, 2018 Snapshot of global photovoltaic markets, 2018, p. 3.

80 Sabotage: Regulator slammed for move to slash solar feed-in tariffs, The Sydney Morning Herald, 3 July 2018, https://www.smh.com.au/environment/climate-change/sabotage-regulator-slammed-for-move-to-slash-solar-feed-in-tariffs-20180703-p4zp7x.html (last date of access 21 April 2020).

81 Poverty Alleviation Will Be Highlight of Chinas 2018 PV Power Policy, Energy Trend, 2 January 2018, https://www.energytrend.com/news/20180102-12118.html. (date of last access 21 April 2020).

poverty alleviation through power development became a major political task. About 70.17 million people spread over 20 million families in China live in poverty, which means they have an annual income of less than 2300 yuan per person (which is about $1 a day per person). To fight poverty, about 3 million families are funded by the government to build photovoltaic plants of 5 kW, generating around 3,000 yuan per year of additional family income through selling the electricity to the grid. This is considered a win-win situation, as the photovoltaic market expands and poor families gain additional income.[82]

Feed-in tariffs as a support scheme are well-suited to establish renewable energies in areas where expansion is still beginning or is still in progress. In other words, feed-in tariffs are a good model for start-up financing. In this way, technologies can be established and developed to market maturity, due to the governmental protective shield. However, since they are very expensive a feed-in tariff based promotion system should be changed to a more competitive promotion system after market maturity of major energy sources.

b) Feed-in premiums (FIP)

Another promotion system for Renewable Energy Sources is a Feed-in premium (**FIP**), which is basically a variation of a feed-in tariff scheme. The producer of Renewable Energies sells the produced energy on the spot market or directly to a third party. In addition to the received market price a further premium is paid. This premium is usually designed as a fixed or a sliding premium. Under a **fixed premium** scheme the plant operator is granted a premium on top of the market price which stays the same over a period of time, i.e., the premium is independent of the revenues generated at the market. Such a fixed-premium is currently in place in **Estonia**. Under that system, the fixed bonus for all technologies added to the market price amounts to € 0.0537 per kWh and is paid by the Transmission System Operator (**TSO**). Nevertheless, changes in the promotion system are expected as the renewable energy sector has been developing faster than expected in Estonia. Hence, drafts of new legislation are currently being discussed in the Estonian parliament. Fixed premiums contain the risk of over- and undercompensating of the plant operator, as they receive high revenues when market prices are high and vice versa low revenues in case of low market prices. To reduce this risk, fixed premiums might be combined with predetermined cap and floor levels for the total achievable market price or granted premium. The **sliding premium** is also granted on top of the market price, but in contrast to the fixed premium the

82 IEA, National Survey Report of Photovoltaic Applications in China, 2017, p. 22, https://iea-pvps.org/wp-content/uploads/2020/01/National_Survey_Report_of_PV_Power_Applications_in_China_-_2017_01.pdf.

premium amount depends on the achieved market price. The premium is calculated as the difference between the average wholesale level and a predetermined reference tariff level. How the reference tariff level is set depends. Sometimes it corresponds to existing feed-in tariffs. In **Germany**, for example, the premium for projects of a certain size is determined in a market-oriented tender since the EEG 2017. Projects which are too small to participate in a tender are still entitled to a classical sliding market premium. In case the achieved market price is higher than the reference tariff level, no premium is paid. Among European Union Member States sliding feed-in premiums are currently preferred. They are used as a promotion scheme among others in **Finland**, **Italy**, the **Netherlands**, **Denmark** (except for offshore wind) and in the **Czech Republic**. Germany used sliding feed-in premiums in the past. The premium was determined by the difference between a statutorily fixed technology specific reference value and the monthly average market price. Since the EEG 2017, the technology specific reference value is no longer statutorily fixed but determined in a tender in the individual case. In this way, a stronger market-based integration of renewable energies is taking place. Other countries using tender based schemes are Denmark regarding offshore wind and Greece.

Feed-in premiums bear advantages in comparison to feed-in tariffs. Feed-in premiums follow a more market-based approach. As energy producers are reliant on the achieved market price to maximise the revenue, the incentive now exists to produce energy when demand is high or production from other sources is low. As a result, renewable energy sources are better integrated into the electricity market and energy supply and demand is combined more efficiently. The market-based approach could help to implement a more efficient grid management by easing pre-existing grid bottlenecks. At last those schemes establish competition among the electricity producers from which the consumers benefit. Nonetheless, feed-in premiums also bear disadvantages. The biggest disadvantage is that they are not equally suited as a promotion mechanism for all forms of renewable energy production. Under a feed-in premium the control of energy supply and the control of production gain in importance when attempting to maximise revenue by supplying and producing in times of high market prices, for example, when demand is high or production from other sources is low. However, this control of supply is not possible for wind and solar energy, for example, as they are dependent on environmental factors (wind force and solar radiation), so additional costs for the procurement of balancing services will arise. Consequently, it is rather unlikely that wind and solar energy are able to adapt the market price signals cost-effectively.

2. Volume-Driven Support Mechanisms

a) Quota obligations

In the quota model, the national government determines a fixed share of renewable energies that must be generated and sold by producers and grid operators over a specified period of time. The adherence to the quota is ensured by green electricity certificates. For each produced unit of green energy, a tradable green energy certificate is issued. By purchasing those certificates the quota obligated consumers are able to prove the adherence to the determined quota. Non-compliance with the quota will be punished by a fine or other sanctions.

The worldwide promotion of renewable energy has increased steadily since the 1990s. For a long time, promotion through price-driven (feed-in tariffs and feed-in premiums) and volume-driven (quota obligations and auction/tender schemes) promotion systems developed nearly equally. In the recent past, a worldwide increase of price-driven schemes and a decrease of volume driven schemes has been observed.[83] This development is surprising since quota systems bear some advantages. A volume model opens up the possibility of achieving the expansion goals of renewable energies precisely. This is rather advantageous. In this way, the society is protected from unnecessarily high costs caused by an excessive expansion of renewable energies. In addition, the statutory climate targets can be achieved more easily. This precise control of costs and the expansion of renewable energies could not be achieved with price-driven schemes. These schemes are characterized by a feed-in tariff or premium granted by the government. Setting the remunerations to the correct level to achieve the expansion goals would be nothing less than a coincidence. Thus, a controlled expansion is not possible under price-driven schemes.

Further advantages become visible by adopting a market economy perspective. Volume-driven promotion systems promote competition, which is not the case for price-driven approaches. Due to the absence of a statutory feed-in tariff, plant operators are forced to sell the electricity on the market at competitive prices and conditions. In addition to the revenue generated from the traded electricity, they also receive the revenue from the certificates, which are also traded on competitive terms. The market for renewable energy, therefore, follows market economy rules. However, in order for individual plant operators to be able to survive in this market, they must realize cost reduction potentials, whereby only the most cost-effective plants and the best locations are used. This in the end leads to cheaper electricity from which consumers benefit.

---

83 Einspeisetarife vs. Quotensysteme, Institut der deutschen Wirtschaft Köln, 13. November 2011, https://www.iwkoeln.de/studien/iw-kurzberichte/beitrag/foerderung-erneuerbarer-energien-einspeisetarif-versus-quotensystem-52729.html.

Nevertheless, volume-driven support mechanisms also have disadvantages. The competition in which the plant operators take part is a curse and a blessing at the same time. The absence of statutory premiums and tariffs reduces the planning and investment security for plant operators, since they cannot rely on constantly high revenues. It is therefore reasonable to assume that price-driven mechanisms encourage a greater expansion of renewable energies. A further disadvantage can be shown by taking a closer look at the need of plant operators to choose the most favorable form of renewable energy production under volume-driven systems. Electricity suppliers would neither buy nor request electricity produced under different conditions, so that the cheapest electricity would always be available. At first glance, this sounds like an advantage, but upon closer look, the impact on the diversification of renewable energy reveals the opposite. In Germany, a price-driven approach has led to a diverse range of renewable energy plants (such as wind, solar, biomass, water and offshore wind). Under a volume-driven approach, such a diversification would most likely not have occurred. Onshore-wind, the cheapest production form concentrated on certain regions, would be the only expanded production form. As a result, advantages arising from a decentralized and diversified renewable energy production would remain unused. High-priced promising technology like offshore wind would not be further developed under a quota model, with the effect that much unused potential would be lost.

Such quota obligations systems, as described above, are among others used by the United Kingdom, Sweden, Poland, Norway, Belgium, Italy, Romania and India. In the following, a brief overview of the support schemes in the UK and Sweden shall be given, as they show some special features.

The UK started the promotion of renewable energies under a quota obligation system. The government set an obligation for licensed energy suppliers to source a steadily increasing share of renewable energies (**Renewable Obligation**). Energy suppliers meet their obligation by presenting Renewable Obligation Certificates (**ROCs**) to the Office of Gas and Electricity Markets (Ofgem). Those suppliers who did not comply with the quota had to make a payment of a fixed amount for each MWh shortfall into a buy-out fund. The funds revenue was paid back to those suppliers compliant with their quota in proportion to the amount of presented ROCs. Since the UK could not reach their targeted expansion rate using the ROC promotion system, discussions arose whether the ROC system was an adequate instrument to reach the expansion targets. This ultimately led to the government's decision in July 2011 to close the RO to new generating capacity from March 31, 2017. Until the closure of ROCs, plant operators had a one-off choice between both support schemes. Thus, a paradigm shift was initiated by the introduction of the Contract of Difference (**CfD**), which is basically a price-driven support scheme on a feed-in tariff basis between the plant operator and a newly formed government-owned company called Low-Carbons Contract Company (**LCCC**) as counterparty.[84] It first opened for applications on October 16, 2016.[85] The CfD is an auction-based support mechanism. Plant operators of projects with a capacity higher than 5 MW are able to participate in a multi-unit, sealed-bid, uniform price auction. In the auction the plant operators bid for the generation costs (**strike price**). The bidder with the lowest strike price is awarded with a CfD. The CfD grants additional revenues from selling electricity in the wholesale power market. The additional revenue is calculated from the difference of the strike price and the wholesale market price (**reference price**). If the strike price is below the reference price the difference is paid as additional revenue to the plant operator. In the reverse case, the CfD requires the plant operator to pay the difference to the counterparty.[86]

Apart from the UK, **Italy** and **Poland** are further countries that will let their quota obligations system expire in the future.[87]

Another country using a quota obligation promotion system is **Sweden**. The quota obligation system was introduced in May 2003 and will run until 2035.[88] Until now it has been used without any major changes. In general, the system works as described above, so plant operators receive revenue from selling the electricity at the wholesale market and receive additional revenue for the sale of the green electricity certificates. The obliged party shows its compliance with the quota obligation by presenting green electricity certificates to the energy agency. A special feature of the Swedish quota obligation system is the common certificate market with Norway (**Nord Pool spot exchange**). Due to bilateral agreements between the countries, a cross-border green electricity exchange is implemented. A major topic on the Swedish renewable energy market was the threat of the end of the common certificate market beyond 2020, since the governments of both countries could not agree on the future of the program. After a long phase of negotiations, the countries' governments reached an agreement permitting certificate trading until April 2046.[89]

---

84 Auctions for Renewable Energy Support in the United Kingdom: Instruments and lessons learnt, p. 6, https://www.researchgate.net/publication/301821658_Auctions_for_Renewable_Energy_Support_in_the_United_Kingdom_Instruments_and_lessons_learnt.

85 Ofgem e-serve Renewables Obligation Annual Report 2015 - 2016, p. 52, https://www.ofgem.gov.uk/ofgem-publications/113760).

86 Auctions for Renewable Energy Support in the United Kingdom: Instruments and lessons learnt, p. 9.

87 CEER, Status Review of Renewable Support Schemes in Europe 2017, p. 10.

88 The electricity certificate system 2012, p. 7, https://www.google.com/url?sa=t&rct=j&q=&esrc=s&source=web&cd=3&ved=2ahUKEwiYqKi7nKffAhUHElAKHWm9ABwQFjACegQIBxAC&url=https%3A%2F%2Fenergimyndigheten.a-w2m.se%2FTest.ashx%3FResourceId%3D2664&usg=AOvVaw29qbiZ7Hp3Y98aK0khsPnk.

89 Sweden and Norway extend joint electricity certificate system for renewables to 2030, PV Magazine, 19 April 2017, https://www.pv-magazine.com/2017/04/19/sweden-and-norway-extend-joint-electricity-certificate-system-for-renewables-to-2030/ (last date of access 21 April 2020).

Finally, quota models are advantageous for the consumer because they ensure the most favorable prices on the market by maintaining competition. However, they only lead to a sectoral expansion of renewable energies and therefore implement the risk of not achieving the targeted expansion rates. In the UK, this led to the paradigm shift described above and significantly higher costs for wind energy than in Germany. The same applies for Sweden, where a slow expansion of renewable energies was observable. In the past years, the renewable energy generation has risen faster in Germany using a price driven support scheme than in Sweden, where a quota system was used. This also led to a very slow expansion of wind energy in Sweden, which accounted for about 10% of the overall energy production in 2017 in Sweden and was even decreasing in the years before.[90] Overall, quota obligation systems are less suitable to implement a comprehensive, cross-sectoral expansion of renewable energies than price-driven mechanisms.

b) Auction/Tender schemes

An upcoming development in EU and non-EU countries is auction/tender schemes. The outcome of the tender is the feed-in tariff, the reference value for the feed-in premium (e.g., in **Germany**), or, alternatively, the basis for a capacity payment per installed kW.[91] By the end of 2017, 13 European states had already implemented a tender scheme, among them **Belgium**, **Denmark**, **France**, **Germany**, **Greece**, **Italy**, **Malta**, the **Netherlands**, **Lithuania**, **Portugal**, **Poland**, **Spain** and the **United Kingdom**. A further five countries already had the respective legislation in place or were about to adopt it, among them **Croatia**, **Finland**, **Hungary**, **Luxemburg** and **Estonia**.[92] This shows that a gradual introduction of competitive bidding processes is in progress. This development is due to the European Commission State Aid Guidelines for Environmental Protection and Energy which state that Member States searching for state-aid clearance shall set up a competitive bidding process for the support of all new plants.[93] As the majority of the tender schemes in Europe and also worldwide follow a **static sealed bid** approach[94] this approach can be highlighted as a trend. In a static sealed bidding procedure each participant makes one bid, while no information regarding the

90 Die Windenergie teht in Schweden vor einem Rekordjahr, Germany Trade ... Invest, https://www.gtai.de/gtai-de/trade/branchen/branche-kompakt/schweden/branche-kompakt-die-windenergie-steht-in-schweden-vor-144162 (last access date 28 April 2020).

91 CEER, Tendering procedures for RES in Europe: State of play and first lessons learnt, 2018, p. 9, https://www.ceer.eu/documents/104400/-/-/167af87c-5472-230b-4a19-f68042d58ea8.

92 CEER, Tendering procedures for RES in Europe: State of play and first lessons learnt, 2018, p. 10.

93 Auctions for Renewable Support: Lessons learnt from International Experiences, 2016, p. 6, http://auresproject.eu/files/media/documents/aures_wp4_synthesis_report.pdf.

94 Auctions for Renewable Support: Lessons learnt from International Experiences, 2016, p. 11.

price or the auctioned product are exchanged between the participants. The best bid wins. This might lead to the scenario that the bid winner undervalues the true project's value, therefore underbids but wins the bid and remains with an unprofitable project. However, due to the low transaction costs and simple execution they remain rather attractive.[95] Although the trend is to use a static sealed bid procedure, as described above, the **Netherlands** use a different tender procedure, containing **a dynamic (ascending) auction procedure**. This form of bidding process goes through several rounds. In each round of the bidding process the auctioneer suggests a lower price than in the previous round, while the bidders make their offer which states the quantity they are willing to produce at the suggested price. The bidding process ends when requested quantities and supplied quantities match. The main benefit of this bidding process is its transparency. Better pricing is achieved, as the bidders can adjust their bids. However, practical experience shows that energy suppliers usually do not adjust their bids during a bidding process.[96] As the only country, **Brazil** uses a **hybrid scheme** between dynamic and static auctions. In the first step, a ceiling price for the project is submitted in advance. Bidders then submit the quantity they would supply at this price. In later rounds this quantity cannot be adjusted. This phase is followed by a further phase of multiple rounds. The auctioneer constantly informs bidders of the new price level and the bidders accept or decline whether they will go on in the auction or not. This phase ends when the overall supply matches the auction's requirement as well as the adjustment factor which is unknown to the bidders. Afterwards, this is followed by the last phase for the remaining bidders. In a sealed bid the bidders offer a price which has to stay under the ceiling price for their quantities offered in the first phase. The lowest tenders will be awarded the contract.[97]

Taking into account the rapid spread of tendering procedures and the demands of the European Commission to set up competitive bidding process to achieve state-aid clearance in their guidelines, tendering procedures may be put forward as the future promotion scheme, at least in Europe. As they allow the control of support costs and volume distribution, this is a welcome development.

---

95 EWEA, Design options for wind energy tenders, 2015, p.7 https://www.ewea.org/fileadmin/files/library/publications/position-papers/EWEA-Design-options-for-wind-energy-tenders.pdf.

96 IRENA, Renewable Energy Auctions: A Guide to Design, 2015, p. 12, https://www.irena.org/-/media/Files/IRENA/Agency/Publication/2015/Jun/IRENA_Renewable_Energy_Auctions_A_Guide_to_Design_2015.pdf.

97 IRENA, Renewable Energy Auctions: A Guide to Design, 2015, p. 14.

5.3.3 Further National Promotion Systems; In Particular State Aid and Tax Benefits

1. Investment Grants/Subsidies

Some countries give grants or subsidise renewable energy projects under certain conditions in addition to promotion schemes. In **Finland**, for example, under the so-called energy aid, grants are given for renewable energy production facilities and related research projects. The granted projects must promote the use or production of renewable energies, advance energy efficiency and the environmental effects caused by energy production and use. The basic condition for funding is that at least 25% of the project funding must come from non-governmental sources. Furthermore, investment aid for renewable energy and new renewable technologies exists, which can be granted against a fixed assets investment. Another incentive can be found in China where the government grants subsidies to poor communities on village level. In terms of feed-in tariff cuts for installed photovoltaic plants the tariffs for plants smaller than 0.5 MW on village-level remained unaffected. This measure therefore has a dual function as it promotes renewable energies while also fighting poverty.

2. Soft Loans

Another approach to promoting the diffusion of renewable energies is finance assistance through soft loans. In this context, the joint project facility of the International Renewable Energy Agency (**IRENA**) and the Abu Dhabi Fund for Development (**ADFD**) stand out in particular. The project aims to support replicable, scalable, potentially transformable renewable energy projects in developing countries by providing soft loans. Further prerequisites for funding are a positive development impact, the improvement of energy access, addressing energy security and governmental support of the project. The projects must be submitted by a member of IRENA, signatories of the statute or states in accession which are listed as developing countries at the Organisation for Economic Co-operation and Development (**OECD**). The ADFD provided $350 million for the project facility. Over seven annual funding cycles projects are selected for funding. $50 million is available for each cycle. The loan amount ranges from $5 to $15 million per loan per financing cycle. The loan period is 20 years, of which 5 years are a grace period. Loan rates are charged at a rate of 1% to 2% per annum.[98] The seventh funding cycle opens for applications on November 12, 2018 and ends on February 19, 2019. The programs of the Brazilian National Bank for Economic and Social

98 IRENA, Accessible Finance for Renewable Energy Projects in Developing Countries, 2018, https://irena.org/-/media/Files/IRENA/Agency/Publication/2017/Dec/IRENA-ADFD_Accessible_Finance_Brochure_2018.pd.

Development (**BNDES**) are also notable. As one of the largest development banks in the world the BNDES runs a climate change fund linked to the Ministry of Environment. It aims to support and finance projects or studies which aim to reduce climate change by supporting the implementation, the acquisition of machinery and equipment as well as the technological development of such projects. As a sub-program, the climate fund also runs a program to finance renewable energies. Another mentionable program is the Brazil Inova Energia Programme. This program offers support by grants and soft loans to enhance knowledge sharing between companies and technology institutes of smart grids, renewable energies and hybrid and energy efficient vehicles. Eligible borrowers could be provided with a loan covering 90% of the project costs while the remaining 10% must come from their own assets.

3. Fiscal Incentives

The promotion of renewable energies can also take the form of tax incentives, as found in the **United States**. Tax credits are granted through a so-called Production Tax Credit (**PTC**) for wind facilities commencing construction by December 31, 2019, and for other facilities like geothermal, closed-loop biomass and solar systems commencing construction by December 31, 2018. An inflation-adjusted per kWh tax credit for electricity generated by qualified energy resources and sold to a third party is granted to the taxpayer for ten years after the facility commenced production. In US law further tax credits apply. A further Investment Tax Credit (**ITC**) of 30% applies to solar, fuel cells and wind. An ITC of 10% also applies to geothermal, microturbines and combined heat and power (**CHP**). Besides tax credits, certain tangible property might also be recovered for tax purposes through annual deductions in the Modified Accelerated Recovery System Depreciation Schedule (**MARCS**). Under MARCS a life time is set for various types of property, during which they may be depreciated. Solar-electric and solar-thermal technologies, fuel cells, microturbines, geothermal electric, wind and CHP properties may be depreciated within five years. The schedule sets the depreciation rate for biomass, marine and hydrokinetic property to seven years. In this way the property owner has the possibility to deduct his tax basis during the depreciation period.

Further tax incentives can be found in **Sweden**. Land owners pay a reduced real estate tax in case a wind energy plant is constructed on the property. Furthermore, a reduced energy consumption tax applies to electricity produced in generators with a capacity lower than 50 kW. Electricity production from wind, wave and solar is rewarded with a higher capacity. In addition micro producers of electricity from renewable energy are rewarded with a tax reduction on the basis of the kWh fed into the grid at the grid connection point during the calendar year.

5.4 Key Requirements for an Investment into National RE Markets

5.4.1 Stability of the Regulatory Framework

Stable legal conditions in the host country are an essential prerequisite for success when it comes to investing in renewable energies. In particular, the security of governmental support mechanisms (i.e., feed-in tariffs) is a key element for the reliable calculation of future revenues of a project. In this context, some countries have experienced so-called retroactive changes ("**RACs**"). These changes are brought upon by laws which are applied to facts that have occurred before the publication of the law. For example, an already granted feed-in tariff for electricity produced by a certain wind farm could be retroactively reduced. This can lead to significant problems in project financing, since revenue streams expected by plant operators are negatively affected, putting the profitability of the project at risk. Furthermore, introducing RACs immediately increases risk premiums for new projects, due to investors becoming more reluctant to invest in the sector similarly to banks that are risk averse and will lend money at higher rates for such projects to compensate for the higher insolvency risk.[99]

In the past, several countries introduced RACs in respect of renewable technologies, creating a harsher investment climate. **Spain** is a stark example of this. After an impressive growth of Spanish renewable capacities as well as the innovative design of the support system and measures for system integration, the situation changed considerably after 2007. The Spanish support scheme for electricity from RE plants in 2007 was based on a system where plant operators could choose between a feed-in tariff or a feed-in premium granted on top of the regular wholesale electricity price. In general, the total revenue per MWh was limited by an upper and lower bound (premium with cap and floor). The support level for PV was comparatively high in 2007 and 2008 according to Royal Decree 661/2007:
- For plants with a capacity of up to 100 kW: 44.0381 €c/kWh for the first 25 years and 35.2305 €c/kWh thereafter;
- For plants with a capacity between 100 kW and 10 MW: 41.75 €c/kWh and 33.4 €c/kWh;
- For plants with a capacity above 10 MW: 22.9764 €c/kWh and 18.3811 €c/kWh.

Alongside these favorable tariffs, several other factors (such as easy access to credit, short approval times and a loophole in support laws, enabling large PV

99 European Renewable Energy Federation, Policy Paper on Retrospective Changes to RES Legislations and National Moratoria, 2013, p. 1 et. seq., http://www.keepontrack.eu/contents/publicationsbiannualnationalpolicyupdatesversions/kot-policy-paper-on-retrospective-changes-to-res-support.pdf.

systems to split their capacity in order to partially be granted the higher feed-in tariffs) played a role in the boom of installed PV capacities.[100] The result was a significant rise in the annual installed solar PV capacity from 103 MW in 2006 to 544 MW in 2007 and 2,708 MW in 2008. In the same period, the electricity tariff deficit (understood as the balance of government expenditure and revenue related to the electricity sector) in Spain increased substantially, due to a slower increase in revenues of 100% between 2005 and 2013 compared to an increase in costs of 221%. In order to decrease this deficit, the Spanish government decided to implement a number of measures – including RACs – in the years after 2007 which included the following:

- **Royal Decree 1578/2008:** Reduction of tariff levels and the support period for new plants to 25 years; annual and quarterly capacity quotas.
- **Royal Decree 1565/2010:** Further tariff decrease for new plants; reduction of the support period to 25 years for existing plants (changed to 28 years by Royal Decree 14/2010). Cap on annual supported full load hours for existing plants.
- **Royal Decree Law 1/2012:** Abolishment of all support for new plants (moratorium).
- **Royal Decree Law 2/2012:** Introduction of a 7% / 22% (for hydro plants) tax on electricity generation for all plants. Abolishment of the fee-in premium option.
- **Royal Decree Law 2/2013:** Reduction of yearly tariff adaption for existing plants by using the core inflation rate as reference, which is typically lower than the previously used consumer price index.
- **Royal Decree Law 413/2014 (and Ministerial Order IET 1045/2014):** Change of the support system for existing plants, which effectively led to a decrease in remuneration for plant operators.

These examples of legal changes include a number of RACs (especially those which are applicable to existing plants) which led to severe loss of revenues for owners of existing plants. In combination with the moratorium for supporting new plants, the changes provided for an almost complete halt for investments in RE and led to closures and mergers of companies engaged in the manufacturing of PV modules. For example, BP's Spanish solar plants closed in 2010, the pioneering company Isofotón was purchased in mid-2010 by Korean investors and the Siliken PV company closed in early 2013. As a consequence, the industry had to deal with severe job losses.[101] Furthermore, for surviving companies, the only way to grow has been to expand into the international market, driving investments away from Spain.[102]

---

100 Directorate General for Internal Policy, Solar energy policy in the EU and the Member States, from perspective of the petitions received, 2016, p. 15 et. seq., https://www.europarl.europa.eu/RegData/etudes/STUD/2016/556968/IPOL_STU(2016)556968_EN.pdf.

101 Directorate General for Internal Policy, Solar energy policy in the EU and the Member States, from perspective of the petitions received, 2016, p. 19.

102 GSI/IISD, A Cautionary Tale: Spain's solar PV Investment bubble, p. 22 et. seq., https://www.iisd.org/gsi/sites/default/files/rens_ct_spain.pdf.

The **Belgian** support mechanisms experienced a similar up- and downhill ride to that of the Spain solar PV industry. In contrast to the majority of support systems, Belgium is characterized by decentralization, giving the three regions (Brussels, Flanders and Wallonia) a wide range of competencies instead of binding rules by the federal government. However, the support system for RE in all three regions is a quota system, where electricity suppliers are obliged to source a certain share of their electricity from renewables. Therefore, they need to either produce renewable electricity themselves or buy green certificates from renewable electricity generators. Each region is entitled to set their own limit in terms of required renewable share by electricity suppliers and minimum prices for green certificates as well as penalties for the non-fulfillment of renewable quotas. Due to favorable price setting, the Wallonian region in particular experienced a boom in PV plants. While the annual installed PV capacity remained relatively constant in 2009 (48,264 kW) and 2010 (43,261 kW), it increased rapidly in 2011 (139,354 kW) and 2012 (272,828 kW) due to the generous support system and a price drop in solar modules. As a consequence of the high growth in PV capacities and the corresponding increase of green certificates issued, an oversupply of certificates was created, leading to low certificate prices and an increasing share of certificates sold at the minimum price to the grid operator ELIA. This price drop endangered the profitability of existing plants and blocked future development in some subsectors (such as biomass).[103] Similar to the Spanish government, Belgium additionally had to deal with rising support costs and falling revenues from the electricity sector and therefore introduced measures to counteract the deficit resulting therefrom. This included a reduction of the support duration (from 15 to 10 years) and scope of support (79% less) for PV plants. It also involved a decrease in the number of certificates received for each MWh of produced renewable electricity as well as the partial integration of a variable support payment instead of a fixed payment to reduce the risk of overpayment in times of low electricity prices. As a result, the annual installed PV capacity in Wallonia dropped in 2013 to 128.918 kW and further drastically declined in 2014 to only 614 kW. These RACs again led to severe turbulences in the RE industry costing jobs and harming future investments, thus, leading to a slower expansion of the technologies.

Italy can serve as another example for the application of RACs and the negative repercussions resulting therefrom. From 2011 to 2013, Italy changed the incentive systems for RE (so-called "Conto Energia") about four times, causing uncertainties among plant operators and investors as well as limiting the access to credit. For example, the retroactive measures included a support reduction in relation to minimum guaranteed prices as well as a reduction in FiTs. On top of that, an additional contribution of 0.05 €c/kWh was introduced in July 2012 to cover the governmental cost for

---

103 Directorate General for Internal Policy, Solar energy policy in the EU and the Member States, from perspective of the petitions received, 2016, p. 22.

management, monitoring and control activities which applied to all existing and future RE plants. For plants already built, this was an additional operational cost that was not budgeted by investors. These RACs were responsible for approximately 8 billion EUR of orders blocked and 20 billion EUR contracts on hold in the solar PV sector alone.[104]

In the **Czech Republic**, investors and operators were also harmed by RACs. Since 2011 the government introduced a series of retrospective measures, creating a severely detrimental environment, especially for PV. The reason behind this was – again – a mismanagement of PV support schemes by the government, leading to an uncontrolled increase in the number of installations and significant additional costs to electricity consumers. The RACs included the abolition of tax breaks, changes in depreciation, the obligation to equip PV installations with remote control appliances as well as recycling fees. One of the most severe measures was a new solar tax introduced in January 2011 applying to nearly all solar systems installed in 2009 and 2010. The tax burdened operators with an additional cost rate of 26–28% depending on the chosen support mechanism (FiT or so-called "green bonuses"). This tax, along with an increased fee for PV plants installed on agricultural lands, has resulted in the collapse of the Czech PV sector. Although the tax meanwhile has been reduced to 10%, a large number of plants still cannot operate profitably, causing investors to struggle with repayments of bank loans.[105]

As the aforementioned examples illustrate, several EU Member States had to deal with serious economic consequences due to RACs. To avoid such detrimental government decisions in the future, the European Commission made a legislative proposal for a **Directive of the European Parliament and of the Council on the promotion of the use of energy from renewable sources** (COM(2016) 767/F2 of April 25, 2017) which includes an Article 6 named "Stability of financial support." In the version last revised on June 21, 2018 by the Council of the European Union, it states that Member States shall ensure that the level of, and the conditions attached to, the support granted to renewable energy projects are not revised in a way that negatively impacts the rights conferred thereunder and undermines the economic viability of already supported projects. This general rule is accompanied by further stipulations which shall ensure the security of investments in the RE sector. For example, Member States shall only be able to adjust the level of support according to objective criteria, provided that such criteria are established in the original design of the support scheme (Article 8 No. 1). Furthermore, Member States shall consider the long-term effects of their support policies by planning ahead and constantly assessing the applicable support system in terms of effectiveness (Article 8 No. 1a and 1b).

104 EPIA, Retrospective Measures at National Level, 2013, p.14 et. seq.

105 EPIA, Retrospective Measures at National Level, 2013, p. 10.

For future prospects, the Directive – provided that it is enacted – could ensure the stability of financial support in the Member states and, thus, make investments in RE in countries who have suffered from RACs attractive again.

The aforementioned examples show that a stable and reliable regulatory framework and governmental policy is a key factor for an investment in renewables. Steady and predictable revenue streams are essential for a valid business case and are – at least until grid parity for all renewables is achieved – dependent on governmental decisions. The EU had to learn this lesson the hard way and is now striving to prohibit the harmful policies of Member States in the future.

5.4.2 Mitigation of Political Risks

In international RE projects, country-specific analysis and risk assessment are indispensable prerequisites for investment decisions. International RE projects are exposed to various risks, whether economic, legal or political. One of the most decisive factors for investment decisions in this field is the assessment of political risks. Political risks must be assessed not only in cases in which investors enter emerging markets, but also for investments in democratic, developed countries, in which it seems rather unlikely that political risks manifest. As a consequence, these risks may lead to export or import restrictions, expropriation, embargoes, breach of contract or currency inconvertibility.

Investors may need to use appropriate risk mitigation measures in order to gain control over political risks associated with their investment projects, such as, for example, risk guarantees or political risk insurance. Active players in this field are multilateral organizations (e.g., World Bank Group's Multilateral Investment Guarantee Agency (“**MIGA**”)), national governments (e.g., Comfort Letters) or private insurers. Another approach for risk mitigation is using ownership structures. Investors could, for instance, involve multilateral development banks or institutions (e.g., the European Bank for Reconstruction and Development (“**EBRD**”) or the International Finance Corporation (“**IFC**”)) as co-owners or co-financiers in their projects, or set up a joint venture with local partners in order to avoid classifying the project as a foreign investment project.

The host states have the primary competence in reducing political risks. The national governments are competent to increase the stability of investment conditions, to ensure constitutional stability and, thus, a stable legal framework. Furthermore, the host states can show their willingness to attract investors by establishing stable conditions by entering into investment protection agreements. However, legal instruments and guarantees are only sufficient if investors' rights have a fair chance to be executed efficiently and in a timely manner. Therefore, it has to be assessed whether host states are equipped with a constitutional system providing a real separation of powers and a functioning judicial system in order to subject administrative and governmental acts and decisions to full jurisdictional control and, if required, revise them. In this context, investors need to consider a number of aspects, including the trustworthiness of courts, particularly, the way in which foreigners are treated by the local courts, the length of court proceedings and, of course, the costs to be borne. Once a court decision or arbitral award has been rendered, it depends on the extent to which that decision is enforceable, the conditions for enforcement and whether the enforcement authorities are reliable at all.

5.4.3 Freedom of Market Access and Regulatory Access Limitations for Foreign Investors

Market access restrictions for foreign investors have to be considered on a national and an international level. At a national level the activity of foreign investors may be restricted by regulations which are justified by national interests. In Germany, such national market access restrictions are found in the German Foreign Trade and Payments Act (*Außenwirtschaftsgesetz*) as well as the Foreign Trade and Payments Ordinance (*Außenwirtschaftsverordnung*). German foreign trade law sets out, for example, notification obligations for foreign investors (i.e., non-EU/EFTA based buyers) in case they acquire at least 25% of the shares in companies residing in Germany which operate in certain business areas. These foreign investors have to notify the Federal Ministry for Economic Affairs and Energy (*Bundesministerium für Wirtschaft und Energie, BMWi*) of the proposed transaction. The mentioned national authority is competent to decide in the course of the investment review procedure (*Investitionsprüfverfahren*) whether the notified transaction threatens essential security interests of the country. If this is the case, the transaction can be declared void or the Federal Ministry is entitled to impose conditions or legal requirements on the transaction.

Typical market access restrictions on the international level are, for example, the United Nations (“**UN**”) sanctions. The UN Security Council is entitled to impose various sanctions, including economic and trade sanctions, on certain states, entities or persons in order to secure the effective implementation of its decisions or to penalise infringements or actions that threaten internationally shared values.

Contrary to market access restrictions on the international level, states are also competent to explicitly grant market access to foreign investors by entering into free trade agreements such as, the Comprehensive and Economic Trade Agreement[106] (“**CETA**”) between the EU and Canada. This agreement prohibits contracting parties from adopting or maintaining any measures that impose limitations

106 Full text available at: http://ec.europa.eu/trade/policy/in-focus/ceta/ceta-chapter-by-chapter/.

on the participation of foreign capital in terms of a maximum percentage limit on foreign shareholdings or the total value of individual or aggregate foreign investments.

5.4.4 Investment Protection

Investments in foreign RE projects may be threatened by regulatory and political risks as well as potential legislative changes to the RE incentives system. Against this background, the existence of investment protection standards may secure the position of the investor and underline the investor's decision to make his investment in a specific country.

1. Supranational Regulations

In the field of international law, investment protection is granted on the basis of investment protection treaties. Nearly 3,000 investment protection treaties[107] have been concluded around the world. There are two types of supranational regulations providing for investment protection measures: Bilateral investment protection treaties ("**BITs**") concluded between two countries and multinational investment protection treaties ("**MITs**") concluded between more than two countries. Although these treaties may differ in detail, they provide for similar basic principles. These guarantees are designed to protect foreign investors against illegal expropriation or nationalization, discriminatory or arbitrary measures, by empowering them with the right to fair and equitable treatment, the right to claim a prompt, adequate and effective compensation, and, in most cases, the procedural right to directly sue the host states' governments before arbitral tribunals.[108]

a) Bilateral Investment Treaties

A bilateral investment treaty is an agreement between two states which sets the legal framework, terms and conditions for investments of nationals and companies of one signatory state in the other signatory state. The first modern BIT was signed

107 The United Nations Conference on Trade and Development (UNCTAD) provides an overview of the concluded investment treaties under http://investmentpolicyhub.unctad.org/IIA.

108 For a more detailed overview of the investment protection concepts, see Rudolf Dolzer and Christoph Schreuer, *Principles of International Investment Law*, 2nd ed. (Oxford: Oxford University Press, 2012), p. 98 *et seq.* and p. 130 *et seq.*; Joern Griebel, *Internationales Investitionsrecht* (Beck Verlag 2008), p. 67 *et seq.*; Bradford S. Gentry and Jennifer J. Ronk, *International Investment Agreements and Investments in Renewable Energy*, undated pre-publication draft, https://www.researchgate.net/publication/242366373_International_Investment_Agreements_and_Investments_in_Renewable_Energy p. 27, 39 et. seq.

by Germany and Pakistan on November 25, 1959 and came into effect in 1962.[109] Despite the early agreement on the first BIT, BITs only became more common in the 1980s. Nevertheless, their provisions vary in essential parts from modern BITs as, for example, investor protection in modern BITs has grown stronger. Treaties from the 1980s mainly included provisions for arbitration between signatory states in case of breach of duties. Thus, investors and companies were not included in the scope of protection of the arbitration.[110] The evolution of BITs becomes evident when the number of ratified treaties is taken into account. While in 1989, 389 treaties had been ratified all over the world,[111] this amount is today almost reached exclusively by Germany (128 BITs ratified), France (95 BITs ratified), Belgium (73 BITs ratified) and Italy (72 BITs ratified).[112] Although BITs are treaties between two signatory states with provisions specific to the two parties, BITs regularly have similar content. This is due to the fact that Canada, India, the USA and China have each drawn up model agreements which provided key concepts and linkages for investments in renewables.[113]

b) Bilateral Investment Treaties

A multilateral investment agreement is an investment agreement concluded between several countries which contains provisions for the protection of investments made by nationals and companies in each other's territories. As they have similar objectives to BITs, the main difference is the number of signatory countries to the agreement. Thus, in particular the agreements contain provisions regarding national treatment, most-favored nation treatment, fair and equitable treatment and compensation in case of expropriation. MITs relevant to investment protection in the field of renewable energy projects are the Energy Charter Treaty[114] and the North American Free Trade Agreement.[115]

---

109 See: UNCTAD https://investmentpolicy.unctad.org/international-investment-agreements/treaties/bilateral-investment-treaties/1732/germany---pakistan-bit-1959-.

110 Bradford S. Gentry and Jennifer J. Ronk, *International Investment Agreements and Investments in Renewable Energy*, undated pre-publication draft, p. 30.

111 Bradford S. Gentry and Jennifer J. Ronk, *International Investment Agreements and Investments in Renewable Energy*, undated pre-publication draft, p. 30.

112 See UNCTAD: http://investmentpolicyhub.unctad.org/IIA/IiasByCountry#iiaInnerMenu.

113 Bradford S. Gentry and Jennifer J. Ronk, *International Investment Agreements and Investments in Renewable Energy*, undated pre-publication draft, p. 30.

114 The English version of the ECT, together with other related documents, is available at: https://www.energychartertreaty.org/treaty/energy-charter-treaty/ (last date of access 21 April 2020).

115 For more general treatments, see Boute, "Combating Climate Change through Investment Arbitration," *Fordham International Law Journal*, 2011, p. 613 et. seq. available at:, https://ssrn.com/abstract=1867663, (last date of access 21 April 2020) Edna Sussman, "Energy Charter Treaty's Investor Protection Provisions: Potential to Foster Solutions to Global Warming and Promote Sustainable Development," ILSA Journal of International & Comparative Law 2008, available at: https://ssrn.com/abstract=1090261.

aa) The Energy Charter Treaty

The Energy Charter Treaty (**ECT**) is a multilateral investment treaty that establishes a legal framework for energy trade, transit and investment between the signatory member states. The treaty's main scope is to promote energy security by promoting the operation of a more open and competitive energy market. Nevertheless, the Treaty respects in particular the principles of sustainable development and sovereignty over energy resources. This scope is achieved through provisions in four key areas: (i) Investment protection of foreign investments, (ii) non-discriminatory conditions for trade in energy materials, (iii) dispute resolution between participating states, which applies in case of investment directly between the host country and the investor and (iv) the promotion of energy efficiency. In the following section, the main consequences of the Treaty for investments in renewable energy technologies shall be outlined.

(1) Background

The ECT was created at the beginning of the 1990s, after the collapse of the Soviet Union. As the successor states of the Soviet Union were rich in energy resources but needed investments to develop them and western European states aimed to expand their sources of energy supply, the treaty was concluded to establish a common cooperation of the States in the field of energy. It was signed in Lisbon in December 1994 and became effective on April 16, 1998. The legal basis for the ECT is the European Energy Charter, which was agreed in the beginning of the 1990s. While the latter is a non-binding political declaration, the ECT has a legally binding character. The ECT also needs to be distinguished from the International Energy Charter of 2015, which is merely a political declaration.

Today, the 53 states are signatories to the ECT, among them the European Union and countries such as Australia and Japan. Russia and Belarus have not yet ratified the ECT but declared to apply the provisions on a provisional basis as far as they are not conflicting with national laws. Italy announced its withdrawal from the ECT in 2014 with effect as of 2016.[116] Although the Italian government justified its decision on the basis of wanting to reduce participation costs in international organizations,[117] one possible reason may be a considerable number of pending investor-state arbitration proceedings against Italy as well as further dispute risks in the future.[118]

116 Compare list of ECT members and observers at: https://energycharter.org/who-we-are/members-observers/countries/italy/ (last date of access 21 April 2020).

117 Italys withdrawal from the Energy Charter Treaty: Which Consequences for Foreign Investors?, Paul Hastings 28 April 2015, https://www.paulhastings.com/publications-items/details?id=e40ae469-2334-6428-811c-ff00004cbded (last date of access 21 April 2020).

118 Italy no longer member of Energy Charter Treaty, hopes to avoid arbitration, 6 January 2016, http://www.globalinvestmentprotection.com/2016/01/06/italy-no-longer-member-of-energycharter-treaty-hopes-to-avoid-more-arbitrations/ (last access date 21 April 2020).

Nevertheless, with regard to investments made before Italy's withdrawal, foreign investors are allowed to rely on treaty protection and pursue dispute resolution procedures contained in the ECT for a period of 20 years. Countries as Canada and the US have an observer status under the ECT.[119] Observer status is given to those who have signed a political declaration, the European Energy Charter and/or the International Energy Charter. Observers are entitled to participate in all meetings and debates of the Charter at working level and can access relevant documents, reports and analyses. This status is intended to familiarise the observers with the Charter and its functions to give them an incentive to ratify the Charter.

(2) Key Investment Protection Principles

The ECT's primary intention is the protection of foreign direct investments in contracting states and the safeguarding of a high standard of investment promotion and protection.

(a) General Treatment of Foreign Investors

According to Article 10 (1), which is a fundamental provision on the general treatment of foreign investors, each contracting state shall create stable, equitable, favorable and transparent conditions for foreign investors of other Contracting Parties to make investments in its area. Such conditions shall include a commitment to accord to investments of foreign investors fair and equitable treatment. Furthermore, investments shall enjoy constant protection and security and no signatory state shall in any way impair by unreasonable or discriminatory measures their management, maintenance, use, enjoyment or disposal. Investments shall not be treated less favorably than required by international law, including treaty obligations (Article 10 (3)). The principle of fair and equitable treatment (**"FET"**) has emerged as one of the most important legal issues in investment protection proceedings.[120]

The described criteria is an indefinite legal concept which needs to be further specified. The ECT itself, thus, does not do this. However, elucidating this principle was a major challenge in the past, which was achieved by international arbitration jurisdiction and the establishment of case groups.

---

119 Compare list of ECT members and observers at: https://energycharter.org/who-we-are/members-observers/. (last date of access 21 April 2020).

120 Global Arbitration Review, Investment Disputes Involving the Renewable Energy Industry Under the Energy Charter Treaty, https://globalarbitrationreview.com/chapter/1142579/investment-disputes-involving-therenewable-energy-industry-under-the-energy-charter-treaty (last date of access 21 April 2020).

The so-called case groups of FET are: (i) the *legitimate expectations* of the investor,[121] (ii) a *stable and predictable legal framework*[122] and (iii) *regulatory* transparency.[123] In relation to the ECT, a further standard of action is expressively provided in Article 10 (3). Those principles have been described above.

Legitimate expectations of the investor contain the host state's duty not to violate the key expectations of the investor's decision to invest. This was further clarified by arbitrational legislation in the case *LG&E Energy Corp and ors. v Argentina.* The court stated that the basic expectations that were taken into account by the investor in order to make the investment may not be affected. Such expectations have the following characteristics. (i) They are based on offered conditions at the host state in time of the investment, (ii) they may not be established unilaterally, and (iii) they have to be existent and enforceable. In the mentioned case, Argentina was sued for having breached the legitimate expectations of investors, as it set up an attractive legal framework and passed regulations that addressed the concerns of foreign investors, in particular, by taking into account the country risks involved in Argentina. As the legislation was considering particular country risks, the investors relied on the key guaranties of the legislation for a specific industry. Major changes of key requirements go against legitimate investor expectations. However, the decision does not state that changes in legislation always go against the legitimate investors' expectations.[124] Under normal conditions an investor cannot have the expectation that the legal framework does not change or will be modified.[125] Breach of legitimate expectations assume that the government did not fulfill a promise or commitment which was essential for the investment.[126]

The provision of a stable and predictable legal framework follows the same rationale of protecting the legitimate expectations of an investor. As the investor has protected expectations, the host state's national framework shall provide that these expectations can be met and implemented.[127]

---

121 LG&E Energy Corp., LG&E Capital Corp., and LG&E International, Inc. v Argentine Republic ICSID Case No. ARB/02/1, Decision on Liability of 3 October 2006 para. 127.

122 CMS Gas Transmission Company v. The Republic of Argentina, ICSID Case No. ARB/01/8, Award of 12 May 2005 para. 276.

123 PSEG Global Inc. and Konya Ilgin Elektrik Üretim ve Ticaret Limited Sirketi v. Republic of Turkey, ICSID Case No. ARB/02/5, Award of 19 January 2007, para. 250.

124 LG&E Energy Corp., LG&E Capital Corp., and LG&E International, Inc. v. Argentine Republic ICSID Case No. ARB/02/1, Decision on Liability of 3 October 2006 para. 127ff.

125 *Charanne B.V. and Construction Investments S.A.R.L. v. Kingdom of Spain*, SCC Arbitration Case No. 062/2012, Final Award, 21 January 2016, paras. 499

126 PSEG Global Inc. and Konya Ilgin Elektrik Üretim ve Ticaret Limited Sirketi v. Republic of Turkey, ICSID Case No. ARB/02/5, Award of 19 January 2007 para. 241.

127 LG&E Energy Corp., LG&E Capital Corp., and LG&E International, Inc. v Argentine Republic ICSID Case No. ARB/02/1, Decision on Liability of 3 October 2006 para. 131.

Lastly, the regulatory transparency consists of the duty of the host states' administration to inform the investor about processes and decisions relating to the investment. In the case ***PSEG Global Inc.*** *and Konya Ilgin Elektrik Üretim ve Ticaret Limited Sirketi v. Republic of Turkey* the arbitral court stated that administrative decisions and concessions which are characterized by a "back and forth" also breach regulatory transparency and thereby fair and equal treatment.[128]

In the recent past, there have been numerous cases in some EU countries such as Italy, Spain and the Czech Republic where support for RE has been reduced or abolished due to the global financial crisis and increasing deficits from the broad promotion of electricity generated from renewable sources (particularly PV in southern Europe). In this regard, the first arbitral award was rendered on January 21, 2016 – on which the court had to decide on the question whether the legitimate expectations of the investor had been violated.[129] The claim was related to the 2010 legislative changes in the Spanish RE support scheme. The arbitral tribunal affirmed in its decision *Charanne* that the *legitimate expectation* of the investor may be derived both from the specific commitments by the host state and from the legal framework.[130] In this case, the arbitral tribunal denied a breach of duty arising from the FET standard on the grounds that there was no specific commitment and, thus, no sufficient basis for a legitimate expectation of the investors.[131] In the other case *Eiser*,[132] in which the Spanish 2013–2014 RE support reductions were challenged, the arbitral award was issued in favor of the investors. Since these changes were deemed very radical compared to the previous changes in 2010,[133] the arbitration court ordered the Spanish government to pay EUR 128 million compensation to the claimants.

(b) Prohibition of Unlawful Expropriation

According to Article 13 of the ECT, expropriation under the ECT is only permitted if prompt and adequate compensation is guaranteed. Expropriation is defined as the

128 PSEG Global Inc. and Konya Ilgin Elektrik Üretim ve Ticaret Limited Sirketi v. Republic of Turkey, ICSID Case No. ARB/02/5, Award of January 2007 para. 247ff.

129 *Charanne B.V. and Construction Investments S.A.R.L. v. Kingdom of Spain*, SCC Arbitration Case No. 062/2012, Final Award, 21 January 2016, the English translation of the Award available at: https://www.italaw.com/sites/default/files/case-documents/italaw7162.pdf.

130 *Charanne B.V. and Construction Investments S.A.R.L. v. Kingdom of Spain*, SCC Arbitration Case No. 062/2012, Final Award, 21 January 2016, para. 489.

131 *Charanne B.V. and Construction Investments S.A.R.L. v. Kingdom of Spain*, SCC Arbitration Case No. 062/2012, Final Award, 21 January 2016, paras. 499, 539–42.

132 *Eiser Infrastructure Limited and Energia Solar Luxembourg S.à.r.l. v. Kingdom of Spain*, ICSID Case No. ARB/13/36, Award, 4 May 2017, available at: https://www.italaw.com/sites/default/files/case-documents/italaw9050.pdf.

133 *Eiser Infrastructure Limited and Energia Solar Luxembourg S.à.r.l. v. Kingdom of Spain*, ICSID Case No. ARB/13/36, Award, 4 May 2017, paras. 369, 387, 389.

taking or modification of an individual's property right by the government. Expropriation can take place in an outright transfer of the title or through measures that leave the title and property untouched but devalue the property de facto.[134] In other words, a measure is also considered an expropriation when it has an effect that is equivalent to a direct expropriation by the host state. Hence, direct and indirect expropriation are covered by the ECT.

As direct expropriations occur rarely, the extent of cases considered to constitute indirect expropriation is of high importance in granting investors protection. Indirect expropriation might occur when governmental measures lead to the effective loss of management or control or to the reduction of the value of investment assets.[135] In this way, the ECT protects the property of the investors' investment. Such clauses are rather typical for BITs and are not a peculiarity of the ECT.

In the above mentioned *Charanne* decision, the alleged violation of an undertaking by the state was, amongst other reasons, based on indirect expropriation. However, not every expropriation is forbidden, as it may be justified. Expropriation is justified if the following four cumulative requirements are satisfied: (i) *Expropriation must be carried out in the public interest*, (ii) *in a non-discriminatory manner*, (iii) *under due process of law and*, (iv) *in addition, prompt, adequate as well as effective compensation must be paid*. The *Charanne* arbitral award rejected the claim of the investors. In relation to the alleged indirect expropriation, the tribunal concluded that the challenged reforms of the Spanish incentive system did not lead to a loss of value that could be equal in its magnitude to a deprivation of the investment and, thus, had no substantial effect on the property rights of the investor. The claimants' argument of a reduction in economic profitability per se was not sufficient to assume unlawful expropriation.[136] The *Charanne* arbitral award proves that RE support reduction cannot automatically be qualified as indirect expropriation.

(c) Principle of Non-Discrimination

The principle of non-discrimination is established in the ECT in Article 10(7) to create a favorable investment climate. It requires the contracting parties to treat foreign investors no less favorably than their domestic investors or investors from other contracting countries or third states. This includes the obligation of host countries to agree to investments of investors of other signatory states and to the related activities according to the investment.[137] In any case, the respective host

134 Energy Charter Secretariat, Expropriation regime under the Energy Charter Treaty, 2012, p. 9., https://www.energycharter.org/fileadmin/DocumentsMedia/Thematic/Expropriation_2012_en.pdf.

135 Energy Charter Secretariat, Expropriation regime under the Energy Charter Treaty 2012 p. 9.

136 *Charanne B.V. and Construction Investments S.A.R.L. v. Kingdom of Spain*, SCC Arbitration Case No. 062/2012, Final Award, 21 January 2016, paras. 461–65.

137 Energy Charter Secretariat, The Energy Charter Treaty: A Readers Guide, 2002, p. 22., https://is.muni.cz/el/1422/jaro2017/MVV2368K/um/ECT_Guide_ENG.pdf.

state shall apply the better standard, as this may be national treatment or most-favored nation treatment. The most relevant consequence of this principle is that investors, independently of whether they are foreign nationals or are nationals of the host state, shall be treated equally if they are all under similar circumstances.[138] Nevertheless, the legally binding obligation of non-discriminatory treatment vis-à-vis foreign investors only refers to established investments.[139] As to the "Making of Investments," Article 10(2) and 10 (3) ECT clarify that the signatory states shall only "endeavour" to accord foreign investors a national or most-favored nation treatment. In this respect, during the negotiation process of the ECT, it was intended to extend the principle of non-discrimination to the so-called pre-establishment phase and include a legally binding obligation regarding this in a supplementary treaty. However, this aim could not be achieved.[140] The signatory states are able to opt for the extension of the non-discriminatory principle to the pre-investment stage on a voluntary basis.

Host states are not allowed any exceptions to the principle of non-discrimination. However, there are three cases where the principle of non-discrimination does not fully apply. (i) Article 21 may allow exceptions regarding taxation matters, as it states: "*nothing in this treaty shall create rights or impose obligations with respect to Taxation Matters of the Contracting Parties.*" Furthermore, (ii) Article 10(8) states exceptions in case a supplementary treaty deals with the principle of non-discrimination concerning grants for technology research and development. Finally, (iii) Article 10(10) provides for exceptions to the principle of non-discrimination when concerning the protection of intellectual property, which shall be governed by the respective international agreements.[141]

(d) Umbrella Clause

In connection with BITs umbrella clauses have become highly relevant for investment protection law. This is shown by the fact that more than two-fifth of over 2,700 BITs contain an umbrella clause.[142] In other words, umbrella clauses have found their way into the ECT but not as a peculiarity of the ECT. Umbrella clauses are clauses in international investment protection agreements that aim to protect the investor by obliging the host state to comply with specific obligations towards the foreign investor. These clauses are, thus, intended to pull the mostly private-law contracts between the host state and the investor into the scope of protection of the

138 Energy Charter Secretariat, The Energy Charter Treaty: A Readers Guide, 2002, p. 22.

139 Energy Charter Secretariat, The Energy Charter Treaty: A Readers Guide, 2002, p. 22 et. seq.

140 Energy Charter Secretariat, The Energy Charter Treaty: A Readers Guide, 2002, p. 23.

141 Energy Charter Secretariat, The Energy Charter Treaty: A Readers Guide, 2002, p. 22.

142 Karimov, "Umbrella Clauses within Energy Charter Treaty in: Baku State University Law Review 4, no.1 p. 80.

international investment protection agreement. Investors are thereby entitled to access the dispute settlement mechanisms laid down in the international investment protection agreements because a breach of contract between the investor and the host state is to be treated as a breach of the international investment protection agreement. In other words, claims from breaches of contract are pulled under the "protective umbrella" of international treaties – an investor state arbitration is introduced. The scope of protection granted to the investor depends to a large extent on the wording of the clause, as BITs are known to cover only "obligations under this agreement" or "any disputes relating investments," alternatively, obligating states to "observe any obligation it may have entered to."[143] As mentioned above, the ECT also contains an umbrella clause, which is at the end of Article 10(1) and states as follows:

> . . . Each Contracting Party shall observe any obligations it has entered into with an Investor or an Investment of an Investor of any other Contracting Party.

Accordingly, the above clause of the ECT covers *any breach of obligation* entered into with an investor or an investment of any other counterparty. The scope of protection is rather wide as any contract concluded between a host country and a subsidiary of a foreign investor in the host country or between the host country and the parent country shall be affected. So under the ECT, any breach of contractual obligation becomes a violation of the ECT and therefore grants the right to the investor and the investor's home country to appeal to the dispute settlement mechanism of the ECT. The scope of this provision is justified by the legal principal "pacta sunt servanda" (agreements must be kept), since most large investments are based on private law contracts between the host state and the investor.[144] Through the umbrella clause under the ECT, investors are protected against political risks in the host state, in particular, against breaches of contract through legislative or administrative acts of the government.[145]

However, not every host state has to stick to the umbrella clause as Article 26 (3)(c) provides an opt-out option by stating: "A Contracting Party listed in Annex IA does not give such unconditional consent with respect to a dispute arising under last sentence of Article 10(1)."[146] Until now four countries are listed in Annex IA of the ETC, which do not allow the submission of disputes to international arbitration, among them are Hungary, Norway, Canada and Australia. The remaining signatory

---

143 Katia Yannaca-Small, "Interpretation of the Umbrella Clause in Investment Agreements," *OECD Working Papers on International Investment*, 2006/03, OECD Publishing, http://dx.doi.org/10.1787/415453814578.

144 Energy Charter Secretariat, *The Energy Charter Treaty: A Reader's Guide*, 2002, p. 26.

145 Karimov, "Umbrella Clauses within Energy Charter Treaty in: Baku State University Law Review 4, no.1 p. 86.

146 Energy Charter Secretariat, *The Energy Charter Treaty: A Reader's Guide*, 2002, p. 26.

states of the ECT provide full investor protection by sticking to the umbrella clause of Article 10 (1).

(3) Dispute Settlement Mechanism

The ECT provides for settlement mechanisms for disputes between an investor and a signatory state arising out of an alleged breach of the latter's obligation regarding the investment promotion and protection provided for under the ECT.

In the event of investor-state disputes, the first step is to try to reach an amicable settlement within three months (the so-called "cooling-off period"). If an amicable settlement fails, the investor party to the dispute has the choice to have recourse to the local courts or administrative tribunals in the host state or to enter into any pre-agreed dispute settlement procedure or a proceeding of international arbitration as provided for by the ECT. The ECT was the first multilateral treaty providing as a general rule the settlement of investor-state disputes by international arbitration.[147] Such an international arbitration proceeding offers foreign investors an alternative to domestic courts and, thus, contributes to strengthening investor confidence.[148]

International arbitration builds on a mutual agreement between the parties on the dispute settlement mechanism. For this reason, each contracting party to the ECT gives its unconditional consent to the submission of a dispute to international arbitration or conciliation. The ECT leaves discretion to contracting states to exclude their unconditional consent for international arbitration in the event the investor has previously brought a claim before a national tribunal (the so-called "fork-in-the-road clause"). More than twenty contracting states (including Hungary, Ireland, Portugal, Spain, Sweden) have made use of this "opt-out" possibility. For reasons of transparency, they were, however, obliged to provide a written statement of their policies, practices and conditions in this regard. Another "opt-out" option concerns the umbrella clause: Contracting states are allowed to exclude disputes arising out of contractual obligations from their unconditional consent to international arbitration. Accordingly, foreign investors of these countries are not permitted to raise treaty claims in case of a breach of contractual obligations.

If the investor opts for international arbitration, investors are entitled to submit the arbitration either to the International Centre for Settlement of Investment Disputes (ICSID), to a sole arbitrator or to an ad hoc arbitration tribunal established

---

147 *Plama Consortium Ltd. v. Republic of Bulgaria*, ICSID Case No. ARB/03/24, Decision on Jurisdiction, 8 February 2005, para. 121.

148 Konoplyanik, "The Energy Charter Treaty: Dispute Resolution Mechanisms and the Yukos Case", Russian Energy and Mining Law Journal, 2005, p. 27, http://www.konoplyanik.ru/ru/publications/articles/388_The_Energy_Charter_Treaty_Dispute_Resolution_Mechanisms%E2%80%93and_the_Yukos_Case.pdf.

under the Arbitration Rules of the United Nations Commission on International Trade Law (UNCITRAL), or to an arbitral proceeding under the Arbitration Institute of the Stockholm Chamber of Commerce (SCC). Practice has shown that investors prefer in particular the ICSID arbitration.[149] The prerequisite for choosing the ICSID arbitration procedure is that both the host state and the home country of an investor are parties to the 1965 Convention on the Settlement of Investment Disputes between States and Nationals of Other States (the "**ICSID Convention**"). Currently, 154 countries have already ratified the ICSID Convention.[150] The advantage of the ICSID arbitration procedure is that, according to Article 54 of the ICSID Convention, arbitral awards are treated as final judgments of domestic courts. This allows investors to enforce arbitral awards without any further steps and thus results in more enforcement guarantees. Furthermore, the preference for the ICSID arbitration can be explained by the fact that the ICSID is an institution within the World Bank Group and states are interested to comply with the ICSID arbitral awards, in order to avoid a bad reputation (e.g., when they need to obtain international credit).

According to the ECT, the arbitral awards are final and binding. As regards enforcement guarantees, it is generally important that the host state is the party to the Convention on the Recognition and Enforcement of Foreign Arbitral Awards of 1958 (the "**New York Convention**"). Nowadays the New York Convention has 159 parties.[151] Consequently, the enforcement of arbitral awards is possible in most parts of the world.

bb) North American Free Trade Agreement ("NAFTA")

Another important treaty for investments in renewable energy projects in the North America region is the North American Free Trade Agreement (**NAFTA**). It was concluded between Canada, Mexico and the US on December 17, 1992 and entered into force on January 1, 1994. The fundamental aim of this trilateral agreement is to remove trade barriers as well as to stimulate cross-border investments between the contracting parties. Contrary to the ECT, the NAFTA does not specifically apply to the energy sector. Nevertheless, since contracting parties to the NAFTA are not party to the ECT, the NAFTA is relevant also for energy investments in the North-American region. Investment-related provisions of the NAFTA offer guarantees similar to those provided by the ECT, such as *national treatment*, *most-favored-nation*

149 Coleman/Innes, Choosing an Arbitral Forum for Investor State Arbitration, 27 January 2015, https://www.steptoe.com/en/news-publications/choosing-an-arbitral-forum-for-investor-state-arbitration.html (last access date 21 April 2020).

150 See: International Centre for Settlement of Investment Disputes, https://icsid.worldbank.org/en/Pages/icsiddocs/ICSID-Convention.aspx (last access date 21 April 2020).

151 See List of Contracting States: http://www.newyorkconvention.org/countries (last access date 21 April 2020).

treatment, the *minimum standard of treatment* in accordance with international law, including *fair and equitable treatment*, *full protection and security*, and the *prohibition of unlawful expropriation*. However, for the interpretation of these terms similar standards apply as already described above.

On May 18, 2017, the US government officially announced its intention to open negotiation talks with Canada and Mexico on the modernization of NAFTA.[152] The background was Donald Trump's pre-election promise to renegotiate or withdraw from NAFTA,[153] considering that it is "the single worst trade deal ever."[154] In the middle of 2018, the renegotiations led to a draft conclusion. The draft foresees the renaming of the NAFTA into United States-Mexico-Canada-Agreement (**USMCA**). Changes will arise in investment protection and dispute settlement in particular. The most relevant change in the treaty will be the withdrawal of Canada from the arbitration mechanisms, as Canada has not signed the required Annexes. Thus, a direct consequence arises for investors out of Mexico and the United States as they cannot bring claims against Canada under the USMCA and vice versa. This limits the potential for investor claims.[155] However, the USMCA still needs to be ratified by the member states. It therefore has not yet come into force, which means that currently NAFTA is still in force. The USMCA treaty was signed on November 30, 2018, but ratification by the respective legislatures could take several months.[156] However, a ratification of the treaty might not be straightforward in the US. This is related to the midterm elections in the US in November 2018, after which the democrats will take control of the House of Representatives from January 2019. No less than the ratification of the treaty depends on the agreement of the Democrats in the House of Representatives. At the present, however, this is anything but certain. The developments around USMCA therefore remain to be seen.

---

152 Compare Letter of the Executive Office of the Presidenct to the Congress, 18 May 2017, http://www.sice.oas.org/TPD/NAFTA/Implementation/NAFTA_Notification_05_17_e.pdf. (last access 21 April 2020).

153 Thoma, Is Donald Trump right to call NAFTA a desaster?, 5 October 2015, https://www.cbsnews.com/news/is-donald-trump-right-to-call-nafta-a-disaster/. (last access 21 April 2020).

154 The New Yor Times, Transcript of the first debate, 27 September 2016, https://www.nytimes.com/2016/09/27/us/politics/transcript-debate.html. (last access 21 April 2020).

155 Kent/Morris/Forrest, NAFTA 2.0: Investment protection and dispute settlement under Chapter 14 of the United States-Mexico-Canada-Agreement, 9 October 2018 https://www.wilmerhale.com/en/insights/client-alerts/20181009-nafta-2-0-investment-protection-and-dispute-settlement-under-chapter-14-of-the-united-states-mexico-canada-agreement. (last access 21 April 2020).

156 Semotiuk, What NAFTA Partners still need to do to launch USMCA, 23 November 2018, https://www.forbes.com/sites/andyjsemotiuk/2018/11/23/attention-usmca-leaders-time-is-running-out/#c4c72a14b92a. (last access 21 April 2020).

5.4.5 Requirements in Respect to the Design of the National Electricity Market

The increasing amount of electricity from renewable sources fed into the grid creates new challenges for the respective national electricity markets. These are related to the substantially different characteristics of the production of energy from renewable sources (such as wind, solar, hydro) and conventional technologies (such as coal, nuclear). The main differences in production can be seen in three characteristics. First, some renewable energy has (i) a **highly variable and uncertain availability** (for example, wind, solar). Second, some technologies have (ii) very **low short-run marginal costs**, which are the costs incurred for the production of an additional energy unit (MWh), compared to conventional generation. Lastly, some renewables are (iii) **nonsynchronous.**[157] Not all renewable energy production forms possess these characteristics necessarily, but each of the individual characteristics implies the need to adjust the design of the electricity market to ensure the best possible integration of renewables into the market, in particular because an increase of the share of renewable energies in the energy production is expected within the coming years.

1. Integration of Highly Variable and Uncertainly Available Technologies

In order to keep the necessary frequency for a safe and stable grid operation, it is important to maintain the balance between the supply and the demand for electricity. This balance needs to be planned for a short period of time and also for years. Since some renewable energy sources are variable and not available with certainty, the flexibility of the other technologies connected to the grid needs to increase to keep the grid stable. Characteristics of a flexible technology are the following: they need to have (i) **fast ramping rates**, which express the ability of a generator to change its output in mW per minute, (ii) **short shut-down** and **start-up times** and (iii) **low minimum rates**, which describe the ability of the technology to produce electricity at a low level without the need of a shut down. Yet already most modern power systems have the technical prerequisites to provide enough flexibility to integrate variable technologies into the grid; currently the International Energy Agency (**IEA**) assumes an integration capacity of modern power systems of 20% to 63% concerning the hypothetical integration of variable technologies into the grid offered by modern hardware.[158] Regardless of the hypothetical integration capacity, a lack of flexibility can be caused by a poor market design that leads to a lack of integration of variable technologies into the grid. To counter this, market design must keep two aspects in mind: First, (i) plant operators should be encouraged to offer

---

157 Riesz/Miligan WIREs Energy and Environment, 2015, p. 280.
158 Riesz/Miligan WIREs Energy and Environment, 2015, p. 282.

their flexibility to the market during operational time frames. This requires a proper design of the wholesale market. Second, (ii) new generators entering into the market should be subject to market signals to ensure sufficient flexibility of new capacity, as developers of energy generators are able to respond to such signals. For example, in the case of an energy-only market (which means that remuneration is only paid for the actually generated energy; as the counterpart to the capacity market, where the provision of the power plant output is already remunerated) producers are exposed to electricity price fluctuations. The price is high when demand is high and low in times of oversupply. Since high and low price phases can switch within the shortest possible time, the producers have to be able to react properly to each different phase to keep revenue high. Therefore, they are exposed to the incentive to build plants as flexible as possible.[159] In order to keep these incentives, market signals should not be dampened by governmental measures.

a) Flexible design of the wholesale market for the best integration of variable energy sources

The design of the wholesale market can have a rather large impact on plant operators to offer flexibility to the electricity market voluntarily. The more variable the renewable energies are, the more flexibility must be guaranteed by the market. Wind and solar energy are variable, since they depend on weather conditions which the plant operator does not control.

The following shall give a brief outline of incentives for a flexible wholesale market design for the best possible integration of renewables. Balancing of supply and demand is of immense importance for the stability of the grid. Usually, a real-time wholesale market helps to achieve this goal. The market is settled when demand and supply are equal, typically at the price set by the last generator dispatched into the grid to meet the demand. The smaller the timeframe to match supply and demand (**dispatch rate**) the higher is the integration of variable renewable energy into the grid at lower costs. The flexibility is given by the opportunity of more re-dispatch. Re-dispatch describes the instruction given by the Transmission System Operator (**TSO**) to electricity producers to postpone electricity production in order to keep supply and demand balanced and, thus, prevent grid bottlenecks and instability. The higher the dispatch rates are the more additional generators must be kept in reserve to manage potential grid instability by re-dispatch. With shorter dispatch rates this can also be done by the power generators involved in dispatch so flexibility arises and costs are reduced.[160] Further, a short period of time from the last offers and bids until dispatch of electricity is essential, as, for example, producers of energy from solar and wind are

159 Riesz/Miligan WIREs Energy and Environment, 2015, p. 282.
160 Riesz/Miligan WIREs Energy and Environment, 2015, p. 282.

able to plan their production better in accordance with the weather forecasts – which also lowers the maintenance costs for additional reserve generators. The electricity should also be dispatched over larger areas. This way costs are reduced by allowing shares of reserve, which offers a larger access to generators that provides flexibility and ensures higher generation and load variability. However, additionally the wholesale market should be designed technology-neutral, which means all technologies can participate in the market due to the same conditions on a level playing field.

b) Flexible design of the wholesale market through implementation of Frequency Control Ancillary Services

Frequency Control Ancillary Services are needed, for example, the reservation of capacity to respond to variations in the system balance on periods shorter than the dispatch interval or variations which were unforeseeable. Such ancillary services are required to maintain grid balance in case of an imbalance of supply and demand in the grid between the dispatch intervals or, if such imbalances occur unexpectedly, by managing minor changes in system frequency and keeping it within the range of normal operating frequency. Therefore, capacity is reserved to compensate for variations in the grid.[161] As described above, the design of the wholesale market can have a rather large impact on the reservation costs to provide ancillary services and, therefore, the required capacity. As these ancillary services are essential to promote grid stability, incentives shall be created so that generators offer the maximum and most flexible frequency ancillary service possible. However, the market design should reconsider the individual technological characteristics to give them the freedom to provide economically and technically efficient frequency ancillary services. In other words a technology-tailored approach should be integrated into the market. Contingency services illustrate this well. Contingency services include those services necessary to compensate the stresses to the grid arising where a generator experiences a forced outage. Raise services include the raise of system frequency while lower services include the reduction of system frequency. Contingency raise services, on the one hand, are economically not feasible for photovoltaic and wind technologies, as this would require their curtailment of the grid over a period of time and would lead to high opportunity costs (costs arising for the loss of alternatives if the other alternative is chosen). On the other hand, those technologies are well suited to provide lower services because they are technically capable of reducing their generation rapidly. On the other hand, some other technologies are better suited to provide raise services. All available technologies at the market should be given the same opportunity to provide those ancillary services which are the most adequate for

161 Riesz/Miligan WIREs Energy and Environment, 2015, p. 283.

them, as a measure of best market implementation.[162] Thus, market design should stick to certain technological specialties regarding ancillary services.[163] The system gains more and more flexibility depending on the determination method of reserve requirements. The more static this method is (e.g., different times of a day, depending on the season), the more difficult it is to perform a demand-oriented analysis of reserve needs that takes into account the system state in a particular dispatch interval. Therefore, the best method to determine reserve requirements would be in a completely dynamic system, taking into account the current needs of the grid.[164]

2. Integration of Technologies with Low Short-Run Marginal Costs

Some renewable energy plants (such as wind, solar) have a very low short-run marginal cost, which means that the costs to produce a new unit of energy are low. For many fossil technologies, these costs are high as they have to provide a generation source (for example, coal). Hence, for most renewable technologies the costs do not rise with increasing energy production as the generation sources are renewable and freely available (for example, wind, solar). Therefore, major generating costs for renewable technologies are the construction costs and maintenance costs, which are independent of the actual generated amount of energy. The low marginal costs apply to wind and solar technologies, for example, but not to biomass technologies as they have to collect, store and process biomass fuel. As a result of the low marginal costs the plant generators can offer their produced electricity at a price close to zero in a competitive market.[165]

In markets with a large amount of energy suppliers from renewable energies the so-called **merit order effect** can be observed, which leads to falling prices reducing the profitability of operating plants. The merit order describes the procedure under which the price for electricity is determined, which is basically by the order of low-short run marginal costs of the plants until electricity demand is covered. The highest low-short run marginal costs of a plant to cover demand reflect the electricity price. However, under the condition of decreasing prices due to low-short run marginal costs nobody would invest into the market. To prevent this, the electricity market must be adjusted accordingly. As an incentive to investments in new capacity and the reduction of risk and uncertainty for investors, capacity remuneration mechanisms (**CRM**) shall be implemented in the electricity market. They foresee a payment for plant operators for keeping electricity capacity available in addition to the revenue from the energy sold at the market. In this way generators can be encouraged to

162 Riesz/Miligan WIREs Energy and Environment, 2015, p. 283.
163 Riesz/Miligan WIREs Energy and Environment, 2015, p. 282 et. seq.
164 Riesz/Miligan WIREs Energy and Environment, 2015, p. 285.
165 Riesz/Miligan WIREs Energy and Environment, 2015, p. 286.

be ready to supply electricity when it is demanded.[166] Nevertheless, CRMs also bear disadvantages. In some cases, their implementation might be complex and might need adjustments with evolution of the market. Furthermore, cross-border effects should be borne in mind as different market models in neighbouring countries might lead to distortions and functional impairments.[167] Despite the existing disadvantages, CRM can contribute to mitigate the falling electricity prices by an increasing share of renewable energies and thus lower short-run marginal costs.

3. Integration of Nonsynchronous Technologies

A third characteristic of some renewable energies is their nonsynchronous connection to the grid (such as wind, solar). Conventional energy generators used to be electromechanically coupled to the power grid, rotating in the synchronous grid frequency. In this way they supply grid inertia. However, as renewable technologies in particular wind and solar do not provide grid inertia and their power output might be volatile, problems for grid stability arise, as imbalances might lead to discrepancies in grid frequency.[168] Electrical inertia is a major property of electrical systems. It describes the property of opposing changes. In a power system, inertia describes synchronous rotating masses of the turbines that are coupled and which deliver the steady system frequency. As frequency imbalances occur, inertia is relevant to resist the grid against fluctuations. So, if an imbalance of supply and demand arises, energy can be transferred between the rotating turbines and the power system to maintain an equilibrium of supply and demand to keep the frequency stable. Problems regarding a constant grid frequency might arise where too many non-synchronous renewable technologies are implemented to the grid, as they do not provide the essential property of inertia. Therefore, a certain amount of synchronous connected technologies as minimum proportion needs to remain connected to the grid in order to keep the grid always operational. However, modern wind turbines, for example, can help to face the problem of sufficient grid synchronicity by synthetic inertia being implemented by the software of the turbines. As they do not have mechanical inertia, modern wind turbine software can use the rotating mass of the blades to replace the above described effect of inertia. This is a very technical topic but the main point to note is that electricity grid operators to keep an equilibrium between synchronic and nonsynchronous technologies to avoid grid failures.[169]

166 Riesz/Miligan WIREs Energy and Environment, 2015, p. 286.

167 Riesz/Miligan WIREs Energy and Environment, 2015, p. 286.

168 Xypolitou, Gawlik, Zseby, Fabini, Impact of Asynchrounous Renewable Generation Infeed on Grid Frequency: Analysis Based on Synchrophasor Measurments 2018, p. 1.

169 Riesz/Miligan WIREs Energy and Environment, 2015, p. 287.

5.4.6 Grid-Related Requirements

The turnaround in energy policy by switching energy production from fossil fuels to renewable energy is steady and regularly a topic of European legislation. Therefore, the European legislator also sets rules regarding national grid-related requirements, as the grid is the key factor for the implementation of renewable energy. The major aspects of the grid-related requirements of European legislation shall now be outlined.

1. The Principle of Non-Discrimination

The **Internal Electricity Market Directive 2009/72/EC** of July 13, 2009 sets rules for the generation, transmission, distribution and supply of electricity on the internal markets. Organization, the functioning of the electricity sector, open access to the market and the dispatch to the grid are among the regulated issues. To achieve the objective of the integration of renewable energy into the grid, certain rules are set for Transmission System Operators (**TSO**). The principle of non-discriminatory access to the electricity grid, *inter alia*, as an expression of the general principle of equality, was set by the Directive. The basic idea behind this principle is linked to the electricity grids as natural monopolies. In a naturally monopoly, the total cost of providing a good is significantly lower if only one company supplies the market and not several. In this way, grid operators have a dominant position on the market. As it would be economically and technically ineffective to construct another high voltage grid, the European legislator set the principle of non-discrimination as a key provision of the Directive. The principle obliges Member States, national regulatory authorities and TSOs to ensure that an abuse of the dominant position of grid operators does not occur. The TSOs shall apply this principle on the basis of conditions and tariffs set by the national regulatory authorities. Hence, access under the same conditions is guaranteed to electricity producers.

The principle of non-discrimination is mandatory to achieve the implementation of electricity from renewable sources to the grid. **Finland**, **Estonia** and **Latvia** stand out in this regard. They implemented the principle of non-discrimination. This means that plant operators are entitled against the grid operator regarding the connection of their plants and the transmission of electricity as soon as the technical and legal requirements are met. All operators, regardless of their chosen energy production form, are entitled to connection due to objective requirements which are the same for all competitors.

2. Priority to Renewable Energy

In **Germany,** technologies producing electricity from renewable sources and mine gas are granted feed-in priority. This priority is granted both temporally and objectively for purchase, transmission, distribution and remuneration. As a result, feed-in priority prevails at all levels of the value chain. In this way, energy from renewable sources is protected against conventional energy sources. The background to this legislation is the **Renewable Energy Directive 2009/28/EC,** which aims at the promotion of energy from renewable sources. Article 16 section 2 of the Directive states that European Member States are obliged either to implement feed-in priority to renewable energy or a guaranteed grid access. Furthermore, the Member States must oblige the TSOs to act in conjunction with Article16 section 2 of the Directive when it comes to the utilization of generation facilities of renewable energies.[170] Therefore, Member States shall require TSOs to ensure that electricity from renewable energy plants is granted priority when dispatching their electricity to the grid (priority dispatch). The TSO shall further guarantee the transmission and distribution of renewable energy in their area. Priority dispatch, guaranteed for renewable energies, describes the obligation of grid operators to feed energy produced by renewable energy plants into the grid and only then fall back on fossil sources in order to cover the demand. Therefore, the Member States have to ensure that system operators inject electricity from renewable energy and Combined Heat and Power (**CHP**) with priority to the grid. The electricity dispatch guarantees grid and system stability. In case of too little electricity in the grid, electricity producers are notified by the TSO to increase production and vice versa limit production in case of too much electricity in the grid. However, if limiting electricity becomes necessary, electricity dispatch from electricity producers with priority dispatch will not be curtailed. By 2020, the TSO will have to grant priority dispatch to all renewable electricity suppliers, which will remain for already existing plants onward. From 2021, the priority dispatch will be phased out for new constructed plants. Instead, new rules for grid curtailment apply, which intend that electricity from renewables will be curtailed last in case of grid congestion and that operators will receive compensation.[171] Exceptions of priority access and dispatch are only permissible to secure the grid security, which has to be safeguarded under all circumstances. Problems for grid security might arise as the grid needs a certain amount of electricity to guarantee safe and stable functioning. As some renewable energy sources are volatile in their availability (such as solar, wind), it is difficult for plant operators to guarantee a certain amount of electricity production amount every day. Hence, for renewable electricity producers it is important to sell their electricity when they produce, as they need a stable predictable income, thus priority dispatch is implemented. Due to this, rejection of electricity from renewables is only permitted for reasons of safeguarding grid stability.

170 Oschmann in Altrock/Oschmann/Theobald, EEG, 4 ed. 2013 § 2 Marginal, 26 et. seq.

171 European Parliament votes to make European electricity market ready for renewables 21 February 2018, https://windeurope.org/newsroom/press-releases/european-parliament-votes-to-make-european-electricity-market-ready-for-renewables/ (last access 21 April 2020).

In 2018, plans of the German government became public regarding the restriction of the priority dispatch due to savings of grid bottleneck costs. A study commissioned by the Federal Ministry of Energy and Economy came to the conclusion that a restriction of the feed-in priority for renewable energies and CHP plants regarding grid bottleneck management would save significant costs. Therefore, the government is currently examining the extent to which such a cut can be justified from the point of network security. A complete abolition of the priority principle is not being contemplated.[172]

Apart from Germany, **Hungary** also implements the priority feed-in into renewable energy. Plants producing electricity from renewable energy must be given a priority connection to the grid and a priority when it comes to the authorization of new plants. Nevertheless, a restriction can apply when Hungary's energy policy goals are threatened or supply security is threatened. Such a restriction needs to be set by the government through the acting minister for energy issues.

The same applies to **Spain,** where renewable energy plants are granted statutory priority access and connection to the grid, as long as the stability and security of the grid infrastructure can be obtained.

5.5 Overview of Typical Securities

5.5.1 Characteristics of Non-Recourse Project Structures

Renewable energy projects are regularly financed through project financing.[173] This is defined as the structured financing of an economically and legally definable economic entity with a limited lifetime. Four characteristics define this type of financing. (i) A company is set up specifically for the project and is dedicated solely to the operation of the project (**single purpose vehicle**). (ii) Further, the loan amount plus interest is refinanced only by the **cash flow** of the project. (iii) There is no recourse to the assets of equity investors or if there is, it is limited in time-, or restricted to certain situations or to a specific amount. Dependent on the extent of recourse to the equity investor's assets the financing is classified as **non-recourse** or **limited recourse** financing. (iv) Finally, there is an appropriate distribution of risks in that the project participant who can best control them bears them.[174] The counterpart to project financing is corporate-credit-rating-based-financing. These two types of financing require an essentially different approach of the lender in terms of securing the loan.

172 Bundesregierung prüft Relativierung des Einspeisevorrangs, PV Magazine, 31 July 2018, https://www.pv-magazine.de/2018/07/31/bundesregierung-prueft-relativierung-des-einspeisevorrangs/ (last access 21 April 2020).

173 See also chapter 5.

174 Rey, BKR 2001, p. 29.

Project finance presents the lender with other challenges than conventional corporate-credit-rating-based-financing. In conventional lending, borrowers do not just operate a single project and, therefore, have access to a larger number of assets that can serve as credit security. As a result, the default risk can be limited by using more assets as security than are available in project financing. Project financing differs substantially from this. It is characterized by a high volume of investment and the limitation of the expected liquidation proceeds. The special purpose vehicle as the borrower has no assets other than the renewable energy plant that could be used as security for the loan. However, further security would be necessary to secure the loan, since the loan amount exceeds the value of the plant and the project development is a costly undertaking. This becomes clear when taking a closer look at the construction of new renewable energy plants, in particular the accruing costs. The plant is the main asset of the single purpose vehicle; however, experience shows that its value is only around 70% of the loan amount disbursed. The remaining investment volume is required for the erection of the infrastructure and project development costs, i.e., particularly, costs of the permit and land securitization. Often, the shareholders of the single purpose vehicle are not willing to grant further security in addition to the invested equity capital. Consequently, the focus of the banks is on the **cash flow** generated by the project. The aim of securitization is to ensure that the project itself is able to bear the entire debt service (**non-recourse**). Such non-recourse projects are characterized by high capital expenditures, long loan periods and uncertain revenue streams. Non-recourse financing mainly aims to isolate cash flow generated by the project to protect it against negative impacts and to control it even in case of a crisis or insolvency of the project company.

As maintaining cash flow in order to secure the repayment of the loan is the main objective of non-recourse financing, the contractual structure of the securities must be adapted to this objective. For this purpose, the lender has direct and indirect security mechanisms at their disposal.

a) Direct Security Mechanisms

Direct security mechanisms aim to use the cash flow as repayment for the loan amount plus interests. Therefore, the lenders are granted direct access to the cash flow generated by the project. In this way, the repayment of the loan amount plus interest is ensured by security assignment of the claims which entitle the plant operator to **revenues from the sale of the produced electricity** e.g., direct marketing contracts, power purchase agreements or insurance contracts.

aa) Security assignments of feed-in revenues

In Germany, the claims of the operating company for the feed-in revenues typically arise from the direct marketing contract and the statutory claims against the grid operator (market premium). Where a corporate PPA is in place, the PPA is the contractual basis for the remuneration claim of the SPV. In order to ensure the recoverability of the assigned claims, the lender has an interest in ensuring that the assigning SPV is also the original claim holder and does not derive its claim from a third party. Therefore, the lender should demand a project structure which provides that the project company itself is directly entitled out of the legal relationship from which the revenue arises. Otherwise, the lender would be burdened with the insolvency risk of a third party on which it has no influence. The lender should also notify the debtor of the assignments. This prevents the lender from losing its assigned claim by a payment of the debtor to the plant operator without the knowledge of the lender.

The difficulties arising from securing the cash flow via security assignment differ according to the feed-in model chosen by the plant operator. Practically, two different feed-in models are commonly used in Germany. A feed-in of electricity directly into the grid of the grid operator/utility, or the involvement of a third party which feeds in the electricity for the plant operator.

In the favorable scenario of a direct feed-in through the plant operator, no major problems arise in respect to the security assignment. There is a direct legal relationship between the plant operator and the grid operator/utility, with the result that the plant operator is entitled to the remuneration. The remuneration claim can easily be assigned to the financing lender.

Sometimes, several plant operators bundle their produced energy and involve a third party (e.g., a transformer station operating company) which is dedicated to the technical process of electricity bundling and feed-in, as well as the processing of feed-in remuneration (**Transaction Company**). This third party involvement makes security assignment more difficult and is therefore a less favorable scenario. As the Transaction Company is dedicated to processing, the ownership of the electricity is commonly not transferred to it. The Transaction Company is acting in the name and on behalf of the plant operator as its representative or agent. Therefore, a security assignment of remuneration claims of the plant operator is only feasible if the electricity fed in by the transaction company is sufficiently determinable. The lender has to pay particular attention to this, since a non-determinable claim is not assignable. Therefore, technical precautions must be taken to ensure sufficient determinability (separated meters for every operator). Once the amount of electricity fed into the grid by the plant operator is recorded individually, the borrower's remuneration claims against the grid operator utility can be assigned to the lender by the borrower as security.

The least favorable scenario is when the third party is entrusted not only with the technical but also with the legal handling of the feed-in process and the plant operator, therefore, transfers ownership of the electricity to the company (**Feed-in Company**). The Feed-in Company, thus, acts in its own name and for its own account and is directly entitled to claim the feed-in remuneration. Hence, security to the lender can only be granted by way of a security assignment of the remuneration claims of the plant operator against the Feed-in Company. In this scenario, the lender bears the credit and insolvency risk of the Feed-in Company.

bb) Security assignment of contractual claims

In the financing of renewable energy projects in Germany, an upcoming trend is the conclusion of Power Purchase Agreements (**PPAs**) which are already standard in other jurisdictions. Particularly in the United States, UK, Norway, and Ireland, PPAs already play an increasing role in the financing of renewable energy projects. A PPA is a long-term energy supply contract between a purchaser and a plant operator. In contrast to the direct marketing structure which provides for the statutory claim for the market premium, no statutory remuneration claims exist in a PPA structure. The contract stipulates commercial terms for the sale of electricity, i.e., the price, payment terms and also the quantity of electricity to be delivered. For the plant operator, the focus lies on stable and predictable revenues from a long-term supply relationship, which leads to planning security and easier future investments. On the other side, the purchaser/offtaker is able to protect its company against price risks on the electricity market and secure long-term electricity delivery.[175] At the present time, PPAs do not play a significant role in the German market, which is still dominated by direct marketing and the use of governmental support. As it is expected that the role of PPAs in the financing of renewable energy projects will increase in the next few years, the security assignment of the remuneration claims from such a PPA will become more and more relevant as security.

cc) Additional securities

Another way of securing access to the remuneration claims for the sale of the produced RE is obtaining control over the creditor of the proceeds. This can be achieved by pledging the shares of the SPV. Depending on the chosen legal form of the SPV, the country-specific and company-specific legal requirements for the pledge agreement may differ. If the German legal form of a GmbH (limited liability company) is chosen, notarial certification of the pledge agreement is necessary.

Pledging the bank account of the single purpose vehicle is also a common security for the loan and lenders commonly demand that the operational account of the SPV is with the lender.

b) Indirect Security Mechanisms

The intent of indirect security mechanisms is securing the project, i.e., the aim for the lender is to have direct access to the project to have the ability to operate the plant himself or through a third party in the event of a project crisis. Through direct access to the project the lender can ensure that cash flow does not dry up in the event of a

175 Hunke/Göß/Österreicher/Dahroug, Power Purchase Agreements: Finanzierungsmodell von Erneuerbaren Energien p.2, (https://www.energybrainpool.com/fileadmin/download/Whitepapers/2018-01-31_Energy-Brainpool_White-Paper_Power-Purchase-Agreements.pdf (last access 21 April 2020).

crisis of the SPV. In other words, cash flow is indirectly secured in these cases. This is achieved by a certain contractual structure combining entry rights into existing project contracts for the lender and rights *in rem* granted for the benefit of the lender.

In the rare case that the plant operator is also the owner of the land on which the plant is located, the material loan security is usually secured by a first ranking mortgage in the amount of the loan. The first ranking mortgage also covers the accessories and components of the land plot, including the plant. Nevertheless, the liability of accessories and components is threatened if the land owner removes them from the land and sells them before enforcement measures are taken.

However, it is more likely that plant operators and landowners are not identical, so that security is granted by the security transfer of the ownership in the plant. How the transfer of ownership by security is to be contractually structured in each case depends on the respective legal system. According to German law, the security transfer of ownership of a plant firmly connected to the ground is complex, since ownership of the land plot is basically connected to ownership of the plant. However, it can be achieved by contractual construction of the lease agreement and also by registering a personal restricted easement (superficies right) stipulating that ownership of the land plot and the plant do not correlate.

The transfer of ownership of the plant for security purposes is worthless in order to maintain cash flow, unless it is ensured that the lender has the option to continue operating the plant itself or through a third party under its control in case of a project crisis (**Continuation Option**). Without a continuation option, the lender would be the owner of the plant but could not use it without delay and incurring high costs. The lender would be forced to rebuild the project assets somewhere else. Therefore, the lender would have to obtain new official permits and usage rights. In other words, a new project development would be required. This would not only take far too long, but would also be very expensive due to new development costs, which are commonly not considered in cash flow models. Furthermore, the cash flow generated by the project would dry out during the period of project development. To prevent this scenario, the land use agreements must be adjusted accordingly. Therefore, the lender should be able to step into the land use agreements and all the other project agreements. If the land use agreements were not concluded at the time of the loan application, tripartite land use agreements can be concluded between the land owner, the lender and the plant operator. Thereby, the stipulations of the land use agreements cannot be revoked or amended unilaterally without the consent of the lender. To achieve this, the land use agreements must be drawn up or adapted in such a way that they contain the irrevocable consent of the landowner that the lender enters into the land use agreements in place of the operator at any time. In addition, the bank shall have the right to replace the plant operator through a third party in the contract of use (**entry clause**).

In order to protect the lender from possible invalidity or termination of the land use agreements, for example, for breaches of statutory formal requirements of the agreements, the landowner must be obliged to enter into an identical use agreement with the lender or a third party designated by the lender in the event of termination of the use agreement for any reason (**obligation to re-conclude**).

Since, the entry clause and the obligation to re-conclude are just contractual obligations, the user of the land would have to sue the land owner in case of a breach of obligations. In order to reduce the litigation risk, the contractual rights are ideally also secured *in rem*.

5.5.2 National Enforcement Risks

The value of securities is to a large extent dependent on whether enforcement is feasible when it comes to realization. It is therefore necessary that enforcement instruments are recognized in the country in which enforcement is to take place and the enforceability of the enforcement instrument is ensured. In case of national enforcement, the aforementioned criteria are governed by the national enforcement law. In case of cross-border financing projects, the recognition of enforcement instruments and their enforceability is dependent on transnational agreements between the respective countries.

In the European Union, the Brussels Ia Regulation (**Regulation No. 1215/2012**) sets out the applicable legal framework for enforcement. It was passed in 2012, replacing Regulation EG/44/2001, and came into force on January 1, 2015. The regulations are directed towards the legal jurisdiction of defendants resident in a Member State of the European Union and the recognition and enforcement of civil and commercial matters from other Member States. The regulation applies to all Member States of the European Union, not to the countries who are members of the European Free Trade Association (**EFTA**). For those countries, Norway, Switzerland and Iceland, with the exception of Liechtenstein, the Lugano Convention is applicable. The scope of the Convention is essentially the same as of Brussels Ia.

Outside of the European Union, the Hague Choice of Court Convention is applicable. It is an international treaty concluded in the Hague Conference on Private International Law. The European Union, Denmark, Mexico and Singapore are parties to the Convention already, while the United States, China, Montenegro and Ukraine signed the treaty but still need to ratify it for it to come in force. The treaty contains regulations on exclusive choice of court agreements and the recognition and enforcement of court decisions in cross-border cases. However insolvency law, antitrust law and parts of tort law are exempt from the Convention. Nevertheless, it remains an important convention for the enforcement of enforcement instruments and might gain in importance in the next years, as more states ratify it.

To minimise the risk in financing cross border renewable energy projects, the lender should ensure the enforcement and recognition of the enforcement instruments are guaranteed by transitional treaties.

References

Agentur für Erneuerbare Energien e.V., 2010: "20 Jahre Förderung von Strom aus Erneuerbaren Energien in Deutschland – eine Erfolgsgeschichte." Renews Spezial 41, https://www.unendlich-viel-energie.de/media/file/171.41_Renews_Spezial_20_Jahre_EE-Strom-Foerderung.pdf (cited as Agentur für Erneuerbare Energien e.V. in Renews Spezial 41: 20 Jahre Förderung von Strom aus Erneuerbaren Energien in Deutschland – eine Erfolgsgeschichte).

Altrock, Martin; Oschmann, Volker; Theobald, Christian (editors), 2013: "EEG – Kommentar", 4th. ed., Munich, C.H. Beck (cited as Oschmann in Altrock/Oschmann/Theobald EEG, 4th ed.).

Amelang, Sören, 2018: "Germany on track to widely miss 2020 climate target – government.", https://www.cleanenergywire.org/news/germany-track-widely-miss-2020-climate-targetgovernment (cited as Clean Energy Wire: Germany on track to widely miss 2020 climate target – government, 13 June 2018).

Barney, Gerald O., 1980: "The Global 2000 Report to the President: Entering the Twenty-First Century.", https://www.cartercenter.org/resources/pdfs/pdf-archive/global2000reporttothepresident–enteringthe21stcentury-01011991.pdf (cited as Gerald O. Barney, The Global 2000 to the President: Entering the 21th Century).

Bellini, Emiliano, 2017: "Sweden and Norway extend joint electricity certificate system for renewables to 2030", https://www.pv-magazine.com/2017/04/19/sweden-and-norway-extend-joint-electricity-certificate-system-for-renewables-to-2030/ (cited as Sweden and Norway extend joint electricity certificate system for renewables to 2030, PV Magazine, 19 April 2017).

Boemke, Maximilian, 2017: "Die Regelungen des EEG 2017 im Überblick." *Neue Zeitschrift für Verwaltungsrecht* (cited as Boemke, NVwZ, 2017).

Boute, Anatole, 2011: "Combating Climate Change through Investment Arbitration", Fordham International Law Journal (cited as Boute, "Combating Climate Change through Investment Arbitration", Fordham International Law Journal, 2011).

Broliden, Caroline, and Linn Regnér, 2015: "On Asset Life Cycle Management for Offshore Wind Turbines – A Case Study of Horns Rev 1." Stockholm. https://www.diva-portal.org/smash/get/diva2:841750/FULLTEXT01.pdf (cited as Broliden/ Regnér, On Asset Life Cycle Management for Offshore Wind Turbines, 2015).

Bundesnetzagentur and Bundeskartellamt, 2017: "Monitoringbericht 2017." https://www.bundesnetzagentur.de/SharedDocs/Mediathek/Monitoringberichte/Monitoringbericht2017.pdf?__blob=publicationFile&v=4 (cited as Bundesnetzagentur/ Bundeskartellamt, Monitoringbericht, 2017).

CEER, 2017: "Status Review of Renewable Support Schemes in Europe." https://www.ceer.eu/documents/104400/-/-/41df1bfe-d740-1835-9630-4e4cccaf8173 (cited as CEER, Status Review of Renewable Support Schemes in Europe, 2017).

CEER, 2018: "Tendering procedures for RES in Europe: State of play and first lessons learnt", https://www.ceer.eu/documents/104400/-/-/167af87c-5472-230b-4a19-f68042d58ea8 (cited as CEER, Tendering procedures for RES in Europe: State of play and first lessons learnt, 2018).

Coleman, Matthew and Ines, Thomas, 2015: "Choosing an Arbitral Forum for Investor-State Arbitration", https://www.steptoe.com/en/news-publications/choosing-an-arbitral-forum-for-investor-state-arbitration.html (cited as Coleman/ Innes, Choosing an Arbitral Forum for Investor-State Arbitration, 27 January 2015).

Corr, Anders, 2016: "Expect Climate Catastrophe: Paris Agreement Lacks Enforcement.", https://www.forbes.com/sites/anderscorr/2016/12/01/expect-climate-catastrophe-paris-agreement-lacks-enforcement/#4fe0605b3313 (cited as Expect Climate Catastrophe: Paris Agreement Lacks Enforcement, 1 December 2016).

Dolzer, Rudolf and Schreuer, Christoph, 2012: "Priciples of International Investment Law", 2nd ed., Oxford, Oxford University Press (cited as Rudolf Dolzer and Christoph Schreuer, Principles of International Investment Law).

Energy Charter Secretariat, 2002: "The Energy Charter Treaty: A Readers Guide", https://is.muni.cz/el/1422/jaro2017/MVV2368K/um/ECT_Guide_ENG.pdf (cited as Energy Charter Secretariat, The Energy Charter Treaty: A Readers Guide, 2002).

Energy Charter Secretariat, 2012: "Expropriation Regime under the Energy Charter Treaty", https://www.energycharter.org/fileadmin/DocumentsMedia/Thematic/Expropriation_2012_en.pdf (cited as Energy Charter Secretariat, Expropriation Regime under the Energy Charter Treaty, 2012).

Energypedia: "Feed-in Premiums." https://energypedia.info/wiki/Feed-in_Premiums_(FIP).

EnergyTrend, 2018: "Poverty Alleviation Will Be Highlight of China's 2018 PV Power Policy." https://www.energytrend.com/news/20180102-12118.html (cited as Poverty Alleviation will be Highlight of Chinas 2018 PV Power Policy, Energy trend, 2 January 2018).

EPIA, 2013: "Retrospective Measures at National Level and their Impact on the Photovoltaic Sector", https://www.qualenergia.it/sites/default/files/articolo-doc/EpiaRestrospective_Measures__at_national_level.pdf (cited as EPIA, Retrospective Measures at National Level, 2013).

European Renewable Energies Federation, 2013: "Policy Paper on Retrospective Changes to RES Legislations and National Moratoria", http://www.keepontrack.eu/contents/publicationsbiannualnationalpolicyupdatesversions/kot-policy-paper-on-retrospective-changes-to-res-support.pdf (cited as European Renewable Energies Federation, Policy Paper on Retrospective Changes to RES Legislations and National Moratoria, 2013).

Directorate-General for Internal Policies, 2016: "Solar energy policy in the EU and the Member States, from the perspective of the petitions received, https://www.europarl.europa.eu/RegData/etudes/STUD/2016/556968/IPOL_STU(2016)556968_EN.pdf (cited as Directorate General for Internal Policy, Solar energy policy in the EU and the Member States, from the perspective of the petitions received, 2016).

EWEA, 2015: "Design options for wind energy tenders", https://www.ewea.org/fileadmin/files/library/publications/position-papers/EWEA-Design-options-for-wind-energy-tenders.pdf (cited as EWEA, Design options for wind energy tenders, 2015).

Fitch-Roy, Oscar, and Bridget Woodman, 2016: "Auctions for Renewable Energy Support in the United Kingdom: Instruments and lessons learnt." https://www.researchgate.net/publication/301821658_Auctions_for_Renewable_Energy_Support_in_the_United_Kingdom_Instruments_and_lessons_learnt, (cited as Auctions for Renewable Energy Support in the United Kingdom: Instruments and lessons learnt).

Fraunhofer Institute for Solar Energy Systems ISE, 2018: "Levelized Cost of Electricity Renewable Energy Technologies." https://www.ise.fraunhofer.de/content/dam/ise/en/documents/publications/studies/EN2018_Fraunhofer-ISE_LCOE_Renewable_Energy_Technologies.pdf (cited as Fraunhofer Institute for Solar Energy Systems ISE, Levelized Costs of Electricity Renewable Energy Technologies, 2018).

Fruhmann, Claudia, and Andreas Tuerk, 2014: "Renewable Energy Support Policies in Europe." *Climate Policy Info Hub*, https://climatepolicyinfohub.eu/renewable-energy-support-policies-europe (cited as Fruhmann/ Tuerk, Renewable Energy Support Policies in Europe, 13 November 2014).

Gentry, Bradford S., Ronk, Jennifer, undated pre-publication draft: "International Investment Agreements and Investment in Renewable Energy", https://www.researchgate.net/publication/242366373_International_Investment_Agreements_and_Investments_in_Renewable_

Energy (cited as Bradford S. Gentry and Jennifer Ronk, International Investment Agreements and Investment in Renewable Energy, undated pre-publication draft).

Griebel, Joern, 2008: “Internationales Investitionsrecht”, 1st ed., Munich, C.H. Beck (cited as Joern Griebel, Internationals Investitionsrecht, 2008).

Gross, Daniel, 2015: “The Paris Agreement Is the Shove the World Needs.” https://slate.com/business/2015/12/the-paris-agreement-wont-punish-countries-that-fall-short-but-its-still-the-shove-the-world-needs.html (cited as The Paris Agreement Is the Shove the Wold Needs, 14 December 2015).

GSI and IISID, 2014: “A Cautionary Tale: Spain’s solar PV investment bubble”, https://www.iisd.org/gsi/sites/default/files/rens_ct_spain.pdf (cited as GSI/IISID, A Cautionary Tale: Spain’s solar PV investment bubble).

Hannam, Peter, 2018:” Sabotage: Regulator slammed for move to slash solar feed-in tariffs”, https://www.smh.com.au/environment/climate-change/sabotage-regulator-slammed-for-move-to-slash-solar-feed-in-tariffs-20180703-p4zp7x.html (cited as Sabotage: Regulator slammed for move to slash solar feed-in tariffs, The Sydney Morning Herald, 3 July 2018).

Hannen, Petra, 2018: “Bundesregierung prüft Relativierung des Einspeisevorrangs”, https://www.pv-magazine.de/2018/07/31/bundesregierung-prueft-relativierung-deseinspeisevorrangs/ (cited as Bundesregierung prüft Relativierung des Einspeisevorrangs, PV Magazine 31 July 2018).

Hirner, Stefan Michael , 2014: “Permissibility of feed-in tariffs for the promotion of electricity from renewable sources under EU State aid law.” *Spektrum der Rechtswissenschaft* (cited as Hirner, SPRW 2014,).

Huneke, F.; Göß, S., Österreicher, J. and Dahroug O., 2018: “Power Purchase Agreements: Finanzierungsmodell von Erneuerbaren Energien“, https://www.energybrainpool.com/fileadmin/download/Whitepapers/2018-01-31_Energy-Brainpool_White-Paper_Power-Purchase-Agreements.pdf (cited as Huneke/Göß/Österreicher/Dahroug, Power Purchase Agreements: Finanzierungsmodell von Erneuerbaren Energien).

ICIS Editorial, 2018: “EU remains on course for 2020 RES target, though some member states see worsening performance.”, https://www.icis.com/explore/resources/news/2018/02/02/10189620/eu-remains-on-course-for-2020-res-target-though-some-member-states-see-worsening-performance/ (cited as ICIS Editorial: EU remains on course for 2020 RES targets, though some member states see worsening, 2 February 2018).

IEA, 2017: „National Survey Report of Photovoltaic Applications in CHINA.” https://iea-pvps.org/wp-content/uploads/2020/01/National_Survey_Report_of_PV_Power_Applications_in_China_-_2017_01.pdf (cited as IEA, National Survey Report of Photovoltaic Applications in China, 2017).

IEA, 2018: “2018 Snapshot of global photovoltaic markets.” https://iea-pvps.org/wp-content/uploads/2020/01/IEA-PVPS_-_A_Snapshot_of_Global_PV_-_1992-2017.pdf (cited as IEA, 2018 Snapshot of global photovoltaic markets, 2018).

Institut der deutschen Wirtschaft Köln, 2011: “Einspeisetarif versus Quotensystem.“, 2011. https://www.iwkoeln.de/studien/iw-kurzberichte/beitrag/foerderung-erneuerbarer-energien-einspeisetarif-versus-quotensystem-52729.html (cited as Einspeisetarife vs. Quotensysteme, Institut der deutschen Wirtschaft Köln, 13 November 2011).

IRENA, 2015: “Renewable Energy Auctions: A Guide to Design, https://www.irena.org/-/media/Files/IRENA/Agency/Publication/2015/Jun/IRENA_Renewable_Energy_Auctions_A_Guide_to_Design_2015.pdf (cited as IRENA, Renewable Energy Auctions: A Guide to Design, 2015).

IRENA, 2018: “Accessible Finance for Renewable Energy Projects in Developing Countries, https://irena.org/-/media/Files/IRENA/Agency/Publication/2017/Dec/IRENA-ADFD_Accessible_Finance_Brochure_2018.pd (cited as IRENA, Accessible Finance for Renewable Energy Projects in Developing Countries, 2018).

IRENA, 2018: “Renewable Power Generation Costs in 2017”, https://www.irena.org/-/media/

Files/IRENA/Agency/Publication/2018/Jan/IRENA_2017_Power_Costs_2018.pdf (cited as IRENA, Renewable Power Generation Costs in 2017, 2018).

IRENA; IEA and REN21, 2018: "Renewable Energy Policies in a Time of Transition." http://www.irena.org//media/Files/IRENA/Agency/Publication/2018/Apr/IRENA_IEA_REN21_Policies_2018.pdf (cited as IRENA, IEA and REN21, Renewable Energy Policies in a Time of Transition, 2018).

Karimov, Elnur, 2018: "Umbrella Clauses within Energy Charter Treaty", Baku State University Law Review 4, no.1 (cited as Karimov, Umbrella Clauses within Energy Charter Treaty in: Baku State University Law Review, 4 no.1).

Kent, Rachael; Morris, Danielle; Forrest, Stephanie, 2018: "NAFTA 2.0: Investment Protection and Dispute Settlement under Chapter 14 of the United States – Mexico – Canada – Agreement, https://www.wilmerhale.com/en/insights/client-alerts/20181009-nafta-2-0-investment-protection-and-dispute-settlement-under-chapter-14-of-the-united-states-mexico-canada-agreement (cited as Kent/Morris/Forrest, NAFTA 2.0: Investment Protection and Dispute Settlement under Chapter 15 of the United States – Mexico – Canada – Agreement, 9 October 2018).

Kirschen, Daniel Sadi, and Goran Strbac, 2019: "Fundamentals of Power System Economics." 2nd ed., Hoboken, NJ, Wiley (cited as Kirschen/ Strbac,Fundamentals of Power System Economics, 2019).

Konoplyanik, A., 2005: "The Energy Charter Treaty: Dispute Resolution Mechanisms – and the Yukos Case", Russian Energy & Mining Law Journal (cited as Konoplyanik, The Energy Charter Treaty: Dispute Resolution Mechanisms and the Yukos Case, Russian Energy and Mining Law Journal, 2005).

Müller, Stefanie Claudia, 2017: "Run auf spanische Wind- und Solarparks." https://www.wiwo.de/unternehmen/energie/erneuerbare-energien-run-auf-spanische-wind-und-solarparks/19933076.html. (cited as Run auf spanische Wind- und Solarparks, Wirtschaftswoche 15 June 2017).

O'Sullivan, Kevin, 2018: "Penalties for missing climate change goals to be less than claimed, Minister says.", https://www.irishtimes.com/news/environment/penalties-for-missing-climate-change-goals-tobe-less-than-claimed-minister-says-1.3508293 (cited as The Irish Times: Penalties for missing climate change goals less than claimed, Minister says, 25 May 2018).

Ofgem e-serve, 2017: "Renewables Obligation Annual Report 2015–16." (March 2017) https://www.ofgem.gov.uk/ofgem-publications/113760 (cited as Ofgem e-serve, Renewables Obligation Annual Report 2015 – 2016).

Parola, Lorenzo; Petronio, Francesca and Cozzi, Fabio, 2015: "Italys Withdrawal from the Energy Charter Treaty: Which Consequences for Foreign Investors", https://www.paulhastings.com/publications-items/details?id=e40ae469-2334-6428-811c-ff00004cbded (cited as Italys Withdrawal from the Energy Charter Treaty: Which Consequences for Foreign Investors, Paul Hastings 28 April 2015).

Patrizia, Charles A.; Profaizer, Joseph R.; Timofeyev, Igor V.; Cooper, Samuel W., unknown date: "Investment Disputes Involving the Renewable Energy Industry under the Energy Charter Treaty", https://globalarbitrationreview.com/chapter/1142579/investment-disputes-involving-the-renewable-energy-industry-under-the-energy-charter-treaty (cited as Global Arbitration Review, Investment Disputes Involving the Renewable Energy Industry under the Energy Charter Treaty).

PV Europe, 2018: "The Spanish PV market has entered into a new phase.". https://www.pveurope.eu/News/Markets-Money/The-Spanish-PV-market-has-entered-into-anew-phase (cited as The Spanish PV Market has entered into a new phase, PV Europe 6 April 2018).

REN21, 2011: "Renewables 2011: Global Status Report." https://www.ren21.net/wp-content/uploads/2019/05/GSR2011_Full-Report_English.pdf (cited as REN 21, 2011: Global Status Report, 2011).

REN21, 2018: "Renewables 2018: Global Status Report." https://www.ren21.net/wp-content/uploads/2019/05/GSR2018_Full-Report_English.pdf (cited as REN21, Renewables 2018: Global Status Report 2018).

Rey, Martin, 2001: “Entwicklung und modernde Tendenzen der Projektfinanzierung”, Zeitschrift für Bank- und Kapitalmarktrecht (cited as Rey, BKR 2001).

Riesz, Jenny and Milligan, Michael, 2015: “Designing electricity markets for a high penetration of variable renewables”, Wiley Interdisciplinary Reviews (WIRES). Energy and Environment, 2015, vol. 4 (cited as Riesz/Milligan WIRES Energy and Environment, 2015).

Semotiuk, Andy, 2018:” What NAFTA Partners still need to do to launch USMCA “, https://www.forbes.com/sites/andyjsemotiuk/2018/11/23/attention-usmca-leaders-time-is-running-out/#c4c72a14b92a (cited as Semotiuk, What NAFTA Partners still need to do to launch USMCA, 23 November 2018).

Streck, Charlotte, Paul Keenlyside, and Moritz von Unger, 2016: “The Paris Agreement: A New Beginning.” *Journal for European Environmental and Planning Law* (cited as Streck/Keenlyside/von Unger, JEEPL 2016).

Sussman, Edna, 2008: “Energy Charter Treatys Investor Protection Provisions: Potential to Foster Solutions to Global Warming and Promote Sustainable Development”, ILSA Journal of International & Comparative Law (cited as Edna Sussmann: Energy Charter Treatys Investor Protection Provisions: Potential to Foster Solutions to Global Warming and Promote Sustainable Develepent”, ILSA Journal of International & Comparative Law, 2008).

Swedish Energy Agency, 2012: “The electricity certificate system”, https://www.google.com/url?sa=t&rct=j&q=&esrc=s&source=web&cd=3&ved=2ahUKEwiYqKi7nKffAhUHElAKHWm9ABwQFjACegQIBxAC&url= https%3A%2F%2Fenergimyndigheten.a-w2m.se%2FTest.ashx%3FResourceId%3D2664&usg=AOvVaw29qbiZ7Hp3Y98aKOkhsPnk(cited as The electricity certificate system, 2012).

The New YorkTimes, 2016: “Transcript of the first Debate”, https://www.cbsnews.com/news/is-donald-trump-right-to-call-nafta-a-disaster/, (cited as The New York Times, Transcript of the first debate, 27 September 2016).

Thoma, Mark, 2015: “Is Donald Trump right to call NAFTA a disaster?”, https://www.cbsnews.com/news/is-donald-trump-right-to-call-nafta-a-disaster/ (cited as Thoma, Is Donald Trump right to call NAFTA a disaster, 5 October 2015).

U.S. Energy Information Administration, 2018: “Levelized Cost and Levelized Avoided Cost of New Generation Resources in the *Annual Energy* Outlook *2018*.” https://www.eia.gov/outlooks/archive/aeo18/pdf/electricity_generation.pdf (cited as U.S. Energy Information Administration, Levelized Cost and Levelized Avoided Cost of New Generation Resources in the Annual Energy Outlook, 2018).

Unknown author, 2016: “Italy is no longer member of Energy Charter Treaty, hopes to avoid arbitration”, http://www.globalinvestmentprotection.com/2016/01/06/italy-no-longer-member-of-energy-charter-treaty-hopes-to-avoid-more-arbitrations/ (cited as Italy is no longer member of Energy Charter Treaty, hopes to avoid arbitration, 6 January 2016).

Volcovici, Valerie, 2017: “U.S. submits formal notice of withdrawal from Paris climate pact.”, https://www.reuters.com/article/us-un-climate-usa-paris/u-s-submits-formal-notice-ofwithdrawal-from-paris-climate-pact-idUSKBN1AK2FM (cited as U.S. submits formal notice of withdrawal from Paris climate pact, Reuters 4 August 2017).

Wigand, Fabian; Förster, Sonja; Amazo, Ana and Tiedemann, Silvana, 2016: “Auctions for Renewable Support: Lessons learnt from International Experiences”, http://auresproject.eu/files/media/documents/aures_wp4_synthesis_report.pdf (cited as Auctions for Renewable Support: Lessons learnt from International Experiences).

Wozniak, Michal, 2019: “Branche kompakt: Die Windenergie steht in Schweden vor einem Rekordjahr”, https://www.gtai.de/gtai-de/trade/branchen/branche-kompakt/schweden/

branche-kompakt-die-windenergie-steht-in-schweden-vor-144162 (cited as Die Windenergie steht in Schweden vor einem Rekordjahr, Germany Trade & Invest).

Xropolitou, Evangelia; Gawlik, Wolfgang; Zseby, Tanja and Fabini, Joachim, 2018: “Impact of Asynchronous Renewable Generation Infeed on Grid Frequency: Analysis Based on Synchrophasor Measurements”, https://www.researchgate.net/publication/325205562_Impact_of_Asynchronous_Renewable_Generation_Infeed_on_Grid_Frequency_Analysis_Based_on_Synchrophasor_Measurements (cited as Xyropolitou, Evangelia, Gawlik, Zseby, Fabini, Impact of Asynchronus Renewable Generation Infeed on Grid Frequency: Analysis Based on Synchrophasor Measurements, 2018).

Yannaca-Small, Katia, 2006: “Interpretation of the Umbrealla Clause in Investment Agreements”, OECD Working Papers on International Investment 2006/03 (cited as Katia Yannaca-Small, Interpretation of the Umbrella Clause in Investment Agreements, 2006/03).

6 Project Finance of a Renewable Energy Project

Jörg Böttcher

6.1 Foundations of Risk Management in Project Financing

In the two following Sections 6.1.1 and 6.1.2, we will describe the main characteristics of risk management within the field of project financing.

6.1.1 Risk and Risk Management

When realizing projects, adequate risk management techniques have to be implemented. Otherwise, all risks will have to be borne by the project company and thus by the project sponsors and the banks. If risks remain unidentified or if they are not allocated according to the risk-bearing capacity and controllability to the individual participants in the project, this may lead to delays and budget overruns during the construction phase of the project due to time-consuming follow-up negotiations or legal disputes. Additionally, risks that have not been adequately assigned to the individual stakeholders can also cause problems during the operational phase. These usually result in a reduction of the projected cash flow. In a worst case scenario, the cash flow is no longer sufficient to service debt service or allow a dividend payment to the sponsors. In the context of the contractual structure, efforts are made by the capital providers, based on all available information regarding the framework conditions of the project, to identify and quantify the risks and to allocate these to other parties involved in the project in the further course of the project.

There are various definitions of the term "risk" in the literature (see section 3). In the following, "risk" is to be understood as the danger of a result deviating from the expected target value due to incorrectly estimated or neglected factors. These deviations can be either positive or negative, whereby the negative deviations represent loss risks in project financing and thus are of real interest to the stakeholders in the project. In order to control the risks associated with projects, along with project development, risk management must also be implemented. Risk management includes all activities, processes, structures and instruments that serve to overcome the risks. The Figure 6.1 shows the risk management process for project financing.

The aim of risk management is to ensure that the projected cash flows upon which the project financing has been structured can be reliably generated, thus ensuring the profitability of the project.

https://doi.org/10.1515/9783110607888-006

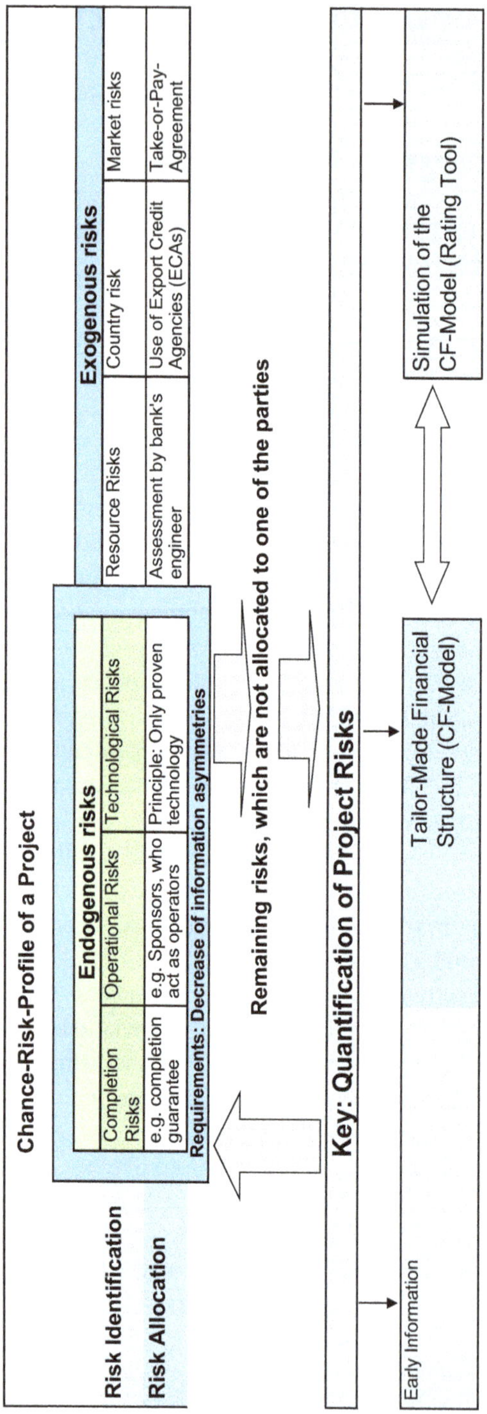

Figure 6.1: Risk management process in project financing transactions (own representation).

6.1.2 Main Risk Management Goal in Project Financing: Sourcing Stable Cash Flows

Identifying and managing risks is the core task for structuring project financing, as the recourse rights of lenders during the operational phase are limited to the project and the cash flow it generates.

The viability and robustness of project financing are determined by its ability to reliably generate the projected cash flows. If the cash flows realized deviate in terms of time or amount from the projected cash flows, adaptation measures are essential in order to prevent the project being at risk. All risk aspects from a project effect the cash flow, so risk management in the case of project financing means controlling and if necessary correcting the factors influencing the cash flow. To understand the importance of risk management within a project financing, it is important to point out the differences between corporate and project financing.

There are two options available to finance renewable energy projects: Sponsors with available financial resources and good creditworthiness may opt for on-balance sheet financing to develop and realize small to medium-sized projects. This means the project investment costs are met from the company's equity or operating cash flow and classical investment loans with the liabilities being secured against the main corporate assets (corporate financing).

Project finance is the raising of funds on a typical non-recourse basis to finance an economically separate investment project. The providers of the finance look primarily to the cash flow of the project – as the source of funds to service loans they may have taken out and to provide the return of the equity they have invested in the project. The different approaches are shown in Figure 6.2:

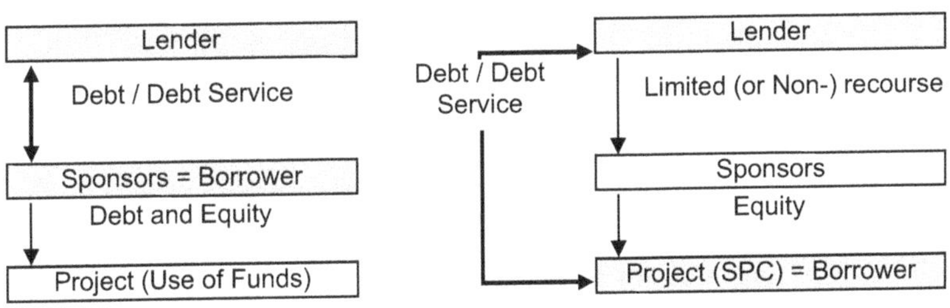

Figure 6.2: Corporate finance versus project finance (own representation).

Utilities or other sponsors with strong financing capacity are able to finance small to medium-sized renewable energy projects using their own cash resources and from their own balance sheets. In this approach, the project's investment costs are met from the corporate financial assets or from the operating cash flows of the sponsoring company, and the project debt is secured against all assets on the sponsor's balance sheet. Debt capital can be raised from either corporate credit lines, bonds or classical project-specific bank investment loans. On-Balance-sheet financing embodies the following characteristics:

- **Simplicity**: Balance-sheet financing is relatively easy and quick to arrange
- **Low cost**: it may be less expensive in terms of arrangement and legal fees as well as the saving of transaction and negotiation costs.
- **Financial structure**: Balance-sheet financing will normally reflect a looser, more flexible financing structure. While still significant, the right network of contracts which creates the risk transfer in project financing is less critical to the lender. In most cases (i.e., the degree of leverage) will be lower than in project-finance transaction.
- **Risk acceptance**: Sponsors are generally prepared to accept the majority of the project risks. Although on-balance-sheet financing structures can also allow for risk transfer, the degree of risk transfer is much lower than in non-recourse project financing.

From both the sponsor's and lender's point of view, the possibility to more effectively protect the RE project from costly agency conflicts is a significant argument for the employment of project financing instead of balance sheet financing. Agency theory analyses information asymmetries between principals and agents. The principal (e.g., the bank) has less information than the agent (e.g., the sponsor), who can use this advantage to act opportunistically. This risk must be excluded by using specific prohibition clauses in the loan contract. Project financing separates the assets from other business activities of the sponsor, isolating and ring-fencing the cash flows generated by the assets. This separation can only be achieved by the setting-up of a new project company (so called SPV, special purpose vehicle) for each individual RE project.

Because of the junior structural ranking of equity providers as compared to creditors described above, it is the owner who bears the risk of negative plan deviations first: The return on their investment deteriorates and it is the project company's entrepreneurial task to implement counter-measures. However, since all project financings are leveraged transactions, creditors are also affected relatively quickly when deviations from the base case scenario occur. In order to protect their contractual repayment claims the lenders require certain control and sanction rights in the case of negative deviations from the base case scenario. In order to limit such deviations various safety elements are implemented: One of these safety elements is to design a financing structure appropriate to the risk profile. The financing structure is designed in such a way that, even in the event of a worst-case scenario, the project will still be in a position to service the debt. The ability of the imminent project cash flow to service the debt service is the essential condition for creditors to get involved in project financing. In addition to servicing operational costs and debt, the cash flow must also include an additional buffer in order to absorb deviations from the plan that are not to be borne by the project participants. Therefore, it is the cash flow and its reliability that determine the viability and debt potential of a project.

6.2 The Financing Process in Four Steps

In the following Sections 6.2.1 up to 6.2.5, we will describe the financing process as a step-by-step approach.

6.2.1 Introduction

Renewable energy projects are developed, constructed and operated along the process chain in Figure 6.3.

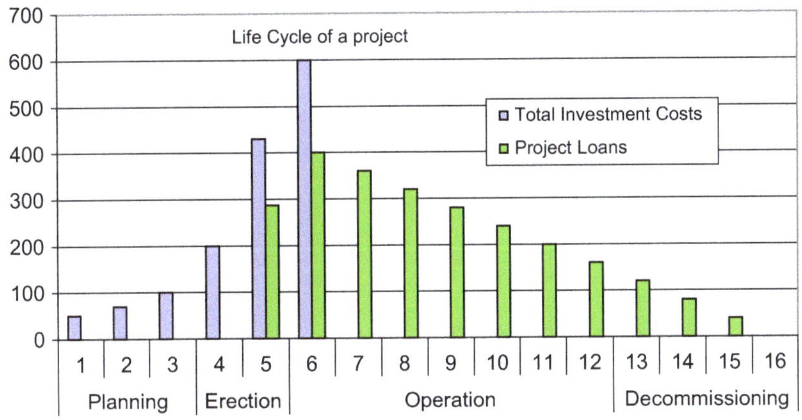

Figure 6.3: Life cycle of a project (own representation).

The negotiation and procurement of the necessary financing is an integral part of the process, and is started as soon as most of the initial project-concept development work (pre-development) has been finalized and a valid operating permit (e.g., concession) has been obtained. The financing phase can be split into four major steps:

- **SPV-contract negotiation**: under the project finance scheme, the sponsor starts the financing process by setting up a project company (also called SPV) as transaction partner for different project contracts.
- **Cash-flow planning**: The sponsor collects all the data relevant to the project which is necessary in order to draw up a business plan that forecasts cash inflows and outflows. The cash flow plan is an important document for negotiations with

prospective lenders and will be thoroughly evaluated by them during the due diligence process.
- **Bankability Assessment, Risk Identification and Risk Allocation**: The bankability assessment is carried out by the lenders and their contracted advisors, and include a general evaluation of the project's economic, legal and technical feasibility and all material risks. It aims at determining the creditworthiness of the project and its ability to meet debt service requirements and other contractual payments.
- **Risk Quantification and Financial Engineering**: Financial engineering is the quantitative and qualitative structuring of a project's financing mix (the right combination and design of debt and equity) in order to reduce default risk and maximize project value. The result are the loan and collateral agreements between the project company (the borrower) and the lender.

Step 1: SPV-contract negotiation

The Figure 6.4 shows a typical commercial structure for a renewable energy project. It is characteristic for most other power projects that use the project finance approach. The project company is the vehicle by which a large number of contractual agreements are concluded. The contracts can be separated into **Investment Agreements, Financing Agreements** and **Operating Agreements**.

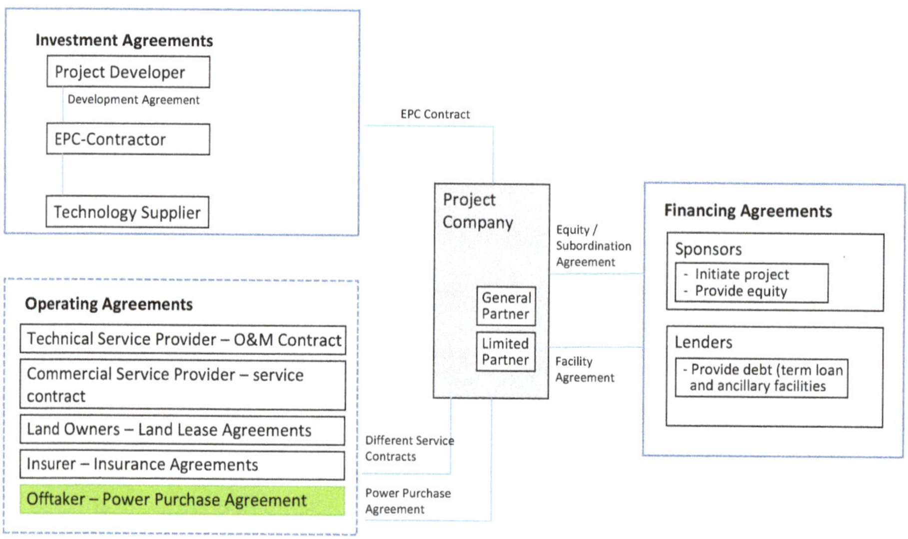

Figure 6.4: Project company and its contractual relations (own representation).

Investment Agreements

The engineering, procurement and construction (EPC) contract: This is an agreement with a project management or a construction company in which the latter agrees to construct the project on a turnkey, fixed-price basis. This agreement can also be split into different agreements that fulfill the same purpose (so called multi-contracting).

Multi-contracting means that the EPC contract is split into different sub-agreements, e.g., a turbine-supply agreement, a development-rights purchase contract and one or more related construction contracts (e.g., for roads, cables, substation, etc.). In EPC contracts, all construction activity is bundled together in the EPC contract. Multi-contracting is more risky for the project company than EPC contracting, but may be less expensive or even without alternative, if no entity would be prepared to act as EPC contractor.

The grid-connection agreement with the local grid operator allows the project to be connected to the electric power grid and to distribute the electricity it produces. Sometimes an additional grid usage agreement is required.

Operating and Financing Agreements

Operating Agreements

- The Power Purchase Agreement (PPA): The PPA is a contract between the project company and a buyer, who agrees to purchase the project's electrical energy or green certificates output. It should ideally contain a defined purchase price for each kWh of generated energy over the project life and a "take-or-pay-clause" that guarantees remuneration of the entire production output. PPAs reduce the offtake risk and are very important in ensuring project bankability.
- Land lease contracts define the relationship with the landowners and ensure access to the project site (in cases where land plots have not been purchased).
- The operation and maintenance agreement (O&M) is a contract with a technical company that operates and maintains the project over its operational life. Often these contracts include explicit guarantees which assure a specific level of availability of the plant to generate electricity.

Financing Agreements

- The Facility Agreement is the loan agreement under which the financing bank provide loans to the project.
- The Shareholder Agreement is concluded between the owners of the project company and defines their rights and obligations, and secures equity funding.

Step 2: Business Planning

The most important step in the business planning of renewable energy projects is estimating the project's future cash flows; these will include both the initial investments and the annual net cash inflows after the project becomes operational. The project cash flows can be separated as follows:

- **Initial investment outlay**: The initial investment includes the up-front cost of the renewable energy technology and all other fixed assets (grid infrastructure, sub-stations, cables, roads, etc.) as well as shipping, installation and project-development costs. The total investment costs have to be covered by the funding sources equity and debt. Funding sources have an impact on the cash-outflow of the project, since the interest and repayment payments form the major part of the operating costs of the project. And an investor will only invest, if the prospective dividends are satisfying his internal investment criteria.
- **Operating cash flow**: The operating income of a renewable energy project is determined by the sales of the generated electric energy minus operating costs, which include cash expenses for operation and maintenance, insurance, land lease payments, management expenses and others. In the following sections, the operating Cashflow will also be called Cashflow Available for Debt Service (CFADS).

For each year of the economic life of the project, the net cash flow is determined as the sum of the cash flows from the two categories. These annual net cash flows, together with the project's cost of capital, can be used to calculate the debt capacity, i.e., the project's ability to redeem the debt service to the bank. Forecasting the future cash flows of a project is not easy, since major input variables such as energy yield, operating costs and potentially prices can be subject to changes and fluctuations. Therefore, the first important issue in cashflow modeling is getting the input assumptions right.

Cash Flow Waterfall Concept

Within project financing, Cashflow positions follow a strict hierarchy, called **Cash Flow Waterfall**. This concept requires annual revenues to cover periodic costs in a pre-defined order.

The first position in the water contains the revenue components, which lead to the cash inflows of the project.

Annual revenues must first cover operational costs that are needed to generate the ongoing revenues – e.g., O&M costs, land lease payments or insurance costs. The next position in the waterfall is occupied by tax payments, eventually leading to a position called "Cashflow after tax." In order to calculate taxes, depreciations of assets need to be factored in as they influence the tax base. However, depreciation is a non-cash item that is not directly included in the Cashflow waterfall.

Table 6.1: Cash flow waterfall (own representation).

	Revenues
./.	Operational Costs and Taxes
=	Cashflow Available for Debt Service (CFADS)
./.	Interest Payments
./.	Debt Repayments
=	Cashflow after Debt Service
±	Increase/Decrease of Debt Service Reserve Account
±	Increase/Decrease of Maintenance Reserve Account
=	Free Cashflow

Rather, it is deducted in the profit and loss statement where the taxes are finally calculated. The resulting tax payments are then deducted in the Cashflow waterfall.

If no further cost occur, the Cashflow after tax equals the **Cashflow Available for Debt Service** (CFADS), redeeming debt principal due to be repaid annually and interest payments. CFADS is a specific cash flow term commonly used in connection with project financing. In practice, lenders expect CFADS to cover the annual debt service by more than 100%.

Calculation of project revenues

The project's revenues are calculated as the sum of all Cash inflows that can be traced to the project.

Table 6.2: Overview of project revenue (own representation).

Revenues	Produced Electricity * Electricity Price
	Produced CO_2-Certificates * Certificate Price
	Interest Income (on Reserve Accounts)

Revenues from electricity sales are calculated by multiplying electricity volume by electricity price. Estimates of electricity output are usually based on expert studies (e.g., of the potential wind or solar resources available) and on the technical specification of the technology to be used. Such expert studies provide an expected electricity production value, and include standard-deviation and related probability distribution functions. This information enables the assessment of probability scenarios (p-cases) for the expected electricity output. The second component of the revenue calculation, the electricity price, depends on the applicable remuneration scheme for the project (e.g., feed-in tariff, market or PPA-price).

In quota-markets, energy produced from eligible renewable sources (e.g., wind, PV or biogas) receives green certificates which can be traded in the market and generate a second revenue stream on top of the revenue from selling the electricity at market prices.

Calculation of operational costs

Following the scheme of the waterfall concept, annual revenues must first cover operational costs, also called operational expenditure (OPEX).

Table 6.3: Overview of operational costs (own representation).

Operational Costs	Operation & Maintenance (O&M)
	Land Lease Costs
	Technical and Operational Management
	Insurance
	Electricity Consumption
	Audit Costs, Bookkeeping
	Taxes

The OPEX of renewable energy projects include land lease payments, operations and maintenance (O&M) costs, insurance costs and grid access fees. Additionally, costs for electricity consumption by the production facility itself and costs for commercial administration and auditing of the project company are usually included.

Renewable energy project operators in many markets are required by law or by contractual agreements to build up decommissioning reserves. These also have to be included into the operational cost budget because building–up these reserves represents a regular cash-outflow.

Operational cost deductions are followed by deductions of taxes payable. Taxation of renewable energy projects is very market-, country and transaction-specific. In order to incentivize investments in renewable energies, some countries have adopted favorable tax-holidays or depreciation regimes that allow renewable energy project companies to postpone tax payments into the second half of the project's life. Taxes payable can consist of corporation taxes (tax on corporation profits), regionally specific taxes such as local business taxes or real estate taxes per turbine.

From CFADS to Free Cashflow

CFADS is predominantly used to cover the project's debt service. This consists of the scheduled annual interest and debt repayments agreed upon in the loan agreement between the bank and the project company. In order to ensure that the debt service can be met even in years with lower than expected cash flows, lenders usually require an additional debt service reserve account (DSRA).

Lenders demand the DSRA according to their risk appetite. This means that they require higher DSCRs for riskier projects. Usually, the DSRA is created by using project's cash flow that remain after servicing the debt service. Depending on the identified project risk, required annual DSRA-levels for renewable energy projects can typically equal the debt service of the next six months (50% of the debt service requirement of the next year). If the annual debt service and DSRA funding have been met by the project company, the remaining cash flow (free cash flow) can be distributed to the shareholders of the project, typically once or twice a year.

The evaluation of future project cash flows is critical to both debt and equity providers, as it enables them to determine their expected returns and financial commitments.

Step 3: Bankability Assessment, Risk Identification and Risk Allocation

The bankability assessment is carried out by the lenders and their contracted advisors. It includes a general evaluation of the project's economic, legal and technical feasibility including the material project risks. It aims at determining the project's creditworthiness and its ability to meet its contractual payments.

A due diligence is a thorough investigation or audit of a potential investment and can apply, for example, to financing through a bank, to a corporate takeover, or to an IPO. Bankability assessment, in particular, examines the transactions from the bank's perspective alone. Thus, due diligence is the overall term which encompasses the bankability assessment. Typical bank advisors are:

- **Legal advisor**: The bank's legal advisor is an international law firm that is contracted to review the legal, tax and regulatory system, as well as the permitting and contractual documents of the project. Often, the Legal Adviser also drafts the credit and security agreements.
- **Lender's engineer**: Lender's engineers are technical advisory firms, who are involved in the independent feasibility study, engineering concept and construction supervision of the project,
- **Insurance advisor**: The insurance advisor reviews contracted insurance cover and confirms its adequacy, and may control payments of insurance premiums during the operational period of the project.

Some banks have the capacity to carry out most of the due diligence process internally, i.e., they have skilled staff who can review project documents and permits, use standardized financing and collateral contracts, and have technical experts who can perform technical evaluations.

If sponsors try to raise financing without recourse to the sponsor's own balance sheet, a substantial amount of project risk is shifted towards the bank. The sponsor's liability is limited to the equity portion that the sponsor has injected into the project company, and the project's creditworthiness and its capacity to debt service depends exclusively on the project's future cash flows.

Debt financing involves a legally enforceable claim with contractual payment obligations in fixed time intervals. Lenders are external partners of the borrower and do not have control over how the project is run. As interest rates are usually fixed at a pre-agreed level, banks do not have "upsides" in the project. That is why only risk mitigation is important for them.

This does not mean that all risks involved in a project have to be reallocated to the project's stakeholders. This is due to the fact that every risk transfer will cost money. Therefore, it is an economic task to determine how much risk should be transferred to third parties, and how much risk has to be borne by the sponsors and by the lenders.

Informational asymmetries are a reason for bankability assessments. Lenders, as external parties, do not have control over how a project is run and are also less informed about a project than the sponsor or the borrower. This information deficit is called information asymmetry. "Agency theory" analyses information asymmetries between "principals" and "agents." The principal (in this case the lender) has less information than the agent (the borrower), and the agent can use its advantage to act opportunistically, e.g., by concealing possible problems a project might be facing. This has consequences for the design of the bank financing contracts: lenders need to draft contract clauses that force the borrower to provide important project-related information (such as information related to operational, technical and financial project performance) in an accurate and timely manner.

Information asymmetries make it difficult to lenders to assess the credit quality and, therefore, the bankability of a project. This can prolong or even prevent a financing transaction form happening. Thus, a bankability assessment is usually required. Bankability assessments are carried out by the lenders and/or specialized external advisors contracted by them.

Information asymmetries can exist either before or after contracting. The asset specificity of RE equipment, for example, can lead to costly agency conflicts between technology suppliers, sponsor and bank, if the delivered and installed technology does not meet the contractually-agreed specifications or quality. Borrowers can increase the knowledge base of lenders by enhancing information "spillover" and providing signalling measures. Banks can also try to harmonize the financial interests of the borrowers with their own interests.

Table 6.4: Ways to decrease information asymmetries (own representation).

Screening	Signalling	Self-Selection
Less informed parties improve their knowledge by Due Diligence:	Better informed parties (e.g., sponsors) provide information by:	Selection of specific parts of contracts lead to a separation between "good" and "bad" risks:
Self-Information	Building up a reputation as borrower	Minimum equity Contributions
Contracting Advisors	Providing Guarantees	Equity is invested before drawdown of the loan
		Accepting Conservative Financial Structures

6.2.2 Risk Identification and Risk Allocation in Practice

Risks in relation to renewable energy projects can be described by a negative impact which possible future events may have in the financial value of a project or an investment. Banks adjust the required interest rate (RIR) that they require from a project depending on the perceived level of risk. In general, the RIR can be calculated as follows:

$$\text{RIR} = \text{Base Rate} + \text{Credit Spread}$$

The Base rate represents the interest rate at which the bank sources money in the bank market (e.g., EURIBOR). The credit spread is regarded as the appropriate compensation for the borrower for the risks which are perceived as being inherent to the project. Its level is determined by the market, i.e., market participants with expectations for such risk compensation. If a project is perceived as "too risky," it can ultimately turn out to be unrealizable.

The purpose of risk analysis is primarily to identify all factors that could have a negative impact on the generation of cash flow. In this context, the risk analysis is not only conducted by the sponsors, but in particular by the credit providers of the project financing. The banks, together with the consultants, have to gain an overview of the risks that could have a negative influence on the successful realization of the project. This is especially important in the development phase of the project, since the project will only produce costs. For the creditors, it is therefore essential that all of the risks are identified and assessed before the financial close and that the risks are distributed according to economic principles.

A number of risks has to be analyzed within a renewable energy project:

Construction risk

Completion risk (also referred to as construction or installation risk) includes all risks that might occur because:

- The renewable energy project has not or has only partly been built according to the required technical design criteria (lack of physical completion),
- The renewable energy project cannot produce the anticipated level of energy due to deficits during the construction phase,
- The renewable energy project cannot produce the expected amount of energy at the assumed unit cost for the time period projected in the business plan, and is therefore not able to meet the financial covenants pre-agreed with the lenders.

Completion risk can be directly linked to technology risk, if, for example, wind turbines – due to technical reasons – cannot be connected to the grid or are not operating in line with contractual specifications. In fact, there are a number of risk factors which can adversely affect the completion:

Table 6.5: Completion risk and potential risk mitigation (own representation).

Risk	Potential Risk Mitigation
Non-Completion	– Turn-Key Contract including completion guarantee and penalties with solvent plant manufacturer – Insurances are available to cover costs of late completion following insured damages
Completion with underperforming parameters	– Performance guarantees (power curve, availability) with solvent manufacturer – Liquidated damage payments
Completion with higher costs	Lumpsum-Turnkey contract with solvent plant manufacturer
Late Completion	Lumpsum-Date-Certain-Turnkey Contract with solvent plant manufacturer

Therefore, "as-built"-compliance of construction works and project completion should be confirmed and certified by an independent owner's or lender's engineer.

Technology Risk

Technology risk exists when a technology, on the scale designed for the project, might not perform according to its specifications or might become prematurely obsolete.

The risk of malfunction of installed renewable energy equipment can be considered a technology risk if the malfunctioning of that equipment could lead to a reduced annual energy yield and therefore to lower revenues, and thus endangers the project's ability to service its debts. Project sponsors try to enhance bankability and reduce technology risk by selecting competent and experienced equipment

Table 6.6: Technology risk and possible risk mitigation (own representation).

Risk	Potential Risk Mitigation
Technology might not achieve the expected performance parameters	– Use of proven technology only (with sufficient track record and certification standards) – Performance Warranties exist on equipment – Adequate Availability Test

suppliers and turn-key contractors who can deliver and install proven technology under fixed-price contracts and deliver the completed and commissioned project at a predetermined date within budget. Proven technology means that the contemplated assets for a project have already been erected and operated successfully in other projects, which can be proven to the client and the bank. The term "proven technology" is also often referred to as "bankable technology" because banks in most cases only finance assets with proven reliability. Otherwise the lenders would face the risk that they have to deal with an unstable cash flow stream due to deficits in the technology.

Proven technology assets are not free of technology risks, but these risks are usually evaluated and managed based on the supply contracts that have been entered into for the project. These should include typical warranty arrangements, in order to increase the "comfort levels" of equipment purchasers and the lenders.

Operational Risk

Operational risks can adversely affect the economic position of banks.

Table 6.7: Operational risk and possible risk mitigation (own representation).

Risk	Potential Risk Mitigation
Poor operational skills may lead to underperformance or even standstill of the project	– O&M contract with an experienced party – O&M contract over project's life time – over- and underperformance will be subject to positive as well as negative incentives – sufficient insurance coverage

The most important operational risks and related management measures are the following:

– **Increases in operating costs** to levels higher than projected (as a result of higher maintenance, insurance or other operating costs than foreseen) can be prevented (internally) by strict cost moitoring and maintenance schedules. Externally, guarantees from technology suppliers and O&M providers can limit the risk.

- **Lower plant availability** and increases in systematic energy losses can be managed internally by including higher discounts in the financial model and by detailed loss calculation, e.g., using transmission loss studies. Externally, guarantees from equipment suppliers and O&M providers can limit the risk.
- **Legal claims:** A project company can sue and be sued by third parties. Reasons could include e.g., higher than expected noise emissions from wind turbines. An internal risk management measure could be a carefully designed contractual structure to enable risk transfers. An external risk management measure could be legal protection insurance.
- Management risk related to **unethical or opportunistic behavior** of key personnel: An internal risk management measure might be auditing and control of key personnel (governance structure). An external measure would be the creation of a stand-alone project company.
- **Force majeure events:** Force majeure or so-called "act of god" risks can normally not be managed. However, certain "acts of god," such as earthquakes, can be insured up to a certain amount.

Market Risk

The generators of renewable energy projects can face the various forms of market and distribution risks listed in Table 6.8.

Table 6.8: Market risks and possible risk mitigation (own representation).

Risk	Potential Risk Mitigation
– Electricity cannot be sold in the expected amount and/or at the forecasted prices – Downtime of transmission lines	– Fixed feed-in tariff (subject to regulatory regime) – Long-term contract with solvent buyer

Distribution risks such as grid downtimes and production curtailments by the grid operator due to transmission line overloads can only seldomly be influenced by the project operator. In the following, we will focus on the main market risks faced by generators who need to trade green electricity because they cannot benefit from fixed feed-in tariff (FiT) regimes. These risks are called price risks. Price risks in renewable energy projects can be twofold:

- Adverse changes in the **prices paid for electricity**, which is determined by supply and demand of electricity on the one hand and by fossil fuel prices on the other.

- Adverse changes in the **prices paid for green certificates**, which is determined in part by supply and demand, but to a large extent also by changes in government policy as well as changes in subsidies and regulations.

Uncertainties in prices due to developments on the world's fossil fuel market are considered to be of lesser importance for wind and PV projects, because their "fuel" is free of charge. In biogas projects a major fuel risk exists (in biofuel projects it is even the most dominating risk) because of possible changes in the cost of the necessary input substrates.

Resource Risk

A project's estimated annual energy production (AEP) can be derived from resource assessment studies. The AEP will be inputted into the financial model when calculating the future cash flows of the project. However, the numerous data-items obtained in the process of making the yield assessment (and the procedure applied to them) contain various sources of uncertainty which may drive the AEP to a higher or lower value. See Figure 6.5 as an example for the variation of solar irradiation in Spain; the standard deviation is slightly above 3%.[1]

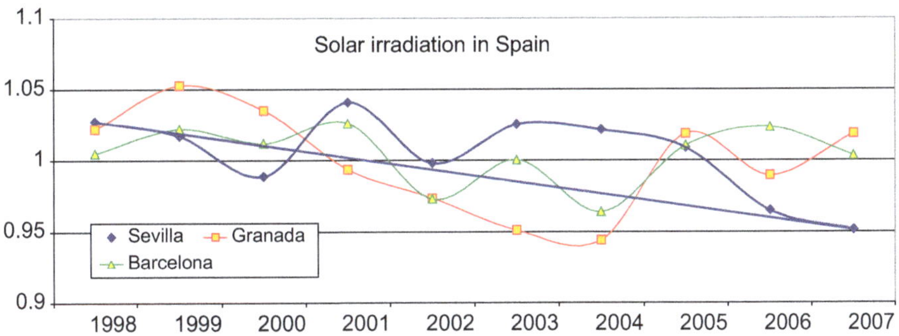

Figure 6.5: Solar irradiation in Spain (own representation).

Moreover, the AEP is considered to be a long-term mean, which will deviate in actual years of production. Because resource risk is an inherent risk that all renewable energy projects face, and which lenders have to deal with.

Sensitivity and scenario analysis are two valuable tools that can help to assess risks in Cashflow models in general, and resources risk in particular. "Sensitivity analysis" refers to the process of varying one factor in the Cashflow model (e.g., the AEP)

1 The y-axis shows the percentage of solar yield compared to a 100%-solar year.

Table 6.9: Resource risk and risk mitigation (own representation).

Risk	Potential Risk Mitigation
– Wind/Solar yield falls below resource assessment study – lack of substrate availability (dimensions: amount, price, quality)	– thorough independent assessment of resource on-site – Wind/Solar assessment by measurements over at least one year – nomination of expert with sufficient experience in this region – for biogas projects: long-term substrate delivery contracts with reputable supplier (if available)

in small incremental steps in order to see how the changes effect the value of the project and thereby seeing what the effects of the resource uncertainty might be.

The main advantage of sensitivity analysis is that it identifies the cash flow model input factors that influence the project's economics the most. In "scenario analysis," on the other hand, a number of key variables are changed simultaneously, so that an alternative Cashflow scenario for the project can be constructed.

Regulatory Risk

Regulatory risk due to changes in renewable energy policy is one of the most significant risk factors, albeit normally not manageable for investors or lenders.[2] Long-term regulatory-policy support is crucial as it provides the security for the planning and operation of facilities, which is necessary for developers and lenders to engage in the business.

Table 6.10: Regulatory risk and risk mitigation (own representation).

Risk	Potential Risk Mitigation
– Change of framework conditions during the project's lifetime – unclear ownership rights – legal uncertainty	– Financing only in countries with a reliable regulatory framework – Use of political risk insurance by Export Credit Agencies – If really in doubt about the regulatory risk, one should refrain from an investment

2 See especially chapter 4.8.

Two dominant support systems are in use, which regulate the monetary compensation of renewable energy production:

Feed-in tariff laws oblige utilities to enable the connection of renewable energy plants to the electricity grid and oblige them to purchase electricity generated by these plants at fixed, minimum tariffs. These tariffs are set by law and are set higher than the regular market price. Tariff payments are guaranteed over a specified period of time.

While feed-in tariff laws establish the price and allow the market to determine the capacity and generation, **quota systems** work in reverse: the government sets a target and allows the market to determine the price. The government mandates that a minimum share of the overall generating capacity or quantity of electricity has to stem from renewable sources. The share required often increases gradually over time, with a specific final target and end-date. Companies producing electricity from eligible renewable resources receive tradable green certificates, and these provide them with additional revenue on top of the revenue obtained from the sale (at market prices) of electricity.

6.2.3 Risk Allocation in Theory

The second cornerstone – apart of cash flow-related lending – is risk allocation.

After the stakeholders and, here in particular, the credit providers of the project, have assessed the risks, the adequate allocation of opportunities and risks among the project participants is managed within the project's contracts. In doing so, the risks of the project are distributed among the individual stakeholders to ensure that all parties have a joint interest in developing and operating the project successfully. Risk allocation is thus carried out with the aim of forming an interest group out of the parties involved in the project.

In the context of risk allocation, it should be ensured that no (one) contracting party is burdened unilaterally, but rather that all parties involved in the project are in a position to bear the assumed risks (the principle of risk-bearing capacity) and that they also have the ability to influence and manage these risks (principle of management of risks).

After the main sources of risk have been identified and the stakeholders in the financing of a project are known, the question is how to allocate the risks. Since the risks of a large project are often too high to be borne by a single stakeholder, it is an essential objective to distribute the risks to all parties involved in the project through an appropriate contractual structure to ensure that the risk-bearing capacity of a single party is not exceeded. Another essential aspect of risk allocation is to ensure that the stakeholders in the project are incentivized by accepting risks to fully support the project because otherwise the party could suffer financial disadvantages. As undetermined risk distributions can subsequently jeopardise the success of the project, the distribution of risks in the context of the contractual structure contributes significantly to the success of the project.

Effectively, risk allocation is also based on the risk appetite and the bargaining power to negotiate a contract of different participants. The second rule of effective risk allocation is to **incentivise each project participant** to work in favor of the project's success. This does not mean that the risk mitigation needs to be all encompassing and it would even be detrimental if it would be all-encompassing: Each risk transfer is also a decision about the costs involved. In most cases, commitments will be limited in scope, amount, and duration.

Basic Aspects of Game Theory

Game theory analyses competition, conflicts and the establishment of cooperation. It implies that the actions of the players are interdependent and the participants know that they are in a strategic situation. Interdependence means that the players are influenced by other players in terms of their options for action and the consequences of their actions, i.e., the players respond to each other. Rational behavior assumes that, in their actions, the players take each other's reactions into account. Game theory provides the necessary analysis instruments for this.

Game theory deals with static and dynamic games: Static games are games in which temporal aspects do not play any role, because all of the players act at the same time or because no information can be extracted from the actions of the others. In the case of dynamic games, it is assumed that players can learn from each other by observing the others' action.

In relation to questions of project financing, there are both static and dynamic elements: In the completion stage, for example, it is about urging one player, e.g., the general contractor, to complete the project on time and in accordance with cost planning. This is so important because successful completion releases the sponsors and the general contractor from their liability to the bank financing the project. This is a one-time – even if it may be longer lasting – interaction between the project and the general contractor, which simply has to work from a project perspective. In the context of the subsequent operational phase, there is a variety of recurring transactions between the project and its customers or suppliers. Even though the financing of a project is

Table 6.11: Examples for application on renewable energy project finance (own representation).

Static Game Situations	– Sponsor urges EPC contractor to complete renewable energy project in time – One-time contracting of a bank for a single renewable energy project
Dynamic Game Situations	– Multi-period contracting of an O&M provider – Repeated contracting of a Bank for several (subsequent) renewable energy project financings

often limited in time, the various stakeholders are mostly established in the industry and must sooner or later give careful consideration as to whether they want to risk their reputation through non-cooperative behavior.

Selection of Contractors in a One-Time Transaction

A major problem in any project financing is choosing the appropriate contractual partners. Reviewing references, economic and technological capability and the seriousness of potential contractors takes up a considerable amount of time during the preparation of financing for a project and incurs considerable transaction costs. In this section, it is intended to show that the structure of the agreements can play an important role in this choice.

There are two types of contractors here: Those who can increase the likelihood that the production plant will be highly efficient through greater care and others who have no influence on this. The analyses are carried out separately for each one, with the result that the latter type should be free of all risks, and on the other hand, one should conclude an incentive agreement with the first type, obliging it to take greater care. Any contractor, when asked what type it is, would naturally count itself among the "good" ones, but this may not reflect the truth.

For the most part, one examines contractual partners very carefully in this situation in order to find evidence that this statement is true. Unfortunately, this cannot always be determined beyond doubt. The ability to take special care is a so-called hidden characteristic, a characteristic of a contractual partner that is key to the contractual relationship but is only known to the contractual partner itself.

Designing the tender correctly can be a means of getting around the information problem associated with this. It must be designed in such a way that the parties reveal themselves through their behavior. The design of a tender thus serves a dual function: It not only informs potential contractual partners about the project and their possible involvement, but also makes it clear to the tendering party what types of contractual partners are available.

Selection of Contractors in Repeated Transactions

In the following, we want to examine the extent to which the choice of partners changes if we are dealing with repeated transactions within the financing of a project. This, for example, is the case during the operational phase, if there are repeated exchange relations between the project company and the other project participants.

Suppose a project company has a choice of two maintenance service providers. In the case of the first contractor (WHITEWATER), the costs can be fairly accurately predicted at kUSD 500 per year. With the other contractor (SCARAMANGA) they are less predictable and may come to only kUSD 250 or may be up to kUSD 750 per year. If both scenarios occur with equal probability, the expected result with SCARAMANGA is also kUSD 500. Which of the two maintenance companies should now be contracted? Even if it goes against one's intuition, the riskier partner is the one that should be brought in: Let us assume that the project is to last for a period of 20 years and it takes one year to determine whether SCARAMANGA will result in costs of kUSD 250 or kUSD 750.

If WHITEWATER is contracted, costs of USD 10 m will be incurred over 20 years. Alternatively, SCARAMANGA could be contracted as the maintenance company. With a probability of 50%, the annual costs will be kUSD 250, resulting in the project having to bear costs of only USD 5 m for 20 years. With the same probability, annual costs in the amount of kUSD 750 may also be incurred, but only for one year, after which the contract is terminated and a contract with WHITEWATER is concluded for the remaining 19 years.

The expected costs for SCARAMANGA are much lower than those for WHITEWATER. It costs USD 10 m, but deciding for SCARAMANGA in the beginning costs:

$$0.5 * (20 * kUSD\ 250) + 0.5 * (1 * kUSD\ 750 + 19 * kUSD\ 500) = kUSD\, 7,625$$

Although the expected costs for the first year are identical for both companies, SCARAMANGA is much more promising. Because the project company can retain it if it developed well and dismiss it if it is not up to the task, the long-term value of SCARAMANGA, the riskier business, is greater. Since the project company can break with "bad" companies, it is worth giving riskier companies a chance.

Conclusive Analysis of Rational Choice in the Contracting Game

If two companies show the same expected value and generate the same costs, it is worth contracting the riskier one. Poor results can be mitigated by dismissal and good results can be reinforced by continued engagement for the entire duration of the project. The value of this "gamble" is often so large that it can also be the better strategy even if the safe company offers lower costs per year.

SCARAMANGA should be chosen over WHITEWATER because the cost of a bad year is overcompensated for by the chance of many good years. Accordingly, the value of a risky candidate decreases for a shorter project term: If the period remaining is insufficient to balance out the risks over time, the value of assuming such risks decreases. The longer the project term, the higher the value of the option. This is why considering the value of risky candidates is particularly relevant if this is done during an early phase of the project and the project duration is long.

The option of letting bad companies go is so valuable for the project company that – for as long as it exists – it is very unlikely for the safe candidate to be the more attractive.

Furthermore: The less time is required to determine the productivity of the contracted company, the more valuable the risky company becomes: If it takes 19 out of 20 years to determine the productivity of SCARAMANGA, its value decreases significantly. In this case, the project company would have to keep it on for 19 years in order to determine its productivity. Because the productivity is not clear beforehand, if it was a good idea to contract it, it would also be a good idea to retain it until the information becomes available. However, it is not a good idea to contract SCARAMANGA under these conditions nor keep it.

With the assumed values, the expected value of the costs over the lifetime of the project would be for SCARAMANGA:

$$0.5 * [(19 * kUSD\,750) + (1 * kUSD\,500)] + 0.5 * [20 * (kUSD\,250)] = kUSD\,9,875$$

Because it is contracted for 19 years, during which it will result in annual costs of kUSD 750, SCARAMANGA is potentially a very expensive candidate. The value of the option to contract and to then terminate quickly if it leads to losses is low, because it can only be terminated after it has already resulted in significant costs.

Table 6.12: Example for choice between Whitewater and Scaramanga (own representation).

	Whitewater	**Scaramanga**		
Cost	**500 kUSD/year**	250 kUSD/year	or	750 kUSD/year
Probability	50%	50%	or	50%
Cost for 20 years	500 KUSD * 20 = 10 MUSD	250 kUSD * 20 = 5 MUSD		**500 kUSD * 19 years+750 kUSD * 1 year = 10.25 MUSD**

Remuneration Strategies in Repeated Transactions

In Figure 6.6 below, the line marked as A describes a remuneration system that starts at 0 and provides USD 2,000 per performance unit (input-based pay). A contractor who provides 50 performance units in one month earns monthly remuneration of kUSD 100. The line marked as B represents a system whereby a monthly fixed remuneration of kUSD 100 is provided (output-based pay). A contractor with a performance output of 40 power units also receives kUSD 100, as does the one who provides 80 output units.

Which system is more advantageous for a project company? This depends on what type of contractor is available. First, we assume two project companies who offer the two remuneration systems above. The project company DINGUS earns revenue from all contractors who provide more than 50 performance units. Because a contractor who produces 100 performance units for example, only costs you kUSD 100, which corresponds to a unit cost of USD 1,000. The same contractor would cost project company MALLARD kUSD 200, which corresponds to a unit cost of USD 2,000.

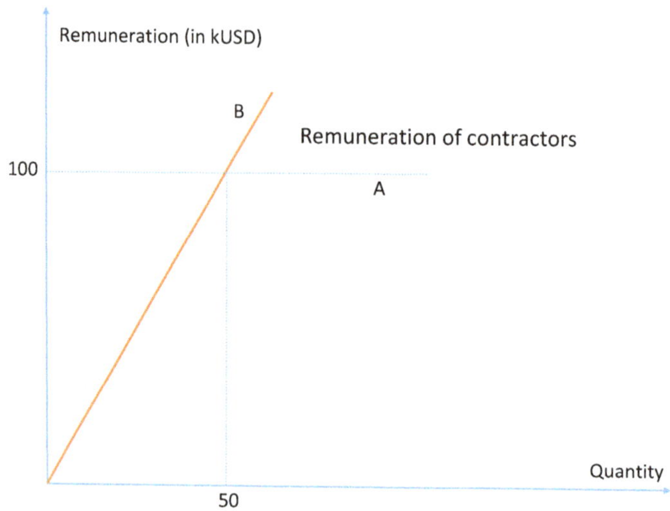

Figure 6.6: Remuneration of contractors (own representation).

However, this is a purely static analysis. In actual fact, the contractors who provide more than 50 performance units will not stay with DINGUS but will instead change to MALLARD, where they earn more money. Thus, DINGUS will just retain the contractors who can only provide 50 performance units or less. Which of the remuneration systems is better for the project companies? Clearly, it is MALLARD. With DINGUS, the best contractor generates 50 performance units per month, the worst not even one, so the average is less than 50 performance units. If this averages 40 performance units, at a total cost of kUSD 100, this results in an average unit cost of USD 2,500 per performance unit. All of the most high-performing contractors go to MALLARD and produce more than 50 power units per month there, e.g., 75 power units. However, the quantity realized does not affect the unit cost at MALLARD, which is set at USD 1,000. To Mallard, it is irrelevant whether a contractor provides an output of 80 performance units or five contractors provide an output of 16 performance units each. The total remuneration cost, in both cases of kUSD 80, corresponds to an average unit cost of USD 1,000. MALLARD's average remuneration for the service provided of USD 2,000 is considerably less than that of DINGUS at USD 2,500, because the contractors with low productivity rates are systematically oriented towards DINGUS.

This is a major reason for giving preference to a result-dependent remuneration system: It moves the more productive contractors to cooperate with the project company and leaves the less productive contractors to competitors who offer fixed remuneration. Therefore, variable remuneration helps to limit the adverse selection risk. The second reason to use result-dependent remuneration systems relates to their incentive effect.

6.2.4 Risk Quantification and Financial Engineering

After the different sources of risks for a project have been identified, the risks are quantified and assessed. By deriving various scenarios in which the individual risk parameters vary, the capital providers verify whether the project cash flows will still be enough even under a stress scenario to service the debt to the creditors and provide the investors with a reasonable return. The banks providing the debt capital are generally more risk averse than the sponsors of the project. The other project participants (such as plant builders, operators, suppliers and customers) will also have to be involved in the further course of the project through contractual assurances and must therefore assess for themselves during the development phase of the project what opportunities and risks are associated with their commitment.

The quantification of risk for all those involved in the project thus aims to determine the viability and capacity of the project and, through the appropriate allocation of risks and opportunities, to develop a project structure that sustainably ensures the success of the project. In the further course of the project, the influence of the risks on the actual cash flow is also monitored based on key performance indicators in order to be able to introduce adaptation measures in time if certain predefined threshold values are exceeded or fallen below.

The source for the payment of debt service and distributions is the generated cash flow of the project. The amount and chronological distribution of these cash flows are subject to uncertainty and therefore cannot be calculated precisely in advance. The capital providers must therefore identify all factors that could influence the project and estimate the effects that variations in individual factors and combinations of these can have on the amount and distribution of future cash flows. Risk quantification is also carried out continuously during the lifetime of the project (see Figure 6.7).

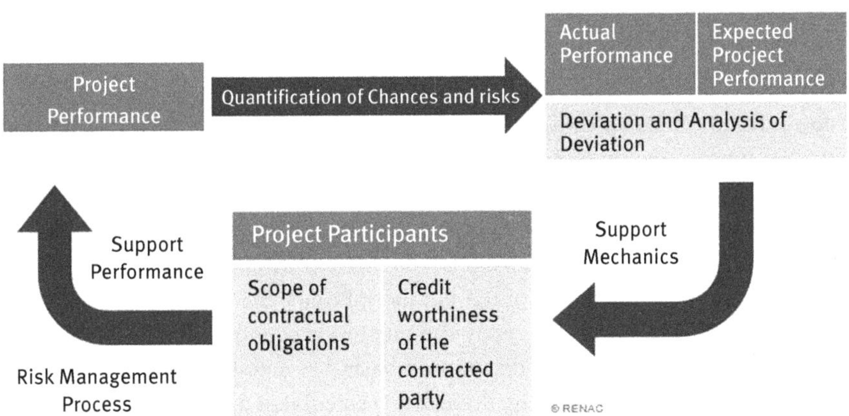

Figure 6.7: Risk quantification and management process (own representation).

Financial Engineering

Designing a project's financing requires careful financial engineering to adjust the payment of interest and loan redemption to the individual Cashflow stream. Lenders test the sustainability of project cashflows using specific financial ratios and apply them in order to determine a project's maximum borrowing capacity.

The **Debt Service Cover Ratio** is a financial ratio that indicates to which extent CFADS exceeds the scheduled debt service in a given period. Target values for DSCRs depend on the bank's risk appetite and higher for riskier or more volatile projects (DSCR > 1.5) and lower for less risky projects (e.g., DSCR > 1.15). DSCR values need to be higher than 1.00 in a Base Case scenario to be bankable (see Figure 6.8). DSCR is defined as follows:

$$\text{DSCR} = \text{CFADS}_t / \text{Debt Service}_t$$

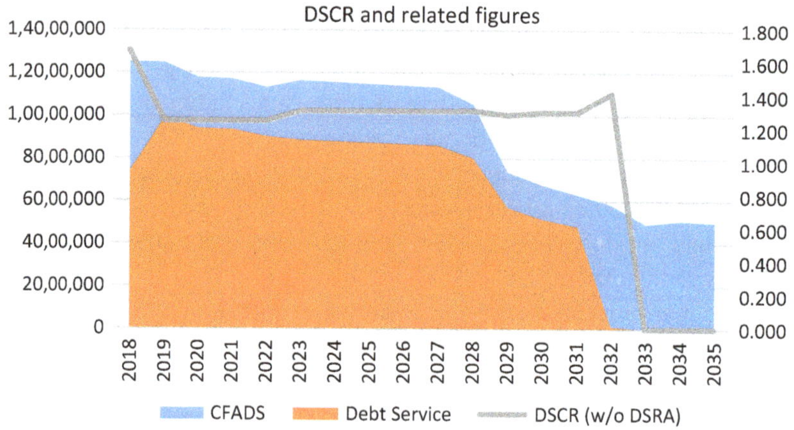

Figure 6.8: DSCR and related figures (own representation).

The **Loan Life Cover Ratio (LLCR)** and the project life cover ratio (PLCR) both take an aggregate view of the project, spreading the present value (PV) of all CFADS and relating it to the outstanding debt. The present value is the nominal value of the future cash flows discounted at the debt interest rate. The PLCR demonstrates additional potential to stretch loan tenures if a loan restructuring is needed.

The LLCR provides a measure of the number of times the project cash flow over the scheduled life of the loan can repay the outstanding debt balance: An LLCR of 1.00 means that the CFADS, on a discounted basis,[3] is equal to the amount of the outstanding debt balance. Generally, the LLCR is calculated as:

3 The discount rate used in the NPV-calculation is usually the cost of debt.

Table 6.13: DSCR, CFADS and debt service (own representation).

	2018	2019	2020	2021	2022	2023	2024
CFADS	12.513.249	12.472.137	11.784.679	11.725.352	11.321.465	11.640.220	11.567.540
Debt Service	7.416.014	9.952.166	9.401.542	9.353.407	9.029.606	8.858.685	8.802.512
DSCR (w/o DSRA)	1,675	1,253	1,253	1,254	1,254	1,314	1,314

$$\text{LLCR} = \text{NPV [CFADS over Loan Life] / Debt Balance}$$[4]

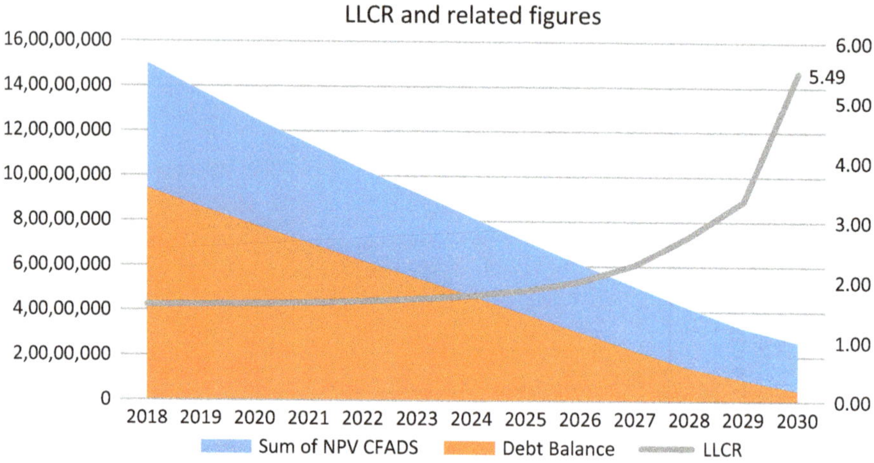

Figure 6.9: LLCR and related figures (own representation).

The LLCR does not pick up weak periods as it essentially represents a discounted average. Comparable to DSCR, the LLCR does not exist during the construction phase. Different from the DSCR, the LLCR at the start of operation is the most meaningful figure (see Figure 6.9). Having said this, the LLCR may become important once a restructuring scenario becomes imminent.

Debt Service Reserve Account

The Debt Service Reserve Account protects a lender against an unexpected drop in CFADS, so that the debt service can be provided although the operational cash flow falls short of covering debt service. These funds are usually established at the end of the construction period or within the first months of operation.

The DSRA releases to bridge a shortfall between the CFADS and debt service. It accumulates and releases according to a predefined target profile and empties out in conjunction with the final repayment of the debt facility. The DSRA is usually dimensioned to be six months of principal and interest payments.

Table 6.15 shows the principle.

---

4 Sometimes you may find variations in LLCR definition: It is not uncommon to find the balance of the debt service reserve account added to the numerator or deducted from the numerator. Caution needs to be applied when assessing the economics of a project where the LLCR is supported with such cash account balances.

Table 6.14: LLCR, NPV of CFADS, debt balance (own representation).

	2018	2019	2020	2021	2022	2023	2024
Sum of NPV CFADS	150.189.063	137.675.814	125.418.185	114.035.390	102.904.686	92.342.229	81.669.165
Debt Balance	94.326.871	85.995.539	78.070.803	70.055.123	62.223.773	54.428.265	46.552.159
LLCR	1,59	1,60	1,61	1,63	1,65	1,70	1,75

Table 6.15: DSRA development (own representation).

	2018	2019	2020	2021	2022	2023	2024
Debt Service	7.416.014	9.952.166	9.401.542	9.353.407	9.029.606	8.858.685	8.802.512
DSRA	4.976.083	4.700.771	4.676.703	4.514.803	4.429.343	4.401.256	4.372.467
DSCR w/o DSRA	1,675	1,253	1,253	1,254	1,254	1,314	1,314
DSCR w/ DSRA	1,675	1,694	1,739	1,752	1,745	1,814	1,812

The Figure 6.10 shows the development of Debt Service and target value of the DSRA as well as the DSCR-values with and without calculation of DSRA. Given the decreasing debt service in this example, the target value of the DSRA also decreases and the difference becomes part of the Free Cashflow. In our example, the DSRA covers six months of the debt service of the following year.

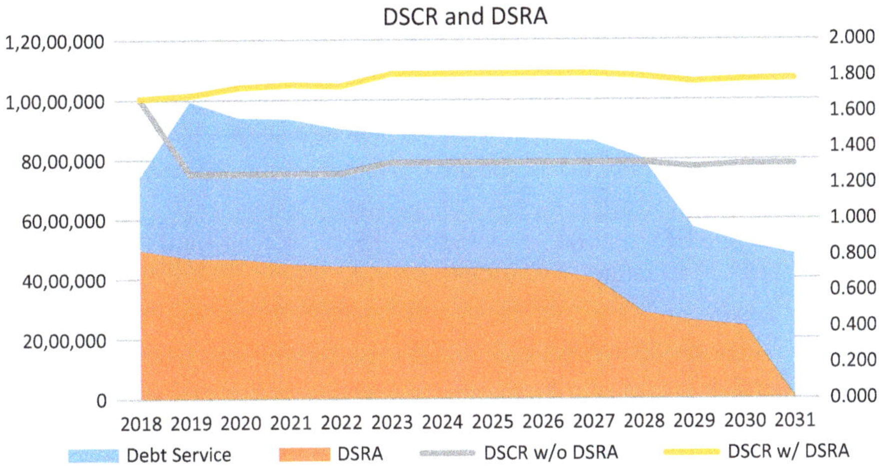

Figure 6.10: DSCR and DSRA implementation (own representation).

Funding of the DSRA is considered part of overall cost of the project. While DSRAs are not funded as part of the initial project costs, they are built up as a priority out of the CFADS in the early operational years. As a third option, lenders may be willing to provide a debt service reserve facility as substitute for a DSRA.

6.2.5 Optimization of a Financial Structure

Leverage Effect and Net Present Value

Two effects are crucial for the optimization of a financial structure within project financing, namely the leverage effect and the concept of net present value.

The **Leverage Effect** describes the effect that the use of debt will increase the profitability of the equity portion, as long as the project's profitability is higher than the debt's interest rate. However, the leverage effect also works the other way round: Losses are also multiplied, and there is a risk that leveraging will result in a loss if the project's profitability falls below the debt's interest rate. Therefore, a lender will limit his credit exposure. So, the leverage effect says something about the credit amount which can be allocated to a project.

The second principle is the concept of **Net Present Value** (NPV): The NPV is the sum of the present value of the project's present and future cashflows. It accounts for the time value of money. The decrease of the current value of future cashflows is based on a chosen rate of return. In the following Table 6.16 we have inserted an example calculation:

The initial equity contribution of 10,000 in t_0 results in increasing dividends in the following eight years. The NPV of all discounted payments is considerably higher than the initial investment, so the NPV of T€ 5,121 gives an advice to invest into this project.

The same cash flow-stream has been used to calculate the Internal Rate of Return (IRR) of the investment – this is the discount rate which produces an NPV of zero. Although this approach has some disadvantages, the IRR-approach is still quite popular.

In general, the NPV-concept as well as the IRR-calculation emphasize the time value of money and therefore an investor is interested in early distributions.

Example: Cash Flow Characteristics for a Wind Farm Project

The central importance of cash flow stability shall be illustrated in the example of project financing in the wind power sector. The example is intended to illustrate that 1. the predictability of the cash flow creates a considerable economic value, 2. what consequences arise when the cash flow is no longer predictable and 3. what conclusions can be drawn for the structure of a regulatory system.

The generation of electricity using wind energy is often supported by the state through industry regulation in many countries. For the most part, this includes a price or quantity regulation. The Table 6.18 shows a sample forecast calculation for a German wind power project.

The Debt Service Coverage Ratio (DSCR) is a key figure from the bank's perspective – it is the ratio of cash flow to debt service, meaning the sum of interest and repayment. If the cash flow is greater than the debt service, the credit commitments can be met in full. In order for this to be sufficiently ensured, the banks regularly demand a DSCR which must be more or less significantly above 1.0. The extent to which the value is above 1.0 significantly depends on the regulatory system and the volatility of the cash flows for this asset class.

The Internal Rate of Return (IRR) is a central assessment figure for investors and, from an economic perspective, represents the growth rate of equity. If the IRR exceeds a certain value specified by the investor, he will invest. The concept of the present value also takes the perspective of the investor: Here, all deposits and withdrawals from a project are subject to a defined discounting interest rate. If this results in a positive capital value, the investment is advantageous.

One can see that the sponsor of this project can expect an Internal Rate of Return of 9.84%, while the lender can realize cover rates of at least 1.18. From the sponsors'

Table 6.16: Example of NPV calculation (own representation).

	1	2	3	4	5	6	7	8
Dividend	1,000	1,500	2,300	2,500	2,600	2,700	2,800	3,000
NPV of Dividend	961.54	1386.83	2044.69	2137.01	2137.01	2133.85	2127.77	2192.07
Discount rate	4.00%							
Initial Equity Contribution in t_0	−10,000							
NPV of Equity	5120.78							

Table 6.17: Example of IRR calculation (own representation).

	1	2	3	4	5	6	7	8
Dividend	1,000	1,500	2,300	2,500	2,600	2,700	2,800	3,000
NPV of Dividend	880.83	1163.80	1571.84	1504.92	1378.60	1261.02	1151.89	1087.09
Discount rate	13.53%							
Initial Equity Contribution in t_0	−10,000							
NPV of Equity	0.00							

perspective, the rate of return on the capital employed is therefore sufficient to invest, and from the debt capital provider's perspective, it can be assumed that the cover rate is acceptable as a sufficient safety buffer for deviations from the plan. Both capital providers thus agree that the realization of the project is worthwhile from their respective risk perspectives and will invest.

Table 6.18: Sample base case scenario for a German wind farm (own representation).

	2018	**2021**	**2024**	**2027**	**2030**	**2033**
Tariff (€c/kWh):	8.96	8.96	8.96	8.96	8.96	8.96
Energy Production (in MWh):	15,393	15,393	15,393	15,393	15,393	15,393
Income in k€	1,380	1,380	1,380	1,380	1,380	1380
OPEX in k€ p.a.	227	243	324	348	421	479
CFADS in k€:	1,153	1,137	1,056	1,032	959	901
Debt Service in k€:	394	960	859	758	397	0
DSCR	**2.93**	**1.18**	**1.23**	**1.36**	**2.42**	**0,00**
IRR	9.84%					
Net Present Value (with i = 6%)	2,643					

Alternative Project Scenario

How does the picture change, if we assume that there is no fixed price system during the term of the project, but instead a coupling of the fees to the electricity price for the end consumer (see Table 6.19)? Both groups of capital providers may fear that the electricity prices will fall in the context of a possible deregulation of the electricity markets by 7.2% per year.

Now the project does not appear to be acceptable either from the investors' perspective or from the debt capital providers' perspective: On the one hand, the declining compensation means that the investment no longer meets the necessary minimum rate of return of the sponsor. On the other hand, the lender also realizes that the debt service – at least from 2023 to 2026 – is no longer covered by the project's cash flow, so that even in the base case, it would be necessary to restructure the commitment. As a result, it is clear at this point that:

1. The stability of the cash flow, both from the sponsors' perspective and the lenders' perspective, is of critical importance, even though both capital providers are affected to different extents due to the asymmetrically distributed opportunities and risks.

2. Clearly, changes in the price system would appear to have a particularly strong impact on the chances of realizing projects. This is due to the fact that project financing is typically very long-term financing, where the tenor of the loans can be 18 years and more. Further, this usually concerns capital-intensive investments, whose risk structure is influenced to a large extent by the price component. This also applies for renewable energy projects, which are characterized by high specific acquisition costs, while the operating costs are usually of less importance (with the exception of biomass projects, though).
3. Targeted changes to the price system also have significant effects on the respective industry: If the capital providers expect the regulatory system to change in the near future, they are more likely to refrain from making investments. This applies in particular if it is not clear whether and to what extent provisions are in place to safeguard existing standards for plants in operation and what any possible transition periods to the new payment system will look like.

Table 6.19: Alternative scenario of the project using decreasing electricity prices (own representation).

	2018	**2021**	**2024**	**2027**	**2030**	**2033**
Tariff (€ Cent/kWh):	8.75	8.12	7.54	7.00	6.50	6.04
Energy Production (in MWh):	15,393	15,393	15,393	15,393	15,393	15,393
Income in k€	1,346	1,250	1,161	1,078	1,001	930
OPEX in k€ p.a.	227	243	324	348	421	479
CFADS in k€:	1,122	1,017	851	743	592	408
Debt Service in k€:	394	960	859	758	397	0
DSCR	**2.85**	**1.06**	**0.99**	**0.98**	**1.49**	**0.00**
IRR	1.61%					
Net Present Value (with i = 6 %)	−2.189					

Optimization of a Financial Structure

Investors and lenders have a uniform interest in a stable project – with the slight, but important difference that the investor strives to increase the economic value of the project, whereas the lender tries to mitigate the risks stemming from the project. This is due to their slight different incentive basis: The investor tries to achieve as much distributions as early as possible, whereas the bank is interested in a swift repayment. This means that the financial structure will always be a compromise between lenders and investors. We will show some examples how a financial structure can be optimized. Therefore, we will analyze variations in IRR and in DSCR.

Change in Maturity

In the following calculation the tenor of the loan is prolonged by two years (Figure 6.11).

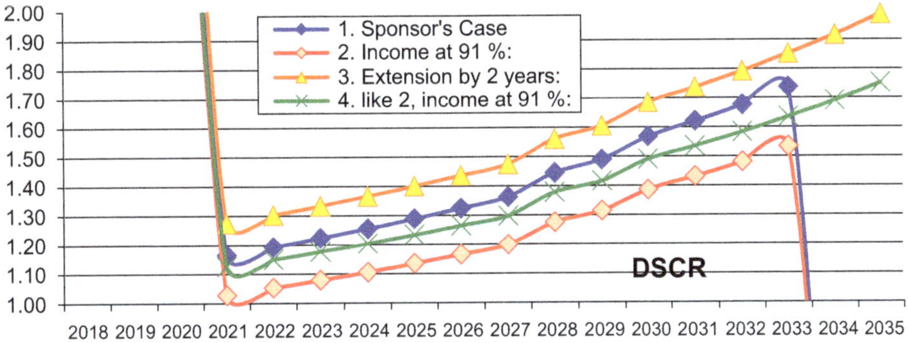

Figure 6.11: Variation of loan maturity (own representation).

Table 6.20: Variation of loan maturity – IRR- and DSCR-implications (own representation).

	Min. DSCR	ø DSCR	IRR
1. Sponsor's Case	1,17	1,76	10,05%
2. Income at 91%:	1,03	1,55	6,42%
3. OPEX plus 9%:	1,14	1,72	9,26%
4. Combination (2+3):	1,00	1,51	5,60%

A longer tenor will lead to higher IRR and to higher DSCR. However, the lender will be reluctant to extend the tenor of the loan over a certain period of time: The main reason is that the economic life of the technology is limited and the maximum tenor of the remuneration regime will set another limit. Usually, lenders expect some buffer.

Grace period

In Figure 6.12 the grace period is amended to one year.

In this new structure, funds are reallocated to repay the loan earlier: this leads to a decrease of IRR and an increase of DSCR-level.

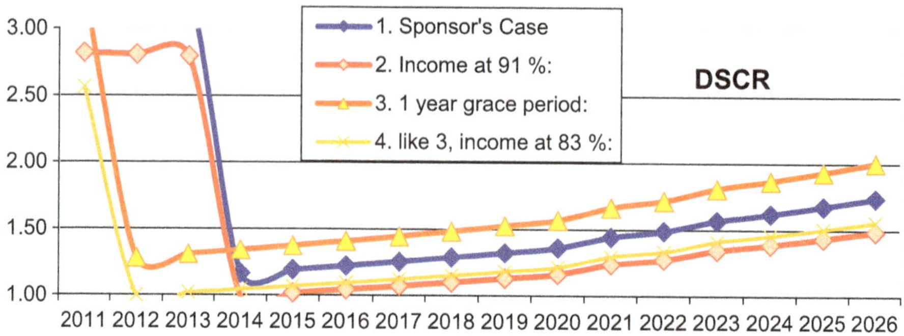

Figure 6.12: DSCR amid a change of the grace period (own representation).

Table 6.21: DSCR and IRR – change in grace period (own representation).

	Min. DSCR	DSCR	IRR
1. Sponsor's Case	1.17	1.76	10.05%
3. 1 year grace period:	1.28	1.69	9.40%

Debt Service Reserve Account

The Debt Service Account (DSRA) is a deposit which is equal to a certain percentage of forthcoming debt service obligations. It works as an additional security measure for lenders when the operational Cashflow is no longer sufficient to cover debt service obligations. The typical target value of DSRA is at 50% of the debt service for the next 12 months.

In the following Figure 6.13 a 6-month DSRA has been implemented:

The implementation of the DSRA will lead to a higher DSCR and a lower IRR. Typically, lenders will almost always require the implementation of an DSRA and borrowers are willing to accept this credit enhancement. This is due to the fact that the financial structure of the project can be stabilized considerably without injecting further equity.

Performance-linked contracts

If operating contracts are income-linked, they offer a buffer, if performance is lower than expected. This characteristic is helpful for the debt sizing, which assess a project under a stress-scenario. The willingness of the contractors to allow performance-linked contracts is quite different according to the asset class and the current competition conditions. In the wind energy market a number of contracts is often performance-linked – sometimes combined with floor payments – whereas such contracts are almost unknown in the photovoltaic project market.

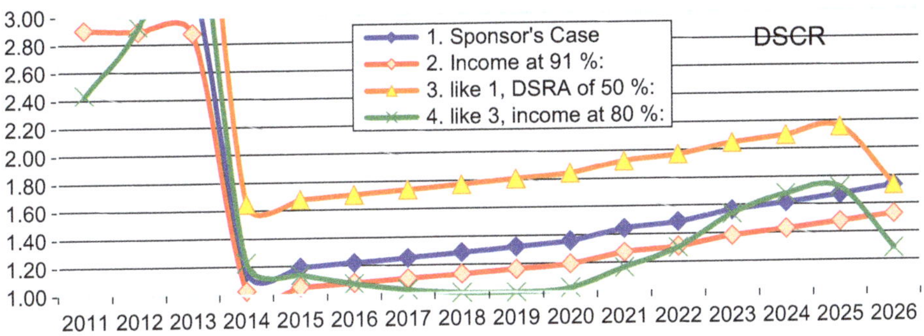

Figure 6.13: DSCR and implementation of DSRA (own representation).

Table 6.22: DSCR and IRR – implementation of a DSRA (own representation).

	Min. DSCR	DSCR	IRR
1. Sponsors Case	1.17	1.76	10.05%
2. Einnahmen bei 91%:	1.03	1.55	6.42%
3. wie 1, SDR von 6 Monaten:	1.65	2.24	9.35%
4. wie 3, Einnahmen bei 80%:	1.00	1.59	1.78%

We have assumed in Figure 6.14 that the O&M-costs are performance-linked.

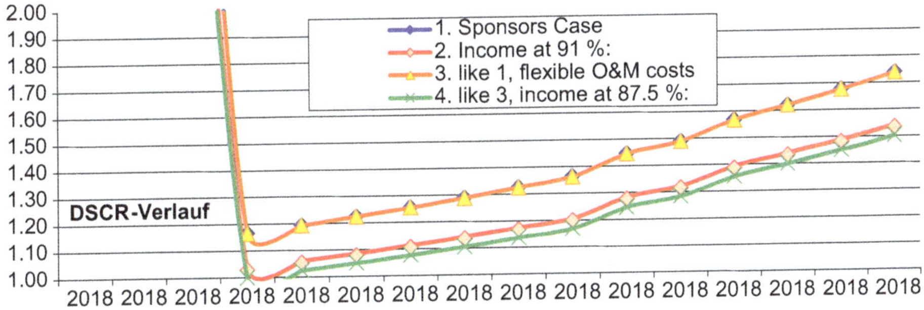

Figure 6.14: Flexibilization of the O&M costs (own representation).

In a comparison of the different base case scenarios, no difference occurs. Only in a downside scenario, IRR and DSCR-levels increase in comparison to a fixed O&M contract. Since this means that part of the risk is transferred to the O&M contractor, he will seek for an adequate compensation like a higher price for the

Table 6.23: DSCR and IRR – effect of flexibilization of O&M costs (own representation).

	Min. DSCR	DSCR	IRR
1. Sponsors Case	1.17	1.76	10.05%
2. Income at 91%:	1.03	1.55	6.42%
3. like 1, flexible O&M costs	1.17	1.76	10.05%
4. like 3, income at 87.5%:	1.00	1.51	5.73%

O&M contract. So, it remains a calculation example which contract structure is preferred.

There are further ways available to optimize the project's financial structure, but the basic principles remain the same.[5] However, one has to keep in mind that an optimization negatively affects the chances for a restructuring.

6.2.6 Project Financing in a Crisis

Project financing is a common method of financing when it comes to realizing large-scale projects that promise a predictable cash flow. Thus, mobile networks, wind farms or privately-operated road projects have, for example, been successfully implemented using this method. However, experience also shows that reality often differs from what was planned and that projects can fall into financial difficulties. What the adjustment measures may look like differs in parts from the procedure used for corporate finance.

An imbalance in a project could look like in Figure 6.15: by the year 2022, the CFADS is sufficient to cover the debt service up to the year 2028. Correspondingly, talks are to be held between investor and bank to resolve measures that compensate for the deficit. Possible measures are just as diverse as the possible causes of the crises.

The following aspects are key in any case:

- Two questions are crucial regarding the options for taking action in the event of a crisis: Has the project reached completion or not? The project is only in a position to generate its own cash flow upon completion, so that the risk position of all parties involved is improved. And the second question: Is the project already insolvent or not? With the opening of insolvency proceedings, the liquidator comes in as a new player, whose objectives may differ from those of the individual stakeholders.

5 If you require further assistance or training on optimization aspects, please do not hesitate to contact me (joergboettcher@gmx.de).

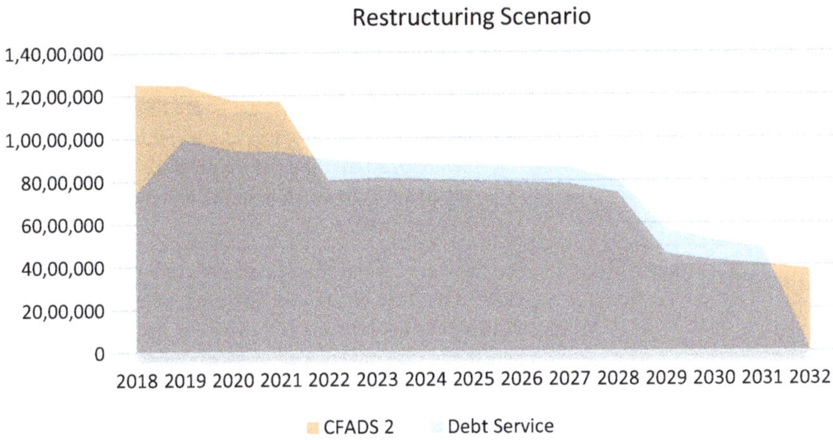

Figure 6.15: Presentation of a cash flow scenario that requires restructuring (own representation).

- It is also of central importance that all stakeholders at contract and relationship level are involved in the project. Errors and deficiencies in internal and external project management cannot be afforded, particularly when matters have become tight in economic terms. And conflicts at the relationship level often make restructuring project financing much more difficult.

Legal and Economic Restructuring Options

Table 6.24: Special aspects of project financing in restructuring (own representation).

Options for project financing are more restricted than for companies:	1.	In the case of project financings, there is often no option to broaden or narrow the business field
	2.	The viability of a project financing is based on long-term contractual relations, which cannot be continued in the case of liquidation.
Distinction between the completion phase and the operational phase:	1.	**Completion Phase:** If a financing gap exists, but the company continues to be viable (after successful completion), supplementary financing should be successful. Both credit providers have an incentive to reach completion, so that both groups often furnish contributions. There is often no economical alternative to subsequent financing: Only the finished project generates cash flow. Therefore, "rescue at any price" is indicated during this phase. All financing parameters are based on the completed project.

Table 6.24 (continued)

	2. **Operating Phase**: The completion risk no longer exists. The returns forecast at the time of the crisis have stabilized (however, at a lower level than planned), so that the risks have become more calculable (how much liquidity is required to cover debt service?).
Number of project participants	The number of project participants are often significantly lower in the case of a project financing, so that the chances of an agreement increase (but there are also exceptions here in the case of very high levels of project financing, financed by a comprehensive banking consortium).
Favorable contractual arrangements for project financing:	The following aspects should already be regulated by financial close: 1. Dividend lock-up to strengthen liquidity in the case of significant negative deviations from the plan concept 2. Reserve accounts (maintenance costs reserve, debt service reserve) or reserve facilities to service the debt (often 50% of the debt service for the following year) 3. Crisis-related termination situations ("events of default"), which in fact allow the lenders to force the initiation of restructuring negotiations 4. Investment cost reserves ("headrooms," "contingencies") to avoid insolvency in the case of construction cost overruns or time overruns prior to completion 5. The repayment of debt capital usually ends several years before the project ends ("tail"); the tail is rarely more than 10% of the duration of the project.

Table 6.25: Structural topics in the restructuring of project financing transactions (own representation).

Ring-fencing	Project financing acts as a separate legal entity and centralises all of the rights and obligations essential to the project.
Project-related financing and collateral structure	The investor tends to want to maximize the Internal Rate of Return, the bank tends towards secure and quick repayment and interest on its loans. Thus, both groups of credit providers are in competition for access to the cash flow available for debt service (CFADS). Nevertheless, a restructuring scenario should not be entirely neglected when defining the initial financing.

Table 6.25 (continued)

Non-recourse financing	There is no obligation on the part of the owners (sponsors) to contribute further resources beyond the equity capital originally agreed or to accept liability for the loans to the project company.
A long term and the importance of correct forecasts	Project financing often runs for terms in excess of 18 years. Because of this, the debt service must be based on the expected cash flow and its volatility.
Additional financial products (e.g., hedging)	Hedging products are often indispensable to mitigate risks, but can lead to significant negative market values, which have also to be taken into account as liabilities in the restructuring.
Management qualification	The question is whether and to what extent the use of interim management is purposeful or necessary in order to bridge a bottleneck.

Table 6.26: Overview of legal actions in transaction restructurings (own representation).

Standstill Agreement	Foregoing the assertion of claims to receivables due for payment and crisis-related grounds for termination (borrower's perspective: The obligation to apply lapses due to insolvency, bank's perspective: by suspending the claim, it does not run any risk of liability (no delay in filing for insolvency)). A **standstill agreement** is only useful in the event of a crisis during the **operational phase** (in the construction phase, a comprehensive solution is required, which also allows for further drawdowns), as time is gained for a start.
Bridging loans (rare in the case of PF)	**Covering the current liquidity needs**. These are only granted if the borrower has commissioned an expert opinion from an independent expert on the restructuring concept
(Temporary) deferral agreements	Subject: **Extension of the repayment profile**. Provides the debtor with greater security in comparison to a standstill. A temporary deferral agreement is seen like a bridging loan, so that here too an expert opinion must confirm the capacity of the restructuring concept. The regulation is often supplemented by an ongoing special repayment (**"cash sweep"**) obligation from the free liquidity.

Table 6.26 (continued)

Subordination	If the existing debt exceeds the equity portion, the bank still has the option if agreeing to the subordination of part of their claims in the insolvency proceedings in order to prevent over-indebtedness. The debt service on the subordinated tranche is left out of consideration for the restructuring forecast. Advantages: 1. In the case of the positive development of cash flows, the creditor can realize its claim in the full amount. 2. In the case of the project financing, the occurrence of an extraordinary income is prevented, which would be taxable. **Practical implementation:** The existing project financing is separated into two tranches, of which the priority tranche reflects the project's debt service capacity in the crisis. The subordinated tranche is repaid through ongoing mandatory unscheduled repayments.
Restructuring loans (rather the exception in the case of project financings)	**In the construction phase:** This scenario tends to be rather unlikely thanks to reserves and fixed price agreements; **in the operational phase:** Improvement of the earning situation through additional investments is not provided for in the case of a PC but there are exceptions (sponsor withdraws; technology must be changed or upgraded). An expert opinion is also required.
Debt-to-equity swap	Acceptance of the equity interest in the PG by the banks can only be an option if the previous shareholder becomes insolvent or has proven to be professionally unsuitable.
Company sale and silent liquidation/ enforcement of collateral	If the company still has a value as an organization, without restructuring appearing realistic, only the sale of the company and final liquidation remain. The enforcement of collateral is no longer used for crisis management. Instead, its aim is to satisfy the claims of the creditors against the project company for repayment of the loans. As a restructuring is no longer the aim, **there is no need to obtain a restructuring report.**
Insolvency plan procedure	This is the exception rather than the rule in project financing, however: In the case of insolvency, this variant is obvious, as the existing contractual relations are continued.

6.3 Summary

The main focus of this article was to find out the prerequisites for banks to finance projects in the field of renewable energies with the project financing model. In particular, it is important to note that the predictability of cash flows and the appropriate involvement of project participants in the project are the key success factors. Basically, the following critical decision-making factors apply to all project financings:
- Stability and reliability of the legal and regulatory environment,
- Appropriate chance-risk allocation for all project participants,
- Use of proven technology,
- Good Site quality (available resources).

Overall, countries with a stable political and legal environment are preferred in project finance. Planning uncertainties are poison for investments that are expected to be successful for a period of more up to 20 years. For most project financings, this also means that central points can appear as contrasting pairs:
1. **Operating contracts – fixed-price or market-oriented flexible?** The possibility to agree fixed prices in important contracts (such as the PPA) gives the impression of high planning security. However, if the relevant market develops in such a way that it becomes uneconomical for the contractual partner to fulfill the contract, the supposed planning security may have disappeared quickly. There is then the possibility that the contract partner fails and we must find replacement on the market – to more unfavorable conditions.
2. **Technology choice – proven or new?** It is a general financing principle that only proven technology should be the subject of project financing, otherwise the cash flow might be unstable. Although this principle is correct, it should not obscure the fact that, on the other hand, no outdated technology should be financed, which may not be competitive any more. This is particularly true if the project has to compete with others in a competitive environment.
3. **Which method of risk quantification: "try to forecast the future!" or "try to be prepared for the future!"?** In many cases, project finance is reduced to cash flow orientation, which also determines the structure of the chosen financing. The practice shows, however, that project financing often develops differently than planned, and that the project company can take advantage of possibilities that were not considered at the start of the project. Thinking in action alternatives – in "real options" – seems to be an essential complement to the traditional method of risk quantification in project financing.

There is no perfect blueprint for the design of a project financing, but it has to be examined specifically for each project which structural configurations are appropriate. It should also be made clear that the success of the project depends not only on the profitability of the project but, in particular, on the shared and implemented understanding of the project participants that the long-term project success depends on fair sharing of chances and risks within the scope of the possibilities of the parties involved. The method of project financing offers the necessary flexibility to implement these growth opportunities.

7 Bankability of Project Contracts: Requirements of the Lender

Daniel Marhewka

7.1 Introduction

Renewable energy projects need financing to be realized.

There are many aspects one needs to consider when realizing renewable energy projects. On the one hand the planning and realization of renewable energy projects has become more and more challenging over the past years. Permitting has become more complex and the requirements to be fulfilled related to those permits are increasingly burdensome and economically relevant. Land owners have become more sophisticated regarding the land lease agreements and more demanding regarding the amount of their financial expectations. Furthermore, while there used to be turnkey projects which were sold after they were planned, constructed and commissioned, the reality today is that renewable energy projects are sold very early, mostly before start of construction.

On the other hand the requirements of a lender need to be fulfilled for the project to receive financing.[1] But contrary to those other requirements of the realization of renewable energy projects which – as just described – have become more challenging over time, my experience is that the bankability of renewable energy projects is not more difficult than it was a couple of years ago. Even more I would dare to say that involved bank have become a lot more professional and experienced and thereby a lot more efficient in the financing of renewable energy projects. More competition on the banking marked for the promising and sustainable renewable energy sector has also led to the streamlining of the financing process of renewables projects. One caveat: New developments in the regulatory framework for renewable energy projects need to be reflected also in the bankability requirements for such projects. For instance, tender processes, the expiring of subsidy regimes and the need for power purchase agreements (“**PPAs**”) will be reflected by financial institutions and need to be dealt with. But apart from such new developments bankability criteria have remained the same. The purpose of this section is to provide an inventory and a guideline for such bankability requirements. My wish would be to set a standard on which all market participants may rely and thereby avoid surprises in the financing process. The market has to decide whether this wish is realistic. At the end of the day, there is nothing more dangerous for the realization of a renewables project if in the process of financing, long after all project

1 See Koh, *Infrastructure Financing*, 235ff., Distler & Sedlacek, Schulz, *Windenergie*, 727ff.

https://doi.org/10.1515/9783110607888-007

contracts are signed the lender requires changes to those contracts which a third party as a land owner refuses to fulfill or asks for a lot of money to do so.

The following paragraphs reflect my experience from more than ten years involvement in renewable energy projects, spending countless hours drafting and negotiating project contract, always bearing in mind what will be required to enable financing. I decided to take a practical approach to this topic based on more than 3,600 MW renewable energy projects in many European countries instead of a theoretical approach. So there might not be as many footnotes as you might expect. But, I assumed that the reader would be more interested in what is relevant in project contract in practice to make them bankable and to fulfill the lenders' requirements.

7.2 Defining Project Contracts

To determine the bankability of project contracts, we first need to define what are the contracts we are talking about in the context of renewable energy projects. Renewable energy projects are complex projects, most of them with various agreements which have to be negotiated and signed to realize such projects. Furthermore, there is not one type of the contractual frameworks that fit all renewable energy projects but the contractual set-up varies depending on the asset class of renewable energy project and the counterparties (see section 7.2.2). And finally, those projects have different phases during their life cycle starting with the development, continuing with construction and commissioning and finally the operation (see section 7.2.1). All of those stages need their contractual background.

7.2.1 Project Contracts during the Life Cycle of a Renewables Project

Development

Starting with the development of a project a project developer will concentrate on finding the right spot for the renewable energy project. While the geographical situation is key to geothermal projects because there are only certain areas of the world in which drilling is promising, for other projects subsidy regimes, political stability and reliability are important points as well.[2] Accessibility of the site, acceptance by neighbours and grid connection are other factors to consider. Once, the right place is identified the project developer will start securing the land. The agreements for securing the land are one essential part of the project contract (see also section 7.2.3).

2 See Goldner & Torwegge in section 5.

Construction

Once the land is secured, permits are applied for and granted, challenges of those permits have been dealt with and tenders have been applied for or won, engineering, procurement and construction (**"EPC"**) is the next focus. Now, it is essential which contractual set up is chosen or is available. In the solar world one counterparty will in most cases provide the whole package and given the burden of such a turnkey obligation in this asset class most of the time can be financially trusted to provide the full package. On the contrary, in the off shore world EPC contracts (from time to time including installation (**"EPCI"**)) are still the exception and only a few players will be trusted by financing banks or investors to have a balance sheet to provide sufficient comfort. In the offshore wind industry issues during constructions may easily turn an EPCI obligation into an insolvency scenario of the contractual counterparty.

The EPC agreements, combined or additionally the procurement contracts for solar modules or wind turbines, the remainder of the project such as the balance of plant works, including infrastructure, substations and others are part of the construction related project contracts of renewable energy projects (see also section 7.2.4). Furthermore, grid connection of the renewable energy project should be achieved at the end of the construction which is regularly dealt with in a grid connection contract (see also section 7.2.5).

Operation

At the end of the construction process there will be (hopefully) commissioning and take over of the renewable project. At such time normally the risk of the project passes to the project company and the operation period begins. The operation is the longest period of time in the life cycle and last generally 20 years plus. In hydro projects or geothermal projects it can even be a much longer expected operating period. The operation phase needs contracts to cover operation and maintenance (**"O&M"**). And again the contractual set-up for O&M predominantly depends on the asset class. While there is mostly one O&M contract for solar projects covering everything, in onshore wind projects there are at least a O&M contract with the turbine manufacturer or another provider for the turbines and a separate contract for the remainder of the project either with the EPC contractor or yet another party (see also section 7.2.7.). During the operation phase the renewable energy project will deliver energy which needs to be injected in the grid (see also section 7.2.5) or sold to a third party (see section 7.2.8) or a combination of both.

7.2.2 Multi-Contracting versus a Full Wrap Turnkey Concept

The risk profile of a renewable energy project is generally defined by two coordinates: The amount of contracts and the financial strength of the counterparties. The more contracts there are the more interfaces exist and therefore the risk is higher. However, in extensive offshore wind projects multi contracting is still state of the art. EPCI structures do exist, with some carve outs, but the amount of potential counterparties that can take the risk of a billion Euro plus project on their books and survive in case if something goes wrong is very limited and the risk premium they will ask to do so might not be acceptable for investors. In onshore wind projects you will most of the time see a turbine supply agreement (“**TSA**”) for the procurement and construction of the wind turbines, if possible including foundations and a separate balance of plant agreement (“**BoP**”)/EPC contract for the rest of the project. The separation of the turbines relates to the fact that the EPC contractors need to rely on the turbine manufacturers and this risk is generally too big for them to take. With solar projects the modules are easily available on the market, there is a worldwide overproduction anyhow, module prices are relatively low compared to the generators in other asset classes and so you do find full wrap turnkey EPC offerings including everything in the solar world. Of course, inclusion of risk always comes at a price. The counterparty taking such risk will ask to get paid for it. So experienced investors may decide to choose a higher risk profile with a multi contract structure to gain a higher percentage of IRR from the projects.

7.2.3 Securing the Land

There is nothing in renewable energy projects as different and therefore country specific as land agreements, depending on the country the renewable energy project is located in. Real estate law is special in each jurisdiction I used to work in. Whether there is a contractual right and a parallel right *in rem* registered in a land register as in Germany[3] or the contractual right itself being registered in the land register as in Sweden or an important role of notaries as in Italy and France controlling the real estate situation, every country and every jurisdiction has its real estate regime which has developed over several centuries and which needs to be complied with when entering into agreements to secure land for a renewable energy project.

Securing the land necessary for the renewable energy project is key for all parties involved, including the lender. The aim must be to secure the land for the whole project life time at a price which fits into the financial model and in a way which survives any insolvency or the enforcement of other creditors of the land lord. The most important provisions in land agreements are generally (i) the term, which has to cover the whole expected life time of the project and prolongation options and related

3 See also (for German projects) Bock in Herbes & Friegen, 137ff.; Reese & Schulz, Schulz, *Windenergie*, 423ff.

termination possibilities, (ii) provisions relating to the ownership of the installed assets and (iii) lease fees/payments.

Often the due diligence review of a renewable energy project identifies rights of third parties secured by rights to the land necessary for the renewable energy projects, for instance through liens. So in the cause of entering into the agreements and rights in rem to secure the land for the renewable energy project the parties need to make sure that there is no risk for the lender if the third party creditor enforces its right in the plot of land. This is normally done by agreements dealing with the ranking of existing encumbrances of the land compared to those established for the lender in the course of the financing of the renewable project.

7.2.4 Construction-Related Contracts

EPC(I)

The EPC is generally the framework for the whole construction process. Furthermore, most of the time the development tasks are owed according to the EPC contract if the developer and the EPC contractor are from the same group of companies. Sometimes, EPC contractors try to split development and other EPC services in two agreements. If this is done the reason behind it is mostly to shift risk to the investor and to the lender by creating an additional interface. So if a development issue leads to problems during the construction process the two counterparties at the other side can point at each other and claim the other contractor is responsible. The investor would have to prove who is responsible which is sometimes hard to do. Therefore, such an artificial split should not be accepted or it should be made clear in the agreements that the EPC contractor is responsible also for the development services if there is an interface issue or a problem of burden of proof on the side of the investor/lender.

Generally, the risk for a lender depends on when the lender provides financing. If there is construction financing, then there is a different involvement in the process than if the financing requires commissioning of the renewable energy project. In case of project financing each step needs to be transparent and include review mechanisms not only for the investor and later owner of the project but also for the lender. The bank will require a bank engineer to monitor partial take over processes which trigger payment steps to be (partially) paid by bank financing and the risk of retention of title must be dealt with if substantial payments are made. In case of a fund investor and a bank the interest regarding the passing over of title is most of the time aligned: For any payment made, the ownership of related services and goods must pass to the investor and therefore to the lender under the existing security assignments as part of the finance documentation (see also section 7.5.2). However, the risk for delivering the whole renewable energy project should remain with the EPC contractor, because until final take over it is the EPC contractor that controls the project in reality.

If the lender only steps in at commissioning and final take over under the EPC contract any process related provisions are less important but the warranties and guarantees provided by the EPC contractor must be transferable and available for and security assignment to the lender in both scenarios (see also section 7.5.4).

In onshore wind projects the construction and procurement of the wind turbines is most of the time done by the turbine manufacturer under the turbine supply agreement ("**TSA**").

Turbine Supply Agreement

The TSA provides for delivery and installation of wind turbines by the turbine manufacturer. With regard to the scope of the TSA it is important to identify whether the foundations for the wind turbines are delivered by the turbine manufacturer or not. The interface between the turbine and the foundation in terms of mechanical loads is a key aspect of the TSA which has to be provided by one counterparty or at least the risk should be borne by one counterparty.

In most projects the TSA is entered into between the EPC contractor and the turbine supplier and will be transferred in total to the project company at a certain point in time or is entered into by the project company and the turbine supplier directly. Sometimes, the EPC contractor will assume the responsibility for the turbines and their installation as well and will only assign the warranty rights, noise, shadow and power curve guarantees later on to the project company.

The transfer of the TSA from the EPC contractor to the project company or the assignment of the warranties and guarantees must be provided for in the TSA (see also section 7.5.4). Otherwise, the discussions with the turbine supplier about such assignment or transfer can become lengthy and complicated and will have to take place in a situation in which they are not welcome. Most of the time such transfer or assignment becomes relevant at or around commissioning of the wind farm and therefore a point in time in which often also the whole renewable energy project is sold and transferred to an investor. While the EPC and the investor try to finalize the sale of the wind farm, it is not the best time to open a discussion with the turbine supplier for the transfer of the TSA since there are normally many other topics to consider at this specific point in time.

Balance of Plant

BoP contracts are normally a feature of onshore wind projects. In small to medium sized onshore wind energy projects they are most of the time subcontracts to the EPC under which the EPC procures the infrastructure for the wind farm as roads, cables and substation. In larger projects it can be a separate contract or even replace the EPC in combination with the TSA completely. In the latter case, the provisions of the BoP often correspond to a classical EPC set up.

Offshore Specific Issues

As already mentioned, offshore wind projects show a very specific type of contract setup.[4] They used to be the prototype of a multi contracting contract setup with between two and seven project contracts in the average.[5] Although, in the meantime EPCI contracts are available for offshore wind they are still the exception. This has two reasons: First of all, as already mentioned, there are only a few providers in the market which are able to show a creditworthiness which makes it plausible that they can survive issues in a billion Euro construction process. Secondly, the risk premium that is asked for such an EPCI contract will have a substantial financial impact on the project and thereby the involved parties may decide to structure a multi contract project instead to save this premium for themselves.

Of course, the interface risk is substantial in multi contract offshore wind projects. However, after the first negative examples of offshore wind farms running out of budget and schedule, there are recent examples that show that the industry has learned from their mistakes and that they can deliver in time and in budget.

All offshore specifics would require a book for itself and such books are available on the market.[6] Therefore, I will not go into further details here.

7.2.5 Grid Connection and Feed into the Grid

Once finalized the renewable energy project needs to be connected to the grid for the feeding-in of the produced power. The only exception to the grid connection requirement is a self consuming island installation, which is the exception for renewable energy projects because of their volatility if we are not talking about biomass and geothermal projects.

Grid Reservation / Grid Connection Agreement

Access to the grid is therefore an essential component for most renewable energy project. Generally, with the start of development of a renewable energy project the developer will seek to obtain a grid capacity reservation. Such grid capacity is in most jurisdictions later on secured by a grid connection agreement. However, in some jurisdictions, as in Germany, there is an entitlement to connect to the grid, even with priority over other generators.

4 Böttcher – Gerhard, Rüschen, Sandhövel, 677ff.

5 See also *Kilgus/Wojtek/von Hoff* in Böttcher, Offshore Windenergie, S. 240, Fn. 402.; *Kersting*, BKR 2011, 47, 60.

6 For example, Böttcher, Offshore Windenergie.

Feed-In Contract

After the grid connection is established feeding energy into the grid either needs to be conducted based on a statutory right or a feed-in contract with the grid operator. Additionally, to the grid connection itself also balancing, metering and the procurement of necessary additional electricity for the operation of the wind farm may be regulated in the feed-in contract.

7.2.6 Other Construction-Related Contracts

Other construction relevant project contracts are (i) inverter and/or substation procurement agreements, (ii) module procurement contracts, (iii) other infrastructure related contracts, e.g., a specific infrastructure EPC contract. Most of the services and items under such agreements should be covered by the EPC and BoP, if not, the comments related to interface risk and burden of proof made in section 7.2.4 apply as well in this case.

7.2.7 Operation Project Contracts

After the construction phase, when the renewable energy project is handed over to the project company and the risk passes over to it the operation begins. The operation period is by far the most important period since this is the time when the project has to produce the energy and operate in line with the planned business model. It is also by far the longest period in the life cycle of a renewable energy project. But, since during planning and construction the most obstacles and issues may arise the phase until operation is a lot more regulated than the operational phase.

Again, depending on the asset class there are different type of operation project contracts. In wind projects a maintenance contract with the turbine supplier for most of the lifetime of the project is the industry's standard. In recent years there are more and more independent providers for maintenance works related to wind turbines. Either, they take over after the maintenance contract with the turbine supplier ends after 15 years or try to provide the maintenance works even earlier. The question that needs to be asked is whether the independent provider has sufficient knowledge, access to the necessary spare parts and the financial background to step in also in difficult cost intensive repair situations. Although, the discussion about the financial capabilities may be asked related to turbine suppliers, given the recent insolvency cases in this sector.

Furthermore, technical management and maintenance besides the turbine is often provided for in a technical operation agreement. Sometimes, the technical management is combined with commercial management so that there is a technical and commercial management agreement.

More often the commercial management is separated or is even done by the project company itself if the organization behind the project company is capable of providing the relevant services.

In solar projects you will find in most cases one O&M contract. The inverter manufacturers do offer maintenance agreements for inverters. Whereas this might be an option for central inverters, in string inverter constellations it is most of the time cheaper to buy a few spare parts and exchange them if they break. Generally, the cost discussions often result in the project company not entering into inverter maintenance contracts.

7.2.8 PPAs, Direct Marketing Agreements

With the subsidies regimes for renewable energy installations coming to an end and market mechanisms being implemented for the produced energy the sale of the produced energy by the renewable energy project has become an essential element of a renewable energy project.

While the sale of the produced energy has been always necessary in some jurisdictions as Norway or Sweden, in other countries as France and Germany the development started with a subsidy regime for each kilowatt hour produced and injected energy which was replaced by a requirement to sell the produced energy at the market. The so called direct marketing agreements are necessary to qualify for the available subsidies.

Full market integration is already necessary in countries in which there is no subsidy regime, where projects need to qualify for a subsidy via tender proceedings and they are not successful or for installations that run out of the subsidy regime. For such renewable energy projects the project company needs to sell the produced energy at the market or to a third party via a PPA.

While the fluctuations in the energy prices make it nearly impossible for renewable energy projects selling their energy at the market to get project financing, the project company needs to find a reliable counterparty buying the produced energy for a predictable price and a certain period of time.

In my experience, ten to 15 years as a term for a PPA is the minimum to achieve a project finance for a renewable energy project if the price risk for selling the energy cannot be covered otherwise. While direct marketing agreements were backed by a certain guaranteed price by a national subsidy regime and therefore the term was not so important, PPAs are a mere market mechanism and have to be judged as such.

The counterparty risk (see also section 7.4.1) is also more important for the same reasons with PPAs than it has been with direct marketing agreements. However, the financial capabilities of a counterparty cannot be secured by a provision in the PPA, unless there are securities provided by the counterparty. Generally, if there is a corporate counterparty is should be made sure that either the project company is contracting with the parent company itself and not a less important subsidiary with a higher insolvency risk or the parent company should issue a guarantee or comparable security.[7]

7.3 Other Transaction Documents

7.3.1 Share Purchase Agreement, Asset Purchase Agreement

If a renewable energy project is sold by the developer to an investor it is either done by a transfer of the shares in the project company through a share purchase agreement (“**SPA**”) or by a sale and transfer of the assets of the renewable energy project through an asset purchase agreement (“**APA**”). Those agreements are not directly project contracts since they do not serve the project itself but they are related to the project and are important for a lender. The acquirer according to the SPA or the APA will be the future owner of the renewable energy project directly or indirectly by holding the shares in the company and therefore the financial soundness of the acquirer plays an important role although the project finance is done on a non recourse basis at the project company level. Furthermore, the owner of the renewable energy project may have given securities to the lender such as a pledge of the shares in the project company and therefore a transfer has also an effect on those securities which needs to be considered.

7.3.2 Shareholder Agreement

Finally, there might be a situation in which the project company or the renewable energy project is owned not only by one company but there is a joint venture or a group of owners. Such groups normally regulate their relationship via a shareholder agreement (“**SHA**”) which includes important provisions for the transfer of the participation, financing and other vital provisions for the project. Those provisions need to correspond to the interest of a lender.

7.4 Concerns of a Lender which Need to Be Considered

The lender provides financing for a certain period of time and expects regular interest for and repayment of such financing over time. This expectation is based on a

7 For a comprehensive market overview of Corporate PPAs please see: https://www.fieldfisher.com/services/hot-topics/corporate-ppas.

financial model of the renewable energy project and therefore it serves the best interest of the lender if the renewable energy project delivers as expected. Of course, this is a very simplistic view but the core of the discussion if we try to find out what could be risks involved in renewable energy projects that could have a negative influence on such expectation and therefor need to be handled in project contracts.

7.4.1 Insolvency of a Party Involved in the Project

First of all, the insolvency of parties involved or related to the renewable energy project is a major risk for the project itself and the repayment of any loan which was granted to finance the project.

Insolvency of the Project Company

Primarily, the insolvency of the project company is the biggest risk. Since, the lender is usually the debtor with the highest claims against the project company it has control over a potential insolvency proceedings. Although, this might not be the preferred commercial solution, the lender may in most cases through extensions of payment terms and deferrals circumvent an insolvency of the project company for a long time. Nevertheless, to safeguard the insolvency of the project company, all project contracts should have step in rights (see section 7.5.5) or should have related direct agreements (see section 7.5.6).

Insolvency of Other Involved Parties

More critical because not within the control of the lender is the insolvency of other parties related to the project, for example the service provider under the O&M agreement. To avoid risks related thereto the following topics should be incorporated into the project contracts: (i) The remuneration paid for the service – also in relation to assumed risk and scope – should be market standard so that there is a substitute for the insolvent party available on the market for this remuneration. (ii) The remuneration should be paid related to acceptable time periods, an insolvency after having paid the whole remuneration for a year is more problematic than if the insolvency occurs after a quarterly payment was made.

7.4.2 Survival of the Project

In a non-recourse financing – the typical case for renewable energy projects – it is the project and the project alone that the lender has to rely on for the repayment of the loan and the regular payment of interest. This will only be possible if the project survives also difficult times. There might be a bad wind year for an onshore wind project, difficulties with the grid, technical issues that lead to a reduced production or other problems that are risks for the expected financial return of the renewable energy project. Those issues can be covered on the one hand by a certain buffer in the returns of the project which are necessary to pay the lender (see also relating to reserve accounts section 7.5.8) but also by providing price security for maintenance works though the right scope of an O&M agreement (see section 7.5.1). Furthermore, availability guaranteed in O&M-Agreements are necessary to respond to this risk. Either from the turbine supplier in wind projects or from the EPC/O&M provider in solar projects, in the latter case combined with performance guaranteed by the module supplier.

7.4.3 Finalization, Transfer of Ownership and Operation of the Project

During construction the main concern is that the renewable energy project gets built (in time) and that the ownership is transferred to the project company. A further risk is that there is a cost overrun during construction. All those risks can be addressed in the construction contracts through a correct and sufficient scope (see section 7.5.1) and a diligent transfer of title provision (see section 7.5.2).

7.4.4 Subcontractors

The subcontractors risk is a variation of the counterparty risk in project contracts. It is usual that contractors, especially in EPC(I) structures do not perform all works themselves but engage subcontractors to perform parts of the work.

Generally, this does not change the responsibility of the direct contractor. But the project company and the lender may want to have a right to reject subcontractors. This can be and should be provided for in the project contract either by establishing a general approval requirement or by introducing a white-list of subcontractors which can be used without such consent.

Normally, there are also further requirements for subcontractors to be checked and assured by the main contractor such as insurance requirements and others.

7.4.5 Contractual Framework for the Duration of the Project

The lender wants to be assured that there is a plan for the operation of the renewable energy project for its whole life cycle. Therefore, the term of an O&M contract is important. Also the PPA, as already mentioned (see section 7.2.8) should cover the majority of the term of the financing.

This sometimes conflicts with the interest of the project owner to remain flexibility for O&M services and have an option to exchange a supplier after a certain period of time if the services are not as expected.

So, the term of the operating project contracts should balance those different interest situations of the owner and the lender.

7.4.6 Security of Subsidies and/or Sale of Energy, Access to the Grid

Subsidies for renewable energy have certain requirements which are specific to each subsidies regime. Such requirements need to be enabled by constructing and operating the renewable energy project in compliance with such requirements. The compliance with the subsidy regime and any permit for the renewable energy project is a key obligation under every project contract for such projects.[8]

If there is no subsidy available for the project the focus is on the PPA, the challenges and requirements of which related to project financing have been already described (see section 7.2.8).

The produced energy must, in most cases, be injected into and transported via the grid. So there must either be a statutory right in the specific country to do so or a sufficient grid contract (see also section 7.2.5) for the life time of the renewable energy project to comply with the needs of a lender.

7.5 Measures in Project Contracts or Related thereto to Safeguard Project Risks

The project contracts must provide for a safeguard and solutions for the risks addressed under section 7.4. Of course, the project contracts related to a renewable energy project do not only cover the concern of the lender but include many more topics. However, in the following the provisions dealing with the described risks shall be the focus.

7.5.1 Scope of Services/Performances

The definition of the scope of a project contract is one of the most difficult and the most important provisions. It is the description of what needs to be delivered and

8 Konrad, PV Anlagen, 107ff.

what is paid for by the agreed remuneration. The aim must be for a future owner and the lender alike to achieve a scope of work that is as inclusive and broad as possible. First of all, to avoid any cost overruns by services or performances that are not covered by the defined scope and secondly to avoid any unnecessary interfaces if specific task are not included in the scope and must therefore be provided by third parties. A first step should be to change a final and conclusive list of services and performances to be delivered according to the project contract by adding " . . . *all necessary services and performances for the construction of the Project, including* . . . " at the beginning of the list. And to add a definition that including only indicates a non conclusive list. Of course, there will then be a discussion around included scope and pricing, but to exclude certain services and performance puts the project company in a much better situation than to make sure that nothing is missing in a conclusive list.

The scope issue is clearly connected to the interface discussion within a renewable energy project. If a contractor is not responsible for certain tasks, because they are not in its scope, a further party needs to be engaged for those performances. And as a consequence the interface between those two providers needs to be regulated.

7.5.2 Transfer of Title

With drawing of funds from the financing and payment to the contractor the title to the goods to which the payment relates should be transferred to the project company. This is not always easy to achieve. Especially, in a TSA the standard provision is that the title to the turbines remains with the turbine supplier until the full price is paid. Sometimes you even find such a provision if up to 5% of the price may be withhold for the two years warranty period which means that title to the turbine stays with the turbine manufacturer for two years after take over of the wind farm by the project company and passing of the risk. This is normally not intended by the parties but not seldom forgotten to amend in the negotiations of the TSA. The starting point however should be, as said, that once there is a milestone payment under the TSA, the EPC or any other project contract, the title to everything that is related to this milestone is transferred.

One other important reason to ensure the passing of title is that any securities provided by the project company relating to any goods can only be valid once the project company has title to such goods. Hence, if there is no transfer of title the normal security structure for renewable energy projects does not work.

7.5.3 Financial Strength of the Counterparty

Commercial Issue

The financial strength of the counterparty to a project contract is something that cannot be provided for in a contract but must be checked independently.[9] In offshore projects this is – as already explained – a major topic. Especially, if a supplier offers an EPCI solution in an offshore scenario the balance sheet of such provider and its robustness amid difficult situations is key.

The financial strength is less relevant if the services and goods are exchangeable. A technical management provider for a solar installation is easy to replace. There are a lot of alternatives on the market.

Market Test for Remuneration, Scope and Term

However, if exchangeability of a counter party in a project contract is relevant, the conditions, especially the payment pursuant to the project contract must be sufficient that a third party provider will deliver the same scope for such price. There might be financial reasons to allocate the over all price for a renewable energy project in a way that there is a higher payment for construction while operation later on is subsidized by the initial payment. In such structures it will not be possible to find later on a provider of operational services for the same remuneration. Therefore, a market standard test of the remuneration to be paid under the O&M and technical and commercial management contracts is required to exclude the counterparty risk in such contracts.

But also scope, assumption of risk and term of the project contract must be offered by other market participants if an exchange of a counterparty in case of financial problems or non-delivery by this counterparty shall be an option.

Change of Control

As already mentioned (see section 7.3.1) renewable energy projects get sold and transferred. And although the project financing is in most cases a non-recourse financing on the level of the project company[10] it cannot be denied that the owner of the project has an important role. If you have a strategic investor in renewable energies it is less likely that it will let the project company become insolvent if there are only temporary issues that can be fixed by some capital injections. Furthermore, as also explained (see section 7.3.1) the owner of a project company is providing certain securities for the lender as a pledge over the shares in the project company. Such

9 For various case studies relating to project financing of renewable energy projects, see Pfarl/Moser, *Projektfinanzierung*.

10 Not in offshore wind projects in which you have most of the time effectively limited recourse structures, whereby the owners enter into equity support agreements to secure to a certain extent the financial situation of the borrower.

securities need to be transferred in case of a project sale. This is even more obvious if the project is transferred via an APA, meaning that the project company which is the borrower and has provided most of the securities for the lender transfers all assets in the renewable energy project and thereby the entity of the borrower changes. Those scenarios are covered by change of control provisions according to which the lender needs to consent to such transfer. Those provisions may cover only a direct change of control, thus the transfer of the assets or the shares in a project company or more often also an indirect change of control on the level of the company holding the project company or even above.

Finally, change of control provisions which normally do trigger a termination right can also be found in real estate agreements, if there is a change of control of the lessee, hence the project company, in EPC or O&M agreements.

There are for example providers of O&M services in the market that express their believe in green energy and their opposition against nuclear energy by insisting on a change of control clause that allows them to terminate the O&M agreement in which they are the service provider if the project company will be acquired by a company directly or indirectly linked to the nuclear industry.

Although, such change of control provisions in project contracts do not directly benefit the lender since the contractual party is the project company, the lender may enforce such provisions indirectly by provisions in the loan documentation providing certain representations about the project contracts and the counterparties.

7.5.4 Securities Related to Project Contracts

The lender in a renewable energy project will require an extensive security package securing the rights to the project.[11] The consequence of a non-recourse project financing is that it is even more important to receive the whole project as collateral for the financing. Relating to project contracts, it is the security assignment of the rights and claims arising out of or in connection with such project contracts that will be assigned.

Assignment of Rights and Claims from Project Contracts

Project contracts normally provide for a non-assignability clause, meaning that no contractual party can assign any rights under the contract without the prior consent of the other party to the contract. It is important to allow assignments to any financing bank or other lenders to facilitate the security assignment of such rights and claims between the lender and the project company.

11 Riede – Gerhard, Rüschen, Sandhövel, 825ff.

Assignment of Insurance Claims
Further, there will be insurances covering various risks of the renewable energy project. The lender will require an assignment of such claims. This must be considered when using proceeds from such claims in any way in the project contracts.

Subcontractor Cut-Through Agreements
I already described the risk related to the performance of works by a subcontractor with whom the project company has no direct contractual relationship with (see section 7.4.4). One further element to make such structures bankable is to establish cut-through agreements. However, to enable this the project contracts must foresee the possibility to establish cut-through agreements, e.g., by the following contract provision:

> The Contractor shall use its best efforts to include a provision in each contract with a subcontractor whereby the Customer and, upon consent of the Customer, the Financing Bank or a party designated by the Financing Bank shall be entitled to assume the Contractor's position under the subcontractor contract under full release of the Contractor from its contractual duties and obligation in the event of (i) insolvency proceedings having been initiated in relation to the Contractor and/or (ii) reasons allowing to file for the initiation of insolvency proceedings having occurred in relation to the Contractor and/or (iii) the financial situation of the Contractor having materially deteriorated ("cut-through contracts").

7.5.5 Step-In Rights

As already explained above the survival of the project is key for any lender (see 7.4.2). To ensure this interest project contracts should provide for step in rights, either directly in the contract or in direct agreements (see section 7.5.6 below). Through such step in rights the lender may take over the agreement instead of the project company or determine a third party to do so. In Germany there is the possibility to include a step in right for the benefit of the lender in a project contract without the lender being a party to the agreement which is obviously a very interesting tool when structuring and negotiating project contracts before the lender is on board.

Generally, the step in right should not only be for the benefit of the lender but also for a third party which can be determined by the lender. A financing bank seldomly will wish to take over a distressed renewable energy project directly but will want to do it via any kind of holding entity to which it should be able to transfer the step in right.

7.5.6 Direct Agreements

Instead of step in clauses which are provided for directly in the project contract it is common to have direct agreements related to project agreements which have the same reason and purpose than step in rights. An example for a standard direct agreement required by lenders is attached as **Annex.**

7.5.7 Best Effort Amendment Clause Related to the Lender

Finally, if the lender and the financing is not yet clear when the project contract is entered into it should include a best efforts clause that the parties will apply those to accommodate later requirements of a lender.

This should for example in an O&M contract also cover the amendment of reporting duties by such information that is requested and required by the lender.

7.5.8 Building Reserves

Building financial reserves is another way to deal with risks related to the project. The principle is clear: Save in good times so you have it for worse.[12]

Building reserves makes sense when a project contract does not cover specific items in the included scope but the contractor may ask for additional remuneration to conduct the required service (see also the explanations relating to the scope of the contract in section 7.5.1). A good example is the maintenance of inverters as already mentioned in section 7.2.6. If there is a commercial decision not to enter into an inverter maintenance agreement, there are arguments to build a financial reserve based on experience with inverter maintenance costs to cover such costs if they arise.

More general, a debt service reserve account may be established at the project company level to cover the financing costs for a certain periods of time if there are operational or technical issues with the renewable energy project that cannot be fixed within an acceptable period of time. Also if the natural resource fuelling the renewable energy project is not available to the expected extent, then such a reserve may help to let the project survive.

From my experience in recent mezzanine projects financings the amount equal to the interest and repayment of such financing for one year is reserved on a pledged account of the project company to serve as security for such "bad times."

Of course building a reserve account is a commercial discussion. Money reserved on this account cannot be paid out to the owners of the project and therefore has a

12 See also Böttcher in section 6.2.5.

negative effect on the profitability of the renewable energy project. Also, if the money is used, generally the reserve account needs to be refilled which again leads to the commercial discussion.

However, reserve accounts are standard in most projects and an easy way to build a certain financial buffer if issues occur. Therefore, they are part of the bankability package of a renewable energy project.

7.6 Conclusion

The requirements of a lender to renewable energy projects can be implemented in project contracts of such projects. The implementation should be done when negotiating those project contracts. The discussion to amend an already signed project contract is difficult.

Annex: Template Direct Agreement

Date___________________________

[●]
as Contractor
- and -

[●]
as Guarantor

- and -

[●]
as Original Employer
- and -
[●]
as Lender / Security Agent

DIRECT AGREEMENT[13]

---

relating to [●]

THIS Direct Agreement is made on 2020
BETWEEN:
(1) [●], (the **Contractor)**;
(2) [[●], (the **Guarantor**)];
(3) [●], (the **Original Employer**); and
(4) [●], (the **Security Agent**).
IT IS AGREED as follows:

1 INTERPRETATION

1.1 Definitions

In this Agreement: [●]

13 This is a general template not tailored to a specific situation and not relating to some general provisions normally required. The usage of the template cannot replace the seeking of legal advice relating to your specific project.

1.2 Relationship to the Contract [and Guarantee]

(a) The rights and obligations of the Employer and the Contractor under the Contract [and the rights and obligations of the Guarantor and the Employer under the Guarantee] shall continue in full force and effect, unless expressly determined otherwise in this Agreement.
(b) In case of inconsistencies between the provisions of this Agreement and the Contract [respectively the Guarantee], this Agreement shall prevail.

2 SUSPENSION

2.1 Contractor Notice

The Contractor [(and, to the extent applicable, the Guarantor)] may not

(a) exercise or seek any right to terminate, suspend or discontinue the performance of any of its obligations under, the Contract;
(b) exercise any right to repossess any asset delivered under the Project; or
(c) apply for Insolvency Proceedings against the Employer or any of its assets,

(any such action: a **Termination Action**), without [the Contractor] first giving to the Security Agent a written notice of its intention to do so specifying the event giving rise to such right of termination or suspension (a **Contractor Notice**). A Contractor Notice must include the date on which the Contractor [or the Guarantor] proposes to take a Termination Action. For the avoidance of doubt, the Contractor is also entitled to issue a Contractor Notice once an Acceleration Notice has been issued.

2.2 Acceleration Notice

The Security Agent is entitled to issue an acceleration notice to the Contractor at any time by giving notice to the Contractor that the facilities under the Facility Agreement will be accelerated (an **Acceleration Notice**). Without affecting the validity of the Acceleration Notice, the Security Agent shall – in relation to the Employer, but not to the Contractor – be entitled, but not obliged, to issue an Acceleration Notice, if an Event of Default has occurred and is continuing.

2.3 Suspension Period

(a) The Suspension Period begins on the earlier of:
    (i) the date on which a Contractor Notice has been issued pursuant to Clause 2.1;
    (ii) the date on which an Acceleration Notice has been issued pursuant to Clause 2.2.
(b) An Acceleration Notice or Contractor Notice issued after the initial Acceleration Notice or Contractor Notice does not cause a new Suspension Period to take effect. For the avoidance of doubt, the Contractor shall be entitled to issue a Contractor Notice based on an Acceleration Notice.

(c) During the Suspension Period, the Contractor [and the Guarantor] may not take any Termination Action.

(d) The Contractor shall promptly submit to the Security Agent and the Employer a list of the Antecedent Liabilities. The Employer may notify the Contractor and the Security Agent, if it believes the list to be incomplete or otherwise incorrect.

2.4 Termination of the Suspension Period

(a) Unless the Contractor and the Security Agent agree otherwise, the Suspension Period shall terminate on the earlier of:
   (i) 120 calendar days after the day on which the Suspension Period commences, unless (A) such period is extended by the Contractor and the Security Agent or (B) the Security Agent has issued a Substitution Notice;
   (ii) the day on which the Contractor withdraws the Contractor Notice, unless the Security Agent has issued an Acceleration Notice or a Substitution Notice;
   (iii) the day on which the Security Agent withdraws the Acceleration Notice;
   (iv) the day on which the Security Agent confirms to the Contractor that the Suspension Period has terminated;
   (v) the withdrawal of a Substitution Notice, which is only permissible prior to the Substitution Date;
   (vi) the Security Release Date; and
   (vii) the Substitution Date.

(b) If the Suspension Period expires without a Substitution taking place and the Contractor has issued and not withdrawn the Contractor Notice, the Contractor [and the Guarantor] is entitled to take Termination Actions, but in any case not earlier than on the date stated in the Contractor Notice.

3 SUBSTITUTION

3.1 Substitution Notice and Substitution Information

(a) During the Suspension Period, the Security Agent is entitled to notify the Contractor of its intention to carry out a Substitution (a **Substitution Notice**). The Substitution Notice must include a Substitution Date proposed by the Security Agent, which shall not be later than 60 calendar days after the date of the Substitution Notice (or as otherwise agreed between the Contractor and the Security Agent).

(b) The Security Agent must inform the Contractor of the identity of the proposed Substitute Employer (including the written consent by the proposed Substitute Employer) and notify the Contractor of the Substitute Security Assignment (the **Substitution Information**). The Contractor may only object to the proposed Substitute Employer, if that person does not fulfill the Substitute Employer

Criteria at the time of the proposed Substitution Date. In case the Contractor gives the Security Agent a reasoned written notice within 5 Business Days after it has received the Substitution Information from the Security Agent that it objects to the proposed Substitute Employer, the Security Agent may propose an alternative proposed Substitute Employer and an alternative proposed Substitution Date in a new Substitution Information to the Contractor. This new Substitution Information shall be made within 10 Business Days of receipt of the written notice of the Contractor's objection (and the Suspension Period shall extend by further 30 Business Days in case of an objection of the Contractor).

(c) In case the Contractor approves the identity of the Substitute Employer or does not respond to the Substitution Information within 5 Business Days of its receipt, the Substitution Date will be the date proposed as such in the Substitution Notice and the Substitute Employer will be the person proposed as such in the Substitution Information. The Security Agent shall confirm the Substitution Date and the identity of the Substitute Employer to the Contractor, the Substitute Employer and the Escrow Agent.

(d) From the date that a Substitution Notice has been issued,
  (i) the Contractor and the Security Agent must co-operate, in particular in negotiating an agreement to adapt the Contract in accordance with Clause 3.2(a)(v) below, and immediately deliver all information that is deemed necessary to effect the Substitution;
  (ii) the Employer must, as and when requested by the Security Agent, fully co-operate to implement the Substitution;
  (iii) the Employer and the Contractor must inform the Security Agent of all payments between the Employer and the Contractor;
  (iv) such payments shall be directed through an account pledged to, or held in the name of, the Security Agent, if so requested by the Security Agent;
  (v) at the request of the Security Agent, the Employer shall refrain from any act or representation insofar as this has not been approved in advance by the Security Agent or its nominee (or any delegates and/or sub-delegates) (acting in the supposed interest (*mutmaßlicher Wille*) of a future Substitute Employer) in writing and, if informed accordingly by the Security Agent, the Contractor shall be entitled to disregard any act or representation of the Employer, unless it has been approved by the Security Agent; and
  (vi) the Employer hereby gives the Security Agent a power of attorney (to be exercised in the supposed interest (*mutmaßlicher Wille*) of a future Substitute Employer), which shall be irrevocable with right of substitution, to perform all acts of the Employer on its behalf until the Substitution Date towards the other parties to this Agreement and towards third parties.

3.2 Substitution

Upon Substitution Date, the following shall apply:

(a) The Substitute Employer automatically enters into the Contract and replaces the previous Employer by way of an assumption of contract (*Vertragsübernahme*) with effect to the Substitution Date under the following terms:

(i) the previous Employer will be released from, and the Substitute Employer will assume,

(A) any obligations or liabilities of the Employer arising on or after the date of the Substitution Date;

(B) any Antecedent Liabilities arising prior to the Substitution Date, provided that such Antecedent Liabilities have been notified to the Security Agent by the Contractor in accordance with Clause 2.3(d). To the extent the Contractor and the Substitute Employer do not agree whether certain liabilities listed by the Contractor according to Clause 2.3(d) are Antecedent Liabilities, this shall be determined between the Substitute Employer and the Contractor in accordance with the Contract; and

(C) for the purposes of this Agreement, the Contract with the previous Employer shall – subject to the terms of this Agreement – be deemed terminated (*gekündigt*) by the Contractor;

(ii) the previous Employer will remain liable for all payment obligations other than (1) as set out in paragraph 3.2(a)(i)(A) and (2) Antecedent Liabilities;

(iii) to the extent not determined otherwise in this Agreement, the Substitute Employer will have the same rights as if it had at all times been party to a contract on the same terms as the Contract in place of the previous Employer;

(iv) any then subsisting ground for termination of the Contract by the Contractor will be deemed to have no effect and any subsisting termination notice will be automatically revoked;

(v) the Contractor shall at the request of the Substitute Employer negotiate in good faith, and enter into, such amendments to the Contract as necessary to the extent the Substitute Employer cannot reasonably perform non-monetary Antecedent Liabilities as agreed under the Contract. The Contractor may not terminate the Contract for any failure to perform such non-monetary Antecedent Liabilities as and when otherwise due until such amendment has been agreed.

(b) The Substitute Employer automatically enters into this Direct Agreement and replaces the previous Employer by way of an assumption of contract (*Vertragsübernahme*) with effect to the Substitution Date. The terms of this Direct Agreement shall remain unchanged (except that the previous Employer is replaced by the Substitute Employer).

(c) The Substitute Employer automatically enters into the Escrow Agreement and replaces the previous Employer by way of an assumption of contract (*Vertragsübernahme*) with effect to the Substitution Date in accordance with its terms.

(d) [The Guarantee shall remain in place for the obligations of the Contractor under the Contract unchanged save that the Substitute Employer shall become the beneficiary of the Guarantee.]

(e) Promptly after the Substitution Date, the Substitute Employer, the Contractor[, the Guarantor] and the Security Agent [(as the case may be)] shall for the purpose of clarification enter into new agreements to replace the Contract[, the Guarantee] and this Direct Agreement under the terms set out above.

(f) The Security Agent and the Substitute Employer shall enter into a new security assignment agreement (the **Substitute Security Assignment**) under the same terms as the Security Assignment (except that the previous Employer is replaced by the Substitute Employer). The Substitution Notice shall constitute notice to the Contractor that under the Substitute Security Assignment, the Substitute Employer assigned (by way of security assignment) in favor of the Security Agent all its rights in respect of the Contract. The Contractor shall, promptly upon the Substitution Notice, acknowledge notice of, and (to the extent required) consent to, the Substitute Security Assignment, under the terms as set out in Clause 4.2 and agrees not to take any action restricting or preventing the enforcement such security.

4 SECURITY AND PAYMENTS

4.1 Notice of Security

This Agreement constitutes notice to the Contractor that under the Security Assignment the Original Employer assigned (by way of security assignment) in favor of the Security Agent all its rights in respect of the Contract.

4.2 Acknowledgement

(a) The Contractor [and the Guarantor] acknowledge[s] notice of, and (to the extent required) consents to, the Security Assignment of the Original Employer and agrees not to take any action restricting or preventing the enforcement of such Security Interest.

(b) The Contractor [and the Guarantor each] confirm[s] that:

  (i) it is not aware of any subsisting Security Interest or, to the extent such consent would be required, has not consented to any Security Interest over the assets of the Original Employer other than pursuant to the Security Assignment and any Security Interest provided for under the Contract; and

(ii) that it has not received any Security Interest for the Employer's payment obligations under the Contract and that it will not request, claim or exercise, any Security Interest, surety or guarantee for the performance by Employer of its obligations under the Contract.

(c) The Contractor [and the Guarantor] shall notify the Security Agent in the event that it becomes aware of any Security Interest referred to in paragraph (b) above.

(d) The Contractor [and the Guarantor] agrees and acknowledges that, notwithstanding anything to the contrary contained in this Agreement, the Employer will remain liable to observe and perform all of the Employer's obligations under the Contract until Substitution and that neither the Security Agent nor any of the Finance Parties will be under any obligation or liability with respect to those obligations by reason of or arising out of this Agreement.

4.3 Payments

(a) On the basis of the Security Interest created pursuant to the Security Assignment, the Contractor undertakes to pay any amounts owed by it to the Employer under or in connection with the Contract to the bank account notified by the Employer or the Security Agent. In the case of inconsistency or conflict between the notice of the Employer and the notice of the Security Agent, the notice of the Security Agent shall prevail. The Contractor shall only be released from its payment obligations under or in connection with the Contract upon irrevocable payment to the designated bank account.

(b) Security Agent and the Employer acknowledge that nothing in this Clause 4.3 affects any right or defences that the Contractor may have under the Contract, including any right of set-off in accordance with the terms of the Contract.

5 REPRESENTATIONS AND AMENDMENTS

[Each of] The Contractor [and the Guarantor] represents and warrants to the Security Agent on the date of this Agreement as follows:

5.1 It is a corporation, limited liability company or partnership with limited liability, duly incorporated or, in the case of a partnership, established and validly existing under the law of its jurisdiction of incorporation.

5.2 It has the power to enter into and perform this Agreement and the Contract [and the Guarantee] and the transactions contemplated by them and has taken all necessary action to authorise the entry into and performance of this Agreement and the Contract and the transactions contemplated by them in accordance with their respective terms.

5.3 This Agreement and the Contract [and the Guarantee] constitute its legal, valid and binding obligations enforceable in accordance with their respective terms and are in proper form for the enforcement in the [German] courts.

5.4 The entry into and performance of this Agreement and the Contract [and the Guarantee] and the transactions contemplated by them do not conflict with:
(a) applicable law or regulation;
(b) constitutional documents; or
(c) agreement or document to which it is a party or which is binding upon it or any of its assets, and will not result in the creation, imposition or enforcement of any Security Interest on any of its assets pursuant to the provisions of any agreement or document, save as provided for in this Agreement.

5.5 No event has occurred which constitutes a default under or in respect of any agreement or document to which it is a party or by which it may be bound which would adversely affect its ability to perform its obligations under the Contract[, the Guarantee] or in this Agreement.

5.6 All consents and other matters, official or otherwise, required in connection with the entry into and performance by it and the validity and enforceability against it of this Agreement and the Contract [and the Guarantee] and the transactions contemplated by them have been obtained or effected and are in full force and effect and all fees (if any) payable in this connection have been paid and there has been no default in the performance of any of the terms or conditions of this Agreement and the Contract [and the Guarantee].

5.7 There is no litigation, arbitration or administrative proceedings against it or with respect to its knowledge to the Project current or pending or threatened which, if adversely decided, would materially adversely affect the ability of the Contractor to perform its obligations under the Contract and this Agreement.

6 CHANGES TO PARTIES

6.1 The Employer and the Contractor

Neither the Employer nor the Contractor [or the Guarantor] may assign or otherwise dispose of all or any of its rights or obligations under this Agreement.

6.2 The Security Agent

(a) Security Agent may only assign or transfer all its rights and obligations under this Agreement to a successor security agent in accordance with the terms of the Facilities Agreement and the other Finance Documents.
(b) References to the Security Agent in this Agreement include any successor Security Agent referred to in paragraph (a) above.

7 MISCELLANEOUS

7.1 Waivers and Remedies Cumulative

No failure to exercise, nor any delay in exercising any right or remedy under this Agreement shall operate as a waiver by the Security Agent, nor shall any single or partial exercise of any right or remedy prevent any further or other exercise or the exercise of any other right or remedy. The rights and remedies provided in this Agreement are cumulative and not exclusive of any rights or remedies provided by law.

7.2 Indemnity

(a) Employer shall, within three Business Days of demand, pay to the Security Agent the amount of all costs and expenses (including legal fees) incurred by the Security Agent in connection with the enforcement of, or the preservation of any rights under, this Agreement.

(b) Security Agent will not be liable for any losses arising in connection with the exercise or purported exercise of any of its rights, powers and discretions under this Agreement, unless that liability arises as a result of the Security Agent's gross negligence or wilful misconduct.

7.3 Severability

(a) The Parties agree that should at any time, any provisions of this Agreement be or become void (*nichtig*), invalid or due to any reason ineffective (*unwirksam*) this will indisputably (*unwiderlegbar*) not affect the validity or effectiveness of the remaining provisions and this Agreement will remain valid and effective, save for the void, invalid or ineffective provisions, without any Party having to argue (*darlegen*) and prove (*beweisen*) the Parties intent to uphold this Agreement even without the void, invalid or ineffective provisions.

(b) Void, invalid or ineffective provision shall be deemed replaced by such valid and effective provision that in legal and economic terms comes closest to what the Parties intended or would have intended in accordance with the purpose of this Agreement if they had considered the point at the time of conclusion of this Agreement.

8 GOVERNING LAW AND DISPUTE RESOLUTION

8.1 Applicable law

This Agreement and any non-contractual obligations arising out of or in connection with it are governed by German law.

8.2 Jurisdiction

(a) The courts of Munich, Germany have exclusive jurisdiction to settle any dispute arising out of or in connection with this Agreement (including a dispute relating to the existence, validity or termination of this Agreement or any non-contractual obligation arising out of or in connection with this Agreement) (a "**Dispute**").

(b) Parties agree that the courts of Munich, Germany are the most appropriate and convenient courts to settle Disputes and accordingly no Party will argue to the contrary.

(c) Clause 8.2 is for the benefit of the Security Agent only. As a result, the Security Agent shall not be prevented from taking proceedings relating to a Dispute in any other courts with jurisdiction. To the extent allowed by law, the Parties may take concurrent proceedings in any number of jurisdictions.

Signatories

Literature

Böttcher, Jörg, *Handbuch Offshore Windenergie: Rechtliche, technische und wirtschaftliche Aspekte* 2013 (cited as Böttcher, Offshore Windenergie).

Gerhard, Markus, Thomas Rüschen, and Armin Sandhövel, *Finanzierung Erneuerbarer Energien*, 2nd ed. Frankfurt am Main, 2015 (cited as Gerhard, Rüschen, Sandhövel).

Herbes, Carsten, and Christian Friege, eds. 2015. *Handbuch Finanzierung von Erneuerbare-Energien-Projekten*. Munich (cited as Herbes/Friege).

Kersting. 2011. *Die Projektfinanzierung eines Offshore-Windparks*. BKR 2011, 57ff. (cited as Kersting, BKR 2011).

Koh, Jae Myong. 2018. Green Infrastructure Financing, Cairo (cited as Koh, *Infrastructure Financing*).

Konrad, Frank, *Planung von Photovoltaik-Anlagen*, 2nd ed. Wiesbaden, 2008 (cited as Konrad, *PV-Anlagen*).

Pfarl, Iris, and Reinhard Moser. Projektfinanzierung als erfolgreiche Finanzierungsform im internationalen Geschäft. Wiesbaden, 2017 (cited as Pfarl/Moser, Projektfinanzierung).

Schulz, Thomas. *Handbuch Windenergie*. Berlin, 2015 (cited as Schulz Windenergie).

8 Special Legal Aspects of Renewable Energy Projects in Emerging Markets

Dr. Daniel Reichert-Facilides

8.1 Introduction

Green banking – roughly understood as the deployment of private capital for the financing of low-carbon and climate-resilient infrastructure[1] – first developed in highly industrialized OECD countries that were gradually moving towards renewable energy generation.[2] As a result, green banking initially benefitted from strong political institutions as a necessary prerequisite to financial incentives and preferential grid access, and from a relative abundance of capital. At the same time, renewable energy projects in industrialized economies had to face high entry hurdles in the form of an oversupply of power and an existing infrastructure that was built around large thermal power plants and nationwide grids run by vertically integrated utility monopolies.

Against this background, renewable energies have long been considered an expensive alternative to carbon and nuclear power generation, whose legitimacy mainly rested on environmental concerns and the related long-term benefits of clean energy to society. It may therefore seem surprising that renewable energies have meanwhile become an increasingly attractive element of the power mix in emerging and frontier markets[3] – i.e., in countries with significantly less financial resources *per capita*. This development, which now even extends to some Heavily Indebted Poor Countries,[4] is of course due to a large extent to the converging global consensus on the dangers of climate change, as reflected in the widespread adherence of non-OECD countries to the 2015 Paris Agreement. But there are also other factors benefitting the roll-out of renewable energies in emerging and frontier markets. Besides the decrease in production costs of renewable energy technologies, these are essentially related to the lower degree of electrification and the corresponding lack of pre-existing infrastructure. Although the magnitude of these

1 https://www.oecd-ilibrary.org/finance-and-investment/green-investment-banks_9789264245129-en.

2 Hydropower occupies a special place both in industrialized economies and in emerging and frontier markets.

3 For that a definition of emerging and frontier as compared to developed markets, see the MSCI Market Classification Framework at https://www.msci.com/documents/1296102/1330218/MSCI_Market_Classification_Framework.pdf/d93e536f-cee1-4e12-9b69-ec3886ab8cc8.

4 See for example Ethiopia, which has run its first round of utility scale solar power auctions in 2017, https://www.iea.org/policiesandmeasures/renewableenergy/?country=Ethiopia. The term Heavily Indebted Poor Countries has been defined by the World Bank for purposes of its debt relief program, see https://www.worldbank.org/en/topic/debt/brief/hipc.

https://doi.org/10.1515/9783110607888-008

factors largely varies both between and within[5] countries, the basic pattern is that renewable energies are often the only, or at least the most easily deployable, source of electric power in regions that are still unconnected to the national grid.

In essence, the lower the electrification rate, in particular in rural areas, the lower the entry barriers for renewable energies. Depending on the scale of the installation, access to electricity solutions for unconnected areas range from individual off-grid units feeding a single battery to low-voltage micro-grids and medium-voltage mini-grids with a capacity of up to 15 MW.[6] The conventional alternative source to renewable energies in these insular solutions is diesel generation. However, while diesel still plays a vital role as a back-up power source in many instances, it has already become much more expensive due to fuel costs. Generally speaking, the high social cost of lack of access to electricity more than outweighs the price of renewable energy, both for political actors and for consumers, even if installation costs are oftentimes not much lower than in industrialized economies.[7]

Even within the reach of an existing grid and without taking environmental merits into account, utility-scale renewable energy is frequently the most attractive source of power generation in emerging and frontier markets: besides being independent from complex fuel logistics, renewable energy generators (notably photovoltaic power units) are typically much easier to deploy and maintain than conventional power plants. In power-hungry rapidly growing economies, these immediate benefits can easily outweigh the specific challenges of higher volatility and storage costs.

In summary, the economic case for renewable energies is actually even stronger in emerging and frontier markets than in highly industrialized countries.[8] This, together with the export-driven growth strategies of many equipment manufacturers and the dearth of capital in most developing economies, makes them ideal targets for green banking.

At the same time, deploying capital in emerging and frontier markets raises a number of additional legal and operational challenges, which are less prevalent or do not arise at all in an OECD setting. While some of these challenges – notably poor grid quality as a limitation to utility-scale renewable energy projects – are specific to renewable energy, most of them are simply reflective of doing business in non-OECD

5 Notably between urban and rural population, which are distinguished as such in the World Bank access to electricity statistics; cf. https://data.worldbank.org/indicator/EG.ELC.ACCS.ZS.

6 For a recent exemplary country overview, see https://sun-connect-news.org/fileadmin/DATEIEN/Dateien/New/Country-Brief-Mozambique.pdf

7 This is notably the case for imported components, which typically constitute more than 50% of overall capex.

8 For a global country-by-country overview of renewable energy policies capturing both developing and developed economies, see https://www.iea.org/policiesandmeasures/renewableenergy/ and http://resourceirena.irena.org/gateway/#.

countries.[9] The following subsectionsaim to provide a general introduction to the specific legal aspects of emerging market projects. The reader must, however, always bear in mind that notwithstanding similarities between the underlying practical concerns, regulation will differ widely across countries.

Generally speaking, the specific legal issues facing renewable energy projects in emerging and frontier markets can be analyzed as belonging to one of two categories. The first category comprises instruments intended to address the (assumed) institutional weaknesses of emerging and frontier markets, i.e., the absence of reliable legislation, an efficient administration and independent courts. This includes bilateral and multilateral investment treaties (1.), implementation agreements (2.), the Equator Principles and IFC Performance Standards (3.), anti-corruption laws and economic sanctions (4.), and the role of arbitration as a preferred dispute resolution mechanism (5.). By contrast, the second category comprises laws and policies that are meant to counterbalance the inherent economic disadvantages and weaknesses of emerging and frontier markets and includes local content requirements and other trade barriers (6.), as well as foreign exchange risks and capital controls (7.). Finally, export credit and investment insurance conceptually fall into both categories, because they often cover not only specific political risks but also the general commercial risk of protracted default (8.).

An additional aspect of renewable energy projects in emerging and frontier markets, which will become evident across most of the following subsections, is the strong role of governmental agencies and inter-governmental institutions. These may provide either technical or financial support and include:

- inter-governmental organizations such as the International Energy Agency (***IEA***),[10] which is established within the framework of the OECD, the International Renewable Energy Agency (***IRENA***),[11] which promotes the development of renewable energy within the UN system, and the Energy Charter Conference, which administers the Energy Charter Treaty (***ECT***)[12];
- international financial institutions (***IFIs***), such as the International Finance Corporation (***IFC***)[13] and the Multilateral Investment Guarantee Agency (***MIGA***)[14] of the World Bank Group, as well as the regional multilaterals, notably the

9 The author is acutely aware of the limits and deficiencies of economic country categorizations such as OECD, developed, developing, emerging, frontier, heavily indebted poor countries, etc., which are all strongly influenced by the vagaries of history and dogmatic preconceptions. Usage in this chapter is not meant to imply that a given country falling into any such category is necessarily facing the issues generally associated with that category, or that countries outside the category do not face the same issues.

10 https://www.iea.org/.

11 https://irena.org/.

12 https://energycharter.org/.

13 https://www.ifc.org/.

14 https://www.miga.org/.

European Investment Bank (***EIB***),[15] the European Bank for Reconstruction and Development (***EBRD***),[16] the African Development Bank (***AFDB***),[17] the Asian Development Bank (***ADB***),[18] the Asian Infrastructure Investment Bank (***AIIB***),[19] and the Inter-American Development Bank (***IADB***)[20];
- (national) development finance institutions (***DFIs***), e.g., KfW Entwicklungsbank[21] and the Netherlands Development Finance Company (***FMO***)[22];
- export credit and insurance agencies, e.g., Euler Hermes,[23] SACE,[24] the Export Import Bank of the United States of America (***EXIM***)[25] and the China Export & Credit Insurance Corporation (***Sinosure***)[26]; and
- development aid agencies, e.g., Deutsche Gesellschaft für Internationale Zusammenarbeit (***GIZ***)[27] and the United States Agency for International Development (***USAid***).[28]

In addition, and reflecting the importance of renewable energy projects to the local economy, the central government of the host country frequently plays a far more active role as compared to highly industrialized countries, which typically rely on decentralized administrative agencies with pre-established procedures.

8.2 Investment Treaties

Investment treaties are inter-governmental agreements regarding the treatment of investments made by individuals or companies from another contracting state by the state where the investment will be made.[29] They aim to facilitate foreign direct investment by providing a basic legal framework that can only be changed with the consent of the home government of the investor and is therefore less vulnerable to policy changes or political pressures in the host state. Investment treaties are

15 https://www.eib.org/.
16 https://www.ebrd.com/home.
17 https://www.afdb.org/en/.
18 https://www.adb.org/.
19 https://www.aiib.org/en/index.html.
20 https://www.iadb.org/en.
21 https://www.kfw-entwicklungsbank.de/.
22 https://www.fmo.nl/.
23 https://www.agaportal.de/en.
24 https://www.sace.it/en.
25 https://www.exim.gov/.
26 https://www.sinosure.com.cn/en/.
27 https://www.giz.de/de/html/index.html.
28 https://www.usaid.gov/.
29 https://icsid.worldbank.org/en/Pages/resources/Investment-Treaties.aspx.

typically negotiated on a bilateral basis,[30] but there are also multilateral agreements, notably the Energy Charter Treaty.[31]

Due to their nature as treaties under international law, the terms of investment treaties vary significantly, reflecting changing trends in foreign direct investment law and variations in standards adopted by different capital-exporting countries. With this qualification, all investment treaties must address the same basic issues, notably:

- What qualifies as an investment, e.g., direct ownership of physical assets, intellectual property, government licenses, contractual rights, share ownership, debt instruments, etc.; for the financing of typical renewable energy projects, the inclusion of indebtedness claims, which is now widely accepted, is the most important issue in this respect;
- Nationality of the investor, notably in respect of corporations and double-nationals,[32] i.e., the requirement of a substantive link between the investor and the state party to the relevant investment treaty so as to avoid "treaty shopping";
  - Substantive protection standards, which may include:
  - National treatment, i.e., non-discrimination as compared to nationals of the host state;
- Most-favored nation treatment, i.e., non-discrimination as compared to nationals of any other state;
  - Protection against expropriation;
  - Protection of repatriation of capital;
- Fair and equitable treatment as an overarching general standard covering procedural fairness, non-retroactivity and similar fundamental, but often elusive, legal concepts; and
- Umbrella clauses that elevate contractual claims under domestic law, e.g., under an implementation agreement, to the level of the investment treaty.[33]

With the exception of umbrella clauses, which are rarely included in modern bilateral investment treaties,[34] all substantive protection standards constitute general principles that are subject to limitations and balancing tests, as reflected by a fast-

30 A comprehensive overview of bilateral investment treaties (***BITs***) can be found at https://icsid.worldbank.org/en/Pages/resources/Bilateral-Investment-Treaties-Database.aspx.

31 https://energycharter.org/.

32 For an overview on treaty shopping through corporate nationality structuring see http://pennjil.com/international-investment-law-and-treaty-shopping-through-corporate-nationality-structuring/. In practice, tax considerations, notably the desire to secure the benefits of a favorable double taxation treaty, usually play a much stronger role in structuring than bilateral investment treaties, which mostly become relevant in a downside scenario.

33 See https://www.oecd.org/investment/internationalinvestmentagreements/WP-2006_3.pdf.

34 See http://arbitrationblog.kluwerarbitration.com/2017/10/13/closing-umbrella-dark-future-umbrella-clauses/.

growing body of published arbitral awards. As such, they are loosely comparable to constitutional rights, which also provide a safety net against abuse of governmental powers rather than constituting a comprehensive system of law.

– Dispute resolution, typically including the right of affected investors to pursue claims for breach of substantive provisions directly against the host government through international arbitration under the auspices of the International Center for the Settlement of Investment Disputes or of another arbitration institution.[35] As a general rule, the investor must have exhausted remedies available under the domestic law of the host state before commencing arbitration and may only pursue compensation for damages rather than restitution if the latter would interfere with public policy of the host state. On the practical side, investor-state arbitration is expensive and enforcing an arbitral award against an obstructive host government can be a daunting challenge.

Over the past few years, both the relevance and the limitations of investment treaties for renewable energy projects have become evident in a series of investor-state arbitrations triggered by the drastic reduction of Spanish feed-in tariffs in 2013 and 2014.[36] Against this background, the main benefit of investment treaties for renewable energy projects in emerging and frontier markets may be less to provide a universal remedy for the legal risks of cross-border projects, but rather – and in the spirit of their original function – to serve as a normative framework for foreign direct investment and a safeguard against populist policies targeted at foreign investors. Moreover, the existence of an investment treaty can be a prerequisite for the availability of coverage by governmental export credit agencies, which are a standard financing source for cross-border onshore wind projects.[37]

8.3 Implementation Agreements

Implementation agreements are often entered into between the project company and the host government in smaller emerging and frontier markets to provide a specific contractual framework for a significant renewable energy project. However,

35 Investor-state arbitration has long been considered as a major improvement for the protection of individual rights, but it has more recently become subject to vigorous criticism for lack of democratic legitimacy, notably in the context of the proposed Transatlantic Trade and Investment Partnership between the United States and the European Union (***TTIP***) and the Comprehensive Economic and Trade Agreement between Canada and the European Union (***CETA***). For a critical but informative overview, see https://isds.bilaterals.org/.

36 For a recent summary account, see https://www.financierworldwide.com/arbitration-cases-in-the-renewable-energy-sector-following-spanish-legislative-changes-at-a-crossroads#.XMGMZVQzbIU.

37 With the exception of China and, more recently, Taiwan, offshore wind has not yet reached emerging markets.

they do not replace or amend the terms of typical commercial contracts required for the implementation of any renewable energy projects, such as power purchase agreements, grid connection agreements, land acquisition agreements, supply and construction agreements, or operation and maintenance agreements. Instead, implementation agreements are meant to specify the mutual expectations of the foreign investor and the host government as to their respective roles and risks assumed in respect of the project.[38]

Many typical terms of an implementation agreement, such as undertakings by the foreign investor to comply with local laws and the standard of care of a prudent operator, or an undertaking by the government to facilitate and support the permitting and licensing processes, would be rather atypical for the OECD context. On the government side, these undertakings may extend to very basic aspects, such as work permits for contractor staff or access to foreign currency. In the context of emerging and frontier markets with limited administrative resources, they are meant to provide comfort to the investor that the project will benefit from the necessary political support, and to reassure the host government that the project will indeed be completed in a timely manner, so as to improve power supply to the population and to ensure that scarce funding for support infrastructure, such as access roads and grid connections, will not be misallocated.

Beyond operational and administrative undertakings, an implementation agreement may also provide for direct commercial support, in the form of a government guarantee for the payment obligation of the purchaser under the power purchase agreement, which is often a state-owned utility. Other terms providing material support for the project can include the assumption of certain *force majeure* risks such as change of law or grid availability by the host government. On the other hand, the implementation agreement may require the investor to share the benefits of a successful refinancing or excessive profits with the utility. Although these aspects could theoretically also be addressed in the power purchase agreement itself, they are often elevated to the level of an implementation agreement in order to adapt to the specific requirements of a cross-border investment, which are typically not reflected in the standardized power purchase agreements used by the local utility.

In addition, an implementation agreement may enable the foreign investor to enter into a direct contractual relationship with the host government. Even if the implementation agreement will typically be subject to the laws and exclusive jurisdiction of the host country, this is typically considered preferable to indirect interaction through the project company and the local utility. Irrespective of the choice of jurisdiction, a breach of the implementation agreement by the host government

38 Examples for typical implementation agreements in the power sector can be found at https://ppp.worldbank.org/public-private-partnership/library?title=implementation+agreement&sort_by=created&sort_order=DESC.

may open up access to international arbitration if the investor benefits from an investment treaty containing an umbrella clause.[39]

In summary, wherever an implementation agreement is available, it should be seen as a helpful addition to the typical suite of project documents, in particular in smaller emerging and frontier markets without a successful track record in the implementation of renewable energy projects.

8.4 Equator Principles and IFC Performance Standards

The Equator Principles are a "risk management framework, adopted by financial institutions, for determining, assessing and managing environmental and social risks in projects and [are] primarily intended to provide a minimum standard for due diligence and monitoring to support responsible risk decision-making."[40] They were developed in response to criticism that international project finance lenders had neither an incentive nor a reliable frame of reference to consider the environmental and social impacts of, e.g., major hydro or pipeline projects in countries lacking the institutions for the efficient enforcement of related policies.

Conceptually, the Equator Principles do not attempt to impose material standards or create material rights, but rather to establish a uniform procedural approach. They are largely built on the performance standards of the International Finance Corporation (***IFC***), which serves as the commercial lending arm of the World Bank Group (***IFC Performance Standards***). Besides benefitting from an existing normative system developed by the most global international finance institution, this approach also reduces the risk of having to apply multiple standards in projects co-financed by the IFC.

Financial institutions that have adopted the Equator Principles (***EPFIs***) are required to implement the following rules and procedures[41]:

- **Review and Categorization**: EPFIs must categorize projects by their magnitude of potential environmental and social risks and impacts. Category A projects represent the most significant risk potential, Category C projects minimal or no impacts, and Category B projects limited and mostly reversible risks and impacts. Except for large dams, which fall into Category A due to their long term impacts, utility scale renewable energy projects typically qualify as Category B or C.

39 See section 8.2 above.

40 https://equator-principles.com/about/; to date, a total of 96 financial institutions from 37 different countries have adopted the Equator Principles. See https://equator-principles.com/members-reporting/.

41 For the complete text of the current version, Equator Principles III (June 2013), see https://equator-principles.com/wp-content/uploads/2017/03/equator_principles_III.pdf.

- **Environmental and Social Assessment**: EPFIs must require their borrowers to conduct an assessment of environmental and social impacts for all Category A and B projects, typically in the form of a comprehensive Environmental and Social Impact Assessment report (***ESIA***) or, for less significant Category B projects, in the form of an audit. In addition, a greenhouse gas alternatives assessment must be carried out for all projects that are expected to emit more than 100,000 tons of CO_2 equivalent annually.
- **Applicable Environmental and Social Standards**: This assessment must in all instances address compliance with all laws, regulations and permits of the host country, and provide a justification for any deviation therefrom. While this is sufficient for so-called Designated Countries,[42] which consist mostly of OECD member states, projects located in Non-Designated Countries must also be evaluated for compliance with the applicable IFC Performance Standards on Environmental and Social Sustainability and the World Bank Group Environmental, Health and Safety Guidelines.
- **Environmental and Social Management System and Equator Principles Management Plan**: For Category A and B projects, EPFIs must require the borrower to develop and maintain an Environmental and Social Management System (***ESMS***) and to prepare an Environmental and Social Management Plan to address issues raised in the assessment. Where the applicable standards are not met, the borrower and the EPFI must agree on an Equator Principles Action Plan (***AP***).
- **Stakeholder Engagement**: For all Category A and B projects, the EPFI must require the borrower to demonstrate effective stakeholder engagement with affected communities and, where relevant, other stakeholders, as an ongoing process. Relevant issues that could come up in the consultations for a renewable energy project may, for example, include the potentially negative impact of renewable energy projects on tourism and the presence of construction companies in a remote area as an opportunity to build or upgrade a school building or community center at a relatively low additional cost.
- **Grievance Mechanism**: For all Category A projects and, as appropriate,[43] Category B projects, the EPFI must require the borrower to establish a grievance mechanism designed to facilitate the resolution of environmental and social concerns as part of the ESMS.
- **Independent Review**: For all Category A projects and, as appropriate, Category B projects, the EPFI must engage an independent environmental and social consultant to carry out a review and produce the relevant assessment documentation, including the Environmental and Social Management Plan

42 https://equator-principles.com/designated-countries/.

43 The qualification "as appropriate" is used in the Equator Principles without further explanation as to the relevant criteria, which must hence be derived case-by-case.

(ESMP), the ESMS, and the Stakeholder Engagement process documentation, as part of its due diligence process. In renewable energy projects, this is often part of the scope of work of the technical advisor.
- **Covenants**: For all projects, EPFIs must require the borrower to undertake to comply with all relevant environmental and social laws, regulations and permits of the host country in all material respects in the financing documentation. In addition, borrowers in Category A and B projects must undertake (a) to comply with the ESMPs and Equator Principles AP in all material respects, (b) to provide periodic reports in a format agreed with the EPFI, and (c) where applicable, to decommission the project facilities in accordance with an agreed decommissioning plan.
- **Independent Monitoring and Reporting**: For all Category A projects and, as appropriate, Category B projects, EPFIs must engage an Independent Environmental and Social Consultant to perform ongoing monitoring after financial close, or require the engagement of an independent advisor for these purposes by the borrower.
- **Reporting and Transparency**: For all Category A projects and, as appropriate, Category B projects, EPFIs must require the borrower to make the ESIA and, if applicable, a greenhouse gas emissions level report publicly available online. In addition, EPFIs themselves are required to report annually on projects that have reached financial close.

8.5 Anti-Corruption Laws and Economic Sanctions

Although corruption and economic sanction risks are by no means limited to emerging and frontier markets, they usually attract higher attention as a lender concern in projects located in these markets. Similar to the rationale underlying the development of the Equator Principles, this is again due to the institutional weaknesses of emerging and frontier markets, which render them generally more prone to corruption.[44] Moreover, economic sanctions currently in place effectively only target non-OECD countries and nationals of non-OECD countries.[45]

As a practical matter, anti-corruption measures and economic sanctions are customarily addressed in the loan and sponsor support agreements for any project finance transaction located in emerging markets. Through these contractual

44 See, e.g., the Corruption Perceptions Index 2018 published by Transparency International, at https://www.transparency.org/cpi2018.

45 See https://www.un.org/securitycouncil/sites/www.un.org.securitycouncil/files/subsidiary_organs_factsheets.pdf for UN Security Council sanctions, https://sanctionsmap.eu/#/main for European Union sanctions, and https://www.treasury.gov/resource-center/sanctions/programs/pages/programs.aspx for US (***OFAC***) sanctions.

provisions, the borrower, and often also the sponsor, makes certain representations with respect to corrupt practices or the breach of economic sanctions, and aims to refrain from engaging in or benefiting from any of these. The basic rationale behind this proactive approach is to avoid legal risks for the project itself, such as the loss of a contract with a public authority or an asset freeze, by making the financing conditioned upon compliance with all relevant laws. Moreover, the possibility to terminate the financing if a breach has occurred provides lenders with an efficient remedy of last resort if they view the reputational and regulatory risks from the project to be excessive. Reputational concerns and the interest in effective prevention are often so strong that the trigger for contractual remedies is shifted from the actual breach of anti-corruption measures or economic sanctions to the mere opening of a formal investigation by the relevant authorities.

Another customary extension of anti-bribery and corruption representations and undertakings that is mostly driven by reputational concerns is to refer not only to the project itself, but also to any other activities of the sponsor. This is often seen critically by sponsors who regularly operate in markets where corruption is a constant concern. Although this is an uncomfortable argument to make, sponsors may therefore take the position that the contagion risk is disproportional to the role of the lenders as providers of capital to a single project. A typical compromise to address these concerns would be to limit representations and undertakings at a sponsor level to the establishment, monitoring and enforcement of efficient anti-bribery and corruption policies by the sponsor for its worldwide operations.

In respect of economic sanctions, effective global policing is typically less of a concern because of the clearly defined scope of the relevant regulations.[46] The main issue here is the conflict between different sanctions regimes, notably between the European Union and the United States of America in relation to Cuba and Iran.[47] In Germany, the risk of a conflict is further increased by the prohibition on any statement whereby a German resident participates in the boycott of a foreign country, except if the same country is subject to economic sanctions imposed by the Federal Republic of Germany, the European Union, or the United Nations.[48] As a result, any unqualified undertaking to comply with, for example, US economic sanctions would expose a German party to the relevant finance document to crimi-

46 At the project level, economic sanctions will rarely affect green banking transactions, because affected jurisdictions are typically associated with political risks that are too high. Where the issue becomes relevant, the lender can invoke illegality or *force majeure* to avoid further disbursements. See, e.g., RGZ 93, 182.

47 See Council Regulation (EU) 2271/96, the current consolidated version of which can be found at https://eur-lex.europa.eu/legal-content/EN/TXT/?uri=CELEX:01996R2271-20180807.

48 See para. 7 of the Foreign Trade Regulation (*Außenwirtschaftsverordnung*).

nal sanctions. At the contractual level, these conflicts are usually avoided to the extent possible by limiting the economic sanctions clauses accordingly.

A general practical issue that often comes up in the negotiation of anti-corruption and economic sanctions clauses are internal guidelines requiring different lenders to use a specific wording. The most simplistic approach in these situations is to allow each lender to agree its own set of policy clauses with the borrower for its own benefit only. While this conceptually increases the overall level of compliance, the resulting level of complexity can make monitoring by the borrower unnecessarily difficult. The better solution, which is in practice also often accepted by IFIs with strong policy commitments, is to seek consolidation of the different wordings along the lines of generally accepted concepts.

8.6 Arbitration

While arbitration is a common feature in construction contracts and joint venture agreements, lenders generally have a preference for domestic courts for the enforcement of their rights under finance documents. The underlying theory is that lenders, after having disbursed the loan, will almost invariably find themselves on the plaintiff side in a later dispute and that arbitral tribunals would tend to encourage compromise even if the borrower is simply unable or unwilling to pay.

Irrespective of the actual merits of these arguments in a domestic or intra-OECD setting, they are usually outweighed by the following considerations for cross-border project finance transactions in emerging and frontier markets:

- Courts in the host country may be biased against foreign lenders, subject to government pressure or simply corrupt;
- Local courts will almost inevitably conduct proceedings in the national language, which can be an additional tactical advantage for the (local) borrower;
- Foreign judgments may not be enforceable without a retrial on the merits, or enforceability may be subject to complex restrictions and significantly more time-consuming than, for example, within the European Union or the European Economic Area;
- On the other hand, the 1958 Convention on the Recognition and Enforcement of Foreign Arbitral Awards (customarily referred to as the ***New York Convention***)[49] provides a well-established regime with almost universal application; and
- By selecting (or having an arbitration institution like the International Chamber of Commerce select) arbitrators with different legal backgrounds and expertise, the parties can neutralize tactical advantages; similar considerations apply for

49 http://www.newyorkconvention.org/.

the language of the proceedings and the place of arbitration, which are typically already agreed in the arbitration clause.

Even if these aspects have made arbitration the preferred form of dispute resolution for project finance transaction in emerging and frontier markets, some important limitations apply:

- Governmental agencies and public utilities in the host country will often insist on jurisdiction of local courts for any contract to which they are a party; in such situations, investor-state arbitration under an applicable investment treaty may become the remedy of last resort, subject to the limitations discussed earlier in this section;
- If necessary, an arbitral award against the borrower will typically have to be enforced through proceedings in the courts of the host country, which may refuse enforcement, *inter alia* on grounds of public policy[50]; and
- Likewise, insolvency proceedings in respect of the borrower would be conducted under the laws of the host country; the same applies for provisional judicial relief such as interim injunctions.

8.7 Barriers to Trade, in Particular Local Content Requirements

As an innovative technology driven by a few highly industrialized economies, the deployment of renewable power generation in emerging and frontier markets is sensitive to trade barriers maintained by the host country for the protection of its domestic economy. Besides tariffs on imported equipment and related administrative formalities, potential trade barriers include procurement rules, licensing requirements for foreign contractors and service providers, and work permit restrictions for seconded personnel.

While tariffs can be quantified in advance, the potential cost and delays resulting from non-tariff barriers to trade are often difficult to assess due to potential knock-on effects. From a lender's perspective, the best protection against this type of risk is careful selection of lenders' advisers, who should have practical experience with the implementation of similar projects in the relevant jurisdiction, and appropriate head-rooms in the banking case.

If the host country is a member of the World Trade Organisation (**WTO**),[51] trade barriers are subject to the WTO rules, in particular the General Agreement on Trade and Tariffs and the General Agreement on Trade in Services. While these prohibit discrimination of foreign products and services as a general principle, remedies for

50 See Article V(2)(b) of the New York Convention.

51 https://www.wto.org/.

breaches of WTO rules can in most circumstances only be pursued by other WTO-member state governments. As a practical matter, governments will only lodge a complaint if the host country market is considered sufficiently important. Trade barriers must, therefore, be treated as part of the applicable regulatory framework for a particular host country even if they have been held to be in breach of WTO rules in a dispute relating to another host country.

In renewable energy projects, this enforcement deficit has notably become evident in relation to local content requirements, which are intended to ensure that a prescribed portion of the goods and services used for the implementation of a product or project is sourced locally. The underlying theory is to maximize the benefit of imported goods and services as a lever for the domestic economy and to encourage the transfer of technologies. For renewable energy projects, local content requirements are usually imposed through the procurement rules for power purchase agreements.

While construction works for the balance of plant will be procured locally in most instances, the power generation components and electrical equipment for renewable energy projects often cannot be sourced locally, because they depend on highly specialized technology. Moreover, buyer credit support for local content from export credit agencies is generally only available for up to 30% of the total contract value.[52] Altogether, local content rules are typically considered costly and inefficient by all project participants other than the host government.[53] They have also been held to be in breach of WTO rules as discriminatory and as a subsidy by the Appellate Body of the WTO dispute resolution mechanism upon a complaint brought lodged by Japan and by the European Union against Canada.[54] Nevertheless, the practice currently persists in slightly moderated forms, e.g., by allowing the local content requirement to be met over the life of the project, thus encouraging the training of local O&M teams. This is typically preferable for operational reasons anyway, which makes the requirement ineffective at best.

Another area where trade barriers often affect renewable energy projects in emerging and frontier markets is insurance. Since the relevant industrial insurance markets are often relatively small, local insurance companies may not be able to provide coverage in line with international standards. On the other hand, foreign insurance providers will typically be precluded from providing cover by licensing requirements for primary insurers. The typical approach to this problem is to stipulate a requirement for full reinsurance coverage by the local primary insurer and to

52 See Article 10(d)(1) of the Arrangement on Officially Supported Export Credits http://www.oecd.org/trade/topics/export-credits/arrangement-and-sector-understandings/.

53 https://www.ictsd.org/bridges-news/biores/news/addressing-local-content-requirements-current-challenges-and-future.

54 https://www.wto.org/english/tratop_e/dispu_e/cases_e/1pagesum_e/ds412sum_e.pdf.

enter into a cut-through agreement whereby payments for total loss and other major insured events are made directly to the lenders.

8.8 Foreign Currency Risk and Capital Controls

Renewable energy projects in emerging and frontier markets are almost invariably exposed to foreign exchange risk. This is due to the fact that the costs for imported equipment, which will account for the bulk of the investment, will be incurred in euros or US dollars, whereas revenues from the sale of electricity will inevitably be denominated in local currency. While this is not entirely different from power sources based on fossil fuels, which are also traded in US dollars, the problem is somewhat exacerbated by the fact that the costs for renewable energy are largely front-loaded and then amortized over 15 or 20 years. As opposed to fuel purchases, exchange rate risk is therefore not compensated by offsetting export gains at a national level.

In particular in highly dollarized economies, the pragmatic approach to this problem is to denominate the power purchase agreement in US dollars. This is of course preferable to a separate currency swap to be entered into by the project company, which may often not even be available for the full tenor of the financing. The inherent risk of this solution is that it relies on the ability of the counterparty, typically the national utility, to source sufficient amounts of foreign currency over the term of the power purchase agreement. In response to these and similar challenges, forward contracts and cross-currency swaps may be available from specialized hedging providers.[55]

Whatever risk mitigation strategy is adopted, foreign lenders must be aware that enforceability of claims for unpaid debt service against the project company will generally be subject to the foreign exchange and capital control regulations of the host country. These will typically require special permits for the repatriation of foreign investments and for the operation of bank accounts held in foreign currency. If possible under the laws of the host country, the conditions under which these permits will be granted can be clarified or even preempted in the implementation agreement.[56] Otherwise, exchange control regulations must be respected, even by arbitral tribunals, because of Art. VIII(2)(b) of the Articles of Agreement of the International Monetary Fund, which provides that:

55 For example the Currency Exchange Fund, which is sponsored by a group of development finance institutions, microfinance investment vehicles, and donors. See https://www.tcxfund.com/about-the-fund/. The benefit of this type of protection as compared to export credit insurance for buyer credits is that it is not dependent on a specific underlying export trade.

56 See section 8.3 above.

> Exchange contracts which involve the currency of any member [of the International Monetary Fund] and which are contrary to the exchange control regulations of that member maintained or imposed consistently with [the Articles of] Agreement [will] be unenforceable in the territories of any member.

Against the background of these restrictions, export credit and investment insurance, which typically covers foreign exchange risk, is often considered a prerequisite component of project financing structures in emerging and frontier markets.

8.9 Export Credit and Investment Insurance

In general terms, export credit and investment insurance comprises a wide range of risk protection for cross-border transactions offered by public and private sector institutions.[57] The three types of protection most often used in project finance transactions are export credit insurance and buyer credit insurance, each provided by public sector export credit agencies,[58] and political risk insurance.

- **Export credit insurance** provides cover for the exporter against purchaser default, including non-payment due to political force majeure events; as such, export credit insurance typically covers the period until the project debt is fully disbursed;
- **Buyer credit insurance** provides cover for lenders, both against political risk and against protracted default, i.e., against general commercial risks.[59] Buyer credit insurance from export credit agencies is only available in connection with an underlying export transaction and is subject to origination rules.[60] In light of the shift of the photovoltaic manufacturing industry to East Asia and the related cost advantages, the current focus of buyer credit insurance in renewable energy projects is on onshore wind turbines and hydropower equipment. Although buyer credit insurance is also available from private political risk insurance providers, the market is traditionally dominated by governmental export credit agencies.

57 For an overview of market participants and products, see the annual yearbook of the Berne Union, the international trade association representing the industry, at https://www.berneunion.org/Publications.

58 For detailed information on cover provided by the German government through Euler Hermes, see https://www.agaportal.de/en; some export credit agencies, notably US-EXIM, provide support in the form of direct loans to the purchaser of exported goods rather than in the form of a guarantee for the benefit of a commercial lender.

59 See https://www.agaportal.de/en/exportkreditgarantien/grundlagen/abgesicherte-risiken.

60 See https://www.agaportal.de/en/exportkreditgarantien/verfahren/auslaendische-zulieferungen.

- **Investment insurance** provides political risk coverage irrespective of an underlying export transaction. It is therefore a more flexible and less standardized instrument. As a practical matter, investment insurance is rarely used in renewable energy projects.

As there are significant differences in underwriting practices, governmental export credit agencies have agreed on a code of conduct for the terms of export credits under the auspices of the OECD, officially titled the Arrangement on Officially Supported Export Credits (***OECD Consensus***).[61] The OECD Consensus contains detailed rules on minimum interest rates for fixed rate loans (commercial interest reference rates (***CIRR***)), minimum premium rates and country risk qualifications, maximum tenor (18 years for renewable energy projects),[62] latest first repayment (starting point of credit) and so forth, so as to avoid a race among export nations for the most favorable support regime.

Although export credit agencies typically evaluate protect finance transactions on a case-by-case basis, they do not accept documentation risk, i.e., the lender taking out the protection bears the risk of enforceability of the finance documents on customary terms. In addition, the cover is subject to a 5% deductible. Notwithstanding these limitations and the additional costs for the cover, buyer credit support from export credit agencies is usually considered an attractive financing tool for renewable energy projects in emerging and frontier markets, wherever it is available.

61 http://www.oecd.org/trade/topics/export-credits/arrangement-and-sector-understandings/.

62 See Annex IV section 5(a) of the OECD Consensus.

9 The Function of Securities within Project Financing

Julian Hoff, Björn Neumeuer

9.1 General Remarks

Securities in project financing have several functions. First of all, securities serve as security for the operation of the renewable energy project. Second – and mainly important for a lender – is the possibility to secure the utilization of the whole project if the beneficiary – i.e., the project company – fails with repaying the loan to the lender. It is very important for the lender that the securities granted to him are very broad and cover the whole project so that the lender is in the position to operate the renewable energy plant and, even more important, to dispose of the project as a whole, in case of a failure of loan repayment. Thus, the lender needs securities with regard to all assets of the project company so that the lender or the purchaser can operate the renewable energy plant by itself or a third operator nominated by him. Securing each asset and not only pledging the shares of the project company is important because in the first case the lender has not to worry about the debt side of the lender's balance sheet and assumes only the assets which enable him to operate the renewable energy plant and to collect the revenues generated by the energy plant.

Typically, a project financing is structured as non-recourse financing so that the lender cannot demand repayment of the loan from third parties, e.g., the holding company of the project company (exceptions will be described below). For that reason, the lender has to ensure that the assets of the project company are sufficient to secure his claims under the loan.

When talking about securities within a project financing, one has first to think about the risk which may occur and which need to be secured. As a renewable energy project is multidisciplinary, risks may result from various facts, such as:

- Technical risks
- Risk of realization
- Economic risks
- Risks due to legal implications, e.g., of being granted with the permit required

Due to such various risks, which primarily affect the project developer and the purchaser of a renewable energy project, also the lender is faced with the risk that the project might not be completed and in consequence the project financing might not be repaid.

The following description of securities is based on German law. Thus, certain aspects might differ under other laws, either that a certain type of security is or is

https://doi.org/10.1515/9783110607888-009

not recognized or that the applicable law contains specific requirements regarding the establishment of the security (e.g., notarization of the respective agreement or filing with the land register, etc.). For that reason, the following section only provides a brief description of the different types of securities in order to get an impression of the issues which might be of importance. However, the section does not describe any requirements or particularities due to German law. In consequence, in each particular case legal advice is required and strongly recommended.

9.2 Types of Securities

When thinking about securities to be requested by one party to a project, it needs to be first distinguished between Material securities and Personal securities.

9.2.1 Material Securities

Material securities are granted by the owner of an object. By granting a material security the beneficiary is entitled to satisfy his claim against his debtor by selling or using the object for himself if a default occurs. Different types of material securities exist which are described in detail below (section 9.4.1).

9.2.2 Personal Securities

In contrast to material securities personal securities do not grant a right to the beneficiary regarding an object. Rather, a third person assumes liability in addition to the debtor in order to secure the beneficiary's claim. The debtor is obliged to arrange for such third party personal security due to the agreement between him and the beneficiary. For further details please cf. below (section 9.4.2).

9.3 Purpose of Securities

A party to a renewable energy project first of all has to identify the risk which needs to be ensured. In order to choose the appropriate security, it has to be distinguished between securities which ensure the project itself (section 9.5.1) and securities which in particular ensure the lender's position (section 9.5.2).

9.3.1 Securing the Project Itself

Securities which serve to ensure the project itself are the basis to realize the project securely. Therefore, it needs to be ensured i. a. that the right to use all plots of land which are required for the transport, erection, installation and operation of the renewable energy plants, are secured, that all securities which are requested by authorities in the building permit are in place, etc. These securities first serve the project company which owns the future energy plant. However, when deciding whether a project financing should be granted and based on which terms and conditions, the potential lender has also to check whether those securities are in place and whether any collateral clauses need to be considered.

9.3.2 Securing in Particular the Lender's Position

Beyond the securities described under section 9.5.1 a lender who grants a loan to the project company needs additional securities which ensure his position as financier. A particular risk for a lender results from the fact that project companies are usually limited liability companies or partnerships with marginal nominal share capital. If the project cannot be realized or it does not generate earnings, the project company is usually not in the position to repay the loan. Thus, a lender needs additional security in this regard. Due to the fact that project financings are typically structured as non-recourse financing the lender cannot rely on a third-party security, e.g., a parent company guarantee or a joint liability of the project company and a parent company which may be a worthwhile security. Thus, securing the lender's claims has to be accomplished in particular by getting hold of the project company's assets.

9.4 Types of Securities

9.4.1 Material Securities

As described above, due to a material security the beneficiary is entitled to realize the security when the circumstances occur for which the security was granted. In the following, the different types of material securities and typical cases in which they are used, are described.

Pledge

A pledge is an encumbrance to an object which entitles the pledgee to seek satisfaction from the object. Physical (moveable) objects as well as shares can be pledged. For the creation of a pledge of physical objects the transfer of possession from the pledgor to the beneficiary is required (under German law). Therefore, a pledge of moveable assets is very rare.

However, also shares can be pledged. A pledge of shares has to be considered as security in particular if the shareholder of a project company holds shares in further companies and these further companies already run their business and generate profits whereas the project company which requires the project financing is only a project developer or has not started running its business.

Mortgage

The mortgage is comparable to the pledge. However whereas only moveable physical objects can be pledged, the mortgage only applies to plots of land. A mortgage entitles the beneficiary to realize his claim for payment of a certain amount by selling the plot of land which is encumbered with the mortgage. A mortgage needs to be registered with the land register to become valid and enforceable.

Assignment for Security

An assignment for security means that the obligor assigns all of his claims against a third party to the beneficiary. By such assignment for security, the beneficiary becomes owner of the claim if the obligor is in default as defined in the agreement which stipulates the terms and conditions of the assignment for security. In this case, the beneficiary is entitled to realize the obligor's claim against the third party for his own account.

In a project financing the lender generally requires an assignment of all claims of the project company. This comprises the ownership of the wind turbine or solar plant, claims against the general contractor, servicers (e.g., for maintenance), banks, insurance companies, etc. In case of renewable energy projects the claim which is furthermore often assigned for security is the plant owner's claim against the grid operator for payment of the feed-in remuneration. If the project company fails fulfilling its obligations towards the lender, the latter becomes entitled to the claim for feed-in remuneration. Based on the assignment agreement, the lender can demand paying the remuneration from the grid operator, i.e., it is not paid to the project company but directly from the grid operator to the lender.

Limited Personal Servitude

A limited personal servitude secures the beneficiary's right to use a third party's plot of land in a certain matter. Typical rights of use are the right to access the plot, to construct, install and operate a renewable energy plant on it, to cross the plot or to use the airspace above the plot as distance space and/or to operate the blades of a wind turbine generator in it. Therefore, the limited personal servitude is very important for the installation and operation of a plant if the owner of the plant is – as mostly – not owner of the plot of land on which the plant is constructed and/or which is needed as distance space.

Note: It always needs to be checked whether adjacent plots of land are required as distance space or to operate the blades above such plot of land. Depending on the size of the plots of land in the particular region, several plots of land might be required. For each plot which is affected, a limited personal servitude is required.

Priority Notice

A priority notice secures a party's right to be registered as beneficiary of a certain right with the land register if a certain event occurs. Thus, a priority notice can only secure those rights which are registered with the land register, i.e., the mortgage and the limited personal servitude. A priority notice is of major importance for a lender as it is generally not entitled to a limited personal servitude. Furthermore, a limited personal servitude cannot be transferred from its beneficiary to a third party. Therefore, the third party – here the lender – has to secure its position by requesting a priority notice which secures its right to be registered as beneficiary of a limited personal servitude if the project company fails with fulfilling its obligations towards the lender.

9.4.2 Personal Securities

Guarantee

A guarantee is a security by which a third party ensures to pay a certain amount or up to a certain amount to the beneficiary instead of the principal obligor. The guarantor is generally entitled to object to the beneficiary's demand to pay by raising objections of the principal obligor. However, the parties can also agree that the guarantor must unconditionally fulfill the beneficiary's claim. In this case, the guarantor has to claim for repayment and has the burden to proof that the beneficiary was not entitled to realize his claim from the guarantee. Often, guarantees are issued by banks. However, also parent company guarantees are common.

Typically, a guarantee is requested by the project company from the seller of the renewable energy plant to ensure warranty claims. Furthermore, usually authorities require to be provided with a guarantee for dismantling costs of the renewable energy plant. Furthermore, a lender might require to be provided with a guarantee of a project company's parent company in order to secure its repayment claim for the project financing loan granted to the project company.

Joint Liability

A joint liability is a third party personal security. The third party agrees to be jointly liable with the principal obligor. Often, a joint liability is requested from a holding company which is the – direct or indirect – shareholder of the project company (special purpose vehicle) which has only limited share capital and no or only less revenues so that it is not in the position to fulfill any payment obligations on its own. The beneficiary often requests that the joint liability is not subject to the fact that the beneficiary cannot realize its claim from the principle obligor. Whereas, the third party who shall become jointly liable often requests the contrary.

9.5 Choosing the Right Security

Each party has the legitimate interest to ensure its position in a project. In particular, a lender has an interest to be provided with a security as he provides the project company with the funds required for the project. However, to choose the right security the lender has to be aware of the risk(s) which need to be secured and he needs to know the different types of securities as well as their field of use.

The following explanations should be based on the following cases:

Case 1:
The company "Wind Project II SPV" was founded as special purpose vehicle (SPV) by its sole shareholder Wind Projects Limited Liability Company in order to erect and operate a wind farm in a certain part of Germany. Wind Project II SPV intends to erect the Wind Farm on a certain plot of land which is owned by a third party (the "Owner"). Wind Project II SPV contacts its bank and asks for a financing of the wind turbines and the erection costs (in total EUR 50m). The bank wants to ensure its position for repayment of the project financing.

Case 2:
During the erection phase the utility "Green Energy Utility" intends to acquire all shares in Wind Project II SPV from Wind Projects limited liability company. Wind Projects limited liability company is furthermore owner of all shares in Wind Project I SPV which has already been operating a wind farm which generates revenues. The financial situation of Wind Project limited liability company's group is tight.

9.5.1 Securities to Ensure the Project Itself

Rent Agreement and Limited Personal Servitude

In Case 1 – which describes the typical situation of a project financing – first the bank needs to assess whether the project itself is sufficiently secured. The bank therefore needs to check whether

- Wind Project II SPV has validly concluded a rent agreement with the Owner of the plot of land on which the wind farm should be erected;
- the Owner has granted a limited personal servitude to Wind Project II SPV which has already been registered with the land register. Thereby, Wind Project II SPV has a right *in rem* regarding the plot of land.

By combining a rent agreement with a limited personal servitude Wind Project II SPV's right to use the plot of land is sufficiently secured, even in case of an insolvency of the Owner.

Contractual Guarantees

Renewable energy projects are often planned and erected by general contractors which involve subcontractors which carry out the different tasks. According to the agreement between the project SPV and the general contractor the general contractor is generally entitled to a down payment prior to carrying out any work, i.e., an upfront payment. Thereby, the general contractor's insolvency risk is shifted to the wind farm SPV. If the general contractor becomes insolvent after receipt of the upfront payment, it will most likely neither carry out the work owed by it nor repay the upfront amount to the project SPV. In order to ensure this risk, a project SPV has to request being provided with an upfront payment guarantee amounting to the upfront payment issued by a bank.

Guarantee for Dismantling Costs

Usually, a project company is obliged to provide a security for the dismantling costs to the land owner and/or the responsible authority. Typically, providing a bank guarantee up to an amount of the estimated costs of the dismantling work is required by the authorities. In order to receive a valid building permit the lender needs to assess whether Wind Project II SPV has arranged for such permit; typically, the bank which is requested to finance the project also issues the guarantee regarding the dismantling costs.

9.5.2 Securities to Ensure the Lender's Position

The securities described in section 9.5.1 above only ensure the project itself. However, beyond that a financing bank or an investor which intends to acquire a project or shares in a project company needs additional securities which secure its position as financier or investor.

Joint Liability

Usually, a project company like Wind Project II SPV is a special purpose vehicle which has only been founded in order to operate a wind farm. Thus, such project company does not generate any revenues prior to the commissioning of the wind farm. Furthermore, if the project fails for whatever reason, the project company can be liquidated by its shareholder easily as it does not have any business relationships, agreements or assets which are of major value. Due to this situation a lender or a third party which concludes an agreement, e.g., for erection works, with the project company often requests from the – direct or indirect – shareholder of the project company assuming a joint liability for any obligations of the project company.

However, due to the fact that most financings are structured as non-recourse financing joint liabilities can mostly not successfully requested by the lender. Only in particular cases, a joint liability is conceivable. A typical situation might be that Wind Projects limited liability company plans to erect another wind farm close to the wind farm of Wind Project II SPV. It is intended that this new wind farm will be operated by Wind Project III SPV (a newly set up project company). In such cases, the purchaser of Wind Project II SPV may request a guarantee from Wind Project III SPV as well as Wind Projects limited liability company to be compensated for any losses caused by the wind turbines of Wind Project III SPV. Both Wind Project III SPV and Wind Projects limited liability company can be held jointly liable for such losses by Wind Project II SPV and/or its purchaser.

However, a joint liability of a project company's shareholder is not in each case recommendable. If the financial situation of the project company's shareholder and/or the whole group is tight (as described in Case 2) a joint liability of the shareholder does not secure the lender's position sufficiently because if the project company fails to repay the loan, it is most likely that its shareholder is not in the position to fulfill such claim instead of the project company. In such case a pledge of shares can be an alternative, as described in the following section.

Pledge of Shares

In Case 2, Green Energy Utility intends to acquire all shares in Wind Project II SPV from Wind Projects limited liability company. However, Wind Project II SPV's wind farm is not fully erected and commissioned yet. Thus, Green Energy Utility has – due to Wind Project II SPV's and its shareholder's financial situation – a severe risk that the wind farm may not be fully erected due to an insolvency. Due to its financial situation neither Wind Project II SPV nor Wind Projects limited liability company is in the position to arrange for third party securities. Furthermore, a joint liability of Wind Projects limited liability company cannot be considered as reasonable security as its financial situation is also tight so that – most likely – executing the claim based on the joint liability only causes the insolvency of Wind Projects limited liability company but does not result in a fulfillment of Green Energy

Utility's claim. In this situation, a pledge of shares in Wind Project I SPV – which has already been generating revenues – by Wind Projects limited liability company to Green Energy Utility is a reasonable security. If Wind Project limited liability company fails to erect the wind farm, Green Energy Utility can exploit the pledge of shares in Wind Project I SPV, i.e., Green Energy Utility becomes owner of the shares in an already revenues generating wind farm company.

Furthermore, a pledge of shares might be necessary for securing the project company's access to the public grid. Often, the access to the grid is managed by a separate legal entity which operates the grid access station and has concluded a grid access agreement with the grid operator. Pledging the shares in such grid access company might be necessary to secure the project company's right to use the grid access.

A pledge of shares is not limited to cases described above. In either case in which a joint liability of a – direct or indirect – shareholder is not of value, a lender or another third party which has a payment claim against Wind Project I SPV a pledge of shares in another company which is already generating revenues should be considered as alternative.

Assignment for Security

To secure the lender's claim for repayment of a loan granted to Wind Project II SPV the lender might furthermore request an assignment for security.

Within the erection phase an assignment of claims against the general contractor and the supplier of the renewable energy plant is recommendable to secure the delivery of the parts and the erection of the wind farm.

After commissioning of the wind farm an assignment of the claim for feed-in remuneration is recommendable. If Wind Project II SPV fails to fulfill the lender's claim for repayment of the loan, the assignment becomes effective and the lender is entitled to request the payment of the feed-in remuneration from the grid operator instead of Wind Project II SPV.

Furthermore, the lender should request an assignment for security of claims, in particular against

- the servicer who carries out the maintenance of the renewable energy plant,
- the financial and technical operations manager,
- the bank which operates the project company's current account,
- the seller of the project and
- the land owners under the lease agreements.

Mortgage

If the wind farm project company or an affiliate owns real estate, a lender may request granting a mortgage on this real estate. However, generally, neither the project company nor an affiliate owns real estate. Furthermore, even if one is actually owner of real estate, the value of said real estate usually does not correspond to the risks which need to be secured.

Right to Become Party to the Rent Agreement and Priority Notice

The conclusion of a rent agreement by Wind Project II SPV and granting a limited personal servitude to it by the land owner as described above in section 9.5.1 does only secure the project itself, but it does not secure the lender's position in case of a credit default. Rather, the lender needs own securities which entitle it to continue the operation of the wind farm after its commissioning. The lender needs the following securities:

- The lender needs the right to become party to the rent agreement concluded between Wind Project II SPV and the land owner or to designate a third party to become party to said rent agreement if Wind Project II SPV fails to fulfill its payment obligations under the loan agreement. In this case, the lender is entitled to become party to the rent agreement instead of Wind Project II SPV. The land owner has to agree in the rent agreement to such possible change of party to the agreement.
- In addition to the limited personal servitude to be granted to Wind Project II SPV the land owner has to grant a priority notice to the lender regarding the registration of a limited personal servitude in favor of the lender or a third party designated by the lender as beneficiary. Thereby, the lender's right in case of a credit failure to operate the wind farm or to designate a third party to do so is secured *in rem*. Thus, also the lender's position is secured in case of an insolvency of the land owner.

9.6 Remarks and Recommendations

Due to various risks which may occur during the various phases of renewable energy projects (erection, commissioning and operation), a lender has to request comprehensive securities. Since a project financing is non-recourse in most cases, the lender will not be able to hold himself harmless on the account of the project company's shareholder. Instead, the project itself has to serve as security for all potential claims of the lender against the beneficiary of the loan, i.e., the project company. The lender's aim has to be securing the unobstructed operation of the renewable energy plant. Therefore, in particular an assignment for security is very important to secure that the lender – or a third party nominated by it – can operate the renewable energy plant if the project company fails to fulfill its obligations towards the lender.

10 Power Purchase Agreements

Claus Urbanke, Jens Göbel

10.1 Power Purchase Agreement ("PPA")

A Power Purchase Agreement ("PPA") is commonly referred to as a long-term power purchase agreement between a generator as seller and an electricity consumer as buyer. The buyer of a PPA secures a long-term power supply at a fixed price and with a specified quality such as the origin of the electricity, interruptibility, volume flexibility, etc. Buyers can be private or public utilities as well as large end consumers or electricity trading companies.

10.1.1 Corporate PPA

PPAs have been around since the dawn of electrification. Prior to the construction of nationwide interconnected power grids, power plants were either built in the immediate vicinity of load centers or industrial companies located themselves near power plants, from which they drew their electricity directly.

In Germany, PPAs have not played a significant role in enabling power plant investments in recent decades. Prior to the energy market liberalization, power plants were built and financed by vertically integrated energy companies. When the electricity market liberalization began, not much changed. Although the newly created wholesale market for electricity provided a platform for short and long-term electricity trading, the price signals created by trading electricity were not much used as a basis for investment decisions in generation capacity but rather used to optimally dispatch the existing power plant fleet.

10.1.2 Renewable Corporate PPA

Also with the advent of wind power, photovoltaics and other regenerative power generation technologies, PPAs played no role in Germany. Although new, independent generators and investors appeared on the scene, the EEG granted them fixed long-term feed-in tariffs, so that PPAs were not necessary to secure the financing of renewable energy projects.

The EEG feed-in tariffs for renewable energy generation projects were initially significantly higher than the generation costs of conventional power plants. However, the recent renewable energy tenders organized by the German regulatory office (Bundesnetzagentur) have shown how competitive wind and solar projects are today: The guaranteed remuneration per megawatt hour from photovoltaics fell to below

https://doi.org/10.1515/9783110607888-010

50 EUR/MWh fixed for 20 years and for onshore wind energy to below 40 EUR/MWh. The result for the German government's call for tenders for the offshore wind farm "He Dreiht" in the North Sea caused a stir in the renewable energy community. The German energy company EnBW plans to set up this project as "merchant project" without state subsidies, remunerated only by proceeds from selling the wind park's production at market prices.

In this context and also because of industry associations such as the BDEW presenting models how the expansion of renewables can increasingly take place without subsidies, i.e., outside the EEG,[1] Renewable Corporate PPAs have become a focal area for many market participants who started to consider Renewable Corporate PPAs as financing tool for renewable projects. Developers and investors are eager to build PPA expertise within their company, to the extent that such capability is not yet available. Financers are preparing themselves for project finance that is not secured by government funding but rather by Renewable Corporate PPAs.

The following sections give an overview of the current PPA market with a focus on Renewable Corporate PPAs from wind turbines. The text references, if not explicitly mentioned, the German electricity market.

10.2 Seller's Motivation to Conclude a PPA

10.2.1 Two or More Cannot Be Wrong

10–20 years ago, during the early phases of electricity market deregulation in Germany, some PPA transactions were reported where an investor had to present a long term PPA of significant size in relation to the total project size to its board in order to reach a final investment decision. Typically, PPA sellers were companies that (a) had not yet made significant investments in generation capacity in Germany before, (b) were trying to realize investments in technologies in which they were not invested in their home market or (c) both of the aforementioned.

10.2.2 Profit Generation

Also during the early phases of the German electricity market deregulation, municipal and regional power supply companies signed long term PPAs for coal or gas generation. The reason for this was the supply companies' realization that they were

1 https://www.bdew.de/presse/presseinformationen/marktkraefte-beim-erneuerbaren-ausbau-staerken/

competing with vertically integrated electricity companies in the sales segment but were relying on them to purchase their supplies. To make themselves independent from the vertically integrated power companies, the supply companies signed PPAs with companies that built and operated state-of-the-art conventional plants for them and made capacity available to each PPA holder in relation to the PPA holders' share in the asset. The PPA writer's motivation for selling PPAs was to generate profit by developing and operating the plant for the PPA holders.

10.3 Prerequisite for Project Financing

There have been some large-scale conventional and renewable power plant projects in Germany in recent years that energy companies and large municipal energy companies have realized without relying on project financing. However, the number of these projects is small in comparison to the number of renewable energy projects which were realized using project-financing during the same time period. For investors in such projects, a PPA or a guaranteed feed-in tariff are key enablers to realize their investment project. The long-term hedged revenues from power marketing ensure the financial viability of the power plant ("bankability"). Thus, the PPA or the guaranteed tariff are necessary conditions for the realization of the power plant. The PPA term required by the project-financing bank will normally correspond to the maturity of the debt.

10.4 Buyer's Motivation to Conclude a PPA: Partial Hedge

Most European electricity markets are characterized by overcapacity in the generation market and stagnant electricity consumption. During the time period for which there is wholesale market liquity most renewables projects cannot yet compete with wholesale prices. Hence, a direct investment in generation capacity that does not feed-in behind the metering point and is thus excempt from grid fees and maybe other levies is usually not commercially attractive for industrial customers compared to a conventional electricity supply contract. Still, long-term supply of electricity, ideally on "favorable terms," seems to be the main driver for the conclusion of a PPA. However, favorable conditions are often a matter of opinion, at least in the long-term view.

If price hedging is the driver for a PPA then one would expect that the PPA duration is either congruent with (i) in the case of an industrial: the budgeting horizon or the liquidity horizion for the hedger's output or (ii) in the case of a power supplier: the duration of the supply contracts.

With this in mind, it seems surprising that industrials as well as supply companies enter into renewable power PPAs that by far exceed the time frames for which they budget, can hedge their outputs or have supply contracts in their portfolio.[2] Such long term commitments might put the PPA buyer into a situation where in the event of lower wholesale power prices in the future, the buyer's competitive position is becoming disadvantagous compared to the competitive position of competitors who have not hedged prices.

It seems that industrials, especially in the Nordic region, are entering into renewable power PPAs in the belief that their competitors in other parts of the world will not be able to secure cheaper power supplies in the future (than them). Supply companies seem to enter into long term PPAs for volumes not greater than volumes representing power customers that they expect to retain no matter what. Moreover, supply companies seem to view the renewable characteristics of power as an asset that will become scarcer going forward. Hence, they are willing to invest in Renewable PPAs relating to production assets with fairly mature technologies at what is perceived to be good locations.

10.5 Carbon Neutrality or Renewable Energy Targets

Non-price elements play an important role in the conclusion of Renewable Corporate PPAs. Self-imposed CO_2 targets or Renewable Energy targets are often drivers for energy supply companies and large energy consumers to conclude Renewable Corporate PPAs. In the case of large corporates or energy supply companies, however, PPAs are in competition with project participation through equity because depending on the structure of the PPA, such contract can have a very similar risk profile compared to an equity investment in a generation asset.

Germany is a pioneer with respect to the energy transition. However, other countries have taken the lead with respect to Renewable Corporate PPAs. The USA could claim to be Renewable Corporate PPA pioneers, especially the big US tech companies. Before they discovered Renewable Corporate PPAs, the big tech companies faced criticism from environmentalists. Growing corporate profits and high energy consumption on the one hand and a self-image to be committed to do good (Google's "Do not be evil") on the other hand, led to a switch to renewable energy sources. The high-tech companies paid particular attention to Additionality, i.e., to enable new projects through Renewable Corporate PPAs.

In line with the foregoing, Google has established itself as the largest buyer of Renewable Corporate PPAs in recent years. Alphabet Inc., the Google Holding Company, now has a total of 2,397 MW of US renewable energy generating capacity

2 https://www.cnbc.com/2018/07/19/norsk-hydro-subsidiary-signs-worlds-longest-corporate-wind-power-co.html. According to the press Hydro Energi AS signed a 29-year wind power PPA that will supply a Norsk hydro Aluminium plant.

under contract and 3,186 MW worldwide, according to news service Bloomberg New Energy Finance (at the time of writing this article).[3] Mathematically, these Renewable Corporate PPAs allegedly cover the entire power consumption of Google. In November 2017, Microsoft announced that it had completed the largest corporate PPA in Europe with 180 MW.[4] Amazon is another major US tech company that has concluded several Renewable Corporate PPAs.

Tax reasons might contribute to the fact that Renewable Corporate PPAs play a bigger role in the US than in other markets. The US American tax system promotes corporate PPAs through Production Tax Credit ("PTC") and Investment Tax Credit ("ITC").[5]

It therefore remains questionable to which companies and to which countries the Google, Microsoft or Amazon examples are transferable. Surely, there are many companies that are in terms of their size and their creditworthiness potential Renewable Corporate PPA buyers. Many of them such as the RE100 companies have set themselves equally ambitious sustainability goals like Google, Microsoft or Amazon.[6] However, this does not hold true for the majority of industrial companies. PPAs are complex contracts with a complicated risk profile. An experienced energy manager should be entrusted with the responsibility for PPAs. However, energy management departments in European industrial companies are often having different focus areas, e.g., shorter-term measures to improve energy efficiency or the short-term optimization of energy costs. Moreover, energy managers in companies whose core business is not energy will face the challenge to get buy-in from their management and supervisory board to conclude PPAs because of the long-term nature and the monetary value of the PPAs. These are hurdles for realizing long-term PPAs with industrial off-takers.

10.6 Characteristics of a PPA

10.6.1 Commodity Related Risk

Price Risk

A PPA transfers long-term price risk from the generator to the buyer. Price risk is generally understood to mean the risk of an adverse change in wholesale electricity prices. For Renewable PPAs, however, the market value risk must also be considered.

3 https://www.bloomberg.com/news/articles/2017-11-30/google-biggest-corporate-buyer-of-clean-power-is-buying-more.
4 https://about.bnef.com/blog/microsoft-signs-largest-corporate-ppa-europe/.
5 http://www.nortonrosefulbright.com/knowledge/publications/139555/renewable-energy-tax-incentives.
6 http://there100.org/.

The market value risk refers to the value of the plant-specific generation profile, i.e., a possible difference between the value of the power production of a plant and the average electricity price on the market (see Figure 10.1).

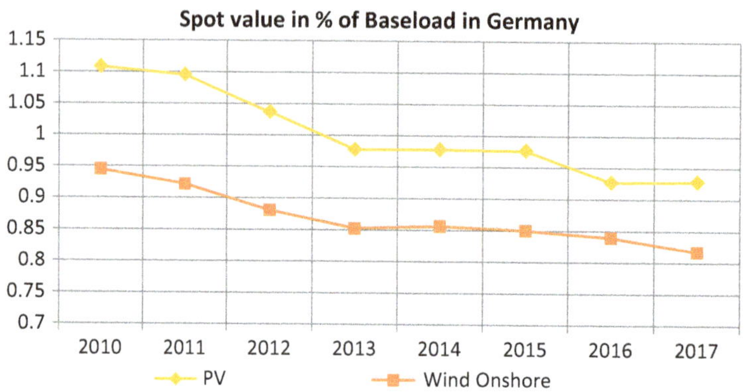

Figure 10.1: Market value in % of German baseload price (own representation).

As long as power generation from wind turbines account for only a small portion of the electricity mix, wind generators theoretically achieve a wholesale price that roughly equals the average price over all hours, the so-called Baseload price. The price of electricity produced by solar systems should even be more expensive than the Baseload price because solar systems generate during the day when prices are usually higher. However, if the share of renewable energy in an electric system increases then there is a cannibalization effect. Whenever strong a wind blows or the sun shines, or both the wind blows and the sun shines, the renewable energy feed-in will be high which results in lower spot prices for electricity. Feed-in performance of renewables and wholesale electricity prices are negatively correlated.

In Germany, wind turbines now generate electricity that covers roughly 20% of the country's electricity demand. The price discount for their generation relative to market price for delivering consistently over all 8,760 hours of the year was 15% in 2013–2015 and 18% in 2017. Even the German solar PV generation has to accept a discount to the Baseload price, even though solar generation is zero during the normally cheaper night hours and only takes place during the normally more expensive day-time hours. The high installed capacity of PV in Germany explains this discount. If the sun shines over large parts of Germany, the solar power yield and the electricity supply are high, however, the electricity prices will then be rather low.

Anyone who has ever negotiated a direct marketing agreement knows that the individual market value of a production facility can differ by up to several Euros per megawatt hour from the average German market value. There are various reasons for different individual generation profiles. Reasons are for example:

- Operating restrictions due to environmental regulations, immission control or shadow strike;
- Bottlenecks in the grid limiting feed-in and consequently triggering down-regulations by the grid operator;
- Local weather phenomena compared to the average weather;
- Age of the plant or technology: Modern plants tend to have a higher market value than older plants or older plant types.

In any case, the forecast of the future development of the individual market value over a longer period of time is as challenging as the electricity price forecast itself. One could argue that the market value risk should naturally remain with the PPA seller. However, if the PPA buyer accepts a fixed price then the market value risk is completely transferred to the PPA buyer. A PPA with a price floor partially transfers the market value risk is to the PPA buyer. The price floor can be seen as the cap for the acceptance of the market value risk.

Another point a Renewable Corporate PPA buyer has to take into account: to what extent the delivery profile from the contracted generation facility fits the PPA buyer's consumption profile. In many cases it will probably not fit very well. Figure 10.2 below demonstrates this for a consumer who has contracted a PV PPA. In this illustrative example, a consumer with an almost flat load pattern turns into a prosumer who both injects and offtakes electricity from the grid. Entering into a solar PPA will radically change the consumers' exposure to power prices. The consumer turns from a baseload buyer into an offpeak buyer and a peak seller.

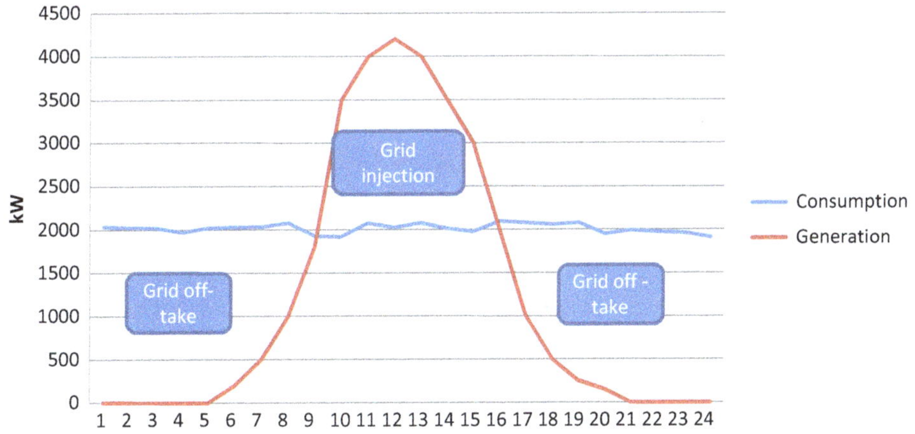

Figure 10.2: Delivery profile versus consumption profile (own representation).

Furthermore, the PPA buyer is responsible for the short-term use of the generating plant, known as Direct Marketing (*Direktvermarktung*) in Germany. The short-term use includes the production forecast, the marketing of production in the day-ahead and in the intraday market, possibly also in the market for regulation capacity, reduction in the event of negative[7] electricity prices, possibly the billing of credits in the event of interventions by the responsible network operator, etc. This activity will remain, even if a renewable energy project is being realized outside the EEG, an important value component for the project as a whole and therefore also for a PPA.

Volume Risk

Electricity supply contracts from renewable plants must contain provisions addressing the possibility that there is an increase or decrease in the performance of a plant. Higher or lower than expected production volumes may have plant-specific reasons or may be due to weather, e.g., wind or hours of sunshine. While technical risk can be reasonably well assessed or insured against, weather risk hedging is not trivial.[8] From the perspective of the PPA buyer, it is problematic if the PPA buyer gets less power delivered than the buyer has contracted (for the possible pricing structures see 3.3). The PPA buyer will therefore most likely only be prepared to accept a fixed price or a price floor for the quantity that will be purchased with a high probability, e.g., the P90 production. The PPA buyer also off-takes any production volumes beyond the P90, however, the P90 excess volumes are bought at spot prices, so that there is no price risk for the PPA buyer for these additional quantities.

From the PPA seller's point of view, the aforementioned off-take structure is acceptable as long as at least the generation volumes are price hedged which are used in the downside scenario of the financing bank, e.g., the P90. For the additional production volumes, the seller receives the spot market price.

Pricing Structures

Pricing a long-term supply of electricity is not a trivial task. The maturity of such a supply contract is usually more than 10 years. Hence it is well beyond the time period for which there is sufficient liquidity in the wholesale market. Price signals from the market are therefore not available for the entire PPA term. Hence, pricing must be negotiated between the PPA buyer and PPA seller based on their market

7 Depending on the market rules, it could make economic sense to continue generating even during negative price hours if other benefits linked to the generation outweigh the losses incurred by the negative spot prices.

8 Weather Derivatives based on weather phenomena that are not related to temperatures are seldomly found in Europe. Because of the limited number of Weather Derivatives based on windspeeds or solar radiation, we will not further expand on them in this chapter.

expectations and project requirements. The following table gives an overview of the most important factors to be considered for PPA pricing.

The energy deliveries can be settled at a fixed price or they can be spot price indexed and thus settled at spot prices (see Table 10.2). A fixed price can be kept constant over the term of the PPA or be adjusted regularly, for example, with a constant rate of increase. Inflation indexation for energy deliveries does not seem to make sense, as wholesale electricity prices have not been correlated with common inflation indices such as consumer price inflation indices in the past. Fixed prices seem to make more sense for the liquid period of the wholesale market. In Germany, there are frequent transactions being observed for the next three to six years with decreasing transaction intensity the farther the delivery year lies in the future. The existence of a tradable wholesale market price facilitates pricing, as well as gives the PPA buyer the ability to manage its exposure by entering into hedging transactions.

For the illiquid second half of the PPA term, a variable pricing structure is more appropriate. Under such a variable pricing structure the PPA seller receives the hourly day-ahead spot price minus either (i) a fee defined as a percentage of the spot price or (ii) a fixed fee in EUR / MWh. This fee covers the costs for market access and balancing energy. In a variable pricing structure, the producer or PPA seller bears the market value risk.

In a variable pricing structure, the long-term price hedging can be accomplished by an annual price floor. With a price floor, each year after the end of a delivery year, the volume-weighted average delivery price that the PPA seller has received is determined. If this price is below the contractually agreed price floor, the PPA buyer will refund the difference to the PPA seller. The price floor is a key element for the bankability of the PPA. Thanks to the price floor there is a secured minimum price, which can be easily used in the risk model of the project-financing bank. The price floor is a type of insurance contract that the PPA seller enters into with the PPA buyer. To minimize the cost of this insurance, the parties may agree that the PPA seller will reimburse the PPA buyer for any (already received) price floor payments in future years, should the electricity prices recover. Another possibility to reduce the insurance premium is embedding a prolongation option in the original PPA. The renewal option can be exercised by the PPA buyer in the event that price floor payments are still outstanding at the end of the original PPA term.

The Figure 10.3 below highlights the functioning of the pricing structures described above. All numbers are chosen such that the example is illustrative.

The price floor guarantees the PPA seller a minimum income. A price cap covers the maximum income of the PPA seller. There are potentially additional revenue opportunities beyond the secured income. These opportunities are subject to uncertainty and of interest to the investor, but not the maximum risk-averse project-financing bank. The PPA buyer may be able to consider the additional revenue opportunities in the PPA pricing. As a result, in the case of a PPA with a price cap,

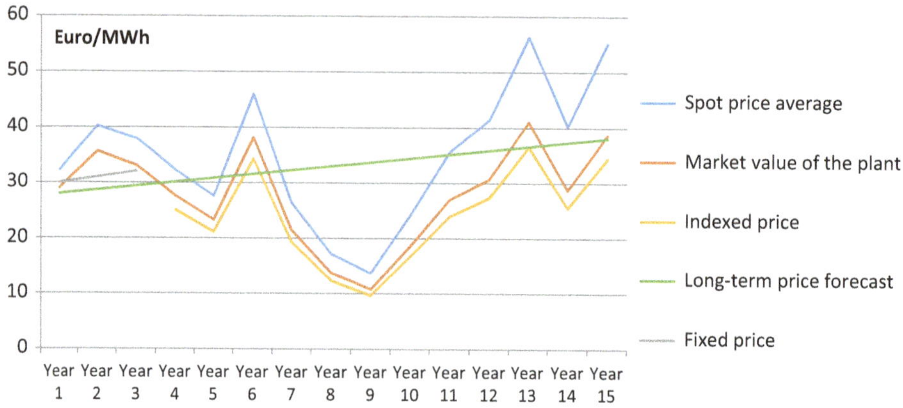

Figure 10.3: Functioning of pricing structures (own representation).

the PPA buyer may be able to increase the price floor, accept a lower discount on the spot price or a lower fixed fee in return for participation in potential price increases.

The project financing banks are not worried about the risk of default in EEG-sponsored investments because the revenue side is guaranteed by the Federal Republic of Germany. In case of project financing without EEG (or a comparable scheme), the project-financing bank will normally require the duration of the PPA to be aligned with the project financing. Moreover, the creditworthiness of the PPA buyer and/or the contract terms for credit protection must be in line with the bank's requirements in order to obtain project financing based on a PPA.

The bank will also usually require the conclusion of a direct agreement governing the triangular relationship between the PPA seller, PPA buyer and the bank, including, but not limited to, the bank's rights in the event of a failure of the PPA seller.

Moreover, the PPA has to be aligned with the relevant terms of the EPC contract and the maintenance contracts.

10.6.2 Non-Commodity-Related Characteristics

Invoicing and Payment

Payments are normally made on a monthly basis. The 20th day of the month following the delivery month has established itself as standard payment target date in wholesale electricity trading. Possible price floor payments are settled and paid in January or at the latest in February after a delivery year. Obviously, hardly any generation asset will go online exactly when the year changes. The price floor, however, refers to the calendar year. Hence clauses laying out rules for the first (fractional) year of the contract as well as for the last (fractional) year of the contract period are required.

Table 10.1: Factors for PPA pricing (own representation).

Market Price Expectation	**What will the market price be beyond the liquid horizon?**
Hedging Cost	Transaction cost; Cost for market access; All other cost related to managing the risk exposure.
Market Value of the Generation Profile	How will the discount of the specific generation profile be compared to baseload prices evolve going forward?
Cost for Balancing Energy	How will the cost for balancing energy evolve going forward?[9]
Cost of Credit	Both PPA buyer and PPA seller are exposed to credit risk that needs to be priced in. If the credit risk can be actively managed – what are the cost for active credit risk management?
Risk Margin	In addition to the aforementioned factors, unspecified or small risks remain for the PPA buyer and PPA seller that are difficult if not impossible to hedge against. These risks are partially offset by difficult to quantify advantages such as e.g., the guaranteed origin of the electricity.

Table 10.2: Representations of possible pricing structures (own representation).

Pricing Structure	**Graphical Representation of the Effects of Pricing Structures**
Spot Price Indexation Market acess only; Price risk completely with the project.	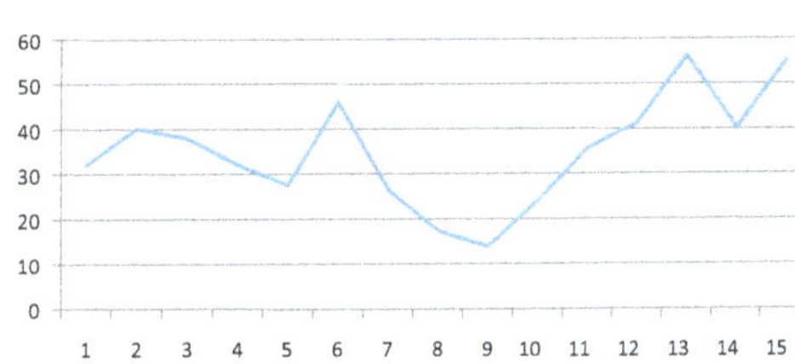

9 It is important to note that a "fee" for providing Direct Marketing is largely determined by the cost for balancing energy.

Table 10.2 (continued)

Pricing Structure	Graphical Representation of the Effects of Pricing Structures
Cap and Floor Guaranteed minimum price ensures bankability; Price cap which reduces the cost for the ensured price floor.	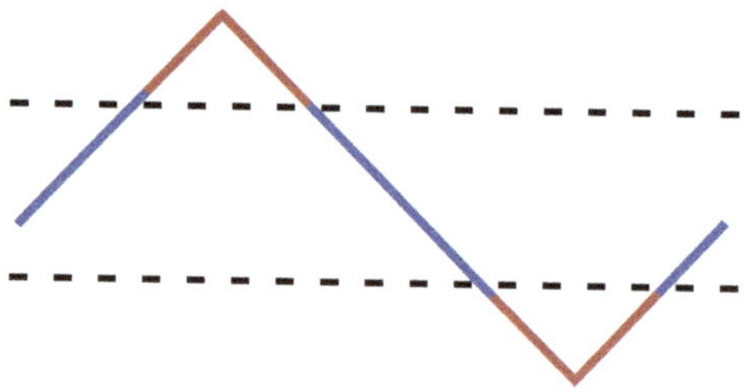
Fixed Price Price certainty; Normally shorter term; Higher familiarity with such a pricing structure among Corporates.	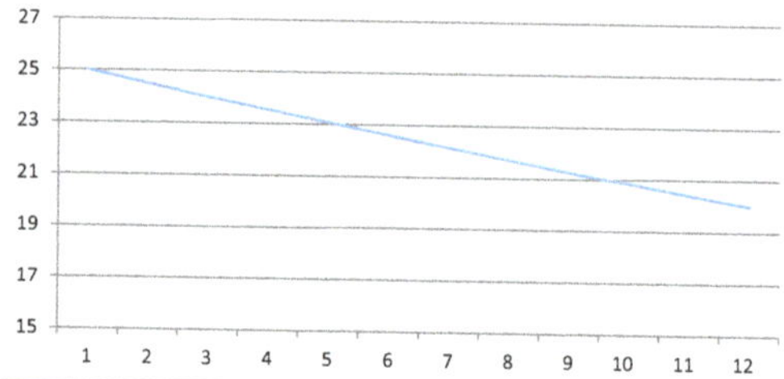

PPA Milestones

The PPA is often negotiated in parallel or prior to the conclusion of the financing agreements and then signed at about the same time with the financing agreements. This implies there is still time left from when the PPA is signed until plant commissioning and delivery of the first megawatt hour occur. The PPA therefore contains clauses that become effective with the contract signature as well as conditions precedent. Condition precedent typically found in PPAs are (in no particular order): the proper accreditation of the generation asset by the network operator including the commissioning of the metering point or provisions of a financial guarantee.

Under the PPA the (regular) delivery period normally commences immediately upon successful completion of the test period during which the generation asset is commissioned by the manufacturer and subsequently handed over. Selling electricity in the spot market might not be feasible during the test period because it is difficult to plan production. Hence, during the test period deliveries to the purchaser's or the direct marketer's balancing group could be cashed out with the prices for balancing energy.

Depending on the agreed pricing structure, after the PPA has been signed, the PPA buyer will start to manage the resulting expected electricity exposures in the wholesale market, meaning the PPA buyer will trade electricity to hedge the value of the PPA. Therefore, the PPA buyer will want to ensure that the electricity deliveries actually start on the agreed date and embed penalties for failure to deliver or delayed deliveries in the PPA.

Ideally, the PPA also already contains provisions addressing a possible increase in generating capacity at the metering point during the term of the PPA. In the case of a wind PPA such increase in generating capacity might be the result of connecting additional wind turbines to the metering point.

Potential Incremental Revenue Streams

During the term of the PPA, it is likely that there will be opportunities to commercially optimize the generation asset. Examples for such commercial optimization opportunities are the asset's participation in the market for reserve capacity or network services or specific certifications of the plant's output. The provision of reserve capacity could have an impact on the operation of the system and thus also on the PPA. The parties should therefore have already agreed on how additional income opportunities will be shared in the PPA. If the PPA buyer is an energy trading company, the PPA buyer is most likely well positioned to realize additional income through such commercial optimizations. If such a PPA buyer has the right to participate in these optimizations, this option value will most likely be considered in the PPA pricing.

Maintenance, Commercial Operations, and Availability

The PPA seller is obliged to agree the maintenance plan with the PPA buyer. Unplanned unavailability of the generation asset must be communicated to the PPA buyer immediately. Typically, the parties will agree on a minimum availability of the generation asset or a one-sided termination right for the PPA buyer, should a certain availability threshold not be reached.

Financial Guarantees

The PPA buyer will be required to demonstrate that a certain investment grade or better credit rating is maintained over the life of the PPA. If the PPA buyer does not fulfill this requirement because the PPA buyer's creditworthiness or the creditworthiness of the PPA buyer's guarantor decreases over time, a security such as a letter of comfort or a bank guarantee must be provided. The level and design of the security is one of the central negotiating points of a PPA.

It is often unrealistic to assume that all revenues stemming from the generation during the remainder of the PPA can be fully covered by collateral. The term of the PPA is likely to exceed the possible timeframe for credit insurance provided by banks or credit insurers anyway. Therefore, the creditworthiness of the PPA buyer is key. Small and medium-sized companies are therefore almost categorically excluded as

PPA buyers (and thus large parts of the total electricity demand in a country). Even with financially (very) strong PPA buyers, the financing bank will consider a default scenario in its long-term view. In such a stress scenario it is examined how a failure of the PPA buyer in an adverse market price scenario (where electricity prices are lower compared to prices when the PPA was agreed) would affect the project ("second way out").

In case the PPA buyer is an energy company, the PPA will typically not be between the parent company and the PPA seller, but rather between a subsidiary, e.g., the parent company's energy trading arm and the PPA seller. This will usually require a parent company guarantee, which will commit the parent company to meet the payment obligations of its subsidiary up to a maximum agreed amount. This maximum agreed amount may be fixed, but it may also change over the term of the contract, e.g., adjusted to prevailing market prices using a predetermined formula. Such a dynamic guarantee scheme would take into account the fact that, should the PPA buyer fail, a replacement PPA can only be concluded at the then possible commercial conditions.

Integration into a Virtual Power Plant

Renewable generation assets are subject to the direct marketing obligation in Germany. The situation is similar in most other international markets where wind and solar generators are subject to the same scheduling and balancing requirements as conventional generators. The market framework and requirements for direct marketing vary between countries. In Europe, it will usually make sense to integrate the renewable generation asset into the Virtual Power Plant of an aggregator who sells the energy in the spot market and takes care of all related activities such as forecasting and scheduling. To calibrate the generation forecast optimally, the marketer requires access to the generation data in real time. If necessary the PPA buyer will send control signals through the Virtual Power Plant to either meet regulatory requirements or to commercially optimize the plant. The direct marketeter will also assume responsibility for processing any interventions by the network operator in terms of data processing and settlement (for example EisMan regulation in Germany).

If the direct marketer and the PPA buyer are different companies, rules governing the interface between the two companies must be included in the PPA. Relevant issues in this context are:

- Where and at what point in time does the ownership of the electricity pass between both companies?
- Is it possible that the direct marketer will never hold the legal title to the electricity but acts solely as service provider?
- How can the cash flows be structured if the electricity is not delivered into the PPA buyer's balancing group but sold directly to the spot exchange?

Change-in-Law

The change-in-law paragraph is often viewed very critically, as at first glance it seems to lessen the reliability of the PPA. The underlying fear is that in the event of a change in the legal or regulatory circumstances, the possibility of extraordinary termination opens up a cheap option out of the contract. However, a change-in-law clause is essential for long-term contracts, as the likelihood of a relevant legislative or regulatory change over ten or even fifteen years is quite high. The intention of the paragraph is that the parties negotiate in good faith so as to obtain a contract adjustment that takes into account the changed circumstances, but does not compromise the balance of commercial results and contractual obligations as of the date of concluding the original contract. Quite often such a paragraph also includes the possibility to consult an independent expert to give advice if the original commercial balance is maintained. Only in the event that the parties cannot agree within a certain time period on contract amendments, a special termination right can be evoked.

Other Characteristics

Moreover, force majeure, termination, insurance, liability, transfer of rights and obligations, confidentiality, jurisdiction and applicable law are important elements of a PPA, but will not be further addressed here.

10.7 Conclusion

Among Renewable project developers in Germany there are many discussions around the questions for how much longer there will be an EEG subsidy and how to prepare for financing renewable energy projects in the post-EEG era.

Many believe PPAs will be the key enabler to finance renewable energy projects after the phasing out of government sponsored funding models. PPAs between renewable generators and large consumers, energy companies and traders will certainly become more prevalent. Because of the credit quality requirements with respect to the PPA buyer, they will not represent an all-inclusive substitute for an EEG-type support. It seems that if all corporates and supply companies that have the capacity and the desire to conclude long term renewable PPAs have concluded their PPAs there will be a gap between renewable energy projects seeking funding and contracted volumes.

Commodity exchanges are positioning themselves to help bridge this gap. If the term for which electricity is traded were longer and if clearing were available for these longer term products it is conceivable that more PPA buying interest would emerge from players that will enter into PPAs and attempt to hedge their commodity exposure by means of (cleared) exchange trades. Such hedging is not without risks. Even if a commodity exposure is hedged with a standard product, there is a mismatch between the standard product and the delivery profile contracted under the PPA. Moreover, in the event of rising electricity prices the PPA buyer must meet the clearing house's marging calls.

The exchange or its Clearing House, respectively, will absorb the credit risk of the long term commodity transaction. The commodity price risk of that transaction will not be absorbed but only intermediated by the exchange. In order to create more liquidity for longer dated products, the exchange must attract long term buyers that cannot or would not conclude long term PPAs but are happy to trade (more standardized products) on exchange. It will be interesting to see which type of actors will assume the long term commodity risk should the exchanges succeed in creating deep long term liquidity.

Irrespective of the exchanges' future role in the context of PPAs and irrespective of whether PPAs will be the key enabler for obtain project financing for Renewable PPAs, it is conceivable that a business model will emerge in which financially strong buyers, e.g., energy suppliers or traders, bundle PPAs upstream and conclude counter-transactions with customers on the downstream side. If there is sufficient term liquidity at exchanges the portfolio size of such players will probably be bigger as they are able to warehouse bigger PPA positions by transferring commodity price risk.

11 Developing a Renewable Energy Project: Dos and Don'ts

Rosa Tarragó

11.1 Introduction: Dos and Don'ts

Like everything in this world, there are certain written (and unwritten) rules when it comes to successful project development. From best practices and guidelines to rules of thumb, project developers, owners and investors are not short of advice or ideas when it comes to their day-to-day duties of bringing projects from the drawing board to financial close.

So what are the basic dos and don'ts of project development? What practices should a project developer embrace and what ones should they avoid in the course of their duties?

This section outlines some of the dos and don'ts in order to successfully develop a bankable renewable energy project.

11.1.1 Renewable Energy Project Demand

A major expansion of power infrastructure is urgently needed and it makes economic, social and environmental sense. In developed economies, the power systems that generate and transmit electricity, as well as the industries, buildings, cities and transport systems that consume it, need to do two things: reduce emissions (both by using low-carbon alternatives like solar and wind power, and by consuming or wasting less power in the first place); and increase their competitiveness with zero subsidies.

The advent of zero subsidies for renewable energy means that renewables are now cheaper than conventional power production across the most developed markets. Wind and solar power producers have been reducing costs and increasing efficiency and reliability for nearly two decades.

Europe is simultaneously facing two challenges: the transition from a fossil- and nuclear-based power generation system to a primarily renewable energy-based power generation system and the changing nature of energy demand. On the one hand, power plants are either too expensive (such as the new nuclear plants under construction in Finland, the UK and France, and the new coal plants in the Netherlands), obsolete (e.g., existing nuclear plants in France), or being phased out for regulatory reasons (such as the national phase-out of nuclear and coal plants in Germany). On the other hand, the accelerated adoption of electric cars and trucks, as well as sector coupling (building heating and power) will further boost electricity demand. The

https://doi.org/10.1515/9783110607888-011

global preference for electrical power will give rise to the decentralization of power generation, the adaptation of the transmission and distribution grids, and the implementation of smart mini-grids in both developed and developing countries.

11.1.2 Challenges Associated with Non-Recourse Project Financing

Non-recourse project financing, without access to guarantees from the project sponsors, requires the treatment of renewable energy projects as hard assets with long-term revenue stability, controllable expenses, a conservative capital structure (typically including long-term, fixed-rate, amortizing debt) and good visibility on long-term cash flows.[1] Nowadays, the ability of a particular renewable energy project to meet these criteria depends largely on its degree of exposure to the main risks in the power sector. Among these key risks are exposure to wholesale prices (in turn influenced by commodity prices, the national power fleet and economic growth), the possibility of regulatory change, and counterparty and country risks.

11.1.3 Opportunities in Developing Countries

Renewable energy project opportunities in developing countries mainly arise as a result of three factors: (i) increasing demand driven by Gross Domestic Product (GDP) (emerging economies are expected to grow by an annual average of 4.6% over the next five years[2]); (ii) the gap in electricity supply and reliable power; and (iii) their ability to sustainably reduce the need for emergency power produced by cost and carbon-intensive heavy fuel oil (HFO) plants.

Developing countries are catching up with developed countries in terms of infrastructure quality and have dominated the improvement rankings over the past decade. Permits, land acquisition and environmental approval policies vary considerably from one country to the next; it is therefore important to consider best country practices

1 The London-based Loan Market Association (LMA) with the support of the International Capital Market Association (ICMA), as well as the Asia Pacific Loan Market Association (APLMA) is launching a set of Green Loan Principles to promote consistency across financing markets. An indicative list of eligible projects includes production and transmission of renewable energy, pollution prevention and control, sustainable natural resources management, climate change adaptation and green buildings. See "Green Loan Principles could define 'new shape of green finance'," *Environmental Finance Magazine*, March 23, 2018.

2 "A Secular Outlook: Emerging markets – home to the next great tech revolution," Pictet Asset Management, July 2018.

when defining the geography of the project.[3] This has a direct impact on the timely and cost-effective delivery of a ready-to-build (RtB) renewable energy project.

11.2 Structure of the Section

This section on developing renewable energy projects is divided into three main sections: the Idea Phase, the Conceptual Phase and the Contractual Phase. In the Idea Phase section, the project dos and don'ts are sorted into three main groups: the dos and don'ts of site selection with regard to technical requirements, the dos and don'ts of choosing a country based on the legal and institutional framework, and the dos and don'ts relating to potential financing and due diligence on partnerships. The Conceptual Phase section outlines the dos and don'ts of assessing the feasibility of the project from a technical, commercial, financial, environmental and social point of view. This phase will give rise to a robust project with a full set of permits. The Contractual Phase section presents the dos and don'ts of Land Lease Agreements (LLAs), Power Purchase Agreements (PPAs), Connection Agreements (CAs), Implementation Agreement (IAs), Engineering, Procurement and Construction (EPC) agreements and Operation and Maintenance (O&M) agreements, even when these agreements are based on bankable templates. Assuming a comfortable insurance package is available, the outcome of this phase will be a RtB and ready-to-finance (RtF) project. Lastly, a summary of these findings is provided at the end of the section.

Lessons learned from projects and additional information are included in boxes.

11.3 The Idea Phase

Perform a realistic assessment to turn an *idea* into a *project* (see Table 11.1). With the liberalization of the power markets, project developers now have more and more opportunities to transform ideas into projects, thus becoming independent power producers (IPPs). In this section, the owner of the idea starts project development from scratch after they have identified the technical requirements, a game-changing legal and institutional environment, and available financial support.

3 The World Bank Group has created the "ease of doing business index." Higher rankings (a low numerical value) indicate better, usually simpler, regulations for businesses and stronger protections of property rights.

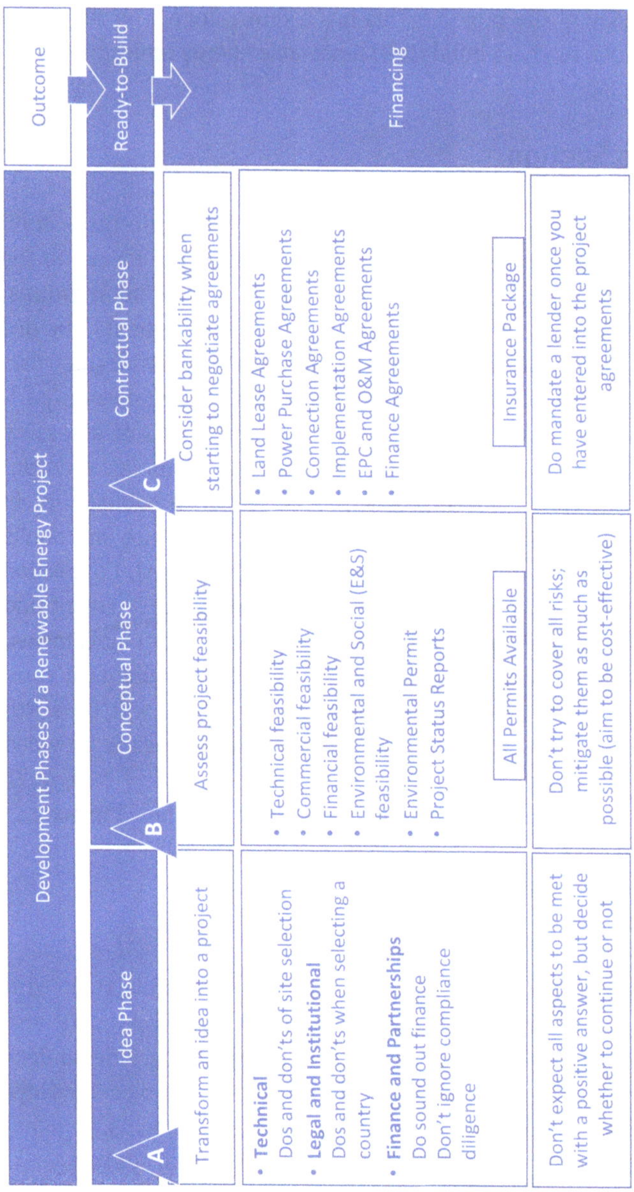

Figure 11.1: Development phases of a renewable energy project (own representation).

Table 11.1: The idea phase: dos and don'ts (own representation).

The Idea Phase Turning an idea into a project		
Technical	DO	Do select a site based on factors such as resource availability, distance to grid and grid availability, site topography and geology, accessibility of the site, as well as environmental and social suitability
	DO	Do ensure a successful renewable energy project by accessing optimised resource data
	DON'T	Don't underestimate grid availability
	DO	Do make sure that the local engineering standards of the grid operator are acceptable and accessible so that you can carry out your own grid capacity study
Legal and Institutional	DO	Do identify typical rules of law and examine the treatment of foreign ownership, shareholder governance, the control of corruption, insolvency proceedings, the opening of bank accounts and taxation in the country in question, as well as time, costs and procedures to start a business
	DO	Do establish a relationship and hold regular meetings with the local authorities
	DO	Do focus on countries where the government and/or donors provide support
	DO	Do remember that figures don't lie, but liars do figure
Finance and Partnerships	DO	Do assess potential for local and international financing
	DO	Do assess financial support in the early stages
	DON'T	Don't trust your business partner without written evidence
	DO	Do run a know-your-customer (KYC) on signatory contractual parties
Don't expect all aspects to be met with a positive answer but decide whether to continue or not		

11.3.1 Technical Dos and Don'ts of Site Selection

Technical site selection will be based on a long checklist considering resource availability, distance to grid and grid availability, site topography and geology, accessibility of the site, as well as environmental and social suitability. Among these various factors, there are two primordial "dos":

First, do ensure a successful renewable energy project by accessing optimal resource data. Natural resources need to be sufficiently available. Next, the quality of the resource data is crucial. Although availability of quantitative and qualitative data on various renewable resources has improved over the past few decades, it is still necessary to install monitoring stations at or close to the project location in line with the applicable norm. In the case of a solar photovoltaic (PV) project, the monitoring duration should be at least one year to adequately correlate the site conditions with those of the nearest locations having long-term historic data.[4] An adequate resource assessment helps to diminish uncertainty regarding the long-term output, improve debt sizing and/or the bid price in a competitive tender, and increase the market value of an asset. In some markets, donors try to cover the data gap by providing technical assistance with investment in meteorological stations.[5]

Second, don't underestimate grid availability. There is a broad range of reasons why grid availability is one of the key criteria for site selection: increased injection of power from various renewable energy sources into the grid, low density of the grid in some markets or changes in national energy policies (e.g., due to the dismantling of the Central Asia unified energy system following the collapse of the Soviet Union[6] – see "Case Study: Grid in Central and West Asian countries" below).

Case Study: Grid in Central and West Asian countries[7]

In Central and West Asian countries (the former Soviet Union's boundaries that included Kazakhstan, Uzbekistan, Turkmenistan, Tajikistan and Kyrgyzstan, and now also Pakistan and Afghanistan), grid security has emerged as a key geopolitical risk with potential to destabilize the region. Although very inefficient, the Soviet Union had an organized approach to coordinating energy supply across upstream and downstream countries. The Central Asia unified energy system was dismantled in the 1990s and individual countries quickly sought to become self-reliant in meeting their growing energy needs. Large-scale grid connection projects are seen as vital to address significant transmission and distribution losses, reinvigorate regional energy trade, and deepen regional co-operation through growth. Distributed renewable energy investments are a crucial component in addressing electricity shortages in Central Asia, Afghanistan and Pakistan. Private investment is needed to meet the capital expenditure requirements of renewable energy plans in the region, but it has been an uphill struggle in state-owned, centrally-controlled systems with minimal distributed energy policies and high levels of fossil fuel and electricity subsidies.

In countries such as Germany where wind and solar power constitute a significant portion of total grid power,[8] wind and solar output need to be managed in ways that the state's grid can handle. Problems include handling a two-way power flow on distribution grids built to handle one-way power only, and a "shadow load" resulting from (mainly) solar-equipped utility customers (prosumers). Developers have the

4 IRENA, "Boosting Solar PV Markets: The Role of Quality Infrastructure," 2017, 144 pages.

5 See the Asian Development Bank (ADB) tender: "Proposed Regional Knowledge and Support Technical Assistance Floating Solar Energy Development," May 2018.

6 Alejandro Litovsky, "China plans super-grid for clean power in Asia as hydropower hits problems," *Financial Times*, December 5, 2017.

7 See also experience from the developer Access Power in "Large-scale solar blossoms in Africa," https://www.pv-tech.org/editors-blog/large-scale-solar-blossoms-in-africa, July 13, 2018.

8 In addition to Germany, read for example: Rebeca Smith, "California grids for electricity woes," *Wall Street Journal*, February 27, 2013.

opportunity (and sometimes the regulatory obligation) to plan more comprehensive projects than in the past, such as wind and solar storage solutions. In other markets, the grid has collapsed because the operators lack the required technical, commercial and financial resources. See “Case Study: Sierra Leone – Gap Analysis on the Grid and Distribution Company” below.

Case Study: Sierra Leone – Gap Analysis of the Grid and Distribution Company[9]

The Electricity Distribution and Supply Authority (EDSA) is responsible for managing the medium and low voltage network and retail operations for its 168,000[10] customers. EDSA is the sole buyer of electricity in Sierra Leone as dictated in the Electricity Act (2011). Although distribution is unbundled from generation and transmission activities, EDSA is state-owned.

In recent years, EDSA has benefited from a significant level of donor funding to upgrade the medium voltage (MV) and low voltage (LV) networks, increase capacity, reduce technical grid losses, improve protection and improve reliability. Projects include funding from the Islamic Development Bank, the World Bank, the African Development Bank and the Japan International Cooperation Agency (JICA). Despite this significant level of investment, it has been estimated[11] that an additional $ 93 million will be required to rehabilitate the grid in the capital city of Freetown alone. Identified gaps regarding the distribution company, EDSA, are:

There is no clear institutional framework for the evolving distribution sector in Sierra Leone

There is no plan to combat illegal connections and meter tampering

Low collection rate for some tariff groups

Power tariffs are below cost recovery

EDSA does not have the capacity to fulfill its role as the single buyer in Sierra Leone

Little preventative maintenance takes place, mainly fault/breakdown maintenance

The full reform process for EDSA is incomplete. Outstanding measures include:

- organizational structure changes
- new business systems and databases
- streamlined business processes and work procedures
- effective human resources management
- appropriate training and capacity building.

Other issues that need to be addressed are:

limited system operation/control, i.e., no proper control equipment

standardized customer service processes are not established

a lack of capacity in commercial operations

a lack of skills in technical operations

a lack of equipment and vehicles to respond efficiently to faults

a lack of a developed accounting system, and

a lack of human resources to plan for, procure and implement (project manage) all the necessary network improvement/expansion projects.

9 Extract from the “Power Sector Roadmap and Coordination Activity. Vision and Gap Analysis Report”, GOPA-Intec GmbH (Bad Homburg, Germany) and Adam Smith International (London, UK), March 10, 2017.

10 Source: EDSA, February 2017.

11 NRECA, *Preparation of the Electricity Network Investment Plan: Draft Final Design Report* (April 2016).

From a technical perspective, **do make sure that the engineering standards of the local grid operator are acceptable and accessible.** They will be determinant in assessing the quality of the information and for drawing up the two studies that are a typical part of project development: the **grid integration study** (or power system analysis), which consists of the static and dynamic modeling of the relevant part of the transmission and distribution system, allowing the developer to identify the grid connection point and verify that the system can absorb the (variable) renewable power adequately at all times and at all points in the grid; and the **grid connection study**, which is usually part of the technical feasibility study and prepares the layout for the electrical equipment needed between the renewable power plant and the existing grid.

Finally, grid usage fees may differ significantly from one connection point to another, grid congestion at a specific point may be quickly reached due to parallel project development activities, or the grid connection permit may be rejected by the operator for no reason whatsoever.

All of these grid related aspects need to be considered when choosing a specific location for a project.

11.3.2 Legal and Institutional Environment

Do a quick check to identify atypical rules of law and to examine the treatment of foreign ownership, the control of corruption in the specific country, insolvency proceedings (for example, Dubai introduced insolvency regulations in 2018), the requirements to open bank accounts, taxation issues, the time, costs and procedures involved in starting a business, and shareholder governance. In addition to this review, three main "dos" should be assessed:

First, **do focus on countries where there is support for renewable energies.** Support can be in the form of targets like in the European Union (EU), guarantees (such as the tariff rate guarantee in Egypt and payment guarantees in Indonesia) or soft loans, among others.

Second, do assess developers' **ability to establish a relationship, and organize and implement regular meetings with the relevant authorities.** In some countries, permits, approvals and land acquisition processes are not timely, predictable or easy to navigate. Thus, regular contact with the local authorities may be necessary in order to obtain the required project licenses on time and in an acceptable form, or to implement the amendments recommended by the financing institutions. These amendments may be considerable if the permit process has not been overseen by a legal expert.

Third, **do remember that figures don't lie, but liars do figure.** In the best-case scenario, statistics from third sources can be used (e.g., to estimate the demand for the power produced by the project). For Africa alone, many institutions try to estimate electricity demand. The International Renewable Energy Agency (IRENA) states that demand will triple by 2030 due to rising living standards, ongoing industrialization and growing electrification rates.[12] With statistics predicting such an exponential increase, you should compare as many sources and studies as possible (e.g., willingness-to-pay studies). Statistical results can vary significantly depending on which figures are extrapolated.

11.3.3 Finance and Partnerships

Do assess the potential for local and international financing. It is advisable to sound out potential lenders as early as possible, including their experience in non-recourse financing and their track-record in the technology sector. Do not rely on unexperienced lenders. Experience is key to achieve financing and avoid high capital costs when implementing a project. High availability of capital at low interest levels has contributed to an increase in project implementation at reduced generation costs over the past few years.

Do apply for financial support early on. According to the definition provided by UNESCO (United Nations Educational, Scientific and Cultural Organization), financial support can take the form of cost coverage during the development phase, sharing expertise and consulting services. Regardless of its form, financial support focuses on the specific needs and priorities identified by the beneficiary (the host country of the project). It is also recommended to diversify the sources of financial support in compliance with the "de minimis Regulation."[13] Once granted, financial support helps to reduce soft development costs, increase credibility regarding the quality of the project (e.g., among potential suppliers, long-term financiers) and speed up project development activities.

There are many instruments available. The German Bank for Reconstruction and Development, KfW, has developed several programs dedicated to medium-sized companies, projects and technologies.[14] The Renewable Energy and Energy Savings program[15] (*Regenerative Energien und Energiesparen*) created by NRW.Bank in the

12 International Renewable Energy Agency (IRENA), "Unlocking renewable energy investment: the role of risk mitigation and structured finance," 2016, 148 pages.

13 "State Aid: Commission adopts revised exemption for small aid amounts (de minimis Regulation)," December 18, 2013, http://europa.eu/rapid/press-release_IP-13-1293_en.htm.

14 In 2017, KfW granted EUR 123 million for solar energy storage appliances to households in Germany. See "KfW: 1150 Zusagen für Photovoltaik-Speicherförderung bis Ende Juli," *PV Magazine*, August 18, 2018.

15 https://www.qinous.de/de/nrw-speicherfoerderung/. This program promotes the installation of storage systems in existing or new photovoltaic projects exceeding 30 kilowatts (kV). Costs relating to performance measurement, monitoring and communication were reimbursed by up to EUR 75,000 under the program. See also https://www.nrwbank.de/export/sites/nrwbank/de/corporate/downloads/presse/publikationen/sonstige-downloads/Mittelstandsbroschuere-Foerderung-fuer-den-Mittelstand-in-NRW.pdf.

German state of North Rhine-Westphalia has been followed by initiatives in other German states such as Thuringia. Climate funds are another good example of financial support. In July 2018, the Irish government launched the Climate Action Fund seeking to fund large-scale projects starting development in 2019 or 2020 and delivering EUR 500 million (approximately £ 441 million) by 2027.[16] Several financial support mechanisms have also been made available[17] within the context of the Paris Agreement. In addition to the latter, a number of other multi-governmental targets (e.g., Agenda2063[18]) incentivise the availability of funds for project development.[19]

Partnerships are another key aspect to be considered during the early stages. In the form of a joint-venture, for example, they can present several advantages: they can facilitate business by providing a local presence, help gain a better understanding of applicable regulations, reduce competition and even be a tender requirement as for the South African RE IPP Program. But not everybody makes a good business partner. Choosing a partner requires a very thorough assessment to avoid any future conflicts in the partnership. Do perform due diligence and **don't trust your joint-venture partner without written evidence**. Ask, inter alia, for the audited balance sheets of your partner.[20] A Know-Your-Customer (KYC) process

---

16 https://www.current-news.co.uk/news/ireland-prepares-further-support-for-climate-change-ambitions, as per July 11, 2018.

17 For instance: in April 2016, the Nordic Development Fund became a shareholder in the African Guarantee Fund (AGF) in a move designed to enhance support for small and medium-sized enterprises (SMEs) investing in green growth and climate-resilient development across Africa. See: "Climate in Focus: A Newsletter from the Nordic Development Fund," issue 1, 2016.

18 On January 30–31, 2015, the African Union (AU) adopted Agenda 2063 at their 24th Ordinary Assembly held in Addis Ababa, Ethiopia. Agenda 2063 strives to enable Africa to remain focused and committed to the ideals it envisages in the context of a rapidly changing world. Energy and Infrastructure is one of the AU's eight portfolios. The member states of the AU are 55 sovereign African states.

19 The "Marshall Plan with Africa" was initiated by the Federal Ministry for Economic Cooperation and Development (BMZ) with the aim of reinforcing African states' own development capacity. The goal is to create favorable conditions to attract private and public investments. The Marshall Plan is not exclusively dedicated to renewable energies, focuses on security, universal access and affordable power supply, in keeping with the targets of Agenda2063. It is thought that the "sun continent" has the potential to significantly expand its energy supply system using renewable energies, without having to resort to environmentally harmful technologies . . . . Within the context of the Marshall Plan, Germany has increased the EulerHermes financing for some of the signatory members of Agenda2063, among other support measures. See "Afrika und Europa: Neue Partnerschaft für Entwicklung, Frieden und Zukunft; Eckpunkte für einen Marshallplan mit Afrika," *BMZ*, January 2017.

20 Also, for non-recourse project financing, lenders may require the balance sheets (and/or credit mirror) of the joint-venture companies. In a recent transaction, lenders required a change of share-ownership of the project as a condition for disbursement due to the high indebtedness of one of the joint-venture partners and corporate lending limits being reached by some of the members of the banking club. Thus, the international partner was obliged to increase their shares in the project

needs to be established and a Political Exposed Person (PEP) test carried out on all of the signatories of agreements in order to avoid compliance risks. Among others, PriceWaterhouseCoopers has elaborated a KYC Quick Reference Guide,[21] a tool providing the key information firms need to cover AML (anti-money laundry) and ABC (anti-bribery and corruption) risks. KYC information requirements should be added to all agreements. Keep in mind John D. Rockefeller's words: "A friendship founded on business is a good deal better than a business founded on friendship."

Don't cut back on legal advisory costs when getting to know your business partner(s)
A project developer can develop a project from scratch or acquire an existing Special Purpose Vehicle (SPV) company with certain project rights (e.g., rights related to a power purchase agreement (PPA) or/and a land lease agreement). When acquiring an SPV, it is crucial to review the historical ownership structure, the contractual parties of the existing company and any notes in the local property registry. Hire local lawyers to discern whether any PEPs (political exposure persons) have been involved, whether personal links exist between the parties (e.g., to ensure that the notary of a document is not a relative of any of the contractual parties, which would generally render the contract invalid), and which local authorities have available relevant information.

In Honduras, the former president Rafael Callejas was declared to be involved in the FIFA (Fédération Internationale de Football Association) scandal.[22] With the election of a new government, public contract awards (including PPAs with the national utility company) signed during the Callejas presidential period were subject to AML investigations. Five years later, former PPA rights-holders were investigated for suspicion of ABC and AML acts and the government confiscated all of their properties. This delayed the financial close of some renewable energy projects until it was legally proven that the former PPA rights-holders were not involved in the projects any more. This shows the importance of performing detailed compliance due diligence on all signatory parties of agreements before acquiring an SPV.

Conclusion: Do assess all critical aspects to decide whether or not to continue with the Project Idea. This will allow you to make a proper decision regarding the project pipeline. Engineering aspects of an idea are relevant, but establishing the commercial and financial priorities are of equal importance in order to ensure the project's successful implementation later on. The outcome of the Idea Phase will be the decision of whether or not to start project development in a specific country, on a specific site and using specific technology.

---

from 33% to 91%. This condition precedent caused a considerable delay with regard to closing, which could have been avoided if financial due diligence of the partner had been performed before mandating the lenders.

21 https://www.pwc.com/gx/en/financial-services/publications/assets/pwc-anti-money-laundering-2016.pdf.

22 https://www.nacion.com/puro-deporte/futbol-internacional/rafael-callejas-expresidente-de-honduras-se-declara-inocente-en-caso-fifa/E6M4PO33VJFFNDZAT7NQ7WWX2M/story/.

11.4 The Conceptual Phase

During the Conceptual Phase, a clear, detailed description of the attributes and benefits of the idea will be drawn up (see Table 11.2). The Project Concept addresses the needs of the targeted power customers (how their needs will be addressed by the project, why they will want to use or buy the power, including a comparison with what is currently available). Project development starts with this phase, during which the technical, commercial, financial and E&S feasibility of the project will be assessed.

Table 11.2: The conceptual phase: dos and don'ts (own representation).

The Conceptual Phase Do assess the feasibility of the project		
Technical Feasibility	DO	Do identify feasible technical solutions and prepare the conceptual design in a sufficiently detailed manner for the selected technical solution
		Do consider hiring an experienced technical advisor to obtain local technical requirements and the bankability of innovative equipment
Commercial Feasibility	DO	Will the commercial feasibility of the project be supported by a favorable regulatory framework? Do assess the regulatory framework
		Do focus on long-term demand (and power price stability)
Financial Feasibility	DO	Develop and then use the financial model to assess the key financial results (equity return on investment, project internal rate of return, debt service coverage levels) and to explore sensitivity
		Do use the advantages of blended finance and don't fear the disadvantages of blended finance
		Do assess the possibility of hedging currencies and interest rates in the long run
E&S Feasibility	DON'T	Don't forget the IFC Performance Standards, the Equator Principles and, in the case of ECA-financing, the OECD Common Approaches
		Don't underestimate the need to involve local stakeholders
		Don't start the environmental and social impact assessment too late to ensure you fulfill local and international requirements. It might take more than one year to compile all required data
Project Status Reports	DO	Do keep Project Status Reports up to date
		Do not underestimate Budget Constraints
Don't try to cover all risks; mitigate them as much as possible (aim to be cost-effective)		

11.4.1 Technical Feasibility

Do define the project layout

A developer should be in a position to realize basic design internally, taking into account several engineering scenarios, so that the ability of the project to adapt to permit constraints (land and community spatial restrictions, grid export bottlenecks, construction permit requirements, logistics) can be identified early on. For the site analysis, it is recommended to seek guidance from an experienced technical advisor. Ideally the technical advisor will be in a position to advise on new technology developments (e.g., bifacial modules, two-compartment string inverters for the connection box and for the power unit,[23] new wind turbine developments), their bankability and engineering benefits (e.g., on grid emulation[24]). A well-known technical advisor will reassure financiers at a later stage. Spending a little money upfront can have a much larger impact on the project costs/viability downstream.

Wind and solar measurement campaigns as well as the energy yield assessment need to be verified by an independent, certified technical advisor. These tasks can also largely dictate the duration of the feasibility study, if not the entire development period. The feasibility study will address, inter alia, the following:

1. Site Assessment
2. Solar and/or wind (or other) Resource Availability
3. Topographical Survey
4. Geological Investigations
5. Technology Review and Selection of suitable technology for the site
6. Conceptual Design
7. Energy Yield Assessment
8. O&M Plan
9. Regulatory Framework
10. Project Organization
11. Initial E&S impact assessment / E&S scoping study / complete E&S study
12. Risk Assessment and Mitigation Measures
13. CAPEX and OPEX Estimation
14. Economic and Financial Analysis
15. Project Implementation Plan
16. Conclusions and Recommendations

---

23 Marian Willuhn, "More strings to the bow," *PV Magazine*, August 4, 2018.

24 Services to simulate grid interconnection before project commissioning to proactively identify issues. The more components leave the factory preconfigured, the faster commissioning work in the field moves. See other examples in "The Future of Solar Commissioning. Faster, cheaper and easier is the goal," *PV Magazine Online*, July 17, 2018.

11.4.2 Commercial Feasibility

Do assess the regulatory framework

Political determination, clear targets and a long-term policy framework that ensures a broad contribution to the energy transformation process are crucial to successfully scale up investment in renewable energies and are therefore also essential for the developers. Governments must commit to creating a stable market environment to secure a bright future for energy in their country. The aim should be to discern whether renewable energy projects will count with the necessary political support and be considered in a considerable portion in the national power mix. Five-years prospects are suggested, at least until the RtB status has been reached. If during development there is a change of law, the project may no longer be feasible (e.g., retroactive tariff changes in Spain in 2010). In some markets, political risk can include anything from nationalization and civil war to currency shortages, or expropriation of assets. In this instance, it is worth considering political risk insurance (PRI). It protects investors and financiers against a range of risks. Under certain circumstances, the PRI can also cover the risk of losing an arbitration case in a PPA dispute.

Do focus on long-term power demand (and power price stability)

The owner of a project needs to be sure that power will be needed, and customers will pay off, for many years to come. In the past, the Integrated Resource Plan (IRP) elaborated by a government or utility was intended to assess what was required to meet customer needs for the next 20 years and was often used as a source. Now, the electricity sector is experiencing a period of unprecedented change. Customers generating their own power on site has made it more challenging to establish estimates in terms of power demand. A company like McKinsey[25] concludes that 80% of the additional power needed by the chemicals sector, industry, buildings and electrical vehicles will be covered by solar and wind energy projects between now and 2050. The ability of these potential offtakers to absorb the energy produced in the long run and at a pre-defined price needs to be considered on a case-by-case basis. The global trend among corporations towards sourcing the majority or even 100% of their electricity needs from renewable energy has been increasing steadily for several years now, helped in part by the work of the RE100, a global initiative run by The Climate Group in partnership with the CDP (formerly the Carbon Disclosure Project).

---

25 Rembrandt Sutorius and Matt Frank, "The drivers of global energy demand growth to 2050," McKinsey & Company, June 2016.

11.4.3 Financial Feasibility

The financial feasibility of the project needs to be assessed from the perspective of potential investors and financiers. Whether or not a project is deemed to be financially feasible will depend on various factors, including investor class, lenders' requirements on debt service coverage level and the market. Feasibility will be assessed by means of a financial model. Figure 11.2 shows a list of the key parameters to be included in a financial model.

One of the main results of the financial assessment is the power tariff (the selling price for the owner and operator of the power plant) at a certain Internal Rate of Return (IRR). If the tariff is fixed, the main outcome of the financial assessment will be the Return on Investment (ROI) with a given debt structure and certain Debt Service Coverage Ratios (DSCRs) to be met during the lifetime of the loan.

In order to assess the robustness of the financial feasibility of the project, ***use the Financial Model to explore sensitivity,*** including: an increase in capital costs, a delay in the start-up of operations, an increase in fuel costs (e.g., in a biomass power plant), a decrease in the power tariff, a decrease in solar radiation/wind speed intensity, a decrease in the technical availability of the plant, an increase in interest rates, an increase in inflation or a change in the foreign exchange rate.

The financial feasibility study will allow you to assess the possibility of avoiding traditional commercial debt financing. In emerging renewable energy markets, the concept of **"blended finance"** is gaining momentum. Blended finance channels donors' and private investors' funds into projects with a public-private-ownership structure (whereas until now most donors exclusively transferred funds to local governments so that the latter could start a procurement process with international competitive bidding). Thus, blended finance is defined as the combination of public finance instruments (equity, grants, concessional loans, state guarantees) with private funds in a public-private-partnership (PPP) structure.

Do use the advantages of blended finance
- Blended finance can help to pay up-front project costs. Example: GET-FIT facility set-up by KfW in Uganda for financing renewable energy IPPs
- Blended finance increases the bankability of the project. Especially when the offtaker is a non-investment grade company and the government is in a high deficit situation; the funds are disbursed into an escrow account from which payments can subsequently be made to the project owner
- Governments tend to support project developers applying for blended finance since it reduces the amount of national funding required to implement a project (or to expand the power fleet)
- The project can easily gain the status of being of national interest

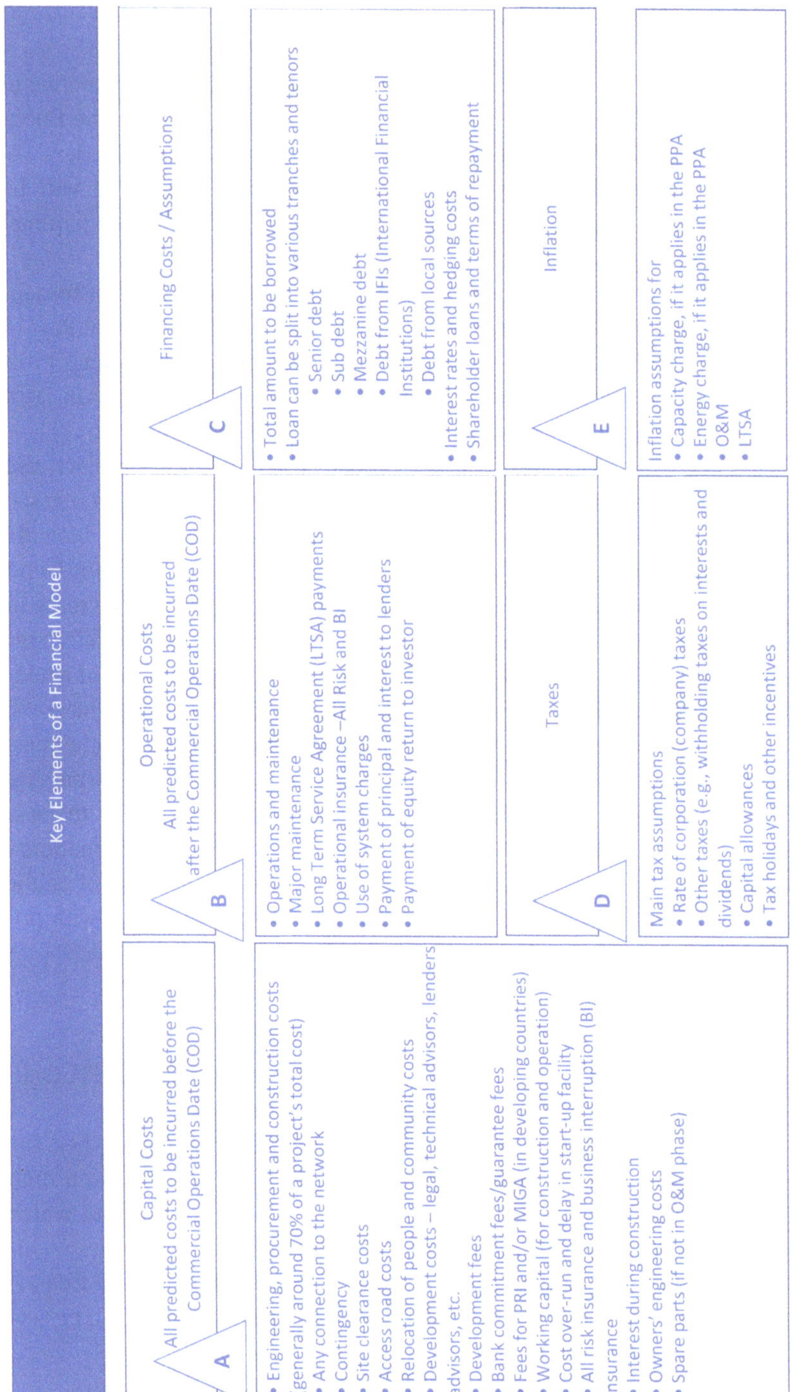

Figure 11.2: Key elements of a financial model (own representation).

- Instead of participating in public bidding, the developer should seek to obtain approval (it will be conditional) for blended finance for the project at an early stage. This provides advantages for the national authority and also for the developer in terms of timing (commitment process to fund the project is faster). Also, it minimizes the risk of exposure to grant shortfalls.[26]

Don't fear the disadvantages of blended finance

- Public sector capacity to manage the combination of public finance instruments and PPPs is still limited
- The grant amount can be at risk if the project is expected to generate net profit. This is due to the existing regulation for multilateral trust funds, whereby if a project is expected to generate net profit, such earnings should be deducted from the eligible project costs. Regulations are changing, thus providing mechanisms to reduce this uncertainty.[27]
- The information requirements for the project tend to be high. These include, at least, estimated project costs, assessment of different project options, cost-benefit analysis, risk analysis, environmental impact assessment and a clear financing plan and timetable. Also of equal importance, the purpose of the project should be in line with the priority areas of the fund(s) providing the grant.

Example of Blended Finance: Sub-national Climate Fund Africa (SnCF Africa)

The so-called R20 Regions of Climate Action (R20), the Leonardo DiCaprio Foundation (LDF) and networks of cities and regions have short-listed over 100 renewable energy, energy efficiency and waste management infrastructure projects with high potential for bankability. BlueOrchard (BO) and R20 have created a customized Public Private Partnership (PPP) to finance the selected projects.

The Sub-national Climate Fund Africa (SnCF Africa), with a target size of USD 350 million, shall invest in low-carbon climate-resilient infrastructure projects that provide energy, waste valorization and municipal lighting services to cities and regions in Africa.

The Fund will predominately invest in minority equity (over 70%) and to a lesser extent in debt investments (up to 30%), selecting 20 to 30 projects with investment costs of between USD 5 million and USD 50 million. Financing at the project level will be combined with tailored capacity building and technical assistance. The Fund shall contribute to the United Nations'

26 Erik Lundsgaarde, "The European Fund for Sustainable Development: Changing the Game?," Discussion Paper 29/2017, Deutsches Institut für Entwicklungspolitik, Bonn.

27 As revenue can be used to help fund the project, grants from trust funds are only available to meet any "funding gap" that remains. The regulations require this gap to be calculated on the basis of cost and revenue projections and in line with a set of conditions that take into account residual values and the use of justified discount rates. This calculation can be complex. While this approach is still available, the new regulation would provide considerably simplified alternatives, using pre-established funding gap rates ("flat rates") for particular sectors. Furthermore, the grant amount, if calculated in this way, is not at risk of subsequent reduction as a result of later, policy-driven, changes in revenue.

Sustainable Development Goals (SDGs) and the Paris Climate Agreement and is expected to reduce up to 2,082,905 tons of greenhouse gases (GHGs) per annum.

Investors in the SnCF will receive support from a dedicated Technical Assistance (TA) facility of USD 10 million, fully funded by grants. The TA facility finances project feasibility studies to bring projects to bankability.

Do assess the possibility of hedging currencies and interest rates in the long run
Hard-currency and interest rate swaps are plain vanilla products in some markets, whereas in countries with high political risk, the premise "***do hedge currencies and rates***" is easy to recommend but harder to implement. The project has to reduce the risks associated with currency (and interest rate) mismatches and thus, risks associated with increasing debt burdens, financial losses, reduced liabilities to repay debt and possibilities of default linked to high currency volatility. To mitigate such risks, there are only a few options. The German and Dutch governments, together with other investor groups, have created funds like the Currency Exchange Fund (TCX).[28]

11.4.4 E&S Feasibility

Don't forget IFC Performance Standards[29] and Equator Principles requirements as well as investor's ESG commitments. E&S regulation tends to be compliant with lenders' Equator Principles[30] requirements and adequate for investors' ESG processes.[31] If E&S feasibility is not given in a project, more and more financiers tend not

---

28 "Private Sector Peer Learning: Mechanism Profiles. Currency Exchange Fund (TCX)," TCX Investment Management Company BV, OECD, July 1, 2016.

29 IFC Performance Standards have become globally recognized as a benchmark for environmental and social risk management in the private sector. In many countries, the scope and intent of the IFC Performance Standards is addressed or partially addressed in the country's environmental and social regulatory framework. The IFC Performance Standards encompass eight topics. See Clemens Schumacher and Rosa Tarragó, "Umwelt- und Sozialstandards in der Projektfinanzierung," EuroForum Seminar Documents at AKA-Bank, May 11, 2017.

30 The Equator Principles are a risk management framework, adopted by financial institutions, for determining, assessing and managing environmental and social risk in project finance. It is primarily intended to provide a minimum standard for due diligence to support responsible risk decision-making.

31 ESG investing is the consideration of environmental, social and governance factors alongside financial factors in the investment decision–making process. Since its founding in 2006, the United Nations Principles for Responsible Investing (PRI) has attracted support from more than 1,800 signatories representing over USD 68 trillion in assets under management as of April 2017. Signatories commit to six voluntary principles, the first of which is the incorporation of ESG issues into investment analysis and decision-making.

to pursue the analysis of the technical, commercial and financial aspects of the project any further.

In some markets, E&S regulation often scarcely exists. To obtain international financing, the project has, inter alia, to be granted with the compulsory local environmental permit and, in addition, has to comply with the IFC Performance Standards, the Equator Principles and the OECD Common Approaches, although the latter only applies if an Export Credit Agency (e.g., EulerHermes) covered loan is being structured. In the E&S feasibility assessment**, do make sure that IFC Performance Standards are addressed early on** and that there is certainty, that at least the four following aspects can be achieved.

First, assess E&S impacts that can stem from the project in the planning, construction, operation and decommissioning phases. Commission an environmental scoping report to gain insight into the project's impact on flora, fauna (biodiversity), water resources, the landscape and visual amenities, and on recreation. Determine the impact on protected areas if affected by the project location, including wetlands and other critical ecosystems and habitats in the region.

Second, pay attention to the potential impact on health and security of the population (disease transmission during construction, particularly HIV/AIDS and waterborne diseases, access to medical treatments, accident risk, noise and air pollution, etc.).

Third, draft the mitigation, management, and monitoring measures to implement an environmentally friendly project without compromising its technical and financial feasibility.

Last, but not least, it will be necessary to consult the local population, stakeholders and potentially affected persons and document their concerns regarding the proposed project. The results of these consultations must be made publicly available.

Above all, don't underestimate the need to involve **local stakeholders.**

Special emphasis should be placed on continuous interaction with the stakeholders (indigenous communities, land owner(s), permit authorities, regulatory authorities, municipalities, etc.). At the end of the day, the project developer and the stakeholders have the most vested interest in the success of the project. As such, the stakeholders should be continuously kept aware of the status and deliverables inherent to the project. Furthermore, while the features (and scope) are defined up front, all things being equal, these may require some "tweaking" as the project moves forward. So, it is important to have the stakeholders re-evaluate the requirements and features as they become available to ensure that their demands match what is being produced.

Site note: IFC Project Classification and specific aspects associated with a photovoltaic project
IFC Performance Standards classify projects into three categories:

Category A: a project is classified as Category A if it has the potential to have significant adverse environmental impacts. These impacts may affect an area broader than the sites or facilities subject to physical works. Category A, in principle, includes projects in sensitive sectors or located in or near sensitive areas (e.g., transmission line projects, offshore wind projects and some onshore projects).

Category B: a project is classified as Category B if its potential environmental impacts are less adverse than those of Category A projects. Typically, these impacts are site-specific; few if any of them are irreversible, and mitigation measures are more readily available.

Category C: a project is classified as Category C if it is likely to have minimal or no adverse environmental impacts.

Inter alia, the following aspects will be evaluated to categorize a solar photovoltaic (PV) project into one of the IFC Performance Standard categories:
- impact on ecologically protected and susceptible areas, with an emphasis on potential bird collisions should they mistake PV installations with a body of water;
- concerns about land degradation, loss of cultivable land or habitat loss;
- usage of water for cleaning or for the manufacturing process of the photovoltaic panels;
- large utility-scale PV installations may have a severe impact on the hydrological resources at the installation site. They may reduce the rate of groundwater recharge, the filtration of pollutants from the air and rainwater, and even increase the likelihood of flooding. These aspects need to be assessed;
- management of hazardous waste (temporary storage, waste transportation, hazardous waste treatment) as well as waste management at the end of the life cycle of a photovoltaic module; and
- visual impact.

In addition to the fulfillment of the IFC Performance Standards, the project will have to obtain the local environmental permit (and be conceptually designed to fulfill social, health and safety requirements). **Don't start preparing the E&S documentation too late. It might take more than one year to compile all of the required data** (e.g., on migratory behavior of the birds). For example, the box below provides a check-list of the usual information required to carry out an Environmental Impact Assessment (EIA) for a PV project.

Environmental Permit Check-List (Example for a PV Project) and Social Requirements
Air quality and noise (mainly during the construction phase):
- Noise, including sensitive noise receptors in the project area, existing noise sources and their potential to influence the project
- Ambient air quality modeling using software
- Air quality, including emissions from stationary and mobile sources, NOx, SOx, wind speed and direction, precipitation, relative humidity and ambient temperatures
- The laboratory used shall be accredited by an internationally-recognized institution such as KAN BSN (National Accreditation Committee, National Standardization Body)

Water quality
- Water quality and sedimentation analysis in the study area

- Tested parameters must refer to the national government or regional government regulations, applicable according to class or water designation

Physiography
- Topographic analysis of land form, geological structure and soil type
- Environmental indicators related to soil stability
- The vulnerability of land forms and geological aid

Hydrology
- Collection of secondary data such as rainfall, climatology, watershed maps, etc. and conducting hydrological analysis
- Analysis of water balances, ups and downs, current waves, reservoir morphology
- Analysis of potential water temperature changes, presented in 3D-modeling so as to show interaction between thermal plumes in the waters surrounding the area of the project
- Potential trends regarding the quantity and quality of biodiversity and fisheries in the project area

Land use
- Land-use assessments covering the identification of protected areas, such as forests and coastal areas

Assessment of biological components
- Flora and fauna, species that are protected, listed or endangered, habitats, ecosystem issues, terrestrial ecology, bird surveys

Water: biotic elements
- Analysis of potential changes in the number and condition of aquatic biota during pre-construction, construction and operation phases due to changes in water quality around the study area of the planned business
- Analysis of equilibrium changes that may occur due to pre-construction, construction and operation phases

Landscape and visual issues

Existing sources of pollution and potential area of contaminated land

Transport and traffic

Existing environmental pressures (including climate adaptation)

Social and socio-economic issues
- Administrative subdivisions and potentially affected communities
- Land use, with a focus on potential existing land rights (whether formal or informal) over the areas to be acquired or leased by the project

Demography
- Activities and occupations, description of livelihoods, with a focus on agricultural activities that may be impacted by the project construction or operation
- Local social and socio-political organization insofar as it is relevant to the project's public engagement efforts
- Vulnerable people

Cultural heritage

Community health, safety and security (during construction and implementation of the project)
- Occupational health and safety
- Labor issues and working conditions

Hazardous material waste
- Temporary storage for hazardous waste
- Transport of hazardous waste by third parties
- Utilization of hazardous waste by project owners and third parties
- Hazardous waste treatment activities

If the outcome of the feasibility study is positive, then permit application should start. See the "Additional Permits and Assessments" box. All steps to obtain permission should be planned, recorded and monitored in a Project Status Report. **Do keep this report up to date.** Use metrics to continuously monitor project status. When projects sleep, it is never a good sign. Sometimes this is unavoidable. Other times, it could have been avoided had the project manager simply been diligent in monitoring the project status through reports and good metrics. Reports not only provide the project manager with information on how the project is progressing, they can also help them to extrapolate the future progress of the project.

The triple constraint (cost, quality and timeline) is one of the most staple concepts in the world of project development and it cannot be ignored. Project adjustments on the fly during the project life-cycle have an effect on the overall timeline and/or cost of the project. Do be aware of the repercussions any changes may have on the project's feasibility.

Additional Permits and Assessments

Within renewable energy development, various permits are required to authorize project construction and operation. The process of obtaining these permits involves contacting many different authorities. Required permits and assessments include, inter alia:

Construction Permits: Construction plans must be submitted for approval. The construction permit application must include maps, profiles, cross sections, data and information regarding the effect on upstream and downstream areas resulting from the proposed construction. Construction, especially of a solar thermal power plant and of a wind project, requires heavy use of local roads. The developer often has to enter into agreements to carry out improvements needed in access roads, repair any damage caused, consult with transportation officials regarding routes, or set up an escrow account to cover potential damages. Where the project will cross or encroach upon existing right-of-ways, **encroachment agreements** may also be beneficial.

Stormwater Permits: The construction permit may also include a permit for stormwater. For sites disturbing several hectares, a permit can be required for discharge of stormwater from construction activities to "waters of the state." Usually an application must include a stormwater pollution prevention plan, detailing steps to protect water quality while construction is ongoing.

Superload & Oversize/Overweight Permits: these authorize vehicles that exceed size and weight limits on a route designated on the permit. This permit may require a bridge analysis and a general liability and auto liability insurance. The route, time of day, and date must be approved (e.g., during festivities of the affected municipalities no transit will be allowed).

Object Marking & Lighting Regulations: Especially for wind energy projects, developers may submit a marking and lighting plan. The wind turbine specialist within the relevant authority will determine which structures should have obstruction lights.

Microwave Beam Path Assessments: Wind farms may adversely impact licensed microwave and fixed station radio frequency facilities due to the chopping or reflection of the beam. Developers may conduct an assessment to determine the presence of any existing microwave paths crossing the property and mitigate any potential impacts.

Decommissioning Agreements: Decommissioning requirements vary depending on the land owner, country and technology. In Europe, decommissioning requirements tend to be a clause within the land lease and/or the construction permit, which regulates the removal of the plant after the technical operational lifetime. From a contractual viewpoint, decommissioning agreements provide security for the decommissioning process (e.g., bonds, contract, escrow, etc.).

Accommodation Agreements: Lay out the groundwork for the mutual development of and cooperation regarding the property. Where property interests are also held by mines or by oil & gas activities (most of these activities are of national interest), accommodation agreements may be beneficial and prevent the construction permits of two different Ministries of a country from coming into conflict. Lessons-learned have been collected in Chile, South Africa, Uruguay.

Conclusion: If the project is feasible, don't try to cover all risks; mitigate them as much as possible (aim to be cost-effective) with the project agreements. And remember, if you won't take a particular risk, the chances are no-one else will either.

11.5 The Contractual Phase

The previous Conceptual Phase sets the basis on which project agreements should be drafted (see Table 11.3). Debt financing without recourse to the assets of the project's shareholders must be based on robust, risk-mitigating long-term agreements that "do what they say on the tin." Assuming that the agreement templates meet bankability standards, this section focuses on specific dos and don'ts to be considered when selecting the negotiation partner, the purpose of the agreements and the rights and obligations of the parties that need to be set out unambiguously so that thorny issues are dealt with at the outset and not fudged in an effort to reach some false deadline for signing documentation. Also, it is assumed that standardized agreement templates will be used as a tool to reduce transaction costs, and to facilitate the aggregation of smaller projects to create larger financial deals.

The minimum set of project agreements required to obtain project financing are the Land Lease Agreement (or Land Purchase Agreement), Power Purchase Agreement, Connection Agreement, Implementation Agreement (in the case of developing markets), the Engineering, Procurement and Construction (EPC) Agreement and the Operations and Maintenance (O&M) Agreement. The sound negotiation of these project agreements will make it possible to attain the ready-to-build status.

Table 11.3: The contractual phase: dos and don'ts (own representation).

The Contractual Phase Do consider bankability when starting to negotiate the agreements		
Land Lease/ Purchase Agreement (LLA)	DOs	Do check in the registry, cadaster or equivalent official source, the land affected by the project in terms of category, ownership and availability
		Do compare the purchase price and/or the annual lease value of the land with the value of the terrain as registered
		Do avoid re-negotiations at debt closing to secure the bankability of the land lease agreements from the very beginning
Power Purchase Agreement (PPA)	DOs and DON'TS	Don't underestimate the time and effort required to develop the schedules – some are complex (tariff schedule, performance testing)
		Do make sure that the agreed fixed power price in a PPA covers operating costs, payment of principal and interest on long tenor debt, and recovery of capital
		Don't sign with non-investment grade offtakers (or without a back-up guarantee of the government in developing markets)
		Synthetic PPA:
		Do consider a financial option (put/call) in the synthetic PPA
		Do make sure that a synthetic PPA is bankable:
		The collateral package
		Termination rights
Connection Agreement (CA)	DOs	Do consider that a Connection Agreement does not alleviate the need to respect the grid codes
		Do negotiate monetary compensation in case ancillary services are not provided as agreed by the grid operator and are curtailed
Implementation Agreement (IA)	DO	IA to ensure the confidence of financiers and governments (local content, transfer of assets/share)
EPC and O&M Agreements	DO	Do prioritize quality, reliability and track record
		Do take part in professional bidding processes
Finance Agreements	DOS and DON'TS	Don't rely on unexperienced lenders (experience in the host country is key)
		Recognize that if equity is to be injected into the project prorata with commercial lenders, then the credit rating of the equity provider will be a key factor
		Set up accounting systems and reporting systems
Do mandate a lender once you have clarity on the signing of the project agreements		

11.5.1 Land Agreement (Lease or Purchase)

Clear and accessible land acquisition legislation is required to ensure both public and private parties are aware when, and by what process, land acquisition is appropriate. Long-term certainty about infrastructure requirements is also important for effective land acquisition, ensuring long lead times for planning and stakeholder engagement on land requirements, and enabling corridor preservation where possible. The OECD's Country Investment Policy Reviews identified significant costs associated with land acquisition when it was not properly included in the project planning and feasibility stage.

Do check in the registry, cadaster or equivalent official source, the land affected by the project in terms of category, ownership and availability. Land affected by the plant and the grid needs to be securitized in project financing. Land securitization can be a time-consuming and cost-intensive task depending on the number of owners and the category of the land (industrial, agricultural or municipal). Two examples of DONT'S are provided in the "Mexico and the challenges with *Ejidos*" and the "Honduras and securitization of the trace parallel to the public road CA-1" case studies. Finally, **do compare the purchase price and/or the annual lease value of the land with the value of the terrain as registered**. If the difference is too high, this agreement might be subject to an intensive review in a lenders' compliance due diligence to justify that there have not been any money laundering issues when renting or acquiring the land.

Do avoid re-negotiations with landlords before debt closing by securing the bankability of the land lease agreements from the very beginning. At minimum, the land lease agreement needs to have a tenor equal to the technical lifetime of the project (or even up to 40 years depending on local regulation) and take into account the entry rights of the lenders. Moreover, the land should be free of mortgage charges and be subject to clear decommissioning rules (if any), among other factors.[32] Communication during lease negotiations is one of the most important aspects, especially in scenarios where the project team is spread out or spans geographic regions where English may not be the first language for all parties.

Case Study: Mexico and the Challenges with *ejidos*
The *ejido* is a peculiar form of land ownership in Mexico that has impeded the implementation of some wind projects in the country, according to the Inter-American Development Bank (IDB).[33] The Mexican Revolution inspired the idea of *ejidos*. One of the main objectives of the

32 R. Tarragó, "Quality requirements for project finance," Symposium on Output- and Quality Assurance in Solar Projects, Meteocontrol, Hamburg, April 25, 2013.

33 "La lucha por la tierra frena inversiones. El conflicto empresas-ejidatarios por adquirir terrenos es constante; los inversionistas se van," magazine *Expansión*, January 30, 2014, https://expansion.mx/expansion/2014/01/14/ ejidos-en-mexico-frenan-la-inversion#article-4.

revolution, reflected in the revolutionary 1917 Mexican Constitution, was to break up large tracts of privately-owned land – *latifundios* – into smaller holdings and return the land to the peasants. The *ejidos* were agricultural land grants, which the new Mexican government issued to farming and ranching cooperatives (mainly made up of peasants) allowing them to use federally-owned property. Members of the *ejidos* were entitled to use and work the land to their benefit but they did not own the property. The government issued these peasants a limited title to the land; they could not sell the land or use it for collateral. The peasants had to continue to work the land or their title would be revoked. The idea was to help peasant farmers get a start in life, and at the same time, bring about an equitable distribution and use of property. In January of 1992 a decree was published in the Official Gazette (*Diario Oficial De La Federación*) stating that Amendment of Article 27 of the Mexican Constitution. With this Amendment to Article 27, it appeared that after nearly 75 years, the dreams of the peasant farmers were to become a reality. Until the new Agrarian Law was passed in February of 1992, *ejidos* were regulated by the Agrarian Reform Law, which strictly prohibited the sale or even the lease of *ejido* property. In other words, a foreigner presently living in Mexico on land leased from an *ejido* before 1992 is doing so illegally.

Since 1992, members of agrarian communities are allowed to buy, sell or lease the land, hire labor and associate with other producers and third parties. They may enter into any type of association or contract including joint-venture schemes, with domestic or foreign private investors, through renewable contracts with a 30-year maximum term. Based on a resolution of an *ejido* assembly, the *ejido* may offer the use of their land as collateral to credit institutions or third parties. After an *ejido* privatization procedure is completed, its members may sell the land.

Nevertheless, do take into account the bureaucracy involved with *ejidos* and try to avoid them. It is difficult to access the names of the land owners, the limits of the land and the ownership registry (*Registro Agrario Nacional*) is not always updated. If only one of the involved *ejidos* is against the project, the implementation will be at risk. There is no expropriation law for *ejidos*.

Case Study: Honduras and securitization of the trace parallel to the Public Road CA-1

In Honduras, according to some legal advisors, public land used by transmission lines does not need to be securitized. Nevertheless, land securitization (on the project site as well as for the trace) is necessary to obtain international project financing. After 12 months of exchanges with the public authority, the 55.7 MWp photovoltaic (PV) project "Fray Lazaro" located in Choluteca, Honduras, obtained such securitization from the respective local authorities, ENEE and INSEP. The securitization was made subject to three main conditions: (i) the line trace had to be in line with the environmental permit (so that the environmental impact assessment was updated), (ii) the replacement of the existing wood posts with concrete towers, 45–55 feet tall, at no cost for the grid operation and (iii) the installation of a double circuit (230 KV) from the Pavana substation to the Fray Lazaro substation, located approximately 5.5 km from the site, using an overhead line running parallel to the CA-1 road on the east boundary of the project.

11.5.2 Power Purchase Agreement

A Power Purchase Agreement (PPA) may be considered the primary commercial and technical document guiding the sale and purchase of power between two specific parties. There are many types of PPAs, which vary depending on the technology used, whether they take into account ancillary services or provide for hybrid remuneration with certificates.[34] In numerous sources, e.g., "Negotiating the fine print" (2014),[35] technical, financial and commercial bankability requirements are specified, though the requirements will differ depending on the type of technology, on what other supporting agreements (i.e., Connection Agreement) are established, in addition to the status of legal codes, regulations to guide technical aspects, etc.

Regardless of the type of PPA, remember: **Don't sign with non-investment grade offtakers (and without a back-up guarantee of the government in developing markets).** Counterparty risk is especially important. In the past, offtaker contracts were typically entered into with governments or highly rated utilities. Now, counterparties include corporate buyers, that are often exposed to commodity prices and other risks:[36] Corporate buyers have started to trade power in an attempt to reduce production costs and although the energy business is rarely considered a "core" activity, the proliferation of RE100 initiatives,[37] and behind-the-meter activities such as demand-side response and time-of-use tariffs, offers projects a large range of offtakers.[38] Thus, it is necessary to understand the counterparty's financial profile, bearing in mind the adage that "*the counterparty of my counterparty is my counterparty*." Understanding a counterparty's economic position in relation to their own exploration and production activity (i.e., production costs and "well economics") becomes an important diligence item.

In countries where national offtakers do not held an investment-grade rating, PPAs shall be underwritten by the Ministry of Finance, ensuring support in the event payment delays are experienced for power, as per an agreement. This, in turn, allows

34 See also chapter 9.

35 Rosa Tarragó, "Negotiating the fine print: PPA's: technical, commercial and financial analysis," *PV Magazine*, January, 2014, 76–79.

36 Dominic Santo, "Corporate PPAs," JLL Energy & Infrastructure Advisory, February 17, 2017.

37 RE100 or RE-Source Platform. The RE-Source Platform aims to raise awareness and accelerate renewable investments and corporate renewable Power Purchase Agreements (PPAs) in Europe. Several deals have been signed in Europe in recent years, providing corporate buyers with reliable and competitively-priced power, but there is huge potential for more deals. In 2017, more than 1GW of PPA deals were signed in Europe. The recent growth of corporate sourcing in European markets, like Sweden, the Netherlands and Norway sees them positioned as "PPA-friendly." Elsewhere in Europe, certain regulatory barriers exist, making it difficult for corporate buyers to procure renewable electricity via PPAs. Google, Microsoft, IKEA Group, BT, Danone, Amazon, Enel, Engie, RES, Iberdrola and Facebook, Inc. have become Steering Group members of the RE100-Source Platform, which pools resources and coordinates activities to promote a better framework for corporate renewable energy.

38 The year 2015 provided record figures with regards to new power traders, with an average of more than 130 power retailers according to "Winning the cost battle: Success factors in digital transformations for energy retailers" written by Tiziano Bruno, Bruno Esgalhado, Blake Houghton, and João Segorbe in June 2018.

for the inclusion of credit risk insurances (CRIs) such as MIGA (Multilateral Investment Guarantee Agency) from the World Bank Group in the finance structure of the project. In some markets, the public offtaker doesn't want to issue bonds or warranties for payments in exchange for energy, but this can hinder the bankability of the project as most international lenders won't invest without a warranty. In developing markets, some corporate PPAs can also be found as supply shortfalls have often motivated the closing of PPAs with the private sector. Example are, Unilever Tea and London Distillers Limited with PPAs signed with off-grid plants in Africa.

An investment grade counterparty for a project is much to be desired, but that, in turn, means a different balance of power in terms of contract negotiation.

In general, a take-or-pay/fixed-fee contract and/or throughput agreements are preferable. Offtakers, however, prefer percentage-of-proceeds contracts, where the power project is more exposed to commodity price and volume risk. Another classification of offtaker agreements is provided by Hamburg Commercial Bank in its report "*Corporate PPA. Green electricity for corporate consumers.*"[39] Among the three contract forms (two forms of "physical PPAs"[40] and a "synthetic PPA") defined therein, the following extract focus on synthetic PPAs and their dos and don'ts.

Synthetic PPAs are the result of project developers being reluctant to sign PPAs with corporate buyers which entail locking in a power price for the next 20 years that may be below projected electricity prices. A synthetic PPA is basically a form of hedge (swap) for a contractually-defined volume of electricity: the project sells its electricity on a merchant basis, but enters into a contract with a PPA buyer that provides a floor under the electricity price. The hedge covers decreases in electricity prices and, depending on how it is structured, may also allow the project owner to earn more if electricity prices rise.

The hedge works in both directions: if merchant prices are below the agreed fixed price (or "strike price"), the PPA buyer pays the difference in price to the project owner. Conversely, if merchant prices exceed the agreed fixed price, the producer has to pay the PPA buyer the difference in price for the contracted power

39 "CORPORATE PPA: Green electricity for corporate consumers," HSH Nordbank, June 2018, 28.

40 With a physical PPA, a renewable energy (RE) producer (the "PPA seller") sells the power they produce to an offtaker (the "PPA buyer") at a long-term price. Here, the physical supply of power is made at precisely-defined delivery points. There are two basic forms of physical PPAs, namely the "direct PPA" and the "sleeved PPA." With a direct PPA, the power is delivered directly from a RE producer to the offtaker; in other words, the offtaker purchases the generated power from the producer behind the buyer's grid connection point (known as "behind-the-meter") and uses it directly without making use of the power grid. With a sleeved PPA, the PPA offtaker buys the power from the producer via an intermediary ("sleeving partner"). This intermediary acts as the PPA buyer's agent, physically taking over the electricity at the producer's grid connection point and feeding it into the power grid. This sleeving partner delivers this volume of electricity to the offtaker's grid connection point. In economic terms, this results in a complete transfer of the purchased power, as well as the associated guarantees of origin from the PPA seller to the PPA offtaker.

production volume. In other words, a synthetic PPA works similarly to a contract for difference (CFD) or to the market premium payment under the EEG 2017 Act (German Renewable Energy Sources Act 2017).

Synthetic PPAs are generally limited to locations where hedging counterparties can be found – therefore, areas that are deregulated and that have liquid spot markets for energy sales that permit the sale of the electricity output into a day-ahead or real-time market.

Also, synthetic PPAs may be appropriate in tender markets and where the commercial start date under a PPA is only allowed in several years into the future to better match anticipated load growth. For such projects that are ready for operation before the PPA starts, a synthetic PPA may let the project generate revenue in the meantime with a floor under the interim revenue so that the project can be financed. A synthetic PPA may also be applied for strings or parts of a wind farm that enter into operation before the complete plant. This way, the term of the PPA (e.g., 20 years) can be prevented from starting to run before the full project is built.

Do consider a financial option (put/call) in the synthetic PPA, involving future revenue derived from the project. In a financial option, the parties have the right to put or call the future cash flows from an actual or hypothetical sale of electricity. The term of these options can range from a few days to several years, and the option may cover only a portion of the output or the entire output from a project. This might help the project to gain liquidity and to cover development costs prior to the operation of the plant.

In a financial option (e.g., a put), the option buyer purchases the right to sell electricity at a certain strike price. If the merchant prices drop below the strike price, then the option buyer will exercise the option to sell its power for more than the market price. Conversely, if the merchant price rises above the strike price, then the option buyer will let the option expire and earn the market price of the electricity. Call options are the opposite of put options where the option buyer purchases the right to buy electricity at a certain strike price. If merchant price rise above the strike price, then the option buyer will exercise the call option and, if not, then they will let the option expire.

Alternatively, the parties can choose to hedge the price of underlying commodities, such as the price of certificates of origin or unbundled renewable energy certificates that are sold separately from the generated electricity.

Termination rights are another focal point when negotiating a synthetic PPA. In order to ensure that the project owner is not subject to differing standards, lenders will want to see the termination rights, as well as termination events under the hedge, as closely aligned as possible with the default events under the loan and intercreditor agreements. Also, lenders may ask for a brief cure period after a default event under the hedge agreement in order to give the lenders a chance to cure any default and thus preserve the value of the hedge.

The short term of a synthetic PPA, typically 10 years or less, is a concern for lenders because it creates a period of unhedged merchant tail and will require the debt to be amortized in a relatively short amount of time. Nevertheless, lenders will finance projects using a synthetic PPA if there is sufficient price protection.

Although it may add further complexity to the agreement, parties to synthetic PPAs may wish to consider whether there is net value than can be captured and shared from particular conditions. For instance, (1) reducing supply to avoid periods of negative pricing and compensate for lost income, (2) reducing demand to take advantage of system constraints, (3) cooperating to maximize any new "green benefits" and (4) achieving flexible redelivery. For instance, Nord Pool allows Google to buy power in Sweden and use it at its Finnish data centers.

Thus, **don't underestimate the time and effort involved in developing a PPA – these agreements and settings are complex (tariff schedule, performance testing, etc.).**

PPA Technical Schedules

These are detailed schedules that describe the power station performance and testing procedures (Performance Testing and Reliability Run). These are critical for testing output power (in KW or MW) and ensuring the power station can produce the contractual output (over 1 to 4 hours), in addition to respecting the grid codes. For instance, the power station must not suddenly disconnect if there is a swing in system frequency: 50 Hz (49.75 Hz to 50.25 Hz) to an extreme high 52 Hz or extreme low 47 Hz. For the Reliability Run, a period of 7 days is typical, but it can cover up to 30 days.

From a commercial point of view, **do make sure that the agreed fixed power price in a PPA covers operating costs, payment of principal and interest on long tenor debt and recovery of capital** with a reasonable return. Operating costs will be subject to escalation due to inflation. Ideally, the power price (or strike price) takes into account at least the same escalation as the operational costs.

Business Case: PPAs in Colombia

Power Purchase Agreements can fulfill many purposes. A peculiar case is Colombia. Electricity in Colombia is mainly generated from hydropower plants (around 77%) with a lesser amount from thermal power plants (around 15%). Thus, the dependence on water supply and weather conditions (e.g., dry seasons during El Niño) generates the need to build reserve capacity. At the same time, the Colombian electricity system requires that power prices absorb (part of) the long-term costs for network and generation capacity expansion to meet national demand. However, water scarcity has led to a drop in power generation and thus in revenue required to expand the power fleet and/or the grid.

Therefore, the national regulator (CREG: *Comisión de Regulación de Energía y Gas*) has renewed the settlement mechanism establishing "Firm Energy Obligations" (*Obligaciones de Energía Firme*), according to which power generation companies undertake to meet supply and demand during periods of power crisis and when power prices on the wholesale market tend to be higher than the "scarcity price" fixed by the regulator.

Power generation companies can tender the "Firm Energy Obligations" to other utilities/IPPs for a pre-defined price and term or invest in new power plants to meet these obligations. The term of the "Firm Energy Obligations" is up to 20 years in the case of new assets. The power price for the "Firm Energy Obligations" is the closing price of the tender under which the generator sold the fixed energy, that is the "Reliability Charge Price" (*Precio de Cargo por Confiabilidad*). During periods of water scarcity for power generation, the generator will obtain the "scarcity price" which is higher than the "Reliable Charge Price." If generation exceeds what is required under the "Firm Energy Obligations," the generator will be reimbursed at the market price.

11.5.3 Connection Agreement

A Connection Agreement (CA) is a legal contract that sets out the technical specifications and parameters of the project to be connected to a public electricity network. Parties of the CA tend to be the transmission (or distribution) operator and the power seller. Under certain conditions, the lenders may be also signatories to the CA (and to the PPA – e.g., through a direct agreement). In some countries, the terms and conditions relating to the use of the connection point and other specific provisions in relation to the grid connection may be integrated in the PPA. But in any case, **don't consider that a Connection Agreement alleviates the need to respect the grid codes**. Table 11.4 below summarizes the main differences between the CA and the grid code:

Table 11.4: Connection agreement versus grid codes (own representation).

Connection Agreement	Grid Code
Details what a specific project / power plant can achieve	Provides technical specifications and requirements to the power plant in order to connect to the grid
Addresses any deviations from the grid codes	Establishes the parameters to ensure safe, secure and economic power supply
Sets out specific payment information (node prices, grid pass-through fees)	Can apply to the power plants, other networks or consumers
Includes commercial terms	

When entering into a CA and a PPA, do make sure that both contracts are aligned. For instance: the duration of the CA should be at least equal to the term of the PPA, including extensions; the CA should allow for plant testing and commissioning time periods; legal and commercial requirements should be consistent (i.e., invoices, billing, payments, insurance, indemnification, force majeure, limitation of liability, provisions on dispute resolutions, applicable law, bank information covenants).

The CA will cover ancillary services. These are the services necessary to support the transmission while maintaining a reliable operational system, capable of meeting fluctuations in load occurring within a scheduling interval, contingency capacity reserve to maintain power system frequency during outages, reactive power support to guard against power system failure through voltage collapse and black start capability to allow restoration of power system operation after complete failure of all or part of the power system. **Do negotiate monetary compensation in case ancillary services are not provided as agreed by the grid operator or are curtailed** (a temporary shutdown, for example, during a period when transmission lines in the area are full so that there is no way to get electricity to the grid). Otherwise, the output estimates in the financial model will have to be reduced.

Case Study: Example of Plant Operating Requirements in a Connection Agreement

- Production may be curtailed if the national hydroelectric reservoirs are full and overflowing;
- The plant is required to automatically regulate voltage at the Point of Interconnection (PoI);[41]
- The plant must be capable of operating at a power factor of −0.96/+0.995 as measured at the PoI;
- The plant will be tripped offline if harmonic currents and voltage exceed IEEE 519 limits at the PoI;
- The plant must have under/over voltage and under/over frequency ride-through capability;
- The plant will be tripped offline for causing voltage fluctuations in excess of Section 3.9 of IEEE 241-1990 limits. Studies or tests on the system should be performed to confirm that these requirements and restrictions will be met;
- The plant must provide 24-hour production forecasts every 12 hours;
- The plant must provide 7-day production forecasts every Thursday; and
- The plant must provide a forecast of "Declared Capacity" on an hourly basis at 23:00 every day.

The example refers to a 55 MWp PV project located in Honduras with an IA granted on January 16, 2014. At the latest, these requirements will be assessed by the Lenders' technical advisor and if not originally considered in the energy yield assessment, there will be a negative impact in the financial model (and thus, in the debt sizing of the loan amount).

11.5.4 Implementation Agreement (IA)

An Implementation Agreement (IA) is typically required when the national power offtaker needs government funding or other support to ensure implementation of the PPA. This is mainly the case in developing markets. The parties of the IA are the government (generally represented by the Ministry of Finance), the project owner

41 See: national document "National Guide for the CND Approval on the Connection of Photovoltaic Projects – OP 15" in Honduras, under which the plant operator has to provide calculations showing the plant can operate over a power factor range as measured at the Point of Interconnection (PoI) during maximum output at peak ambient temperature.

(developer) and the national utility. **Do use the IA to ensure the confidence of financiers and governments.** The general legal provisions of an IA will include, inter alia, the applicable law, anti-corruption clauses, no third-party rights, confidentiality, representations and warranties, modification/survival, good faith provisions, costs and counterparts. Specific legal provisions will refer to the financial commitments of the offtaker (i.e., payment obligations under the PPA), visas, work permits, land access, import/export equipment, repatriation of funds generated by the project, no expropriation, remedies for events of default or specific requirements for the use of services, goods and/or local employers.

11.5.5 EPC and O&M Agreements

The EPC and O&M Agreements are two core agreements in a project. This Section mentions dos and don'ts for the selection of EPC and O&M service providers. Generally speaking, lenders will require the following elements to be included for an agreement to be considered "bankable": a fixed completion date, a fixed completion price, no or limited technology risk, performance and availability guarantees, liquidated damages for both delay and performance, security from the EPC contractor and/or its parent, sufficient caps on liability, restrictions on the ability of the contractor to claim extensions of time and additional costs. An EPC Contract delivers all of the requirements listed above in one integrated package.[42] This is one of the major reasons why they are the predominant form of construction contract used on large-scale projects. Lenders have become comfortable with the interface risk arising in a split EPC structure and will focus on the remedies for underperformance.

Do prioritize the quality, reliability and track record of the EPC contractor and O&M service provider. The EPC contractor's credentials will be a good gauge of their quality, creditworthiness and bankability. Do agree on a certification process for the EPC contractor to ensure their compliance with prevailing standards and state-of-the-art skills. The EPC contractor is liable for the material and workmanship during the construction phase.[43] The O&M operator is liable for the material and workmanship in relation to their services. Missing or poorly expressed warranties in the EPC and O&M agreements are a risk for the owner since the quality can't be properly assessed. The performance warranties along with the applicable pass/fail criteria

42 In some cases, multi-contracting is a valid option (e.g., in an onshore wind project, a turbine supply agreement plus a balance of plant contract ensures that both contractors play to their strengths). If the project relies on one main contractor for execution, the owner distances himself from managing the project, can lose control and risks challenges in the event of the default of the EPC-contractor.

43 For examples of guarantees in EPC Agreements under German Law, see Andreas Kleefisch and Jens Reiermann, "Was Garantien wirklich Wert sind," *PV Magazine*, July 4, 2018.

should be clearly expressed in the EPC and O&M agreements in order to reduce the risks of the project owners. The component manufacturer must meet the warranty and performance guarantees and disposal guarantee for their products; if they fail to do so, the EPC and O&M suppliers are responsible for making a claim with their providers. Mandatory and optional insurance policies can cover financial risks caused by external or internal factors, but O&M companies' awareness of the consequences of inaccurate maintenance should be raised in order to prevent safety issues and performance drops. For all risks which are not covered by the above measures, the owner/operator of the PV project will be held responsible with their equity capital. Banks are last in the risk transfer chain and only get involved in cases of creditor default.

EPC companies need to discern which suppliers are truly bankable, which suppliers have a level of manufacturing quality control that is acceptable, which products are reliable, have a fully-audited bill-of-materials and, perhaps more pertinent, how many of these companies will be solvent 2 to 3 years from now and able to honor 20- to 30-year product performance guarantees.[44]

An obvious option to improve Return on Investment ("ROI") estimates of a project is to select cheaper components to drive down costs, but it is essential that there's no compromise on component quality which could affect the lifetime or durability of the project. Quality components must be used to ensure the expected project lifetime (usually 25 years) while retaining a robust business case; however, quality doesn't necessarily equate to higher costs. Do carry out component testing prior to installation; and do practice advanced monitoring for early fault detection and implement preventive maintenance for fault avoidance.

Since EPC and O&M agreements provide the framework for the whole project lifecycle, it is important to ensure that all technical aspects of EPC and O&M contracts are based on best-practice quality. Do use official checklists[45] validated by recognized donors or work hand-in-hand with an experienced owners' engineer when negotiating these agreements.

Do take part in professional bidding processes, especially if the project should be part of a tender. Costs estimates need to be based on a well-structured competitive bidding process. If needed (e.g., due to ECA requirements, insolvency cases and/or the redefinition of pricing terms close to the start of construction), this will facilitate the exchange of equipment and service suppliers and will allow the project to qualify for certain sources of debt financing. Especially in developing countries when closing bilateral agreements with a Public-Private-Partnership Unit (PPP U), some lenders like the European Investment Bank (EIB) require evidence that suppliers and services

44 Finlay Colville, "New module suppliers and technologies to create more opportunities and risks to developers and EPCs," July 13, 2018.

45 Example for EPC and O&M Agreements fulfilling bankability requirements for PV projects can be downloaded at http://www.solarbankability.org/home.html, an initiative funded by the Horizon 2020 Framework Programme of the European Union.

providers have been selected on the basis of competitive bidding. Details on competitive bidding processes are compiled in the "Guide to Procurement for projects financed by the EIB." An example of what can happen if no professional bidding is carried out, is explained in the "EPC Bidding Processes – First regional tender in Pernambuco, Brazil" box.

Make the Tough Decisions Early. As tempting as it may be, if the contracting parties are associated companies, don't try to make the construction or operating contracts too onerous on the project company. A construction contract or operating contract that has not been properly negotiated and prepared (as if between two truly independent parties) will not pass muster with financiers who will seek to renegotiate a clearly one-sided contract – often resulting in a far tougher contract than might otherwise have been necessary.

A bankable contract is a contract with a risk allocation between the contractor and the SPV that satisfies the lenders. Lenders focus on the ability (or more particularly the lack thereof) of the contractor to claim additional costs and/or time extensions, as well as the security provided by the contractor for its performance. The less comfortable the lenders are with these provisions, the greater amount of equity support the owners will have to provide. Obviously, price is also a consideration, but it is usually considered separately to the contract's bankability because the contract price (or more accurately the capital cost of the facility) has a more direct impact on the project's capacity to provide debt service or not.

EPC Bidding Processes – First regional tender in Pernambuco, Brazil

The first regional photovoltaic auction in Pernambuco (Brazil) on December 27, 2016 granted the winners a 20-year PPA indexed to escalation. Two out of the three winning projects (each amounting to 30 MW in size) could not be built. Among other reasons, because the bid price, based on an aggressive EPC-price, could not be achieved. The EPC contractor that submitted an unbinding offer (at a price of USD 1 million per installed MW) refused to accept the contract award without strong corporate guarantees when the project developer won the tender. Alternative (low) EPC offers could not be collected after the result of the price-auction was made public. Local import taxes in Brazil were also to be assessed. Luckily, the project developer managed to recover the bid bond (about USD 3 million) from the Pernambuco regional government. Therefore, it is fair to say that professional bidding processes are a "do" when it comes to obtaining financing in a bilateral agreement with a public authority, as is the need to submit realistic bid prices in an auction or tender.

Conclusion: In contracts, do share risks with suppliers and service providers.

11.5.6 Finance Agreement

Know Your Financiers. The previous sections should have helped you to recognize lenders specific needs, to think ahead and do the preparation work for a project without having to repeat simple steps two or three times. Once all of the permits are available, contracts can be negotiated and insurance bids collected; it then makes sense to mandate a financial entity willing to structure a non-recourse project loan. When selecting the mandate lead arranger (MLA), don't rely on unexperienced lenders (experience in the host country is key).

Prepare in advance for meetings. Much of the time spent negotiating financial agreements is due to unwillingness to try to understand the hopes and aspirations of the lenders ahead of large-scale, all-party meetings. All too often, the developer responses to suggestions made by the lenders are dismissed without any real consideration and, as a result, when explanations are given as to why such a suggestion was made, time is lost. Constructive dialogue can be achieved during meetings and internal approvals can be sought ahead of time. Good advisers will be able to understand much of what is being asked for, and what to look out for when reviewing commentaries/approaches being adopted.

Recognize that if equity is to be injected into the project pro rata with commercial lenders then the credit rating of the equity provider will be a key factor. If a bank letter of credit (LC) is required, start working on obtaining this early on in the development phase. Do not wait until two days prior to financial close when you finally read the conditions precedent (CP) to the loan and discover that you need to negotiate specific forms of LC to comply with lender requirements; otherwise you will have to seek unnecessary and complicated waivers for non-compliant LCs.

Set up accounting systems and reporting systems on day one in a manner that should satisfy the lenders and then take the time to read the information sections of the credit documentation carefully.

11.6 Conclusion

The development of renewable energy projects is a comprehensive activity involving several fields: engineering, financial, legal, environmental and social. The level of complexity depends on the technology, country, site and partners involved. Project development costs tend to exponentially increase along with progress on ready-to-builds. Financial liabilities (bid bonds, grid connection bonds) tend to be the norm in the permit process. Timewise, the project development period can be as short as one year (best-case scenario in a mature market such as Germany) or last more than ten years (e.g., in Ethiopia).

It can take years to solve the multitude of unforeseen situations with which a project developer can be confronted. That is why a list of major rules of behavior ("dos") and practices to be avoided ("don'ts") has been compiled, starting from the very early stages. They take into consideration the energy transition that many countries are pursuing and the deployment of renewable energies in countries with low rates of electrification.

Electrification, power supply and flexibility needs are one key aspect. At the other end, compliance criteria when selecting a country have also gained importance since the Panama Papers scandal. Regardless of the project, it is now mandatory to run a know-your-customer process on potential business partners, signatory parties of contracts and former right-holders. Compliance checks together with the Equator Principles and the IFC Performance Standards are fast becoming the first criteria a project has to pass before a lender starts the technical, commercial and financial diligence process. Corporate entities with Environmental, Social and Governance (ESG) targets are on the rise and thus, driving the growth of the green economy and the increase in power generation from renewable energies.

Energy resource estimates, grid availability and the engineering feasibility of the project remain the factors that increase the technical quality of an asset. From a commercial point of view, remuneration structures used in renewable energy projects are experiencing a radical transformation requiring higher qualifications among market participants than in the past: power demand, price volatility, and offtaker creditworthiness need to be properly assessed over a long period of time in a corporate power purchase agreement (PPA) and if the project is subject to public tender. Although grid parity has been reached for most of renewable energy technologies, the sector needs more national policies to promote a stable, transparent and well-defined legal environment.

Naturally, financing is still a necessity. Blended finance instruments and government commitments like the Paris Agreement or Agenda2063 should facilitate the deployment of renewable energy projects in countries where electricity access has been rather limited. A variety of permits (environmental permits, construction permits, grid connection agreements) are required for a project to achieve ready-to-build status. Some of them need to be developed for the first time in countries with low installed capacity. Once the permits have been obtained, project agreements (i.e., core agreements such as PPAs, EPC agreements, O&M agreements, but also Implementation Agreements) can be finalized in order to share project risks with involved parties as much as possible. Risks shall also be covered by a comprehensive insurance package, one of the requirements to achieve a non-recourse loan.

Non-recourse financing granted by experienced lenders, who are familiar with the technology, capable of properly assessing the risks affecting a market, and have a credit-process adapted to the new norm (synthetic PPAs and similar), continues to be key.

12 Cost of Capital for Renewable Energy: The Role of Industry Experience and Future Potentials

Florian Egli, Dr. Bjarne Steffen, Prof. Dr. Tobias S. Schmidt

12.1 Introduction

In 2017, global energy investment accounted for roughly 2.2% of global gross domestic product (GDP), with the electricity sector taking the largest share, surpassing oil and gas investments (OECD/IEA 2017). Within the electricity sector, renewable energy technologies (RETs) are on a growth path and accounted for the largest share (ibid.). In the course of the expansion of renewable energy investments, the predominant types of investors have changed. While energy assets used to be the domain of vertically integrated utilities, the advent of RET assets has changed the investor landscape. Between 2010 and 2015, the share of institutional investors in European wind projects for example increased from 6% to 36% (OECD 2016). In early RET markets, such as Germany, 59% of renewable energy investments were undertaken by institutional and strategic investors in 2012 already (Trend Research 2013). The arrival of institutional investors in the RET market points out that RETs – at least in certain markets – are considered a mainstream asset with a reasonably low risk profile. This section sheds light on the effect of the mainstreaming of RET assets on financing costs. It investigates how much and why financing costs have decreased and discusses whether there are remaining potentials for (financing) cost reductions in Europe.

From a financing perspective, the essential difference between most RETs and fossil fuel based technologies (FFT) is the RETs' higher share of capital expenditures (CAPEX) compared to operating expenditures (OPEX).[1] CAPEX mainly consist of the initial investments in capital equipment (e.g., wind turbines), which need to be financed, whereas OPEX occur during operation over the lifetime of the asset (e.g., fuel costs or maintenance) and typically do not need upfront finance. The relation of CAPEX to OPEX is commonly termed capital intensity. As no fuel costs occur for RETs (with the exception of biomass plants), they are more capital intensive than FFTs (Schmidt 2014; Hirth and Steckel 2016). Consequently, the effect of higher costs of capital is asymmetric across technologies, affecting RETs more than FFTs. High costs of capital therefore not only increase the levelized costs of electricity (LCOEs) for RETs,

1 With biomass projects as an exception from the rule.

Florian Egli, Dr. Bjarne Steffen, Prof. Dr. Tobias S. Schmidt, Energy Politics Group, Department of Humanities, Social and Political Sciences, ETH Zurich, Switzerland

https://doi.org/10.1515/9783110607888-012

but also increase CO_2 abatement cost (Schmidt 2014; Ondraczek, Komendantova, and Patt 2015) and can decrease the deployment of RETs (Iyer et al. 2015). Schmidt (2014) demonstrates that the initial investment and the capital service make up only about 15% for FFTs, but up to 91% for RETs.

Figure 12.1 shows the cost components of solar PV, onshore wind and FFTs. The cost of debt denotes the interest payments on the debt raised to finance the project, the cost of equity denotes the dividend payments (i.e., return) to the project shareholders and together they constitute a project's financing costs. CAPEX denote the initial expenditure (i.e., investment) into the asset and OPEX denote the expenditures to operate the asset throughout its lifetime.

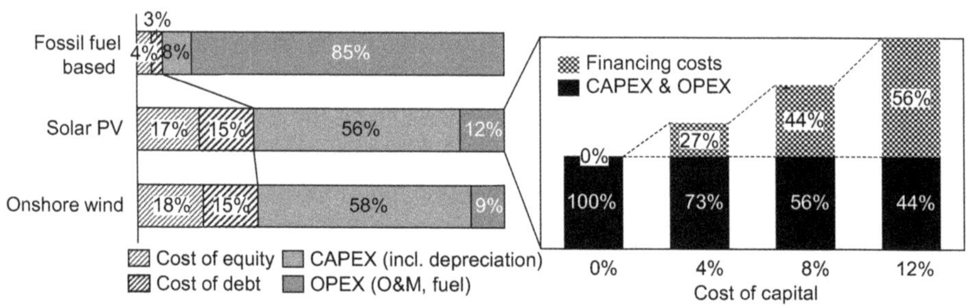

Figure 12.1: The different LCOE cost structures of RETs and FFTs (left-hand) and the sensitivity of solar PV LCOE to changes in the cost of capital (right-hand).[2]

The LCOE of RETs is highly sensitive to the cost of capital. The cost of capital is a function of the cost of debt, the cost of equity, the project leverage (i.e., ratio of debt to total project volume) and tax (omitted in Figure 12.1). Figure 12.1 (right-hand) shows the sensitivity of solar PV LCOE to different costs of capital for the LCOE of solar PV. For RET projects in Europe, the cost of capital is typically between 4% and 12% (Angelopoulos et al. 2016), whereas 12% has long been a lower bound for projects in many emerging or developing economies, such as India or Kenya (Shrimali et al. 2013; Waissbein et al. 2013). At a cost of capital of 12%, more than half of the solar PV LCOE stems from financing costs (cf. Figure 12.1). Hence, high costs of capital are a main barrier to widespread RET deployment. However, by the same logic, lowering the cost of capital (overall or specifically for RETs) opens an interesting space to navigate for policymakers to further reduce the LCOE of RETs, even for technologies where the investment costs might not decrease much further. In other words, low-cost finance can play a crucial role to enable the low-carbon energy transition.

2 The left-hand figure is based on the low financing cost scenario in Schmidt (2014), assuming 5% cost of debt, 10% cost of equity. Fossil fuel based is the average of diesel, hard coal and natural gas. The right-hand figure is based on the LCOE parameters used in Egli et al. (2018).

Recent empirical evidence on the development of costs of capital and other key financial indicators (leverage, debt service coverage ratio, loan tenor) suggests that indeed finance can play an enabling role for RETs (cf. Egli, Steffen, and Schmidt 2018). In a study analyzing solar PV and onshore wind projects in Germany between 2000 and 2017, Egli et al. (2018) find substantially improved financing conditions for both technologies in 2017 compared to 2000. These improved financing conditions in turn helped lowering the LCOEs and making solar PV and onshore wind viable alternatives to FFTs. The next two sections summarize key findings for practitioners from the study. In section four, we build on Egli et al. (2018) with an outlook for investors on potential cost reductions for solar PV and onshore wind in other European countries. The section ends with a conclusion, discussing implications for investors and policymakers.

12.2 Lessons from the Past

This section describes the evolution of the financial conditions for RET projects. Deriving lessons from the past in RET markets comes with two problems. First, RETs deployed at scale are a rather recent phenomenon. Finding evidence of changes over time is therefore limited to few early markets. Second, observing changes in financing conditions for RET projects requires RET project data, which is not publicly available. Financing details are often treated confidentially because large RET investments are typically set up in project finance structures. However, this setup comes with an advantage too. In project finance, each project is a separate legal entity, set up for the project's lifetime, often called a special purpose vehicle (SPV). The project sponsors hold equity in the SPV, and banks provide loans (i.e., debt) to the SPV with no recourse beyond the project (Steffen 2018). The isolation of an SPV from other projects or a balance sheet means that each SPV is realized with individual financing conditions that are tailored to the project's risk and return profile. Hence, the costs of capital reveal unbiased information about the underlying investment project (cf. Gatti 2013).

Egli et al. (2018) analyze solar PV and onshore wind projects in Germany, one of the first RET markets worldwide. Germany added more solar PV capacity than any other country in 13 years between 2000 and 2016 and more onshore wind capacity in eight years between 2000 and 2016 (IRENA 2018). Additionally, utility-scale renewable energy investments in Germany are mainly financed by private actors and realized in project finance structures, as it is the case in many other countries. Working directly with the most important RET investors in Germany, Egli et al. (2018) assembled a RET project database covering 133 projects between 2000 and 2017. The projects are similar in terms of size and technology by corresponding to a reference project with an investment sum of €20 million, using standard technology from established manufacturers.

Figure 12.2 shows the aggregate changes in the cost of capital for solar PV and onshore wind projects. The cost of capital is calculated by averaging the cost of debt, the cost of equity and the leverage by technology across all projects for the indicated years. It includes the corporate tax rate in Germany. The stacked bars for 2000–2005 and 2017 should be read as the after-tax cost of capital. The unleveraged cost of debt and equity are indicated in Table 12.1. Three main points can be concluded from the data in Figure 12.2. First, the cost of capital decreased substantially for both technologies. While it used to be between 4.5% and 5.1% in the early days of RET deployment, the projects have been financed with a cost of capital of just 1.6% to 1.9% in 2017. The 2017 costs of capital correspond to a low-risk corporate bond of a financial service firm (BB+ to BBB). Second, the decrease happened on the cost of debt as well as the cost of equity, with a slightly larger effect on the former. Third, the dynamics of the cost of capital meant that the technology difference between solar PV and onshore wind reversed. Put differently, financing a solar PV project in the early days of RET deployment (2000–2005) was more expensive than an onshore wind project. In 2017, however, the opposite was true and financing a solar PV project became cheaper than financing an onshore wind project.

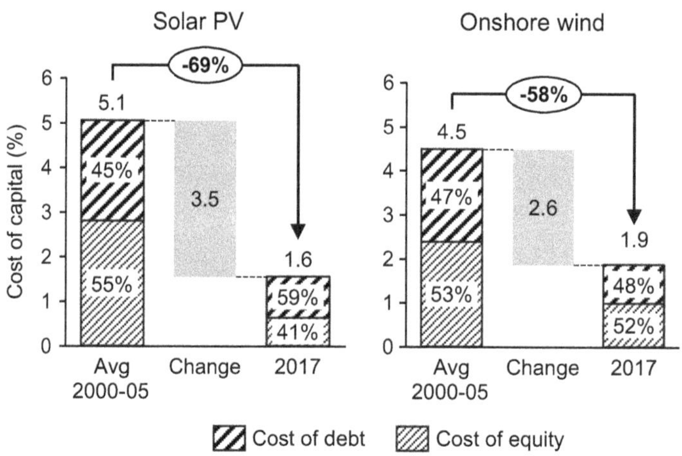

Figure 12.2: Empirical observation of changes in the cost of equity, the cost of debt and the cost of capital (own representation).[3]

3 Empirical observation of changes in the cost of equity, the cost of debt and the cost of capital for solar PV and onshore wind projects (N = 133) in Germany between 2000 and 2017, reported in percentage-points. Based on Egli et al. (2018).

To complement Figure 12.2, Table 12.1 reports the changes for each component of the cost of capital and adds the changes in the debt service coverage ratio (DSCR) and the loan tenor. Both additional financial indicators confirm the observed changes in the cost of capital. DSCRs decreased and loan tenors increased, indicating a higher confidence level of investors for solar PV and onshore wind projects.

Table 12.1: Costs of debt and equity, leverage and tax rate. Based on Egli et al. (2018).

	Solar PV		Onshore wind	
	2000–2005	**2017**	**2000–2005**	**2017**
Cost of debt	5.5%	1.5%	4.8%	1.6%
Cost of equity	9.3%	4.8%	9.5%	5.4%
Leverage (debt share)	70%	87%	75%	82%
Corporate tax rate	41%	30%	41%	30%
Other financial indicators				
DSCR	1.24	1.13	1.28	1.16
Loan tenor	16 years	19 years	15 years	17 years

In total, the changes in costs of capital contributed 5% to the decrease in the LCOE of solar PV and 20% to the decrease in the LCOE for onshore wind (Egli, Steffen, and Schmidt 2018). Together with lower technology costs (i.e., CAPEX), the changes in financing conditions sped up RET deployment and contributed to a self-reinforcing cycle of cost decreases. As solar PV and onshore wind assets were being deployed, developers, financiers and users were able to learn from experience, which in turn made technology improvements and cost decreases possible and led to even more deployment due to lower costs. This effect is well known for many technologies and especially RETs. It is commonly termed technology learning and expressed empirically with a constant learning rate. The learning rate describes the percentage cost reduction in CAPEX for each doubling of cumulative global capacity. For solar PV, this rate has been estimated at approximately 23%, for onshore wind at approximately 12% (Rubin et al. 2015). The following section sheds light on the question whether the observed improvements in financing conditions are due to a learning effect (similar to the technical improvements), or whether other factors drove the observed changes.

12.3 Reduction of Cost of Capital: Luck or Experience?

While the reduction in costs of capital for RETs is stark, it remains open whether the reduction is specific to RETs or whether it reflects a broader trend in the economy. More specifically, the 2008 financial crisis and the subsequent period of low interest rates for the entire economy fall into the period of study. Hence, the question is whether the deployment of RETs worked out so well thanks to a favorable coincidence with a period of low interest rates or whether the finance industry learned from experience with RET projects, reducing investment risk and hence the cost of capital.

In interviewing leading RET investors, Egli et al. (2018) identified drivers of the changes in costs of capital on three levels: the economy, the renewable energy sector, and the renewable energy finance industry. Economy-wide drivers are mainly linked to the low interest rate environment leading to low-cost liquidity and lower return expectations, partly due to a lack of viable investment projects. On a sectoral level, the increasing availability of performance data proved that solar PV and onshore wind are reliable technologies with low default rates. At the same time, investors perceive the German support policy for RETs (i.e., feed-in tariff) and hence future project revenue streams as reliable, which has also been confirmed in other studies. On the lowest level, the renewable energy finance industry, drivers are related to increasing in-house expertise and experience with RET risk assessments. Moreover, the increasing number of RET projects created incentives to standardize deal structures and contracts and to establish networks of trusted project partners. Both effects were substantially reinforced by the arrival of new investor types such as institutional investors (e.g., pension funds) or large banks. These investors helped professionalize the industry, streamline processes and lower deal costs by putting pressure on the margins. In sum, the first level points to an important driver external to the RET industry, while the second and third level point to drivers internal to the RET industry (i.e., improvements as experience grows).

In trying to quantify the effect of the internal drivers, Egli et al. (2018) use debt margins as a metric for the project-specific risk above a general country-specific investment risk. Indeed the paper finds quantitative evidence that experience plays a role in reducing debt margins. For both solar PV and onshore wind, the debt margin decreases by approximately 11% for each doubling of cumulative global investment in the respective technology. These results are robust to a number of different specifications, including using European instead of global investment. However, weighing the importance of the experience effect in reducing the cost of capital against the importance of the changes in the general interest rate level, the latter comes out on top. Specifically, comparing the experience effect with the yield on 10-year German government bonds, a common proxy for the baseline country-specific investment risk, the paper finds that the general interest rate level was responsible for a reduction in cost of debt about four to five times as high as the investment experience. Nonetheless, the absolute contribution of the experience effect is substantial at 1.0%-points and 1.5%-points for onshore wind and solar PV, respectively, both between 2000 and 2017. Hence, the German effort to deploy RETs at scale benefited greatly from the low interest rate environment but, at the same time, was able to leverage an experience effect in the renewable energy finance sector. The following section expands the analysis beyond Germany and discusses to what extent future cost reductions in RETs are possible in other European countries if they were able to reduce the RET risk margins to a level observed in Germany at present.

12.4 Potential for RET Cost Reductions in Europe

In this section, we build on the analysis of the German RET market by Egli et al. (2018) and develop a potential outlook for 26 European countries. The existence of an experience effect means that country- and technology-specific risk margins are not static. Currently, risk margins for solar PV and onshore wind differ across countries. For investors, this indicates that there may be a potential to enter new markets (i.e., countries) and exploit experience effects to drive down the cost of capital. If there is a financial cost reduction potential, how substantial is it in reality? While the potential is most likely highest in developing and emerging economies, there are large variations in risk margins across European countries too. Figure 12.3 illustrates this potential across 26 European countries (all EU countries except Luxemburg and Malta). The figure shows the current LCOE, a potential LCOE if the technology risk premium were at the level of Germany in all other EU countries and a potential future LCOE if – additional to the change in risk premium – the technologies became cheaper (i.e., CAPEX reductions) according to historically observed rates of cost reductions (i.e., learning rates, see above).

For the first value in Figure 12.3 (LCOE, current cost of capital), we use the most recent data on CAPEX, OPEX, asset lifetime, full load hours and learning rates for Germany (Fraunhofer ISE 2018). For simplicity, the analysis abstracts from differences in CAPEX, OPEX and full load hours. While the level of the LCOE displayed in Figure 12.3 thus needs to be treated with caution, the approach allows focusing on the effect of a change in costs of capital. In other words, the percentage reduction when risk margins are reduced and technology learning is accounted for, which is the main point of Figure 12.3, remains valid. In order to estimate the current country- and technology-specific cost of capital, we use the data from the EU Horizon2020 research project DIACORE, which has collected EU-wide costs of capital for onshore wind (Angelopoulos et al. 2016). To calculate the cost of capital for solar PV, we use the evidence from Egli et al. (2018) and assume that solar PV receives a 0.3%-point discount compared to onshore wind in all European countries (cf. 2017 numbers in Figure 12.2).

For the second value (LCOE potential), we use the same technology data, but adjust the cost of capital. Specifically, we define the country-specific (i) and technology-specific (j) cost of capital according to Equation (12.1), where K_E denotes the cost of equity, K_D denotes the cost of debt, E and D denote the equity and debt

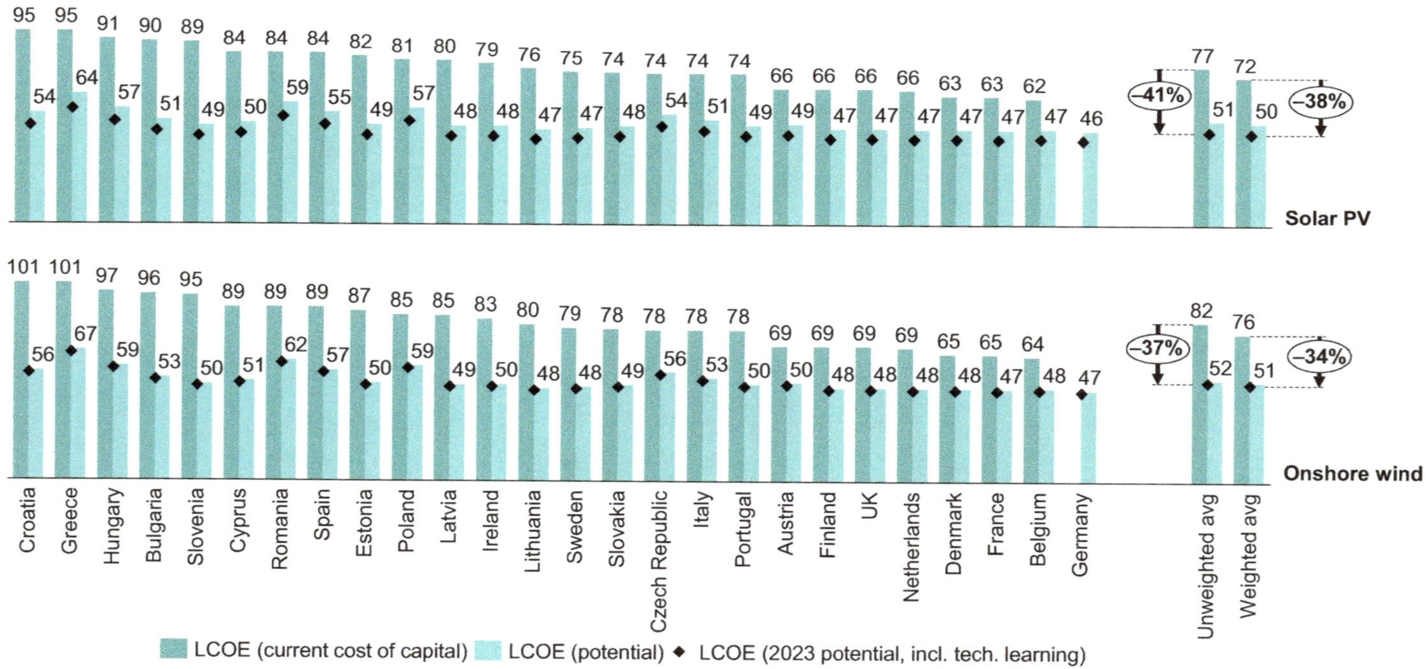

Figure 12.3: Potential for LCOE reduction in 26 EU countries (own representation).[4]

4 Country-specific tax rates are from OECD (2018). For Bulgaria, Croatia, Cyprus and Romania the OECD source does not provide tax rates, which were obtained from KPMG (2018).

investment, V denotes the total investment volume and T denotes the tax rate[5]. All country-specific variables, namely the cost of equity, the cost of debt and the tax rate are adjusted to calculate costs of capital for both technologies j in all countries i. We hence assume that projects across Europe are financed with identical capital structures (E, D and V), debt margins and equity premiums.

$$CoC_{ij} = K_{E,ij}\frac{E_j}{V_j} + K_{D,ij}\frac{D_j}{V_j}(1 - T_i) \tag{12.1}$$

To calculate the cost of debt in each country, we define the cost of debt as a baseline country risk with a technology-specific risk margin on top as shown in Equation (12.2) (Elton et al. 2001). We use the average yield on a 10-year government bond (govbond) from Eurostat (2018b) as a proxy for baseline country risk. We assume that investors finance RET projects in all EU countries with the same technology-specific risk premium (margin) as in Germany in 2017, i.e., 1.0% for solar PV and 1.5% for onshore wind (Egli, Steffen, and Schmidt 2018).[6]

$$K_{D,ij} = govbond_i + margin_j \tag{12.2}$$

To calculate the cost of equity in each country, we assume an equity premium over the cost of debt as commonly assumed in the energy finance literature (Donovan and Nuñez 2012). We use the equity premium for German projects in 2017, i.e., 3.3% for solar PV and 3.8% for onshore wind (cf. Table 12.1) from Egli et al. (2018) for all countries.

$$K_{E,ij} = K_{D,ij} + equitypremium_j \tag{12.3}$$

Lastly, for the third value in Figure 12.3 (LCOE, 2023 potential, incl. technology learning), we add expected technology cost reductions up to 2023 to the calculation using the same costs of capital as before. We use the main case RET deployment scenario from the IEA (IEA 2018) and 2017 RET capacity from IRENA (IRENA 2018) and calculate future technology costs using a one-factor learning curve with learning rates commonly used in the literature (Fraunhofer ISE 2018).

Figure 12.3 shows an unweighted average across all 25 countries except Germany and an average weighted with the electricity production in each country to account

5 For Estonia, no data on 10-year government bonds was available. The yield was calculated using the German 10-year government bond as a baseline and adding the country risk premium for Estonia to this (Damodaran 2016).

6 Potential for LCOE reduction in 26 EU countries with improved financing with and without technology improvements up to 2023. Note that for Germany, we report only the potential LCOE, which is identical to the current LCOE. Note that we report the cost of capital displayed in Figure 12.2 from Egli et al. (2018) for Germany because it is more accurate than the calculation described in Equations (12.1–12.3).

for market size (Eurostat 2018a). These averages need to be read with caution as they describe hypothetical cost reduction potentials and it is unclear whether European countries will be able to reduce risk margins for RETs to the extent that Germany has in the past. However, it is also possible that the risk margins observed in 2017 in Germany do not represent a lower bound and will decrease further. Above all, Figure 12.3 shows large differences between European countries and – for some countries – a possibly large cost reduction potential via lower RET risk margins. The weighted averages point to a gap of 38% for solar PV and 34% for onshore wind between the best-in-class (Germany) and the other 25 European countries considered. The difference between the two technologies is due to a larger technology learning effect for solar PV due to an expected faster deployment between 2018 and 2023. The largest cost reduction potential occurs in countries with currently high costs of capital. It is important to note that this analysis only reduces the risk margins on top of differences in government bond yields. That is, this analysis for example still assumes that the Greek country risk, which is currently very high (6% yield on a 10-year government bond), remains constant. Hence, the analysis may underestimate the potential for cost reduction in countries with currently high government bond yields (i.e., high country risk). The five countries with the highest reduction potential (in percentages) are Slovenia, Bulgaria, Croatia, Spain and Estonia. With the exception of Estonia, all of these countries have solar irradiation potentials above the EU-28 average (i.e., above-average expected full load hours for solar PV) (Breyer and Gerlach 2013). While this does not change the percentage reduction potential, it would lower the absolute value of the LCOE substantially. Future analyses could investigate potential in terms of the level of the LCOEs in more detail.

12.5 Conclusion

This section has demonstrated that costs of capital are highly relevant for the LCOE of RETs and hence their cost-competitiveness. It has further summarized recent literature, showing that the costs of capital for solar PV and onshore wind have decreased substantially in the past, leading to RET cost reductions. The reasons for the decrease in costs of capital were both external to the RET sector (general interest rate level) and internal (experience and market development), while the former effect was by approximately four to five times larger than the latter. However, the experience effect has allowed reducing risk margins in the German context to very low levels. If other European countries were able to reduce their risk premiums for solar PV and onshore wind projects to similar levels, the LCOE of solar PV could fall substantially. The hypothetical cost reduction potential amounts to approximately 38% for solar PV and 34% for onshore wind LCOEs. Reaping these potentials for cost reductions by lowering risk margins and hence the costs of capital is therefore a promising avenue to make RETs cheaper.

To deliver such cost reductions, there are implications for investors and policymakers. Investors may find markets with currently high costs of capital (i.e., risk margins) interesting as future experience may allow reducing those margins. In order to reduce risk margins, knowledge transfers between markets are crucial. Importantly, large financial institutions that are active in various markets may find a competitive edge by transferring knowledge effectively from one market to another within the institution. Such knowledge may include project assessment and data management skills, due diligence frameworks, contract templates, or trusted partner networks (supplier, developer, law firm, etc.). It may however also include better familiarity with the regulatory environment, the credibility of public support schemes and the requirements for project completion. To the extent that this knowledge hinges on individuals, in person exchanges and deliberate training of local staff will be required. Investors may also find it interesting to set up partnerships with other investors (or players in the investment ecosystem such as law firms, policymakers or technical experts) in order to assess market potentials and project proposals more efficiently. Especially, the establishment of international partnerships where the local experience in RET markets of one actor helps another one to enter a market quicker seems promising.

Action from policymakers may be needed too to facilitate knowledge sharing in the financial sector and to build up local RET investment ecosystems, which promise to reduce the cost of RETs. An example of facilitating knowledge transfer on a systems level could be the open sharing of project data (both performance and financial) across Europe. Some state investment banks (SIB) have played leading roles in providing data and technical expertise necessary to evaluate RET projects and secure financing. SIBs in Australia, Germany and the UK for example were shown to have enabled learning in the financial sector by diffusing knowledge, creating technology track records and thereby trust in these projects among investors (Geddes, Schmidt, and Steffen 2018). In addition to an active role of SIBs, streamlining RET regulations across Europe would certainly also be helpful in facilitating fast and efficient knowledge transfers. Such knowledge transfers and the resulting improved financing conditions for RETs may also help policymakers transitioning to more flexible support regimes for RETs that expose investors to more market risks (e.g., from a feed-in tariff regime to an auctions for premium regime). Finally, gradually improving financing conditions for RETs across Europe may help absorb potential negative cost shocks on RETs following a recovery of record low interest rates in Europe.

References

Angelopoulos, Dimitrios, Robert Brückmann, Filip Jirous, Inga Konstantinaviciute, Paul Noothout, John Psarras, Lucie Tesniere, and Barbara Breitschopf. 2016. "Risks and Cost of Capital for Onshore Wind Energy Investments in EU Countries." *Energy & Environment* 27, no. 1. SAGE PublicationsSage UK: London, England: 82–104. doi:10.1177/0958305X16638573.

Breyer, Christian, and Alexander Gerlach. 2013. "Global Overview on Grid-Parity." *Progress in Photovoltaics: Research and Applications* 21, no. 1. John Wiley & Sons, Ltd: 121–36. doi:10.1002/pip.1254.

Damodaran, Aswath. 2016. "Country Risk: Determinants, Measures and Implications – The 2016 Edition." *SSRN Electronic Journal*. https://papers.ssrn.com/sol3/papers.cfm?abstract_id=2812261.

Donovan, Charles, and Laura Nuñez. 2012. "Figuring What's Fair: The Cost of Equity Capital for Renewable Energy in Emerging Markets." *Energy Policy* 40. Elsevier: 49–58. doi:10.1016/J.ENPOL.2010.06.060.

Egli, Florian, Bjarne Steffen, and Tobias S. Schmidt. 2018. "A Dynamic Analysis of Financing Conditions for Renewable Energy Technologies." *Nature Energy* 3. Nature Publishing Group: 1084–92. doi:10.1038/s41560-018-0277-y.

Elton, Edwin J., Martin J. Gruber, Deepak Agrawal, and Christopher Mann. 2001. "Explaining the Rate Spread on Corporate Bonds." *Journal of Finance* 56, no. 1: 247–77. doi:10.1111/0022-1082.00324.

Eurostat. 2018a. "Electrical Energy Available for Final Consumption." http://appsso.eurostat.ec.europa.eu/nui/show.do?dataset=nrg_105a&lang=en.

Eurostat. 2018b. "EMU Convergence Criterion Bond Yields." *EMU Convergence Criterion Series – Monthly Data*. https://ec.europa.eu/eurostat/web/products-datasets/-/teimf050%0A.

Fraunhofer ISE. 2018. "Stromgestehungskosten Erneuerbare Energien."

Gatti, Stefano. 2013. *Project Finance in Theory and Practice: Designing, Structuring, and Financing Private and Public Projects*, 2nd ed. Waltham, MA: Academic Press.

Geddes, Anna, Tobias S. Schmidt, and Bjarne Steffen. 2018. "The Multiple Roles of State Investment Banks in Low-Carbon Energy Finance: An Analysis of Australia, the UK and Germany." *Energy Policy* 115: 158–70. doi:10.1016/j.enpol.2018.01.009.

Hirth, Lion, and Jan Christoph Steckel. 2016. "The Role of Capital Costs in Decarbonizing the Electricity Sector." *Environmental Research Letters* 11, no. 11. IOP Publishing: 114010. doi:10.1088/1748-9326/11/11/114010.

IEA. 2018. "Renewables 2018 Market Analysis and Forecast from 2018 to 2023." https://www.iea.org/renewables2018/power/.

IRENA. 2018. "Renewable Capacity Statistics 2017." http://resourceirena.irena.org/gateway/#resource-search.

Iyer, Gokul C., Leon E. Clarke, James A. Edmonds, Brian P. Flannery, Nathan E. Hultman, Haewon C. McJeon, and David G. Victor. 2015. "Improved Representation of Investment Decisions in Assessments of CO2 Mitigation." *Nature Climate Change* 5: 436–40. doi:10.1038/nclimate2553.

KPMG. 2018. "Corporate Marginal Tax Rates – By Country." http://pages.stern.nyu.edu/~adamodar/New_Home_Page/datafile/countrytaxrate.htm

OECD/IEA. 2017. *World Energy Investment 2017*.

OECD. 2016. "Fragmentation in Clean Energy Investment and Financing." In *OECD Business and Finance Outlook 2016*, 141–76. Paris: Author. http://www.oecd.org/investment/investment-policy/BFO-2016-Ch5-Green-Energy.pdf.

OECD. 2018. "Statutory Corporate Income Tax Rate." http://stats.oecd.org/index.aspx?DataSetCode=TABLE_II1.

Ondraczek, Janosch, Nadejda Komendantova, and Anthony Patt. 2015. "WACC the Dog: The Effect of Financing Costs on the Levelized Cost of Solar PV Power." *Renewable Energy* 75. Elsevier Ltd: 888–98. doi:10.1016/j.renene.2014.10.053.

Rubin, Edward S., Inês M L Azevedo, Paulina Jaramillo, and Sonia Yeh. 2015. "A Review of Learning Rates for Electricity Supply Technologies." *Energy Policy* 86. Elsevier: 198–218. doi:10.1016/j.enpol.2015.06.011.

Schmidt, Tobias S. 2014. "Low-Carbon Investment Risks and de-Risking." *Nature Climate Change* 4, no. 4. Nature Research: 237–39. doi:10.1038/nclimate2112.
Shrimali, Gireesh, David Nelson, Shobhit Goel, Charith Konda, and Raj Kumar. 2013. "Renewable Deployment in India: Financing Costs and Implications for Policy." *Energy Policy* 62: 28–43. doi:10.1016/j.enpol.2013.07.071.
Steffen, Bjarne. 2018. "The Importance of Project Finance for Renewable Energy Projects." *Energy Economics* 69: 280–94. doi:10.1016/j.eneco.2017.11.006.
Trend Research. 2013. "Definition und Marktanalyse von Bürgerenergie in Deutschland."
Waissbein, Oliver, Yannick Glemarec, Hande Bayraktar, and Tobias S. Schmidt. 2013. "Derisking Renewable Energy Investment: A Framework to Support Policymakers in Selecting Public Instruments to Promote Renewable Energy Investment in Developing Countries." New York, NY.

13 The Role of Green State Investment Banks in Financing Low-Carbon Projects

Anna Geddes

13.1 Overview

The deployment of low-carbon technology, such as renewable energy and energy efficiency projects, is necessary in order to mitigate climate change (Geddes et al. 2018; IPCC 2014; Schmidt et al. 2012). However there is concern that the required finance for these projects will not flow, either quickly enough or where it is most needed (Geddes et al. 2018; IEA 2014, 2016). Many of these projects and technologies are still perceived as too risky by investors, and developers face many barriers to sourcing the finance they need (Geddes et al. 2018). These barriers vary by technology, project size and local context setting, such as high construction risk and large upfront capital requirements for offshore wind in Germany and the UK or fuel supply risk, revenue uncertainty and novel technology risk for waste-to-energy plants in Australia (for examples of barriers, see Geddes et al. 2018; OECD 2016). Although public finance has a role to play, public financial support is currently limited; hence there are calls to use what little is available to leverage in private finance (Geddes et al. 2018; Schmidt 2014; Steffen 2018).

13.2 Introducing Green State Investment Banks

It is in this context that several governments have recently established new public finance institutions, or refocused existing finance institutions, to help green their economies and leverage in private finance for low-carbon projects. Here we refer to these banks as green state investment banks (SIBs) but they are also referred to as green investment banks (GIBs), national development banks (NDBs), government owned banks and public banks. The OECD defines a green investment bank as a publicly capitalized entity established specifically to facilitate private investment into domestic low-carbon, climate-resilient infrastructure and other green sectors such as water and waste management (OECD 2015, 2017). SIBs tend to operate in the deployment and diffusion phase of a technology's development, downstream on the innovation chain, rather than upstream where research and development occurs. It is here that many developers still struggle to source finance, even for what are considered to be "commercial ready" projects and it is this phase that is most important for the rapid deployment of low-carbon projects (Grubb 2004; Karltorp 2015; Mazzucato and Semieniuk 2017).

https://doi.org/10.1515/9783110607888-013

The OECD lists 13 green investment banks or green investment bank-like entities that operate at either a country or state level (OECD 2015, 2017). However it should be noted that there are several other publicly funded banks that have been heavily involved in financing low-carbon projects, both at a country or regional level, even though their mandates are not strictly focused on low-carbon sectors. Hence their activities in these areas should not be ignored when investigating the role of green SIBs. These banks include Germany's KfW (Kreditanstalt fuer Wiederaufbau or Reconstruction Credit Institute), the EBRD (European Bank for Reconstruction and Development) and the EIB (European Investment Bank). Table 13.1 presents a list of green SIBs.

Table 13.1: Green SIBs and SIBs with notable low-carbon activities.

	Location
California CLEEN Center	California, United States
Clean Energy Finance Corporation (CEFC)	Australia
Connecticut Green Bank	Connecticut, United States
Green Energy Market Securitization (GEMS) (Hawaii Green Infrastructure Authority)	Hawaii, United States
Green Finance Organisation	Japan
Green Investment Group, Macquarie (privatized in 2017, previously the UK Green Investment Bank (GIB))	United Kingdom
Malaysian Green Technology Corporation (GreenTech Malaysia)	Malaysia
Masdar	United Arab Emirates
Montgomery County Green Bank	Maryland, United States
New Jersey Energy Resilience Bank (ERB)	New Jersey, United States
NY Green Bank	New York, United States
Rhode Island Infrastructure Bank (RIIB)	Rhode Island, United States
Technology Fund	Switzerland
SIBs with notable low-carbon activities	
European Bank for Reconstruction and Development (EBRD)	Various
European Investment Bank (EIB)	Various
Kreditanstalt fuer Wiederaufbau (KfW)	Germany and abroad

(Source: Author's own research and OECD (2015)).

In addition to leveraging private finance for low-carbon projects, governments have various parallel motivations for establishing, or repurposing, SIBs, including the desire to create a more sustainable, resilient and/or innovative economy, economic growth, meeting emissions and renewable energy targets, improving energy security and independence, lowering energy costs, improving market efficiency, stimulating local business and manufacturing, creating jobs, etc. For example, The Green Finance Organisation in Japan supports local communities in order to address issues around an ageing society and to stimulate economic growth, the Rhode Island Infrastructure bank implemented its clean energy programs to reduce energy prices and create employment whereas the UK's Green Investment Bank was established to help the country meet its ambitious and legally binding emissions targets (Geddes et al. 2018; OECD 2017).

The NRDC (National Resource Defense Council) has identified common characteristics displayed by SIBs, namely that they share a narrow mandate (generally focusing on low-carbon sectors such as renewable energy, energy efficiency and low-carbon vehicles, for example), are publicly funded but operate as independent institutions, must leverage in private finance while being cost effective and accountable and are designed to have the greatest impact by addressing local market needs (NRDC 2016). Investments are usually held to different performance standards, with SIBs tracking performance data such as leverage ratios of private investment mobilized per unit of public investment, emissions saved, number of co-investors drawn, jobs created and of course acceptable losses, rates of return and other standard financial performance data (CEFC 2016a; GIB 2016; KfW 2017; OECD 2017). SIB mandates define target markets, sectors and technologies, target beneficiaries (developers, households, municipalities etc), appropriate levels of investment risk, allowable instruments, programs and financing channels and performance criteria. An SIB's mandate and its particular performance requirements determine how and how well an SIB can operate and should be designed carefully (Geddes et al. 2018).

13.3 SIB Instruments, Programs, and Financing Channels

SIBs offer a wide variety of instruments, programs and financing channels in order to address different barriers to financing. Some SIBs offer ***grants*** in order to reduce the overall project cost while providing some long-term financial certainty. Grants feature minimal administration, are a cost free financing option for developers and can help leverage in private finance (Lindenberg 2014). Usually grants are provided earlier in the project development phase when risks are higher, and are often reserved for projects that contain more innovative aspects and hence are struggling to source private finance (Lindenberg 2014). However many SIBs only offer limited grant funding or none at all as they prefer to offer instruments that are considered less market distorting and/or have a greater capacity to leverage in private finance.

Some SIBs provide **equity**, taking a higher risk position in a project than as a debt provider. By offering equity these SIBs not only reduce the risk to other investors in that project, but by taking a high risk position, it also sends a signal that the project is worth investing in, which eventually leads to further investment. The UK's GIB provided equity to successfully leverage in private investment to biomass and waste-to-energy projects. More SIBs are starting to consider providing equity where local contexts require it but they more commonly provide **debt**. Some SIBs offer concessional debt at lower than market interest rates to help reduce the cost of the project and in turn reduce the risk of defaulting on repayments, de-risking projects to help leverage in private finance. However other SIBs determine that offering market rate debt can have a greater impact as it sends a signal that the project is viable and ready for market, and the lack of concessionality reduces any potential for crowding-out private finance and/ or creating market distortions. SIBs can also take a subordinated position within a syndicate of debt providers (some SIBs also offer mezzanine finance), taking a higher risk position, which similarly reduces other participants' risk and sends a signal of project viability. In particular it should be noted that when SIBs offer equity or debt, it is not just the capital but also both the **long-term nature** and any **fixed-rate features** of this finance that are of importance to developers and other potential investors, as both of these features play a de-risking role. The CEFC commonly provides long-term and fixed-rate debt to wind and solar PV developers, helping to de-risk these projects and attract private finance.

Financial Instruments and Flexibility

Founded in 2012 the UK's GIB (now privatized and known as the Green Investment Group) aimed to help the UK meet its ambitious emissions targets by investing on commercial terms and mobilizing private finance into low carbon projects (Holmes, 2013). The UK's GIB supplied a variety of financial instruments in order to support the UK's low-carbon project development sector. The GIB offered equity products (including bridging equity loans), long-term, market rate debt products (taking either senior or sub-ordinated positions where required), mezzanine products and securitization/aggregation products. Developers reported that this flexibility, where the GIB was able and willing to offer a variety of finance types, was extremely valuable as it helped to address particular barriers and fill the financing gaps for each unique case. Overall the ability to be flexible in their approach meant the GIB was seen to address the local market's needs well. (Geddes et al. 2018; GIB 2016).

SIBs can provide **guarantees** in order to help address certain risks, such as off-take and counterparty risk guarantees. Where an SIB is unable or unwilling to offer guarantees itself, they have been seen to encourage others within the marketplace to offer guarantees. The GIB encouraged waste-to-energy equipment manufacturers to provide guarantees on their technology so that developers could more easily attain finance (Geddes et al. 2018). Guarantees help to reduce or transfer risk within a project.

SIBs have also created several **aggregation/securitization products** and/or funds to address a mismatch between project size and the amount of capital investors are willing or able to invest, and to help reduce transaction costs. Large scale projects can require very large amounts of up-front capital, too much for smaller, and even some larger investors to participate, and small scale projects are considered too small for many investors, especially considering transaction costs remain the same regardless of project size. KfW and the GIB established wind funds that allowed investors with limitations on their portfolios to invest in large-scale wind projects. The GIB and CEFC also provided tools and funds to allow the aggregation of smaller scale renewable and energy efficiency projects in order to attract investors who usually do not invest in small projects. KfW also issues climate and green bonds allowing smaller investors to invest in projects they could not have accessed previously. Finally, **technical assistance**, where an SIB uses its expertise to provide non-financial support to projects developers and investors alike, plays a very important role. Technical assistance can take the form of standards, due diligence processes, training and advice. SIBs employ both technological and financial experts who can help "investors better assess risk and become familiar with new projects while supporting developers with due diligence in order to reach financial close" (Geddes et al. 2018).

Sectors and Programs: A Wider Focus

The CEFC was established in 2012 by the Australian government in order to "mobilize and leverage the flow of funds for commercialization and deployment of renewable energy, low-emissions and energy efficiency technologies necessary for Australia's transition to a lower carbon economy" (CEFC 2016b). Since its establishment, the CEFC has built on the success of its early projects to widen its focus to support more sectors via a variety of programs. It has made investment commitments in sectors including energy, agribusiness, infrastructure, transport and property. Programs and funds include the venture capital-like Clean Energy Innovation Fund that helps to accelerate the commercialization of a range of low carbon technologies and businesses, the Sustainable Cities Investment Program focusing on precinct-scale clean energy, green buildings, next-generation transport management systems and affordable housing, and the Reef Funding Program to support the long-term health of the Great Barrier Reef. The CEFC also provides support for the purchase of hybrid electric vehicles and provides specific technical advice for energy intensive manufacturers. (CEFC 2018)

SIBs have created various **programs, funds and financing channels** that help them focus their efforts on particular sectors and to achieve their mandates while also ensuring they are fit for the local market. Examples include the CEFC's Clean Energy Innovation Fund, which focuses on earlier stage technologies, and KfW's Energy Advice program to support SMEs to access externally accredited advisors.

SIBs disburse their finance via various channels such as direct investment in projects (usually co-investing with other investors in larger projects), on-lending via local credit intermediaries, own and third-party managed investment funds and green or climate bond investment or issuance. Co-investing via syndicates has the advantage that SIBs can pass on their expertise to new investors during the process. On-lending via local banks is usually accompanied by provision of standards and risk assessment processes, ensuring local banks become familiar with assessing projects and their risks independently. It can also be seen as a more efficient way of disbursing funds to a wider range of beneficiaries as local banks are more familiar with their local customers and they also take on some of the administrative and transaction costs for the SIB. SIBs use third party managed funds in order to harness specialist expertise in certain sectors.

Financing Channels and Local Impact

KfW, originally established in 1948 to aid Germany's development, supports the country's energy transition through its Energy Turnaround Action Plan. KfW has made extensive use of the financing channel known as on-lending. KfW provides concessional fixed-rate, long-term debt to Germany's extensive network of local banks, who then in turn on-lend this finance to local clients. KfW uses its expertise and knowledge of the risks of low carbon projects to create and provide standardized project due diligence and risk assessment processes, which are provided to the local banks to use when assessing loan requests. The local bank takes a fee for processing a transaction and also has the option of providing part of the loan on its own books. In this way, the local bank becomes familiar and comfortable with the risks involved, while KfW uses the local banking network's knowledge of the local market to more easily access clients without incurring high transaction costs. SMEs, public and municipal authorities, community co-operatives and homeowners are then able to access cheap and appropriately sized and structured finance for small to mid-sized projects. In this way KfW has helped build local capacity in the local banking network for assessing and financing projects and has managed to disburse finance to a wide range of beneficiaries as well as a range of smaller and medium sized projects. (Geddes et al. 2018; Hall et al. 2016; KfW 2017).

13.3.1 The Roles of Green SIBs and How They Offer Additional Value

By means of their instruments, programs and financing channels, SIBs perform a range of roles in order to address barriers and crowd-in finance for low-carbon projects (for more detail on SIB roles see Cochran et al. 2014; Geddes et al. 2018; IDB 2013; NRDC 2016; Whitney and Bodnar 2018). SIBs take a **capital provision role** to address structural barriers such as investment gaps for projects with very large up-front capital costs (e.g., large scale off and onshore wind) or gaps that arise during times of economic downturn such as the 2008 financial crisis (Geddes et al. 2018; Mazzucato and Penna 2016; Whitney and Bodnar 2018).

However, many low-carbon projects are not financed because they exhibit, or are perceived to exhibit, high risks. **De-risking** approaches aim to reduce, share or transfer risk and many of the instruments mentioned in the previous section are deployed with these aims in mind (Cochran et al. 2014; Geddes et al. 2018; IDB 2013; NRDC 2016). De-risking instruments include counterparty risk guarantees, insurance and technology guarantees. Examples of de-risking approaches incorporating capital include grants, concessional finance, equity, mezzanine products, long tenure and/or fixed-rate finance and co-investment and on-lending activities (risk sharing). When SIBs take a de-risking role, reducing or redistributing the project risk, the overall risk/return profile of the project is improved and private finance can be leveraged in.

SIBs also take a **size transformation role** to address mismatches between the amount of capital investors are able or willing to invest and the amount of capital required for projects (Geddes et al. 2018; IDB 2013; NRDC 2016). By providing certain instruments and funds, SIBs have allowed investors who could not previously participate in certain projects to now do so.

SIBs also take an **educational role** by diffusing knowledge throughout the sector, where they educate and support investors and developers (Cochran et al. 2014; Geddes et al. 2018; NRDC 2016; Whitney and Bodnar 2018). They use their internal expertise to create standards (instruments, paperwork and processes) so that investors can more quickly, and better, assess risk and become comfortable with new projects, bringing down costs of due diligence and arranging. These standards allow investors and other relevant stakeholders, to follow standardized forms and processes, sidestepping any lack of knowledge or experience and reducing the time, costs and barriers associated with obtaining the knowledge from scratch. In addition, by participating in syndicates or other co-investment setups, SIBs are able to disseminate their knowledge and experience directly, exchanging ideas and information with the other investors, enabling a "learning-by-co-investing" environment. SIBs also use their expertise to support developers with due diligence processes in order to help them meet investors' requirements, attract the necessary finance and reach financial close.

SIBs are also known to take an **industry co-ordination role** where they use their experience and knowledge to help identify weaknesses or gaps in services and products within a sector (Geddes et al. 2018; IDB 2013). In less developed sectors there may be absences that are a barrier to finance, for example, if original equipment manufacturers do not yet supply technology guarantees. SIBs can use their position to negotiate and co-ordinate between stakeholders in order to fill these gaps and help remove said barriers to finance.

SIBs have developed a reputation for expertise in accurately assessing risk and identifying and investing in bankable projects, and hence their decision to invest in a project has a signalling effect to other investors; it indicates that this project is legitimate and worth investing in. This **signalling role** is especially important for bringing finance to projects that contain something innovative or unproven (Geddes et al. 2018). We also see SIBs take a **demonstration role** by demonstrating that a project can be developed successfully (Geddes et al. 2018;

Whitney and Bodnar 2018). A successful demonstration, or preferably several, creates a track record for that project and anything novel that it contains, such as a new technology or developer. Track records are essential for crowding-in private finance as they allow investors to concretely observe and assess any risks relating to those projects.

Finally Whitney and Bodnar (2018) show that an SIB can take a **role as an enabling environment accelerator** where SIBs "create a tight feedback loop to governments on how they can unlock capital flows through policy reforms, since as the sole/primary shareholder of a GIB and guarantor of its green bonds, the government has a strong vested interest in its successful deployment and return of capital."

13.4 Lessons Learned and the Path Forward

There are some issues that policymakers should take into account regarding SIBs. The threat of crowding-out needs to be considered. Crowding out occurs when public finance either displaces or reduces the participation of private finance, distorting the development of a healthy and effective private sector market for financing projects (Cumming and MacIntosh 2006). This is, in fact, in complete opposition to what SIBs are trying to achieve by using public finance to crowd-in private finance. When an SIB invests in more mature markets, particularly via concessional finance, it may lead to crowding out. Hence automatic checks and appropriate strategies to scale back distortionary support should be built in to an SIB's mandate and operation (Rodrik 2014; Stiglitz 1993). Checks and redesign strategies should also be built in to ensure SIBs' provisions are in line with the current needs of developers and the local market, rather than offering tools and support that are out of date and no longer required. In the case of the UK's Green Investment Bank, the government saw its success in the UK marketplace as an indication that it was time to privatize the bank, simultaneously reducing government debt. Whereas other SIBs that are effective have been instead allowed to refocus and redesign their tools and strategies to target other emerging low-carbon sectors and areas in need, e.g., the CEFC created a new innovation fund and added equity to its list of provisions in response to its own success and changing local market requirements.

SIBs can be important actors in the development of a country's low-carbon sector and hence an important component within a country's energy and climate change policy mix. Geddes et al. (2018) showed that the roles taken by SIBs have managed to have an impact on supporting the development of local renewable and energy efficiency projects. Mazzucato and Penna (2016) found that SIBs can have a market shaping and creating role, rather than merely fixing market failures and Mazzucato and Semieniuk (2017) showed that public finance institutions have taken on many higher risk low-carbon projects. There is also evidence that SIBs help reduce financing costs (Geddes et al. 2018; OECD 2015). Whitney and Bodnar (2018) highlighted that green SIBs display a model that is transferable across advanced, emerging and developing economies alike and that they have "emerged as among the most inclusive and flexible type of institution exclusively focused on financing the low-carbon transition." If designed well, green SIBs can be a powerful tool to leverage in private finance, enabling the investment needed to support the energy system transition.

References

ADDIN EN.REFLIST CEFC. 2016a. *CEFC Annual Report 2015–2016*. Clean Energy Finance Corporation, Sydney, Australia.

CEFC. 2016b. *CEFC Investment Policies*. Clean Energy Finance Corporation, Sydney, Australia.

CEFC. 2018. *CEFC Annual Report 2017–18: Investing for Impact and Innovation*. Clean Energy Finance Corporation, Sydney, Australia.

Cochran, Ian, Romain Hubert, Virginie Marchal, and Robert Youngman. 2014. "Public Financial Institutions and the Low-carbon Transition: Five Case Studies on Low-Carbon Infrastructure and Project Investment." *OECD Environment Working Papers*, 0_1.

Cumming, Douglas J., and Jeffrey G. MacIntosh. 2006. "Crowding out private equity: Canadian evidence." *Journal of Business Venturing* 21, 569–609.

Geddes, Anna, Tobias S. Schmidt, Bjarne Steffen. 2018. "The multiple roles of state investment banks in low-carbon energy finance: An analysis of Australia, the UK and Germany." *Energy Policy* 115, 158–70.

GIB. 2016. *UK Green Investment Bank plc Annual Report and Accounts 2015–2016*. London, UK.

Grubb, Michael. 2004. "Technology Innovation and Climate Change Policy: an overview of issues and options." *Keio economic studies* 41, 103–32.

Hall, Stephen, Timothy J. Foxon, and Ronan Bolton. 2016. "Financing the civic energy sector: How financial institutions affect ownership models in Germany and the United Kingdom." *Energy Research & Social Science* 12, 5–15.

Holmes, Ingrid. 2013. *Green Investment Bank: The History*. E3G.

IDB. 2013. "The Role of National Development Banks in Catalyzing International Climate Finance". Inter-American Development Bank, Washington, DC.

IEA. 2014. *World Energy Investment Outlook 2014*. International Energy Agency, Paris.

IEA. 2016. *World Energy Investment 2016*. International Energy Agency, Paris.

IPCC. 2014. *Climate Change 2014: Mitigation of Climate Change. Contribution of Working Group III to the Fifth Assessment Report of the Intergovernmental Panel on Climate Change*. Cambridge University Press, Cambridge, UK and New York, NY.

Karltorp, Kersti. 2015. "Challenges in mobilising financial resources for renewable energy: The cases of biomass gasification and offshore wind power." *Environmental Innovation and Societal Transitions*.

KfW. 2017. KfW and its mandate. Author.

Lindenberg, Nannette. 2014. Public Instruments to Leverage Private Capital for Green Investments in Developing Countries.

Mazzucato, Mariana, and Caetano C. R. Penna. 2016. "Beyond market failures: the market creating and shaping roles of state investment banks." *Journal of Economic Policy Reform* 19, 305–26.

Mazzucato, Mariana, and Gregor Semieniuk. 2017. "Financing renewable energy: Who is financing what and why it matters." *Technological Forecasting and Social Change*.

NRDC. 2016. *Green & Resilience Banks*.

OECD. 2015. *Green investment banks: Leveraging innovative public finance to scale up low-carbon investment, Policy Perspectives*. Author, Paris.
OECD. 2016. *Green Investment Banks: Scaling up private investment in low-carbon, climate-resilient infrastructure, Green Finance and Investment*. Author, Paris.
OECD. 2017. *Green Investment Banks: Innovative Public Financial Institutions Scaling up Private, Low-carbon Investment*. Author, Paris.
Rodrik, Dani. 2014. "Green industrial policy." *Oxford Review of Economic Policy* 30, 469–91.
Schmidt, Tobias S. 2014. "Low-carbon investment risks and de-risking. Nature Clim." *Change* 4, 237–39.
Schmidt, Tobias S., Malte Schneider, Karoline S. Rogge, Martin J. A. Schuetz, Volker H. Hoffmann. 2012. "The effects of climate policy on the rate and direction of innovation: A survey of the EU ETS and the electricity sector." *Environmental Innovation and Societal Transitions* 2, 23–48.
Steffen, Bjarne. 2018. "The importance of project finance for renewable energy projects." *Energy Economics* 69, 280–94.
Stiglitz, Joseph E. 1993. "The Role of the State in Financial Markets." *The World Bank Economic Review* 7, 19–52.
Whitney, Angela, and Paul Bodnar. 2018. "Beyond Direct Access: How national green banks can build country ownership of climate finance." Rocky Mountain Institute. Boulder, CO.

14 Renewable Energy Finance by Multilateral Development Banks

Dr. Bjarne Steffen, Prof. Dr. Tobias S. Schmidt

14.1 Renewable Energy Projects in Developing Countries

The rapid expansion of power generation capacity is a key priority for policymakers in the developing world. Unlike in many industrialized countries, in developing and emerging countries the electricity demand is growing rapidly, driven not only by electrification but also by population growths, urbanization, and economic development. Accordingly, there is a tremendous investment need, estimated at $ 2,700 billion during 2017–2025 (International Energy Agency 2017). Increasingly, energy utilities and investors turn to renewable energy technologies (especially wind turbines and solar PV) given the large negative externalities of fossil fuel-based plants (such as climate change-causing carbon emissions, and particle emissions causing smog and local health impairments). Beyond providing clean energy (and thereby addressing the sustainable development goal [SDG] No. 7), renewables can also contribute to other development goals such as decent jobs (SDG 8), industrial development (SDG 9), and of course climate action (SDG 13).

Given the many virtues of renewables, and following massive cost reductions, renewable energy deployment has become a global phenomenon. More than 80 developing countries had at least one utility-scale solar PV, wind, or biomass plant as of 2016 (Steffen, Matsuo, Steinemann, & Schmidt 2018). Renewable energy investment in developing countries overtook that in developed countries in 2015, though it is quite concentrated in certain countries, particularly China and India (McCrone & Moslener 2017). Many other developing countries struggle to realize projects at scale, and more than 70 developing countries lacked any utility-scale renewable energy plant as of 2016 (Steffen et al. 2018).

There are several barriers for renewable energy projects in developing countries, many of which apply to long-term infrastructure investments in developing countries more general, such as macroeconomic instability, political and regulatory uncertainties, currency risk, the risk of corruption, access to qualified staff, and access to financing (Steffen & Papakonstantinou 2015). Further barriers apply specifically to low-carbon technologies, such as public institutions that were designed for traditional high-carbon paradigms (Granoff, Hogarth, & Miller 2016). Taken together, these barriers increase the cost of renewable energy projects in developing countries, particularly the cost of capital (Komendantova, Schinko, & Patt 2019;

Dr. Bjarne Steffen, Prof. Dr. Tobias S. Schmidt, Energy Politics Group, ETH Zurich, Switzerland

https://doi.org/10.1515/9783110607888-014

Schmidt 2014; Waissbein, Glemarec, Bayraktar & Schmidt 2013), often to a degree making projects unviable from an economic point of view.

To address these challenges, the international community has established a number of international financial institutions, out of which the group of multilateral development banks (MDB) is particularly important. This section discusses the landscape of MDBs (section 14.2), their activities in the area of renewable energy (section 14.3), as well as specific offerings and a typical project cycle for MDB support (section 14.4). Drawing on recent academic research, expert interviews, and practical experience of the authors, the section aims at informing project developers, financiers, and other actors that consider working with MDBs. It provides an initial overview of the roles that MDBs can take. References throughout the text point towards articles and reports that provide further details.

14.2 The Landscape of Multilateral Development Banks (MDBs)

Starting with the establishment of the World Bank in 1944, countries have set up multilateral development banks (MDBs), that is, financial institutions with the purpose of eradicating poverty and fostering development. MDBs are jointly owned by national states and governed by international law. They borrow on global financial markets (typically with an AAA rating) and then provide finance as well as technical assistance to member countries. To fulfill their mandate, the MDBs' activities span various development-related sectors, including agriculture, health, education, and energy. Most MDBs provide finance for both the public and the private sector, often through different branches (Steffen & Schmidt 2017).

Concerning renewable energy projects, three groups of MDBs are relevant (compare Steffen & Schmidt 2018): First, the globally-active **World Bank group**, which consists of IBRD and IDA (mainly public-sector lending and policy advise), IFC (private sector lending), and MIGA (private sector investment guarantees), amongst others. These banks have been financing conventional power generation projects since more than 50 years, and since the late 1990s started to finance non-hydro renewable energy projects as well. With large subscribed capital and significant political lever, the World Bank institutions are among the most important renewable energy lenders in many of their countries of operation.

Second, a number of **regional MDBs** that emerged during and after decolonization, including the African Development Bank (AfDB), the Asian Development Bank (AsDB), and the Inter-American Development Bank (IADB). Following the collapse of the Soviet Union, the European Bank for Reconstruction and Development (EBRD) was created to foster the transition towards market-oriented economies; hence, it has a slightly different mandate that nevertheless includes private energy projects. Finally, the EU's European Investment Bank (EIB) primarily aims at developing the internal market of the EU but also has specific mandates for activities in developing countries where energy project are being financed.

Third, a special case are so-called **"South–South" MDBs** that do not include donor countries from the Global North among their shareholders and boards. These include the Development Bank of Latin America (CAF) and the Islamic Development Bank (IsDB) which is active globally in Islamic countries.

Renewable energy activities of these banks are discussed below. Besides, several further MDBs exist, often on a sub-regional level (e.g., East African Development Bank), but so far their focus has been on sectors other than energy. Recently also two newly formed banks started operation, namely the New Development Bank (NDB), which operates in the BRICS countries, and the Asian Infrastructure Investment Bank (AIIB). As they started operating in 2016 only, their numbers are not yet included in the retrospective figures in this section.

14.3 MDB Activities in Renewable Energy Finance

Given the importance of electricity for economic development, all three groups of MDBs dedicate substantial finance to power generation commitments. Since roughly 2006, non-hydro renewables thereby play a significant role, with varying (but generally increasing) importance between individual banks and regions (see details in Steffen & Schmidt 2018). Figure 14.1 shows the split of commitments that goes to different technologies for the three groups of MDBs, differentiated between their public and private sector branches. As the numbers illustrate, the role of non-hydro renewables (e.g., wind turbines and solar PV) differs markedly between the branches, especially for the regional MDBs and South-South MDBs. While about half of all private sector commitments of these groups are dedicated to non-hydro renewables (56% and 47%, respectively), the share among the public sector commitments is much lower (18% and 3%, respectively). MDBs in general try to increase the share of clean energy investments in their portfolio. An important reason why the share is nevertheless low in public sector lending is that investment priorities of local public authorities (e.g., ministries of energy) are not necessarily aligned with these MDB objectives. Instead, the borrowing countries might prefer fossil fuel-based power plants for various reasons. This is less of an issue for MDBs' private sector branches, which lends to a dynamically evolving industry of project developers that seem to be swift in presenting bankable projects for MDB financing (compare Steffen & Schmidt 2018). Hence, private sector lending developed into an important channel for MDBs to increase their renewable energy commitments.

Zooming into private sector commitments, Figure 14.2 shows which renewable energy technologies received financing. Since 2006, wind turbine projects make up the largest share in most years, which reflects the fact that the technology has reached technological and commercial maturity earlier than other renewables

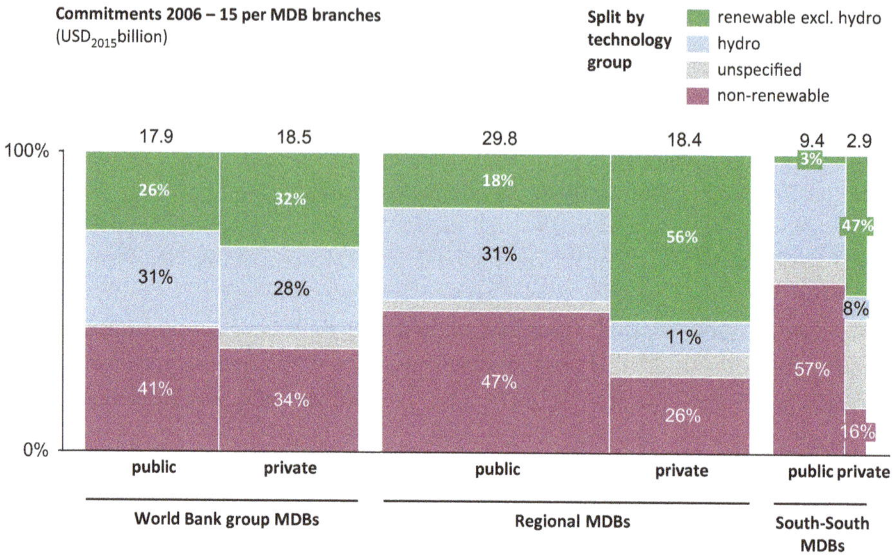

Figure 14.1: MDB commitments 2006–2015 (based on data from Steffen & Schmidt, 2018).

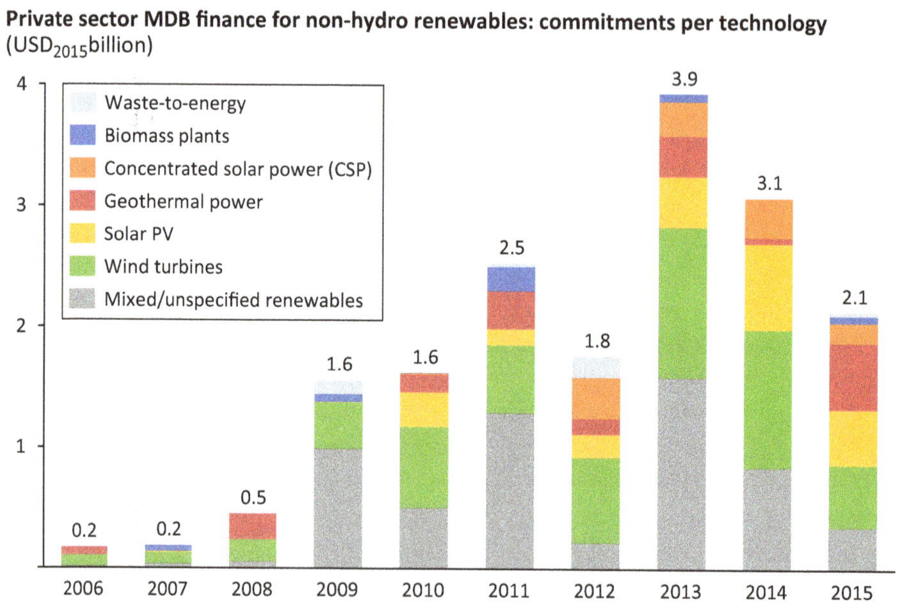

Figure 14.2: Private sector MDB commitments (based on data from Steffen & Schmidt, 2018).

(Steffen et al. 2018). Solar PV has received significant commitments since 2010, with a generally growing share over the years. Further technologies with significant financing volumes include concentrated solar power (CSP), geothermal power, and biomass plants. Finally, it is noticeable that a large share of financing is labeled as "mixed/unspecified renewables" – which are mainly commitments for renewable energy facilities and frameworks for which the individual projects (and hence their technologies) are not yet determined at times of the commitment by an MDB.

14.4 Financial Instruments and the Project Cycle

In renewable energy finance, MDBs are flexible to offer different financial instruments, as per the requirements of individual projects. Figure 14.3 provides an overview of commitments during 2006–2015 for non-hydro renewable energy projects. Clearly, loans (senior and subordinate) make up the lion's share, with 81% of commitment volumes in that period. While conditions differ between banks, lending in the sector typically comes with a maturity between 5 and 20 years, and is based on Libor plus a contractual spread, service charge, and potentially a commitment fee. Both foreign and local currency loans are offered. An important subgroup are so-called "concessional loans" that draw on specific funds to offer subsidized debt (in some cases also combined with a grant component).

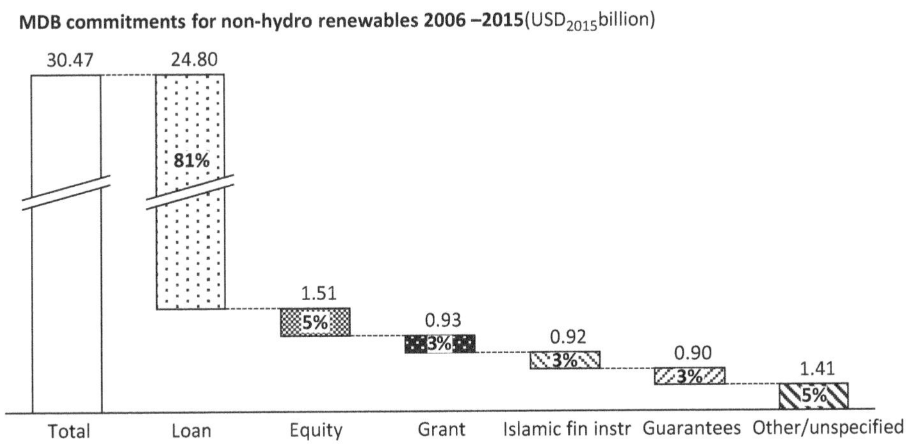

Figure 14.3: Financial instruments of MDB commitments for non-hydro renewables 2006–2015 (based on data from Steffen & Schmidt, 2018).

Besides loans, MDBs engage with equity (5%), e.g., for larger portfolios of renewable energy projects in a certain region. Grants make up 3%, as do specific instruments compliant with Islamic law (e.g., Istisna'a and leasing). Finally, guarantees are being used (3%), most importantly political risk insurance and credit enhancement guarantees from the World Bank group's MIGA (Multilateral Investment Guarantee Agency). Guarantees from MIGA are available for five different risks: currency inconvertibility and transfer restriction; government expropriation; war, terrorism, and civil disturbance; breaches of contract; and the non-honoring of financial obligations. Premiums typically range between 0.5% and 1.5% of the investment amount per year and insured risk.

For all types of instruments, potential investment projects are rigorously screened, and, if approved, continuously monitored until full repayment. Compared to commercial banks, the MDBs thereby put additional emphasis on aspects such as compliance with social and environmental safeguards, as per their sustainable development mandates. While details vary between the MDBs, the overall project cycle is comparable, and described as a stylized process in Figure 14.4. Following initial project preparation, several gates have to be cleared before the final decision of an MDB's board. Compared to commercial banks, many MDBs have significant technical knowledge in-house, supporting with the appraisal of projects, but also offering for instance technical assistance to develop necessary institutional capacity in the country of intended investments. The entire cycle typically takes 4 to 8 months, even though there are also shorter and much longer processes depending on the individual circumstances. Particularly drawing on a specific facility for concessional loans or grants typically requires extra time, as further approvals from the body that governs the facility (e.g., the Green Climate Fund GCF, or the Global Environmental Facility GEF) might be needed.

14.5 Conclusion

Overall, this section illustrated that renewable energy projects have become an important lending area for MDBs, which significantly increased their commitment amounts over the last decade. Like other public banks, they thereby draw in additional private investment for the projects in which they participate. Over the last decade, all MDBs built up significant sector knowledge, such that their participation now often sends a "quality signal" to potential co-investors, further leveraging their role in supporting low-carbon development. Hence, working together with MDBs is well worth considering for potential renewable energy investors in developing countries, and can help to realize projects in contexts where a purely commercial structure would be unviable.

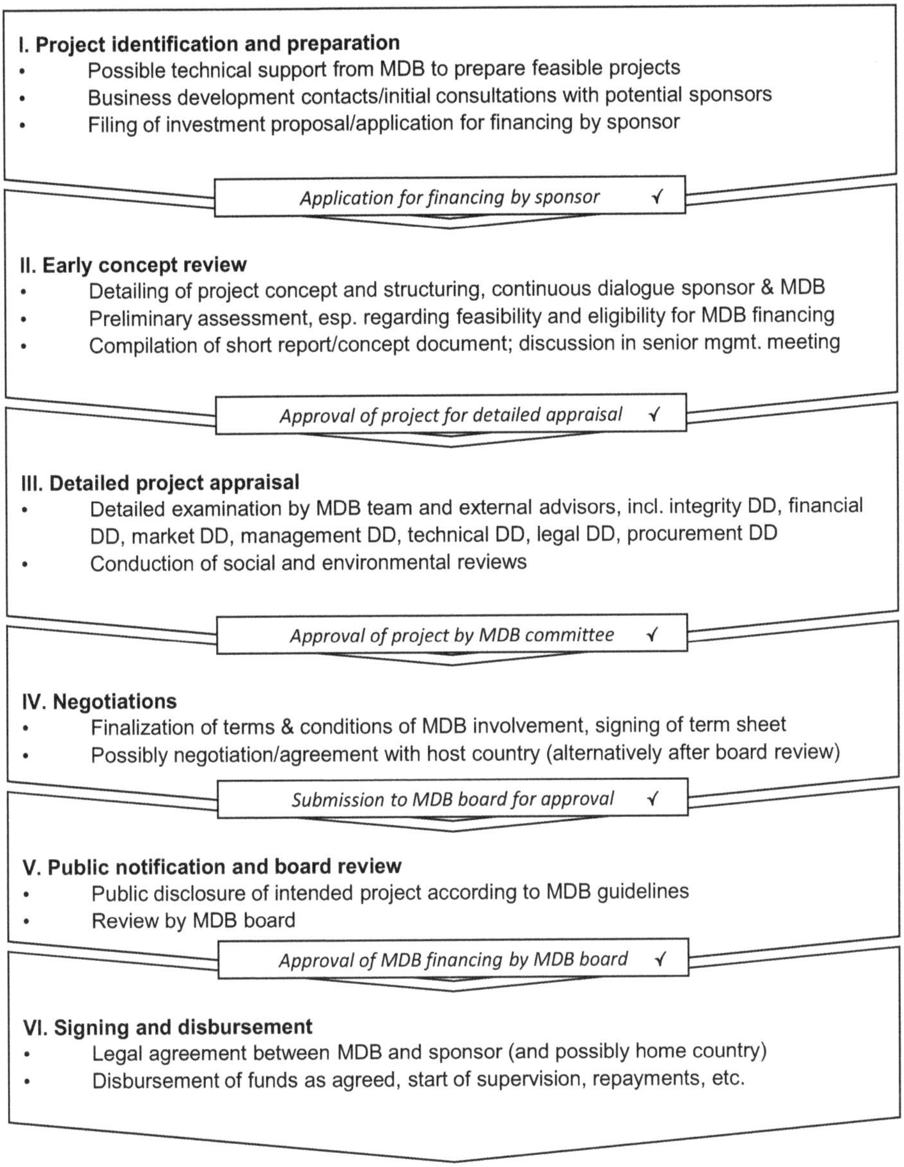

Figure 14.4: Stylized project cycle at multilateral development banks (own representation).

References

Granoff, Ilmi, J. Ryan Hogarth, and Alan Miller. 2016. "Nested barriers to low-carbon infrastructure investment." *Nature Climate Change* 6, no. 12: 1065–71. https://doi.org/10.1038/nclimate3142.

International Energy Agency. 2017. *World Energy Outlook 2017*. OECD/IEA.

Komendantova, Nadejda, Thomas Schinko, and Anthony Patt. 2019. "De-risking policies as a substantial determinant of climate change mitigation costs in developing countries: Case study of the Middle East and North African region." *Energy Policy* 127: 404–11. https://doi.org/10.1016/J.ENPOL.2018.12.023.

McCrone, Angus, and Ulf Moslener. 2017. *Global Trends in Renewable Energy Investment.*

Schmidt, Tobias S. 2014. "Low-carbon investment risks and de-risking." *Nature Climate Change* 4, no. 4: 237–39. https://doi.org/10.1038/nclimate2112.

Steffen, Bjarne, Tyeler Matsuo, Davita Steinemann, and Tobias S. Schmidt. 2018. "Opening new markets for clean energy: The role of project developers in the global diffusion of renewable energy technologies." *Business and Politics.*

Steffen, Bjarne, and Vangelis Papakonstantinou. 2015. *Mitigation of Political & Regulatory Risk in Infrastructure Projects.* Geneva: World Economic Forum.

Steffen, Bjarne, and Tobias S. Schmidt. 2017. "The role of public investment & development banks in enabling or constraining new power generation technologies." *IEEE Conference Proceedings*, International Conference on the European Energy Market (EEM), 1–6. https://doi.org/10.1109/EEM.2017.7981949.

Steffen, Bjarne, and Tobias S. Schmidt. 2018. "A quantitative analysis of 10 multilateral development banks' investment in conventional and renewable power generation technologies from 2006 to 2015." *Nature Energy* (forthcoming).

Waissbein, Oliver, Yannick Glemarec, Hande Bayraktar, and Tobias S. Schmidt. 2013. *Derisking Renewable Energy Investment.* New York: UNDP.

15 Choice of Adequate Insurance Coverage

Dr. Michael Härig

15.1 Introduction

This section is about risk transfer to insurances. Focus is on property insurance, which is taken out to protect own investment and to cover the consequential financial loss (loss of revenue, additional costs, take or pay, etc.).

In the field of renewable energies, project financing is a widely used financing instrument. The energy projects are to a large extent externally financed. Given the numerous contractual obligations of the project (especially operating expenses and debt service), there may not be sufficient funds available to cover the costs of a big damage.

Usually, banks are risk averse and in project financing they expect special insurance conditions:

- Long term contracts
- Broad insurance cover and only few exclusions
- The consequential financial loss must be insured already during the construction phase (delay in start-up, advanced loss of profit).

The insurance industry has developed special covers:

- New technologies which are difficult to insure
- Bacteria in biogas
- Exploration risk in geothermal energy
- 25-year long-term performance guarantee for photovoltaic modules
- Wind and sun guarantees

The insurance industry thus contributes to the economic success of the project companies and to the success of the energy transition.

Although the focus of this article is on property insurance, liability insurance must not be neglected. Liability insurance has a passive legal protection function, since it covers the legal claim of the third party.

Technical insurance brokers have an important task. In the contracts between the parties involved in a project (investors, operators, plant manufacturers, grid operators, etc.), the risk situation and the resulting requirements for insurance must be analyzed at an early stage. In the second step, the insurance cover is designed according to the risk situation. Risk and insurance management complement each other and insurers and brokers play an important role in the energy transition.

https://doi.org/10.1515/9783110607888-015

15.2 Core Issues of Risk and Insurance Management

The following subsections describe the different issues which have be to managed with regard to insurances within project financings.

15.2.1 What Can Be Damaged?

In property insurance, buildings and technical equipment and components as transformers, photovoltaic modules, motors for biogas plants, gearboxes of wind turbines and more are immediately considered.

The policyholder is obliged to prove that a property damage exists. From an insurance perspective there is a material damage if there is a change in substance leading to reduced usability or to reduced value. Typical examples are fire damage, broken rotor blades in a wind turbine or hail damage of PV modules.

Defects and deficiencies are not insured by property insurance. However, the property damage resulting from the defect should be insured. What does this mean? If after a short period of operation of a fermenter it is found that there is no coating on the concrete, this can only be assured if there is no doubt that the fermenter originally had a coating. However, if the fermenter was never coated, this is an uninsured deficiency. The insurer will not pay for the recoating. The consequential damage to the concrete, however, should be a property damage, because the substance has changed.

The height of the consequential loss depends on the standstill time of the power plant. Fixed costs as personnel costs or debt service from project financing have to be paid also in times when no revenue is generated. It has to be considered that the damage is unexpected and there are neither personnel nor spare material. Therefore the business interruption will take longer than a planned repair under optimal conditions.

15.2.2 When Do the Risks Occur?

The greatest risks occur during the construction and operation of the plants. Even in "turnkey" projects there remain risks for the employer. The general contractor is usually not liable during the construction phase for damages caused by force majeure. Especially these damages can cause total loss. With progress of the construction, the risk of total loss becomes greater and greater. For this reason, it is recommended that the employer takes out the construction and erection insurances. All further parties involved in the project are also insured (see also section *Who should insure?*).

15.2.3 Prevention Measures

Typical measures are:

- Fire protection measures
- Training of employees
- Theft protection (especially for photovoltaic systems)
- Adjustment of supply and service contracts so that each party bears the risks that it can manage. As an example, theft on the construction site is allocated to the contractor not to the employer.
- Maintenance contracts and guarantees. Most wind energy projects close long term maintenance contracts with guarantees for availability. This reduces the insurance premium up to 90%. It is important whether there is a liability limit and whether all major components are included without exception.
- Special obligations for operation and technology due to loss experience. For example in biogas plants this includes maintenance contracts for the motors, but also measurements of the operating parameters, compliance with gas quality and oil analysis.

15.2.4 Who Bears the Risks?

The risk depends on many factors. As stated above, even in a turnkey project many risks remain during the construction at the employer. These perils can also lead to a total loss.

If a damage occurs during operation, which is not covered by a warranty or guarantee, the plan owner will usually have to bear this risk. Depending on the insurance situation, the cause of the loss must be clearly assigned to one party. This becomes very difficult if many parties are involved.

15.2.5 Which Insurances Should be Taken Out?

Property insurance covers unforeseen property damage to the insured property.

During the construction phase of the project the construction and erection insurance should be taken out by the employer (owner controlled insurance program) as mentioned in section *Who should insure?*

Property damage during construction often results in a delay. The consequential financial loss can be insured with *Delay in Startup* or with *Advanced Loss of profit* insurances.

In most cases the transport insurance is only important for the employer if components with long delivery times are assembled. The *Transport Business Interruption* insurance covers the financial loss by the delay after transport damage.

During the operation phase, all-risk insurance concepts are recommended. Contrary to classic programs they do not separate in fire and machinery insurance. The difference between the concepts is described in section 15.3.5. Financial loss resulting from property damage is covered through All Risk- of Fire- or Machinery Breakdown- Business Interruption insurance.

While property insurances cover damages of the own system, liability insurance cover injury of persons or damage of third parties or to the environment. The most important task of liability insurance is to prove whether the claims of third parties are justified at all. This corresponds to a passive legal protection.

In the field of renewable energies, many plants are not run and operated by the owners, but by commercial and technical operating companies. The liability insurance of the operating company is only limited liable for damage to the system itself because the operator is not considered a third, external party. For the management company it is important that it is co-insured in the property insurance of the plant owners and recourse is largely excluded.

As already stated, there exist special insurance solutions with regard to exploration, solar and wind guarantee as well as to the bacteria in biology. These insurance policies are usually extensions to the property insurance during construction and operation phase.

15.2.6 Who Should Insure?

Projects always involve several parties. In principle, the party with the greatest interest should insure the investments. This is almost always the owner or investor of the project. This also applies to the construction. During the construction, the later owner as employer should take out the project insurance. Interests of all involved parties should be included. This is for the following reasons:

- Only the party that has taken out the insurance can be sure that the insurance is still in force and has not been terminated due to outstanding premium payments or damage to other projects.
- The policyholder has the right to receive the indemnification. Thus he is informed of any damage and does not run the risk that another recipient will file for bankruptcy shortly after receipt of the compensation.
- One insurer is responsible for all damages. There will be no discussions which party is liable for the loss.
- No interfaces exist with insurance gaps or expensive double insurance.
- The financial loss resulting from late start-up, which particularly affects the client, can only be insured against the material damage at the same time.
- Lenders insist on Delay-in-Startup or Advanced Loss-of-Profit insurance of the employer. The consequential financial loss can only be placed together with the property insurance.

15.2.7 How to Insure?

The height of the deductibles, the extent of insured risks and the quality of cover in general depend on the risk philosophy of the company as well as on the requirements of other parties, such as e.g., banks and investors. These factors determine the premiums and the scope of insurance must therefore be chosen wisely.

The loss experience in recent years shows that for premium reduction it is better to increase the deductible than to exclude certain hazard groups. Large deductibles can be planned and kept from the beginning. Of course, the height must fit to the company. A company that has been specially created to finance a project on renewable energy projects (SPV, special purpose vehicle) has often limited funds and strict contractual obligations – and cannot carry too much deductible.

Wherever manufacturers and service companies offer comprehensive maintenance and guarantee services, the insurance cover may be correspondingly lower. In many cases, only damage from the outside and own operating errors are to be insured. The rest is covered by the guarantees of the maintenance companies. The guarantee conditions are to be analyzed exactly if there is a compensation limit. If they are actually limited or even some components are excluded, the insurance company must compensate the damage beyond the limit of the guarantees. Technical insurance brokers are specialized in analyzing the interface between maintenance contracts and insurance contracts.

15.3 Property Insurance

A typical property damage is indemnified if
- an insured thing
- at the insurance location
- in the insured period
- with insured interest
- is damaged through an unforeseen insured peril.

The lines correspond to the conditions for indemnification. The different insurance concepts differ in the design of these individual conditions. With broad cover wordings, many discussions about damage can be avoided.

15.3.1 Insured Items

Insured should be everything that is necessary for the operation and maintenance. If insurers insist on special lists of insured items, they must be complete. In the event of damage, the insurer checks whether the damaged part is included in the list. In the case of flat-rate approaches, it is agreed that all items required for operation and maintenance are insured, and only exceptions are explicitly stated. Here it is for the benefit of the policyholder, if the list is incomplete through an error.

The determination of the insured item is not only important for the repair of the property damage. The insurer only pays the consequential financial loss if the damage occurs to an insured item.

The experience of many damages shows that the following components should be insured (which is not always the case, unfortunately):

Biogas plants
- The gas storage hoods, which, however, exclude many insurers due to great damages.
- Biology in the biogas plant: If the biology is not co-insured, the insurer indemnifies the financial loss after fermenter damage only up to the time when the fermenter is repaired again. The period up to the previous gas production as before of the loss is not compensated. In most cases of fermenter damage, the loss of revenue is greater than the actual property damage. Biology should therefore be included in the insurance.

Photovoltaic systems in addition to the modules and inverters
- The substation, the electronic anti-theft devices and the fence.

Wind energy parks
- The periphery, such as the wiring between the plants and substation.

Geothermal projects
- The drill, as long as the customer, is liable to the drilling company for the equipment.

Biomass power plants
- Concrete foundations of steam turbines.

Prototypes/Unproven technology
Concerning new technology prototypes have to be observed. Insurers have exclusions for a product or a performance that is carried out for the first time. Development risks are not accepted because they are to be taken over by the manufacturer.
- This can be the design of the plant, or a component
- It can also be the kind of production, e.g., a new kind of welding
- Or the kind of welding may be well known but it is carried out for the first time by the contractor.

Insurers only accept proven technology. And for this reason, the prototype character must be defined clearly. A risk analysis has to be carried out. What is really new?

15.3.2 Insured Location

Damages are only indemnified if they occur at the place stated in the insurance contract. In order to ensure insurance cover in principle, policies with broad coverage state that everywhere is insured location if there is an insured item (and even transports are covered). With this clause components remain insured e.g., during a revision transported and stored in other locations.

15.3.3 Insured Period

Construction Phase

The construction and erection insurance usually begins with the unloading of the insured items at the construction site. If there are pre-assembly places, it must be included.

The insurer should be liable until the end of the building including the test run. In many projects, the successful end of the tests means the transfer of risk and PAC (Provisional Acceptance).

The construction and erection insurance ends only with the completion of the entire project. Under no circumstances should insurance end up in accordance with individual sub-works or be terminated by the insurer after an insured damage.

Operational Phase

Successful test run is required for the start of operational insurance as Fire or Machinery Breakdown. Even if the contract was concluded and paid at an earlier stage, there is no insurance coverage. The beginning of the insurance must be considered especially if suppliers have cited an earlier transfer of risk in their contracts.

15.3.4 Insured Interest

Usually, only the owner is insured during the operational phase. This means that he must be affected directly by the property damage. Damage for which suppliers or repair shops are liable (for example, warranties) is generally excluded. The insurers also offer special premium discounts, because the guarantees reduce the risk. In cases where the supplier or repair shop denies their duty of entry, the insurer should first compensate. In negotiations with the supplier or through the process, the insurer can then try to reimburse the costs.

15.3.5 Insured Perils

The insured dangers are with the most important properties of insurance. As mentioned above, we recommend the all-risks insurance for the entire system instead of the classic separation in fire and machinery insurance. Insured are all unforeseen losses and losses that were not caused by an explicitly excluded risk.

The exclusions can usually be limited to the following:

- Intent of the insured
- Defects that were known when the insurance was taken out
- Damage (as stated in Section: *Insured Interest*) in the responsibility of the supplier or repair workshop. This exclusion must be deleted in the business interruption insurance for consequential financial loss, as suppliers and repairers are liable only for material damage.
- Immediate consequences of the continuous effects of the operation (this is among other things wear and tear, which is not unforeseen in many cases).
- War
- In the Federal Republic of Germany the replacement of nuclear damage is governed by the Atomic Energy Act.

Examples of the insured dangers that can not be enumerated are:

- Fire, lightning, explosion
- Machinery Breakdown due to material, design or manufacturing failures
- Natural hazards
- Operating errors

In addition to property damage, special insurance policies have been developed especially for renewable energy projects that cover other special risks:

- In the case of biogas plants: poisoning of the fermenter biology from the outside (this can be, for example, the entry of poisoned material). The system has no property damage, but does not produce further gas.
- For photovoltaic and wind energy plants less solar radiation or wind velocity as predicted resulting in less energy yield.
- In the case of photovoltaic systems: degradation of the modules and reduced yields, although usually wear and aging are not insured.
- For geothermal projects the exploration risk, which means that the thermal water production rate is insufficient or that the temperature is too low.

Compensation/Indemnification of Property Damage

The insurer should replace the costs for restating the damaged items into the state before the damage occurred.

These are

- Repair and spare parts, including disassembly and reassembly
- Freight costs
- Other costs related to the repair
- Especially if there are large financial losses, the insurer will also pay acceleration measures such as Sundays, public holidays and night-time work.

The insurer will pay the sum insured at the most, which usually corresponds to the replacement value. Since additional costs occur after a total loss, so-called First Risk Sums should be agreed:

- Cleaning costs and costs for earthworks
- Clean-up, demolition and disposal costs
- Movement and protection costs
- Rescue costs, e.g., fire extinguishing costs
- Additional costs for official rebuilding restrictions

The sum insured should be equal to the amount required to restore the asset after a total loss. If the original investment costs are taken as a basis, one-off costs such as planning costs or land acquisition do not have to be included in the sum insured.

Indemnification of Business Interruption Damage

The revenue situation has to be analyzed carefully, because all kind (electricity, heat, gas sales and more) should be included in the insurance. If delivery or acceptance obligations are entered into, it is not necessary to insure lost sales, but the additional costs incurred in the performance of the contract. This can be other electricity or gas procurement and heat generation.

15.4 Liability Insurance

In addition to the previously treated property insurance, liability insurance must be taken into account. It provides insurance cover if claims are made by third parties for personal, property or resulting financial loss.

The main tasks of the insurer are (as stated above):

- Proof of liability
- Defense against unjustified claims (legal protection function)
- Indemnification of claims

Not insured are:
- Damage caused by intent
- Damages arising from contractual obligations
- Damage to own things

Especially the last point has to be considered. Often energy parks are operated by external service providers (technical and commercial managers). It is a common error that liability insurers pay damage to the managed equipment.

The plant owner still needs comprehensive property insurance, because
- the liability insurer will prove carefully for each damage whether the service provider alone is liable (was he informed by the owner of all circumstances?)
- the liability conditions usually have an exclusion or a limit for claims to property under care, custody and control. Maintenance contractor is not owner but he works with the property. Therefore no third party is affected.

External service providers should therefore agree in the contracts with the park owners that their interests are co-insured and that the insurer, with the exception of intent or gross negligence, is not allowed to take recourse.

15.5 Summary

Comprehensive and consistent risk management means the combination of mitigation measures and insurances. Although the effects of damage are reduced through insurances, it is always better to avoid a damage. Therefore, in the recent years banks and insurers have consistently demanded and enforced improvements in the technical risks of all types of energy production.

Technical insurance brokers have the experience of many comparable projects and the know-how to tailor the insurance conditions precisely to the risk, taking into account guarantees, technology used, etc.

16 The Debt Financing Process in Project Financing

Jörg Böttcher

16.1 Introduction

Renewable energies have been shown stable growth for years: While this growth was initially driven by the political support to pave the way for new, eco-friendly energy production, aspects of security of supply and cost-effective energy supply became more and more important as market maturity increased. At the project level, this success was only feasible because a reliable regulatory environment and proven technology allowed the use of project financing. Project financing allows a risk limitation for the investors and an investment opportunity for lenders in projects with long-term, stable cash flows.

In order to realize project financing within an industry, at least two conditions have to be fulfilled:

1. The technology must allow a stable and predictable output in the long term and
2. the host country must provide a clear, predictable and reliable legal and regulatory environment, which gives investors and lenders sufficient planning security to operate viably.

In accordance with the market maturity of renewable energy technologies, specific financing standards have been developed in the banking industry in the meantime. In this context, one should be aware that the use of renewable energy sources is in the midst of an ongoing process of change: Their increasing technical efficiency allows the legislator to increasingly expose them to competition, which in turn effects financing practices.

The purpose of this section is to highlight the requirements that have to be met on the part of the lender in order to realize financing for a large renewable energy project using the project financing method and what steps have to be taken until the conditions precedent for a drawdown of the funds are fulfilled.

16.2 Project Documentation, Structuring, Credit Analysis, Rating, and Credit approval

16.2.1 Bank-Internal Credit Decision Process

The bank must make the decision to participate in a project in the form of a loan within a collaborative process: In doing so, the credit process initially depends heavily on which financing methods are available, i.e., whether it is a **corporate loan** or a **project loan** (see Figure 6.1).

https://doi.org/10.1515/9783110607888-016

The second question is which loan amount is assigned to the respective project financing from the bank's perspective: There are often very bank-specific rules, which one must inquire about individually. However, the general rule is that projects with a relatively large volume of credit or a high-risk content require an approval which is higher in the approval hierarchy of a bank. Normally, this question is resolved quickly.

In order for a bank to be able to make a sound credit decision, the available documents and agreements must be examined and assessed in a near-final form. Experience has shown that decision makers find it difficult to decide amid alternative scenarios or an uncertain framework. Finally, at the end of the internal credit decision process, a decision is made in favor of or against lending.

Nevertheless, it is useful from the project perspective to engage in talks with the bank already in the planning phase of the project: This allows the project to find out the bank's requirements for the subsequent granting of a loan and enables the sponsor to avoid additional negotiations just because it later turns out that the agreements originally concluded do not comply with the requirements of the capital providers.

16.2.2 Information Memorandum

An Information Memorandum ("IM") is intended to inform the bank or banks in condensed form about the project and its opportunities and risks. It is often prepared by the sponsors or the project company and, within the context of a syndication, partly by the lead bank itself.

The relevant bank is interested in obtaining a well-founded overview of the opportunities and risks profile from its perspective as quickly as possible. This means that the IM also serves the central function of gaining the bank as a credit provider. Conversely, the bank will expect the information provided in the IM as accurate and complete and will also check this as part of its due diligence. It is therefore recommended that all aspects stated in Table 16.1 should be addressed in detail, so they can withstand a later review.

16.2.3 Letter of Intent: Flower Letter

Sometimes the sponsor of a project requires a letter of confirmation from a bank, in which the bank states that it is considering the financing of the project ("flower letter"). This is the case, for instance, if certain project rights are granted by public institutions and the guarantor wants to make sure that a bank has already seriously considered the project's debt financing.

In this context, the following sample declaration may be issued at a very early stage:

The factors above are compiled as a key figure using a scorecard system, which is added to the rating for qualitative factors. Ultimately, however, it is the level and stability of future cash flows that essentially determine the rating result.

16.2.6 Fulfillment of Covenants: Achieving First Loan Disbursement

Once the bank has reached its credit decision, it or its consultants examine the underlying agreements in order to verify whether they correspond to the grounds for the decision and the economic assumptions made therein. Insofar as these correspond to the assumptions made and the project can be achieved and operated according to plan, the conditions precedent for a drawdown are fulfilled.

As soon as the project setup begins, the financial resources are paid out according to the progress of construction. The credit providers have to ensure in regard to construction financing that the necessary payment conditions are observed and the temporal and budgetary plans as well as other agreements that are complied with. The consequence of non-compliance is that the agreed debt service to the debt capital providers and distributions to the sponsors are at risk. Both the construction phase and the subsequent operational phase at project level are therefore supervised through financial controlling by the credit providers. The aim of financial monitoring is to control the economic situation of the project during the term of the loan. For this purpose, key financial figures are defined in the loan agreement, which the project may not exceed or fall short of during the term of the loan. These key financial figures are also referred to as ***financial covenants***. In addition to the financial covenants, the loan agreements also set contractual assurances and documentation that have to be complied with during the term of the loan. These are also referred to as ***legal covenants***. Compliance with the covenants is, as a rule, essential to ensure that a loan can be disbursed. If the borrower cannot comply, it is in breach of the credit agreement. Banks define this as an ***Event of Default*** and reserve the option to call in the loan in such a case. This does normally not happen, because the borrower has the option of requesting an amendment of the contract (a so-called ***Waiver Request***) from the lead arranger, which the bank consortium has to agree to by the majority stipulated in the loan agreement in order to allow the contract amendment to take effect.

16.3 Project Loan Documentation: Overview

The **Loan Agreement**, as the central financing document, provides the legal basis for the granting of a loan. The focus here is on defining the costs for the borrower (interest and other charges), as well as the borrower's commitment to repay the loan at the agreed points in time and in the agreed amount. The loan agreement for project financing also includes numerous other ancillary obligations on the part of

Table 16.1: Important contents of an Information Memorandum (own representation).

Aspect	Contents
Executive Summary	Here, the essential aspects of the project are summarized on a maximum of two pages
Presentation of the Project	Typically, the project is presented here (plants, rated power, annual energy yield, location, remuneration or regulatory system, central project stakeholders and their roles, status of the contractual structure design, cash flow overviews (mostly base case and downside scenarios)). The individual aspects are usually addressed in detail in the individual sections.
Presentation of the risks and the risk mitigating agreements	The risks of the project are usually described based on the aforementioned project risks. For the most part, in addition to the risks, the characteristics and the risk mitigating measures are described.This can appear as follows: "Completion is planned for 30/09/2018. The general contractor is committed to this latest deadline and shall pay a penalty for each day of delay in the amount of . . ., which represents sufficient incentive for timely completion."
Presentation of the necessary facilities and the financing structure	In this section, the different credit tranches are described, as well as the presentation of the equity capital and external resources structure.
Disclaimer	It is often pointed out that the information memo is not a sales prospectus and the banks should form an independent opinion on the project.

> According to the current plans, the project consists of a total of 11 wind turbines with a nominal capacity totalling 37.95 MW, with an annual net energy production of 113.3 GWh. The total investment costs for the project come to USD 65 million. We are prepared to provide long-term loan resources to the project in an amount of up to USD 50 million. Our declaration of willingness to provide financing is subject to a satisfactory legal, economic and technical due diligence as well as the approval of our committees.

However, a reliable statement can only be released later on. The bank will want to avoid entering into a credit commitment if the conditions for this do not exist yet. Nevertheless, flower letters can help the bank's credit clients when they negotiate with their renewable energy technology suppliers and want to demonstrate that the financing process is already quite advanced.

16.2.4 The Term Sheet

A Term Sheet reflects the major material credit characteristics of the financing of a project. It is the precursor to a loan agreement which, in addition to the Term Sheet, contains even more detailed provisions regarding reporting obligations, obligations of the project, grounds for termination and general loan and credit terms and conditions.

Such a Term Sheet can be structured in one of two ways: Either in short form (sometimes referred to as the "Short Form Term Sheet" or "Heads of Terms", see Table 16.2), which essentially only contains the financing structure and the essential economic parameters of financing, or as a detailed "Long Form Term Sheet," which also contains extensive legal clauses that are to be implemented in the financing documentation. In the case of small volume financing, in particular in the area of biomass, onshore wind and solar, a "Short Form Term Sheet" may be advised: The parties thus concentrate on the essential economic parameters without having to "overburden" the Term Sheet negotiations with legal issues and possibly controversies. For more complex or larger projects and financing, it is advisable to include the essential guarantees, ancillary obligations and reasons for termination in the Term Sheet negotiations.

Similar to the Information Memorandum, the Term Sheet is understood as a basis for the bank's financing offer. As soon as the parties have reached agreement on these aspects, the basic credit decision is made by the financing bank(s) and the Mandate Letter together with the Term Sheet have been signed, the actual "hot phase" of the financing negotiations, the documentation phase, begins. During this phase, the agreements that represent the legal basis for financing are drafted and negotiated.

The Term Sheet phase is completed upon signing (see Table 16.3). Financing is generally considered to be "focused on documentation" as soon as it exceeds a certain volume. This assessment is essentially correct – numerous documents have to be drafted and agreed even in the case of what initially appears to be relatively "simple" project financing, which are also in part of considerable length and complexity.

16.2.5 Rating of Renewable Energy Project Loans

The cash flow model and the rating procedure are two interlinking methodological procedures that aim to determine an appropriate risk structure for the project on the basis of individual risk aspects.

In this respect, the cash flow model serves as an initial estimation of the project capacity and viability, and the rating process then allows the cash flow progression to be evaluated within a simulation process and thus the probability of failure of the project can be determined. The rating result corresponds to a risk pricing. Insofar as this deviates from the risk pricing used in the cash flow model, which is initially only an estimation, the model must be adapted and the simulation calculation repeated. If necessary, this process has to be repeated until the cash flow model and rating

Table 16.2: Categories and contents of a Term Sheet (own representation).

Category	Contents
Project Description and purpose of the loan	This illustrates what the project involves and what tranches will have to be made available. Special features of the project can also be mentioned.
Loan Facilities	This section lists the individual loan facilities. Essential components include: the term and grace period, the face interest rate, the margin, the repayment procedures including mandatory and unscheduled repayments (cash sweeps).
Reserve Accounts	Agreement of reserve accounts: A debt service reserve account is often agreed, sometimes with an additional maintenance costs reserve account.
Covenants	Here, mandatory financial key figures are defined. If the key figures fall below the pre-defined threshold, a dividend lock-up comes into effect or the bank may even have the right to terminate the loans (event of default).

procedures provide the same information. In this respect, the cash flow modeling and evaluation using a rating tool form an iterative process.

The objectives pursued using a rating tool can be described as follows:

1. Objective and standardized risk assessment of a project.
2. Calculation of an overall risk for project financing – determining the probability of default (PD), which in turn is relevant for the risk pricing.
3. Regulatory requirements, in particular the capital adequacy requirements, can be met.

The rating tool simulates the major risk drivers under a certain set of assumptions and taking account of the macroeconomic factors, such as interest rates, exchange rates and inflation assumptions, as well as industry-specific assumptions based on a random walk approach which uses historical volatilities and correlations.

In this context, two volatilities have to be distinguished: On the one hand, there is the volatility of supply of resources in the case of an renewable energy project, and on the other hand the forecast uncertainty specified by the expert evaluator. The volatility of the basic supply is typically presented in the form of site-specific expert opinions.

In addition to the quantitative parameters, the project is also qualitatively assessed in the context of a rating procedure with regard to its structure and the involvement of the project participants. For example, these include the project structure and an assessment of the involvement of project parties, an evaluation of the competitiveness of the project and the market environment, and the complexity of the transaction.

Table 16.1: Important contents of an Information Memorandum (own representation).

Aspect	Contents
Executive Summary	Here, the essential aspects of the project are summarized on a maximum of two pages
Presentation of the Project	Typically, the project is presented here (plants, rated power, annual energy yield, location, remuneration or regulatory system, central project stakeholders and their roles, status of the contractual structure design, cash flow overviews (mostly base case and downside scenarios)). The individual aspects are usually addressed in detail in the individual sections.
Presentation of the risks and the risk mitigating agreements	The risks of the project are usually described based on the aforementioned project risks. For the most part, in addition to the risks, the characteristics and the risk mitigating measures are described.This can appear as follows: "Completion is planned for 30/09/2018. The general contractor is committed to this latest deadline and shall pay a penalty for each day of delay in the amount of . . ., which represents sufficient incentive for timely completion."
Presentation of the necessary facilities and the financing structure	In this section, the different credit tranches are described, as well as the presentation of the equity capital and external resources structure.
Disclaimer	It is often pointed out that the information memo is not a sales prospectus and the banks should form an independent opinion on the project.

> According to the current plans, the project consists of a total of 11 wind turbines with a nominal capacity totalling 37.95 MW, with an annual net energy production of 113.3 GWh. The total investment costs for the project come to USD 65 million. We are prepared to provide long-term loan resources to the project in an amount of up to USD 50 million. Our declaration of willingness to provide financing is subject to a satisfactory legal, economic and technical due diligence as well as the approval of our committees.

However, a reliable statement can only be released later on. The bank will want to avoid entering into a credit commitment if the conditions for this do not exist yet. Nevertheless, flower letters can help the bank's credit clients when they negotiate with their renewable energy technology suppliers and want to demonstrate that the financing process is already quite advanced.

16.2.4 The Term Sheet

A Term Sheet reflects the major material credit characteristics of the financing of a project. It is the precursor to a loan agreement which, in addition to the Term Sheet, contains even more detailed provisions regarding reporting obligations, obligations of the project, grounds for termination and general loan and credit terms and conditions.

Such a Term Sheet can be structured in one of two ways: Either in short form (sometimes referred to as the "Short Form Term Sheet" or "Heads of Terms", see Table 16.2), which essentially only contains the financing structure and the essential economic parameters of financing, or as a detailed "Long Form Term Sheet," which also contains extensive legal clauses that are to be implemented in the financing documentation. In the case of small volume financing, in particular in the area of biomass, onshore wind and solar, a "Short Form Term Sheet" may be advised: The parties thus concentrate on the essential economic parameters without having to "overburden" the Term Sheet negotiations with legal issues and possibly controversies. For more complex or larger projects and financing, it is advisable to include the essential guarantees, ancillary obligations and reasons for termination in the Term Sheet negotiations.

Similar to the Information Memorandum, the Term Sheet is understood as a basis for the bank's financing offer. As soon as the parties have reached agreement on these aspects, the basic credit decision is made by the financing bank(s) and the Mandate Letter together with the Term Sheet have been signed, the actual "hot phase" of the financing negotiations, the documentation phase, begins. During this phase, the agreements that represent the legal basis for financing are drafted and negotiated.

The Term Sheet phase is completed upon signing (see Table 16.3). Financing is generally considered to be "focused on documentation" as soon as it exceeds a certain volume. This assessment is essentially correct – numerous documents have to be drafted and agreed even in the case of what initially appears to be relatively "simple" project financing, which are also in part of considerable length and complexity.

16.2.5 Rating of Renewable Energy Project Loans

The cash flow model and the rating procedure are two interlinking methodological procedures that aim to determine an appropriate risk structure for the project on the basis of individual risk aspects.

In this respect, the cash flow model serves as an initial estimation of the project capacity and viability, and the rating process then allows the cash flow progression to be evaluated within a simulation process and thus the probability of failure of the project can be determined. The rating result corresponds to a risk pricing. Insofar as this deviates from the risk pricing used in the cash flow model, which is initially only an estimation, the model must be adapted and the simulation calculation repeated. If necessary, this process has to be repeated until the cash flow model and rating

Table 16.2: Categories and contents of a Term Sheet (own representation).

Category	Contents
Project Description and purpose of the loan	This illustrates what the project involves and what tranches will have to be made available. Special features of the project can also be mentioned.
Loan Facilities	This section lists the individual loan facilities. Essential components include: the term and grace period, the face interest rate, the margin, the repayment procedures including mandatory and unscheduled repayments (cash sweeps).
Reserve Accounts	Agreement of reserve accounts: A debt service reserve account is often agreed, sometimes with an additional maintenance costs reserve account.
Covenants	Here, mandatory financial key figures are defined. If the key figures fall below the pre-defined threshold, a dividend lock-up comes into effect or the bank may even have the right to terminate the loans (event of default).

procedures provide the same information. In this respect, the cash flow modeling and evaluation using a rating tool form an iterative process.

The objectives pursued using a rating tool can be described as follows:
1. Objective and standardized risk assessment of a project.
2. Calculation of an overall risk for project financing – determining the probability of default (PD), which in turn is relevant for the risk pricing.
3. Regulatory requirements, in particular the capital adequacy requirements, can be met.

The rating tool simulates the major risk drivers under a certain set of assumptions and taking account of the macroeconomic factors, such as interest rates, exchange rates and inflation assumptions, as well as industry-specific assumptions based on a random walk approach which uses historical volatilities and correlations.

In this context, two volatilities have to be distinguished: On the one hand, there is the volatility of supply of resources in the case of an renewable energy project, and on the other hand the forecast uncertainty specified by the expert evaluator. The volatility of the basic supply is typically presented in the form of site-specific expert opinions.

In addition to the quantitative parameters, the project is also qualitatively assessed in the context of a rating procedure with regard to its structure and the involvement of the project participants. For example, these include the project structure and an assessment of the involvement of project parties, an evaluation of the competitiveness of the project and the market environment, and the complexity of the transaction.

The factors above are compiled as a key figure using a scorecard system, which is added to the rating for qualitative factors. Ultimately, however, it is the level and stability of future cash flows that essentially determine the rating result.

16.2.6 Fulfillment of Covenants: Achieving First Loan Disbursement

Once the bank has reached its credit decision, it or its consultants examine the underlying agreements in order to verify whether they correspond to the grounds for the decision and the economic assumptions made therein. Insofar as these correspond to the assumptions made and the project can be achieved and operated according to plan, the conditions precedent for a drawdown are fulfilled.

As soon as the project setup begins, the financial resources are paid out according to the progress of construction. The credit providers have to ensure in regard to construction financing that the necessary payment conditions are observed and the temporal and budgetary plans as well as other agreements that are complied with. The consequence of non-compliance is that the agreed debt service to the debt capital providers and distributions to the sponsors are at risk. Both the construction phase and the subsequent operational phase at project level are therefore supervised through financial controlling by the credit providers. The aim of financial monitoring is to control the economic situation of the project during the term of the loan. For this purpose, key financial figures are defined in the loan agreement, which the project may not exceed or fall short of during the term of the loan. These key financial figures are also referred to as ***financial covenants***. In addition to the financial covenants, the loan agreements also set contractual assurances and documentation that have to be complied with during the term of the loan. These are also referred to as ***legal covenants***. Compliance with the covenants is, as a rule, essential to ensure that a loan can be disbursed. If the borrower cannot comply, it is in breach of the credit agreement. Banks define this as an ***Event of Default*** and reserve the option to call in the loan in such a case. This does normally not happen, because the borrower has the option of requesting an amendment of the contract (a so-called ***Waiver Request***) from the lead arranger, which the bank consortium has to agree to by the majority stipulated in the loan agreement in order to allow the contract amendment to take effect.

16.3 Project Loan Documentation: Overview

The **Loan Agreement**, as the central financing document, provides the legal basis for the granting of a loan. The focus here is on defining the costs for the borrower (interest and other charges), as well as the borrower's commitment to repay the loan at the agreed points in time and in the agreed amount. The loan agreement for project financing also includes numerous other ancillary obligations on the part of the borrower, which define the loan as a continuing obligation until full repayment. The document under "further reading," *Project Loan Agreement*, provides a comprehensive overview of the contents of a loan agreement for renewable energy projects according to LMA standard.

Credit collateral serve in the context of project financing a totally different function than in corporate financing: The project partners are only willing to a limited extent or not willing at all to issue guarantees for the equity capital invested in the project. In the absence of a broad credit basis, an increased need to limit and control the business risks arises, which entails the restriction of a defined field of business. The profitability of the project therefore depends to a large extent on the expected cash flow in this business field. This applies even more for renewable energies projects whose viability continues to depend on statutory tariffs. The traditional role of credit collateral in the financing of companies therefore shifts to a perspective focused on risk control and cash flow-backup in project financing.

A risk-reducing function is also added through the conclusion of **subordination agreements**, through which claims by the lender are guaranteed priority over the subordinated claims of the shareholders or other parties close to the project in the case that the project company becomes insolvent.

16.4 The Concept of "Collateral" in Project Finance Transactions

The economic and legal characteristics of project financing demand that the main objective is to protect the cash flow of the project against risks and also to sustain the project in the case of a crisis. Protection of the cash flows against risks cannot be achieved solely by the constituted collateral, but instead requires close controlling of the project operation throughout the entire term of the loan[1].

Risks that concern the behavior of third parties require a risk-fencing of the project company. To serve this purpose, satisfying external demands should be given priority, insofar as this is necessary to maintain operation and the cash flow, e.g., land leases, maintenance service charges and taxes. The remaining risk that can materialize, especially through the exclusion of senior legal claims of third parties such as banks, is expropriation risk. This risk can barely be controlled. However, external risks that cannot be controlled by those involved in the project and the bank – insofar as these are insurable – can be often allocated to an insurer.

Further motives for collateralization come from the economic and financial spheres: The extent to which the bank has to use equity capital for its commitment depends on the assessment of the collateral. This aspect has become more important with the increased capital requirements of banks following the financial crisis. In

1 See also chapter 8.

order to manage one's own credit risks through syndication of a commitment and open up refinancing options, the bank relies on offering its potential syndicate banks a contract and collateral structure that is acceptable on the refinancing market.

16.4.1 Aims of Collateral Agreements

The primary objective of credit protection in project financing is the continued operation of the project and continuation of the future cash flow until the loan repayment has been occurred.

This objective requires primary collateral securing of all plant components and areas of land required to operate the project and a structure that allows for effective controlling of the generated cash flow. The objective of providing sufficient collateral for the liquidating recovery is secondary to this, though without becoming meaningless.

In particular, the classical collateral securities grant the bank privilege in the case of insolvency proceedings and allow for various options in order to maintain the operation and control of internal and external risks. Protection against measures of enforcement by third parties can, however, be reinforced in parallel through debt agreements in the loan agreement, such as payment cascades, for example.

Basically, the same collateral is available to project financing as normal corporate financing: In the case of renewable energy projects, these include classical collateral securities on land and property-equivalent rights. In the case of plants on land owned by the operator, this is the mortgage. On third party sites, the mortgage comes into question if the plant operator holds the lease. For projects, however, the agreement of a ground lease is only rarely enforceable, so that alternative solutions have to be applied. Perhaps the most common solution is the limited personal easement, whereby the plant operator is entitled in rem to use the site to construct and operate its facilities.

16.4.2 Typical Collateral Agreements in Renewable Energy Project Financing

As **material moveable collateral**, in project financing, the focus is on the collateral assignment of plant components. This applies in particular to plants on third-party soil.

For **receivables**, individual claims cessions and global cessions of the project company's receivables from the essential project agreements are common. These are primarily land use agreements, general contractor and plant delivery agreements, maintenance and management agreements as well as network connection and direct marketing agreements. Pledges are made on the accounts of the project company and on the shares in the company.

Insofar as recourse to third parties is possible (limited recourse) for the financing of a project, this is often done in the form of sureties, guarantees, letters of comfort or contractually shared liability, for example by the equipment manufacturer for its local distribution company.

Third parties are also integrated into project financing through contractual arrangements for collateral. In the project agreements that the borrower concludes with partners involved, it is common for these partners to be obliged to grant the financing bank an entry option in the event of termination, which often goes hand in hand with information obligations. These agreements are concluded either between the bank, the project company and the third party as so-called **direct agreements**, or the admission rules are incorporated into the project agreements as agreements to the benefit of a third party, the bank. This form has now become common practice in site use agreements for renewable energy plants.

In the case of projects whose operation depends on how reliable the logistic chains are, both in regard to the fuel supply and disposal, the conclusion of **supply-or-pay or take-or-pay agreements** is sought. The delivery or acceptance obligation in these agreements approximates a delivery or acceptance guarantee, in that the project company's contracting partner is obliged, in the absence of its services, to provide certain agreed compensation payments, even if it is not responsible for non-performance.

Insurance policies that financially secure the assets of the project against events of damage are also described as collateral in the broader sense.

16.5 Syndication

In order to be able to address further potential debt capital providers on the market, the bank responsible for the arrangement prepares an **Information Memorandum** which presents all of the essential information on the project. This is forwarded to other banks, who can then decide based on this information whether they want to participate in the financing of the project. Furthermore, the arranging bank plays the leading role in the formation of the bank consortium and the syndication on the market. The aim of syndication is to raise the required credit volume to finance the project as well as to spread the risks of lending across the participating banks. In doing so, the banks that form the consortium assume different functions: The bank that has been mandated as the lead arranger is responsible for the further structuring and administration of the financing. In order to provide the required credit volume, further major banks are sought as co-arrangers, who underwrite the credit amount in the first instance together with the lead arranger. The borrower thus receives the assurance of the arrangers that the requested credit volume will be provided in full amount (fully underwritten proposal). As the lead and co-arrangers hereby assume large credit packages and therefore a high level of credit risk, they will seek additional banks in the further course to become participants in the financing commitment and to assume credit packages from them, so that the financing risks can be further dispersed within the banking market.

As soon as the required credit volume can be raised on the market, the agreements are drawn up within the context of the documentation and signed by the contractual partners during the financial close. The financial close comes at the end of the development phase of the project, because this milestone makes the financial resources available for the set-up phase.

Chronologically speaking, syndication is usually sought at the end of a credit process: The banks approached receive prepared project documents from the syndicating bank and can then decide whether they want to participate or not within a relatively short period of time. Options to renegotiate the project agreements at the request of individual banks are usually no longer possible.

Table 16.3: Documentation of a Loan Syndication (own representation).

Document	Function
Mandate Letter	In the mandate letter, the arranger is given the order to organize the syndication process
Term Sheet	In the Term Sheet, the essential terms of financing that the contractual partners have to negotiate are presented schematically
Information Memorandum	The Information Memorandum provides essential information about the project. This is made available to the banks with the objective of obtaining participation in the consortium.
Fee Letter	In the Fee Letter, the fees for the banks participating in the syndication are determined.
Syndicated Loan Agreement	This is the negotiated syndicated loan contract, which is signed by the contracting parties at financial close.

16.6 Credit Monitoring and Re-Rating

Credit monitoring of the financing of a project is done throughout the entire term of the loan on the basis of statutory and contractual obligations.

Materially speaking, the statutory monitoring only plays a subordinated role in the financing of a project here, as submission of the annual financial statements reports on a matter in the past, which no longer leaves any room to react to deviations from the plan.

What is much more important for the monitoring and control of a project financing is the expected future development of the project:

Set-up phase: Before drawdowns under the individual credit tranches can be made, the bank checks whether the conditions precedent agreed in the loan agreement are completely fulfilled.

Furthermore, in the **operational phase,** the planned and the actual performance are continuously compared. In the event of a shortfall, talks begin to determine whether this is a one-off event or an ongoing disruption and whether and which adjustment measures are required.

In parallel to project monitoring, an internal presentation of the transaction is carried out within the bank. It is essential for the bank to incorporate the project into the cash flow model against the background of actual experiences and re-evaluate it using the rating procedure.

The following principles apply for the incorporation into the rating model:

- In principle, the project is assessed based on its actual performance and the actual contractual rights or obligations.
- If there is an event of a unique nature, this event is eliminated for the preparation of the rating in order to continue to ensure a fair, long-term assessment of the project.
- Otherwise, a re-rating does not differ from the approach taken in the initial project rating process.

16.7 Due Diligence: Documenting a Project for Credit Assessment

16.7.1 Introduction to Due Diligence

A due diligence process within the context of renewable energy project financing differs in scope and in terms from the due diligence review in the context of a company acquisition. The focus here is on **legal due diligence**. This is not least due to the fact that the essential economic aspects, such as the level and reliability of remuneration, feed-in options as well as manufacturer guarantees and insurance policies, are also protected by statutory provisions or contractual arrangements.

As many renewable energy projects (especially onshore wind and photovoltaics) have also come to be seen as proven, standardized and therefore robust technologies from a financing perspective by the financing bank, a **technical due diligence** is often omitted. It is more common here for technical information to be obtained regarding certain individual questions that arise from the expert opinion submitted. However, for more complex renewable energy projects – such as hydropower projects, offshore wind energy projects and bioenergy projects – comprehensive technical due diligence are a standard procedure.

Tax due diligence, which overlaps with **financial due diligence** in some areas, focuses on the tax situation of the project company. From the point of view of the lender, this tax due diligence is not about a tax analysis of the business structure, but rather about current tax obligations that may even have originated in the past. Depending on the scope of the agreements already concluded with the operating company at the time of the review and the age of the company, the tax due diligence may be necessary.

The basis for achieving the financial close from the perspective of all participants is a positive due diligence process. Depending on the internal policies of the financing bank and the size of the project, this process is prepared and carried out either internally by the bank itself or by external consultants. Due diligence reviews for large wind farm projects, for instance, are usually carried out by external consultants.

Table 16.4: The renewable energy project due diligence in six steps (own representation).

1	**Signing of the Term Sheet (bank – borrower)**
2	Definition of scope of work for the due diligence advisors
3	"Beauty contest" of advisors
4	Selection and formal mandate of advisors
5	Analyzing of renewable energy project documentation by mandated advisors
6	Submission of due diligence "red flag reports"

16.7.2 Due Diligence: Process and Roles

The due diligence process usually begins upon conclusion of the Term Sheet between the financing bank and the project company/sponsor (see Table 16.4).

The financing bank asks one or more consultancy assignments out to tender for the various areas of the due diligence process in agreement with its client. In the area of legal due diligence, the consultancy assignments to be awarded by the financing bank also cover all further questions that arise in the context of the intended project financing and in particular the preparation of the complete credit documentation, in addition to the review of the project contracts. The resulting external costs of the due diligence process are to be borne by the project company.

In many financing transactions, the project sponsor is also the buyer of the project to be financed and has, within the context of the purchase negotiations, already had comprehensive due diligence carried out by its own external consultants. In this case, the project will endeavour to make the results available to the financing bank. If this due diligence has been carried out in accordance with the catalogue of requirements of the lender, the lender may limit itself to reviewing the results obtained by the buyer. In some cases, the financing bank receives a guarantee as to the accuracy and completeness of the buyer's due diligence report from the authors of the due diligence report on the basis of a specific liability agreement (***reliance letter***). However, this approach is not the rule in practice, as consultants often only extend reliance letters as a privilege to selected clients or certain projects. Alternatively, existing due diligence reports can be handed over to third parties on the basis of a ***non-reliance-letter***, albeit then with explicit liability exclusion of the consultant (see Table 16.5).

Table 16.5: Reliance versus Non-Reliance Letter (own representation).

Reliance Letter	Non-Reliance Letter
Financing Bank may ask consultant(s) for liability extension related to existing DD report(s)	Consultants prepare DD reports on behalf of project sponsor that are later forwarded to third parties (e.g., banks)
Reliance Letter contains clauses i. a. dealing with liability amounts & confidentiality	Non-reliance-letter contains liability exclusion of consultant(s) and confidentiality clauses
Consultants need to present proofs of professional liability insurance cover amounts	Letter is signed before report may be circulated to the bank

Due Diligence: Scope and Completion

After awarding the due diligence assignment, the consultant and the financing bank agree on the aspects to be covered by the review (review catalogue, e.g., based on the headlines outlined in the figure below – ***scope of work***) and the requirements for the individual aspects (standard of review) as the basis of the due diligence review.

Before conclusion of the review process, the project company or the sponsor assure that they have provided all project-related documents and information in accordance with the scope of review to the consultant in full up to the end of the review (***completeness declaration***).

The result of the review process is recorded in a due diligence report. This is submitted to the financing bank and is a prerequisite for payment of the investment loan applied for by the operating company. This is a decisive milestone for the project to fulfill the conditions precedent.

What is essential for the further progress of the project is whether correction of the defects found in the project represent a condition precedent for the financing bank or whether these can be remedied later on, i.e., after partial or full payment of the loan ("conditions subsequent"). In this case, the obligation to remedy this defect is determined in the loan agreement, in the form of a condition that must be met by the operating company within an agreed period of time, and is executed by the contracting parties following the financial close. The purpose of the report is both to provide the financing bank with a basis for assessment and decision-making and to act as the basis for optimal structuring of the loan agreement (***recording of assurances and warranties***).

Loan Conditions and Covenants

In the loan agreement, the lender is granted various control and co-determination rights, which can be divided into ***loan conditions*** and ***loan covenants***. While in the loan conditions i. a. the essential elements of the collateral structure for the financing of a project *before* completion are defined, the loan covenants serve a security function *after* project completion.

Within the loan conditions, credit usage and payment conditions in particular effect the credit provider's control rights. In the case of loan covenants, the capital structure requirements, the restrictions on disposal and the credit provider's information and inspection rights are relevant in this context. The following essential rights are to be distinguished:

Condition for payout of the loan amounts is the proof of conclusion of the agreements, warranties and approvals required under the financing conditions. Furthermore, assurance is to be given that the loan amounts will only be used for the agreed purpose (credit usage and payment conditions).

The aim of the capital structure requirements ("***financial covenants***") is to keep the existential risk of the project within the framework agreed on upon conclusion of the loan agreement. For this purpose, the requirements regarding the creditworthiness of a borrower are set out in requirements, compliance with which is meant to ensure the agreed fulfillment of the loan agreement. Capital structure requirements are divided into those that are to ensure the liquidity of the borrower and those that concern the composition of the capital sources.

Disposal restrictions occur in the form of distribution conditions and requirements concerning the sale and encumbrance of assets. Co-determination rights arise in particular from the requirements which bind the borrower's disposal of parts of the fixed assets or financial assets to the agreement of the credit provider. By setting limits for expenditure, which can only be exceeded with the agreement of the lender, this makes it possible for the creditor to have at least partial control of the budget.

The ***information obligations of the borrower*** relate to the periodic submission of annual financial statements and interim performance reports during the operational phase and construction progress reports during the completion phase. In addition, there is a general obligation to make all information that may be of interest accessible to the credit provider.

In the event of a contractual breach or unforeseen difficulties in the execution of project financing, lenders usually reserve the right to take over the management of the project company by appointing a management of their own choice.

16.8 Summary

The main focus of this section was to find out the prerequisites for banks to finance projects in the field of renewable energies with the project financing model. In

particular, it is important to note that the predictability of cash flows and the appropriate involvement of project participants in the project are the key success factors. The following critical decision-making factors apply to practically all project financing:
- Stability and reliability of the legal and regulatory environment,
- Appropriate opportunity-risk allocation for all project participants,
- Use of proven technology,
- Site quality (available resources).

Overall, countries with a stable political and legal environment are clearly preferred in project finance. Planning uncertainties are poison for investments that are expected to be successful for a period of more than ten years.

Further Reading

Böttcher, Jörg. 2009. *Finanzierung von Erneuerbare-Energien-Vorhaben* (Financing of renewable energy projects). Oldenbourg, Munich.

Böttcher, Jörg, ed. 2014. *Geothermie-Vorhaben* (Geothermal projects). Oldenbourg, Munich.

Böttcher, Jörg, ed. 2013. *Handbuch Offshore-Windenergie* (Handbook of offshore wind energy). Oldenbourg, Munich.

Böttcher, Jörg, ed. 2013. *Management von Biogas-Vorhaben* (Management of biogas projects). Springer, Berlin.

Böttcher, Jörg. 2012. *Möglichkeiten einer Projektfinanzierung bei CSP-Vorhaben* (Options for project financing of CSP projects). Peter Lang, Hamburg.

Böttcher, Jörg, ed. 2011. *Onshore-Windenergie* (Onshore Wind Energy), Oldenbourg, Munich [2nd ed. in 2019].

Böttcher, Jörg, ed. 2015. *Rechtliche Rahmenbedingungen von EE-Projekten*, vol. 1 (Legal framework conditions of renewable energy projects). Berliner Wissenschaftsverlag, Berlin.

Böttcher, Jörg, ed. 2011. *Solarvorhaben* (Solar projects). Oldenbourg, Munich.

Böttcher, Jörg, ed. 2014. *Stromleitungsnetze* (Power line networks). Walter De Gruyter, Munich.

Böttcher, Jörg, ed. 2015. *Wasserkraftprojekte* (Water power projects). Springer, Berlin.

Böttcher, Jörg, and Peter Blattner. 2010. *Projektfinanzierung* (Project Financing), 2nd ed. Oldenbourg, Munich.

Böttcher, Jörg, and Anja Wiebusch, eds. 2017. *Krise und Sanierung von Projektfinanzierungen* (Crisis and Restructuring of Project Financing). Walter De Gruyter, Berlin/Boston.

Gröhl, Matthias. 1990. *Bankpolitische Konsequenzen der Projektfinanzierung: Lösungsansätze für bankbetriebliche Probleme bei der Einführung von Finanzdienstleistungen für große, rechtlich selbständige Investitionsvorhaben* (Banking policy consequences of project funding: Solution approaches for operational banking problems when introducing financial services for large, legally independent investment projects), PhD diss. Marburg.

Hupe, Michael. 1995. *Steuerung und Kontrolle internationaler Projektfinanzierungen* (Managing and controlling international project financing), PhD diss. Peter Lang, Frankfurt am Main.

Thommen, Jean-Paul, and Ann-Kristin Achleitner. 2009. *Allgemeine Betriebswirtschaftslehre: Umfassende Einführung aus managementorientierter Sicht* (General business administration:

A comprehensive introduction from a management-oriented perspective), Springer, 6th ed. Wiesbaden.

Wolf, Birgit, Mark Hill, and Michael Pfaue. 2011. *Strukturierte Finanzierungen: Grundlagen des Corporate Finance, Technik der Projekt- und Buy-out-Finanzierung, Asset-Backed-Strukturen* (Structured finance: Basic principles of corporate finance, techniques for project and buy-out financing, asset-backed structures), 2nd ed. Schäffer Poeschel, Stuttgart.

Offshore Wind Energy

1 Technology of Offshore Wind Energy Turbines: Current Status and Developments

Uwe Ritschel

1.1 Introduction: Why Offshore Wind Energy

The transition from fossil to renewable energy sources will be one of the main global transformation processes of the coming decades until about 2050. As argued for example recently (Schellnhuber, 2016) this is the only viable way to keep the global warming below 2° and, thus, prevent irreversible damage to our climate. In a cooperative study of several German research institutes (Schmid, 2011) a detailed scenario for the transition was provided. Wind energy always plays a major rule in such scenarios contributing about one fifth of the global primary energy corresponding (under certain assumptions explained in the study) to 28.000 TWh/a.[1] This would correspond under certain assumptions[2] to a wind power capacity of 7000 GW compared to about 600 GW that have been installed during the past 30 years. A substantial part of the needed capacity will certainly come from OWT.

Why should we go offshore with wind turbines (WT) to generate electricity? There are a number of disadvantages and challenges when one works offshore. Conditions are much harsher than on land, the salty air leads to fast corrosion and OWT are much more difficult to access than turbines based on land. This has an impact also on costs and is the reason why OWT have been too expensive in the past and have been – depending on the political framework for the energy transition – driven up the electricity costs for consumers.

On the other hand there are also many advantages of offshore wind energy. The wind resource is much better over water than over land. Wind speeds are higher and turbulence is lower. Since the power of the wind depends on the third power of wind speed, the energy production at an offshore site is much larger than at a land site given the same power rating and rotor diameter of the WT. Concerning the distance to consumers many large cities and densely populated areas are close to the

1 Somewhat lower figures for wind power are provided for instance by the Global Wind Energy Council (Sawyer, 2016).

2 An average capacity factor of 0.45 has been assumed. This is too high for present day turbines but taking into account the present trends it might be realistic. The capacity factor is explained in section 1.2.3.

Uwe Ritschel, Chair of Wind Energy Technology, University of Rostock

https://doi.org/10.1515/9783110607888-017

sea. As stated in (Koebe, 2014) the large scale deployment of OWT could also entail a great economic benefit for those areas.

Another important advantage of working offshore is that size is essentially not a limiting factor. On land there are certain transport limits that determine the size of components and modules for land-based WT. For offshore application weight, length and other geometric properties are not limited as long as they are fabricated near the harbor can be handled there and on site. As a consequence, during recent years a number of large wind turbines have been developed specially for off-shore application. Even some manufacturers produce exclusively OWT, while others have stopped to work on OWT. So effectively we presently observe a segregation of WT in offshore and land-based types, while in earlier days, some 20 years ago, certain types of WT where used for both applications.

Presently a lot of research is done for offshore wind energy, both by the industry and in academic research facilities, often in cooperation projects. This has led to a fast development of the technology with respect to reliability, size of OWT and cost reduction. For example during the present year, 2019, we will see the installation of WT with more than 10 MW rated power, and 20 MW is in sight. With a little optimism one can assume that in the coming decade energy from OWT will have the same cost level as land-based WT or other crucial renewable generation methods like utility-size photovoltaic power plants. And even in regions where on land wind speeds are too low, WT on nearby offshore sites can generate electrical power in an economically feasible way.

The purpose of the present text is to describe those aspects of wind energy technology that are different from land-based wind energy. In the introductory part the offshore wind resource will be discussed and it will be explained how the energy production of a modern large OWT can be obtained under rather simple assumptions.

Most prominent there are the large new OWT which will be discussed in some detail in section 1.3. There are interesting new concepts that might dominate the future of offshore wind. Especially the transition from traditional geared WT to direct-drive technologies will take place much faster offshore than on land. The most recent developments will be discussed in some detail.

Another main topic in the present text is substructures for OWT. Most land-based WT are installed on simple concrete slabs. OWT can be either floating or fixed to the seabed. Both solutions are presently more expensive than foundations on land. Installation is more difficult and hampered by wind and waves which also increases the cost of energy. Substructures and the installation process are topics where a lot of research is being done with the aim to reduce the costs of energy significantly. Some of the ideas and results will be discussed below.

Offshore wind energy is a fascinating and very extensive field of work. So not all aspects and developments can be treated in such a contribution. There are good accounts of the topic in some books about wind energy in general (Hau, 2013)

(Burton, 2011) (Gasch, 2012) and about onshore wind energy in particular (Anaya-Lara, 2018). We refer to these references for more details.

1.2 Basics about Offshore Wind Energy

1.2.1 Why All Wind Turbines Have Three Blades and a Horizontal Axis

There is a long history of using wind energy for various purposes. A good overview is provided in (Hau, 2013). WT can have a vertical or horizontal axis of rotation and operate on drag or lift. Almost all utility-size WT on the other hand have three blades, are of lift-type and have a (nearly) horizontal axis. What is the reason why all other concepts have not been successful when it comes to large WT?

Firstly, horizontal axis WT (HAWT) with aerodynamically well designed rotor blades have a high power efficiency. The efficiency is expressed by the power coefficient CP, the share of power that can be extracted from the wind. With modern rotor blades one can reach 0.5 or even more, not far from the theoretical limit 0.59 according to Betz (Hau, 2013).

Secondly, for HAWT a relatively small amount of aerodynamically inactive material, the hub, is needed to keep the blades in position. Only a small area near the center, in the order of 1% of the rotor disk, is not active. This also means that with little structural material (hub) really long aerodynamically active elements (blades) can be kept in their position.

Thirdly, the high CP can be achieved with relatively little material compared to a large rotor area. It is possible to use a small number of blades and making them quite slender and still have CP=0.5. The area of the rotor covered by the blades divided by the rotor area is called the solidity. Lower solidity means that the rotor speed, more precisely the tip-speed ratio, needs to increase keeping the performance on the same level. This is one of the main trends in blade design during the last 10 years or so. By using carbon fiber in highly loaded parts of the blades and/or optimizing structural concepts, the blades are not only much longer but also more slender than 10 or 20 years ago. The solidity of the rotors is decreasing. In this way the costs of the rotor per area have been reduced. Solidity is the essential setting wheel for cost reduction.

Now, the question which number of blades, three, two, or even one, is an old one. From the mechanical point of view there is a big difference between two and three blades. Technically speaking, the three-bladed rotor (also rotors with more blades) has the same inertia with respect to any axis perpendicular to the axis of rotation. This is not the case for the two-bladed rotor. Due to this the three blades are dynamically more benign than two, and this probably is the main reason, why almost all WT have three blades.

Another reason for three instead of two blades is the tip speed. If we use two blades with the same dimensions as in the three-bladed case the solidity of the rotor is reduced and the tip speed has to go up. This causes more noise and poses a problem for WT at least on land. In spite of this, there are the famous early two-bladed experimental WT[3] and also new proposals for WT with two blades (see also section "New and alternative technologies").

An alternative that also comes with high CP and low solidity is the lift-type VAWT. There are new attempts to push the vertical-axis type for offshore application (see section "New and alternative technologies"). The most important advantage of the VAWT is that they operate on any wind direction while with the HAWT the rotor axis has to be aligned with the wind direction. On the other hand, the structural parts needed to form the rotor with an area comparable to a HAWT with, say, 180 m rotor diameter become large and heavy. Structural dynamics will be an issue and it might be challenging to create an economic design for a large VAWT to compete with the present-day OWT.

1.2.2 Offshore Wind Resource

The lowest layer of the atmosphere up to several hundred meters is determined by the friction between air and ground. In the language of fluid mechanics this is called a boundary layer. The properties of the ground, characterized by the so-called roughness length, are responsible for wind speed and turbulence in a certain height, at least under certain atmospheric conditions. By modeling the boundary layer one finds that the speed is proportional to $log(z/z_0)$ where z is the vertical distance and z_0 is the roughness length. Somewhere between 500 m and 1000 m above ground the wind speed is independent of surface properties. This is called the geostrophic wind.

Different roughness lengths lead to a significant difference between wind speeds above water and above land. A comparison is shown in Figure 5.14. The graphs show the windspeed rescaled with the value in 750 m which has been assumed as the speed of the geostrophic wind. The difference in the relevant range is about 10–15.

Wind in the boundary layer is turbulent such that the logarithmic dependence holds for an average over a sufficiently long time span as for instance a 10-minute average value. Without going into details here the turbulence shows the inverse behavior, it is proportional to 1/log. So it decreases with height and is smaller at sites with low roughness.

Unfortunately the simple picture shown in Figure 1.1 is distorted somewhat in reality. The lower atmosphere can be stable, unstable or neutral. We cannot go

3 See (Hau, 2013) for more details.

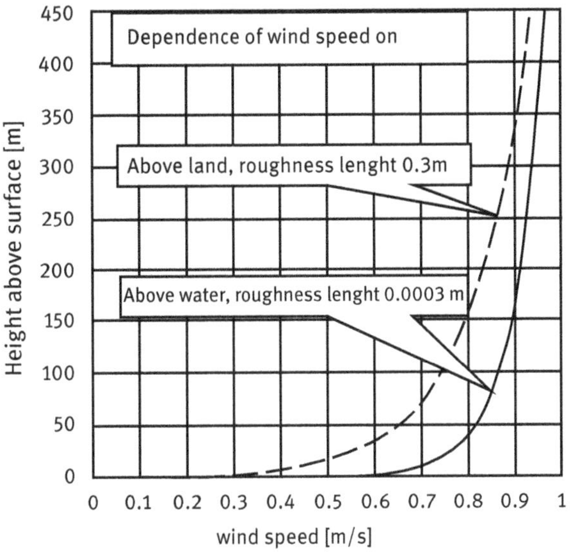

Figure 1.1: Wind speed rescaled with geostrophic wind above land and water (586).

into the details here but to summarize briefly one can state that in case of a stable atmosphere (stable layers with little vertical exchange) the dependence on height is generally stronger while in the case of unstable atmosphere (convection) the height-dependence is less pronounced (Sathyajith, 2012). The form shown in Figure 1.1 only holds for the so-called neutral atmosphere, which divides the stable from the unstable region.[4] For higher wind speeds the atmosphere tends to be neutral but in the low and medium wind-speed range up to 10 or 12 m/s there occur frequently unstable and stable situations.

The offshore wind resource is not distributed equally over the globe. The large-scale wind motors on earth are global circulation zones that are powered by the sun. In Figure 1.2 the zones with high wind speed schematically displayed as red stripes. This provides a rough picture. Reality is more complex. Above land the picture is more distorted by the local orographic features. Above the oceans however, the wind speeds are ruled to a larger extent by the circulation cells.

Highest average wind speeds are found at latitude of 40–60° (northern and southern). At a height above ground of 100 m the annual averages are typical 10 m/s or above. At latitudes of 10–20° north and south wind speeds are also high. Low annual wind speeds are found in the equatorial region, ± 10° and between 20 and

4 Normally the temperature of the atmosphere is decreasing with height above ground. In the neutral atmosphere this decrease is equal to the one that would come from adiabatic expansion when a volume of air is lifted over a certain vertical distance.

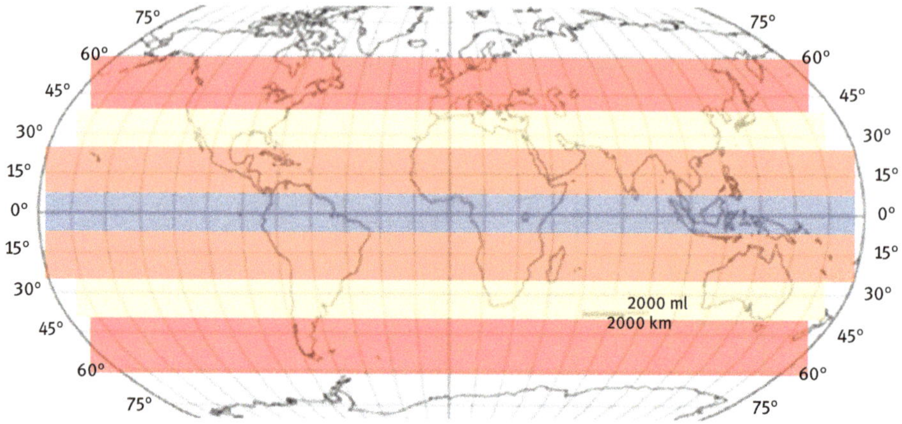

Figure 1.2: Zones with low and high wind speeds (own representation).

40° north and south. At offshore sites in these zones average wind speed can be 6 m/s or even less in 100 m height. The zones beyond ± 60° are not discussed here.

Looking at the map one can state that Europe and North America as well as Asia beyond 40° are in the northern belt with high wind speeds. At the same time a significant part of the world population is living in this area. The southern high-wind belt, however, is largely unpopulated.

For certain countries and regions offshore wind potentials have been assessed. Interesting is the technical potential that could be used for OWF. The study by NREL of 2016 (Musial, 2016) finds based on a generic 6 MW OWT the technical potential for offshore wind energy of 2,000 GW capacity. The AEP of this capacity would be 7,200 TWh/year corresponding to approximately twice the electrical energy consumption of the United States in 2014.

For Europe similar results have been obtained for the offshore potential in Atlantic, North Sea and the Baltic (Hundleby, 2017). The technically feasible potential is estimated to be more than 10.000 TWh/year while the total electricity consumption in the European Union is approximately 3000 TWh/year.

1.2.3 Energy Production of a Large Offshore Wind Turbine

How can we obtain an estimate for the annual energy production (AEP) of a WT? Basic ingredients needed are the power curve of the WT and as wind data the distributions of wind speed and the wind direction. The latter is the basis to account for shadowing effects between WT.

Since WT are based on the same aerodynamic concepts (lift-type HAWT) and use blades with similar aerodynamic properties as for instance lift-to-drag ratios or stalling properties, a rough estimate for power curve and energy production can be easily obtained. As stated in section 1.2.1 the aerodynamic efficiency is about 0.5. Taking into account all other mechanical and electrical losses the overall efficiency (from wind to electrical power measured by the grid operator) is about 0.45, such that the approximate power curve is

$$P = \begin{cases} 0.45\frac{\rho}{2}Av^3 & v < v_R \\ P_R & v \geq v_R \end{cases} \tag{1}$$

where ρ is the air density, A is the rotor area and v is the wind speed. For wind below rated we speak about partial power or partial power regime, above we have rated power. Power regulation is done by pitching the blades. The transition from partial to rated power in the power curve is oversimplified in this model. The real power curve does not have a cusp but is smoothly varying. The precise form depends on turbulence and the controller. But for the present purpose the equation above is sufficient.

The rated wind speed where the turbine reaches rated power is given by the approximate formula

$$v_R = \left(\frac{4\ P_R}{9\ A\ \rho}\right)^{1/3} \tag{2}$$

Let us consider as an example a WT with 8 MW rated power and 164 m rotor diameter. The rotor area of this turbine is 21,124 m^2 and the approximate rated wind speed is 11.2 m/s.[5] From the above equation one can see that rated wind depends on air density ρ and the ratio P_R/A which is called specific power of the WT.

Besides the power curve also the wind speed distribution is needed. From the wind-speed distribution the time (in hours for example) can be obtained with wind speed assuming a value within a certain wind bin, for instance from 8 to 9 m/s. The wind speed distribution can be described by a Weibull function (2)

$$F(v) = 1 - exp\left(-(v/A)^k\right) \tag{3}$$

with parameter A and k which can be used to fit a measured wind speed distribution. $F(v)$ expresses the probability that the wind speed is below v.

For the special case $k = 2$ the Weibull function is also called Rayleigh function. For many real sites where OWF are installed presently, the frequency distribution can be fitted with a Weibull function with k near 2. So when we need a quick estimate one can just use the Rayleigh function.

Combing the wind speed distribution and the power curve, the result can by displayed in a diagram like Figure 1.3. Since time in bins is expressed in hours and

5 The data are derived from the simple model described in the text above. The power curve of a given WT will normally be measured by a certified institute and provided to customers by the manufacturer.

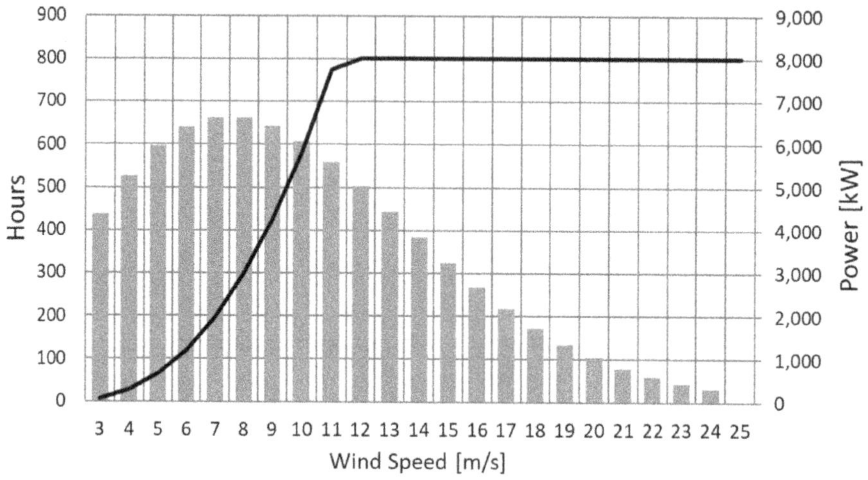

Figure 1.3: Wind speed distribution (bars) versus power curve (solid line) of WT with 164 m rotor and 8 MW rated power.

power in kW one can easily obtain the number of kWh generated in a given bin by multiplication. For the AEP calculation an availability of the turbine of 97% has been assumed.

The black line is the approximate power curve. The grey bars represent the time (hours) the WT operates at a certain wind speed. The model can be made more precise and sophisticated, but this does not change the results very much. The result for the AEP is 38.5 Mio. kWh or 38.5 GWh which the turbine generates at a site with 10 m/s mean wind speed at hub height.

An important quantity in this context is the capacity factor (KAPPA). It is defined as the ratio between the AEP and the energy produced with wind turbine always at rated power. The latter is 8,000 kW times 8,760 hours (per year) corresponding to 70 GWH, such that KAPPA=0.55. The same can also be expressed in terms of full-load hours which is the time needed to generate the AEP at rated power. In our example we have 4,815 full-load hours.

KAPPA depends on the wind speed at the site and on the specific power. Clearly more wind leads to higher KAPPA. In addition the factor is increased by lowering the specific power discussed in the context of equation (2).

Figure 1.3 illustrates that the maximum of the frequency distribution is well in the partial power regime. This is the case for most WT. But with lower specific power the power curve is shifted to the left towards the maximum which explains the growing AEP with declining specific power.

In our example the specific power is 380 W/m^2. In the past the specific power of OWT was often higher, for instance 500 W/m^2. Going to lower specific power has been one of the trends of WT and OWT for many years. This trend is not independent of the trend to lower solidity. The longer more slender blades make it possible to increase the rotor area in an economically feasible way.

Which specific power is recommended can be discussed. From the perspective of a utility we would like to have high KAPPA. This can be reached by increasing the rotor at given power rating or reducing the power rating. Given the rated power of 8,000 kW, if the rotor is increased to 180 m the AEP will be 40.8 GWh and KAPPA increases to 0.58. Taking the rotor diameter as 150 m the AEP goes down to 36.0 GWh with KAPPA = 0.51. For comparison at a site on land with 7.5 m/s at hub height the 164 m turbine would generate 26.2 GWH with KAPPA 0.38. So the benefit from going offshore is significant.

1.2.4 Cost of Energy

For any power plant the cost of energy is an important figure. Normally it is measured in EUR-Cents/kWh, EUR/MWh or in other relevant currencies. The cost of energy have to be compared with the amount for which the energy can be sold. The latter should be higher than the former. The cost of energy is determined by two factors, the investment costs also called capital expenditures (CAPEX) and the operational expenditures (OPEX). Since a certain amount of money is not the same now and in 10 years, say, one also has to take into account a yearly discount rate that relates quantities from the future to the present. The result is called the levelized cost of energy (Kost, 2018). Neglecting for simplicity the discount rate, the cost of energy is written in the form:

$$\text{Cost of Energy} = \frac{\text{CAPEX} + \sum_{\text{years}} \text{OPEX}}{\sum_{\text{years}} \text{AEP}} \tag{4}$$

where the sum extends over the years of operation of the WT.

Of course the CAPEX is very important. For land-based WT CAPEX is dominated by the WT itself which is about 70% of the investment. Other costs are for foundation, grid connection, planning, etc. In reference (Skiba, 2012) some figures are given that can be considered as typical for projects carried out in the recent past. In an offshore installation the WT is only about 30% of the CAPEX. Other large contributions to CAPEX are installation (18%) and substructure/foundation (26%). Under the bottom line, the investment is about 1 Mio EUR per MW installed for land and 2–3 Mio EUR per MW for offshore, where the CAPEX for offshore are decreasing rapidly. OPEX values can be very roughly estimated as a certain percentage of the CAPEX, something between 5 and 10% per year with a tendency to decrease.

Using the above equation and the result for the AEP for the 8 MW turbine obtained in the previous section, assuming 10% OPEX costs and 25 years lifetime of the turbine, one obtains cost of energy of about €c 10 /kWh. This is a level that has

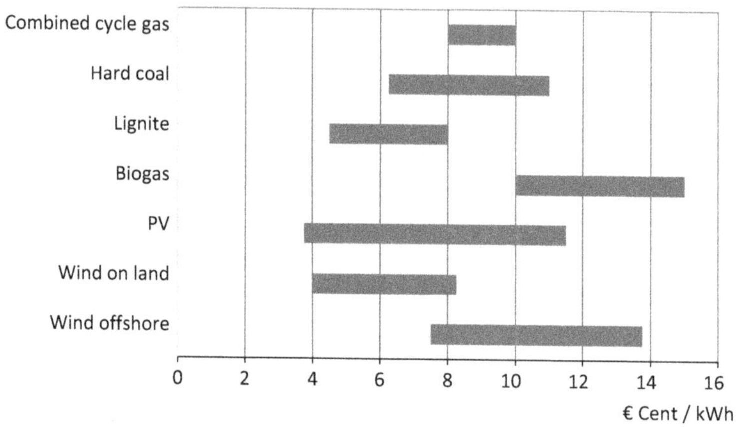

Figure 1.4: LCOE for electricity generation from renewable and other sources according to (Kost, 2018).

been achieved in recent projects. In Figure 1.4 the results for LCOE obtained a study of Fraunhofer ISE published in 2018 (Kost, 2018) are shown. Offshore wind energy is roughly between 8 and €c 14 /kWh.

There are several levers which can be considered for cost reduction:

- The AEP can be increased with larger rotors/longer blades. The challenge is that the ratio CAPEX/AEP is getting smaller.
- Another way to lower COE is to increase the lifetime of the WT. This is in fact one of the trends in wind energy technology. WT were designed for 20 years service life for many years. In view of the relatively large CAPEX this is short. Conventional power plants are designed for much longer lifetime. OWT are now designed for 25 years. 30 years have at least been discussed. One has to bear in mind however that the extension of lifetime is not for free. Fatigue plays an important role in the design of WT. So increasing of service life should run parallel to reducing fatigue loading.
- CAPEX costs as such need to be lowered. The main levers here are the substructures and the installation process. Some ideas to reduce these costs are discussed below.
- OPEX costs can be lowered by improving service concepts and reliability of WT.
- The so-called scale of commerce might be most important in this context. Processes in each sector that are relevant for offshore wind energy become more cost-efficient with increasing experience and larger projects. Competition among OEM and companies of the supply chain also leads to lower costs. Standardization of components would also contribute to lowering costs.

Various researches predict a fast decline of LCOE in the future. A summary of several studies can be found in a communication of the Danish Ministry of Energy, Utilities and Climate.[6] In conclusion the CAPEX and OPEX are expected to come down to 50% or even less compared to present day values until 2030. This would lead to LCOE of 5 or 6 EUR Cents/kWh, about the same as present day land-based WT.

1.3 Offshore Wind Turbines

1.3.1 Elements of an Offshore Wind Turbine

An example for an offshore wind turbine (OWT) with monopile foundation is shown in Figure 1.5. The WT consists of the rotor, the nacelle and the tower. Commonly rotor and nacelle are called rotor nacelle assembly (RNA). The part of the OWT below the tower that is partly in the water is by definition called substructure. In Figure 1.5 the substructure is composed of a transition piece and part of the monopile. This is by far the most frequently used technology for OWT.

The monopile is driven into the seabed thus providing the foundation of the OWT. The combination of substructure and tower is sometimes called the support structure.

In the case of floating substructures the connection to the seabed is provided by mooring lines. Different types of substructures will be discussed below.

In case of OWT normally the tower (relative to the rotor diameter) is lower than for WT on land. The reason for this is low turbulence close to the water surface. The rotor needs not to be lifted much above the surface.

To provide an example for the dimensions of state of the art OWT we consider the MHI Vestas V164. In the wind farm Horns Rev 3 this WT was installed on a monopile foundation.[7] Some data are available.[8] The hub height is 105 m. The transition piece ends about 15 m above the mean sea level. So the distance of the blade tip to the sea surface is 25 m. The maximum blade tip height is 185 m which is lower than the tip height of most recently installed WT on land. The height of the substructure depends on the water depth. The latter in this project is 6 to 13 m.

1.3.2 Evolution of Technology

The following account is not complete and biased by the personal experience of the author. The first commercial offshore wind farms were installed in the early nineties

6 ens.dk/sites/ens.dk/files/Energibesparelser/note_on_technology_costs_for_offshore_wind_turbines.pdf.

7 See: corporate.vattenfall.dk/globalassets/danmark/vores_vindmoller/horns_rev_3/hr3_nyhedsbrev_01.pdf.

8 Press release from MHI Vestas Offshore Wind (2017), http://www.mhivestasoffshore.com/burbo-bank-extension-inauguration/.

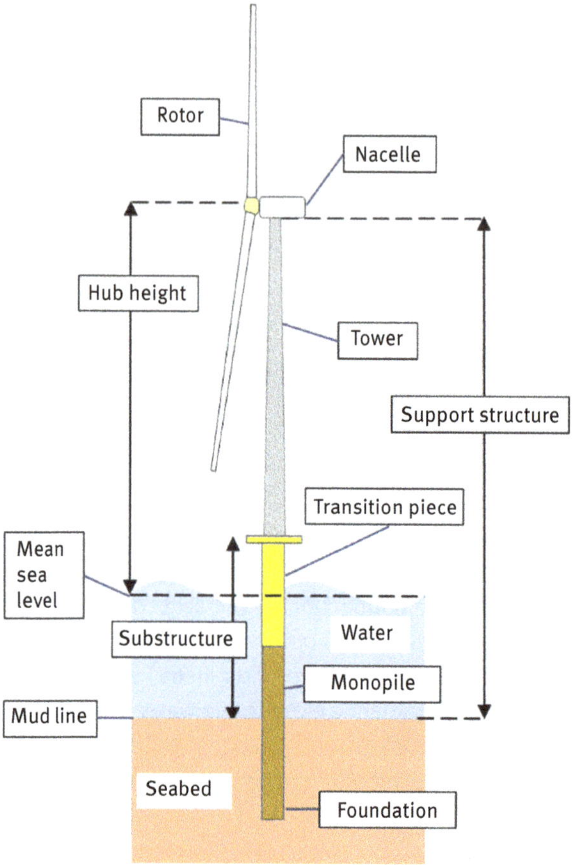

Figure 1.5: Schematic sketch of an OWT on monopile. Details described in the text.

near the shores of Sweden, Denmark and the Netherlands. The WT had power ratings of a few hundred kW and rotor diameters of about 40 m. Moreover the WT were largely identical with land-based models with some minor modifications for offshore application. Also the sites of the early offshore wind farms are typically close to the shore.

Around 2000 some manufacturers and engineering firms started OWT development projects. An example is the NOK (Norddeutsches Offshore Konsortium) formed by the companies Nordex, Jacobs Energy and pro+pro that started to develop a 5 MW WT with about 110 m rotor diameter. After one year Nordex stepped out of the consortium and the newly formed Repower continued the development that finally led to the Repower (now Senvion) 5M.

An important milestone was the installation of 80 Vestas V80 (2 MW rated power) in the year 2002 in the Horns Rev I wind farm near the Danish west coast.

Similarly one year later 77 WT of AN Bonus (2.3 MW rated power) where erected in the wind farm Nysted in the Baltic Sea. AN Bonus shortly after was taken over by Siemens such that this model is usually referred to as Siemens SWT 2.3 80.

One can assume these two wind farms paved the way for the dominance of Siemens and Vestas in the OWT market. Together the companies have now a cumulative market share of about 80%, a tough situation for competitors.

At the beginning of the present century, WT with 5 MW rated power and somewhat more than 100 m rotor diameter were thought to be the future OWT. This is sometimes called the second generation of OWT. Prototypes of Areva, Repower and Bard were installed around 2005 in Germany at or near the shore. However, the market success of these models was limited. The major wind farm projects were mainly supplied with much smaller WT of Siemens and Vestas. Siemens 3.6 MW with 120 m rotor and some variants and Vestas 3 MW with 90 m and 112 m rotor.[9] Both WT are based on models originally developed for installation on land.

An important step for offshore wind energy was the German pilot wind farm alpha ventus with 12 OWT with power rating 5 MW, six Repower 5 M and six Areva Multibrid. The project was accompanied by research done with public funding under the Acronym RAVE.[10] Also important in this context was the installation of three research platforms Fino1 to Fino3, two in the North Sea and one in the Baltic Sea. These platforms brought a wealth of information on environmental conditions at offshore sites that was not available before.

In 2013 also the offshore wind farm (OWF) BARD I was completed. BARD, the project developer, had also its own WT design with 5 MW rated power. After completion of the first project, the company went bankrupt, contributing now still 2.1% of installed power capacity in OWF.

From about 2010 on a number of manufacturers started to develop larger OWT thus giving rise to a third generation of OWT. The step from 5 MW to machines with power rating of 6 to 8 MW and rotor diameters of 160 to 180 m was taken.

Siemens Wind Power, the company with most offshore experience, decided to change their drivetrain concept and move to a DDG in the SWT 6–154. Vestas decided after detailed feasibility studies for a concept sometimes called hybrid drive train using a medium speed generator. More industry companies entered the offshore competition. General Electric (GE) made a first attempt that ended with a prototype, a concept with DDG at the downwind side of the tower. In 2014 GE took over the power division of Alstom and in this way acquired the Haliade concept with 6 MW, 160 m rotor and DDG.

Other companies started new development projects. For instance Samsung as well as other Korean companies also developed large OWT. More recently also

9 Data from (Wikipedia, 2018).

10 Details under www.rave-offshore.de.

Chinese manufacturers started to design new turbines. The Chinese offshore wind capacity is increasing rapidly and catching up with European countries concerning the yearly installation rates (GWEC, 2019).

1.3.3 Drivetrain Concepts

The basic concept of a WT consists of the rotor (aerodynamic rotor) that drives the generator (generator rotor). In comparison to many other concepts for electricity generation the speed of the aerodynamic rotor in a large machine is low. As discussed in section 1.2.2 above, the rotor speed of a WT like the Vestas V164 is – at rated conditions – at about 10 rpm such that either a generator is needed that is designed for such low speed or one needs a gearbox to convert the speed to a higher value. As a consequence WT come in two different types, the geared WT and the direct-drive WT.

Electrical machines for many applications have a low number of pole pairs and, thus, are effectively designed for relatively high speed rating at or near synchronous speed. This means for example 1000 rpm or 1500 rpm in the 50 Hz grid. When a converter is used to obtain speed variability, the generator speed is not directly determined by the grid frequency, but still the generator has to be operated in a range near the synchronous speed. The generators with speed rating at 1000 rpm or above are called high-speed generators (HSG).

As a consequence a turbine with a HSG needs a gearbox that in the case of the large OWT would need a gear ratio of 100 or 150 to convert the 10 rpm to 1000 or 1500 rpm. Such a gear ratio can be designs with a sequence of planetary and/or spur gear stages. Typical gear ratio of a single stage is around 5, such that with three stages one can achieve a gear ratio of 125. This would make the combination of the large aerodynamic rotor with a high-speed generator designed for 1000 rpm feasible. The advantage of this concept is that the generator in such a WT is a relatively inexpensive component. The costs of the electrical machine at a given power rating are largely determined by the torque it generates. Torque is reduced by the gearbox to 1/nG of its original value. So the gearbox has been a very attractive solution especially for WT with smaller rotors. Most of the older models of WT used gearboxes.

Of course the gearbox itself is also a demanding mechanical device. It contains many parts that have to be fabricated with high precision. Lubrication has to work properly. When wind industry started to use gearboxes there was ample experience with this technology from others fields like for example automotive. Nevertheless the use of gearboxes in WT due to the different environment and loading was burdened by many problems. There were many premature gearbox failures such that WT without gearbox with a direct-drive generator (DDG) became increasingly attractive.

For a long time until about 10 years ago only the German WT manufacturer Enercon was really successful on the Market with DDG. Since that time more manufacturers like

Goldwind, Siemens, and General Electric came up with direct drive, while Enercon, still one of the major WT manufacturers, has withdrawn from offshore wind energy.

The DDG designed for low speed have a large number of poles. They can be either electrically excited or equipped with permanent magnets. The poles are located on a ring with a relatively large diameter that, depending on the individual design, has typically diameters of 5 to 10 m. The generator rotor can be either outside the stator or inside the stator, inner or outer rotor. In all these machines the air gap between the electrically active material (copper windings or permanent magnets) of stator and rotor needs to be very tiny compared to the ring diameter, for example 5 mm compared to more than 5 m. The challenge in such a DDG concept is to provide a stable air gap. When the WT is operating deformations in the drive train will occur. So one has to design the drive train such that the loads do not affect the air gap in such a way that rotor and stator get in contact and get damaged.

The air-gap stability can be achieved either by using a massive and therefore stiff generator structure that leads to a heavy nacelle or by designing the drive train such the loads are not affecting the air gap. As shown below there are solutions for the air gap issue but the technical risk coming with a new DDG concept was the reason that wind industry continued to use geared concepts and will still do so in the future, at least in the land-based sector.

Additionally to the classical geared type and the DDG concept there is a drive train concept that is sometimes called hybrid drive train. This concept does not use a classical three-stage gearbox but one or two planetary stages only. With such a concept one needs a so-called medium-speed generator (MSG). Let us assume the gearbox provides a gear ratio of 30, with the aerodynamic rotor working at 10 rpm one needs a generator designed for 300 rpm. Such a MSG is much smaller and lighter than the DDG. Since both gearbox and generator are rather compact concerning their axial dimension they can be flanged together to form a single unit. For instance the MHI Vestas V164 and its variants are based upon such a concept.

In conclusion, there are three different basic concepts without and with gearbox and with direct-drive, medium-speed or high-speed generator. In each group are many different variants of the arrangement of the mechanical components.

An important point that has impact on the rest of the drive train is the rotor bearing concept. The rotor bearing is also called main bearing. In the first place the main bearing supports the rotor. The rotor can be carried by a shaft or by a non-rotating axle.[11] The bearing has to support the weight of the rotor and the forces and bending moments that are product by the wind. In present-day WT the bending moments are normally dimensioning for the components at the low-speed side of the drivetrain. Without gearbox, of course, there is no high-speed side.

11 The axle is often also called king pin.

The main bearing concept may consist of two bearings as for instance a combination of a two-row spherical roller bearing and a cylinder roller bearing that are assembled in a certain distance in the axial direction. Also two tapered roller bearings in a certain distance that are prestressed against each other inside a joint housing can be used. Alternatively a moment bearing can be used. The moment bearing is a unit where the two rings are close to each other with a large diameter. A popular variant of the moment bearing is the two-row tapered roller bearing.

An important issue is the degree of integration in the drivetrain. This means that different functions are taken over by one component. Often bearings are integrated. In most of the concepts with DDG the generator does not have an extra bearing but the generator rotor is supported by the main bearing. Of course this has an impact on the generator design and one has to do a careful analysis concerning air gap stability.

Another example of integration is that the bearing of the first planetary stage of a gearbox can be used as the main bearing. Similarly the loads transferred to the gearbox need to be known very well and if this is not the case it might entail problems with the gearbox. So integration is often also considered a technical risk.

The main motivation for integration is certainly cost reduction. Bearings are expensive components that in addition need maintenance such that both CAPEX and OPEX can be reduced by integration. Another aspect is reduction of the size of the nacelle in axial direction. The so called separated drive train without integration is rather long in the axial direction. A more compact drive train might entail advantages concerning transportation. If we look in the past, most of the OWT have been of the classical gear-type with separated drive train. More details can be found in (Hau, 2013) and other text books.

The potential technical risks coming with integration sometimes lead to the opposite move that deliberately certain functions are separated. The objective of such design variants is to protect either generator or gearbox from unwanted loads, mainly the bending moments from unequal blade loads. If this bending moment is supported by two bearings it is converted to two forces in lateral direction, perpendicular to the rotation axis, often called off-axial loads. The objective of the decoupling is to transfer only torque to the generator or gearbox and guide the off-axial loads directly guided to the tower. An example of such a decoupling is the Haliade concept of General Electric.[12]

Looking at the 10 biggest WT[13] that are presently built or planned for offshore projects worldwide there are only 4 left with HSG. Five of these WT are manufactured by European companies. There is only one, the Senvion 6.2 MW 152, with a classical gearbox concept. There are two MSG and two with DDG.

12 www.ge.com/renewableenergy/wind-energy/turbines/offshore-turbine-haliade.

13 www.windpowermonthly.com/10-biggest-turbines.

1.3.4 Electrical Concepts

The power generation system modern WT consists of a generator, the converter and some additional components like filter, a transformer, etc. There are three concepts for the power generation the systems that are presently used.[14]

- The double fed induction generator with partial converter
- The induction generator the full-size converter and
- The synchronous generator with full-size converter that can be either permanently or electrically excited

The first two concepts have so far not been used in the context of medium- or low-speed machines, such that all hybrid or direct-drive WT work with synchronous generators. In addition generators can be classified according to the direction of the magnetic flux in the air gap. In principle the flux can be radial, axial or transversal with respect to the orientation of the drivetrain. Although many concepts have been proposed, for commercial WT only generators with radial flux have been used.

For direct-drive turbines there is another distinction possible. The radial flux concept allows for outer and inner rotor, where outer and inner refers to the radial position of the rotor relative to the stator. Electrical machines with radial flux commonly work with inner rotor. The low-speed high-pole generator typically have an overall disk-like shape. Due to this geometric property the bearing and the support structure of the generator rotor can be one-sided and open to the other side. This makes the outer rotor feasible, first used in the Genesys project (Klinger, 2004). It is now used in all Goldwind turbines and also by Siemens. It will be explained in more details below.

Besides the generator the converter is the most important electrical component in modern WT. With the converter it is possible to adjust the speed to a value with optimum power at wind speed below rated. For higher wind speeds pitching of the blades is used to regulate or limit the power to its rated value. The basic concepts used for OWT are the same as on land. So I will not go into the details at this point.

Another issue is the voltage level used in the power generation system. Traditionally a voltage of 690 V was used. The advantage is that 690 V is regarded as low voltage such that safety and insulation efforts are still moderate. Service people do not need special training to work in the nacelle that would be needed for medium voltage. The disadvantage is clearly the large cross-sections of the cables needed at higher power rating. Especially when the converter is located at the tower

14 Altogether four concepts have been used so far. The directly coupled induction generator was used in the old Danish concept. In present-day utility-size wind turbines it is not used anymore and will not be discussed here.

bottom, the cable loop that connects nacelle (yawing) with the tower (not yawing) needs a lot of copper.

As a consequence there is a trend to work at higher voltage. Concepts for generator and inverter that work on a level of 3.3 kV are available. The planned model Haliade X of General Electric works on a voltage level of 6 kV.

Alternatively the big cables can be avoided by installing the transformer to medium voltage in the nacelle. This means that the complete power generation system including the converter is located on top of the tower. Since service personal is normally transported by helicopter to the turbine, the location of the main components in the nacelle can be regarded as an advantage. Disadvantage is that the converter and transformer add to the weight of the nacelle what, in turn, will increase the costs for the tower somewhat to provide the necessary dynamic properties. These additional costs have to be compared with the savings reached with smaller cables and the other aspects mentioned.

Concerning the efficiency both the generator and the converter are in the range of 96–97%. The transformer has an efficiency of 99%, such that from the electrical system we have losses in the range of 7–9%. The losses might be somewhat higher in direct-drive generators. If a gearbox is used the additional mechanical losses amount for approximately 1% per stage.

As a rule of thumb one has 10% loss from the aerodynamic power to the electrical power fed in to the medium voltage grid. In the large OWT like the V164 the 10% correspond to 800 kW thermal output which require efficient cooling concepts for gearbox, generator and converter.

1.3.5 General Electric, MHI Vestas, and Siemens Gamesa

In this section we will discuss in more detail the concepts that are used by the leading manufacturers for OWT. It is very likely that Siemens Gamesa (SG), MHI Vestas (MV) and General Electric (GE) will be the major players in the European and American markets. In the Asian markets also Chinese companies like Goldwind and other will be important.

As stated previously, in OWT the trend is clearly towards direct-drive and hybrid designs SG and GE propose direct drive. MV propose a design with gearbox and medium-speed generator. Let us have a closer look at the different concepts.

The SG concept used in several variants of the turbine is based on a permanently excited generator with outer rotor. The concept is shown in schematic form in Figure 1.6. A moment bearing is used for both the aerodynamic rotor and the generator (integration). The hub is directly connected to the generator rotor that has to be open backwards. The bearing concept could be different, for instance two separate bearings mounted on an axle. But the moment bearing has a number of advantages – one of

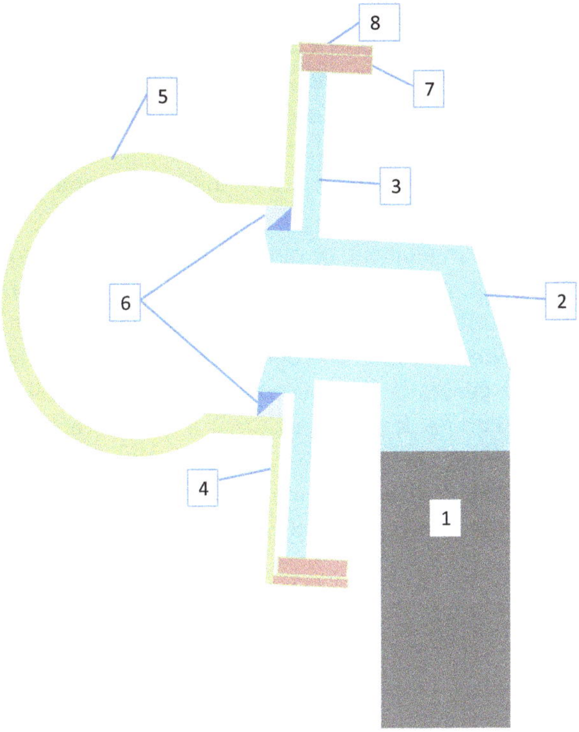

Figure 1.6: SG concepts with outer rotor and moment bearing.[15]

them is that axles or shafts are not needed anymore, the reason why this bearing-type is used in many new wind turbine designs.

One might object that such a design is unbalanced concerning the heavy items rotor and generator. But this only entails that the yaw bearing is somewhat more loaded than in the situation when the generator would be installed at the down-wind side of the tower. With this solution a shaft is needed to transfer the torque from up- to down-wind side and the generator needs an extra bearing. The resulting design would be certainly heavier and more expensive than the SG design.

A serious issue for which a reliable solution is needed is air-gap stability. As mentioned above we have the 5 mm air gap while the overall diameter of the generator at air gap radius is up to 10 m. Now the bending moment (discussed in the previous section) acts on the generator rotor and through the bearing on the axle. The loads inevitably cause a certain amount of deformation of the arrangement and thus a change of air gap thickness. The challenge for the SG design is to keep the

15 Tower (1), main frame/axle(2), stator structure (3), rotor structure (4), hub (5), bearing (6), stator coils (7), outer rotor/magnets (8), own representation.

relative deflection of the generator rotor with respect to the stator small and to develop a model of the structural design which allows a precise prediction of the air gap response to the loading. Quite obviously the former is achieved by keeping the axial distance between the rotor and the stator small. For the latter the state of the art is to design a detailed finite-element model that takes into account all relevant properties of bearing, axle and other structural items, allowing to analyze the structural response in detail.

The SG design can be used with axle moment bearing also for an inner rotor generator. This is the generator bearing concept of the GE Haliade 6 MW. In this WT, however, the hub is not directly attached to the generator rotor by a bolt connection. Instead generator and aerodynamic rotor have both their own bearing. The transfer of torque from the hub to the generator is achieved with a special coupling using elastic material. The coupling can be designed such that it is relatively stiff with respect to torsion but much softer with respect to bending such that the generator rotor can be largely decoupled from the bending moment. This is the so-called "pure torque" concept of the GE Haliade shown schematically in Figure 1.7.

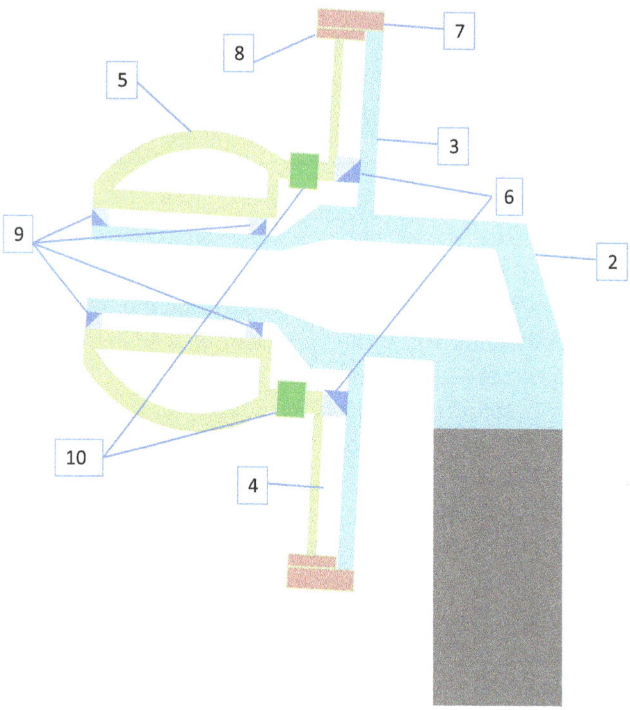

Figure 1.7: GE "pure torque" concept with inner rotor and separate bearing for generator and rotor. New compared to items in Figure 1.6 are rotor bearing (9) and elastic coupling (10).

The off-axial loads are of course acting on the bearings (9) and will lead to bending of the axle. This should not have any influence on the air gap since the generator bearing (6) is not affected by the off-axial loads. Any deflection of the axle and machine frame will lead to a deflection of the whole generator but does not influence the air gap. The cost of the pure-torque concept is an additional bearing, a coupling that has to transfer large torque and an axle that is several meters longer than in the SG design.

For the planned 10–12 MW turbine Haliade X whose first prototype will be installed in 2019 it has not yet been disclosed whether the pure torque concept will be used or not. One might guess that for cost reasons the Haliade X comes with a drive train concept that is more like the one of SG only with inner rotor.

Last but not least the MV concept will be discussed. As displayed in Figure 1.8 the concept has a main shaft supported two bearings. Attached to the main frame (2) is also the gearbox and the generator. The torque is transferred from main shaft to gearbox by an elastic coupling (8). In this way the off-axial loads are supported by the bearings (6) and are largely decoupled from the gearbox (4). Depending on

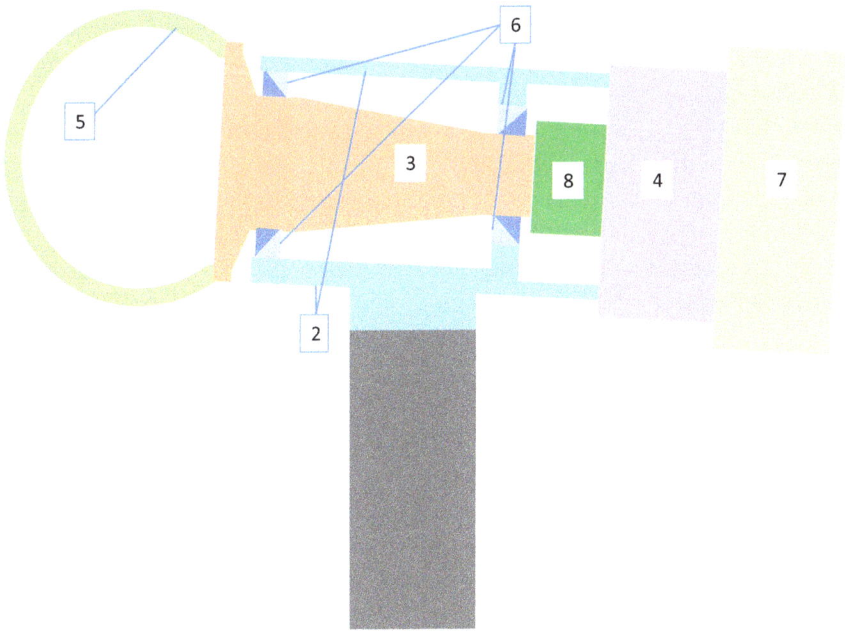

Figure 1.8: MV concept with gearbox and medium speed generator.[16]

16 Main frame (2), main shaft (3), gearbox (4), hub (5), rotor bearing (6), generator (7), coupling (8), own representation.

the bending stiffness of the coupling, the overall deformation and the precision of the alignment of the components along the drivetrain axis some residual off-axial loads or constraint loads might still be transferred to the gearbox.

The level of integration in the MV drivetrain is relatively low. Gearbox and probably also generator have individual bearings. A main shaft is needed which is a relatively costly component in such a large machine. The protection of the gearbox against off-axial loads is on the cost of an extra coupling that has to be designed for the torque in the low-speed shaft.

It is stated by MV (Bach Andersen, 2011) that the combination of gearbox and medium-speed generator is less costly than a direct-drive generator of this dimension. One has to take into account, however, that the gearbox needs a large quantity of oil that is absent in the SG and GE concepts. Further the elastic coupling, comparable in functionality to the one of GE "pure torque" is a costly component. Also the rotor bearing concepts of GE and MV are very much comparable in terms of extra effort only that GE uses the axle (not rotating) and MV a shaft (directly connected to the hub and rotating).

Compared to GE, the generator structure of the SG machine should be somewhat heavier since the air gap needs to be stabilized with respect to higher off-axial loads. However, the stability can be achieved by an intelligent design with detailed control of loads and deformations, such the extra effort made by GE "pure torque" and MV seems questionable.

As said already, these three concepts might dominate the market during the next years. The Goldwind concept (also DDG with outer rotor) is very similar to SG such that even from global perspective the three concepts described might be the ones used in most OWT during the next 5 or 10 years. Which one is better will be decided by many factors and with time. For land-based turbines the number of different drivetrain concepts is larger.

1.3.6 Loads on OWT

Extracting power from the wind generates loads on the rotor blades, not only a propulsion force that provides the torque but also thrust on the rotor area that has to be supported by the tower. Moreover due to turbulence and, related to this, the increase of average wind speed with height above the sea source, the aerodynamic forces are not balanced which causes bending moments with respect to the axis of rotation. Due to lower turbulence intensity these loads are lower in OWT than on land but are still large enough to be dimensioning for some components of the drive train. As mentioned already below, the bending and also forces that are oriented perpendicular to the axis of rotation are the so-called of axial loads in contrast to thrust in axial direction and torque.

In addition the off-axial loads are fluctuating. In 3-bladed WT they come to some extent with 3-fold rotor frequency, then also called 3-p loads. Why 3-p can be easily explained. Consider a gust that goes through the rotor area but affects only the upper part of the rotor. Each blade runs through the gust possibly several times. As a consequence of this so-called "gust slizing" the aerodynamic force on a blade changes during each passage thus giving rise to thrust on the rotor that varies with 3-fold rotor frequency.

Loading that is not immediately related to the wind can be effected by ice. Under certain conditions ice can occur on the surface of the rotor blades that might cause temporary loading of the blades. In the wake the wind is more turbulent that the ambient wind. So in farms this added turbulence due to neighboring rotors needs to be taken into account.

Now for OWTs also loads on the substructure have to be taken into account. The main impact certainly comes from waves. At particular cites, in German waters for instance in the Baltic sea, in addition ice impact on the substructure has to be considered. Further there may be currents exerting loads on the substructure. Wave loads may to some extent also be influenced by marine growth. Certainly for floating OWT the marine growth has to be considered.

Another phenomenon that affects the foundation is scour. Scour is caused by currents and the result is that material surrounding the foundation (the monopile in Figure 1.9) are removed that either has to be prevented by scour protection or has to be taken into account in the foundation design.

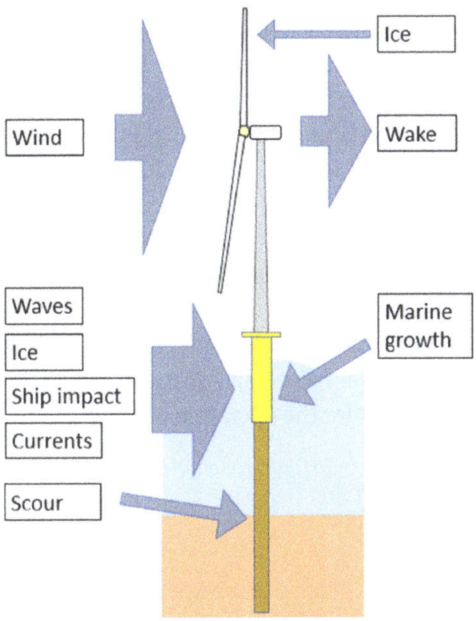

Figure 1.9: Different impacts that contribute to the loads on OWT.

Aerodynamic and wave loads are of unsteady or even periodic nature. The structure elements are flexible to a certain extent (blades, support structure) and wind and waves may cause vibration or in general a response of the structure. When designing the WT the structural dynamics has to be well known and under control. This is achieved with simulation codes that are taking into account the relevant dynamics of the WT and the relevant impacts shown in Figure 1.9. Within the simulation model it is even possible to optimize the control procedures such that the response of the structure to external impacts is kept small and also transient states of the WT like start or stop procedures do not increase the loading too much.

1.3.7 Wind Turbine Control and Load Mitigation

The WT controller monitors and controls hundreds of parameters. Essential parameters that determine the state of the system are rotor speed, torque/power and blade pitch angle. The basic control concept of all recent WT is variable speed and power regulation by pitching the blades. Variable speed is used to optimize the power generation at wind speed below rated. The blade pitch is used to regulate the power to rated power above rated wind. These procedures equip the WT with a power curve shown in Figure 1.3.

If pitch and torque could not be controlled, the WT would just be a large elastic structure passively reacting to wind and waves. With pitch and torque one can generate a counter force stabilizing the WT or damping vibrations. One direction that is pursued by many WT manufacturers and researchers is individual pitch control (IPC). As explained before gusty wind causes off-axial loads that increase fatigue loading and thus have a significant impact on the design and the cost. By measuring blade loads or deflection, with a suitable algorithm it is possible to change the blade angle such that the thrust on the individual blades is more balanced. Some progress in this direction has been made recently, for a publication see (Shan, 2013).

Rotor thrust fluctuations due to turbulence and waves cause vibrations of the support structure in back-and-forth direction. The pitch has an immediate effect on power and thrust of the WT and can be used to damp tower vibrations in the back-and-forth direction (Burton, 2011). Further by controlling the torque one can generate effectively damping of drive train vibrations and vibrations in the sideways direction. These methods are in particular used for instance for floating substructures where the dynamical phenomena are even more important for the operation of the WT.

1.3.8 Special Requirements for Offshore Wind Turbines

Compared to WT on land, OWT operate in a much harsher environment. Especially salt water and humid and salty air cause corrosion. Surfaces that are directly exposed have to be protected by coatings that are used also for ships and other offshore structures. They are thicker than the ones used on land. For parts of the structure that are only exposed to the water and not to the air, in recent projects coating was not used. They are dimensioned in such a way that corrosion is taken into account. Also sacrificial anodes are used for corrosion protection.

Inside the tower and the nacelle it is more challenging. The interior the WT cannot be simply sealed from outside air. At least not according to the present state of the art. The cooling system transports heat to the outside air via heat exchangers. A certain amount, roughly 10 to 20% of the waste heat dissipates via the surface of components to the air inside the tower or the nacelle. This is true for mechanical and electrical components. As a consequence one needs exchange of air at a relatively high rate. State of the technology is to remove moisture and salt from the air with special equipment before it is brought to the interior. For WT on land this is normally not needed.

1.3.9 New and Alternative Technologies

So far the focus was on commercial OWT. The history of wind energy is full of innovative concepts. Only few of them have been commercially successful. For OWF nowadays large investments are necessary to develop new technology to the commercial stage. Still there are many ideas for new technologies on the market. Having not time and space to discuss all new and alternative technologies, here only two directions will be mentioned.

Publicly funded research projects have been carried out on next-generation OWT. The rationale behind funding such projects by tax-payers money is that the technology is relevant for future energy supply and for individual companies it might be too risky to develop innovative technology at the scale of an OWT. One example of a project where several research institutes and companies from industry cooperated is Innwind (Hjuler Jensen, 2017) funded by the European Union.

In this project many possible conceptual solutions for the next-generation OWT have been analyzed. All parts of the OWT have been treated, the blades, the drive train, the power generation system, etc. One direction of research is passively pitching blades. As already mentioned the blade pitch is used to regulate power and to start and stop the WT. For the power regulation at wind speeds above rated wind small changes of the blade angle are needed to keep the power at rated. The idea is that small changes can be done by designing the blade structure in such a way that increasing loads on the blade automatically leads to pitching, the so called coupling of bending and torsion. The objective is that short-term fluctuations can be regulated passively, such that something similar to individual pitch control would work passively without using the drives or measuring the blade loads.

In the Innwind project also new drivetrain concepts were explored. An interesting idea is to arrange the generator in front of the rotor. With such a solution no additional shaft for transferring the torque would be needed but the generator, in case of damage, in principle could be replaced without dismantling further majors part of the WT or even the complete RNA. So far this work had little impact on the technologies of the major industrial players described above. The three WT described in the previous section do no use Innwind concepts. So one has to wait for a new generation of WT to come in 5 or 10 years.

Another idea for OWT is to revive the two-bladed rotor. Presently practically all WT are three-bladed. In the history of wind energy there was a time – 30 or 40 years ago – when the two-bladed rotor was considered as most promising for the future. Obviously two-bladed models have not been very successful commercially so far. But after many years of very little activity in this sector, in recent years several companies have invested in the development of two-bladed OWT.

One nice potential feature of a two-bladed design is a teeter hinge. This idea is quite old and was used in the mentioned experimental prototypes (Hau, 2013). In one of the recent projects[17] the teeter hinge is inside the hub such that to a large extent the bending moment is not transferred to the drive train. So besides the active and passive individual pitching this is another concept to reduce unwanted off-axial loads.

Last but not least also VAWT have been proposed as OWT. With VAWT working on lift, called Darrieus turbines, one achieves a good power coefficient, something like 0.4 aerodynamically according to text books. The great advantage of the VAWT is that they do not have to be turned into the wind direction due to the aerodynamic concept. The SeaTwirl is such a concept.[18] The SeaTwirl is a so-called H-Darrieus rotor, where the blades, the aerodynamic active components, are kept in position by horizontal or slightly inclined arms. This concept is quite successful for small WT. The challenge for the large OWT is to obtain structural stability, i.e., keeping the aerodynamically active blades in a stable position with a reasonable amount of structural material (tower and arms).

Concerning the alternative concepts that are proposed mainly by small companies and startups it will be very difficult to compete with the established technologies in any OWF project. There could be niche markets for these concepts. Alternative technologies could also have a chance after 20 or 30 years, when the present-day installations have to be replaced.

1.4 Offshore Wind Farms

1.4.1 Layout of OWF and Efficiency

WT in a wind farm need to have a certain distance to their neighbors. The reason for this are the rotor wakes. In the wake that extends downwind from the rotor the

17 seawindtechnology.com.

18 seatwirl.com.

wind speed is decreased and the turbulence is increased. Thus the power production of a nearby neighbor operating in the wake is reduced and the impact due to turbulence is increased. The increased turbulence causes fatigue loading so there is a minimal distance between turbines that has to be kept just to make sure that fatigue loading is not destroying the WT.

How much individual WT are affected, depends on the direction to the neighbors in relation to the wind direction distribution (often also called wind rose). Typically there is a main wind direction and in addition the mean wind speed might be also highest in main wind direction. This has to be taken into account when the sites of WT are determined. The plan for WT sites is called the layout of the wind farm.

With increasing distance from the WT the wake widens up and the speed approaches the ambient value (undisturbed by WT). The dimensions of the wake are proportional to the rotor size such that it makes sense to quantify the distance between the WT in multiples of the rotor diameter D. The distance where the wake effects have reached an acceptable level is 5 D. The distance where wakes have essentially vanished is 10 D, although especially offshore under certain conditions the wakes may be quite stable.

Another aspect that plays a role in selecting sites is the length of the cables. So even if there was sufficient area available the distances were typically not be chosen arbitrarily large to minimize costs for cables. As a result the distance between WT in OWF lies in the range from 5 to 10 D in main wind direction. It can be below 5 D in other directions.

In many OWF the layout of OWF follows a geometric pattern with constant spacings in main and secondary direction. For instance in the case of the famous Horns Rev 1 project the distance is 7 D.[19] The OWT are arranged in an area that has the shape of a parallelogram, with equally spaced rows.

In a recent example, Horns Rev 3, the installation was completed in 2018. The owner of the wind farm is the Swedish power company Vattenfall. The wind farm consists of 49 MV turbines with 164 m rotor and 8.3 MW rated power. The area is 88 km^2. The distances between turbines in this layout was chosen between 1.1 and 1.5 km corresponding to 6 to 9 D.

The layout in the context of wind speed and directional distribution determine the efficiency of the OWF. A member in the interior of the OWF will have a lower AEP than a member at the edge of the area. As a consequence the AEP of the farm will be lower than the one of the same number of WT under ambient conditions. For instance for Horns Rev 1 an efficiency of 87% has been determined.

19 See www.researchgate.net/figure/Layout-of-the-Horns-Rev-offshore-wind-farm_fig1_263895202.

1.4.2 Substructures and Foundations

Depending on the water depth there are different types of substructures an foundations. A recent review on substructures is provided in (Arshad, 2013) and also in the textbooks (Burton, 2011), (Gasch, 2012), (Hau, 2013).

The deeper the water the more difficult it becomes to design a stable and sufficiently stiff support structure that at the same time is not too heavy and expensive. For shallow water below 10 m depth also gravity foundations have been used. The extension of this technology to larger water depth was proposed but not adopted so far in OWF projects. The gravity foundation shown schematically in Figure 1.10 is inspired by the design used in the Nysted wind farm, where the WT is directly connected with the concrete structure.

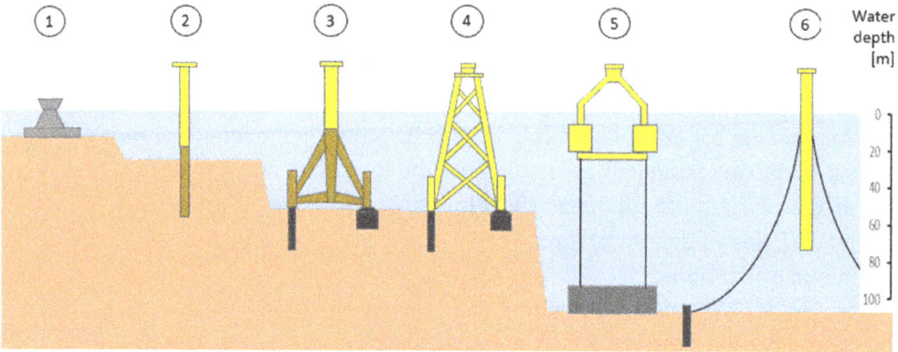

Figure 1.10: Examples for offshore substructures and foundations. 1. Gravity foundation, 2. Monopile, 3. Tripod, 4. Jacket, 5. TLP, 6. Spar buoy. For 3. and 4. it is shown that the foundation can be a pile (left side) or a suction bucket (right side).

The monopile, number 2 in Figure 1.10, is by far the most frequently used foundation. It consists of a steel tube that is rammed into the seabed. Most WT with monopile have in addition a transition piece. It is fixed to the monopile by a special concrete (grout) such that it is possible to adjust the WT tower to the vertical direction in case the rammed pile has a certain deviation from the vertical. With better installation methods the transition piece has been discarded in some recent projects, such that substructure and foundation consist of one long steel tube. Secondary steel and other items on the substructure are boat landing and a working platform at the tower bottom with some lifting equipment.

For water depths of 30 m and beyond, monopiles are getting to their limit. Increasing the diameter and shell thickness increases the stiffness. So-called XXL monopiles with tube diameter of 8 to 10 m are used for water depth up to 40 m. For instance for the OWF project Borseele III–IV monopiles manufactured by the Dutch company SIF Holding will be in water up to 38 m for MHIV 164.[20] One monopile has a mass of nearly 1000 t.

For larger water depths other concepts are needed. When the turbine is fixed to the ground for instance tripods (number 3) and lattice-type structures called jacket substructure (number 4) have been used. In principle such a technology can be used even in deeper water, but costs are increasing such that in deeper water fixed substructures are too expensive. So OWT fixed to the seabed are constrained to a certain range of water depth mainly by economic reasons.

In Figure 1.10 above (number 3 and 4) it is shown schematically that the foundation, the connection to the seabed, can be achieved with piles (left) and with suction bucket (right). In the suction bucket a vacuum is generated such that the structure is sucked to the seabed. The advantage of this technology is that it is easy to remove the substructure after the service lifetime.

The promising solution for deeper water is a floating OWT (5 and 6 in Figure 1.10). As shown in the figure the floater is fixed by mooring lines to keep it in its position. There are three different concepts for floating substructures, the spar buoys, the semi-submersibles and the tension-leg platform (TLP). Only the TLP (5) and the spar buoy (6) are displayed.

The most advanced of them concerning practical experience is the spar buoy. It is a long pile that is not driven into the seabed but floating in vertically oriented with ballast at the lower end in order to generated restoring forces when the OWT is tilting. In 2017 the first wind farm near Scotland with turbines of the type SG 6MW/154 m have been installed.

Catenary mooring lines are used to hold the OWT in its position. Catenary refers to the fact that the shape of the line is caused by gravity. The semi-submersible is stabilized by buoyancy. Also in this case catenary mooring lines are used. The third concept, the TLP, is stabilized by pre-stressed mooring lines. The TLP is known from oil and gas industry and has been used there for platforms in water depths up to 1000 m.

The advantages of floating WT are that sites can be harnessed beyond the depth limit of fixed substructures. There is a huge offshore wind potential accessible for floating OWT. The second advantage is that the floater can be also used for transportation. This will be discussed in more detail in the following section.

1.4.3 Installation

As said in section 1.2.4 the installation process for OWT is one of the cost drivers. The OWT has to be assembled from modules of suitable size at the site. Special equipment is needed. Weather plays a more restrictive role than for WT on land. Seasons with much wind and waves are excluded from installation of OWT.

20 OWF will be installed in 2019. Press release: http://hugin.info/174277/R/2185845/844829.pdf.

Only exception is the gravity foundation that has been used in shallow water that can be either prefabricated and transported to the site or even casted from ready mixed concrete at the site with a sheet pile wall. This technology has been used for projects in shallow water and does not play an important role currently.

For other types of foundation the installation process is not done from a floating device but from a so-called jack-up rig that consists of a buoyant barge with four movable vertical legs. The legs can lift the barge over the water surface such that a fixed platform for the installation process is provided. The rig can be self-propelled or moved by tug boats. Recently large jack-up ships have be built for transport and installation.[21]

Figure 1.11: Installation of the rotor in the OWF alpha ventus with a jack-up rig (own representation).

First step in in the installation process is the substructure and foundation. The monopiles are rammed into the seabed. This process is very noisy and can be harmful for marine live to be discussed below.

21 See, for example, www.dnvgl.com/expert-story/maritime-impact/Fresh-breeze-for-offshore-wind-farms.html.

The process for other fixed substructures like jacket or tripod is similar. The foundation is provided by piles that are connected to the substructure. For instance the jacket has a tube at each edge enclosing the pile (giving rise to the name jacket). After preparation of the seabed and placing the jacket on the site the piles can be driven into the ground. After the substructure is installed at the site, the cables of the OWF can be laid. The cables are inserted through a tube to the interior of the WT, called the J-tube.

Next step is the installation of the WT. Suitable modules of the turbine will be transported the construction site. Then tower, nacelle, and rotor are installed (see Figure 1.11). The rotor might be lifted to the turbine in one piece. This is called the "star" installation. Alternatively the nacelle including the hub is lifted on the tower and the blades are installed one by one, called single-blade installation.

A lot of development concerning these logistic and installation issue in the context of OWF took place in recent years. In some projects the components for several WT where transported on the jack-up vessel to the sites and installed one after the other. In spite of high costs for the jack-up vessels and the installation process, this is presently the most cost effective procedure for the installation of OWT with fixed substructure.

It has been suggested to transport the complete WT, assembled in the harbor, to the site and lift it on the substructure (see Figure 1.12). But this seems to cause more costs than the modular concept. One exception is the Hywind project mentioned already in section 1.3.2 where the complete turbine was installed on the spar buoy with the help of a large floating crane. The procedure was carried out inside a Norwegian fjord that provided the necessary water depth and a calm water surface. But this can be regarded as a special case that will in general not be feasible technically nor economically.

A great advantage of the floating WT is that they open up new perspectives concerning the installation process. The WT can be installed in the harbor, such that the complete assembly consisting of substructure and WT can be brought to the site by tug boats. An exception, of course, is the spar buoy. In vertical position this substructure needs a water depth of 100 m or so which is not available neither in the harbor nor in the waterways near the harbor. So concerning installation one has to find new cost-effective concepts for the spar buoy to make it an economically feasible offshore substructure. But for semi submersibles and the floater of the TLP the transport described in the following paragraph is technically feasible.

In a recent research project (Adam, 2017) the TLP is used in connection with a gravity anchor (Figure 1.10). The gravity anchor is a hollow concrete structure and designed such that it can be used a floating panel for substructure and WT. After arrival at the site, the anchor is floated and lowered to the ground with the mooring lines. Finally the anchor is filled with sand and the mooring lines are stressed providing the foundation for the WT.

Figure 1.12: Visualization of WT assembled in the harbor and pulled to the OWF by tug boats.[22]

1.4.4 Grid Connection

The solution for grid connection depends on the factors like total power of the OWF and distance to the shore. An important issue is also the availability of power lines on land of sufficient capacity to evacuate the power from the OWF. Also the question who has to pay the costs for grid connection is an issue. Certainly not all the aspects can be discussed in the present text.

For the connection of OWT to the power grid on land several voltage transformations are needed. All cables used are subsea cables. In all OWF power from individual turbines is collected in a substation. Electricity in this network is AC and voltage is medium voltage in the range 30 to 60 kV. In the substation the electricity is transformed to high voltage up to 220 kV. If the wind farm is near the shore a second conversion is not be needed and the electrical power is transport to the shore.

For large OWF or several OWF in a certain area, as for instance in the German Bight, another concept is used. Several substations are connected to a HVDC converter station. At the converter station AC is converted to DC. For longer distance transport of electrical energy, DC is more efficient. Of course the conversion steps from AC to DC and back to AC on land with power electronic converters leads to losses of some percent of the generated energy. It is subject to detailed analyses when the HVDC connection is more cost effective than the common high-voltage AC lines.

22 Video: www.youtube.com/watch?v=t7cIcBYRs5Q.

1.4.5 Operation and Maintenance

Like in the previous section also for this topic few important aspects will be highlighted. Reliability of the technology, the mechanical and electrical components and the controller are important for WT in general and for OWT even more. The reason is that service is costly or might be even not possible due to adverse weather conditions. Very important in this context is the controller. The control of the WT is based on hundreds of sensor data, where the most important are speed, power, pitch angle and some more, discussed already in previous sections. For automatic operation over long time periods like several months, reliability of the controller and its sensors is very important and, thus, the sensor system should be to some extent redundant.

OWF but also WT on land run automatically but with digital control and communication quickly developing WT nowadays use supervisory control and data acquisition (SCADA) to control the WT in certain respects and obtain information about their operational state. Mandatory for OWT are also condition monitoring systems (CMS). The CMS monitors bearings, the gearbox (if there is any) and other components to detect damages in an early stage. The purpose of the CMS is that unplanned service and larger damages are avoided.

Regular service on WT takes place in intervals of six months or one year. There are two independent ways to access the OWT that have impact on the logistics of spare parts and even on the arrangement of components in the WT: One way is the access from the water by boats as depicted in Figure 1.13. The substructure has a boat landing taking also into account different water levels due to tides. Due to waves the access for people and the transport of spare parts is difficult. This will be possible only for low waves. Another argument for the transport of service personal by boat is the travel time. Boats are slow and so a lot of time is needed for the trip to the OWF and back to the harbor.

The alternative that has many advantages is the use of helicopters. The helicopters are not landing on the WT but hoisting people to the so-called heli-hoist deck. Thus the OWF needs this deck on the roof of the nacelle in a sufficiently large distance from the rotor. The hoisting action is shown in Figure 1.14. A big advantage is that the helicopters can be maneuvered even at high wind speed up to 20 m/s and more.

1.4.6 Offshore Wind Farms from 1990 to Now

(Wikipedia, 2018) provides a list of OWF with power rating, number and type of WT, etc. With these data one can illustrate the development and main trends in offshore wind energy.

Figure 1.13: Boat landing at OWT in wind farm alpha ventus (own representation).

The power rating and rotor diameters of turbines used in various projects are displayed in form of scatter plots in Figures 1.15 and 1.16 in dependence of the year of commissioning. Derived from these data the specific power can be obtained and is shown in Figure 1.17.

As discussed in some detail in section 1.2.3 above, the specific power plays an important role, determining the kappa at a given site. In Figure 1.17 one can see that the trend goes to lower specific power while there is a large spread in this quantity during recent years.

Figure 1.14: Hoisting service personal from the helicopter to the OWT in alpha ventus (own representation).

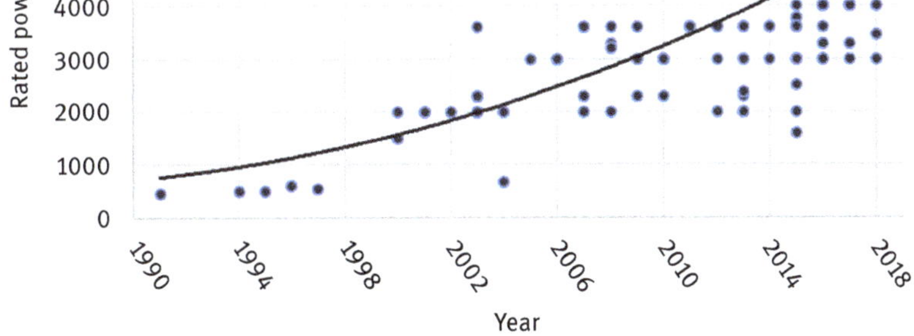

Figure 1.15: OWT rated power used in offshore projects depending on year of installation (own representation).

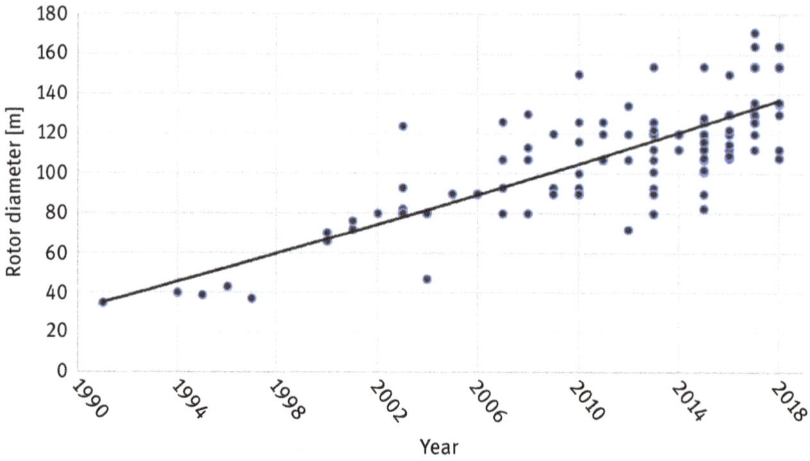

Figure 1.16: Rotor diameters of OWT depending on year of installation (own representation).

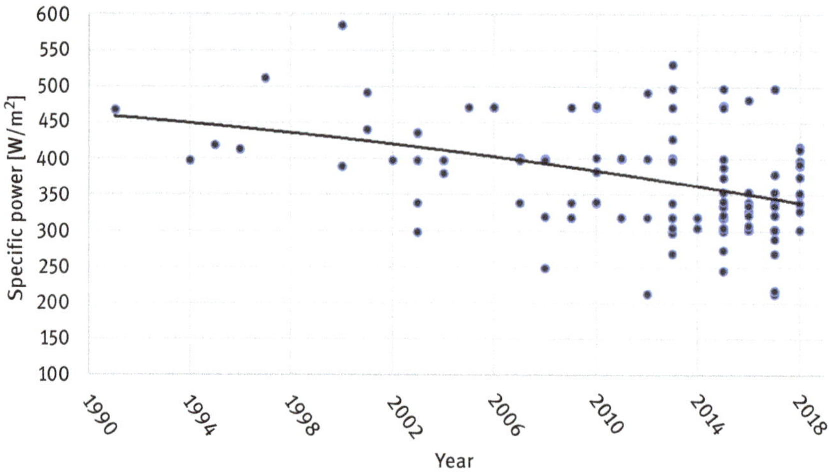

Figure 1.17: Specific power of OWT depending on the year of installation (own representation).

In Figure 1.18 the total power of the OWF is shown. The size of OWF is increasing over the years with small projects in the early days and large projects greater or equal 500 MW since 2012.

Figure 1.19 shows the number of turbines within a range of power ratings (see also Figure 1.20). The peak in the range from 3.25 to 3.75 MW. This illustrates the dominance of the Siemens 3.6 MW model. On the other hand several models with 5 MW have reached a total number of less than 400 only.

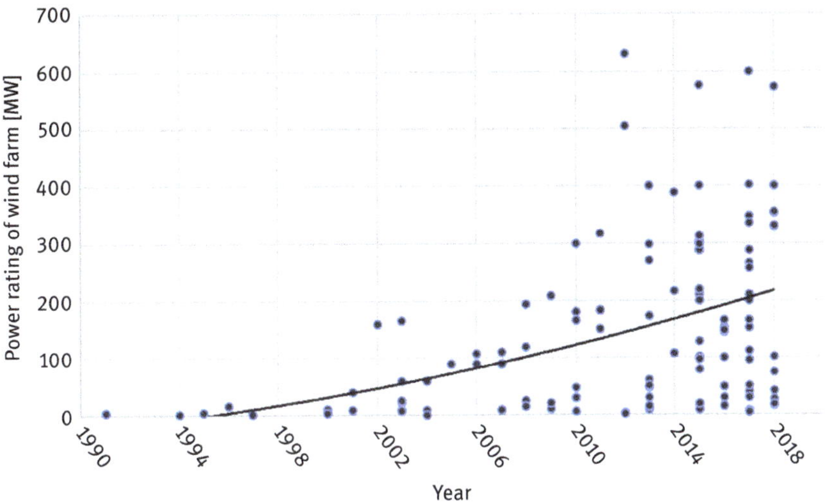

Figure 1.18: Size of OWF in MW depending on year of completion of wind farm (own representation).

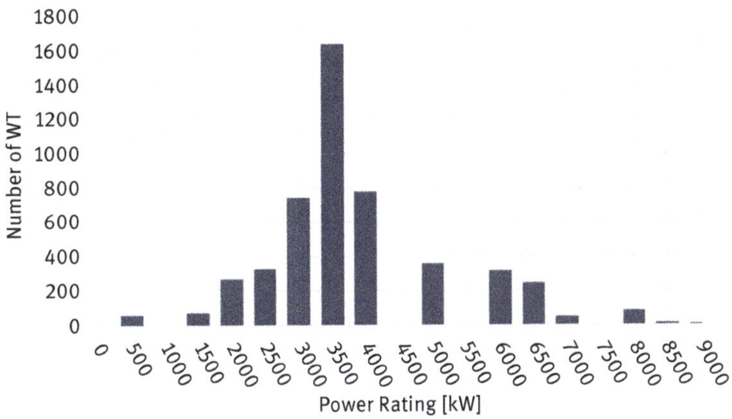

Figure 1.19: Number of OWT vs. power rating (own representation).

The total capacity of OWF installed until end of 2018 was 23,140 GW (GWEC, 2019) The new installation in 2018 was 4,496 GW. For the first time China was the leading market for offshore installation. The countries with most offshore wind capacity are United Kingdom with 7,963 GW, Germany with 6,380 GW, China with 4,588 GW and Denmark with 1,329 GW. Details can be found in the cited GWEC report (GWEC, 2019) that is updated every year.

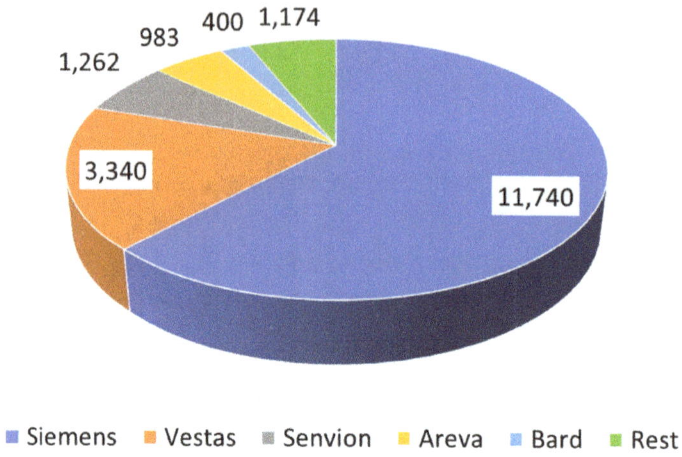

Figure 1.20: Cumulative installed offshore-wind capacity (in MW) of major manufacturers from reference (Wikipedia, 2018).

1.5 Other Topics

1.5.1 Certification and Standards

Certification is the examination and approval of a WT or a wind-farm project by an independent accredited entity called the certifier. There are a number of companies that are accredited like the German Lloyd, the TÜV Nord, and others. Certification increases the safety of the design and reduces the risk of major technical problems when the WT is in operations. Thus certification plays an important role for bankability, in other words, that banks provide the money for a OWF project.

WT technology has to comply with specific standards. Most important currently is the IEC standard. Relevant for WT is the group of standards IEC61400. Especially IEC 61400–1 contains design requirements for WT in general and -3 adds special requirements for OWT. These scheme is presently transformed to the new IEC renewable energy scheme. For the design process also other standards and guidelines are used. A famous guideline for WT is the DNV GL guideline, formerly simply called GL guideline.

The certification process relevant for wind energy projects can be divided in two main categories, type certification and project certification. In the type certification process a certain type of WT is examined. The type is characterized by its main parameters like power rating and rotor diameter, but also by technical details like main frame and generator design. Essentially all technical details that are relevant for the safe operation of the WT need to be clear and unchanged for a specific type.

The type certification process consists of the following steps

- Examination of the design documents. The WT design is reanalyzed in great detail in this stage before the production process starts, partly even before the prototype is installed.
- Examination of the manufacturing process. Personal of the Certifier visit the manufacturing plant and check the processes, especially whether the company uses the design that was checked in step 1.
- Check of the quality management system. A more formal step that makes sure that systematic procedure to assure quality are applied by the manufacturer.
- Prototype testing. Tests and measurements are carried out on the WT. Tests are witnessed by the personal of the certifier. Results are used to validate the assumption made in the design process for instance for the loads. For WT with gearbox also a gearbox prototype needs to be tested on a test bed.

In case all the steps are carried out successfully the type certificate for the given type of WT is issued. For a new WT the type certification means a lot of work and costs. Sometimes several variants are considered like slightly different blades from different blade manufacturers or slightly different rotor diameters. Such variants also can be included in an extended type certificate if they are needed later on.

The project certification is done for larger wind farm projects. Most OWF projects go through project certification. Many aspects of the OWF project are double-checked by the certifier. An example is the question whether a certain WT type is suitable for the wind farm project examined. For type certification assumption have to made concerning external conditions like wind and waves or the type of substructure. This is the basis of the simulation model providing the loads on which, in turn, the WT design is based. The assumption must be general enough since the product should be feasible for many potential sites and substructures. They must not be too general, however, since a WT that fits all sites would be not competitive. As a result, in the project certification process a simulation of the WT is done with site-specific wind and waves and the particular substructure, to compare with the data used for type-certification.

1.5.2 Approval Process

The potential sites of OWF are located mainly in the territorial waters and the exclusive economic zone. The territorial waters extend to 22 km (12 nautical miles) from the coast and the exclusive zone to 370 km (200 nautical miles). The approval process includes all stages of the OWF, like exploration of the site, planning, installation, operation and maintenance and dismantling. Aspects that are important in the approval process are safety of waterborne traffic, environmental impact and potential conflicts with other interests for example of fishing industry. A more detailed account on this topic is given in (Hau, 2013).

Since offshore wind energy is considered an important future energy resource in many countries worldwide, the legal framework for OWF is developing rapidly with the objective to streamline the approval process.

An example is the “Promotion of Renewable Energy Act” introduced in Denmark 10 years ago.[23] According to the Danish regulation the parties active in offshore wind have to work with one responsible authority, the Danish Energy Agency. The agency is responsible for all aspects of project approval and operation of the OWF including the feed-in conditions for the electrical energy.

In Germany a similar law has been enacted in 2017, the “Offshore Wind Energy Act.”[24] As stated in there: “The aim of this act is to increase the installed capacity of offshore wind energy installations to a total of 15 gigawatts between 2021 and 2030. This increase is to take place steadily, cost-efficiently and taking account of the grid capacities needed for the purchase, transmission and distribution of the electricity. The expansion of offshore wind energy installations and the expansion of the offshore connections needed to transmit the electricity generated in them are therefore to be coordinated, also taking into consideration the onshore grid connection points, and an alignment of the respective planning, approvals, construction and commissioning is to be achieved.” If the moderate pace of deployment will be realistic in view of a progressing climate change is highly questionable.

1.5.3 Environmental Impact, Acceptance, and Possible Synergies

OWF like other industrial plants have impact on the environment and in particular on living creatures. It was mentioned already that during installation one has to take care that no harm to marine mammals is done. Sound due to ramming the piles can be damped by bubble curtains, a ring of air bubbles in the water surrounding the construction site. Other methods to avoid noise are under development or have been applied already. An example is a recent wind farm project where the monopiles were vibrated into the soil.[25]

When the OWF is in operation mainly birds may be affected and in the worst case killed by colliding with the rotor. There are a number of studies concerning the impact of OWF on birds. An example is (Kahlert, 2005) where the impact of the wind farm Nysted on sea birds was studied. Most of the birds where eiders living in

---

23 See: ens.dk/en/our-responsibilities/wind-power/offshore-procedures-permits.

24 English version: www.bmwi.de/Redaktion/DE/Downloads/E/windseeg-gesetz-en.pdf.

25 See: www.4coffshore.com/news/heerema-vibrate-monopile-into-place-nid7926.html.

the coastal area near the Danish coast. The flight trajectories of the birds were monitored by radar. The results of the study can be summarized as follows:
- The birds avoid to enter the OWF. Thus one effect is that the habitat of the birds has become smaller after installation of the OWF.
- If birds enter the wind farm the trajectories are mainly in the middle between two rows.
- It was observed that bird trajectories are below and, during the night, above the rotors.
- The increase of annual mortality was estimated to 1%, which can be regarded as a low value.

It was emphasized in the report that these results are specific for the situation in Nysted and cannot be extended to other OWF and species.

Another issue in the context of OWF is acceptance. Wind energy in general is under criticism for spoiling the view of the landscape. In Mecklenburg West Pomerania, a state in the north east of Germany at the coast of the Baltic Sea, land based wind farm project were stopped due to encirclement. Nearby resident would have seen WT in all directions. In the same area protests against OWF took place which the argument that the WT can be seen from the beach and this would have a negative effect for the local tourism. Now most of the projects, especially those in the North Sea, are in a distance from the coast that they cannot be seen.

1.6 Final Remarks

As said in section 1.2.2 above, wind energy will be an important contribution to the future primary energy mix. According to various scenarios for the energy transition one fifth to one quarter of primary energy will come from wind. There are unknowns in these scenarios, of course, like the future development of the global primary energy demand. But certainly several thousand GW of wind power installation are needed globally to provide the necessary contribution to the primary energy. The 50 GW/year that we see presently (GWEC, 2019) are not sufficient. With pressure from climate change increasing we are going to see an accelerating deployment of wind energy converters during the next two decades.

Currently offshore-wind technology is developing fast in many respects. Concerning the technology wind turbines become larger and more efficient. New models are all direct-drive or hybrid designs. Cost of energy are rapidly declining, more rapidly than forecasted previously. Another development – this indeed has been forecasted correctly – is a concentration process of the WT manufacturers. Only a few large manufacturers like Siemens Gamesa, MHI Vestas and General Electric have the financial resources to carry out the needed research and development work, install the prototype, build manufacturing plants, etc.

But under the bottom line this development will lead to extremely competitive electrical energy from OWF. So it seems likely that the contribution from offshore wind to the primary energy mix in 2050 will be much larger than expected by studies carried in recent years.

Abbreviations

AC	Alternating Current
AEP	Annual energy production
CAPEX	Capital Expenditures
CP	Power coefficient of wind turbine
DC	Direct current
DDG	Direct-drive generator
GE	General Electric
HAWT	Horizontal axis WT
HSG	High-speed generator
HVDC	High-voltage direct current
KAPPA	Capacity factor
MV	MHI Vestas
MSG	Medium-speed generator
OPEX	Operational Expenditures
OWF	Offshore wind farm
OWT	Offshore wind turbine
SCADA	Supervisory control and data acquisition
SG	Siemens Gamesa
VAWT	Vertical axis WT
WT	Wind turbine

References

Adam, F. et al. (2017). One-step installation of a TLP substructure – requirements, assumptions, issues. *Proceedings of the ASME 2017 International Conference on Ocean, Offshore & Arctic Engineering OMAE.*

Anaya-Lara, O. et al. (2018). *Offshore Wind Energy Technology*. Hoboken: Wiley.

Arshad, M. et al. (2013). Offshore wind-turbine. *Energy*, 139.

Bach Andersen, A. (2011). *Selecting the Optimum Drive Train*. Vestas Wind Systems A/S.

Burton, T. et al. (2011). *Wind Energy Handbook*. Chichester: Wiley.

Gasch, R. et al. (2012). *Wind Power Plants*. Heidelberg: Springer.

GWEC. (2019). Global Wind Report 2018. www.gwec.net.

Hau, E. (2013). *Wind Turbines*. Heidelberg: Springer.

Hjuler Jensen, P. et al. (2017). *LCOE reduction for the next generation offshore wind turbines*. Report, www.innwind.eu. Retrieved from www.innwind.eu.

Hundleby, G. et al (2017). Unleashing Europe's offshore wind potential. *Wind Europe Report.*

Kahlert, J. et al (2005). Investigations of birds during operation of Nysted offshore wind farm at Rødsand: Results and conclusions. *NERI Report.*

Klinger, F. (2004). *GENESYS 600, Eine neue Generation hocheffizienter Windenergieanlagen*. HTW Saarland.

Koebe, K. (2014). *Regional Policies for Offshore Wind: A Guidebook*. German Offshore Wind Energy Foundation.

Kost, C. et al. (2018). *Levelized Cost of Electricity – Renewable Energy Technologies*. Fraunhofer ISE.

Musial, W. et al. (2016). 2016 Offshore Wind Energy Resource Assessment for the United States. *Report NREL/TP-5000-66599*.

Sathyajith, M. et al. (2012). *Advances in Wind Energy Conversion Technology*. Berlin: Springer.

Sawyer, S. (2016). *Global Wind Energy Outlook 2016*. Global Wind Energy Coucil (GWEC).

Schellnhuber, H. J. (2016). Why the right climate target was agreed in Paris. *Nature Climate Change*, 649.

Schmid, F. et al. (2011). *Energy Concept 2050 for Germany with a European and Global Perspective*. Berlin: ForschungsVerbundErneuerbare Energien (FVEE).

Shan, A. (2013). Field Testing and Practical Aspects of Load Reducing Pitch Control Systems for a 5 MW Offshore Wind Turbine. *European Wind Energy Conference*.

Skiba, M. et al. (2012). Offshore-Windkraftwerke: Marktentwicklung und Herausforderungen. *Energiewirtschaftliche Tagesfragen, Vol 10*, 31.

Wikipedia. (2018). Liste der Offshore-Windparks. *German, accessed 11/2018*. Retrieved 03 2019

2 Project Contracts of an Offshore Wind Farm

Matthias Hirschmann

2.1 Introduction

The successful realization of an offshore wind farm depends to a large extent on the design of the project contracts that will provide the legal basis for the project's development, construction, operation – as well as for the dismantling of the wind turbines.

Against the background of the (legal and technical) complexity of offshore wind projects, various experts are required and parties need to be involved in the realization: First, there is the project owner, being highly interested in the profitability of the offshore wind farm over its whole lifecycle and in certainty of the investment. In the first instance it is crucial for the project owner that the project will be commissioned in time and in the form and manner as agreed.

Then, there are the contractors – parties that will be responsible for one or several parts of the project, with the aim of achieving the highest possible profit with the realization of the project. Apart from the profit, it is also of utmost importance for the contractors that they receive the agreed payments on time.

The purpose of the project agreement is to harmonize the differing interests of project owner and contractor as well as to allocate the risks. Said risk allocation is in particular necessary with a view to third "big player" in offshore wind farms: banks and financial institutions will demand a clear risk horizon that enables them to assess the venture of the investment. Unclear liability regulations and risk allocations make it difficult, even impossible, for banks to assess the risk of their investments in such a way that project owners will receive funds on reasonable terms.

That being said, it should be noted, that the German civil law does not know the contract type "project contract." However, it is highly important to match the project contract with one of the contract types that the German Civil Code (*Bürgerliches Gesetzbuch* – "**BGB**") provides for, mainly because the provisions on statutory warranty differ between the several contract types. Besides this, the national law also sets the legal framework when it comes to the interpretation of contracts and the closing of contractual loopholes. Therefore, it is often necessary to assign the project contract to a contract type provided for in the BGB. When it comes to offshore wind farms, there are three contract types pursuant to the BGB that set the legal framework: purchase contract (*Kaufvertrag*), work contract (*Werkvertrag*) and service contract (*Dienstvertrag*). Often, a project contract combines these contracts or parts of them into one agreement.

The following pages are intended to outline the specific characteristics of project contracts in the offshore wind energy sector.

https://doi.org/10.1515/9783110607888-018

2.2 Contract Design

Since every energy project is unique, also the project contracts are different in every single case. One of the most important factors when drafting the contractual framework is the number of parties that will be involved in the realization of the project, since this will determine if and to what extent the contract structure can be limited to only a few agreements or whether the conclusion of numerous individual agreements may become necessary.

The number of parties to be involved in an offshore wind farm project depends on the choice of a certain project development design. Thus, the project owner must decide if and to what extent it can or wishes to conduct certain work by itself, taking into account the associated risks. Any remaining works and services that the project owner will not conduct on its own will require external expertise and assistance.

2.3 General Contractor Agreements (EPC – Engineering, Procurement and Construction)

The development of an offshore wind farm is characterized by many different works and services that are necessary until commissioning of the wind farm. For example, technical planning, the supply of numerous parts and components as well as their assembly will become required throughout the completion phase.

From the project owner's point of view, it may be preferable to bundle the works and services under one contractor. The risk allocation is clear in this constellation: all risks associated with the various works services will be allocated to the general contractor. Needless to say, the technical, logistical and general planning challenges make offshore wind farm projects rather complex. This complexity and the resulting interfaces lead to an increased risk in each of the mentioned individual areas. Further, there is a risk of adverse weather conditions possibly slowing down the construction works. Besides this, the often used pilot technologies in the offshore wind energy sector may entail risks that are not yet foreseeable.[1]

For the project owner it may be attractive to shift the responsibilities and risks connected with the interfaces and challenging circumstances of the project's development to a general contractor. Eventually, the project owner will receive a turnkey wind farm. Until the handing over of the wind farm, the general contractor will most likely make use of subcontractors, since the general contractor does in most case not have the capabilities and expertise to develop the project without third

1 *Schulz/Rohrer* in Schulz (Hrsg.), Handbuch Windenergie, Kapitel 5 Rn. 26.

party support. The decisive advantage of this constellation is that the project owner has one key contact instead of several different counterparties.

What makes a general contractor agreement attractive for the project owner on the one hand, makes it a challenge for the general contractor on the other hand. In practice, there is only a limited number of potential general contractors that have the capability to develop a turnkey wind farm. Since the general contractor agreement concentrates the majority of responsibilities on the general contractor's shoulders, general contractor agreements are rarely to be found on the market. Hence, this concept is rarely applied in practice, at least in its pure form.[2]

2.4 Multi-Contracting

As an alternative to the general contract agreement, the project owner can also opt for a so-called multi-contracting concept. By choosing this concept, the project owner will have to negotiate the different project agreements individually with several contractors.

The project owner will remain responsible to coordinate the different services and works – the project owner will also bear the risk of defaults on the contractors' side. Each contractor only owes the performance of the services and works it committed itself to. The coordination of the different interfaces is the project owner's responsibility. If an individual contractor will not perform, perform poorly or with delay and other services cannot be provided in time as a result, the project owner is the party bearing this risk.

In most cases, contractors will exclude their liability for indirect damages. In case a contractor's default prevents other contractors from completing their works on time, the claims against the defaulting will often not be sufficient to compensate the project owner.

Whereas the multi-contracting concept allocates several risks and responsibilities with the project owner, it also opens potential for savings. When opting for a general contractor agreement, the project owner will have to remunerate the general contractor for taking over the risk of breaching or defaulting subcontractors.

The project may also be able to bundle at least a number of different works and services under one "small" general contract. This variation of the multi-contracting concept can be more attractive for the project owner, as reduces the interface risk from several different contract to just a number of general contracts. Each general contractor will then be responsible for the fulfillment of its "small" general contract. This bundling of various works and services is also referred to as

---

2 Vgl. *Kraft/Sethmann* in Böttcher (Hrsg.), Handbuch Offshore-Windenergie, S. 180, *Busch*, NZBau 2011, 1 (2); *Schulz/Rohrer* in Schulz (Hrsg.), Handbuch Windenergie, Kapitel 5 Rn. 26.

the "Island Approach."[3] In practice, the multi-contracting is frequently seen on the offshore wind market.

2.5 Alliance Contracting

Even though this concept is rarely seen on the market (almost never in the offshore wind sector), the so-called alliance contracting should not remain unmentioned. The model of alliance contracting origins from Australia. It tries to harmonize the interests of the project owner and the contractor by making the project's development a joint task. The economic success for both sides, project owner and contractor(s) depend on the overall success of the project.

The economic success for both sides therefore depends on the overall economic success of the project. Both sides have an interest and an intrinsic motivation to avoid delays and other actions that could put the project's realization at risk. A so-called alliance board signs responsible for the clarification of contentious issues and disputes. Since this board consists of representatives of both the project owner and the contractor, consensual solutions can be promoted.[4]

2.6 General Terms and Conditions (GTCs)

Sections 305 et seqq. BGB provide for the framework regarding the control of certain contractual provisions. This regime is rather strict in order to safeguard a party that is confronted with GTCs. If GTCs are not compliant with section 305 et seqq. BGB they are not effective – making GTCs to a major factor of uncertainty in legal disputes.

Section 305 para. 1 BGB does stipulate when a contract or provision is actually considered to be a GTC: GTC are all contract terms pre-formulated for more than two contracts which one party to the contract (the user) presents to the other party upon the entering into of the contract. It is irrelevant whether the provisions take the form of a physically separate part of a contract or are made part of the contractual document itself, what their volume is, what typeface or font is used for them and what form the contract takes. Contract terms do not become GTCs to the extent that they have been negotiated in detail between the parties.

The assessment of GTCs' effectiveness is intended to protect the party which does not provide the GTCs from particularly detrimental agreements in order to compensate for existing power inequalities.[5] It is easy to find potential inequalities in contractual

---

3 *Schulz/Rohrer* in Schulz (Hrsg.), Handbuch Windenergie, Kapitel 5 Rn. 15.

4 Vgl. *Kraft/Sethmann* in Böttcher (Hrsg.), Handbuch Offshore-Windenergie, S. 182; ausführlich dazu *Bücker*, Alliance Contracting – Streitverzicht beim Bauvertrag, NZBau 2007, 609ff.

5 *Schmidt*, in Bamberger/Roth/Hau/Poseck – BeckOK, § 307 Rn. 1.

relationships between consumers and entrepreneurs. But also the relations between entrepreneurs in question of offshore wind farm projects (Business-to-Business – "**B2B**") can show these inequalities. German law on GTCs also applies to B2B contracts, albeit with certain differences to Consumer to Consumer ("**C2C**") contracts.

In general, provisions in GTCs are ineffective if, contrary to the requirement of good faith, they unreasonably disadvantage the other party to the contract with the user. An unreasonable disadvantage may also arise from the provision not being clear and comprehensible. This standard is adjusted in accordance with section 310 para. 1 BGB when GTCs are provided to entrepreneurs. Sections 305 para. 1, 2, 308 numbers 1, 2–8 and 309 BGB do not apply in these cases. These prohibitions remain only fully and directly applicable if the GTCs are utilized vis-à-vis consumers.

However, the clarification in section 310 para. 1 sentence 2 BGB also shows that the provisions in the sections 305 para. 1, 2, 308 numbers 1, 2–8 and 309 BGB have to be taken into account within the framework of the content assessment according to section 307 BGB. Hence, it is common that the assessment of identical clauses in B2B and C2C contracts come to similar results. Therefore the various contracts for offshore wind farm projects often have to be assessed against German law on GTCs.

In principle, section 307 para. 1 sentence 1 BGB provides that clauses of GTCs shall be invalid if they unreasonably disadvantage the contractual partner contrary to the requirements of good faith. In the offshore wind energy sector there is often a need for extensive liability limitations or indemnifications. However, such provisions in the project contracts often cannot withstand the content check according to section 307 BGB. Even if it is stated in the literature that less stringent standards would have to be applied in the B2B sector,[6] this corresponds to the jurisdiction of the German Federal High Court of Justice.[7]

In order to exclude clauses and agreements from the content check of GTCs, it is occasionally proposed to implement arbitration clauses. According to this opinion, the agreement can be excluded from the content assessment by choosing an arbitration tribunal using German law under the exception of section 305 to 310 BGB.[8] The controversial admissibility of such agreements left aside,[9] as already mentioned above, GTCs do not exist as far as the provisions of a contract have been negotiated between the parties in detail (section 305 para. 1 sentence 3 BGB). Such individual agreements represent a further (and more certain) possibility to bypass the strict standards of German law on GTCs.

---

6 *Cloppenburg*, Die Lieferung und Errichtung sowie Wartung von On- und Offshore Windenergieanlagen, ZfBR-Beil. 2012, S. 3 (4); *Stadler*, in Jauernig (Hrsg.), BGB, § 307 Rn. 5.

7 Vgl. BGH, BeckRS 2017, 121112.

8 *Pfeiffer*, Die Abwahl des deutschen AGB-Rechts in Inlandsfällen bei Vereinbarung eines Schiedsverfahrens, NJW 2012, 1169ff.

9 Siehe hierzu: *Schulz/Rohrer* in Schulz (Hrsg.), Handbuch Windenergie, Kapitel 5 Rn. 57.

It should be noted that the requirements for said individual negotiations are relatively strict. The German Federal High Court of Justice (*Bundesgerichtshof*) requires the party using GTCs to show that it is seriously willing to dismiss the corresponding clause in a way that gives the other party the opportunity to actually influence the contract's content.[10] The burden to prove the occurrence of said negotiations is with the party using GTCs. In practice, it can be rather challenging to prove negotiations for every single clause. On the other hand, it is easy for the other party to deny the occurrence of negotiations. In any case, the negotiation of individual clauses does not necessarily lead to the conclusion that the GTCs in dispute have also been subject to such negotiations.

In the B2B sector in particular, regulations are often adopted unchanged in order to strengthen the negotiating position in other areas. In such cases, a collective solution is negotiated, but German jurisdiction,[11] contrary to widespread criticism,[12] does not consider this to be sufficient and points out that at least thorough negotiations have to be taken place beforehand.

Accordingly, German law on GTCs has a considerable influence on the practice of drafting project contracts (not only but also in the offshore wind energy sector). However, the following explanations assume that the corresponding regulations are not subject to German law on GTCs in order to have a closer look on possible problem areas and possible approaches for project owners and contractors when entering into negotiations.

2.7 The Different Stages of a Wind Farm Project

The various phases in the life cycle of an offshore wind farm project are reflected in the different project contracts. First of all, a distinction must be made between the construction phase and the subsequent operating phase. In the following, this time line differentiation is intended to illustrate the contract contents in the individual phases, contract types and possible problematic areas. The dismantling phase following the operating phase must also be taken into account at the end.

2.7.1 Phase 1: Construction

At the very beginning of every offshore wind farm is the planning and construction of the various elements. In addition to the construction of the individual turbines, this

10 BGH, NJW 2013, 856 Rn. 10.

11 BGH, NJW 2013, 856 Rn. 10.

12 *Schulz/Rohrer* in Schulz (Hrsg.), Handbuch Windenergie, Kapitel 5 Rn. 47.

also includes the logistical planning and realization. E.g., transport vessels will have to be provided which are technically capable of transporting the relevant components and assembling them on site. In addition, there is the necessary transport and accommodation of the offshore workers. The necessary plants include foundations, wind turbines, cabling within the wind farm and an offshore transformer platform. These challenges must be taken into account during the construction phase of the contract and must be coordinated in the best possible way.

The Use of Sample Contracts

Instead of drafting projects contracts on the drawing board, project owners have the opportunity to use already existing sample contracts. In Germany, the VOB/B (*German Construction Contract Procedures Part B: General Terms and Conditions for the Execution of Construction Work*) is used for this purpose in some cases. The VOB/B is a continuously updated set of rules for construction contracts, to which the balanced consideration of conflicting interests in the B2B sector is attested.[13] Besides this, the German civil law considers the VOB/B as a privileged set of rules, which are indeed GTCs, but according to section 310 para 1 sent. 3 BGB not subject to the content assessment. This shall only apply if the VOB/B have been included in the contract completely and unchanged in their current version. Parties may therefore wish to consider to use the established standards of the VOB/B and at the same time, by using VOB/B, to avoid the content assessment according to the German law on GTCs.

In an international context, parties would rather opt for FIDIC templates. The initial and continuing strong hesitancy using FIDIC templates is in particular the result of open questions regarding the extent to which the FIDIC regulations are able to exclude the agreement from the content assessment under German law on GTCs.[14] If parties can overcome this difficulty and uncertainty, the FIDIC templates constitute a reasonable basis for offshore wind farm projects with an appropriate risk allocation.[15]

There are different FIDIC standards: with the Yellow Book, the Red Book and the Silver Book three obvious versions should be mentioned, which differ in particular by the area of application and the intended risk distribution. All of them were recently updated in 2017.

For example, the Yellow Book states that the contractor is responsible for the planning and execution of the project. However, certain central risks remain with the project owner.[16] The Silver Book differs significantly in this regard: It allocates

13 Vgl. BGH, NZBau 2008, 640.

14 Vgl. *Bonke/Stumpf*, Das FIDIC Yellow Book 2017: Neuer Vertragsstandard für den Anlagenbau im Lichte des deutschen AGB-Rechts, NZBau 2018, 449.

15 *Müller-Helle*, Die Gestaltung von FIDIC Verträgen für Offshore-Windparks, RdE 2014, S. 53.

16 Vgl. *Schulz/Rohrer* in Schulz (Hrsg.), Handbuch Windenergie, Kapitel 5 Rn. 66f.

the risks of the completion of the project on time with the contractor as far as possible. Considering the reluctance of potential contractors to offer extensive turnkey solutions on the market mentioned above, the applicability of the Silver Book for offshore wind farm projects is also arguable.[17] A characteristic feature of the Red Book is that the project owner remains responsible for the planning of the project.

Details of the Construction Contract

If the contracting parties decide against FIDIC templates, they are required to elaborate the different agreements in individual negotiations. Whether there is a comprehensive agreement with only one contractual partner within the framework of a general contractor agreement or whether many individual contractual partners of the project owner participate together in the construction depends on the choice of the contract design as outlined above.

Legal Classification

To what extent the construction contract can be assigned to a certain contract type under German civil law cannot be answered generally. This question will have to be answered on the basis of the respective contents of each contract. The allocation of the construction contract to one of the legal contract types can become relevant since German law provides for different rights and obligations for the contracting parties depending on the type of contract. To name just one among other differences, the law applicable to sales contracts provides for an obligation for entrepreneurs to give notice of defects (section 377 German Commercial Code (*Handelsgesetzbuch* – "**HGB**")). This mechanism is unknown to the law on contracts for works and services.

The construction of the turbines and other systems of the wind farm or of the entire offshore wind farm requires not only installation works but also production and delivery in the first place. In addition, there is also the preceding complex planning phase.

When the construction contract has to be categorized, a differentiated view becomes necessary: In case of a general contractor agreement, an overall view of the various contract components is necessary in order to categorize the agreement. In multi-contracting structures, the allocation is easier since the contractor has only committed himself to a clearly defined partial performance. The categorization is based on the focus of the service to be performed.[18]

In most cases, the potential contract types are the sales contract and the works contract. The assignment of the project contract to one of those types is based on an overall assessment, considering the type of item to be delivered, the value ratio

---

17 Zu diesem Ergebnis kommt auch *Müller-Helle*, Die Gestaltung von FIDIC Verträgen für Offshore-Windparks, RdE 2014, S. 53 (55).

18 BGH, NZBau 2004, 326.

of delivery and assembly and the special features of the result owed.[19] When series-produced components are delivered without significant installation costs, a sales contract was usually concluded. If the delivery of a movable object to be manufactured is the subject of the contract, the sales law (section 650 BGB) also applies.

If, on the other hand, the contractual relationship is characterized by a certain work to be performed by the contractor (e.g., due to necessary adaptations to the special conditions of the project or complex installation work), the law on works contracts is applicable.

In 2018, the legislator introduced a new form of the works contract. Section 650a BGB provides for the construction contract applicable to the construction of buildings. Hence, at least if the project contract covers the construction of the foundation of the wind turbine, a construction contract is likely to be assumed.[20]

Content of the Construction Contracts

Definition of the contractual performance

The definition of the performances owed under the agreement is the core piece of any (project) contract and the relationship of the parties. When it comes to a dispute, the provisions regarding the contractually owed performance will be critical for the court's decision. For both parties it is therefore important to clearly define the subject matter of the contract.

From a legal point of view, functional performance descriptions have to be distinguished from comprehensive service specifications. A functional performance description defines the final result of the work or service as agreed in the contract and sets specific target conditions of the product. It is basically up to the contractor how it can reach this target condition. Service specifications on the other hand define the technical specifications of the work or service from the outset; the project owner does not hand over the planning work.

Securing On-Time Fulfillment

In the energy sector, delays in the project development often cause considerable revenue losses. In addition penalty payments and the withdrawal of the tender award (cf. sections 60 et seq. Offshore Wind Energy Act (*Windenergien-auf-See-Gesetz* – "**WindSeeG**")) are possible. Hence, the project owner has to assure the on time fulfillment of all project contracts.

For this reason, it is of particular importance for the project owner to be assured of the timely performance of services by its contractual partners. By implementing a

19 BGH, NZBau 2004, 326.

20 *Cramer*, in Messerschmidt/Voit, Privates Baurecht, 3. Auflage 2018, I. C. Rn. 26.

strict sanction system, the project owner can urge the contractor to provide the works and services as agreed in the project contract.

Under statutory provisions, the contractor becomes liable if it is in default (sections 280, 286 BGB). The due date is determined by the time of performance defined by the parties. If the project owner asserts this claim the contractor will not be released from its obligations under the project contract. Pursuant to section 249 para. 1 BGB, the contractor must restore the state that would have existed if the delay had not occurred. The potential damage can therefore be significant, especially since there is no liability cap.

This statutory liability regime is often adjusted for several reasons. Most importantly because its unlimited liability is not acceptable for the contractor and because the burden of proof regarding any damages lays on the project owner. Therefore, parties often enter into an adjusted liability regime, comprising contractual penalties, lump-sums and liability caps.

When the parties agree on lump-sum penalties, other claims for the same reason may be excluded. It is common practice to link the amount due and payable to the number of days of defaulting due to the contractor's breach of contract.

The contractor will seek to exclude as many risks as possible from such penalty payment, especially when it comes to external factors. The precise description of the scope of risks that are taken over by the contractor is therefore crucial. To safeguard the project owner's interest, it is often agreed that delays due to external risks lead to a prolongation of the respective time frame but will not discharge the contractor from its obligation to undertake the works and services agreed between the parties.

Usually the project owner agrees to certain liability caps in favor of the contractor. In practice, this limit is often a percentage of the total volume of the project. In order to consider also the project owner's interest, the parties may agree on an extraordinary termination right for the project owner if the cap is reached.

Definition of Adverse Weather

Especially in the offshore wind sector, adverse weather can become a severe danger to the schedule of project developments

The risk of adverse weather is one of the few factors during the project development that cannot be controlled by either party. Therefore, project contracts should clearly allocate adverse weather risks clearly between the parties.

As far as they are predictable, adverse weather risks are often considered in the schedule. However, as it is in the weather's nature, most events are not predictable. Therefore, it is in the contractor's interest that the project contract provides for deadline extensions and reimbursements in case of delays due to adverse weather.[21] On the

21 Regarding the controversial question, if there is a payment entitlement according to § 642 BGB given a bad weather incident: *Diehr*, ZfBR 2011, 627.

other side, the project owner will try to limit said reliefs to a certain contingent of "adverse weather days." Such contingent solution is often seen in the market.[22]

It is obvious that a contingent solution could be used by the contractor to gain deadline extensions by claiming adverse weather conditions even if they are not given. Hence, it is necessary to clearly define the term "adverse weather," e.g., by defining certain levels of wind speed, swell, visibility, etc.

Warranty

Both, the project owner and the contractor will have an overwhelming interest to agree on a clear warranty regime. The warranty provisions of the BGB for defects are the basis for the contractual warranty regime.

The provisions for purchase contracts and works contracts are similar in many respects. A defect within the meaning of these provisions is given if the object or work does not meet the agreed quality (cf. section 434 para. 1 sentence 1, section 633 para. 2 BGB). But also the non-suitability for the use intended by the contract or the usual customary use constitutes a defect.

In case of a defect, the customer (i.e., the project owner) is entitled to various warranty rights. Primarily, the customer can demand subsequent performance in order to ensure that the product eventually meets the agreed quality standard. The contractor is obligated to make the necessary improvements, to produce a new work or to deliver a defect-free item.

The German law on works contracts also provides for a right of the customer to take actions itself after demanding improvements unsuccessfully. In addition, in the event of an unsuccessful demand for subsequent performance, the customer shall have the option of reducing the price or withdrawing from the contract.

Although these possibilities can often satisfy the interests of the project owner, especially if the obligation to subsequent performance is fulfilled immediately, other possibilities encounter difficulties in practice. For example, the reduction of the contractor's remuneration can, in some cases, hardly ever be able to compensate for the project owner's economic losses.

The legal provisions of the BGB are not exclusive though. Parties may agree on amendments to this framework. The project owner will try not to reduce its rights under the legal framework, but rather to extend it in its favor. On the project owner's side, it is not only itself who will demand and push forward the appropriate contract designs. The banks that finance the project will also make similar demands on the contract design.

22 Vgl. *Schulz/Rohrer* in Schulz (Hrsg.), Handbuch Windenergie, Kapitel 5 Rn. 189.

Performance Guarantees

In addition to the statutory warranties, the project owner will in most cases request the contractor to guarantee that the corresponding plants will meet certain performance parameters in operation, considering the dependence of the profitability of the whole project on the amount of electricity generated. On the one hand, this includes a power curve that describes the power at certain wind speeds. On the other hand, it also includes availability commitments that guarantee a certain number of operating days per year.

Liability

In addition to the above-mentioned liability cases for default or warranty claims, the project contracts should also take other possible liability cases into account. On both sides, breach of various kinds is imaginable, which constitute claims for damages. In addition, there are possible claims for tort. These claims are based on the condition that the other party is at fault. According to section 276 BGB, this exists if the obligor has acted intentionally or negligently. However, an attribution of fault can also be possible. Limitations of liability which exclude liability are a frequently used way of adapting the liability regime to the characteristics of the sector.

Interface Management

The fact that multi-contracting structures dominate the offshore wind energy sector necessarily leads to a situation in which the services of the various parties have to be coordinated separately and arising risks at the interfaces have to be dealt with as effectively as possible.[23] Interface management involves the technical coordination of the commissioning of the individual turbines and systems. But also the logistics and the general scheduling of the project development require detailed arrangements. Whereas the explanations above where focused on the relationship between the individual contractor and the project owner, interface management involves various contractors. Basically, there are two different approaches available to the project owner to consider the necessary elements of an effective interface management.

Multiparty agreements with all contractors

One possible approach is to negotiate a common agreement with all other parties involved in the project. The advantage is that the contractors can be forced to coordinate their services with each other. The project owner can limit the resource-intensive coordination work. However, the large number of parties will make the negotiations difficult. Hence, this concept is rarely seen in practice.

---

23 Vgl. *Schulz/Rohrer* in Schulz (Hrsg.), Handbuch Windenergie, Kapitel 5 Rn. 11.

Consideration in individual contracts

The project owner can also take manage the interface by way of coordinating the individual contracts with the contractors. This requires that the content of all contracts in the construction phase, which relate to a specific interface, are harmonized with each other. A complete exclusion of all interface risks can rarely be achieved in practice, but at least a far-reaching minimization is possible.

2.7.2 Phase 2: Operation

The construction phase is followed by the operating phase.

Maintenance Contract

The technical maintenance of the installed turbines is supposed to ensure a constantly high operational availability of the wind farm. Since the profitability of the entire project depends on the turbine's availability and functionality, securing maintenance work is particularly important from a financing point of view.[24]

Maintenance contracts can be designed as full service contracts and thus also include unplanned maintenance work. Contracts that only cover regular maintenance work, on the other hand, only provide for basic service. Any extraordinary repairs or measures would have to be ordered and paid separately.

Legal Classification

As already mentioned in the case of the construction contracts, the classification of the maintenance contracts depends on the individual case, whereby the main focus lays on the services to be conducted. Besides elements of sales and works contracts, there will be a strong focus on services (characterizing such maintenance contracts often as service contracts).[25]

The contracts usually run for several years. They are continuous obligations, premature contract terminations are usually neither in the interest of the project owner nor the contractor. The project owner does not know whether he can commit a new partner on acceptable terms. The contractor has regularly made investments which will only be amortized over time.

24 See also chapter 5.

25 Regarding the classification of contracts, which offer permanent services, see BGH NJW-RR 1997, 942 (943).

Content

The main focus of the operating phase is on ensuring availability of the offshore wind farm. The contractor usually warrants a certain availability of the wind farm. This is one of the main reasons why maintenance works are often done by the contractor who installed the turbines, because it knows the installation works best and is most likely willing to warrant a certain availability. The risk of taking over responsibility for another's installation work is usually remunerated with considerable price surcharges.

Benchmark for an availability guarantee can be the entire wind farm or individual turbines. The project owner is interested in receiving an availability guarantee for each individual turbine. Should an individual plant not provide the agreed performance, the project owner would be entitled to compensation for this reason alone. The contractor, on the other hand, could spread default risks if the entire wind farm was used as a benchmark.

Needless to say, days with adverse weather or regular maintenance work a usually excluded from a availability guarantee.[26]

Management Contract

In addition to the maintenance contracts, general management also becomes relevant in the operating phase. As in the construction phase, these services can also be taken over by the operator itself. Often, however, projects are owned by project companies without any employees.

Legal Classification

As the maintenance contracts, the operating management contracts are designed for a term of several years. They are also continuous obligations. Typologically, the contracts are agency agreements with a service contract character.

Content

Operating management requires detailed technical and commercial planning. It must be ensured that necessary technical adaptations are identified and that the required work is then carried out.

In order to identify the need for action, the central task of the operator is the continuous monitoring of the entire offshore wind farm. Among other things, this is done by recording and managing the operating data on a regular basis. However, on-site inspections must also be made. In any case, there is a need for action where technical adjustments to the turbines are required in order to ensure operation or to modernize

26 *Busch*, Ausgewählte vertragsrechtliche Fragen bei der Instandhaltung von Offshore-Windparks – Teil 2, NZBau 2011, 85 (88).

the wind farm. Management contracts may also cover the accounting and communication with authorities and network operators.

2.7.3 Phase 3: Dismantling

So far, a third phase, the dismantling of offshore wind turbines, has rarely been considered in detail in the literature. On the one hand, this is due to the fact that the implementation of offshore wind farm projects has only started significantly in the past 10 years. In conjunction with expected operating times of more than 20 years in some cases, dismantling has not been a topic of high importance. Looking at the permits, however, the Federal Maritime and Hydrographic Agency requires the plants to be dismantled after the operating phase. Here, too, offshore conditions make the processes complex and cost-intensive. The exact planning and consideration of the financial effort are therefore crucial for the success of an offshore wind farm project.

As in the construction and operating phases, there is the question which parties are potential contractual partners of the project owner. On the one hand, these can be companies that are specialized on the dismantling of offshore wind turbines and thus take over the entire dismantling process. On the other hand, certain services may be taken over individually by other companies involved, such as logistics. Furthermore, another factor is whether the entire plant or individual parts still have a market value. Buyers of such items can also be involved. Whether multi-contracting structures or general contractor concepts predominate the market cannot yet be assessed.

The dismantling contract is most likely a works contract under German law. A certain success is owed, namely the dismantling of the plants. If the dismantling is followed by the sale of the plant or the materials, elements of the sales contract may also be important when it comes to the potential sale of used turbines or systems. However, due to the dimensions of the individual systems, reutilization after a decommissioning elsewhere is often not profitable. The possible savings potential will often lag behind the transport and assembly costs that will again become necessary. In addition, the dismantling effort and consequently the costs also depend upon the extent to which the system must remain functional after dismantling. Often the most cost-effective option will be the demolition of the entire system. Nevertheless, there are often customers for older offshore wind turbines all over the world.

3 The Completion Risk in Offshore Wind Construction Projects: How Good Risk Management Adds Value to Large Asset Construction Projects

Peter Frohböse

3.1 The Motivation and Importance of Risk Management

3.1.1 Why Risk Management At All?

Planning an offshore wind farm development or construction project calls for plenty of tasks to be done in an appropriate and explicit manner in a limited amount of time. Therefore, you should weigh each task carefully with respect to the benefit for the final and long-term objective of the offshore wind farm project.

The implementation and execution of a risk management system into a project organization and project plan will certainly require time and resources, but the added value will be visible from day one onward as the return period and value generation is straight forward and will not require a maturation or evolution period.

3.1.2 Why Is Completion of Construction Projects a Risk?

The planning, design, fabrication and finally the construction and commissioning of major projects, such as large assets or infrastructure projects, often suffered from deviations of completion on time, budget and with the right quality in the past.

There are various examples on single cases as well as the attempt to collect very diverse projects in a uniform statistical database. Examples are given in [R Singh] and [C Koch].

A famous example for miscalculation is the “Elbphilharmonie” Opera House in Germany’s “wind capital” Hamburg, which has become a renowned landmark for Hamburg already. In that case the actual figures for finalization and budget very fast deviated from the planned and officially agreed figures that were used to find financial agreement within the federal state of Hamburg. For this reason, an assumed mismanagement was discussed widely in the public during the whole renovation and construction period [Wiki 2019–02].

Similarly, in the offshore wind sector are many examples of projects throughout the European countries that have largely exceeded both, budget as well as completion time. Additionally, quality deviations are common, but often not revealed in detail in the public debates as quality deviations are more complex to compare. The

https://doi.org/10.1515/9783110607888-019

budget and time schedule in contrast often is a single monetary value and a single datum. Respectively deviations on those parameters are often easily visible without looking into the projects in detail. Informed experts will recognize that quality is an important issue in many cases when projects have a time and budget challenge to solve. Quality deviations often come hand in hand with budget and time constrains, but quality issues will evolve and become visible over time and not as clearly as the budget exceedances and schedule changes.

The significance of the completion risk(s) can obviously not be ignored, with the consequences on budget, time and quality being to evident and the relation between the risks and the (positive) project outcome being clearly visible to all stakeholders.

3.1.3 Which Benefits Can a Risk Management Offer?

Why risk management and what is the additional benefit compared to the typical project management approach [PMI Guide], which requests and offers more than plenty reporting and planning duties to be performed?

A good structured and fully implemented risk management will have several benefits that will exceed the typical project management benefits. First of all, the objective of the risk management needs to be defined and understood:

- A risk management creates the needed awareness for project stakeholders to identify potential risks for the project and to follow up with the appropriate mitigations in a responsible manner.
- A risk management is a supporting tool for the project stakeholders and project management to ensure the delivery of the project on time, on budget and with the planned quality level.
- A risk management will make usage of the collected data in the risk register ensuring a structured way to analyze, predict and report the technical and commercial status of the project towards internal and external stakeholders.

These objectives are extremely important as risks will change over the project lifecycle and time. With changing characteristics and the nature of the risk, the mitigation will change and in most of the cases become more difficult and expensive. For a simplified illustration see Figure 3.1.

Looking at the consequences of the completion risk and the objectives of the risk management, the benefits can be stated in a simple and straight forward manner:

Based on the three main pillars budget, quality and time the project completion phase is the phase in which the different pieces of the project are coming together, and the execution will prove if all the detailed planning was sufficient to make things work.

A risk management will repetitively ask the questions “What is the project objective?” and “What can go wrong while archiving this objective?” This will create

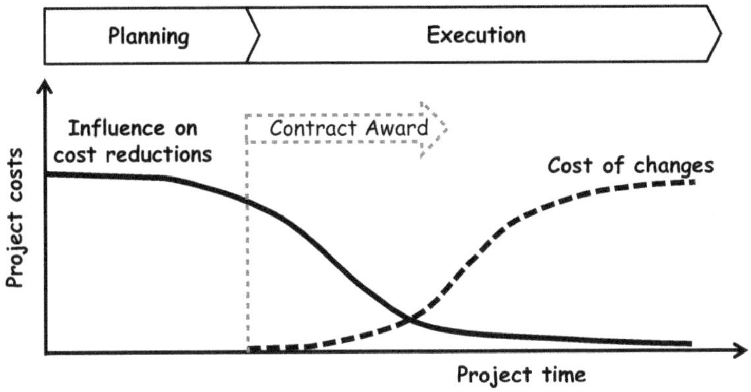

Figure 3.1: Mitigation costs increase with time (own representation).

an open atmosphere amongst all stakeholders to early identify, structure, organize and follow up all risks during the project development and execution.

As early mitigation will be beneficial for the effect on the risk (and such project cost, time and quality), a risk management will lead to better outcome of the project results.

The benefits, which are also defined in the ISO 31000 standard [ISO 31000] can be condensed to the following main benefits:

- Risk management aims to create and protect value(s).
- Risk management forms an essential part of the decision making.
- Risk management provides a methodology to specifically and explicitly address uncertainty.

In addition, risk management will reflect on the risk distribution and risk sharing of all stakeholders. This provides the basis for very large offshore projects (that are also projects that involve a great financial outlay) in order that these projects can be realized. This is done by distributing both the opportunities and the risks appropriately to all project stakeholders. This allows all stakeholders to recognize their benefits in bearing the risks.

3.2 The Basic Terms and Ideas

3.2.1 The Risk

A risk can have several appearances depending on the nature of the project and project objectives. However, there is a clear definition on the term and the usage of the term risk to avoid the confusion with other terms, which is often seen in the day-to-day language.

The definition according to the dictionaries e.g., [Wiki 2019–03] is:

> Risk is potential of losing something of value.

This is a simple and straight forward definition, but obviously very general and "open."

This definition is also in line with the more completion risk and risk management focused definition of the relevant industry standard on Risk Management ISO 31000 [ISO 31000]. Nevertheless, the standard definition is more specific on the objective and is as follows:

> Risk: effect of uncertainty on objectives.

In addition, the ISO Standard gives guidance on several aspects of the used term in that definition amongst which the effect explanation is worth mentioning. The effect is a deviation from the expected and in addition it allows a deviation in both directions positive and/or negative. As such the term risk is also applicable for changes often referred to as a "chance," a possible positive change of the expected.

In science and engineering risk has been reduced to a very simple equation that refers to two (2) main parameters that have an influence on the risk. Here the definition with the consideration of the parameters is:

A risk is the chance of something happening multiplied by the resulting outcome on the objective

Which leads to the following definition in a mathematical equation:

$$\text{Risk} = \text{Likelihood x Consequence}$$

The Likelihood

In this equation the likelihood is the chance of something happening and it can be expressed in various units depending on the objective of the application of the term risk. As such likelihood will be given as percentage (%), occurrences per year, occurrences per item or occurrences per project (etc.) or a combination of the previous.

The Consequence

The consequence is the loss or the benefit, which is most commonly expressed in the unit of money, as such EUR, USD, or other applicable. If the objective of the risk management suggests other units also a different definition can be a good choice, e.g., destroyed units, incidents, etc.

Finally, this will also lead to a unit for the risk figure based on the two main parameters defined above. In the common way it will lead to a cost per project figure (e.g., EUR/project completion). This definition may seem obsolete or self-explanatory, but when it comes to assessing the individual risks of a project it is of utmost importance to have a joint understanding of the units and as such the contest of the assessed risk input parameters.

The Completion Risk

The term completion risk has been adopted by the offshore wind energy sector from other industrial sectors (e.g., plant construction and building construction).

In the offshore wind energy industry, three main topics regarding the delivery for an offshore wind farm are discussed, which significantly influences the projects objective:

- Budget
- Time
- Quality

It is misleading to use the term "completion" to refer to the installation phase only. The build-up phase is merely the "grand finale" of a long development, manufacturing and assembly process that is all part of the completion process.

3.2.2 The Methods of Risk Assessment

The difference of qualitative and quantitative risk assessment has been touched in the risk definition already. Both approaches are shortly described in the following to make clear how to distinguish and when to use which approach.

Qualitative Risk Assessment

The qualitative approach is best used for risk assessments on a limited data basis. It is a less formal and less structured (as such less reproductive results) approach that should only be used in cases where Likelihood and Consequence cannot be numerically expressed or estimated [Wiki 2018, 11]. In that cases the risk is assessed by using rather vague, verbal descriptions of "qualifiers" for the risk as the result or the Likelihood (e.g., high likelihood, low likelihood, etc.) and the Consequence (e.g., severe, very severe, low, etc.). Be careful as these verbally descriptions can lead to lack of clarity and mixing cause and result (e.g., likelihood, consequence and risk). Therefore, the qualitative assessments should be applied with great care and in cases where a quantitative assessment is not possible. Thus, the application is mostly limited to early screening or pre-assessments when, for example, a benchmarking of multiple cases or choices is needed or when a sufficient database or estimation is not possible [Wiki 2019–01].

Quantitative Risk Assessment

The quantitative risk assessment (often referred to as "QRA") is the method that will result in quantitative estimates of risks. This method is requiring the quantitative assessment of the defining parameters as such specifically likelihood and consequence.

In the context of project execution and completion risk the quantitative risk assessment in most cases includes a calculation of a single loss expectancy of mostly a monetary value of a project (e.g., deviation from the planned investment budget).

Special considerations are needed to statistically combine the multiple single risk items into one single project value of significance (e.g., [Wiki 2019–03] and [Wiki 2019–01]). This has been solved in the offshore wind sector by employing the so called "Monte-Carlo-Simulation" method. This method is both mathematically correct and easy to integrate in simple software tools or even spread sheet applications.

3.2.3 The Risk Register

A risk register is a list or table of context and project related risks including the definition and values of the risk specific parameters such as likelihood and consequence. It is the single point of source for all risks to have full interface coverage and transparency. The risk register further serves as a source for project reporting and as the basis for a statistical assessment and analysis. It will include the responsibilities for both the risks and the mitigation actions and have a basic record to allow tracking of the individual risks and their mitigations. The risk register can in addition be used to be an important part of the reporting to the senior management or project directors. The risk register is best filed accessible for all participants involved in the risk management process. As a recommendation the following parameters should be included for each of the risks:

Further the risk register is needed to assess the risks for the project in a macro assessment, e.g., to quantify the risks via a Monte Carlo Simulation into a single statistic and a very focused set of results. The details will be discussed in section 3.4.

3.2.4 The Risk Manager

In principle the risk manager facilitates the whole risk management process throughout the project life time. The risk manager must train and create the awareness amongst the project team and has to implement and update the risk review process. He supports the updates of the risk register based on the findings in the regular risk reviews (see Table 3.1). The responsibility of the risk identification, the risk assessment as well as the risk description and the details of the risk mitigation are preferably with the risk owners and not the duty of the risk manager.

Table 3.1: Recommended Parameters of the Risk Register (own representation).

ITEM	DESCRIPTION
ID	Some risks may have exchangeable names or risks may reappear over time as such an individual Risk ID, number or other code is deemed beneficial to be clear and precise.
NAME	Item short name or short description. This is just to have a catchy name to refer to in day-to-day treatment, as not all people involved will keep the precise IDs in mind.
DESCRIPTION	The risk description is more detailed than the name allowing the reader to understand the context and challenge of the risk. It is a brief but also comprehensive description, that must discuss all factors. As such the following items must be discussed: Likelihood, Consequence; Mitigation and risk context.
LIKELIHOOD	The likelihood is a quantitative description of the risks associated likelihood (as per definition a probability per project, etc.). Keeping it simple the figure could only come as a percentage (%). It is recommended to be accompanied by a description how this percentage value was assessed and if it is understood to be conservative, moderate or progressive.
CONSEQUENCE	The consequence is a quantitative description of the risks associated consequence (as per definition a range, a distribution (e.g., statistical function and the parameters)) Keeping it simple the figure could only come as a monetary value (for example a single € value as the 50% mean). It is recommended to be accompanied by a description how this consequence was assessed and if it is understood to be conservative, moderate or progressive.
OWNER	The risk owner is the person responsible to take action and inform on this particular risk including mitigation. In many cases the risk owner will have the possibility to delegate the daily treatment of the mitigation plan, however ownership should be based on responsibility and the power to take action (budget, resources, etc.)
MITIGATION	The risk mitigation is the detailed description of the mitigation and mitigation plan. As such this should elaborate on whether the likelihood or the consequence will be mitigated or both. The mitigation description should allow for the reader to understand the context and rational behind the risk. It is a brief but also comprehensive description, that must discuss all factors and the effect on the risk. As such the following items must be discussed: Effect on Likelihood, Effect on Consequence; Effect on Risk in total and Budget/Cost for the mitigation plan once executed as well as time schedule and due dates for the mitigation actions.
STATUS	This status is required for reporting and analysis purposes. It needs to be deviated between "active risks" and "historic risks." This will be a multiple choice for example "Open" or "Closed" or any other status required.

3.2.5 The Typical Types of Risks

The most important and most general distinction of risk types is with respect to the knowledge and thus the predictability. In terms of predictability of a risk or a certain set of risks a decision can be made towards risks that are well known and risks that are fully unknown at the time of investigation. The risks that are more transparent are those that are well understood and that respectively can be predicted and assessed with a reliable basis. The other area is risks that the stakeholders are not aware of and as such cannot assess or even predict. This distinction can be done in a 4 x 4 matrix as given in Table 3.2:

Table 3.2: Types of risks in a 4 x 4 matrix (own representation).

	Easy to assess	Difficult to assess
High awareness	**Known Knowns:** the associated risks are based on things that we know that we know; general knowledge, well understood and good awareness.	**Known Unknowns:** the associated risks are based on things we know that we don't know. Not understood but aware of the potential risk. (it might be also that we are aware, but we don't know their potential risks.)
Low awareness	**Unknown Knowns:** the associated risks are based on things that exist and have been influencing our approach to reality, but we are unaware of knowing them. (it might be we do not realize their value or worse we refuse to acknowledge knowing them.)	**Unknown Unknowns:** the associated risks are based on things we don't even know that we don't know. They can lead to serious and unexpected impacts. The worst of the 4 groups. Not understood (not assessable) and not aware (no warning time).

There are several other types and definitions of categories that one can think of and that can be applied if considered useful in the context of a certain project. These are for example the types based on the consequence (budget, time, quality) or the types based on allocation (external or internal).

3.2.6 The Life Cycle of a Risk

The perception and knowledge of the risks will change over time as such it is useful to understand that 1. the likelihood and 2. consequence of a risk will change over time and these changes need to be monitored and tracked.

As has been indicated in the previous sections there are risks that are well understood and that can be estimated on a good basis. In contrast there are many risks that will not be visible at all and there is a number of risks that lie in between and either have bad visibility or can only be badly assessed.

As a result, if time proceeds the predictability will change over time as knowledge is gained on the parameters of the risk such as consequences and likelihood. This is a typical learning curve that can be stated on a risk evolvement path form unknown to identified to assessed, mitigated and then budgeted and finally solved.

In the concept of risk management and budget planning with a certain contingency in place the risk can be seen in 2 points in time.

- Before identification (unknown) (Time 1)
- after identification and assessment (in the risk register, Time 2) and
- in the appeared stage (in the budget) (Time T3)

The following Figure 3.2 serves as an illustration:

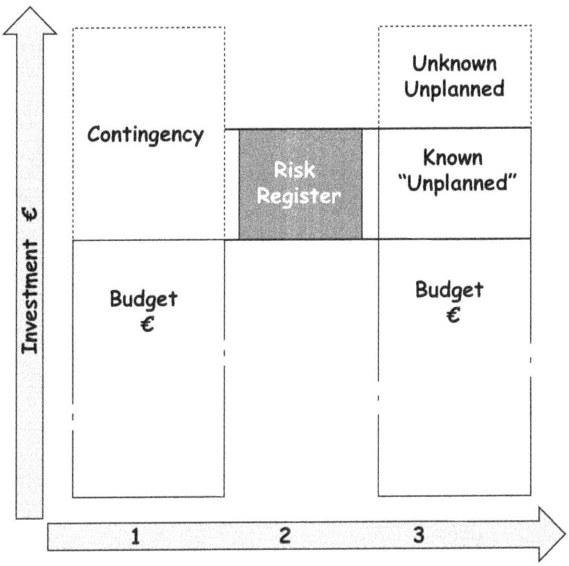

Figure 3.2: Risk development over time (own representation).

3.3 Technology, Stakeholders, and Phases

3.3.1 The Elements of a Typical Offshore Wind Farm Project

This section outlines the main components that are typically employed in an offshore wind farm. This description shall allow a specific set of defined terms for the main components and associated subcomponents to be used in this article.

As this description is specifically limited to highlight the technical elements for the discussion of risks, the technical definition and description within this section is not comprehensive. There is literature available to refer to for further exploration and information on offshore wind assets as well as the wind turbine generators (for example [R Gasch] and [E Hau]) which are much more comprehensive.

In general, typical offshore wind farms can be split into the broad main components that are visualized in the following simplified illustration (Figure 3.3):

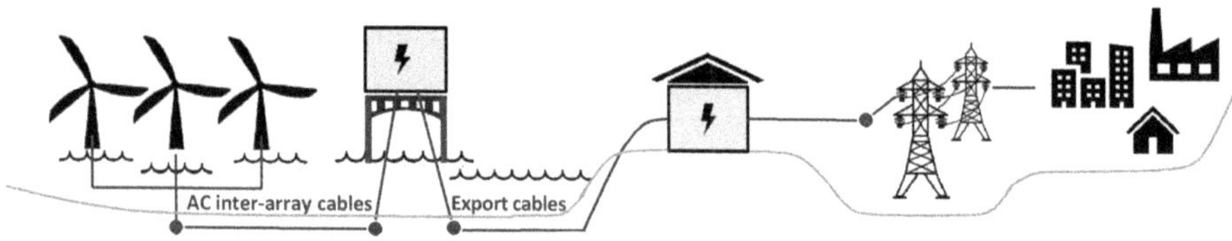

Generation	Collection	Transform	Transmission	Grid connection	Consumption

Wind Turbines	Strings	Offshore Sub Station	Onshore Cable	Onshore Station	Grid connection	End User

Inter Array Cables	Export Cable	Onshore Cable	Onshore Grid

The wind velocity conversion to torque and then electrical power is done via the wind turbine generators.	The power collection is done via inter array cables connecting the individual turbines to strings and then the strings to the offshore substation.	The power will be gathered from all wind turbines and converted from one voltage level to a higher voltage level for more efficient transportation to the next connection point or to the grid.	The connection to the onshore grid is done via export cables and maybe a converter station. This can potentially include downward adjustment of the voltage levels to grid connection level.

Figure 3.3: Technical elements of a modern offshore wind farm (own representation).

3.3.2 The Stakeholders

For defining the risk assessment objective and context, it is required to understand the perspective of the stakeholders, project partners and relevant participants that are involved in the project. The most important part of this stakeholder and participant discussion is to gain a precise understanding of the objective, motivation, scope of work, responsibilities, capabilities and intention of the different stakeholders.

According to the Project Management Institute [PMI Guide] the term stakeholder is used for individuals, groups, or organizations, that may affect or be affected by (or only perceive to be affected) by any kind of decision, activity, or outcome of the project. Due to this interaction between the project and the stakeholders, the stakeholders must be considered as parties that have an interest in the project.

Stakeholders can be separated according to their organizational location (inside or outside the wider project team). These stakeholders are introduced briefly to understand the interests and capabilities of these parties. In the design and construction phase, the following project stakeholders are the ones who are actively involved in the project realization. It needs to be stated that "double roles" are not uncommon. For example, the operator can also be involved with a share of equity in the project. The split is intended only to clarify the different interests of the stakeholder groups.

Supply: Marine Coordination and Logistics

The installation of wind turbines and substructures requires large crane ships and transport ships. These ships must be able to transport and install the large components. The offshore wind energy industry relies on ships developed specifically for the offshore wind market but also oil and gas offshore market. This also means competition with the prices paid in the oil and gas industry.

Suppliers: Main Components

Most suppliers of the main components (substructures) come from the classical engineering, shipbuilding or supplier spectrum that have mostly a history in the oil and gas sector. It is only in recent years that companies have emerged that specialize in delivering primarily to the offshore wind energy industry.

Suppliers: Wind Turbine

In the early years of the emerging offshore wind market in Europe, the wind turbine manufacturers have had a very dominant role in the offshore wind market. However, this role has changed and nowadays does not apply to all wind turbine manufacturers. This is due to the fact that in addition to special technical features of a wind turbine, special requirements are needed on the wind turbine manufacturer as contractual partner. An ideal wind turbine manufacturer must be able to support (prefinance) projects of a certain size and be able to process them. Furthermore, it must be ensured that the supply of spare parts is always possible over a period of 20 to 30 years (project operation). The larger the series of wind turbine type, the more likely it is to deliver and adequately stock spare parts. As a result, market dominance has focused primarily on high-turnover and profitable manufacturers.

Equity Investors and Lenders

Above all, the investor (banks and / or investors) has the interest to recover the capital invested and to earn his margin (interest). He only has a conditional influence on the design of the project as part of a so-called due diligence or as defined in the conditions of contract.

Developer, Owner, Operator

The project owner and operator will assess the project primarily according to its characteristics during the operational phase. Respectively these factors are the ongoing costs for maintenance, repairs and operational management. The Operator is responsible for influencing the costs and revenues of the project by actively designing towards the operating phase. This also includes to ensure a steady cash flow to have always sufficient cash flow in the projects revenue stream to meet current obligations (e.g., towards investors and lenders).

In slight deviation the project developer if he is focused only on a pure development and flipping strategy, his objectives are slightly different and are aiming high return once the project sale is completed. For example, this can lead to a simple goal to create a very attractive project with as little effort as possible in order to maximize the profits from the development.

Insurance Body

Since the individual project participants in the design and construction phase are difficult to bear all of the potential risks in full consequence, an insurer is a good solution to transfer some of the major risks and to meet the need for protection of the other stakeholders.

Regulators and Authorities: Permit, Consent, Grid

For the regulators (legislators, authorities, etc.) the specific economic interest of a single project is of low importance. The regulator will aim towards a best match of macro-economic benefits in the mid to long term while safeguarding the health and safety of the involved personal and public as well as the environment.

Consultants and Advisors

Consultants are rather the ones that are used inside the project or inside a supplier's organization to cover a specialist topic or to cover a lack of own resources. As the consultants are working for a specific stakeholder they will follow the stakeholder's objective. Advisors are often supporting the Investors and Lenders.

3.3.3 The Phases and Processes

The Development and Construction Phases

As mentioned in the terms and definitions the construction phase that has the completion risk inherent, is merely the "grand finale" of a long development, design, engineering, procurement, fabrication and assembly process. The following Figure 3.4 illustrates the construction phase in the whole life cycle of the project.

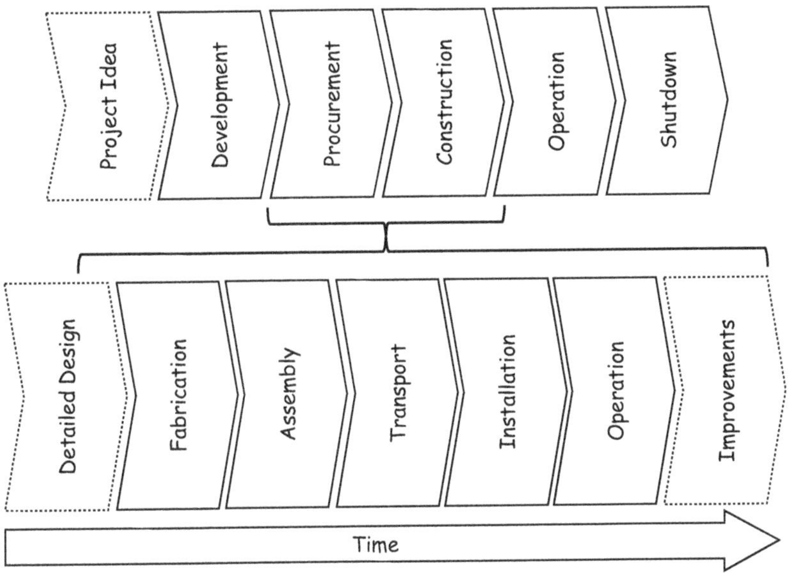

Figure 3.4: High level time schedule and project phases (own representation).

The construction phase must be understood to cover the complete detailed design, fabrication, assembly and construction and erection of the offshore wind farm. As such broadly speaking all phases that follow the final investment decision after the project financing has been agreed. These phases cannot be limited to the pure installation work of the offshore wind asset as engineering and fabrication are crucial phases. This focus on the construction phase is driven by the fact that all work in this phase is highly dependent on the previous tasks and works. This includes the tasks production, transport and assembly, as these form the preparation process for the offshore installation.

As an approach for splitting the construction process into distinguished phases is to follow the different activities. For most of the technical components and elements, the project will be required to do the following:

- Design and Engineering
- Fabrication and Manufacturing
- Assembly and Pre-Assembly
- Transportation and installation
- Fabrication Testing and On-site testing
- Installation
- Commissioning

3.3.4 Risk Distribution and Risk Allocation

Offshore projects are too complex to give a single person and even a single project stakeholder complete capability to handle, manage and mitigate all risks. For this reason, it is expedient to commission different stakeholders with risk management for different specialist areas.

For the planning or during the active project, the following questions must be clarified to allow a smooth cooperation of the participants:
- Which Stakeholder has what interests and goals?
- Which Stakeholder owns which skills and opportunities?

This makes it easier to determine:
- Which project work packages and tasks can the project stakeholder control or influence?
- Which risks can a project stakeholder assess and possibly bear?
- Which possible and potential unidentified risks may be brought up by the various stakeholders?

The answers to those questions will ease to entrust the stakeholders involved in the project with a certain set of specific risks. This needs to ensure that they are able to control or in a worst-case scenario accept and buffer this risk. As a second point it may be beneficial for some stakeholders to bear a risk as they will also benefit from positive developments. This will have a motivational effect to those stakeholders and lead to a beneficial outcome for the project.

In the second step, it must then be ensured that each of the actively involved stakeholder receives the risks as acceptable but still has a high level of interest in the project's common objectives.

Contracting Strategy

The risk allocation exercise is seamlessly connected to the actual contractual strategy and also to the risk allocation within the individual supply and execution contracts.

The contracting strategy will have a major impact on the successful outcome of the project. This planning process requires:
- distributing the risks as fairly as possible, and
- clearly defining the potential risks to make responsibilities clear.

As potential risk takers it may be considered anyone who is actively involved in the project or who can benefit from the project's common objective.

This risk distribution usually takes place in the contract structure and contract design in the procurement phase. In most cases, construction companies are formed under subcontracting of experienced and high-performance suppliers. The contractual strategy should not leave any gaps at the interfaces of the individual works and tasks. This strategy must assure the predictability of the risk allocation but should still allow an optimization of the collected experience during execution of the project.

It is recommended that the owner undertakes a full and detailed risk assessment with senior management and the project team to develop the best contracting strategy for the project. This needs also to reflect the external conditions of the market – for example, early evaluation of the stakeholder's appetite for certain risks or benefits of the project.

An important decision is needed ahead of the risk allocation to define the risk distribution between the employer and the contractor(s). For example, for a strategy that has a more turnkey like approach (low risk allocation at the project owner) or to go with a more open multi-contract strategy (more interface risk and coordination effort at the project owners' team).

3.4 The Risk Management Process

3.4.1 General

The objective of this section is to describe the minimum requirements of a risk management system for a typical offshore wind farm project and the associated project management team and the project stakeholders. The requirements are defined with respect to management of risks within the project execution during construction phase and construction management of the project.

Risk management is an important part that needs to come hand in hand with the standardized project management principles. Risk management must be a cornerstone of the project's control mechanisms for budget, time and quality. It is the objective to control the risks the project is exposed to.

All managers, directors and technical experts are expected to understand the concept and importance of risk management and to implement this in their areas of responsibility where applicable.

The process will describe the key steps in the risk management process and the required main activities that need to be carried out.

Minimal Requirements

Before the detailed implementation of a risk management and the activities on a task level are discussed the requirements are summarized to allow the risk management to unfold its full potential. This means the project management should:
- ensure that required resources (human and financial) are provided.
- ensure commitment and participation of all stakeholders, in particular the package managers, to ensure that the risk management objectives are achieved.
- proactively seek to predict risks which can negatively affect the projects objectives.
- emphasis a state-of-the-art quantitative risk assessment methodology is required and applied.
- review the risk assessments on significant new ventures and activities.
- review the risk summary on a project or predefined stakeholder level.
- ensure that risk mitigating measures are applied and needed resources are available.
- assign responsibilities to each respective mitigation measure to ensure the initiative is being executed according to plan.
- participate in re-evaluating the risk profile on a regular basis to ensure that the overall risk exposure of the project is effectively managed and that the residual risk is acceptable.
- actively seek to learn from past events to minimize the probability of such event to reoccur, and to limit the consequence should such events still occur.
- actively seek to learn from other offshore projects of similar nature (offshore wind energy, as well as oil and gas or other major projects) to minimize the probability of such event to occur within the project itself.
- actively use findings from the risk management process as input to the operational planning process to ensure that potential risks can be mitigated through initiatives driven by the project director, the package managers or the technical experts in charge.
- support regular trainings of the project key stakeholders to ensure an appropriate level of understanding and basis for the risk owners to fulfill their role.

3.4.2 The Step by Step Process

The Risk Management Process described here is aligned to the principles and guidelines in ISO 31000 [ISO 31000] as well as the Offshore Code of Practice [VdS OCoP] and the PMI guide to project Management [PMI Guide].

Based on the above literature and the reduction to the most important steps and tasks the risk management process can be summarized in four essential steps that are to be undertaken in a repeating manner therefor the circular respective illustration is a good display of the "never ending activity of risk management." The four essential steps are:
- Risk identification
- Risk assessment and analysis
- Risk mitigation and steering
- Risk control and management

The detailed content of the steps will be discussed in the following sub sections. The steps are to be applied in a repetitive manner during the lifecycle of the project and as such the circular illustration (Figure 3.5 and 3.6) serves a good and representative recap.

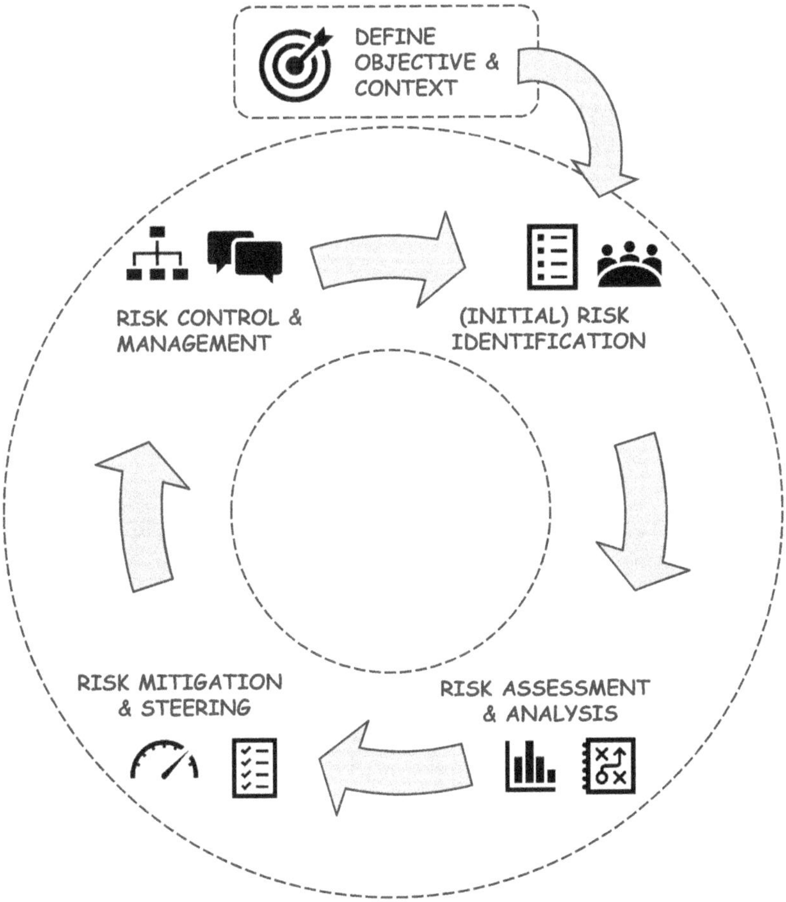

Figure 3.5: The essential steps of the risk management process (own representation).

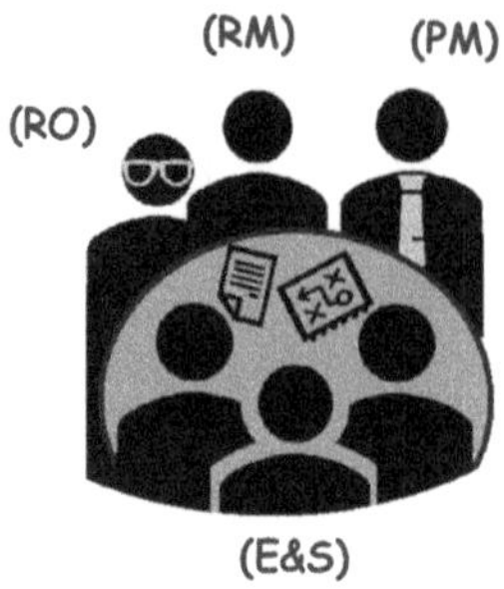

Figure 3.6: Roles and responsibilities (own representation).

3.4.3 Initial Step: Objective and Context Definition

However, before the first step and before the initial risk identification can be started a definition of the project objective and also the context of the risk management in a reflective manner needs to be performed. This may be simple as the cornerstones of the project plan can serve as a good source for this definition. Nevertheless, this initial task should not be overseen as it may reduce the alignment and discussions in the day to day activities of the risk management process.

3.4.4 Risk Identification

The first step of any risk management process is an (initial) identification of all possible risks towards the project's objective. During the course of the risk management this risk assessment will be done repeatedly to review the new conditions the things that have changed and find any new risk. In principle the following points need to be done:

- Review the project objective and the risk management context
- Analysis of the project details to identify the existing and possible risks and start documentation in a professional and appropriate manner (risk register and reports).
- The identification will include the consideration of communication, contracts, information memorandums and Variation Orders / instructions and other relevant documents.
- The implemented risk management process will be based on the actual findings out of the project management and construction monitoring processes.

For risk identification the ISO 31000 provides a summary of possible activities and methods to gain the best results possible. In addition, the European Standard IEC/ISO 31010 gives further guidance and illustration on various techniques that can be used and applied. A few very practical methods and tools are described in the following sections.

Risk Review: Meetings and Interviews

The risk management shall perform a regular "risk-review", which is best undertaken in meetings and interviews or group interviews with the relevant stakeholders.

The approach to schedule formal risk review meetings that are held on a (at least) monthly basis is the best way to do this. This review should include the review of the project, the project packages as well as external factors.

The Risk Meetings shall include the repeated risk identification, the assessment of the risks, risk mitigation, appointment of a risk owner and the mitigation/control and adjustment of the existing risks and mitigation plans.

Within the risk meetings at least the responsible managers and external and internal technical experts are to be interviewed and their opinions are to be considered respectively.

The tracking of the mitigation measures is part of the risk reviews meetings.

Identification, evaluation and assessment of the risks should best be done in a multidisciplinary working group. It is recommended to include topic specific verifiers to avoid a tunnel view of the daily involved experts.

A valid approach would make use the knowledge and experience of many experts. The following roles and responsibilities for the risk review meetings must be considered for the process:

- Specialists to the specific problem or area (commercial, technical, legal or management experts)
- Responsible person for project or sub-task (project manager, package manager or responsible mitigation manager)
- Responsible person in charge for the specific risk discussed (risk owner)
- Moderator and risk method specialist (risk manager)

The roles can overlap, but conflicts need to be assessed and investigated up-front.

3.4.5 Risk Assessment and Analysis

As already discussed in the step 1 the assessment of the risks can already be done in conjunction with the risk identification. As soon as you identify a risk you will have a certain understanding of the risk, the underlying parameters and their quality. From this to a quantitative assessment it is an easy exercise.

For the assessment it is important that the assessment in different groups/settings and meetings follows the same approach in order to allow the combination of results and comparison of the assessments.

The precision can often serve as a barrier in practical applications. The experts and team members want to be very precise which may lead to time consuming and ineffective debates or background research. The solution here is to refer to ballpark figures only and the effect that individual risks will only occur in combination with each other make a difference to the project's overall assessment. As such better a fast and less precise result and a regular review than an unassessed risk.

The step will assess the individual risks based on consequence and probability of occurrence. This automatically specifies the risks in their significance and in most cases their allocation within the project's structure.

As an associated result you will obtain a micro assessment of the risks and this can be used to conduct first a prioritization of the risks based on the compared rating.

However, the final objective is to conduct the macro assessment: The assessment is meant to create a result on a project basis by taking into account all risks that have been identified. For this task the risk register can be used to model and evaluate the Budget and as such the capital investment after project completion including all risks.

3.4.6 Risk Mitigation and Steering

A more global perspective is available following a first micro assessment on a risk by risk basis and relative macro assessment of all risks against each other. This will allow the identification and focus on the most relevant risks for the project. Obviously the most important risks are the ones that would have the most severe effect on the project objective. However, both criteria – the likelihood and the consequence – need to be considered for this conclusion. As a result, the mitigation actions undertaken must focus on those most critical risks, which then gives you the best candidates for starting to evaluate the mitigation measures.

The discussion, assessment, evaluation and choice of different mitigations for the individual risks are required and should be conducted by the project team and the responsible risk owner respectively. This should also include a review of the mitigations with respect to their relevance and applicability. Finally, all mitigations need to be integrated in the risk register including their effect on the probability and consequence. As a consequence, the risk assessment needs to be done once again.

Mitigation Planning and Types

In order to mitigate a risk, there are only two choices as a risk consists out of two parameters. As a result, the risk can only be mitigated by reducing one or both of the following:

- Likelihood
- Consequence

Depending on the type of risk you will find that one option is more suitable or if the risk is of utmost importance that you need to approach both parameters.

The principle mitigation strategies are limited to the following set of possibilities:

- **Acceptance**

The risk will not be mitigated at all and needs to be accepted as a risk for the project objective.

- **Avoidance**

The activity that leads to the risk is not done as such the consequence cannot appear or the consequence is reduced to zero.

- **Limitations**

Likelihood and consequence can be reduced resulting in a lower risk or a limited risk to the project.

- **Transference**

The risk is transferred to another stakeholder as such the responsibility is not with the project anymore. Also, an insurance is a typical transfer measure.

- **Other**

Combination of the above; Insurance

The mitigation measures often come as a mitigation plan and should be treated accordingly. In many cases a mitigation is treated as a small task or project itself. Frequently major project risks end up being run as a separate sub-project with the objective to control and reduce the risk accordingly. Time and budget as well as resource planning applies accordingly.

Most important is that all mitigations and decisions need to be put into action in the project management activities.

3.4.7 Risk Management and Control

The activity management and control are to be understood as a follow up and review activity of the current project and sub packages with regard to the development of the identified risks and mitigations over time, but also emerging risks. In addition, it is required to gain a global picture, meaning that the individual risks that have been assessed on a risk by risk basis now need to be combined and accumulated on a project level to a set of results that is more aggregated towards a limited number of results (Figure 3.7).

This global result is usually generated by risk cumulation techniques such as Monte Carlo Simulation or other combination technics, see below sub section for details.

Further the risk management and control step will be the point for generating the detailed and summary results and initiate the required reporting and result interpretation. Combined with a recommendation for the next iteration round.

Finally, this step will finish the cycle and then start the new cycle for the next round following again the same four steps. It will be a re-loop of the process

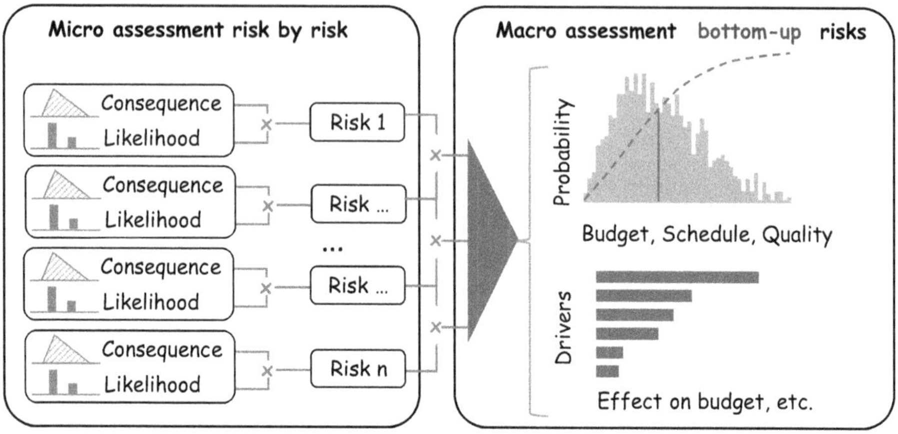

Figure 3.7: Micro and macro assessment in the risk management (own representation).

starting again from "Step 1 Risk Identification," but re-assessing will be faster and easier. However, starting again will also mean to carefully review the mitigation plans and mitigation actions implemented and check if the desired outcome and effect is visible in the project.

Reflection of Process and Context

When finishing the circle, the risk management objective, the initially agreed context and the implemented processes need to be reviewed and reflected against any occurred changes inside or outside the project. It needs to be checked if all the implemented processes are still appropriate and if the context is valid. If major changes to the objective are made this needs to be understood and taken into account. If changes are found these need to be discussed with all stakeholders and teams participants. This task is basically looking at the risk management from a bird's eye perspective and to assess if the overall setting still is appropriate.

Risk Modeling, Simulation and Consolidation methodology

As discussed above the objective is to perform a quantitative risk assessment for each of the individual risks. Based on the quantitative risk assessment approach of the single risks a mathematical approach to consolidate the risks on a project level (and the package and sub package level) is needed.

This methodology is found in the so-called Monte Carlo simulation approach that in a statistically correct manner. This approach allows the aggregation of independent and non-correlated risks within a certain project context. Thus, the project can consolidate and assess for example possible future investment and budget values on a statistical basis as for example exceedance levels such as 10%, 50% or 90% based on all the events in the risk register.

Based on the outcome of the findings and discussion on the bottom up approach new assessments or mitigations can be implemented into the risk register and the risk assessment can be rerun accordingly (bottom down). This will create a solid basis for the generation of the final global results.

3.5 The Summary and Hands-On Guidance

In this article the basic vocabulary was introduced and defined as well as difference was made clear towards the non-scientific usage of the risk management language.

The importance of the project objective and context setting and the awareness of both as well as the scope of the risk management was explained. Respectively the clear distinction between risk that are controlled by the project and risk that are not in control of the project was pointed out. This rationalization lead to the rational of the risk allocation and the importance of the right stakeholders being in charge for the corresponding risks.

As the core of the explanations a simple and easy to implement risk management step by step process was explained and introduced. This process being conformed to the international standard for risk management the ISO 31000 [ISO 31000] and aligned with the VDE Guideline on offshore risks [VdS OCoP].

Risk Management in a Nutshell: The Six Questions!

In order to create a risk management mindset and to have the required awareness for the monitoring and identification of risks there is a very simple and straightforward recipe that can be applied. As the risk identification is all about having the context in mind under which to repetitively consider "things" that can go wrong the easy to use formula is asking questions! The following six questions will serve the mind setting and guide through the process:

What is the project objective and context?

Be clear with your targets! Be able to answer the question: What am I trying to archive? The Context setting and clarity on the overall objective is an important step that is often overlooked. Only if you have targets you can have risks!

What might affect me?

What will help or hinder me achieving the objectives and is there anything that could change the context dramatically? Identify all possible risks. Use various techniques and – most important – always be open, reflective and honest. Involve the project team and experts to ask open questions. Do not hesitate to be disturbing.

Which of those affecting things are most important?
Go through a robust quantitative risk assessment and use the results to prioritize. How likely are the risks and what is the severity of the consequence? Is there low probability and high consequence risks that hide in the results. Check them and treat them with attention.

What am I going to do to mitigate it?
After prioritization of the risks start the mitigation planning. Ask the question: What can you do to prevent the consequence or to reduce the likelihood to the responsible experts? Further be able to think out of the box and indicate if there is a risk that needs to be transferred or accepted.

Did my mitigation plan work?
Be sure you implement the mitigation plans and be sure you track the execution. If that is done repeatedly ask the questions: Did the mitigation work? Can we do more to protect the project objective? Are the people in charge motivated to execute the plan? Is the initially assessed risk reduced according to plan? Make sure this assessment of the mitigation (actually the re-assessment of the risk) gets into the risk register.

What has changed?
Once you have gone through this loop: you need to restart . . . from 1. Do loop these six questions again. "Life" is changing thus stay ahead of any unknowns! Be able to predict the unknown knowns and to uncover the hidden risks. Reduce the surprises to a lowest minimum.

References

[R Singh] Singh, Ram. 2009. "Delays and Cost Overruns in Infrastructure Projects – An Enquiry into Extents, Causes and Remedies." Centre for Development Economics, Delhi School of Economics, Working papers.

[C Koch] Koch, Christian. 2012. "Contested overruns and performance of offshore wind power plants." *Construction Management and Economics* 30: 609–22. 10.1080/01446193.2012.687830.

[Wiki 2019–02] Wikipedia contributors (28.02.2019). "Elbphilharmonie." Wikipedia, The Free Encyclopaedia. https://en.wikipedia.org/wiki/Elbphilharmonie.

[PMI Guide] *A Guide to the Project Management Body of Knowledge (PMBOK Guide)*. 3rd ed. Newtown Square, PA: Project Management Institute, 2004. Print.

[ISO 31000] International Standard; ISO 31000 Second edition 2018–02; Risk management – Guidelines; Reference number: ISO 31000:2018(E).

[Wiki 2019–03] Wikipedia contributors (05.03.2019). “Risk.” Wikipedia, The Free Encyclopaedia. https://en.wikipedia.org/wiki/Risk.

[Wiki 2018–11] Wikipedia contributors (19.11.2018). “Qualitative risk analysis.” Wikipedia, The Free Encyclopaedia. https://en.wikipedia.org/wiki/Qualitative_risk_analysis.

[Wiki 2019–01] Wikipedia contributors (13.01.2019). “Qualitative risk assessment software.” Wikipedia, The Free Encyclopaedia. https://en.wikipedia.org/wiki/Quantitative_risk_assess ment_software.

[R Gasch] Gasch, Robert, ed. 1993. *Windkraftanlagen, Grundlagen und Entwurf*, 2nd rev. ed. Stuttgart: Teubner, 1993.

[E Hau] Hau, Erich (1996). *Windkraftanlagen: Grundlagen, Technik, Einsatz, Wirtschaftlichkeit*, 2nd rev. ed. Berlin: Springer, 1996.

[VdS OCoP] International Guideline on the risk management of offshore wind farms; Offshore Code of Practice (OCoP); VdS 3549en 2014–01 (01).

[IEC 31010] European Standard IEC/ISO 31010:2009 EN 31010, Reference number EN 31010:2010 E Risk management – Risk assessment techniques (IEC/ISO 31010:2009), European Committee for Electrotechnical Standardization, May 2010.

4 Energy Yield Assessments

Dr. Volker Barth, Dr. Beatriz Cañadillas, Dr. Patricia Chaves-Schwinteck

4.1 Introduction

One of the first steps in planning an offshore wind farm is to estimate the available wind resource. This determines the possible yield and therefore forms the basis of the entire economics. The wind farm design also depends crucially on the wind conditions in order to use the available wind supply as efficiently as possible at a minimum level of wear and tear. This results in high demands on the quality of the calculations to assess the wind potential at the wind farm location – especially offshore, where the investment sums are significantly higher than onshore.

In this section we first describe the basic characteristics of the wind conditions at sea, and which measurements and databases are available to estimate the wind supply. The focus here is on North Sea conditions, for which the greatest historical experience exists, but the methodology can in principle be applied worldwide. Next, we look at the wind flow within the wind farm, because the reduction of the wind speed behind a wind turbine ("wake") plays a central role offshore, both for the energy yield and for the loads imposed on the wind turbines. With this information and some more turbine specific data the energy yield can be calculated. We describe the commonly used method based on measured wind data, discuss possible causes of loss and sources of uncertainty and give some hints on how these can be reduced. The section ends with an outlook on energy yield assessments based on production data, which can be expected to grow in importance given the increasing number of operational wind farms.

4.2 Wind Resources Offshore

Offshore wind conditions are characterized by high wind speeds, which are not disturbed by obstacles or topographical features. Therefore the wind flow is generally steadier and less turbulent than over land. In this section, we discuss the essential characteristics of the atmosphere above the sea, describe common methods for wind measurements, and present existing databases and modeling approaches, which are frequently used when determining the yield of offshore sites.

4.2.1 Structure of the Marine Atmospheric Boundary Layer

The atmospheric boundary layer is the lower part of the troposphere where the wind speed increases from zero at the ground to the wind speed of the undisturbed

https://doi.org/10.1515/9783110607888-020

geostrophic wind at about 1–2 km altitude. Above lies the free atmosphere, which is considered to be unaffected by earth's surface. The height of the atmospheric boundary layer varies depending on the weather and solar irradiation. For unstable stratification and the resulting strong vertical exchange it is slightly higher, while it is lower for stable stratification. Over land, the boundary layer reaches up to approx. 1–2 km height. Offshore, this height is reduced to only about 0.5 km. Under very stable conditions, the offshore boundary layer can even be as low as only 50–100 m in extreme cases.

The marine atmospheric boundary layer can be divided into three layers: the wave layer, which is strongly influenced by single waves; the Prandtl layer, which is dominated by surface friction, and the Ekman layer, where the surface friction impact gradually decreases as height increases (see Figure 4.1).

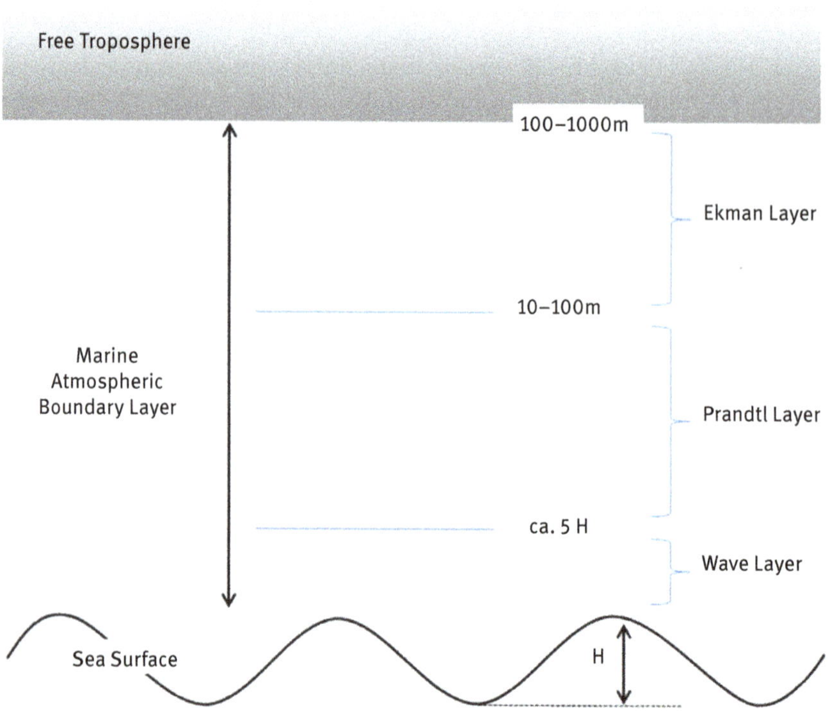

Figure 4.1: Structure of the marine atmospheric boundary layer (Source: UL International GmbH, adapted from Emeis and Türk, 2009).

The Prandtl layer comprises about 10% of the thickness of the atmospheric boundary layer. In the Prandtl layer, the wind speed typically increases with height following the logarithmic wind profile. Vertical flows of energy and matter are constant with height. Apart from turbulent fluctuations, the wind direction in this layer mainly depends on terrain and surface conditions.

In the Ekman layer, however, wind veer is a characteristic feature. Above the atmospheric boundary layer the geostrophic wind moves along the isobars due to the large-scale pressure gradients and Coriolis force, which may differ significantly from the surface-dominated direction in the Prandtl layer. The transition occurs in the Ekman layer, and the wind direction change can easily amount to 30–45°. On the northern hemisphere the wind direction turns to the right (clockwise) with increasing altitude.

4.2.2 Logarithmic Wind Profile

In the Prandtl layer, the increase in wind speed is mainly determined by surface roughness. For neutral atmospheric stratification a logarithmic wind profile applies:

$$U(z) = \frac{U_*}{\kappa}\left(\ln\left(\frac{z}{z_0}\right)\right)$$

with U(z): wind speed at height z, U_*: friction velocity, κ: von-Karman's constant (κ=0.41), and z_0: roughness length. The roughness length is a heuristic measure of the effect of the surface roughness on the wind profile, i.e., it is higher in "rough" areas like cities than above the "smooth" sea. Typical values for sea are 0.1 mm, while typical onshore values are about two orders of magnitude larger (meadows: ca. 1 cm, cities: ca. 1 m) (Troen 1990). Computationally, z_0 is the height above ground at which the wind speed has virtually decreased to zero. Due to the low roughness above sea, the vertical wind speed gradient is initially rather strong when moving upward, but decreases strongly above some 20 m (see Figure 4.2).

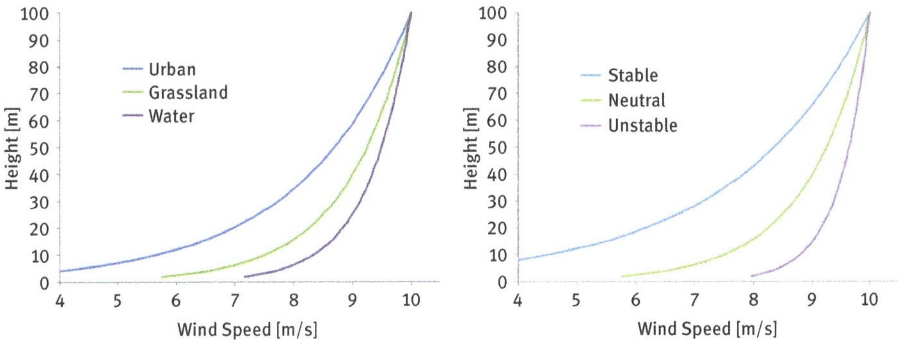

Figure 4.2: Wind profiles for various levels of surface roughness (left) and atmospheric stratification (right) (Source: UL International GmbH).

Although the roughness length above water is generally low, it is obviously connected to the wave height and thus shows some dependency on wind speed.

4.2.3 Atmospheric Stability

Atmospheric stability is determined by the vertical exchange of momentum and heat. For stable stratification, vertical exchange is small and air layers are more or less decoupled from each other. The airflow is laminar. On the other hand, unstable stratification is characterized by strong vertical exchange and associated with enhanced turbulence.

While the exact level of atmospheric stability cannot always be determined easily, the vertical temperature gradient usually serves as a good first approximation. This gradient results from the fact that an (adiabatically) ascending air parcel expands and loses temperature. For dry air the temperature lapse rate is approx. 1K/100 m. Condensation reduces this rate for humid air, therefore the average lapse rate in the troposphere is only 0.65K/100 m. If the actual vertical temperature gradient is smaller than the temperature reduction rate in an adiabatically ascending air parcel, this is referred to as stable stratification: any adiabatically ascending air parcel will be colder (and thus heavier) than the surrounding air. The air parcel is thus prevented from ascending further and there is little vertical mixing. If, on the other hand, the vertical lapse rate is greater than the temperature reduction of an ascending air parcel, the air parcel is always warmer than the surrounding air. Its ascent continues and mixing is enhanced, therefore the stratification is considered as unstable. Under neutral conditions, the vertical temperature gradient exactly meets that of an ascending air packet. In this case, airparcels stay where they are, as there is no net vertical force, neither for ascending nor for descending.

Over land, unstable stratification conditions occur particularly during daytime when the sun heats up the ground and the air directly above. Locally, this leads to the formation of warm air parcels, which eventually detach from the ground and ascend. At night, on the other hand, stable conditions prevail.

Water surfaces do not heat up as rapidly as land, therefore this daily stability cycle is hardly observed offshore. In mid-latitudes, there is a seasonal variation with rather stable stratification in spring, when the water is still cold, while warmer air is already advected from land. Conversely, there is a tendency towards unstable stratification in autumn, when the water is still warm and cold air masses are still being blown across the sea.

4.2.4 Turbulence Intensity

Turbulence is the temporal and spatial fluctuation of the wind speed. Turbulence intensity (TI) is defined by the ratio of standard deviation σ_v and mean value v of the horizontal wind speed:

$$TI = \frac{\sigma_V}{V}$$

Turbulence is either thermally driven (vertical air displacement), or induced by surface conditions, or a combination of both. At low wind speeds, thermal turbulence sources predominate. At higher wind speeds, surface effects become more important, and turbulence intensity tends to decrease (besides the fact that v is in the denominator).

The low offshore roughness results in a number of special features: (1) Turbulence intensity is much lower than onshore. (2) Together with often weak temperature gradients over sea, much less mechanical turbulence is produced compared to onshore sites. For this reason, atmospheric stability is expected to be the decisive parameter governing the generation of turbulence. (3) Offshore surface roughness is related to wave height; therefore TI at offshore sites typically increases again for higher wind speeds. Figure 4.3 shows the turbulence intensity at FINO1 for an undisturbed wind direction sector at FINO1.

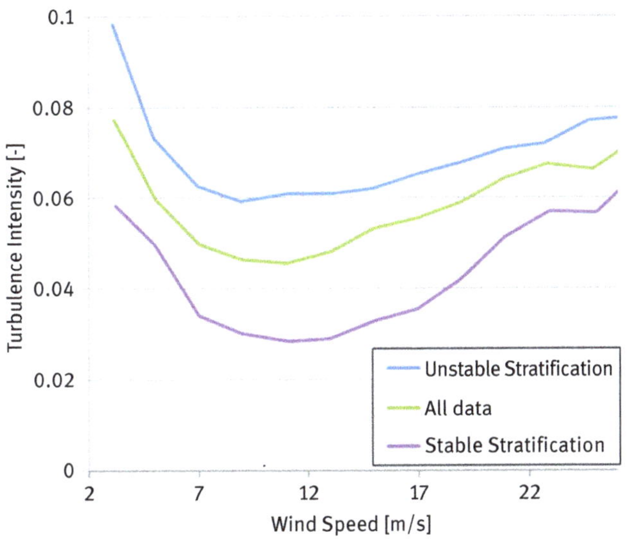

Figure 4.3: Measured turbulence intensity at FINO1 for south-westerly wind directions during 2010–2011 (Source: UL International GmbH).

4.2.5 Wind-Related Implications for Offshore Power Generation

Compared to onshore sites, offshore wind conditions are usually characterized by high average wind speeds (e.g., around 10 m/s at a height of 100 m in the German North Sea). These high wind speeds ensure significantly higher energy yields than onshore, but also a high level of combined wind and wave loads at the offshore wind turbines.

Due to the low surface roughness over sea and the associated steeper wind profile, high wind speeds are already found at relatively low heights above sea level. While onshore turbine tower heights are constantly increasing in order to achieve higher yields, the additional energy yield gained from increased tower heights is much smaller offshore. Therefore, offshore hub heights rarely exceed the rotor diameter plus a security offset of some 20–25 m.

In general, the relatively small average vertical wind shear offshore reduces the respective mechanical loads on the wind turbines and thus allows for smoother operations. On the other hand, "low level jets" may occur at very low altitudes in some offshore regions like the North Sea. These meteorological events occur over surface layers with extremely low turbulence and lead to extremely strong vertical wind speed gradients above the surface layer. Offshore, this increase may already start at around 100 m; in this case the wind turbine rotor will experience high wind shear.

The lower levels of turbulence intensity imply that wind turbine wakes decay much slower than onshore. There is less impulse exchange with the undisturbed wind above and to the sides of the wake region, so a longer distance is required until the original wind speed is restored. Therefore, larger distances between the wind turbines are typically considered for offshore wind farms.

In contrast to onshore conditions, where rapid warming of the ground can lead to pronounced daily variation of wind speeds and stability, there are very little daytime variations at offshore sites. In mid-latitudes, however, there are typical annual cycles with low-wind summers and windier winter months.

4.3 Offshore Wind Data

4.3.1 Measurement Towers

Despite the rapid improvements in LiDAR ("Light Detection And Ranging") technology in recent years, measurement masts are still widely considered as the most reliable data source for offshore wind resource assessments. In particular for turbulence intensity calculations, there is no alternative yet for cup anemometer data from met towers.

Typical examples of high quality offshore measurements are the three FINO platforms installed in the German North and Baltic Sea. One of the main features of every FINO platform is its lattice mast reaching up to more than 100 m above the sea level, which is equipped with several meteorological sensors (see Figure 4.4). In addition to temperature, humidity, air pressure and radiation sensors, the wind speed and wind direction measurements are of decisive importance for wind energy purposes. The used sensors are typically best-in-class industrial systems with extensive track records to ensure highest quality and the important comparability to the measurements and databases existing on land.

Figure 4.4: The FINO1 platform in the North Sea is in operation since 2003 (Source: UL International GmbH).

Wind speed is measured using cup anemometers, which provide very good proportionality between wind speed and rotation frequency. Cup anemometers are installed at several heights, at least every 20 m to allow for proper assessment of the vertical profile. Many towers are equipped with more than one anemometer at each height, pointing in different directions. This setup allows to use only those data with the least mast impacts for a given wind direction in order to improve the measurement uncertainty. Wind direction is usually measured at two or three heights, and other wind speed measurement devices (e.g., ultrasonic devices) may be installed additionally.

The accuracy requirements for wind measurements are extremely high, as measurement errors have a direct effect on the predicted energy yield. For this reason, new calibration procedures and requirements have been developed for cup anemometers. However, as offshore masts require relatively massive tower constructions, measurements typically suffer from greater mast effects and generally do not meet the standards for onshore towers (e.g., IEC 61400-12-1). These mast effects can in many cases only partly be corrected by data processing. Therefore, even high quality offshore met towers typically have slightly higher measurement uncertainties than good onshore measurements.

The high investment costs significantly limit the number of existing offshore towers. In some countries, platforms were built on public funding, e.g., in Germany or the Netherlands. In these cases, the obtained data are often available from public data bases (see http://fino.bsh.de/ for the German FINO data base, or https://www.windopzee.net/ for several Dutch measurements). Besides that, other (and often proprietary) measurement data may still be available from third parties.

It should be noted, however, that only few offshore wind measurements meet the high standards required for wind energy purposes. In particular, wind data obtained at fire ships, hydrological buoys, oil platforms or helicopter stations are generally not sufficient: the anemometers are rarely calibrated, the measurement height is not high enough, and the disturbances from the platforms are usually too large to be corrected.

4.3.2 Wind LiDAR Data

Wind LiDAR devices are measurement systems based on coherent laser light. They use the physical effect of the Doppler frequency shift to determine the wind speed at a target distance. Laser light with a fixed frequency is emitted into the atmosphere and is usually reflected with a slightly different frequency by small particles that move with the air (e.g., aerosols). The difference between the frequency of the reflected signal and the frequency of the laser source is detected and converted into the wind speed along the beam direction (Line of Sight, 'LOS'), as the frequency change is directly proportional to the wind speed.

LiDAR technology has proved to produce highly reliable wind profiles (Peña 2009), earning in recent years the acceptance of the wider wind-energy community for a broad range of applications (e.g., wind resource assessment, verification of wind turbine power curves, wind-profile monitoring for wind-farm development and operations, etc.). Typical LiDAR systems allow measurement of offshore wind-speed profiles up to 200 m, providing valuable information of the flow, while encompassing the rotor diameter of the current generation of offshore wind turbines.

1. Vertical Beam LiDAR Sytems

The most widely used LiDAR systems are installed on the ground and "look" vertically upwards (actually, several laser beams are emitted on a cone around the vertical). Offshore, these systems can be deployed on both fixed platforms (e.g., existing met mast platforms as in Figure 4.5, oil rigging or helicopter platforms, wind turbine transition piece, etc.) and floating platforms like buoys or ships (Cañadillas 2017). Floating LiDARs appear as a cost-effective and more flexible alternative to conventional fixed meteorological masts (e.g., Pichugina 2012, Gottschall 2014). However, the influence of the platform motion on the wind LiDAR measurements has to be corrected in order to obtain accurate wind speed and direction data. Moreover, such a system demands extremely robust, autonomous and reliable operation of all measurement, power supply, data logging and communication systems due to the remoteness of its deployment.

Figure 4.5: Ground-based wind LiDAR at FINO1 platform (Source: UL International GmbH).

To date, several floating LiDAR systems (FLS) are available in the market. The Carbon Trust's "Offshore Wind Accelerator" (OWA) initiative provides a good overview of those systems and their deployment campaigns (OWA 2018a). The OWA Floating LiDAR Systems Roadmap (OWA 2018b) provides guidance for the adoption and use of floating LiDAR systems at different stages of maturity, and establishes prerequisites for floating LiDAR systems to satisfy these defined stages of maturity.

So far, no standard for the use of FLS in wind resource assessments is available. However, recommended practices are detailed in OWA (2016), which provides helpful guidance for the use of FLS as a data source in wind resource assessments.

2. Scanning LiDAR Systems

Unlike the systems mentioned above, scanning LiDAR systems are designed to send laser beams in virtually any direction (e.g., to obtain a full 360° scan around the device), and at larger distances (up to 10 km). This offers additional flexibility as the LiDAR no longer needs to be positioned directly at the wind farm site, but can be located on a fixed platform a few kilometers away or even at the coast (see Figure 4.6). The range of possible measurement heights is also enhanced. However, both the temporal and spatial accuracy may be reduced for larger distances. Besides the use as "virtual" met mast, other possible applications include measurements of the spatial variation in wind resource offshore, power curve measurements, or wake measurements.

Figure 4.6: Scanning wind LiDAR at an offshore wind turbine transition piece (Source: UL International GmbH).

To date, many offshore commercial projects are using scanning LiDAR measurements as a flexible alternative. However, there is no standard or recommended practice yet to guide the use of this system as a data source in wind resource assessments.

4.3.3 Long-Term Databases

In addition to the data sets described above, most of which are intended directly for wind energy use or research, there are a number of other databases that can be used at least to a limited extent for estimating the wind energy potential of offshore sites.

In many countries, national meteorological offices run networks of weather observation stations. Such data can usually be purchased directly from these offices. Others are distributed via publicly accessible databases, like the global station network of the U.S. National Oceanic and Atmospheric Administration (NOAA) or the National Center for Atmospheric Research (NCAR). However, the wind measurement data from these stations are generally not suitable for determining the energy yield of wind turbines directly, as the measurement height is usually only 10 m or less, and the measurement interval is often only recorded on hourly or less frequent intervals. Nevertheless, such stations can be useful for the long-term correction step during the AEP calculation (see section 4.5.3).

In recent years, global weather model calculations have made impressive advances both in accuracy and in resolution. Those reanalysis data sets are calculated from large amounts of measurement data, originating from weather stations, radiosondes, satellite measurements and others. These data are used as input for a global model of the atmosphere that calculates the current state of the atmosphere on a regular grid covering the globe. While initial reanalysis data sets were only available on coarse grids of 2.5° x 2.5° and every 6 hours, the recently released ERA-5 data are available hourly on a 0.28° x 0.28° grid. Despite these impressive improvements, reanalysis data are still far too uncertain to be used as the sole basis for wind farm energy production assessments, but they are frequently used to extrapolate short term measurement data to longer time horizons, and can also be useful for correlation purposes.

Traditionally, the focus of reanalysis data sets has been on weather description, therefore new data sources have been constantly added over time, so that the quality of data simulated for recent years is much better than for earlier years. With this approach, however, the internal consistency of some reanalysis data sets is only conditionally guaranteed, so that long-term statements require thorough examination and comparison with other data sources. To overcome these consistency problems, dedicated data sets like the Merra and Merra 2 projects (Modern Era-Retrospective Analysis for Research and Applications) have been launched. Here, particular attention has been given to the highest possible level of long-term consistency when selecting data sources, in particular satellite data.

4.3.4 Mesoscale Models

The horizontal resolution of current global reanalysis data is bounded from below to some 30 km. Structures that occur at finer scales cannot be resolved and require additional tools. For this purpose, the standard approach is to use mesoscale models, which allow horizontal grid sizes down to about 1 km x 1 km. These models are thus often used for wind farm micrositing.

Mesoscale models are numerical weather prediction models, solving the conservation equations for mass, momentum, internal energy and other relevant parameters such as water vapour. The input data for mesoscale simulations are usually provided by global reanalysis data; in a sense the mesoscale simulation allows for a close-up view on a certain region within the global model. Typical simulation areas range from 50 km x 50 km up to 3000 km x 3000 km (see Figure 4.7); temporal fluctuations are resolved in the range of 1 to 12 hours. Note that several small-scale atmospheric processes cannot be modeled explicitly and have to be approximated by parameterizations, e.g., the effect of turbulent vertical mixing in the planetary boundary layer.

In the recent past, various mesoscale models have been implemented for wind energy purposes, most widely used is the WRF (Weather Research & Forecasting) model (Skamarock et al. 2008) but others like COSMO (Baldauf 2016) are also found occasionally. While some providers already offer their data products based on mesoscale models for site assessment, the typical error range for wind speed data is still in the order of 0.5 m/s. While this may be already sufficient for initial scoping studies, mesoscale models generally still need to be calibrated by on-site measurements from a mast or LiDAR to reach bankable uncertainty levels. However, the error in relative wind speed differences between one location and another is typically much smaller. Therefore, if measurement data exist within the modeled area, but only at some distance from the actual wind farm site, mesoscale models are often used to extrapolate from the measurement location to the wind farm site. Note, however, that the reliability of this horizontal extrapolation is strongly reduced in land-sea transition zones, like coastlines or around islands.

4.4 Wind Flow in Offshore Wind Farms

As already mentioned, the offshore environment with smooth surface and reduced thermal effects leads to reduced turbulence compared to onshore sites. Therefore, the wakes downwind of operating wind turbines are more stable and extend farther than onshore. In typical offshore wind farms with 40–80 turbines, wakes are the dominant reason for wind speed reductions and energy losses in offshore wind farms, and thus require much more attention than for onshore sites.

In this section we will briefly discuss the formation of near and far wakes, and present various calculation models for wind farm losses that are currently used.

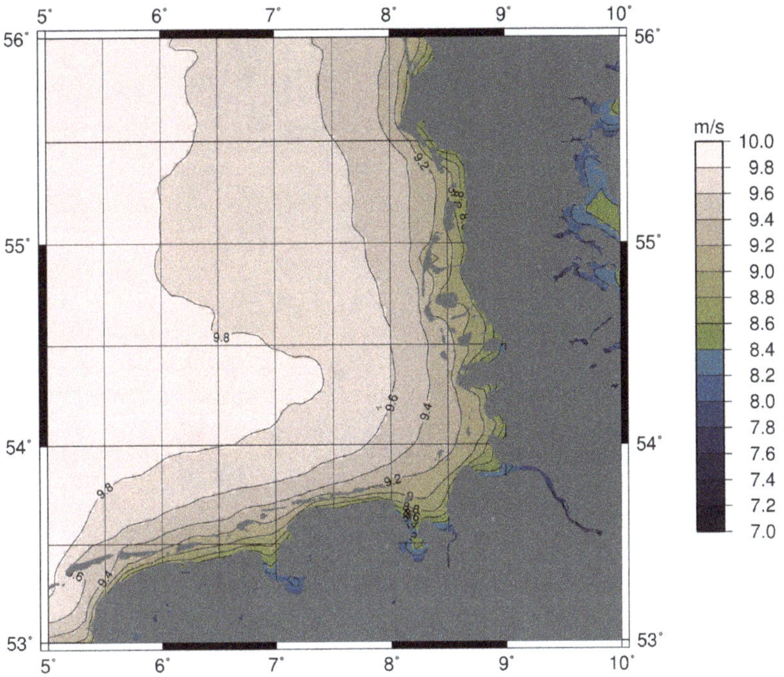

Figure 4.7: Mean wind speed in the German Bight in 100 m height as calculated by a mesoscale model (Source: Durante 2012).

4.4.1 Wakes

1. Near-Field Processes

The wake flow behind a wind turbine can be separated into the "near" wake some 0–3 rotor diameters (D) behind the turbine, the "intermediate" wake (3–5 D behind the turbine), and the "far" wake (> 5 D), which are governed by different processes inside the wake.

An air parcel traveling through a wind turbine experiences an increase of wind speed and pressure directly in front of the rotor. In the rotor plane, pressure and wind speed drop suddenly corresponding to the extraction of momentum by the wind turbine. Directly behind the rotor plane, this leads to the formation of a wind component against the direction of rotation of the rotor corresponding to the torque of the turbine. Wing tip vortices "roll away" and form spiral paths. If these vortices are still narrow, i.e., near the turbine, these can be thought of as a cylindrical shear layer with reduced wind speed in the center and undisturbed wind speed outside. The pressure difference between inside and outside is further enhanced by the centrifugal force which drives the streamlines radially away from the center (see also Figure 4.8).

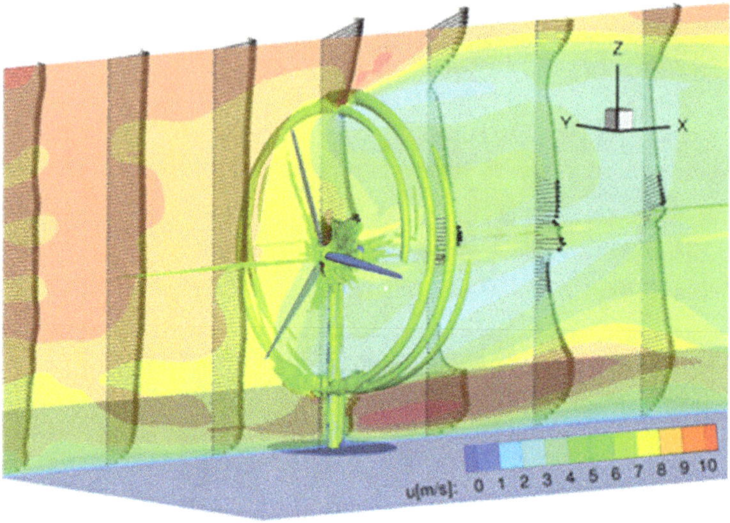

Figure 4.8: Simulation of the relative wind speed in the wake of a wind turbine. (Source: Meister et al., 2010).

Within a distance of 1 D downstream the turbine, the shear layer widens due to turbulent diffusion and the pressure starts to recover. Wind speed remains slow until the pressure is back to ambient pressure. High turbulence occurs mainly in the shear layer, due to the strong wind speed gradient. Here, one finds a ring-shaped area with increased turbulence intensity in the cylindrical shear layer. The shear layer expands in radial direction and eventually reaches the wake center (usually at distances of 2–5 D). This indicates the end of the near wake area.

2. Far-Field Processes

In the "far" wake area, starting at approximately 4–5 rotor diameters behind the wind turbine, the wake flow is fully developed. The small scale regions from different localized processes that governed the near wake have now mixed, and the wind speed deficit and the turbulence level inside the wake can now be described by statistically. The wake grows symmetric to its axis, thereby becoming weaker. The wake evolution in the far field can thus be described by relatively simple models like those of Jensen or Ainslie (see section 4.4.2), which are commonly used for energy yield assessments.

The far field is of particular interest when determining the wind farm energy yield, as offshore turbines are usually located at distance of 5D or more.

4.4.2 Wind Farm Models

1. Simple Engineering Models

Obviously, the actual effect of wakes on turbines inside a wind farm cannot be measured before the farm is built, but plays a crucial role for the economic performance of the farm. Hence, a number of models with various degrees of complexity have been developed for this task.

The Jensen or Park model was developed by Jensen and Katic at DTU (Jensen 1983, Katic et al. 1986). It is very simple, though relatively accurate when calculating the annual energy production, and thus still one of the most commonly used wake models. It is a simple analytical model that takes into account conservation of mass and momentum. Wake effects directly behind the system are not considered, therefore the model is only valid for downwind distances of more than 3–4 D.

The wind speed deficit in the Jensen model is calculated from the turbine's thrust coefficient (c_t) and is assumed to be constant inside the wake. At the radial wake edge, the wind speed jumps to the undisturbed wind speed outside. The wake diameter increases linearly as the distance from the turbine grows; this widening is described by the wake decay constant. The wind speed deficit inside the wake decreases as the wake gets wider, until the ambient wind speed is reached. The wake decay constant is determined empirically. While for onshore locations a value of 0.07 is often used as default value, this value is significantly lower for offshore sites. A value of 0.04 is widely accepted when the Jensen model is used standalone without additional models. If a wind turbine is only partially in the wake, an average wind speed is determined. If it is in the wake of several wind turbines, then the wind speed deficit is added quadratically.

The Ainslie model (also known as Eddy Viscosity model) offers a more exact representation of the wind speed deficit inside the wake than the Jensen model. It is based on an axial symmetric solution of the time-averaged Navier-Stokes equations, using several simplifications. The equations were developed by Ainslie (Ainslie 1988). Conservation of mass and momentum are taken into account. The turbulent shear stress between the slow wind inside the wake and the undisturbed wind outside is described by the introduction of a vortex (Eddy) viscosity. From a distance of 5D onward, the model results in Gaussian-shaped wind speed profile across the wake diameter, which depends on the turbine's thrust coefficient and ambient turbulence.

2. Internal Boundary Layer Models

Models of the Jensen or Ainslie type only consider the direct wake effects. Wind farms, however, also constitute a source of roughness. For onshore wind farms, this contribution is usually marginal compared to the surface roughness. For offshore wind farms, however, this effect is frequently considered by models that simulate the formation of an internal boundary layer (IBL), depending on the wind farm size and layout. The wind farm energy production is then determined by the combination of both the direct wake model (Jensen/Ainslie) and the IBL model.

3. More Elaborate Models

Much more complex is the determination of the wind farm flow with flow simulations. CFD (Computational Fluid Dynamics) models solve the Navier-Stokes equations numerically. These equations describe the movement of liquids or gases under consideration of mass, momentum and energy conservation. As solving the full set of Navier Stokes equations is extremely time-consuming and computationally expensive, the Navier Stokes equations are frequently solved as time averages using the RANS (Reynolds averaged Navier Stokes) approximation. This allows to reduce the computational effort significantly, so that solutions can be obtained in reasonable time even without a supercomputer.

The turbulence terms of the equations of motion are considered by simplifying closure approaches, e.g., the k-ε turbulence model, in which two transport equations, one for the turbulent kinetic energy k and one for the dissipation rate ε of the turbulent kinetic energy are solved. The results are stationary calculations, where the wind turbines are usually represented as so-called actuator discs. This approach assumes that momentum is extracted from the wind flow homogeneously over the entire rotor surface according to the incoming wind speed and the thrust coefficient (c_t) curve.

For research purposes, even more complex models are used. Non-stationary CFD calculations for example offer the advantage of simulating the wind field with rotating rotor depending on time and location. With Large Eddy Simulations (LES), the turbulent wind field is modeled with high temporal and spatial resolution. Here, larger vortices are no longer parameterized, but the turbulent flow is calculated directly up to length scales of a few meters. Only smaller turbulence elements are parameterized. The high resolution of LES models even allows to represent individual rotor blades as "actuator lines."

4.4.3 Efficient Wind Farm Design

The wake of individual wind turbines not only reduces the wind speed and thus the energy yield of the wind turbines in the slipstream. The rotating air and the wind speed gradients across the wake also cause additional turbulence, which may add significantly to the ambient turbulence of the free wind. Turbines inside a wind farm therefore experience increased mechanical loads compared to a single, isolated turbine. The "effective" (or "design-equivalent") turbulence at each turbine position must be taken into account when designing the farm, towers and foundations. As it cannot be measured in advance, and as the impact is highly dependent on the actual layout and turbine type it is generally calculated by the model developed by Frandsen (2007), which is also included in IEC 61400–1 Annex D.

1. Effective Turbulence: The Frandsen Model

Modeling the actual loads directly from the wind data time series and the wind turbine construction detail is a very complex effort and can often only be justified during the development of a wind turbine. At the end of its development, each turbine is certified to meet the limits of certain load classes, usually those laid out in IEC 61400–1. In practice, the question is rather to determine whether the turbulence values at the turbine site exceed the turbulence class limits of the respective turbine. One efficient method to estimate these design-related turbulence loads is the model by Sten T. Frandsen, which was developed around the turn of the millennium at Risø DTU and which has also been adopted by IEC 61400–1 standard.

This model uses a simple linear parameterization to describe the turbulence in the wake of a wind turbine. In order to calculate the turbulence intensity experienced by a given wind turbine at a given wind direction, it is therefore decisive whether it is currently inside a wake. Central parameters of the model are therefore the distance to the wake-generating wind turbine, the rotor diameter of that wake-generating turbine, and the wake decay constant, which determines the opening angle of the wakes. The thrust coefficient (c_t-value) of the wake-generating WTG also plays a role.

To calculate the design-relevant turbulence intensity at a given wind turbine site, the incoming turbulence is averaged over all directions, taking the actual wind direction frequency distribution and the direction dependence of the ambient turbulence into account, if possible. Since the Frandsen model focuses on loads, the turbine material is considered using the so-called Wöhler slope m. The Wöhler slope is a material constant, which describes how many load changes a material can withstand before it breaks. Ultimately, stiffer materials such as glass fibre reinforced plastics ($m \approx 10 \ldots 14$) have higher values of the design-relevant turbulence intensity (and are thus closer to the limits of the turbine's turbulence class) than tougher materials such as steel ($m \approx 3 \ldots 5$).

2. Wind Farm Geometry and Layout Optimization

For an optimal energy yield an efficient alignment of the WTG is essential. An optimal layout delivers maximum yield while taking all boundary conditions (e.g., administrative obligations, seabed conditions, etc.) into account and also avoids unacceptably high loads on the wind turbines in the farm and its neighbors due to turbulence in the wakes.

Generally, the external boundaries and the maximum number of turbines of the wind farm are specified by the approval authority. Many of the limitations that affect onshore wind farms are irrelevant for offshore farms: distances to settlements and shadows are no problem and noise only matters during construction. However, the seafloor conditions are more difficult to explore, and often a helicopter corridor and/or relatively wide spacing zones from underwater cables and pipelines impose additional constraints.

In general, the simple rule of layout design is to provide as undisturbed inflow in the main wind direction for as many wind turbines as possible. Onshore, especially in areas with very dominant main wind directions, this often leads to wind farms which, depending on the terrain, stand in one or a few rows perpendicular to the main wind direction. This approach has also already been realized offshore, for example in the iconic Middelgrunden wind farm off Copenhagen, Denmark.

In many offshore cases, however, this is less practical or even impossible for three reasons. On the one hand, the designated areas often have an east-west extension that is comparable to the north-south extension, so that wakes from turbines in the same wind farm are the major source of shading. Secondly, offshore wind farm areas are often located as "clusters" to simplify spatial planning and to allow for shared power export infrastructure, so that neighboring wind farms also determine the wind inflow. And finally, in many regions the main wind direction is not very sharply defined; for example in the North Sea the main wind direction is southwest, but almost similar frequencies are found over a sector of some 120°.

The result is that a layout with very regular wind turbine arrangements rarely delivers optimum yields. Apart from possible advantages in cable layout, layouts that are "staggered" in as many wind directions as possible often provide the best yield. Obtaining such a layout usually requires the use of numerical optimization algorithms, which are contained in a number of common software tools for wind farm design.

These algorithms require the definition of the type of wind turbine, the wind farm boundaries and the areas in which no wind turbines may be located. For example, existing subsea cables and pipelines have safety corridors where no turbines may be deployed. Often, helicopter corridors must also be considered. In order to minimize harmful turbulences in the wake flows, inter-turbine distances should not be smaller than approx. 5–6 D in the main wind direction and 4.5 D perpendicular to the main wind direction (D: rotor diameter). Due to its computational advantages, the Jensen/PARK model is often used during optimization, even though the final energy yield figure may be derived from a different model. Also compliance of the obtained layout with the applicable turbulence limits should be checked according to the Fandsen model.

Optimization usually aims at maximizing annual energy yield while taking all boundary conditions into account. Unfortunately, the underlying problem of multidimensional optimization does not ensure that there is one single distinct global optimum of energy yield. In effect, usually multiple layouts exist with very similar yields, and the obtained results may thus differ depending on the starting conditions and the algorithm used.

4.5 Energy Yield Calculation from Wind Data and Power Curve

4.5.1 Long-Term Correction of Measurement Data

Since most wind measurements at wind farm sites cover only one or a few years, these short term data need to be related to the average wind speed during the typical operating period of a wind farm (20–25 years). Because one cannot look into the future, one looks into the past and then assumes that the wind climate will not change on a long-term average.

In order to relate the short-term data to the average wind conditions in the past, the measured time series is compared with long-term measurements in the region, such as meteorological stations or model data. If these correlate well with the on-site data during the short term measurement period, it is assumed that this good correlation also existed in the past. The course of the long-term data series can then be used to estimate to what extent the average wind speed during the measurement period overestimates or underestimates the long-term mean. The measured time series can then be scaled accordingly so that its mean value corresponds to the long-term mean value. Only such long-term corrected time series or wind statistics should be used for yield forecasts.

Alternatively, more complex time series correlation methods known as MCP (measure, correlate, predict) can be used to obtain long-term corrected wind speed data. This allows to also adjust the wind direction to the long term, but introduced additional uncertainties due to the correlation procedure. Experience shows, however, that the quality of the long-term correction depends more on the proper selection of the long term reference data set than on the actual correlation method. It should be noted that the value of the long-term mean changes with each additional year, so that it is recommended to renew yield forecasts after each additional year of measurement data.

4.5.2 Power Curves

1. General Features

In theory, the available mechanical power of the wind (P_W) is proportional to the third power of wind speed and can be expressed by the following formula:

$$P_W = \frac{1}{2} \rho A v^3$$

where ρ is the air density, A is the rotor area and v is the wind speed.

Due to this dependency on the third power of wind speed, even small variations in wind speed can lead to large variations in power output. This is the reason why the exact description of the incident wind across the rotor area is so important.

The electrical power (P_e) generated by a wind turbine from the undisturbed wind is given as:

$$P_e = C_p P_w$$

where C_p is the total coefficient or power coefficient of the wind turbine, which is usually dominated by the aerodynamic efficiency $c_{p,Aero}$.

The power coefficient C_p describes the proportion of wind energy that can be converted into mechanical work by the wind turbine. It has a theoretical maximum value of 16/27 ≈ 59% (Betz 1926), but is always lower in practice due to various loss factors (such as air friction). C_p is a turbine parameter and varies with wind speed (≈ 0.5 at 6–10 ms^{-1}, depending on the design of the wind turbine). At higher wind speeds, the value is deliberately reduced by the turbine design in order to keep the mechanical power of the rotor constant above rated wind speed (see Figure 4.9).

While the power coefficient is important when comparing the efficiency of single turbine types, the most important data set for determining the annual energy production (AEP) of a turbine is its power curve. It relates the incident wind speed to the electrical power generated by the wind turbine. Figure 4.9 shows the hypothetical power generated by an offshore wind turbine and the power coefficient of the wind turbine (C_p). The minimum wind speed at which a wind turbine generates usable energy is referred to as cut-in wind speed, usually between 3 and 5 ms^{-1}. At higher wind speeds, the power output increases quickly until rated power is reached i.e., the maximum power that a turbine can generate. Rated wind speed is the minimum wind speed where rated power is produced.

Present-day wind turbines are controlled by adjusting the blade angles with respect to the incoming wind (pitch control). Around rated wind speed the turbine starts to extract only less than the theoretically available power, so that the C_p value decreases, while generated power remains constant above rated wind speed. Even though the relative extraction declines, the forces acting on the turbine at very high wind speeds continue to increase, so that at a certain point there is a risk of structural damage. Turbines are therefore switched off at a cut-out wind speed, typically around 25–30 ms^{-1}.

While onshore turbines still often follow the traditional way of simply switching off the turbine at cut-out wind speed, this is less favorable offshore for two reasons. Firstly, shutting down a turbine from full power to zero (and the subsequent re-cut-in at a slightly reduced wind speed) results in significant mechanical loads and should thus be avoided. At many offshore sites, however, wind speeds of 25 m/s are quite frequent, so that this shutdown cycle with its adverse effects on turbine lifetime would often be encountered. Secondly, this simple on-off behavior means that a passing storm front may remove the full wind farm from the grid within a few minutes. Given typical offshore wind farm capacities of 0.5 GW, such a situation is difficult to manage from a grid operator's point of view.

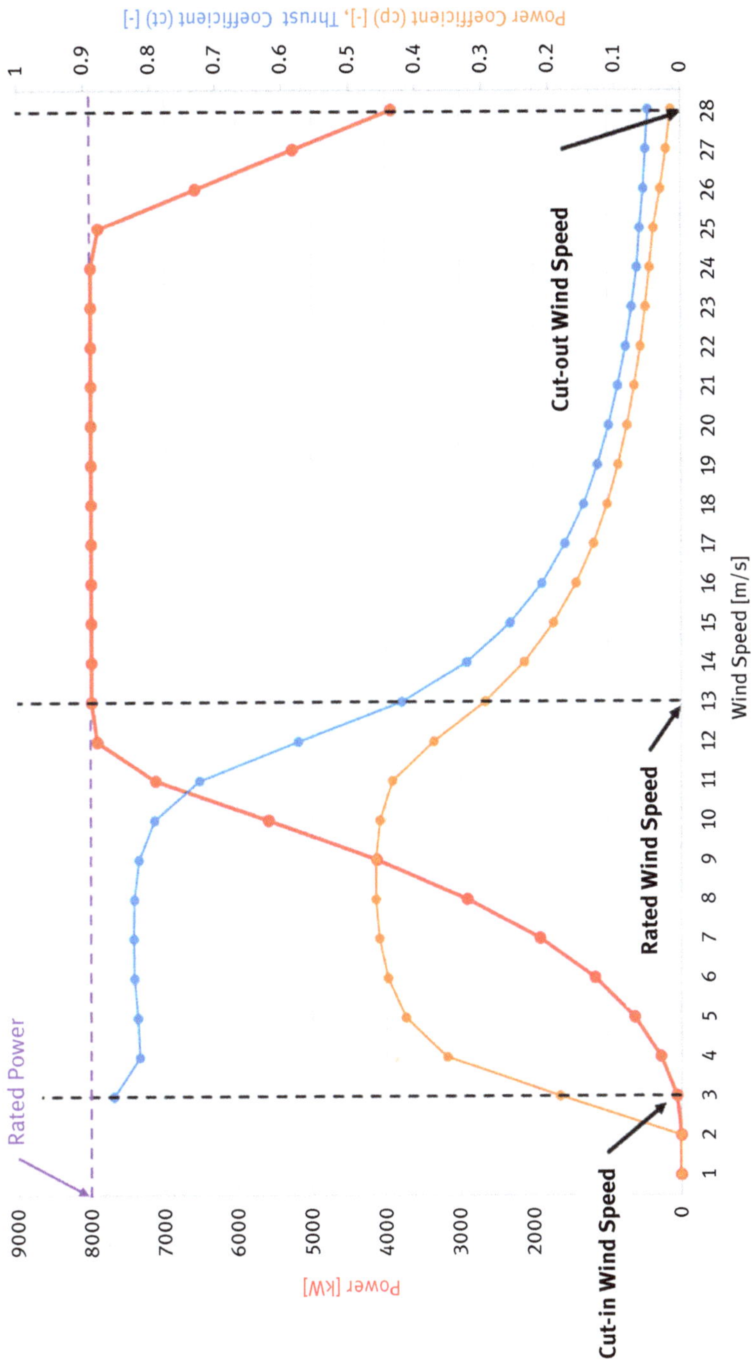

Figure 4.9: Example of a wind turbine's power curve and its power coefficient C_p (Source: UL International GmbH).

Therefore, most modern offshore turbines offer mechanisms to gradually reduce the power output down to about 50% or 30% of rated power, before switching off completely. Besides reducing the adverse effects just described, this feature also offers additional energy yields to the operator and is thus widely implemented in recent wind farms.

2. Measurement of Power Curves

Onshore experience shows that the power curve of actual turbines usually differs more or less from the theoretical power curves provided by the manufacturers. Therefore, measured power curves are commonly used for AEP calculations of onshore farms. Offshore, however, measured power curves are less frequently used during pre-construction energy yield assessments, mostly for two reasons. First, the measurement process is more difficult to perform under true offshore conditions, as a mast or LiDAR needs to be installed very close to the turbine. Onshore measurements are sometimes performed, but transferring the results to offshore conditions is subject to enhanced uncertainties due to the different atmospheric conditions. Second, due to the rapid developments in offshore turbine technology in recent years, measured power curves often were simply not yet available. Loosely speaking, developers have usually been planning with the next generation of turbines, while the current generation has just completed its prototype phase.

Nevertheless, offshore power curve measurements are carried out for two different reasons:

- Performance check: Performance measurements are used to check whether a system corresponds to the performance curve guaranteed by the manufacturer.
- Type tests: A measurement of the prototype of a particular plant model provides the power curve required for type testing as part of the certification process.

There are various national and international standards and guidelines according to which measurements, analyses and reports on the measurement of power curves of individual wind turbines can be carried out. In international context, the most important standard is IEC 61400-12-1. However, none of these standards and guidelines have been developed specifically for offshore installations. Therefore, the general approach is still to measure the turbine's power output and relate it to the wind measured by a high quality met mast less than 4 D away from the turbine (D: rotor diameter). LiDAR devices are only permitted when monitored by a separate cup anemometer at the lowest tip height of the rotor, so that the costly mast installation is still required. Therefore, fully IEC compliant offshore measurements are still not expected to become available in the near future.

If IEC compliance is not strictly required, nacelle-based LiDAR devices offer a more flexible solution, in particular for offshore installations. These allow to measure the incoming wind field directly in front of the rotor plane. Various approaches are currently in use:

- “Two-beam” LiDARs are mounted at hub height on the nacelle and probe the upstream air through the rotation rotor blades. Examples are the commercially available Iris or Vindicator type LiDARs. With these systems the wind speed is directly measured at hub height in front of the turbine.
- Scanning LiDARs measure the wind speed at several points in front of the rotor plane so that three-dimensional information about the inflow of the rotor plane can be obtained. These systems are currently on the transition from research into commercial operation. In contrast to nacelle based LiDAR devices at hub height, these systems allow to determine the wind speed distribution in the rotor plane. Scanning LiDARs can also look upward and can thus also be installed on the transition piece between the turbine foundation and the tower, or on a nearby substation.

4.5.3 AEP Calculations

The annual energy production (AEP) is usually calculated from the long term corrected wind distribution at the wind turbine site and the power curve. The wind speed distribution is converted into hours per year for each wind speed bin. Since the power curve describes the power output of the wind turbine as a function of the wind speed, the annual energy yield at this wind speed is then obtained by multiplying the number of hours per year during which a certain wind speed occurs by the corresponding power. Integration over all wind speeds results in the annual energy yield of the WTG. In practice, discrete distributions are used, thus the integration is replaced by summation over all wind speed intervals.

On top of this basic methodology for the AEP of a single turbine, wind farm calculations require additional models. Most important is the wake model, which describes the shading by upwind upstream turbines. For each wind speed and each wind direction, the wake model describes the wind speed reduction at a given turbine site. This results in a new frequency distribution depending on the wind direction, which then becomes the starting point for the yield calculation.

Furthermore, the power curve must be corrected to the correct air density at the site, since air with a higher air density contains more molecules per volume unit, and thus more kinetic energy can be extracted by the turbine. The procedure is defined in IEC 61400-12-1 and uses the following equation

$$P = \frac{\rho}{2} v^3 A,$$

to correct the wind speed v of the power curve for given power values (P: power, ρ: air density, A: rotor area).

Finally, the shutdown behavior of the turbine in strong winds must also be taken into account. As mentioned earlier, turbines shut down when the cut-out wind speed is exceeded to prevent damage. As a rule, the turbine control system allows the turbine to re-start only if the wind speed has dropped significantly below the cut-out wind speed. This approach shall prevent the turbine from switching on and off continuously at wind speeds around the cut-out speed, which would lead to enormous mechanical loads. Therefore, the wind speeds between the cut-out and the re-cut-in wind speeds do not contribute to the energy yield when the storm is fading, even though they are included in the wind statistics (because the measurement does not switch off when the storm is fading). The resulting reduction in yield can be taken into account either by interpolation AEP results obtained from different cut-out wind speed settings, or by heuristic methods of power curve correction, or by more or less flat-rate deductions. It should be noted that modern turbines with gradual power reduction technology often have rather high cut-out wind speeds. On many locations, these turbines therefore shut down very rarely during the most extreme storms, so that energy losses due to storms are greatly reduced.

4.5.4 Systematical Losses

In addition to the losses already mentioned due to wakes and storm shutdown, a number of other effects reduce the energy measured at the grid connection point compared with the theoretical energy yield calculated using the procedure described above. It should be noted that different perceptions exist in different markets (mainly between Europe and the USA), whether some effects are considered as a loss or rather as an uncertainty. The following list describes the main loss factors that are usually considered in European markets.

1. Availability of wind farm and turbine components: This is usually the largest loss factor of an offshore wind farm, as repairs at sea cannot be carried out as quickly as onshore due to weather conditions and distance. Experience shows that 5–7% losses are not uncommon, in particular in the early months of operation. Well-tailored concepts for O&M and emergencies can achieve significant improvements.
2. Planned maintenance work also requires turbines to shut down. In contrast to unplanned failures, however, these can often be deliberately carried out in times of low wind speeds and ideally also prevent unplanned failures.
3. Electrical losses in the wind farm cables and in the transformer substation are also significant. Here the design of the cable layout (cable lengths and interturbine distances), the deployment (cable unbundling) and the manufacturing of individual components (cables, transformers) play a role.

Disconnecting the wind farm from the grid by the grid operator is a realistic scenario in some countries, depending on the grid capacities available in coastal regions. As disconnections due to grid overload tend to occur during profitable high wind seasons, significant losses may be the consequence. In addition, accidental grid failures (e.g., due to damage to the submarine cable) can never be ruled out.

Over the operating life of the wind farm of 20 years and more, the aerodynamic profile of the rotor blades is not expected to remain in its original condition. While icing, insects and dirt probably only play a minor role in most offshore wind farms, recent studies indicate that rain and sea water droplets can have a strongly deteriorating effect on the leading edge of the rotor blades (Sareen et al. 2014). Yet, additional research is required to fully assess the potential losses of this phenomenon.

4.5.5 Uncertainties and Possible Reduction Measures

AEP calculation is based on measured quantities and simplifying models, which are all subject to error. The resulting energy yield is thus also subject to uncertainties. The individual uncertainties are usually assumed to be normally distributed around the calculated value, which therefore has a probability of 50% to be exceeded, hence the calculated value is called P50. For risk assessment, however, it is important to also know the width of the distribution and thus to be able to calculate the energy yields that will be exceeded with 70% or 90% probability. Therefore, the uncertainties must be identified and quantified in detail. The main uncertainties considered in European markets are explained below.

1. First of all, the wind measurement itself is afflicted with a number of uncertainties. These include the quality of the used instruments and the measurement setup, as well as the quality of the data recording and data processing, including any necessary corrections. The long-term correction should be considered separately, because it requires a number of statistical extrapolations which may strongly influence the uncertainty of the time series.
2. The extrapolation from the site and height of measurement to the wind turbine location and hub height is usually also carried out with models or on the basis of assumptions whose uncertainty must be estimated.
3. The uncertainty of the wind resource at the wind turbine site determined in this way translates directly into an uncertainty of the energy yield. Essentially, the gradient of the power curve at the average wind speed determines how sensitive the energy production responds to fluctuations in the wind. If the average wind speed is still the partial load range of the power curve, this dependency is generally high, whereas the sensitivity becomes smaller the when the average wind speed meets or exceeds rated wind speed.
4. The power curve itself is also subject to technical uncertainties, which may easily exceed 5% for calculated power curves that are not confirmed by measurements. The uncertainties of measured power curves, on the other hand, can be determined experimentally and are usually in the range of 3–5% for typical average offshore wind speeds.

5. Additional uncertainties result from the wind farm shading, which is determined by the park layout and the thrust coefficients of the shading wind turbines. On top of that, the uncertainty of the used wake models and their influence on the calculated energy yield also needs to be estimated.

4.6 Energy Yield Assessments Based on Production Data

4.6.1 Why an AEP Estimation Based on Production Data?

The development of an offshore wind farm project and its subsequent construction demands a very high investment. The first commercial offshore wind farms installed after the year 2000 had a high risk profile, since both the technology as well as the required construction efforts were then new and largely unproven. Although project financing was already a well-established way to raise funds for onshore wind farm projects by that time, lenders were extremely careful with offshore wind. In recent years, this picture changed as a result of the continuous developments of technology and the supply chain, as well as project sponsors' increased experience.

As indicated by WindEurope (see Figure 4.10), the amount of new assets relying on project financing achieved before the start of construction has been steadily increasing over the last years. Lenders are continuously gaining confidence. This development diversifies the range of players in the landscape of offshore wind financing,

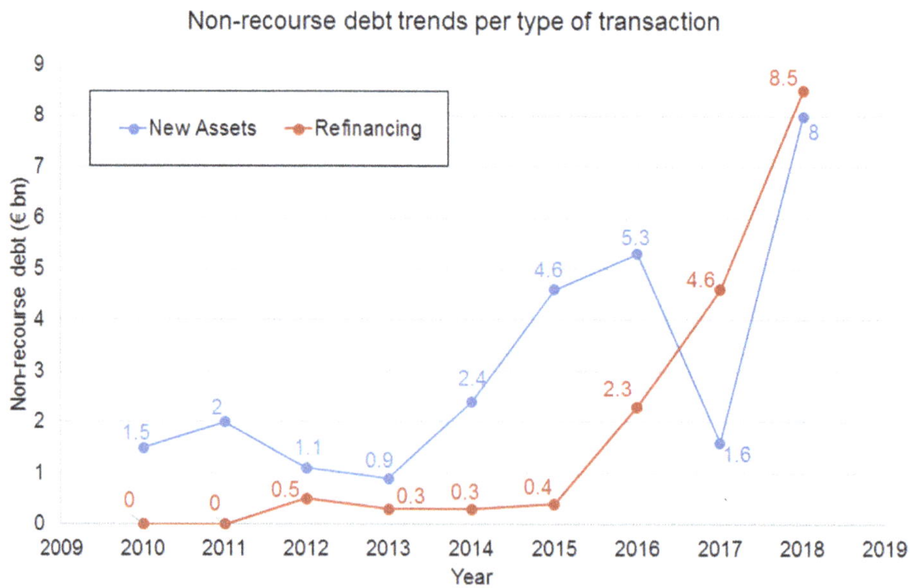

Figure 4.10: Non-recourse debt trends – offshore wind in Europe (Source: Windeurope 2019).

and is a key aspect to achieve a sustainable reduction of energy costs. Nevertheless, self-funding the construction and securing a loan and/or divesting part of the asset after the start of commercial operation through refinancing is still common practice.

One of the advantages of re-financing a wind asset after a few months of operation is the possibility to forecast the energy yield, and consequently the revenues, based on the real operational data of the wind farm instead of short term wind measurements and assumed losses. Yield estimations based on real operational data are therefore subject to different sources of uncertainty than pre-construction estimations. The re-assessment can lead to the adjustment of the exceedance probability values (P-values) to a more realistic long term performance of the asset – an effect very welcomed by owners procuring a lending bank or willing to divest part (or all) of the asset.

4.6.2 Advantages and Limiting Factors

A reliable estimation of long term energy yield (Annual Energy Production, AEP) based on operational data requires at least 12 months of data on production, availability and other information related to plant performance and losses such as periods of grid curtailment, shutdown for scheduled maintenance of the turbines, and balance of plant (cables, substation), etc.

The 12 months are needed to cover a full annual cycle in order to avoid biased data with rather discrete events of extraordinary or poor wind conditions and/or plant performance. Given the interest to understand how the wind farm will perform on a long-term basis, the original data needs to be filtered to reflect the operation under realistic and most likely conditions to occur within the operational life of the asset. For this reason, all events leading to unusual shutdowns and high losses (e.g., repair/replacement of big parts such as gearboxes, blades) during the reference period of operation shall be diligently documented.

The efficient management (acquisition, storage and monitoring) of the operational data, especially in the first months after commissioning of the wind farm is a pre-condition to a high quality energy yield assessment based on the production data. Practice shows that the quality of the available operational data frequently challenges their analysis and is clearly a limiting factor to their accuracy. However, even if conditioned to a reliable data basis, the estimation of energy yield based on operational data still presents clear advantages in comparison to pre-construction assessments due to the following aspects:

- **Modeling vs. real operational data**: Pre-construction assessments are largely based on measured wind data. Even if of high quality and covering several years of observation, the measurement devices (meteorological mast or remote sensing such as LiDAR) are positioned in one determined spot of the wind farm area. Therefore, the wind conditions determined with such measurements must be extrapolated to the exact turbine position (horizontal extrapolation) and to the turbine hub height (vertical extrapolation). This extrapolation requires, as state of the art, models which are nowadays pretty much advanced and accurate, but which are still models relying on several assumptions. Even when those assumptions have been properly validated within several research initiatives and by different institutions, the extrapolation of the wind conditions to the turbine position still carries uncertainties. The same applies to the estimation of the wake losses, one of the key issues of concern of developers and investors. In a pre-construction assessment, the wake losses are modeled, while the real production data already includes these losses (also blockage effects), which therefore do not need to be discounted explicitly from the future yields.

- **Systematical losses**: Following the same principle, losses connected to the operation of the wind turbines such as availability, electrical (cable and substation) losses, grid availability, maintenance and others related to specific environmental conditions (e.g., icing) or permitting obligations are largely estimated according to site specific assumptions during the pre-construction phase. Even if these assumptions have been validated based on past experience, and compensation can be received in some cases, the unpredictable nature of some of these events still brings uncertainty to the net production of the wind farm and consequently to the project's cashflow. A detailed assessment of the individual losses of the wind farm as a whole or of a single turbine can be a powerful tool not only to identify deviations from what has been expected, but also to increase the accuracy of future yields.
- **Performance review**: Although not directly related to the estimation of future yields, another advantage of the analysis of production data is the assessment of the performance of the operating turbines. Experienced wind farm operators include for example, the review of the turbine's power curves according to SCADA data on the regular routine of the operational monitoring. This practice identifies the need of specific adjustments or a more detailed investigation of eventual deviations on a timely manner avoiding unnecessary production losses. Even if the assessment of the SCADA data of the turbines is normally within the scope of operators, an independent review of this data with an estimation of the long term energy yield is helpful not only to identify possible power curve deviations (which should be considered somehow in the estimation of the long term yield). It also allows flagging other issues leading to underperformance caused by for example, a change in the O&M concept (from full service contract to independent service provider).

4.6.3 Assessment Methodology

Differently from pre-construction Energy Yield Assessments, a specific guideline for the estimation of the long term energy yield based on production data is not available. Nevertheless, a very similar procedure is followed by the various experts on this area. Figure 4.11 shows a general methodology of assessment.

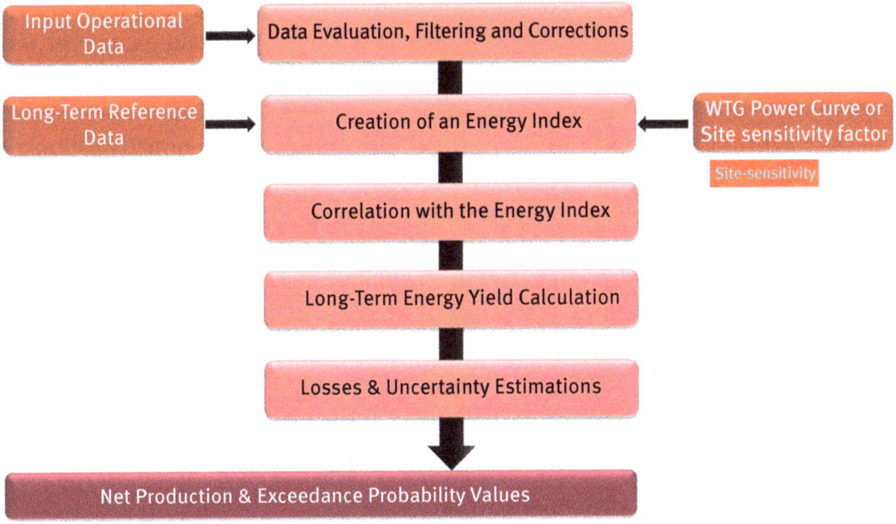

Figure 4.11: Energy yield assessment from production data – general methodology (Source: UL International GmbH).

The resolution of the input data required for the assessment (production, availability and any other data related to the performance of the wind farm) depends on the extension of the analyses. An assessment based on SCADA data with 10 minutes time resolution enables a deeper screening of faulty or unreliable production values. However, the interest is usually on the behavior of the production on a month by month basis, to define a seasonal and yearly profile of production. Therefore, the input data, even if available in 10 minutes resolution, is normally converted into monthly values before going to the evaluation, filtering and correction steps.

As the goal of the assessment is to provide a realistic estimation of future energy yields, the input data need to be corrected by availability downtimes, faulty values or any other issues that do not represent the likely performance of the turbines on a longer term. To be representative for the long term, the corrected input data is checked against a long term reference of meteorological data (e.g., Merra2) firstly for plausibility and secondly for long term correction purposes.

The long term meteorological reference data relate to wind speed, while the input data (short term production) relate to produced energy (kWh). Therefore, the long term reference is used to create an energy index, either based on the power curve of the turbines, or on the site sensitivity factor which indicates the relationship between wind speed and energy (dE/dv). The relationship between the real production and the created energy index is then analyzed through regression analysis. The long-term energy yield is then obtained by combining the index with the regression results.

Finally, the losses likely to occur during the future operation such as availability, electrical losses (cable and substation), downtimes for maintenance or any other related to permit conditions or events such as icing, or aging of the turbines (e.g., blade degradation) need to be taken into account.

Once operational data is available, the electrical losses are normally estimated through the assessment of the dispatched energy from the turbine and the energy effectively reaching the point of connection to the grid. Similarly, other systematical losses, originally estimated based on experience values, can be verified with the past production. The same however, does not apply to wake losses.

As mentioned earlier, the wake losses of an operational wind farm are already included in the production data. Nevertheless, this data includes the losses in line with the current site or cluster configuration. Therefore, once extensions or new wind farms are to be built in the surroundings of the operating site, the additional wake losses related to such extensions need to be modeled and accounted for in the net production.

Although bundled to lower uncertainties than the uncertainties of a pre-construction energy yield assessment, the estimation of long term production based on the assessment of production data includes uncertainties related to the input data and the future behavior of the wind resource.

The uncertainty associated with the input data is dominated by the quality of the data available for analysis. Longer period of reference production, with lower gaps either due to lower downtimes (e.g., availability related) or better data management, usually lead to lower uncertainties. The uncertainty related to the behavior of the wind resource is intrinsic to the question to which extent long term reference data sets do really represent future wind conditions. This question cannot be fully ruled out and needs to be taken into account when assessing future yields. The level of uncertainty is however, largely influenced by the quality of the correlation to the input data. Therefore, it is common practice to evaluate the correlation of the corrected (by availability, faulty values, etc.) production data to different sets of long-term references.

References

Ainslie, J. F. 1988. "Calculating the flowfield in the wake of wind turbines." *Journal of Wind Engineering and Industrial Aerodynamics* 27: 213–24.

Baldauf, Michael, Jochen Förstner, S. Klink, Thorsten Reinhardt, Christoph Schraff, Axel Seifert, and Klaus Stephan, 2016. "Kurze Beschreibung des Lokal-Modells Kürzestfrist COSMO-DE (LMK) und seiner Datenbanken auf dem Datenserver des DWD", Version 2.4. Deutscher Wetterdienst, Geschäftsbereich Forschung und Entwicklung, Offenbach.

Betz, Albert. 1926. "Windenergie und ihre Ausnutzung durch Windmühlen." *Naturwissenschaft und Technik* 2.

Cañadillas, Beatriz, Friedrich Wilts, Hauke Decker, Christian Krüger, and Tom Neumann. 2017. "Floating Lidar measurements: use a Lightship in the North Sea to retrieve long-term wind profiles." DEWEK conference, Bremen.

Cowan, Marie-Anne, 2019. "How are LiDAR products driving wind farm development and supporting resource assessment?" https://blogs.dnvgl.com/energy/how-are-lidar-products-driving-wind-farm-development-and-supporting-resource-assessment.

Durante, Francesco, Annette Westerhellweg, and Barbara Jimenez. 2012. "Comparison of a Mesoscale Model with FINO Measurements in the German Bight and the Baltic Sea." *DEWI Magazin* 40.

Emeis, Stefan, and Matthias Türk. 2009. "Wind-driven wave heights in the German Bight." *Ocean Dynamics* 59: 463–75.

Frandsen, Sten Tronæs. 2007. "Turbulence and turbulence-generated structural loading in wind turbine clusters." Risoe Research Center, Denmark. Risø-R-1188-(EN).

Gottschall Julia, Gerrit Wolken-Möhlmann, Thomas Viergutz, and Bernhard Lange. 2014. "Results and conclusions of a floating-Lidar offshore test." *Energy Procedia* 53: 156–61.

International Electrotechnical Commission (IEC). 2014. "International Standard IEC 61400-1 Wind Turbines – Part 1: Design Requirements, Edition 3.1." April.

International Electrotechnical Commission (IEC). 2017. "Wind turbines – Part 12-1: Power performance measurements of electricity producing wind turbines." IEC 61400-12-1 Ed. 2. March.

Jensen, N. O. 1983. "A note on wind generator interaction." Technical Report m-2411. Risø, Roskilde, Denmark.

Katic, I., J. Højstrup, and N. O. Jensen. 1986. "A Simple Model for Cluster Efficiency." European Wind Energy Association Conference and Exhibition, Rome. October 7–9.

Meister, Konrad, Thorsten Lutz, and Ewald Krämer. 2010. "Consideration of unsteady inflow conditions in wind turbine CFD simulations." DEWEK conference, Bremen.

OWA (Offshore Wind Accelerator). 2014. "Remote Wind Measurements Offshore Using Scanning Lidar Systems."

OWA (Offshore Wind Accelerator). 2016. "Floating Lidar Recommended Practice."

OWA (Offshore Wind Accelerator). 2018a. "Floating Lidar Repository: Deployments of Floating Lidar Systems."

OWA (Offshore Wind Accelerator). 2018b. "Roadmap for commercial acceptance of floating Lidar Version 2.0 and floating Lidar recommended practices. V2.0."

Peña Alfredo, Charlotte Bay Hasager, Sven-Erik Gryning, Michael Courtney, Ioannis Antoniou, and Torben Mikkelsen. 2012. "Offshore wind profiling using light detection and ranging measurements." *Wind Energy* 12, no. 2: 105–24.

Pichugiña, Yelena L., Robert M. Banta, W. Alan Brewer, Scott P. Sandberg, and R. Michael Hardesty. 2012. "Doppler Lidar-based wind-profile measurement system for offshore wind-energy and other marine boundary layer applications." *Journal of Applied Meteorology and Climatology* 51: 327–49.

Sareen, Agrim, Chinmay A. Sapre, and Michael S. Selig. 2014. "Effects of leading edge erosion on wind turbine blade performance. " *Wind Energy* 17: 1531–42.

Skamarock, William C., Joseph B. Klemp, Jimy Dudhia, David O. Gill, Dale M. Barker, Michael G. Duda, Xiang-Yu Huang, Wei Wang, and Jordan G. Powers. 2008. "A description of the advanced research WRF version 3." NCAR Tech. Note NCAR/TN-475+STR.

Troen, Ib, and Erik Lundtang Petersen. 1990. *European Wind Atlas*. Risø National Laboratory, Roskilde, Denmark.

WindEurope. 2019. "Offshore Wind in Europe – Key trends and statistics 2018." February.

5 Operation and Operating Experience

Jan Engelbert

5.1 Introduction

Operation of offshore wind farms has more than twenty-five years of history, however, the learning curve is still quite steep. The industrialization of offshore wind has just begun, as wind farms become bigger and distance to shore increases. While the early projects were just a few hundred meters from shore, current projects like "HornSea 2" in the UK will be erected at a distance of approximately 100 kilometers from shore. Similarly, current wind farms are incomparably larger than early ones: "Vindeby" in Denmark, consisting of eleven 450 kW turbines, had a nameplate capacity of less than five megawatts (MW) in total, while "HornSea 2" in the UK will reach almost 1,400 MW, with each of its planned 165 eight MW turbines exceeding the total "Vindeby" capacity.

This demonstrates the rapid development of offshore wind in general, but also suggests that previous operating concepts have little in common with those of modern wind farms. Still, the knowledge and experience which has been gained over this period is an important basis for the development of today's logistics, methods for performing annual service as well as spare part concepts.

With subsidies slowly coming to an end for future wind farms and many construction-related optimizations already being realized, efficiency of offshore wind farm operations is getting more and more attention. This section describes the most important factors for the commercially successful operation and maintenance (O&M) of offshore wind farms (see also Figure 5.1 which depicts the main cashflow streams during the entire lifecycle of an offshore wind asset).

5.2 Health, Safety, Environment (HSE)

Health, safety and environment (HSE, sometimes written in another order) is the number one topic when it comes to development, construction and operation of an offshore wind farm. The health and safety of the personnel and the protection of the environment from negative impacts is of utmost importance for the industry. Given the distance and travel time to hospitals, the focus is on avoiding situations which require medical assistance as well as securing the best possible emergency plans and assistance should an incident occur. The same is true for negative impacts on the environment, such as oil spills, which could lead to the authorities ordering any work to stop immediately.

With each new offshore wind farm, the number of technicians being exposed to often harsh environmental conditions and challenging working conditions increases,

https://doi.org/10.1515/9783110607888-021

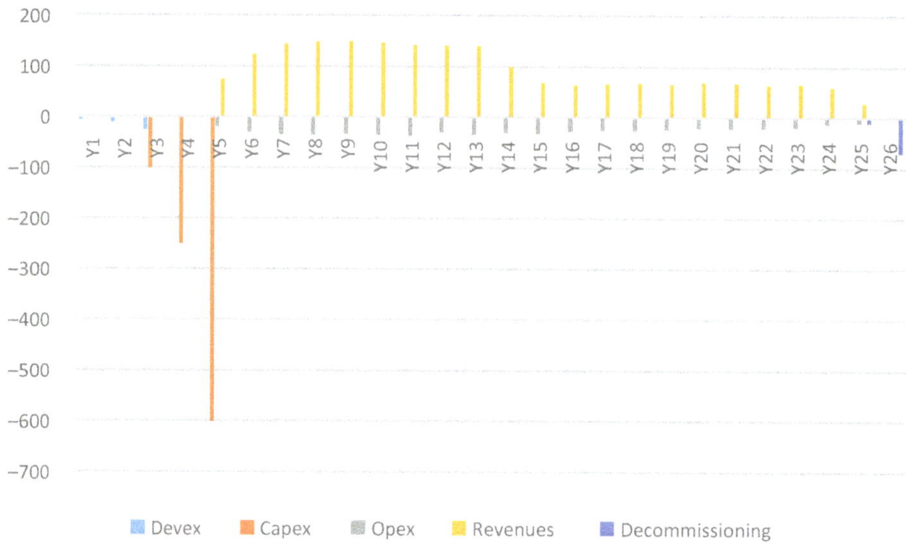

Figure 5.1: Lifetime cash flow distribution of an offshore wind farm (sample assuming subsidies during operational years 1–10), own representation.

as does the likelihood of incidents requiring medical treatment or evacuation. To date, medical rescue has been organized to a large degree by the individual wind farm operators themselves. However, it is expected that in the future this will be coordinated industry-wide involving national or regional authorities. Individual wind farms would then be expected to contribute to their regional programs according to a pre-agreed cost-sharing scheme.

Due to the importance of HSE, various key performance indicators ("KPIs") are crucial tools in optimizing wind farm operations. Well-known KPIs are for example "lost time injury frequency" (LTIF), or "total recordable injury rate" (TRIR). As in the oil and gas industry, the offshore wind industry records all observations, near misses and actual incidents in corresponding databases. This allows for detailed monitoring and analysis of events and accelerates improvement processes.

5.3 History

Some countries and local energy players decided to invest in small scale demonstration projects before investing substantial amounts in the new and risky technologies of offshore wind energy. These early projects provided essential lessons for subsequent industry-scale investments.

Denmark became the first offshore wind pioneer when it constructed its first near-shore wind farm "Vindeby" with a capacity of five MW in 1991 (the wind farm was decommissioned in 2017). The second country to jump into the water was the Netherlands. Their "Lely" wind farm consisted of four 500 kW turbines installed in the Ijsselmeer. In the UK, the first project called "North Hoyle," was commissioned several years later in 2003, with a significantly higher nameplate capacity of 60 MW. What all these projects have in common is that they are nearshore sites with only few hundred meters distance to shore, meaning that logistics during operation differ relatively little from those of onshore wind farms.

The first offshore wind farm with a significantly higher distance from shore was developed in Germany, where seabed conditions and the national park area "Wattenmeer" provide little room for nearshore wind. In addition, increasing the distance from shore results in both higher average wind speeds, higher top wind speeds and more steady wind resource availability. For many sites in the German North Sea, average wind speeds of around 10 m/s and full load hours of 4,000 to 4,500 are normal. This compares to onshore windspeeds of 5 to 7 m/s and full load hours of around 1,600 in Germany.

In 2006, a consortium consisting of the three energy companies EWE, E.ON, and Vattenfall was formed to construct a proof-of-concept wind farm in a test field in the German North Sea. In 2010, the goal was achieved with the commissioning of "alpha ventus," a wind farm comprising twelve wind turbines of two different manufacturers and a combined nominal capacity of 60 MW. The field is located 60 km off the East Frisian coast in Lower Saxony and thus required the first real offshore logistical and operational concept.

Construction of the first commercial offshore wind farm in Germany, "BARD 1," started in 2009. It is located approximately 90 km from the nearest land (the island of Borkum), almost twice as far as "alpha ventus." Due to various challenges, construction of "BARD 1" was not completed before mid-2013.

Not surprisingly, distance to shore has a major impact on the choice of the logistical setup, which is described further below. But first, we will explore some common contractual set-ups used to govern the operation of offshore wind farms.

5.4 Contractual Framework and Practical Implications

This section intends to provide a high-level overview of common contractual setups used during the operational phase and, based on that, puts a spotlight on situations which require special attention in practice.

5.4.1 Operations and Maintenance Agreement

An Operations and Maintenance Agreement, or OMA, is an overarching contractual framework which governs all operations and maintenance activities provided by an

O&M service provider. It acts as an umbrella for the Service and Warranty Agreement with the turbine supplier or its affiliated service organization (described in more detail further down) as well as covering the service and maintenance for all other components of the wind farm, such as foundations, array cables, and the offshore substation(s). Having a single contract covering all these aspects is meant to incentivize and enable the O&M service provider to monitor interfaces and realize synergies between service activities of the various sub-suppliers or relevant specialists. In short, the main task of the O&M service provider is to secure optimal operation of the asset, while understanding and ensuring best asset integrity as well as adhering to the relevant authorities and regulations that the wind farm interacts with or is built under.

Multiple variants of this setup exist in the market, depending on the preferences and capabilities of the respective owners. In some cases, the operating company coordinates all maintenance activities, except for contracting the wind turbine service activities to the turbine supplier for a defined period. In other cases, the operator only has a core management team and engages third party interface/project managers who then subcontract the necessary activities to different suppliers. In any case, it is strongly recommended that the core knowledge of the wind farm's main contracts and interfaces are kept close to the owners, to minimize dependency on external advisors or interface/project managers.

A very important fact which is often not fully reflected in the respective agreements is, that the operational phase does not start on one specific date. In fact, the commissioning phase of a wind farm usually lasts several months. This means a seamless integration of contracts governing the construction phase with those governing the operational phase is essential. For projects with a time-based feed-in tariff it is particularly important to ensure proper maintenance of the operating turbines from achievement of first power, as this marks the starting point of the tariff period. Cases have been reported where turbines achieved first power but were not handed over to the O&M service provider due to pending contractual hand-over. Without an O&M service provider, the turbines were not operating in a stable manner, thereby eating into the subsidy period without producing power – sometimes for weeks or even months. Even when the turbine manufacturer is contracted for both the construction of the wind farm and the operational phase starting immediately thereafter, a thorough interface management is required to support a smooth transition.

The above example demonstrates the importance of well-defined legal and practical interfaces between the construction-related activities and the O&M activities. Generally, the first turbines of a wind farm are put into operation while the construction phase continues for weeks or months thereafter. This leads to a situation where two quite different organizations, with often very different HSE requirements and logistical setup, are working simultaneously at the same wind farm. In practice, it can therefore make sense to define one specific date on which the overall responsibility for the site moves from the construction organization to the operations organization. The respective other organization will continue to work in the field during this transition phase but instead act as a subcontractor. After the handover date, the roles will reverse if the construction organization still has activities to carry out on site.

5.4.2 Service and Warranty Agreement

The service and warranty for the most important component of the wind farm, the wind turbines, is ensured through the Service and Warranty Agreement (SWA). This contract is generally concluded between the turbine supplier (or an affiliated company) and the wind farm owner. A common alternative is that the contract is concluded with the O&M service provider. In the latter scenario, the most important arrangements in the SWA are usually passed on to the wind farm operator through the OMA.

The Turbine Supply Agreement (TSA) and the SWA are usually concluded with the same company (or group) with the goal of seamless integration of these two agreements. This integration is key to supporting maintenance of the manufacturer's warranty and preventing downtime. However, most turbine suppliers are large corporations with several different divisions. It is advisable to closely monitor these interfaces as if these were two different contractors.

The minimum term of the SWA depends on individual considerations such as requirements from the lenders if project financings is in place, or from the owners if the project is funded in some other way. Terms vary between five and fifteen years, with certain price and scope adjustment clauses after the initial (five-year) term.

The warranty start-date is usually the individual taking-over date of the specific turbine, while the end-date is generally harmonized so that all turbines of a wind farm have the same warranty termination date. This date is often calculated as a specific number of years, e.g., five years, after the average date of the individual taking-over dates of the specific turbine.

5.4.3 Availability Warranty

An important part of the warranty is the availability warranty which is normally linked to the term of the SWA. While in the past this was a time-based warranty, nowadays the turbine availability is generally production-based. A time-based availability of e.g., 96% only guarantees that a turbine is ready to operate approximately 8,410 out of 8,760 hours per year, not necessarily meaning that these are average wind-speed hours. In practice, the actual yield can be significantly below 96% if the turbines are available during low wind periods and not available during periods with high wind. Production-based availability, on the other hand, means that the O&M service provider or SWA provider warrants that 96% of the possible production is either realized or compensated.

A production-based availability level of 95 to 96% is fairly standard for offshore wind turbines after the ramp-up period. This is approximately 1 to 3% below the expected levels known from onshore turbines as can be expected due to more challenging accessibility and environmental conditions.

Various criteria for exclusion from the availability warranty exist, e.g., grid unavailability, adverse weather situations, or downtime resulting from balance-of-plant unavailability like the offshore substation in case this is not attributable to the turbine supplier or covered by the SWA.

5.4.4 Offshore Substation

Turbines in nearshore wind farms are often directly connected to (onshore) assets belonging to the transmission system operator. However, with increasing distances to shore as well as increasing sizes of offshore wind farms, it is better to collect the power from the turbines in an offshore substation (OSS) first (see Figure 5.2). Here, the power from the turbines is stepped up in voltage (e.g., from 33 to 155 kV) and then transmitted to the grid to minimize electricity losses in the cables.

Depending on the specifics of the respective market, the OSS can either belong to the wind farm or the transmission system operator. For offshore wind farms in the Netherlands, e.g. "Borssele 1+2," the OSS is generally owned by the transmission system operator, however, certain components on the OSS are owned by and in the control of the wind farms such as the wind farm control system.

In most wind farms in the German North Sea, the OSS is part of the wind farm. However, the transmission system operator owns and remotely operates a relatively small compartment on the OSS in which the power is taken over from the wind farm before it is transmitted to a converter platform nearby. These converter platforms convert the AC power from the wind farms to DC power before it is transmitted to shore, as electrical losses on AC cables increase with cable length. As a rule of thumb, transmission losses on cable systems longer than 100 km make it feasible to invest in AC/DC-offshore converters. Onshore, the DC power is converted back into AC before it is fed into the grid.

The OSS is not naturally part of the SWA with the turbine supplier. The OSS is a complex separate asset, comprising not only the electrical equipment to transform power from e.g., 33 kV to 155 kV but also a large variety of other systems like the wind farm control system, auxiliary systems like diesel generators, air conditioning, lighting, helicopter platform, safety systems and the like. Often, the supplier of the steel structure of the OSS, sometimes in a joint venture with an electrical specialist, is contracted for the delivery of the overall system/structure, including most subsystems. However, all of the hundreds of components come with maintenance instructions from each individual supplier and are often commissioned by several subcontractors.

Figure 5.2: CTV pushing on to "Gode Wind 2" OSS foundation (Ørsted).

Due to the diversity of the systems, neither the O&M service provider nor a single OSS operations and maintenance provider is capable of servicing all components of the OSS themselves. Therefore, it is key to appoint a very professional O&M service provider who is capable of managing all interfaces to the numerous subsystem suppliers of the OSS. This not only includes management of the extensive documentation but also management of complex sub-supplier contracts and collaboration as well as timely follow-up of maintenance requirements, including e.g., proactive monitoring of offshore training of the respective technicians.

Many suppliers of these systems not only deliver their equipment to onshore customers but also service their products normally onshore. Some cases have been seen where only when service intervals were reached or, much worse, when system break-downs occurred and immediate repair was required, it became obvious that the supplier's service technicians did not have the respective offshore certificates, whereby they were not allowed to work offshore. It is a costly experience when a full wind farm cannot export power due to e.g., a broken cooling system on the OSS until a service technician has completed the necessary training. In the past, this issue has been fixed by granting extra-ordinary work permits. However, this is no longer possible as the industry is becoming stricter, requiring technicians to present the respective training certificates before being allowed to go offshore. In addition to portraying the importance of proper management of subcontractors and technician training, this also shows the improved focus on health and safety in the industry.

5.4.5 Maintenance Types and Optimization

O&M concepts are – or should be – heavily influenced by the revenue profile of the respective wind farm. For example, wind farms with a front-loaded subsidy scheme, leading to increased revenues over e.g., the first eight years of operation as in Germany, should consider postponing major overhaul campaigns until after the subsidy period to the extent possible as these can cause significant downtime. At least the aim should be to minimize downtime by optimizing maintenance campaigns.

To date, however, most maintenance programs are defined primarily by specifications from the suppliers of the various components and less so by the revenue profile, which could be considered either by the subsidy scheme, or simply by the wind profile.

Thus, it is advisable to introduce an incentive scheme which rewards the O&M service provider for optimizing the maintenance program so production-based availability and therefore revenues are maximized. One way of achieving this is by sharing revenues above a contractually defined level with the O&M service provider.

5.4.6 Scheduled Maintenance and Regular Inspections

As mentioned above, the maintenance specifications of the component suppliers more or less dictate the maintenance schedule. Generally, most major components require annual service intervals, with warranty instructions only allowing for small deviations in order to ensure component warranties and asset integrity. The biggest part of the annual service campaign is thus determined by the turbine maintenance. In wind farms which include an OSS, servicing the OSS is the second biggest aspect of the service planning due to the complexity and number of different systems it comprises.

Foundations and array cables need less maintenance but do require regular inspections. This scope should also be regarded as part of the annual service campaign.

5.4.7 Condition-Based Monitoring and Preventive Maintenance

Modern wind farms continuously collect thousands of data points from countless sensors in the turbines and on the OSS. These data points are not only used for the analysis of failures occurring in the wind farm but also for preventive maintenance.

Predictions about the remaining lifetime of components allows a prudent operator to order and exchange spare parts as part of scheduled maintenance and prevents longer outages of turbines due to component failure. Further, it allows the operator to plan and carry out these works when the weather conditions are favorable. Both of these strategies minimize production losses due to downtime.

"Big data" has just begun to influence how wind farms are operated and maintained. Historically, a wind farm has been a large collection of individual assets with numerous individual and non-integrated monitoring systems, sensors and the like. With the possibilities of integrated data collection and analysis tools, combined with external data points from e.g., other wind farms or external weather data, significant efficiencies can be harvested by these synergies in the future.

All these measures aim to reduce unscheduled maintenance, as these are the most expensive O&M activities and, at the same time, very often lead to downtime of essential components during high wind periods. While there are certainly areas for improvement with complex assets such as offshore wind farms, unscheduled maintenance can most likely never be eliminated completely.

5.4.8 Unscheduled Maintenance

Unscheduled maintenance or troubleshooting, as the name suggests, is not planned but a reaction to unforeseen failures of critical components. Failures of non-critical components will most likely be dealt with in a (fairly) planned maintenance activity, if the turbine can continue production. The urgency to react can either result from asset integrity risks to avoid consequential, and more severe damages to other components, or to minimize substantial revenue losses due to turbines being stopped. Time-based subsidy regimes significantly increase the pressure on the O&M service provider to bring turbines back into operation even when e.g., the weather conditions are not favorable for service operations, as otherwise the subsidy period continues without power production. In volume-based subsidy regimes, this risk is much lower as the subsidy will only be postponed and not lost.

5.4.9 Logistical Concepts

As mentioned earlier, logistics concepts vary significantly, depending mainly on the distance to shore – or, more precisely, the distance to and accessibility of, the O&M hub, meaning the onshore facilities of the O&M service provider. In this section, the focus is mainly on those offshore wind farms which are considered "far shore" sites. Another determining factor for the choice of the most suitable logistical setup is the type of O&M activity at hand. Scheduled maintenance or annual inspections have different requirements than ad-hoc repairs or troubleshooting.

1. Overview

Offshore wind farms can be serviced using a variety of access methods. Most commonly, sites with an acceptable sailing distance (generally less than two hours) deploy crew transfer vessels, or CTVs. With increasing distance to the O&M port, the feasibility of CTVs decreases, and service operation vessels, or SOVs, become more attractive. These vessels often are equipped with a helicopter platform, which facilitates the combination of SOVs and helicopters in a joint service set-up. For even greater distances to shore, accommodation platforms are generally deployed.

While the aforementioned methods of accessing the wind farm cover the standard operations and maintenance scope, jack-up vessels are used for the exchange of major components which cannot be handled by smaller vessels or helicopters (e.g., blades, gearboxes, or nacelles). Below, we will describe the above-mentioned transportation types in more detail.

2. Crew Transfer Vessels

Crew transfer vessels (CTVs) are meant to transport service technicians and their equipment to offshore wind farms on a daily basis. The majority of the vessels used today are purpose-built and optimized for wind farm logistics. As it is vital that technicians arrive at their workplace ready to work, CTVs are equipped with comfortable suspensions seats, reducing the risk of seasickness. The vessels also have comforts like TVs and even small kitchens. The standard capacity is 12 passengers ("pax"), however, newer CTVs can carry 18 or 24 pax, reflecting increasing wind farm sizes and the drive to optimize logistics costs. Transportation capacity for tools, spare parts, diesel, fresh water, usually ranges from four to 25 tons.

To transfer technicians to turbines or offshore substations, CTVs push on to specially designed turbine access ladders attached to the foundations, using 60 to 70% of their maximum thrust. This pressure stabilizes the vessel, enabling it to remain stationary while the technicians step across to the ladder.

A number of different vessel shapes exists. Older CTVs most often have a monohull shape while new-built vessels often have a double-hull, or catamaran, shape. The latter sail much more steadily and cause less seasickness in passengers and crew.

Due to their relatively small size, the operability of CTVs is limited to significant wave heights under approximately 1.2 to 1.5 meters. Therefore, with increasing distances to shore and thus increasing incidence of larger waves, the feasibility of CTVs declines unless the size of the CTV is correspondingly increased.

3. Service Operation Vessel

Service operation vessels (SOVs) were originally used during the commissioning of the wind farms when a relatively large number of technicians need to stay in the construction field for several weeks. But with increasing distances to shore, their advantages for the operational phase have become quite obvious. Modern SOVs are more than 70 m long and offer accommodation for up to 60 technicians, including leisure and fitness rooms, as well as large storage areas and workshops. They are equipped with a comfortable walk-to-work solution as well as a helicopter platform for crew exchange or emergency evacuations. Further, SOVs are equipped with boat landings for CTVs so that they can flexibly support a combination of all transportation means. Last but not least, the use of an SOV, equipped with a modern walk-to-work solution as described further below, has a significant positive impact on HSE as transfers from CTVs to platform ladders can be eliminated or at least reduced.

The major advantage of SOVs is that they can stay in the wind farm for weeks, thereby minimizing travel time for technicians. With their dynamic position systems, they have a much higher operability window than CTVs and can stay in the field during high-wind events. This allows for a significantly accelerated annual service campaign duration, which can be better planned during low wind periods and thus cause reduced production loss.

On the other hand, a significant disadvantage of an SOV is the high operating cost which will only pay off if the lease can be limited to an accelerated annual service campaign of some six to ten weeks, depending on the wind farm's size. Thus, compared to an annual service carried out more continuously throughout the year using CTVs, an SOV campaign is much more compressed. This automatically leads to a more condensed impact on turbine availability during the service campaign. Therefore, it is important to ensure such campaign is carried out during low wind periods in summer. If a cluster of wind farms shares an SOV and the schedule dictates that some annual maintenance must be performed during high wind periods, the impact should be shared (e.g., by alternating which wind farm is serviced during the high wind season).

4. Walk-to-Work Solutions

In recent years, several walk-to-work solutions have been developed. Installed on the deck of an SOV, they allow access to turbines or offshore substations in significantly higher wave conditions than CTVs by providing stabilizing walkways which automatically adjust to wave and vessel movements.

Walk-to-work solutions can be a fixed part of the SOV or be leased and attached to the vessel more or less as a plug-and-play solution. The most commonly used solutions are the so-called Ampelmann and the UPTIME. The Ampelmann solution provides a fully three-dimensional motion compensation and works up to a significant wave height of 4.5 meters, significantly decreasing weather waiting times as compared to CTVs. The UPTIME uses telescopic technology to compensate for sea or vessel movements and comes in various sizes. For SOVs, walkway lengths of 22 to 30 meters are most commonly chosen. The wave height compensation varies correspondingly between four and five meters.

Figure 5.3: SOV "Wind of Change" with walk-to-work solution, drawing (Ørsted).

5. Helicopters

Helicopters are frequently used during the construction phase, but they also play an important role in the operational phase of many offshore wind farms. However, a number of prerequisites need to be fulfilled to make helicopters a cost-effective addition.

First, the distance to shore needs to be within certain limitations. Most helicopters offer a maximum flight duration between 2.5 and 3.5 hours. For wind farms far offshore, either large helicopters with a corresponding range can be deployed or a refueling station must be provided en route. Refueling, however, is a significant cost factor, as very strict requirements for fuel storage, hangar, and fire protection need to be fulfilled. To add to the business case of including a helicopter, the operating costs are roughly EUR 1,000 per hour. Therefore, only large wind farm with revenues for a turbine exceeding these costs will benefit from the flexibility that the helicopter provides. Finally, either the OSS needs to be equipped with a helicopter platform and/or the turbines need to have a hoisting area on top of the nacelles. The latter is, however, quite standard when looking at the large 6+MW offshore turbines that are used in the modern offshore wind farms.

Costs for deploying a helicopter are high compared to other access methods. Thus, they are mainly used for troubleshooting activities where either assets or significant revenues are at risk. In addition, helicopters are used for medical evacuation where time and not money is the decisive factor. Helicopters used for emergency evacuation are, however, quite different to the ones used for troubleshooting. The biggest advantage of helicopters over all types of vessels is their ability to transfer even in situations with wind speeds of 20 m/s or more.

Helicopter services are normally subcontracted by the O&M service provider. Contractual models vary depending on the specific needs. Often a certain number of hours per month is covered by a base fee while additional hours are charged based on actual use.

All passengers using the helicopter need to be trained according to international standards (most often GWO). This includes helicopter underwater escape training (HUET) and hoisting training. Very few exceptions to this requirement are granted, so everyone planning to go offshore should complete and refresh all certificates in due course.

Different types of helicopters are available in the market. Most often, helicopters with eight to twelve passenger seats are chosen. This provides flexibility in regard to personnel and allows for a hoisting device to be attached to the helicopter.

In future wind farms where subsidies play only a minor or no role at all, careful assessment will be necessary to determine if expensive transportation means like helicopters are still feasible.

6. Accommodation Platforms

Accommodation platforms are chosen when the wind farm is relatively far from shore, and when an SOV concept is not feasible e.g., due to lack of cluster effects, or when the platform also hosts further technical equipment (see Figure 5.4). Accommodation platforms were also deployed before SOVs were introduced to the market. Their advantage is that they are available any time while for example the mobilization of an SOV generally takes some time. Ideally, accommodation platforms are located so they can service more than just one wind farm.

Accommodation platforms provide comfort similar to an SOV, but without the flexibility to transfer directly to specific turbines. If constructed as depicted below with a fixed walkway to the OSS, they provide a very high accessibility to the core of the wind farm. For shuttling to the turbines, either CTVs or helicopters are deployed. Accommodation is most often provided by a separate hotel platform as shown. However, solutions where the accommodation is integrated into the OSS can also be found.

Technicians and platform staff usually stay offshore for two consecutive weeks, then they are off-duty for two weeks. Facilities on the platform include sports and leisure rooms, TVs, a canteen and, most importantly, internet access.

7. Jack-Up Vessels

Jack-up vessels are used for the exchange of larger components which cannot be carried out by CTVs or helicopters (e.g., gearboxes, blades, or complete nacelles; see Figure 5.5). These vessels generally have four or six legs and can jack-up to stand on the seabed. This enables them to operate independently from wave

Figure 5.4: "Horns Rev 2" OSS and accommodation platform, Denmark (Ørsted).

impact. They are equipped with one or two cranes and current models provide a lifting capability of up to approximately 1,500 tons.

Due to their specialization, only a few jack-up vessels are available on the market, leading to correspondingly high charter rates in the six-digit Euro range per day. Therefore, O&M activities requiring jack-ups are normally planned carefully and the industry tries to avoid ad-hoc need as much as possible. Mobilization lead times are rarely below three months.

8. Combining Access Methods for an Integrated Logistics Concept

Often, it makes sense to combine different types of logistics means in an integrated logistics concept. For example, the annual service of the wind farm can be carried out from an SOV supported by one or two daughter crafts (CTVs) while a helicopter is used for troubleshooting activities. The following diagram provides an example of a concept which combines CTV, SOV and helicopter use, bringing the combined accessibility of the wind farm to approximately 90% of the time throughout the year (see Figure 5.6).

9. Drones

Drones are a comparatively new means for carrying out services on offshore wind farms and are particularly used for inspections where access is limited or poses a significant safety risk. The latest generation provides sufficiently long operating

Figure 5.5: Jack-up vessel bold tern (Fred. Olsen Windcarrier) installing a blade in "Borkum Riffgrund 2" (Ørsted).

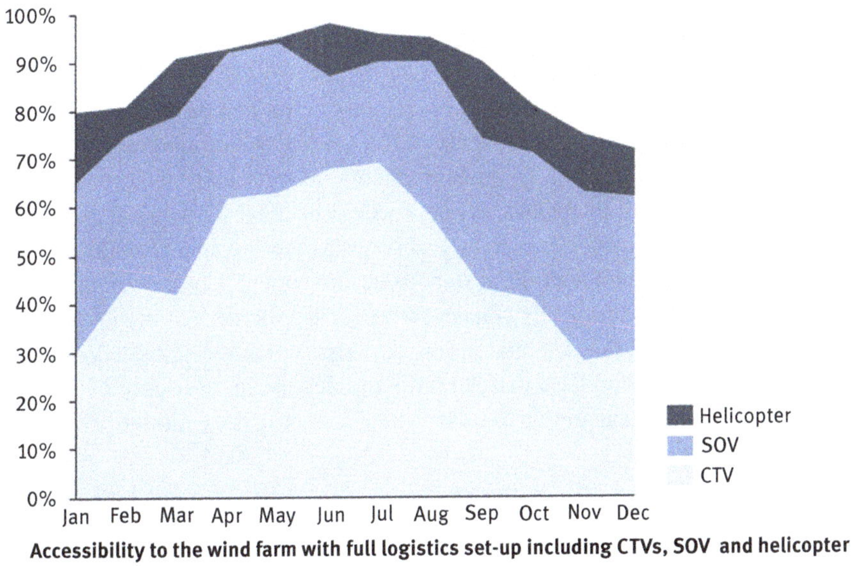

Figure 5.6: Accessibility to the wind farm with full logistics set-up (own representation).

times as well as operating stability for offshore conditions. Combined with high resolution cameras or even small tools, they facilitate activities like blade inspections as they significantly reduce the need for rope access by service technicians. The advantage of drone inspections inside the blades is even more obvious when comparing it with time and effort for technicians accessing confined spaces. These two examples illustrate that drone inspections can not only have a positive effect on the precision of inspections, but also on inspection-related downtime of the turbines and reduction of HSE-related risks for the employees.

For statutory inspections, drones are not yet permitted in all countries as more proof is required by some authorities to document the same quality level as with human inspections. The main argument for this is that drones currently only inspect the surface of the component, whereas manual inspections can include endoscopic inspections and other types of thorough analysis. However, it seems likely that the importance and the use of drones will continue to increase in the future, and thereby continue to reduce maintenance costs and exposure to HSE risks.

10. Remote Control

The most comfortable and efficient means to control proper operation of wind farm components is via remote control from an onshore control room. This is generally provided by the Supervisory Control and Data Acquisition (SCADA) system. The SCADA system can either be supplied by the turbine manufacturer or a specialized third-party provider. Due to the amount of data traffic, this system requires broadband or glass fiber communication to shore. The SCADA system is the central tool for communication with the turbines. It controls the turbines' power production, collects failure codes and monitors the turbines' performance. Thus, it is a key source for planning maintenance works.

It is crucial that the SCADA system works reliably and offers the highest possible availability. However, due to the complexity of the system, the number of interfaces, and the geographical distribution of its components onshore and offshore, a 100% availability level is difficult to achieve. While it would be ideal for the overall system to have a redundant lay-out, this is extremely difficult to achieve and, in reality, rarely provided. Given the importance of the system to ensure commercially stable and reliable operation, one should carefully consider a respective increase of the investment costs (capex) compared to the potential production losses of a less stable SCADA system. This will vary from wind farm to wind farm and depend on the specific business case but is a necessary consideration to make when designing the wind farm.

5.4.10 Personnel

1. Turbine Technicians

When it comes to offshore wind farm operations, turbine technicians are to date the most important resource for executing maintenance and repair works (see Figure 5.7). Technicians often specialize in a certain turbine type and cannot be allocated to another turbine model without proper training. Thus, if a new turbine type is introduced to the market, sufficient lead time needs to be planned for training the personnel and allowing them to gain experience on the specifics of the new equipment. This is often underestimated, especially if a number of wind farms with the same new turbine type enter the operational phase within a short time period.

In this context, it should be mentioned that different levels of turbine-specific experience are required for different service and maintenance works. For example, only the technicians qualified to the highest level are allowed to do troubleshooting works. Attaining this level requires several months of theoretical and practical training. These highly trained technicians can therefore become a scarce resource, particularly during the ramp-up phase from construction to operations, or after an outage of the wind farm, where all turbines need to be restarted immediately. Their availability is key to keep power production high in the early phase after commissioning, where cash flows have the highest impact on the net present value of a wind farm investment.

Figure 5.7: Technician with PPE, climbing a foundation ladder (Ørsted).

With numerous offshore wind farms becoming operational in various countries, the demand for a skilled workforce is constantly increasing. As some of the O&M hubs are located in "weak" regions, when considering infrastructure and population number, this can easily become a bottleneck. Challenging shift patterns add to this (e.g., 14/14, i.e., 14 continuous offshore working days with 12 hours shifts, followed by 14 days off work). To ensure a sufficient supply of new technicians, the industry will need to increase its efforts in educational programs and local cooperation with schools, job training centers and suppliers.

As operations and maintenance programs develop over time, shift patterns will be required to change accordingly. Thus, it is advisable to include as much flexibility as possible in all labor contracts. On the other hand, both trade unions and works councils see an increased need to protect the technicians against too demanding working conditions. In essence, creating a win-win situation which ensures both optimal availability and performance of the wind farm and motivation and flexibility of the technicians should be the end goal for all.

2. OSS Technicians

The OSS is both the heart and the brain of many wind farms, and it requires a high level of attention. The availability of its systems influences the commercial success of the wind farm significantly, as an issue on the OSS can bring the whole wind farm out of operations, as compared to issues on the turbines where often "only" one position is affected and the revenue impact therefore minimal in comparison. However, as explained above, no single technician can service all systems of an OSS, so a combination of different skillsets and competencies needs to be present on site or at least available on very short notice. It is therefore important to employ a crew with sufficiently diverse skills and training, to ensure that most issues can be managed immediately. In addition, it is advisable to implement a thorough contract management setup regarding the maintenance requirements on the OSS as well as subcontractor service agreements with the possibility for immediate mobilization.

3. SCADA Experts

An often-underestimated role is that of a SCADA expert. As the SCADA system can be regarded as the nervous system of an offshore wind farm, the impact of malfunctions can easily result in considerable financial losses. In such a scenario, it is vital to ensure minimal reaction times and a thorough understanding of the complexity of the SCADA system.

4. Switching Authorized Persons

In Germany, like in most other countries, switching of high voltage equipment like that on the OSS may only be performed by experts with proven electrical and technical expertise. They usually have an electric engineering background and are key for the safe operation of the wind farm.

5. Other Specialists

From time to time, other specialists may be needed for less frequent or more specialized tasks. While it normally does not make sense to keep these resources on the payroll throughout the year, well-established relationships with external advisors or specialists will help reduce lead times in case of urgent repairs.

6. Hub Selection

Many offshore wind farms are erected within reasonable sailing distance from shore, so the maintenance concepts are primarily based on the use of CTVs as transportation means. As sailing time is a key factor for the efficiency of operations and maintenance activities throughout the lifetime of the asset, the hub location should be carefully selected.

A number of considerations should be taken into account in making this decision. In addition to the sailing distance, suitable harbor facilities including sufficiently large and flexible storage areas also need to be present. One possible solution is to exclusively rent quay space on a long-term basis so that the onshore and offshore logistics interface can run smoothly and planned throughout the lifetime of the asset. In addition, it is worth assessing potential tidal restrictions on the planned logistics setup. When making a final selection, it might be worth considering how difficult it will be to add on more elements to the wind farm's logistical solution in the future. For example, it is beneficial to ensure that tides do not restrict access to the wind farm, and in case an SOV or helicopter operations are added to the O&M concept, sufficiently large harbor and mooring facilities as well as a nearby heliport would be needed.

Additionally, as mentioned in the Personnel section of this section already, the local infrastructure is also crucial to acquire and retain skilled workforce. It is advisable to establish a long-term strategy with local authorities as well as cooperation with schools or job training centers to ensure that, for example, electricians or mechanics are qualified according to the standards needed in the offshore wind industry.

5.4.11 Training and Standards

1. Oil & Gas Standards

Some of the standards in the offshore wind industry are based on those from the oil and gas industry guidelines with its long-lasting offshore experience, such as sea survival or helicopter trainings. Others are specific to the wind industry, such as working at heights.

2. GWO Standards

The Global Wind Association, or GWO, has defined the most commonly used training standards in offshore wind. Courses include working at heights, sea survival, manual handling, fire awareness, first aid, helicopter underwater escape training and others, depending on the professional focus of the individual. These courses need to be refreshed regularly. A proper system for monitoring the training certificates and deadlines for renewal is key to avoid situations where urgently required technicians do not have proper work permits or are refused by the helicopter service provider.

3. Interface Challenges

Wherever interfaces are present, there is a risk that communication breaks down, or information gets lost. If, for example, the grid operator needs to access the wind farm's OSS but has different training requirements than the wind farm operator, there is a risk that important service works could be delayed until either exemptions from the rules are granted or the required training certificates can be presented.

5.4.12 Spare Parts

With the offshore wind market maturing steadily in the various regional markets, operators are beginning to focus on synergies between different wind farms via portfolio strategies instead of seeing each wind farm as an individual asset. Synergies could arise from regional strategies where, for example, one SOV could support the annual service campaign of a number of operating wind farms in a circular pattern. Another example are turbine (or platform) related synergies. Operators with a fleet of similar turbines could keep a central – or regional – stock of spare parts, which can be shipped to the wind farm when needed, rather than keeping decentral spare parts for each wind farm. Such strategies can significantly reduce storage costs and minimize money tied-up in strategic spares kept for each wind farm without compromising performance and availability.

The same principle can be applied for spare array cables. Array cable failures lead to significant revenue impacts, as often a full string of turbines is impacted (usually five to eight turbines). Main reasons for cable failures relate to installation problems, issues with the connectors or exceeding the minimum bending ratio. With production lead times of many months, having spare array cables on stock is likely to be a good business case. An often-used solution is to keep the excess cable from the construction phase for emergency array cable issues.

5.5 Operational Challenges

Despite all the progress that has been made in recent years, offshore wind is still at a relatively steep part of the learning curve compared to more mature industries. Naturally, the optimization of the construction phase is a few years ahead as capex risks have been weighted higher than "opex" (operational expenditure) risks in the past. However, the industry is becoming increasingly aware of the influence of optimized operations on the revenue generation.

5.5.1 Interface Risks

One of the biggest challenges in this regard is the optimization of interfaces. A key interface from an operator's perspective is the interface between construction and operation. The operator has a keen interest (or at least should have) in getting a handover that allows them to seamlessly take over after commissioning completion (which is generally carried out by the construction teams) and to keep availability high from day one.

However, turbine manufacturers often have an organization with separate construction and operations departments. As an external customer, it is not easy to manage this interface between construction and operation. It is highly recommended to actively involve the operations organization as early as possible in the commissioning phase and ensure a proper ramp-up of operations resources. This can also be helpful when experiencing grid-related challenges, as a good cooperation between construction and operations in the transition phase can help ensure that turbines are restarted at the earliest opportunity after a grid outage.

5.5.2 Example of Grid-Related Challenges

Significant challenges can result from delayed, unstable or defective grid connections. A number of cases have been reported where the grid connection was either delayed or was not operating in a stable manner (for example due to an export cable failure or damage), resulting in the wind farm being off-grid for several weeks or even months after planned grid availability. Most turbines are not prepared to stand still for an extended period of time, and so diesel generators may have to be deployed in order to exercise the nacelle or rotor to avoid standstill marks or standstill-related problems (e.g., with batteries, moisture inside the turbine or similar). Logistics of refueling as well as commissioning and decommissioning of diesel generators pose a major challenge to any operations team. In such scenarios, it is recommended to outsource these extraordinary activities and involve experts to ensure a professional and timely reaction. This also helps protecting the rest of the organization so that they can continue their regular activities during the generally stressful ramp-up period and further secures that the asset integrity will not be at risk.

5.5.3 Defects and Serial Defects

As can be expected for a relatively new industry, defects cannot be avoided, and any rectification work must be performed in adverse environmental conditions. Prudent developers and operators will therefore carefully consider defects and defect mitigation, not only during operations but also during the development of a wind farm. Additionally, the major manufacturers of offshore wind equipment have established continuous improvement processes to avoid defects or at least simplify their rectification.

Despite all these efforts, due to the fast development pace of new technology and continuously growing turbines, defective components cannot be completely avoided. In practice, different parts of many turbine types have been affected by more or less substantial failures.

Fortunately, failures of large components, requiring an expensive jack-up vessel for exchange, like gearboxes, blades, or generators, do not occur on a regular basis, but they do occur from time to time. During the warranty period, the exchange campaign is generally planned, executed and paid for by the O&M service provider in connection with the turbine manufacturer. After this period, this exercise will come at the owners' cost.

Even within the warranty period, defects can occur which are not clearly attributable to lack of quality of components, for example turbine blades which are struck frequently by lightning. To mitigate potential damage, blades are equipped with lightning protection systems (LPS). These systems have been developed in a laboratory environment and are constantly being improved based on practical learnings. Turbine supply contracts generally stipulate the standards according to which LPS need to withstand lightning strikes, but it is designed for impact of lightning strikes within a standard range, and an extraordinary weather phenomenon can expose the blades to more severe impacts at any time, where the LPS is insufficient. In such cases, it might become necessary for the owners to commission a blade exchange campaign on their own, and to investigate the root cause for the blade defect after it has been exchanged and brought ashore.

The above examples relate to specific cases which rarely occur, and only on specific turbines. Some defects may occur on several turbines and even be linked to a specific turbine platform. These are referred to as "serial defects" and are a special category altogether. If the turbine supply contract contains a serial defect clause (generally only possible if the purchaser has strong negotiating power), the owner can more easily request the supplier to exchange a defective part across the whole wind farm. This requires an agreed defects percentage on the specific part to be exceeded, which is often in the range of 5%. Ideally, the parties should also align on a time window in which even a smaller percentage of defects would trigger the clause.

Based on a serial defect clause, the owner can force the supplier to exchange the part in question, even on turbines where it has not yet failed. This allows for coordinated exchange campaigns, bundling with other regular maintenance, and optimization of turbine downtime due to the exchange while avoiding longer standstill period due to turbines failing with this defect.

Serial defects are not unheard of, and in fact have been observed in many components. In one example from the earlier days of offshore wind, the grouted connection between the monopile and the so-called transition piece failed and led to so-called pile slipping, so that the transition piece slipped down the monopile some centimeters. As this was an uncontrolled movement, it put the integrity of the tower at risk. More recently, bolts connecting the nacelle housing with the tower have proven to be too weak, forcing the respective supplier to develop a plan to inspect or exchange all such bolts installed in this turbine type. Due to the corresponding HSE risks, a large number of turbines was stopped for several weeks, causing significant consequential losses for the owners until the relevant risk assessments were ready and approved by the authorities.

Less dramatic but still costly serial defects have affected generator bearings, resulted in oil leakages or shown up as blade defects. With regards to the latter, a variety of blade issues have been observed in the market, although negotiations are still ongoing as to these being serial defects or regular wear and tear.

Rotor diameters have continuously increased, multiplying the loads on the blades both at the root and at the tip of the blade. With current blade lengths of 80 meters, resulting in diameters of more than 160 meters, the blade tips travel around 300 kilometers per hour for more than 4,000 hours per year. Considering the harsh environmental conditions offshore with salty air and heavy rain, there is no doubt that this puts maximum stress on the materials. On the other hand, as blade repairs are costly and come with HSE risks, there is a significant pressure on the suppliers to develop and apply high-tech materials which can withstand these forces for many years. Specialized coating producers are constantly improving their blade protection technology. Despite these improvements, a drawback is that the protection is only as good as the overall process. The best product, if not applied following strict specifications, will not deliver the desired result, and could cause significant operational costs for repair or even blade exchanges.

5.5.4 Communication Challenges: TETRA Radio, Mobile (Data) Network

Offshore communication presents a completely different challenge. It is vital that all technicians can both be reached and reach out to team leads or offshore coordinators, most importantly in case of HSE issue, but of course also during normal working conditions. TETRA radio (terrestrial trunked radio) is a platform standard for communication commonly used in many industries including the offshore wind industry. Inside the turbines, or more precisely inside the towers, this technology reaches its limitations as the radio waves are blocked by the steel walls of the towers. It is recommended to plan for repeaters inside the turbines already when designing the wind farm. The same is true for Wi-Fi or 4G/5G connections. As applications on the technicians' handheld devices require stable connections to support efficient data exchange, it is important to ensure stable coverage of the wind farm with 4G/5G.

5.5.5 End-of-Warranty Inspections

End of Warranty activities should be carefully planned standard tasks during the first operational years but have sometimes been underestimated or neglected. Well in advance of the end of the warranty period – generally five years for the turbines and often less for other balance-of-plant assets – the inspections need to be planned and executed as well as any claims submitted. It is recommended to precisely define the scope and sample size of inspection activities. Logistics like helicopter flights or vessel transfers, availability and transportation of inspection equipment, offshore certificates or weather contingency planning require significant lead times. In this context, it should be noted that often minimum lead times prior to the end of the warranty are agreed with the manufacturers which should be carefully observed.

Further, the inspection quality is only as good as its documentation. To avoid or at least minimize disputes, it is recommended to ensure that the inspection results are documented according to necessary standards. Following these standards should allow the documentation to be accepted by the manufacturer and ensure that inspections do not need to be repeated. It might be necessary to ensure that inspections are done jointly with the manufacturer or by inspectors, however, a representative from the operator should always participate for quality assurance on behalf of the owners.

The end-of-warranty inspections are normally not carried out by the operations service personnel on site, but by internal or external experts, mainly due to potential conflicts of interest. It is recommended that the inspection teams agree well in advance with the operations service provider on their inspection schedule so that regular maintenance works are impacted as little as possible and additional turbine downtime is minimized as well.

5.5.6 IT Security

With an increasing share of the energy mix coming from offshore wind farms, they will soon become part of the critical energy infrastructure of the respective countries, which increases their attractiveness for hackers and cyber-attacks. Thousands of cyber-crime attempts are reported on a monthly basis, so it is key for the operators to deploy a robust IT security system. Given the number of sub-suppliers of various IT-based components in the turbines, the OSS and the SCADA system, this is a challenging exercise. Therefore, it is even more important to have a tested redundancy system in place, enabling the wind farm to quickly recover and restart operation after a potential cyber-attack.

5.5.7 Pandemic Crisis Management

The COVID-19 pandemic painfully demonstrates the vulnerability of human beings as well as the global economy and its production chains. At the time of writing, the full effects of the crisis on the operation of offshore wind farms have not yet materialized. However, some initial considerations on crisis management shall be described in the following.

It is crucial to immediately activate a crisis response team which closely interacts with the company's top management, to ensure fast decision making and responses to immediate threats. This team should consist of senior representatives from operations, HSE, IT, sourcing, communications and other relevant functions. It needs to have access to a so-called "situation room", which is connected to all relevant internal and external resources and thus facilitates informed and fast decisions. However, in a pandemic situation, robust and secure remote working abilities are of equal importance.

Strategic decisions need to be taken in this forum, based on the best available knowledge, for example if planned maintenance shall be continued to ensure stable operation at any time, or if services shall be limited to troubleshooting only.

Several disease control and prevention centers publish guidelines for businesses, for example the Centers for Disease Control and Prevention (CDC) in the UK (https://www.cdc.gov/coronavirus/2019-ncov/community/guidance-business-response.html). It is advisable to constantly monitor their websites for most up-to-date information, checklists etc.

Further, frequent top management communication to the entire workforce is of key importance, explaining major decisions and supporting a "can do" team spirit.

Close communication with key contractors is of equal importance. A crisis like the COVID-19 pandemic could cause contractors to declare a force majeure event under their respective service contract. If this is justified, liability for lack of performance under the contract is limited. However, generally, these clauses require very specific substantiation and a concrete impact of a force majeure event on the performance required under the contract. As offshore wind farms produce power, they can be classified as part of the critical infrastructure. This classification may help overcome certain challenges affecting other industries or parts of the society, for example travel restrictions, as traveling technicians maybe equipped with letters confirming that they operate critical infrastructure and are thus allowed to travel. In this case, general travel restrictions on their own would not constitute a force majeure event allowing the contractor to suspend services. The picture might change if technicians are sick or quarantined, or if works cannot be carriedout due to lack of spare parts as a direct consequence of the pandemic and the various restrictions it brings. It remains to be seen what impact on sourcing and stockholding the COVID-19 crisis might have. In general, low-cost items which might be affected by global supply chain interruptions and which can affect turbine availability, should be stocked in sufficient numbers. Authorities generally support the stable operation of infrastructure assets, while they are – of course – also concerned about the health and safety of offshore personnel. It is key for the offshore industry to be able to demonstrate that safe procedures which protect workers from being exposed to health risks can be implemented quickly. Such procedures should be captured in writing in business continuity plans and need to be tailored to the individual situation, logistics setup and concrete physical limitations resulting, for example, from available seating space or actual cabin size on service vessels. A key aspect in the offshore environment is to ensure and demonstrate that the rescue chain remains intact and reliable, so that the overall situation does not pose any inacceptable risks to offshore personnel.

As opposed to blue collar employees, white collar employees can generally carry out their job as well from the office as remotely from home. A very specific case is the control room for the permanent monitoring and remote access to wind farms, however, which is usually manned permanently. In this case, strict access limitations, including avoidance of overlapping shifts, need to be defined or remote handover procedures need to be implemented. Again, stable and secure remote working capabilities are essential to be able to continue safe operations in case the control room gets contaminated. Leerzeichen Sharing best practices across the industry can be facilitated by industry associations, who can also channel communication with relevant authorities and thus support a structured approach across the industry to react professionally in an unprecedented situation.

5.6 Outlook

The offshore wind industry will remain on a solid growth path internationally for many years to come. As most of these wind farms operate in challenging environmental conditions as well as decreasing subsidy levels, the pressure towards automated O&M concepts increases. It can be expected that the number of technician working hours per wind turbine, or per MWh produced, will decrease significantly.

A number of technologies have already become available, or will become available soon, to reduce the need for humans working offshore, which we have touched on in this section. This will for example be due to redundancy of components, proactive maintenance, as well as drones, robots, and remote control of many devices.

The development of robots or robotic features in wind turbines has just begun but could soon allow automatization of a variety of standard maintenance tasks, like oil change. This is expected to contribute significantly to reduced maintenance downtime of turbines as no humans are endangered by being in close proximity to electrified components.

Another very promising area to optimize on the time humans spend in the turbines is augmented reality (AR). AR is already being tested on some sites with promising results. Technicians are equipped either with tablets or smart-goggles which show for example maintenance manuals or procedures in a very practical way in parallel to the technician's real-time view of the respective component. This will help less experienced technicians becoming faster, thus driving down the time spent on annual service significantly, but also has the potential to improve safety.

Adding the commercial perspective of declining subsidies to the picture, it becomes obvious that there is an enormous pressure on the O&M service providers to make use of such latest technologies – at the same time offering an enormous potential for them to increase wind farm availability and, thus, to participate in the corresponding upside.

6 Supportive System for Offshore Wind Energy: The Example of Germany

Thoralf Herbold (Partner), Thorsten Kirch (Associated Partner), both GÖRG Partnerschaft von Rechtsanwälten mbB

6.1 Introduction

The first offshore wind farm in Germany was commissioned in 2010.[1] By the end of 2017, 1,169 wind turbines had been installed and offshore wind energy made up 2.7% of the power production mix in Germany.[2] Compared to 2016, the production capacity from offshore wind farms had increased by 31%,[3] making offshore wind energy the fastest-growing source of renewable energy in Germany.[4] Today, Germany is second in the world after the United Kingdom with regard to the offshore wind power market.[5]

This significant development was largely based on an extensive system of state support. The supportive system for offshore wind energy changed repeatedly[6] to encompass the industry development and the provisions under EU law.[7] The latest amendment of the Renewable Energy Sources Act (EEG) in 2017 marked a turning point, as the statutory claim to state funding was replaced by a competitive model based on auctions. Additionally, in a more formal sense, most questions concerning offshore wind energy are now laid down in a separate law, the Offshore Wind Energy Act (WindSeeG 2017).

1 http://www.offshore-windindustrie.de/windparks/deutschland.

2 Benjamin Wehrmann, "German offshore wind power – output, business and perspectives," FactSheet, https://www.cleanenergywire.org/factsheets/german-offshore-wind-power-output-business-and-perspectives.

3 Deutsche WindGuard GmbH, Status des Offshore-Energieausbaus in Deutschland 2017, p. 1, https://wind-energy-network.de/files/downloads/Factsheet_Status_Offshore-Windenergieausbau_2017.pdf

4 Benjamin Wehrmann, "German offshore wind power – output, business and perspectives," FactSheet, https://www.cleanenergywire.org/factsheets/german-offshore-wind-power-output-business-and-perspectives.

5 Benjamin Wehrmann, "German offshore wind power – output, business and perspectives," FactSheet, https://www.cleanenergywire.org/factsheets/german-offshore-wind-power-output-business-and-perspectives.

6 Main amendments of the EEG in 2000, 2004, 2009, 2012, 2014 and 2017.

7 Christian Bauer and Korbinian Kantenwein, EnWZ 2017, 3 (3).

https://doi.org/10.1515/9783110607888-022

6.2 Legal Framework/Regime before the 2017 Amendment

Since the entry into force of the EEG in 2000, the main instrument of state support for renewable energy sources in Germany had been a statutorily fixed feed-in tariff and the priority grid connection and feed-in to the grid system. Anyone who produced energy from renewable sources was allowed to feed in this energy and had a statutory right for a fixed remuneration for 20 years. This provided an incentive to invest in renewable energies.

In recent years, the supportive system was primarily altered to facilitate and stimulate the market integration of renewable energies. Under the EEG 2014, the supportive system was two-fold: Producers of renewable energy generally received market funding, in exceptional cases however a claim to a feed-in tariff still existed.[8] Market funding entitles the installation operators to a market premium in addition to the market price if they sell the energy at the EEX exchange.[9] This ensures that selling energy directly is as profitable as receiving the feed-in tariff,[10] promoting the transition from a fixed remuneration to a market price. A claim to the feed-in tariff remained only in the exceptional cases laid down in Sec. 37, 38 EEG 2014. The supportive system was so effective, that negative power prices occurred repeatedly at the EEX exchange and the steady increase of the EEG surcharge (EEG-Umlage) led to increasing energy prices.[11] The German legislator even began to fear excessive funding.

6.3 Changes in the EEG 2017

To encompass the industry development and the European Commission's Guidelines on State aid for environmental protection and energy 2014–2020, the 2017 amendment of the EEG provides for a system change: Though the funding is still awarded by way of market funding, the claim to funding and its level are now determined in auctions instead of being statutorily fixed.[12] Only an operator who received a funding award in an auction will be supported by the state.[13] The claim to funding has thus become contingent upon the issuing of a funding award.[14] By establishing more competition, this paradigm change intends to slow down the expansion of renewable

---

8 Steffen Herz and Florian Valentin, EnWZ 2014, 358 (358); Guido Wustlich, NVwZ 2014, 1113 (1117); Sec. 2 SubSec. 2 EEG 2014.

9 Herz/Valentin, EnWZ 2014, 358 (358).

10 Andreas Hinsch and Jan Reshöft, in Jan Reshöft and Andreas Schäfermeier, EEG, 4th ed., 2014,§ 33 g Rn. 4; Volker Lüdemann and Manuel Christian Ortmann, EnWZ 2014, 387 (387).

11 Larissa Bahmer and Sophia Loers, GewArch 2017, 406 (406).

12 Bahmer/Loers, GewArch 2017, 406 (406).

13 https://www.next-kraftwerke.de/energie-blog/eeg-2017-ausschreibungen.

14 Sandra Pflicht, EnWZ 2016, 550 (551).

energies, allowing for its synchronization with the grid extension.[15] Moreover, the auctioning system aims at the prevention of excessive promotion of renewable energy, which would lead to an increase in the energy price.[16]

From a formal point of view, the major change was that most rules on offshore wind energy installations are now encompassed in the WindSeeG. It covers sectoral planning, auctions and the approval, construction and operation of such installations. By including these rules, the Act replaced the Sea Installations Ordinance (SeeAnlV).[17] However, some questions like the connection to the grid system are still governed by the Energy Industry Act (EnWG) and the EEG 2017 is applicable where the WindSeeG does not provide for specific provisions.[18]

According to Sec. 1 WindSeeG, its aim is to expand the use of offshore wind energy, increase the installed capacity of offshore wind energy installations and coordinate the expansion of such installations and the offshore grid connections.

The WindSeeG applies to installations that are commissioned after January 1, 2021, Sec. 2 Subsec. 1 WindSeeG. However, pilot offshore wind energy installations and installations with an installed capacity of up to and including 750 kilowatts are exempted, Sec. 22 EEG 2017.

6.3.1 Auctioning Model

Sec. 22 Subsec. 5 Sentence 1 EEG 2017 regulates that the entitlement to the market premium or the feed-in tariff, shall apply to the electricity generated in offshore wind energy installations only as long and to the extent that an award issued by the Federal Network Agency (BNetzA) to the installation is effective.[19]

The auctions will determine both the entitled party and the value to be applied[20] for the electricity generated in these installations, Sec. 16 WindSeeG. In the end, the funding will be awarded to the applicant who applies for the lowest federal funding.[21] BNetzA is responsible for the performance of the auctioning process, Sec. 34 WindSeeG. BNetzA plans to achieve a an increase of 500 megawatt per year in 2021 and 2022, 700 megawatt per year between 2023 and 2025 and 840 megawatt per year between 2026 and 2030.[22]

---

15 Bauer/Kantenwein, EnWZ 2017, 3 (3).

16 Pflicht, EnWZ 2016, 550 (551); BT-Drs. 18/8860, 158.

17 Maximilian Uibeleisen, NVwZ 2017, 7 (7); BT-Drs. 18/9096, 379.

18 Thomas Schulz and Markus Appel, ER 2016, 231 (231).

19 The same provision can be found in Sec. 14 SubSec. 1 WindSeeG.

20 The value to be applied is the value, which is the basis for the calculation of the market premium and the feed-in tariff and is determined by the BNetzA in auctions, Sec. 3 Nr. 3 EEG 2017.

21 https://www.next-kraftwerke.de/energie-blog/eeg-2017-ausschreibungen.

22 https://www.bmwi.de/Redaktion/EN/FAQ/EEG-2017/fragen-und-antworten-zum-eeg-2017.html.

The system laid down in the WindSeeG differs depending on the commissioning date of the respective wind farm. For commissioning dates before January 1, 2021, the funding will still be determined statutorily by the EEG. For commissioning dates between January 1, 2021 and December 31, 2025 a transitional model will apply. Starting on January 1, 2026, the central auctioning model will be applicable.

6.3.2 Commissioning Date before January 1, 2021

A statutory exemption from the contingency of the claim on the issuing of a funding award applies to installations that were given an unconditional grid connection confirmation before January 1, 2017 pursuant to Sec. 118 Subsec. 12 EnWG or connection capacities pursuant to Sec. 17d Subsec. 3 EnWG as applicable on December 31, 2016 and were commissioned before January 1, 2021.[23] For these installations the funding will still be statutorily determined by the EEG.[24] The same exception applies to pilot offshore wind energy installations according to the WindSeeG, Sec. 14 Subsec. 2 WindSeeG.

6.3.3 Commissioning Date between January 1, 2021 and December 31, 2025: Transitional Model

The transitional model provides for two auctions in which only existing projects can participate, Sec. 26 Subsec. 1 WindSeeG. The limitation to existing projects accommodates the extensive lead time of offshore wind farms.[25] According to Sec. 26 Subsec. 2 WindSeeG existing projects in this sense are projects for which a plan has either been approved or an approval has been issued according to the SeeAnlV or a hearing was held according to the Administrative Procedure Act. Additionally, these projects have to be located in Clusters 1 to 8 in the North Sea or Clusters 1 to 3 in the Baltic Sea pursuant to the respective offshore federal sectoral plan. For projects that do not fulfill these criteria, all ongoing planning approval procedures or approval procedures to construct and operate offshore wind energy installations end on January 1, 2017, Sec. 46 Subsec. 3 WindSeeG.

The bid deadlines are set for April 1, 2017 and April 1, 2018 and concern offshore wind energy farms that will be commissioned starting in 2021. The auctioning volumes will be 1,550 megawatt per bid deadline, Sec. 27 Subsec. 1 WindSeeG. However, on the bid deadline of April 1, 2018, the volume of the auction shall increase to the

23 Pflicht, EnWZ 2016, 550 (551); BT-Drs. 18/8860, 159.
24 Uibeleisen, NVwZ 2017, 7 (8).
25 BT Drs. 18/8860, 157.

extent to which funding awards pursuant to Sec. 34 were issued for less than 1,550 megawatts on the April 2017 bid deadline, Sec. 27 Subsec. 2 WindSeeG. As a matter of fact, the volume of the auction in 2018 was set at 1,610 megawatt, because 60 megawatt had not been subject to an auction in 2017.[26]

The auctions have to be announced at least six calendar months before the bid deadline, Sec. 19 WindSeeG. The announcement has to include the maximum value for bids, Sec. 19 No. 8 WindSeeG. In the transitional model, the maximum value is set at €c 10/kWh, Sec. 33 WindSeeG.

Bid Requirements and Security

In the transitional model, the bidder has to own an existing project in the aforementioned sense. He has to deposit a security with the BNetzA. This shall ensure that the winning bidder will in fact realize the project.[27] The security can be deposited through a guarantee issued by a bank or a credit insurer or by paying the sum to a custodial account of the BNetzA, Sec. 31 Subsec. 3 EEG 2017. The amount of the security equals the bid quantity multiplied by 100 euros per kilowatt of capacity to be installed, Sec. 32 WindSeeG. The security will be returned without delay if the bid is unsuccessful.

Bidders can provide alternatives to the bid. They can either provide a minimum bid quantity or an alternative bid, where the latter means a bid for a smaller quantity at a higher price. As a consequence, the bidder can provide for a situation in which the auctioning volume or the grid connection capacity are not sufficient to issue a funding award in the full amount.[28]

Award Procedure

Sec. 34 outlines the award procedure for the auctions: BNetzA sorts the bids in ascending order by value, beginning with the bid with the lowest bid value. If there are two bids with the same value, the bids have to be sorted in ascending order beginning with the lowest minimum bid quantity; if both these criteria are identical, the order has to be decided by lot as far as it affects the issuance of funding awards. Starting with the lowest bid, all eligible bids are issued an award in the full amount of their bids until the auctioning volume is exhausted, Sec. 32 Subsec. 1 Sentence 4 EEG 2017.

Right of Subrogation

An important feature of the transitional model is the right of subrogation. It is conferred upon owners of an existing project who were not awarded funding in the

26 BNetzA, press release, "BNetzA startet zweite Ausschreibung für Offshore-Windenergieanlagen," January 30, 2018, p. 1.

27 Bahmer/Loers, GewArch 2017, 406 (407).

28 Uibeleisen, NVwZ 2017, 7 (10).

transitional auctions, Sec. 39 Subsec. 1 WindSeeG. If the right is exercised, the funding award issued to the bidder for the site, which has been subject to a preliminary investigation and is affected by the right of subrogation, is fully transferred to the owner of the existing project. The subrogation right is supposed to mitigate the negative effects of the duty to hand over data collected during the development of the project in the auctions pursuant to Division 2. It is limited to a funding award issued pursuant to Sec. 23 until December 31, 2030. The right of subrogation is the only compensation that the WindSeeG offers for owners of existing projects that do not receive a funding award. It can be transferred to another natural or legal person until the day of the announcement of the auction for the site, which has been subject to a preliminary investigation, Sec. 39 Subsec. 3 WindSeeG.

Results of the 2017 and 2018 Auctions

The 2017 auctioning process illustrated how considerably the confidence in the innovation and profitability of offshore wind energy farms had grown: three out of four projects that received a funding award auctioned for €c 0.00/kWh,[29] meaning that they are planning on building and operating the offshore wind farm without any state funding.[30] The average award value for the auction was €c 0.44/kWh (compared to between 15.4 and €c 19.4/kWh under the EEG 2014). Even the BNetzA was surprised by this outcome.[31] The 2018 auction had a more moderate outcome with an average award value of €c 4.66/kWh. Again, there were bids for €c 0.00/kWh. In comparison to the first auction in 2017, the situation slightly differed because only existing projects that were not awarded funding in the 2017 auction were allowed to participate. Furthermore, at least 500 megawatt had to be awarded to existing projects in the Baltic Sea. Although the development towards lower state funding is beneficial for energy consumers, experiences in other countries have shown that the profitable operation of wind energy plants with such low state funding can be problematic.[32]

6.3.4 Commissioning Date starting January 1, 2026 – Central Model

For offshore wind energy installations that are commissioned starting January 1, 2026, the so-called central model pursuant to Sec. 4 et seq. WindSeeG will apply. In this model, auctions will be held annually on September 1, starting in 2021. While

29 https://www.erneuerbareenergien.de/drei-projekte-ohne-eeg-foerderung-erhalten-zuschlag/150/434/101902/.

30 https://www.welt.de/wirtschaft/article164749952/Doch-noch-Hoffnung-auf-eine-kluge-Energiewende.html.

31 BNetzA, press release, "BNetzA erteilt Zuschläge in der ersten Ausschreibung für Offshore-Windparks," April 13, 2017, p. 1.

32 Bahmer/Loers, GewArch 2017, 406 (408).

the sites auctioned off in the transitional model have been developed by the bidders themselves, the central model applies to sites that have been evaluated by the authorities. Accordingly, the capacities that are auctioned off are tied to the sites. The volume of the auctions will be between 700 and 900 megawatts each year, Sec. 17 WindSeeG. The auctions will be announced by BNetzA . In the announcement, BNetzA will also publish the maximum value. This value equals the lowest successful bid in the 2018 auction, Sec. 22 WindSeeG. Due to the high number of €c 0.00/kWh-bids, BNetzA might make use of its right to determine a deviating maximum value by means of a determination, Sec. 22 Subsec. 2 WindSeeG.

Bid Requirements and Security

Sec. 20 et seq. WindSeeG lay down additional requirements for bids compared to Sec. 30 EEG 2017. The bidder has to agree that documents may be used by the Federal Maritime and Hydrographic Agency (BSH) and BNetzA if the planning approval decision becomes invalid. This is supposed to facilitate a project on the same site by a new operator. Furthermore, the bid quantity must equal the share of the volume of the auction for the site for which the bid is submitted. Alternative bids are not foreseen.

As in the transitional model, the bidder has to provide a security for the bid, Sec. 31 WindSeeG. The amount of the security equals the bid quantity multiplied by 200 euros per kilowatt of capacity to be installed, Sec. 21 WindSeeG. If the bidder is not issued a funding award, it will be returned without delay.

Award Procedure and Legal Consequences

BNetzA will issue the funding award for each site to the bid with the lowest bid value, Sec. 23 Subsec. 1 WindSeeG. The award entitles the winning bidder to implement a planning approval procedure, and gives him a claim to the market premium pursuant to Sec. 19 EEG 2017 to the extent of the bid quantity awarded funding on the site, to connection to the offshore connection line to the same extent and to the assigned grid connection capacity on the offshore connection line, Sec. 24 WindSeeG.

6.3.5 General Provisions for All Auctions

The aforementioned specific requirements are complemented by some general provisions.

Once a funding award has been issued, there is no right to return the award, Section 62 Subsec. 1 WindSeeG, except in the cases of Sec. 62 Subsec. 2. If the installed capacity falls behind by more than 5%, a penalty must be paid. Additionally, the funding award has to be revoked to the amount of the lack of capacity, Sec. 60 Subsec. 3 WindSeeG. However, the bidder awarded funding may not return the funding award unless one of the exceptions put forward in Sec. 62 Subsec. 3 WindSeeG applies.

Funding awards may not be transferred to installations on other sites, Sec. 63 Subsec. 1 WindSeeG. However, funding awards may be transferred to other persons. With the transfer of the award, all legal consequences of the funding awards are transferred as well.

Introduction of provisions for power-to-x offshore

The most recent law concerning the sector is the so called Collective Energy Act (EnergiesammelG) of November 2018. Amongst other amendments in the renewables sector, the law establishes the regulatory framework for offshore energy production concepts operated without direct or indirect connection[33] to the general supply network, notably for installations using offshore "power-to-x" technologies. The provisions concern the law of sectoral planning.[34] No financial support will be granted for these installations. In addition, a new regime will be set up to determine the location of such projects.

Moreover, the explanatory memorandum to the Collective Energy Act mentions that the government will request the competent federal office to present additional expansion scenarios concerning offshore wind farms for 15 to 20 Gigawatts until 2030.[35]

33 Cf. Sec. 1 SubSec. 2 Sentence 1 No. 3, Sentence 2 SeeAnlG, Sec. 3 No. 8 WindSeeG.

34 Cf. Sec. 2 SubSec. 1, Sec. 5 SubSec. 3 Sentence 2 SeeAnlG; Sec. 4 Subsec. 3, Sec. 5 Subsec. 2a WindSeeG.

35 BT-Drs. 19/6155, 6.

7 Renewable Energy in Belgium: The Support Regime for Offshore Wind Farms

Dieter Veestraeten, Nino Vermeire

7.1 Introduction

With Belgium being n° 11 on the global list of coastal countries with the shortest coastline, i.e., 66.5 kilometers in total, one would not expect much from offshore wind production in Belgian waters. However, over the last ten years Belgium has obtained an important position as a European frontrunner in offshore wind energy and continues to do so.

30 kilometers off the Belgian coast, a zone of approx. 260 km^2 in the North Sea is reserved on the Thornton Bank for offshore wind generation. Electricity production started in early 2009 with the C-Power wind turbine project, followed by Belwind, Northwind, Nobelwind and Rentel. In 2018 alone, these projects produced 3,408 GWh of electricity. This corresponds to the annual electricity consumption of approx. one million Belgian households.[1]

By 2020, three more wind turbine projects will be realized: Norther, Northwester 2[2] and Seamade.[3] Once all the projects have been completed, the total capacity will amount to 2262 MW,[4] and the offshore wind energy will cover half of the households' electricity consumption (or no less than 10% of the country's total electricity needs).[5]

This fast evolution to renewable energy is made possible by a comprehensive legal framework, which includes an elaborate support mechanism that makes it appealing for developers and operators to invest in such vast projects. This support mechanism will be briefly explained in this contribution.

1 https://www.belgianoffshoreplatform.be/nl/news/2019-wordt-recordjaar-voor-windenergie-in-de-belgische-noordzee/.

2 Northwester 2 will have the world's largest wind turbines. There will be 23 wind turbines of the new model V164 from the manufacturer Mitsubishi Vestas. With a capacity of 9.5 MW, they are the most powerful ever. By way of comparison, the turbines of the Belwind, which is about ten years older, had a capacity of merely 2.5 MW: https://www.tijd.be/ondernemen/milieu-energie/belgie-krijgt-s-werelds-grootste-windturbines-op-zee/10056212.html.

3 Seamade has two separate zones: Seastar and Mermaid.

4 Or as many as 2 nuclear power plants.

5 https://www.tijd.be/ondernemen/milieu-energie/belgie-krijgt-s-werelds-grootste-windturbines-op-zee/10056212.html.

Dieter Veestraeten, Nino Vermeire, Lawyers at ASTREA Law, Antwerp, Belgium

https://doi.org/10.1515/9783110607888-023

7.2 The European Backdrop: Policy and Targets

Promoting renewable energy production is an important political and economic item, mostly driven by the European Union. According to the European "2020 climate & energy package," EU member states have taken on binding national targets for raising the share of *renewables* in their energy consumption by the year 2020, under the Renewable Energy Directive.[6] These targets vary, to reflect countries' different starting points for renewable energy production and ability to further increase it. The overall effect will enable the EU as a whole to reach its 20% target by 2020 and at least 27% by 2030.[7]

Belgium's target for its share of energy from renewable sources in gross final consumption of energy by 2020 is 13%.[8] It goes without saying that offshore energy production is important for Belgium to achieve its EU 20-20-20 targets.

7.3 The Belgian Legal Framework: Competence and Regulation

In order to meet these targets, the Renewable Energy Directive provides that EU member states may establish a support mechanism.

Belgium is a federal state, which results in a distribution of competences between the different governments. Although the regional authorities[9] are in principle competent for "*new energy sources, except those linked to nuclear energy*,"[10] their competences do not extend beyond the borders of their territory, thus not to the Belgian territorial sea, the Belgian continental shelf and/or the Belgian exclusive economic zone in the North Sea.[11]

Therefore, the regulation with regard to offshore (wind) energy is a competence of the federal government.

The Federal Electricity Act of April 29, 1999 and the Royal Decree of July 16, 2002 on the establishment of mechanisms to promote electricity from renewable energy constitute the general regulatory framework in this respect. The Belgian support mechanism that the federal government has worked out for offshore energy

---

6 Directive 2009/28/EC of the European Parliament and of the Council of April 23, 2009 on the promotion of the use of energy from renewable sources and amending and subsequently repealing Directives 2001/77/EC and 2003/30/EC, *Pb. L.* 140, June 5, 2009, 16–62.

7 Brussels, October 24, 2014 (OR.en), EUCO 169/14, CO EUR 13, CONCL 5, https://www.consilium.europa.eu/uedocs/cms_data/docs/pressdata/en/ec/145397.pdf.

8 Art. 3 *juncto* Annex I, A of said Directive.

9 Flanders, Wallonia and Brussels Capital.

10 Art. 6, § 1, VII, f) of the Special Law of August 8, 1980 on institutional reform.

11 See in this respect T. Chellingsworth and D. Vanherck, "Er beweegt wat op de zee. Over de hervorming van het ondersteuningsmechanisme voor offshore windenergie," *MER* (2015), 187.

production installations is based on two pillars: green certificates and subsidies for the submarine cable connection.

7.3.1 Green Certificates

On the basis of article 7 of the Federal Electricity Act, the Belgian government can adopt market organization measures, including the establishment of a system (managed by the Commission for Electricity and Gas Regulation or *CREG*)[12] for the granting of green certificates for renewable electricity from offshore wind farms, as well as imposing an obligation on the transmission system operator (TSO) (which is Elia on federal level), to purchase these green certificates at a certain minimum price.[13]

The Royal Decree of July 16, 2002 contains more detailed rules on the procedure and conditions for the granting of green energy certificates and the value of such green certificates.

Granting Procedure and Conditions

An application for the granting of green certificates needs to be addressed to the CREG. Within a month, the CREG verifies whether the applicant meets the conditions for the granting of green certificates and notifies the applicant of its decision.

The applicant must be a producer of renewable energy who holds a domain concession,[14] as well as a certificate of guarantee of origin.[15]

The TSO (Elia) records and controls the production of green electricity on the basis of measurable data made available by the producer.

One green certificate shall be issued for a quantity of green electricity corresponding to one MWh.[16]

However, since there isn't a real market for green certificates, the TSO (Elia) is obliged[17] to provide minimum support by ways of an obligation to purchase the green certificates it gets offered at a fixed price.

Elia, obviously, does not bear these costs by itself: Elia (partially) passes these costs on to the end consumers of electricity through the transmission grid tariffs in order to finance all or part of the net burden that arises from the mechanism of

12 The Belgian energy market monitoring organisation.

13 And to sell them, in order to ensure the sale on the market, at a minimum price.

14 A permit, granted by the federal government, that is valid as authorisation to use the public domain of the government for an economic (private) activity.

15 The certificate of guarantee of origin proves that the produced electricity is green electricity and that the produced quantity is calculated according to the applicable measurement standards.

16 Article 7 of the Royal Decree of July 16, 2002.

17 As part of its public service obligations.

offshore green certificates. Each year, the Federal Minister of Energy takes a decision by means of a Ministerial Decree to establish the surcharge to be applied by the TSO for the purpose of compensation of the net real cost resulting from the obligation to the purchase and sale green certificates. The surcharge during the year 2019 is fixed at € 7.2875/MWh.[18]

From Fixed to Variable Support

The production of renewable energy from offshore wind turbines was originally subject to a fixed, guaranteed support mechanism. This mechanism consisted of granting a fixed amount of € 107.00/MWh for the production of electricity generated from the first 216 MW of installed capacity and € 90.00/MWh for the production of electricity generated from any additional capacity installed.

Since the Royal Decree of April 4, 2014,[19] this support mechanism has been changed because it was considered too expensive and to be granting a too large return on investment.

The old support mechanism only still applies to the wind turbine projects who had their domain concession and *financial close*[20] before May 1, 2014. Thus, the green certificates earned on these wind turbine projects can still be sold at these fixed minimum prices to the TSO (Elia).

Offshore wind turbines projects with financial close after May 1, 2014, are entitled to flexible support based on the Levelised Cost of Energy (LCOE) in order to ensure a stable return on investment without granting excessive support.

LCOE

The idea of flexible support is that the price of green certificates is linked to the electricity price.

The principle of the Royal Decree of April 4, 2014 was that the minimum price for one green certificate is calculated by deducting the electricity reference price and a correction factor off the LCOE:

$$\text{Minimum price} = \text{the LCOE} - [\text{electricity reference price} - \text{correction factor}].$$

18 Ministerial Decree of December 6, 2018 to establish the surcharge to be applied by the TSO for the purpose of compensation of the net real cost resulting from the obligation to the purchase and sale green certificates, *Official Gazette*, December 11, 2018.

19 *Official Gazette*, June 4, 2014.

20 The Electricity Act defines "financial close" as the time at which the most important contracts concerning the investment costs, financing costs, operating costs and income from the sale of electricity and green certificates of a wind turbine project are officially concluded.

The Royal Decree of July 16, 2002 defines the LCOE as: the total annual cost, calculated over a period of 20 years and standardized on the basis of a generally applicable technological reference framework, required to produce 1 MWh of electricity and also includes the cost of investment, exploitation, maintenance and financing. The latter costs are calculated taking into account an update of the financial flows and a return on investment of 12% each year.

For wind turbine projects who had their financial close between May 2, 2014 and April 30, 2016, the LCOE was fixed at € 138,00/MWh.

The electricity reference price is determined each year by the CREG on the basis of the nominations of the ICE Endex Belgian Power Baseload Futures. The correction factor was set at 10% of this electricity reference price.

For wind turbine projects who had or will have financial close from May 1, 2016 onward, the Royal Decree of February 9, 2017[21] changed the calculation of the minimum price for one green certificate again to further reduce the risk of over subsidization.

The minimum price is now calculated by the following formula:

$$\begin{aligned}\text{Minimum price} = {} & \text{the LCOE} - [(\text{electricity reference price} \times (1 - \text{correction factor}) \\ & + \text{the value of a guarantee of origin}) \times (1 - \text{grid loss factor})].\end{aligned}$$

For every wind turbine project whose financial close did not happen before March 4, 2017, the Federal Minister of Energy determined the LCOE individually. In the cases of Rentel and Norther, the LCOE is fixed by Royal Decree at € 129.80/MWh for the Rentel project and at € 124.00/MWh for the Norther project.

On the moment of writing this contribution, a new amendment has been approved but did not yet enter info force.

The legislator confirmed the aforementioned formula for future wind turbine projects who had or will have financial close after June 30, 2018, but moved away from the system of individual determined LCOEs. The minimum price of green certificates for these wind turbine project is calculated with a fixed, but noticeable lower LCOE of € 79.00/MWh.[22] Additionally, the Government imposes a firm commitment on the operator of these wind turbine projects to produce at least a volume of electricity corresponding to 63,000.00 hours of production at full capacity. These operators must commit to it in order to get green certificates.[23]

---

21 *Official Gazette*, February 22, 2017.

22 Article 1, 2° of the Amending Royal Decree of August 17, 2018, *Official Gazette*, August 27, 2018. This amendment has not yet entered into force on the date of writing this contribution.

23 Article 2 of the Amending Royal Decree of August 17, 2018, *Official Gazette* August 27, 2018. This amendment has not yet entered into force on the date of writing this contribution.

The value of the minimum price can be reviewed if there are important changes to its constitutive elements.[24] The producer must provide relevant information to the CREG every three years for evaluation, who can change the value of the minimum price for the next period.

Extra Support

Article 7, § 2 of the Electricity Act also provides for an increase of € 12.00/MWh for wind turbine projects whose financial close took place between May 2, 2014 and December 31, 2016, which were allowed to not connect to the (offshore) installation for the transmission of electricity and therefore have their own submarine cable to land (see further under 4. CABLE SUBSIDY). However, this system has never been applied.

No Support

In 2017, the federal legislator developed a system to set the minimum price for the green certificates at zero if the market prices are negative. The Council of Ministers believes it does not make sense to subsidise electricity production when there is too much electricity on the grid.

The minimum price shall be set at € 0.00 per MWh if production takes place (i) at a time when the imbalance tariff[25] applicable to a positive imbalance is equal to or less than – € 20 per MWh, or (ii) if the *day ahead* price of a Nemo[26] is below € 0.00 per MWh for six consecutive hours, and this for the whole period considered.

The minimum price shall only apply during the first 288 quarter hours (or first 72 full hours), in the same calendar year, during which the imbalance tariff for a positive imbalance is equal to or lower than – € 20/MWh and from which the periods shall be deducted in which, in the same calendar year, the minimum price of € 0.00 per MWh is applied.[27]

This system only applies to wind turbine projects who had their financial close after May 1, 2016.

7.3.2 Support Period

The obligation to purchase green certificates, which applies to the TSO (Elia), starts with the commissioning of the production installation.

---

24 Not retroactively.

25 This imbalance tariff shows *in real time* (per 15 minutes) the situation of the Belgian control area.

26 The Royal Decree of July 16, 2002 defines Nemo as: a Belgian electricity market operator appointed in application of Regulation (EU) 2015/1222 of the European Commission of July 24, 2015 laying down guidelines on capacity allocation and congestion management.

27 Article 14, § 1*quinquies*/1 of the Royal Decree of July 16, 2002.

Due to changes in the support mechanism, the support period has been shortened two times.

The initial support period was twenty years. This support period only still applies for those wind turbine projects who had financial close before May 1, 2016.

Wind turbine projects who had their financial close between May 1, 2016 and June 30, 2018, will benefit from a support period of nineteen years.

If a wind turbine project had or will have its financial close after June 30, 2018, the support period is limited to seventeen years.[28]

Finally, it is the goal of the federal government to have all wind turbine projects up and running by January 1, 2021. In any case, the support period will end on December 31, 2037, which is seventeen years later.

7.3.3 Cable Subsidy

Offshore wind turbine projects are entitled to a "cable subsidy," intended to partially cover the costs a producer must make to connect its project to the onshore transmission grid.[29]

For the oldest projects – with a domain concession granted before July 1, 2007 – the TSO (Elia) was obliged to finance one third of the cost of the submarine cable to connect offshore wind turbine projects to the onshore electricity transmission grid, with a cap of EUR 25 million for a project of 216 MW or more. The cap is proportionally reduced, if the capacity of the offshore wind turbine project is less than 216 MW.

The obligation not only includes the purchase, delivery and installation of the submarine cable, but also extends to the connection installation, equipment and connections. The financing will be spread over five years, at a rate of one fifth per year from the beginning of the works. The TSO (Elia) will conclude a specific contract with the offshore wind operator to set out the further terms and conditions of the subsidy.

If after five years from the start of the construction works, the projected 216 MW capacity has not been attained, an amount proportional to EUR 25 million can be reclaimed by the Federal Minister of Energy, after advice from the regulator CREG.

Offshore wind turbine projects, of which the domain concession was granted after July 1, 2007 and financial close happened between May 2, 2014 and December 31, 2016, can only benefit from a contribution for the submarine cable by the TSO (Elia),

28 Article 1, 3° of the Amending Royal Decree of August 17, 2018, *Official Gazette*, August 27, 2018. This amendment has not yet entered into force on the date of writing this contribution.

29 Art. 7, § 2 Electricity Act.

when they are granted an explicit exception by Royal Decree allowing them to connect directly to the onshore grid. In that case, TSO Elia must also finance one third of the cost of the submarine cable to connect offshore wind turbine projects to the onshore electricity transmission grid, with a cap of EUR 25 million.

The more recent projects – which have had or will have financial close after May 1, 2016 – benefit from a *differentiated* cable subsidy. The subsidy (by means of a raised minimum price per green certificate) is determined per project individually by the regulator CREG and is intended to cover the total (real) costs of the financing of the submarine cable to land.

Offshore wind turbine projects, of which the domain concession was granted after July 1, 2007 and financial close happened or will happen after December 31, 2016, must in principle connect to the Modular Offshore Grid (MOG, see further under 5). These projects will merely receive a subsidy (by means of a raised minimum price per green certificate) that covers the (real) cost of the submarine cable between the project and the MOG.

7.3.4 MOG: Modular Offshore Grid

Historically, offshore wind turbine projects are connected individually to the onshore transmission grid via a radial connection. However, the Federal Electricity Act was amended in 2017 in order to create a legal framework for a Modular Offshore Grid or MOG.

It must be noted that the Belgian Modular Offshore Grid (BOG) is currently under construction (see Figure 7.1). TSO Elia is responsible for the construction[30] and exploitation of the BOG, which is basically an offshore electricity hub (or a so called "socket at sea"), and it is scheduled to be operational as of September 2019.

The BOG will bundle 2.000,00 tons of electricity, coming from four different projects,[31] and will bring it to shore in a more efficient way, rather than to have all wind turbine projects have their own separate submarine cable.

Offshore grid development also has an international aspect to it: by building interconnectors between the transmission grids of different EU member states, the internal energy market can be further completed.

After the realization of the BOG, the offshore wind projects in the North Sea will look as follows:

30 The construction was outsourced to Heerema and costed EUR 400 million.

31 Rentel, Seamaide (Seastar and Mermaid) and Northwester 2.

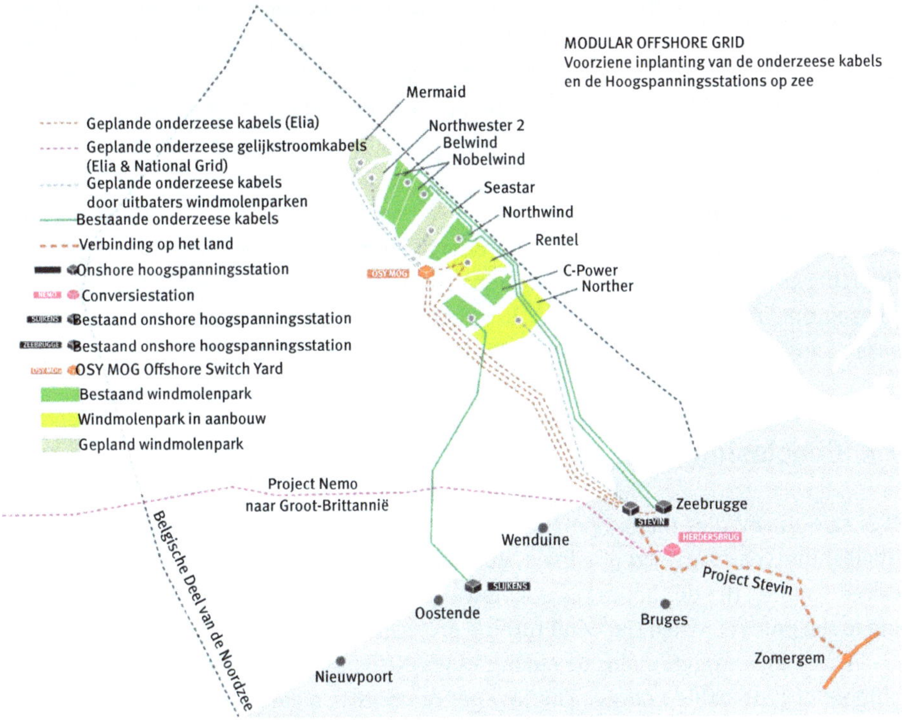

Figure 7.1: Modular offshore grid (Source: Elia).

7.3.5 State Aid?

European member states can more or less design their own support mechanism, but also need to consider the European state aid rules.

In the past, the European Commission has decided that the notified (original) support mechanism did not constitute *state aid* within the meaning of Article 87(1) of the EC Treaty.[32] The EC based its position on the lack of transfer of state resources.[33] This changed when the amended support mechanism and the individual support to Rentel and Norther were notified to the European Commission. In its decision of December 8, 2016, the EC decided that the Belgian support mechanism does qualify as *state aid*, but that it is compatible with the validity conditions applicable to such measures.[34]

32 Decision of the European Commission C(2002)2904-fin of August 2, 2002, n° 14/2002.

33 Taking into account the Preussen Elektra case law of the Court of Justice of the European Union (ECJ 13 March 2001, C-379/98).

34 Decision of the European Commission C(2016)8426-fin of December 8, 2016, 14, § 67.

The Belgian government has declared that it intends to better integrate offshore wind energy within the energy market, and that it will therefore align the support mechanism with the "Guidelines on State aid for environmental protection and energy 2014–2020."[35] From January 1, 2017 onward, the aid is to be granted in a competitive bidding process on the basis of clear, transparent and non-discriminatory criteria.[36]

The Guidelines also mention that it is to be expected that in the period between 2020 and 2030 established renewable energy sources will become grid-competitive, implying that subsidies and exemptions from balancing responsibilities should be phased out in a degressive way.[37] It remains currently unclear to what extent offshore wind energy will be considered grid-competitive by 2020.[38]

7.4 Conclusion

It is safe to say that the support mechanism has undergone some major changes in the last five years. Instead of a fixed, guaranteed minimum price according to the produced volume, the minimum price is now determined to the LCOE, that varies according to the date on which the wind turbine projects had or have their financial close.

These amendments aim to reconcile investors and project operators with consumers of renewable energy. The level of support is steadily going down. A lower LCOE is the result of technological progress. Competitive bids organized abroad (e.g., in the Netherlands) have highlighted this downward trend. It remains to be seen if and how this debate will further evolve in Belgium. The evolution of electricity prices is likely to play an important role in the future.

The support mechanism for the submarine cable subsidy was also subject to a number of fundamental amendments. To date, the starting point has been a direct connection of each individual wind turbine project to the onshore grid, with substantial compensation from TSO Elia.

The next generation of wind turbine projects will be connected offshore to the MOG. International interconnectivity of energy is a technical and legal challenge, of which we haven't seen the last yet.

---

35 Policy Declaration of December 9, 2014, *Parliamentary Documents* Chamber of Representatives 2014–15, no. 20/54, pp. 4–5.

36 § 126 Guidelines.

37 § 108 Guidelines.

38 C. Degreef and W. Geldhof, "Offshore energy and the Belgian legal framework: All at sea?," *TRNI* 2015, n°1, 66.

Onshore Wind Energy

1 Technology of Onshore Wind Energy Converters: Current Status and Developments

Alois Schaffarczyk

1.1 Introduction

Wind Energy has been very successful over the last 30 years [1]. By the end of 2017 (2018) 539 GW (not far from 600 GW) were seen with a constant increase of at least 60 GW per annum [6]. That is why wind energy in on the right track to reach for the next goal to exceed hydropower, world largest renewable energy source today. As is well known, technology has developed in equal speed if measured in size growth and production cost decrease for one MWh electricity.

Today, the largest turbine – probably erected in 2019 – will be GE's Haliade-X offshore turbine with 220-meter rotor diameter and "powered by 107-meter-long" LM107 blades. Nevertheless, although this huge growth, onshore wind energy still has a far larger market share.

For a general introduction to wind turbine technology, with emphasis to offshore, see section 1 of Uwe Ritschel.

We here give a short account of what changes have occurred since 2014, when [1] appeared. An interesting and very readable view from an economic and political point of view of the last 10 years gives [10]. We will not discuss price issues like production costs here. We feel that prices of electricity from renewable sources (photovoltaics and onshore wind) have proven to be in the same range like those from fossil sources (lignite or hard coal, oil and natural gas). The reader has to bear in mind that production costs are around (or even less then) 50 €/MWh but private consumers may pay up to 300 €/MWh – at least in Germany.

1.2 Current Onshore Wind Turbine Technology

The trend for offshore wind turbines is a further all-component growth or simply: up-scaling [2, 3]. Onshore turbines follow a different line. Power-density (measured in W/m^2) of wind in most regions is much smaller than the solar constant of about 1 kW/m^2, as a result onshore turbine diameter only grows to reach for comparable small values around 200 W/m^2 and these turbines rightly are called "low-wind-turbines." At the time of writing, Nordex' N149/4.0–4.5 MW, according to Wind power monthly [8] "turbine of the year 2018," reaches for 230 W/m^2. It has to be added that a team of students in 2016–2017 [7] reached for even lower values of 200 W/m^2 with their design *Optimus 150*.

https://doi.org/10.1515/9783110607888-024

In a comprehensive and detailed study up to 2015 Serrano-González and Lacal-Arántegui [11] emphasized the regional and wind-class dependent lines of evolution.

In February 2019, Vestas, the leading Danish wind turbine manufacturer announced an even larger on-shore wind turbine than seen before the V162-5.6MW. Figure 1.1 shows a nearly doubling of rotor diameter each 10 years, starting with D = 10 m in 1979.

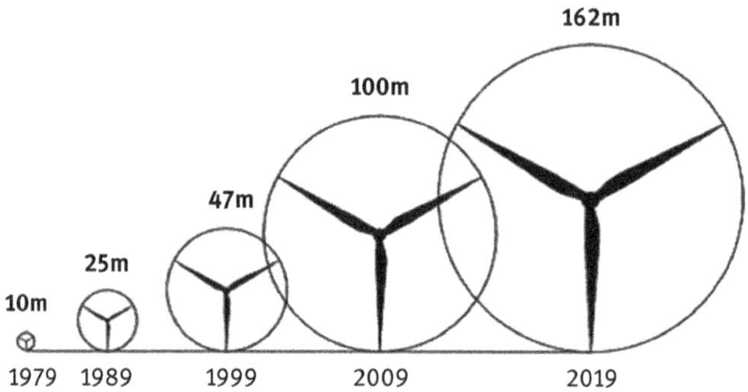

Figure 1.1: Upscaling of onshore wind turbines from manufacturer VESTAS (1979 to 2019) in steps of ten years (own representation).

If asked how to define a state-of-the-art wind turbine one may follow recent textbooks like [1, 5] or with slightly more emphasis on future developments Peter Jamieson's "Innovation in wind turbine design" [9] or trends seen in big fairs like Hamburg Wind Energy.

Variable (rotational) speed and active control is now common while the drive train – with or without gearboxes – has a larger variability. It may be surprising that the driving argument for not using gearboxes was a presumed better durability of inverters, but more detailed investigations [4] showed that electrical subassemblies as well might suffer from premature failure as it was much too often seen from gearboxes.

1.2.1 Towers and Wind Turbine Blades

Towers

If one divides a wind turbine into parts, tower and rotor blades have the largest share to the amount of materials used. Costs may be regarded as approximately proportional to mass. For the tower three concepts are available:

- Steel,
- Concrete,
- Hybrid (first part concrete and upper part steel).

Towers up to 160 m height have been manufactured so far; half of it using concrete. Very recently a trend to fully steel construction seems to be visible.

The total supporting structure comprises the tower and the foundation. The foundation depends on the ground conditions and the total mass of the plant. A special feature compared to other "structures" are much higher dynamic loads during lifetime from 20 to 35 years.

The tower carries the nacelle, which still accommodates all essential parts of the turbine at hub height, and brings the rotor to as favorable a "wind height" as possible.

The following tower types are used: lattice towers as for high-voltage lines, steel towers in tapered construction and concrete towers, e.g., used by Enercon.

At first glance, lattice towers seem to be your first choice due to their lower material consumption, but the long-term maintenance costs seem to partially cancel out the advantages. Surprisingly, tubular steel towers [1] can be manufactured using the same material as lattice towers if they are designed in the so-called "soft" finish. The tower is called "soft," when the first natural frequency of the plant (= tower + nacelle) is below the p-fold speed of the rotor (p = number of blades). When the system is brought up to the rated speed range, a potential resonance point must therefore be passed through. Fortunately, this does not seem to jeopardize the stability of the systems in these versions.

The concrete construction method is preferred above all by Enercon. If one again uses their E-126 as an example, then material masses of approx. 3000 tons each for foundation and tower with a tower head mass to be carried of approx. 605 tons are mentioned here. A comparable steel tube construction with the same nominal power (Repower 5M, now Senvion 6.XM) has a mass of approx. 750 tons, with a tower head mass of approx. 410 tons.

Rotor Blades

Wind turbine blades serve to "harvest" the energy from the wind to feed the electrical generator with torque. In 2019 we have seen blade lengths up to 107 m with an estimated mass around 60 tons. Figure 1.2 gives an overview how blade mass scales with length (roughly the same as rotor radius, shown there).

The notorious price-driving "square-cube-law" (visible as solid tend lines and confirmed by more details studies from UAS Kiel [12] and Sandia, USA [13]) obviously can be circumvented by modern technology (as indicated by points LM, SSP and others).

The Upwind project (ending 2011 [14]) so far resulted in a detailed design with largest length (123 m) and mass (161 tons). Figure 1.2 indicates that is was designed along the guideline of traditional scaling.

For an approximate estimation the price per kg is now well below 10 €/kg. Material costs roughly are half of it the rest being labor costs which differ significantly around the world.

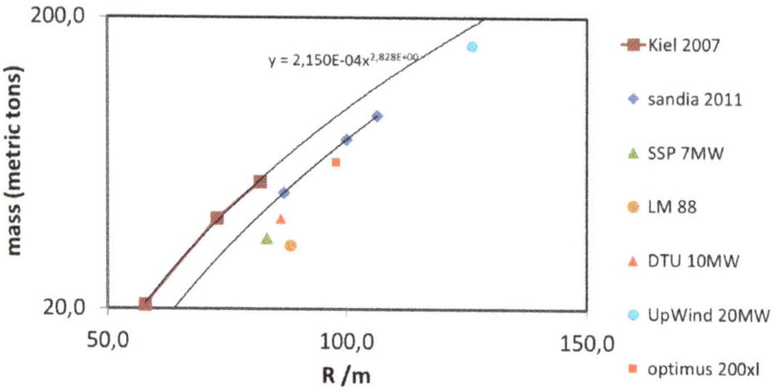

Figure 1.2: Upscaling of blade masses of wind turbine for very large turbines.[1]

1.2.2 Drive Train

Mechanical components include the rotor, the nacelle with the drive train and the electric generator.

The state of the art can be seen in the three-blade system with horizontal rotation axis.

Although systems with a vertical axis of rotation were developed as Darrieus rotors in the improved version up to the 90s with prototypes with a rated output of up to 4 MW (Éole-C, Canada), they were not able to compete with the rapidly improved horizontal systems. Only recently does interest seem to be reviving, both for very large offshore turbines (20 MW, deep wind [8]) and for small wind turbines (rotor area < 200 m^2). In [9], turbines with vertical axis of rotation up to 200 kW (rotor area 26 × 24 m^2) are discussed.

The number of blades in the majority of the turbines is now three, only a few are still selling or developing two-bladed turbines. The reasons for this can simply be summarized: Due to the vertical wind speed profile, turbines with two or fewer blades show strong imbalances, which lead to increased fatigue loads. In turbines with more than three blades, the blade depth must be reduced proportionally to the number of blades for aerodynamics reasons [1], so the blades become even slimmer and thus even more susceptible to vibration.

An essential distinguishing feature, which affects both mechanical and electrotechnical components, is the use of a gearbox.

If a wind turbine blade is designed as close as possible to the Betz limit value using the usual blade element method [2], the speed of the rotor in the optimum

1 Lines indicate estimates from early investigations. Dots are from more detailed investigations or even manufactured blades. Both scales are logarithmic to account for easy recognition of poten-tial lows m ~ Rn. Straight lines indicate exponentials not much lesser than 3 (trivial scaling or "square-cube-law").

performance is directly proportional to the instantaneous wind speed. The consequence of this is that the speeds in the now usual 2–3 MW class are around 10 to 15 rpm. However, electric generators must generate alternating voltage at 50 (Europe) or 60 (USA) Hz. This frequency must be strictly observed and forces the generator to a speed of 3000/n rpm. Here n is the number of pole pairs in the generator. If a generator is to be coupled directly to the mechanical rotor, i.e., without gears, a high number of poles is required. This concept is pursued, for example, by Enercon. On the other hand, generators with a low number of poles as so-called asynchronous machines are widely used and technically very sophisticated, so that the use of a gearbox is unavoidable when using them. Until recently, systems with gears accounted for more than 80% of the systems sold. Gearboxes usually manage this speed change of 1:100 in several, usually three stages. Gears of this type are masterpieces of mechanical engineering. In a 5 MW version, such a gearbox from Winergy AG has a mass of over 60 tons. However, it must be admitted that the gearboxes must be held responsible for a large proportion of premature damage. The wide range of dynamic loads is usually used to explain this. Systematic and more comprehensive studies can be found, for example, in [10].

Multibrid technology occupies a position between systems with and without transmission. Although a gearbox is used here, the transmission ratio is only about 1:10, so that only one or two gear stages are necessary. As a result, the medium-speed speeds of the generator are only 50 to 150 rpm. The companies Adwen Wind (Germany, France), WinWindD (Finland) and the even more compact SCD (= Super Compact Drive) design by aerodyn, Rendsburg are examples of this. In the meantime, there are prototypes up to 6 MW.

As for the case of blades also for the drive a trend to more compact systems can be seen. Now, aerodyn's SCD Technology ® (= super-compact-drive) is the most pronounced. For example, the 3 MW "basic" system is announced with 114 tons tower head mass only.

A more systematic overview [1], section 6 shows that drive trains further may be distinguish between the number and type of support: one point, two point or torque support.

1.2.3 Electrical Parts

The electrical components include the generator and the necessary devices for controlling and operating the system. As mentioned above, the choice of concept (gearbox yes or no?) strongly influences the characteristics of the electric generator. While in the initial phase of the modern use of wind energy (from approx. 1985) there was hardly any influence on the selection of components, this has changed very much in favor of wind energy, especially after the collapse of some parts of typical mechanical engineering companies in the course of the 2008 financial crisis. Many of them are prepared to develop and manufacture components specially designed to meet the needs of wind energy. This can now be seen particularly impressively in the electrical engineering sector with the introduction of so-called synchronous generators with electrical excitation by permanent magnets [11].

Electro-mechanical energy conversion was introduced at the end of the 19th century, primarily for the long-range distribution of electricity for lighting lighthouses and buildings. The physical principle, Faraday's law of induction, allows electrical voltages to be induced by time-varying magnetic fields, which in turn mobilize electrical charges. The product of electric voltage and electric current (= flowing electric charge per time unit) represents a power in its original mechanical definition.

The following distinguishing features can be specified in the technical realizations [11, section 3.2]. Based on the so-called three-phase current technology, in which electrical power is transmitted by three partial currents of the same frequency, each phase-shifted by 120 degrees, the mechanically driven rotor and the electrical rotating field can rotate with the same frequency (= synchronous) or slightly different frequency (asynchronous).

As a further distinguishing feature, synchronous generators have excitation by permanent magnets or electromagnets fed from the outside.

Only recently has the introduction of relatively inexpensive permanent magnets using rare earth metals (Cobalt, Samarium, Iron-Neodymium-Boron) made it possible to advance the development of such permanently excited synchronous machines.

However, this is only possible if so-called frequency converters are used [11], while at the same time the speed variability of the mechanical rotor is required. These electrical components make it possible to change the frequency and voltage of the generator over a wide range. In view of stricter grid connection rules, this design also offers the possibility of increasing the quality of the electrical power generated.

Asynchronous machines are designed as so-called squirrel-cage rotors or slip-ring rotors. If the squirrel cage rotor has the advantage of a simple mechanical design, it is easier to intervene in the exciter circuit with the slip ring rotor in order to cause or react to speed changes.

In a particularly concise version of the DFIG (= Double-fed induction generator), this is probably still the most frequently used generator concept at present.

1.3 Outlook into the Future

Wind Turbine Technology will undergo many changes in the near future. At the moment a trend to merging of manufactures as predicted in [10] is seen. This for sure offers an opportunity for larger line-production and even lower prices but also a danger to less competition is given.

From the point of innovation Peter Jamison's [9] gives a good outlook based on recent non-standard technology.

1.4 Summary and Conclusions

Wind energy has undergone a stormy development in the last twenty years and still grows fast, which is manifested both in the development of this technology and in its dissemination.

Since 2011, the installed capacity has more than doubled from 238 GW to about 600 GW. Although the offshore installed share grew faster (from 4 GW in 2011 to 19 GW in 2017), it only accounts for a share of just under 4%.

The driving forces behind this development are easily identified: on the one hand, fossil fuel resources are limited with growing demand, especially from Asia, and on the other hand, CO_2-free- and low-risk, i.e., non-nuclear-technologies must be increasingly used.

This trend is supported by the constantly falling prices for electricity produced by wind power.

References

[1] Alois Schaffarczyk, ed., *Understanding Wind Power Technology: Theory, Deployment and Optimisation* (Chichester: John Wiley & Sons, 2014).

[2] Alois Schaffarczyk, *Introduction to Wind Turbine Aerodynamics* (Berlin and Heidelberg: Springer-Verlag, 2014).

[3] Georgios Sieros, P. Chaviaropoulos, John D. Sørensen, B. H. Bulder, and Peter Jamieson, "Upscaling wind turbines: theoretical and practical aspects and their impact on the cost of energy," *Wind Energy* 15 (2012): 3–17.

[4] F. Spinato, P. J Tavner, G. J. W. van Bussel, E. Koutoulakos, "Reliability of wind turbine subassemblies," *IET Renewable Power Generation* 3 (2009): 387–401.

[5] Trevor M. Letcher, ed., *Wind Energy Engineering* (London: Elsevier/Academic Press, 2017).

[6] Global Wind Energy Council, *Global Wind Statistics* (2018).

[7] Team Optimus 150/200, OPTIMUS150/200, Flensburg (2016, 2017), unpublished.

[8] https://www.windpowermonthly.com/article/1521599/turbines-year-2018-onshore-turbines-3mw-plus.

[9] Peter Jamieson, *Innovation in Wind Turbine Design*, 2nd ed. (Hoboken, NJ: Wiley, 2018).

[10] Ben Backwell, *Wind Power – The struggle for control of a new global industry*, 2nd ed. (London: Routledge, 2018).

[11] Javier Serrano-González and Roberto Lacal-Arántegui, "Technological evolution of onshore wind turbines – a market-based analysis," *Wind Energy* 19 (2016): 2171–87.

[12] Benjamin Hillmer et al., "Aerodynamic and Structural Design of MultiMW Wind Turbine Blades beyond 5MW." *Journal of Physics: Conference Series* 75 (2007).

[13] D. Todd Griffith and Thomas D. Ashwill, "The Sandia 100-meter All-glass Baseline Wind Turbine Blade: SNL100-00," *Sandia Report*, SAND2011-3779 (June 2011).

[14] Johan Peeringa et al., Upwind 20MW Wind Turbine PreDesign Blade design and control, ECN-E–11-017 (2011).

2 Energy Yield Assessment

Lars Tallhaug

2.1 Introduction to Wind

In order to identify and document a profitable wind energy project, it is crucial to understand the complexities of the wind. The wind is one of several parameters in a wind energy project that cannot be controlled, it can only be understood. The purpose of this section is to give a short introduction to how the wind behaves by giving an overview of how it varies within and between wind farms in addition to how the wind varies over time on different time scales.

2.2 Variability

It is obvious to all that the wind speed varies over time. Wind varies most obviously from day to day, but there are also differences from year to year. This longer term variability presents one of the greater challenges when utilizing wind as a source for producing electricity. The variability must be understood and taken into account when calculating both the expected production and the degree of uncertainty in the production.

Figure 2.1 shows the variability of horizontal wind speed on different time scales presented by Van der Hoven in 1956 [1] and is called the Van der Hoven spectra. The area under the graph is proportional to the overall variability of the wind. It means that when there is a peak, a large part of the total variability in the wind speed comes from that frequency. The peak to the left is called the Synoptic peak and is the typical time it takes for a low pressure system to pass, which is usually around 4–5 days. The small peak to the right of the synoptic peak is the diurnal peak, showing the variability from day to night. The last peak to the right is the turbulent peak, showing the variation in the wind speed caused by the interaction between the air and the surface of the earth. Turbulence is variation in the wind speed with a time scale in the order of a few minutes and down to seconds and less.

The variability of the wind speed will be different in different areas. The height of the Synoptic peak, for example, will vary between regions. Some regions like the Mediterranean tend to have stable weather and thus a lower Synoptic peak. The Diurnal peak will be more visible on southern latitudes compared to northern latitudes. The diurnal pattern is driven by the variation of the heating from the sun during the 24 hours of the day, where the heating and cooling of the ground can introduce wind. A good example is the coast of California where a large number of wind turbines were installed in the 1980s which are largely driven by sea breeze. The sun heats up the land during daytime, which makes the air expand and rise,

https://doi.org/10.1515/9783110607888-025

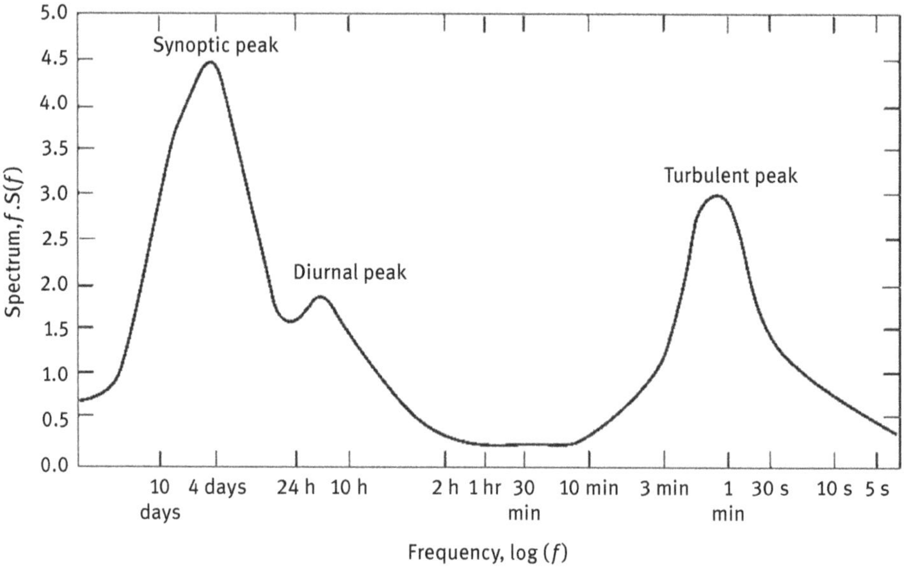

Figure 2.1: Spectrum of horizontal wind speed at Brookhaven Laboratory [1].

resulting in lower pressure close to ground. The air above the sea does not warm up as quickly. This causes a pressure difference between land and sea, and a resulting wind blowing from the sea towards land in the afternoon, a phenomenon called sea breeze. Due to the rotation of the earth, the sea breeze will rotate clockwise in the northern hemisphere. On a coastline with a north to south direction and the sea on the western side, the sea breeze will turn into a northern wind in the afternoon.

Since the turbulent peak is driven by the interaction between the wind and the surface of the earth on a rather short horizontal scale, the turbulence can vary between different wind turbine positions in a wind farm. Buildings, vegetation and topography can introduce turbulence, which can be perceived as vortexes in the wind. The size of the vortex is proportional to the length scale of the turbulence. There is also a clear connection between the time scale and the length scale of the turbulence, so that turbulence with a very short time scale will also have a very short length scale. Turbulence plays a very important role in the utilization of wind energy and is one of the most important parameters for the life time of wind turbines. If the length scale of the turbulence is similar to the size of the wind turbines, it can introduce vibrations and movement of the structure which reduces its life time.

The last and probably most important time scale for wind variability for wind energy purposes is the year to year variability. Knowing the yearly variability is important for the understanding of the uncertainty in the expected energy production in a normal year, and how much the production can vary from one year to another.

The most commonly used parameter to describe this variability is the standard deviation of the annual mean wind speed. The map in Figure 2.2 shows the standard deviation of annual mean wind speed for the southern part of Scandinavia. It can clearly be seen that the standard deviation varies a great deal within this area. The largest variability is around 7% of the annual mean wind speed, and the lowest around 3% [2]. A similar pattern can be found for instance in the Mediterranean, where the largest variability of around 8% is found on the coast close to Monaco and the lowest variability close to the southern end of Greece with a variability of less than 3% [3].

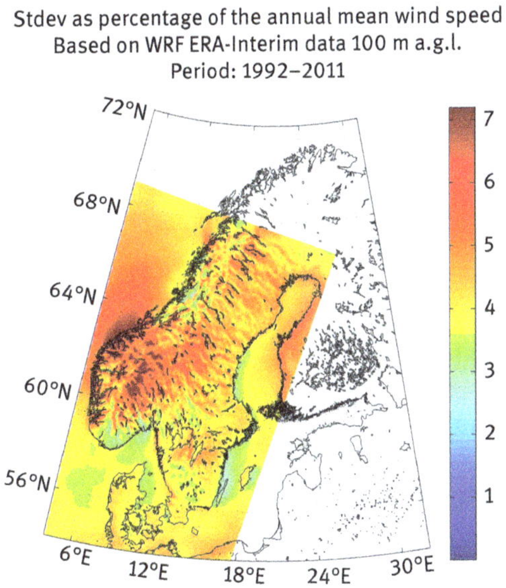

Figure 2.2: Standard deviation of annual mean wind speed [2].

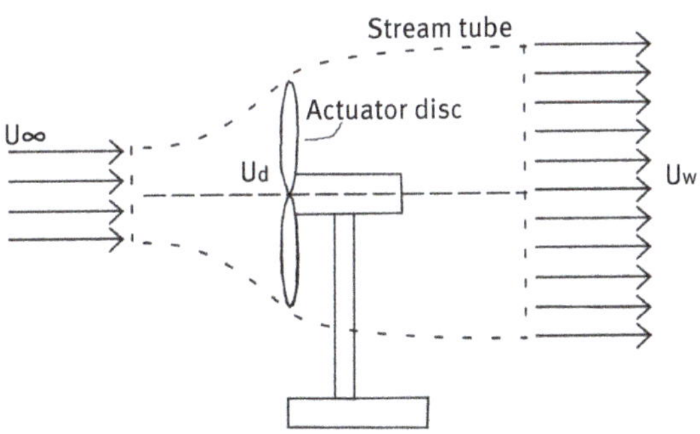

Figure 2.3: Illustration of the flow of air through a wind turbine (own representation).

For a wind farm at a site with 7% standard deviation of the wind speed, the worst year in a 25 year life time of a wind turbine can have a production that is 30% lower than in an average year.

The annual average wind speed is the single most important parameter for calculating the expected energy production for a wind farm. For the life time of the turbines, the turbulence intensity and the average wind speed are the two most important parameters. Before installing the wind turbines, the expected extreme wind speed events during the life time must also be determined. For wind farms, there are two main parameters that need to be established. The highest 10 min average wind speed and the highest 3 second gust (extreme wind speeds), both with a 50 year return period. A 50 year return period means that over a very long period of time, the given wind speeds are expected to be exceeded once every 50 years on average.

A good wind farm site is categorized by:
- High annual average wind speed.
- Low turbulence intensity.
- Low standard deviation of the annual mean wind speed.
- Low extreme wind speeds.

2.3 Geographical Variations of Wind

In this section we will focus on how the annual average wind speed varies from one location to another.

In basic terms, winds are created because the sun heats the surface of the earth differently due to both the rotation and the shape of the earth. Close to the equator, the heating is strong and close to the poles the heating is weak. The heating close to the equator makes the warm air rise and the cooling closer to the poles makes the air sink. In total the air circulates and winds occur. Due to the rotation of the earth, the Coriolis force affects the air and rotates the wind direction. The non-uniformity of the earth's surface with its pattern of land masses and oceans ensures that this global circulation pattern is disturbed. These variations interact in a highly complex and non-linear fashion to produce a chaotic result and an inevitable uncertainty in the daily weather forecast for any given location.

The annual average wind speed is highly affected by the topography and distance to the sea. Even the roughness of the surface influences the wind speed. High roughness areas like forests slow the wind speed down in the lower parts of the atmosphere, while open water areas like oceans and lakes with low roughness, have less of an influence on the wind speed. Coastal areas have a higher annual average wind speed compared to inland due to the sea breeze and the short distance to a large area with low roughness.

Topography plays a very important role when placing onshore wind turbines. In elevated locations, the wind speed is usually higher due to both the altitude itself and the fact that the ridges and mountains tend to accelerate the wind as it flows over the topography. The best wind farms are typically located on mountain ridges that are perpendicular to the prevailing wind.

There can be large differences in wind speed within a wind farm area. In complex terrain it is common that the least windy locations are having an annual mean wind speed less than 90% of the average wind speed in the wind farm, whereas in flat terrain the differences can be within a few percent. For complex sites, the energy production for the best turbine can be more than 50% higher than the turbine with the lowest production.

The average vertical gradient in the wind speed is mainly dependent on the topography and the roughness of the surface. On a ridge with low roughness, the change in wind speed with height is very small at hub height level. The profitability of installing high turbine towers at such a site is therefore very low. In flat, forested areas the wind speed increases rapidly with height at hub height level. An increase of hub height from 100 m to 130 m will typically give a 10% increase in annual mean wind speed.

2.4 Introduction to Energy Capture from a Wind Turbine

A wind turbine extracts energy from the wind by slowing down the wind speed. Because the air is not compressed when it flows towards a wind turbine, the upstream area of the air going through the wind turbine is smaller than the disc that is described by the tip of the blades. The pressure of the air in front of the disc increases towards the disc. The opposite happens downstream of the turbine as illustrated in Figure 2.3. Behind the disc, the pressure is lower than in the free stream. The affected area downstream of the disc with lower wind speed is larger than the disc area and increases downstream as the velocity picks up towards the free stream velocity.

The instantaneous power of a wind turbine is proportional to the pressure difference between the upstream and downstream side of the disc (ΔP) and the velocity of the wind through the disc (V_{disc})

$$Power \sim \Delta P \, V_{disc}$$

The equation above shows that a large difference in pressure leads to a large power output. Since a large pressure difference will lead to lower wind velocity through the disc, a balance between pressure difference and velocity through the disc is needed in order to maximize the power output. When taking the diameter of the rotor (d) and the density of the air (ρ) into account, the power output can be calculated. In addition to the physical properties, a power coefficient (C_p) is needed to present the real power output of a wind turbine. In the formula below, V_{disc} is replaced with V_{∞}. V_{∞} is the free stream velocity.

$$Power = C_P \frac{1}{2} \rho V_{\infty}^3 \frac{\pi}{4} d^2$$

The power coefficient (C_p) is a measure of the effectiveness of the wind turbine. In 1926, the German physicist Alfred Betz published an article [4] showing that the maximum value of C_p is 16/27≈59% (Betz limit) independent of turbine technology. The Betz limit is still valid. Modern wind turbines have a power coefficient close to 50%. The power coefficient is usually at its maximum around a wind speed similar to the annual mean wind speed. For lower and higher wind speeds, the power coefficient is lower.

All commercially used wind turbines must be delivered with a power curve showing the power output at different instantaneous wind speeds. It is common that the customer requires that the power curve is measured by an independent and accredited institution. An example of a power curve is shown in Figure 2.4.

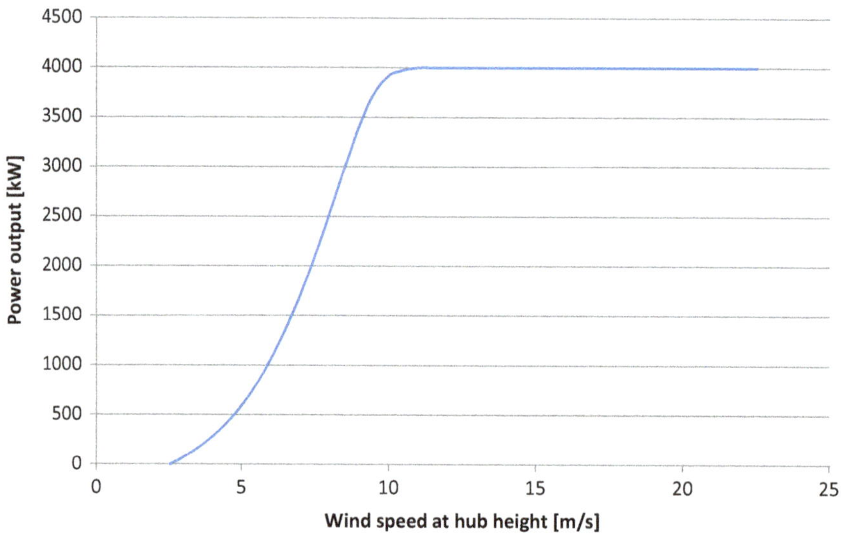

Figure 2.4: Example of power curve of a modern wind turbine (own representation).

The annual energy production of the wind turbine in Figure 2.4 can be calculated if the wind speed at all time steps during a 20 year period is known for the location of the turbine. For the efficiency of the calculations it is more common to present the wind speed as a distribution, as seen in Figure 2.5, rather than a time-series.

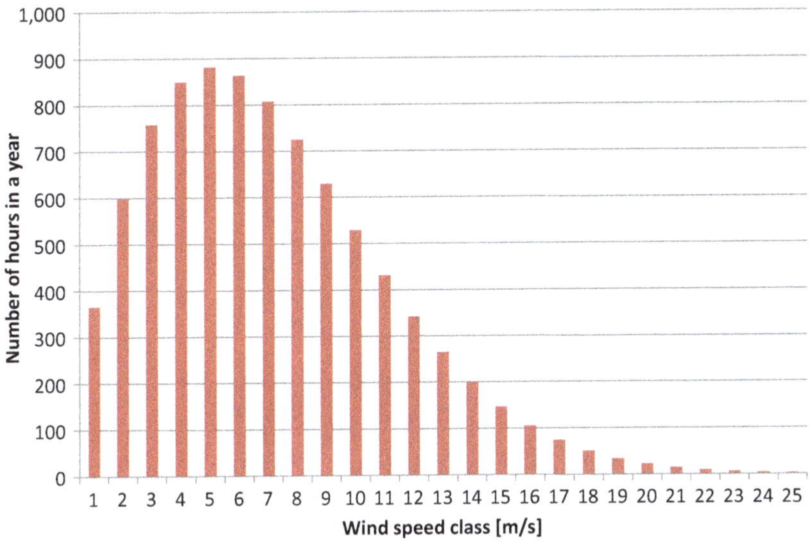

Figure 2.5: Example of distribution of wind speeds at a typical wind turbine site with an annual mean wind speed of 7 m/s (own representation).

Figure 2.6: A typical cup anemometer used in wind resource assessment (Picture: Kjeller Vindteknikk AS).

Figure 2.7: A met mast used in wind resource assessment in Sweden (Picture: Kjeller Vindteknikk AS).

2.5 Methods for Wind Resource Assessment

To be able to finance a wind farm, the expected production must be well documented using reputable methods. There are many recommendations and guidelines available, but there is no standard specifically for how to perform wind resource assessments. Examples of guidelines are the German TR 6 issued by FGW [5] and the Measnet guideline [7].

This section gives a short introduction to the available methods for wind resource assessment.

2.5.1 Anemometry

Anemometers are the most accurate instrument for the measurement of wind speed. Anemometers can either be cup or ultrasonic. In the wind industry, the cup anemometer is recommended. A cup anemometer for wind resource assessment should be of the highest standard according to for instance the classification system given in IEC 61400–12. Each individual anemometer needs to have a calibration certificate issued by a reputable institution, such as MEASNET.

Common practice is to place the upper anemometer in a met mast at least at 2/3 of the hub height. The method used when mounting the anemometer is very important; some of the largest issues in the history of wind resource assessment are related to how the mounting affects the anemometers. Speed up effects are most commonly found, which will introduce a positive bias in the estimates of the production for the entire wind farm. This positive bias may lead to a significant overestimation of possible energy production. The standard for Power Curve Measurements, IEC 61400-12-1 [6], describes how to install anemometers in a met mast well.

An anemometer is also the best instrument for measuring turbulence intensity, which is one of the most important parameters to understand when estimating the life time of the wind turbines. Turbulence intensity has great impact on wind farms, especially in complex terrain. .

A met mast will usually have more than one anemometer. Good practice is to have two anemometers at the top of the met mast, one main anemometer and one anemometer for the redundancy. In addition, the met mast should have anemometers at different height levels in order to calculate the wind shear.

For a small wind farm, one met mast is usually sufficient. If the wind farm is large and if the terrain is complex, more than one met mast is recommended. Guidelines for locating a met mast can for instance be found in the MEASNET procedure “Evaluation of Site specific wind conditions” [7]. The most important factor is that there are measurements representative of all the turbine positions in the wind farm. A wind farm project must therefore present documentation on the validity of the measurements for the different turbine positions. A rough rule of thumb from the MEASNET recommendations is that no turbine should be located more than 2 km from a met mast in complex terrain. Met masts should be placed to cover the terrain variation of the site, taking varying roughness, height and complexity into account. The diversity lowers the risk for introducing biases in the production estimate.

2.5.2 Remote Sensing

An alternative measurement technique to anemometry is remote sensing. There are two different remote sensing techniques available for wind resource assessment:

SODAR and LIDAR. SODAR (Sonic Detection and Ranging) uses sound pulses and LIDAR (Light Detection and Ranging) uses laser light.

Both LIDAR and SODAR measure the radial wind speed along the pulses. When located on the ground, the instrument will therefore have to measure at an angle to be able to decompose the radial wind into vertical and horizontal winds. Both techniques use more than one beam to be able to calculate both wind speed and wind direction. The instrument beams are usually angled 15–30 degrees from the vertical axis.

The advantage of remote sensing is that it is not necessary to install a mast, and that it is possible to measure the wind speed up to 200 m above ground. The installation will usually not need a building permit and the equipment is easy to install.

The disadvantage is lower accuracy in complex terrain; in flat terrain, the accuracy of remote sensing is very high. Since the remote sensing device uses beams traveling at an angle, the wind speed will be measured in a volume and not a single point. In complex terrain remote sensing can be used in combination with a met mast, either for vertical extrapolation to higher heights than the met mast or to increase the number of locations in the wind farm with observations. Measurements from met masts and remote sensing must be compared and the result from the remote sensing devise must be adjusted if the discrepancy is significant.

Figure 2.8 shows a LIDAR installed in Nordic climate. The LIDAR is installed on a 2 m high mast to avoid snow to interfere with the measurements. The LIDAR itself is also covered with a small tent to protect it from wind and snow.

2.5.3 Long-Term Correction

The expected production in an Energy Yield Assessment, EYA report shall be representative for a normal year. The period when the measurements have been performed will normally not be representative for a normal year. The wind speed might be too high or it might be too low.

To account for the variation of the wind speed from year to year, the measurements must be long-term corrected. To do that, an independent source for the wind speed for a long period of time must be available. There are usually two alternatives for such independent wind data, also known as reference data:
- Long-term measurements from a met station or an airport.
- Historical data from weather models.

The challenge of using long-term measurements is partly their validity to represent the temporal wind variation in the planned wind farm. A large distance, a different elevation or a different type of terrain might make long-term measurements less suitable than data from weather models. For long-term measurements to be useful it is necessary that it can be documented that the data is homogeneous throughout the period. It means that the measurement mast must not have been moved in the

Figure 2.8: A lidar installed in wind climate. (Picture: Kjeller Vindteknikk AS).

period, the instruments should have been of the same type, a proper maintenance should have taken place and the surroundings of the mast should have been as unchanged as possible throughout the measurement period.

There are a large number of weather model data sets available for long-term correction. As for the measurements, it is important that the data set is as homogeneous as possible throughout the period. The most commonly used global data sets for long-term correction are:

- MERRA. Modern Era Retrospective-analysis for Research and Applications (MERRA) is a reanalysis data set produced by the Global Modelling and Assimilation Office (GMOA). The data set is available at a resolution of 1/3 degree longitude and ½ degree latitude with one hour temporal resolution. MERRA data is available from 1979.

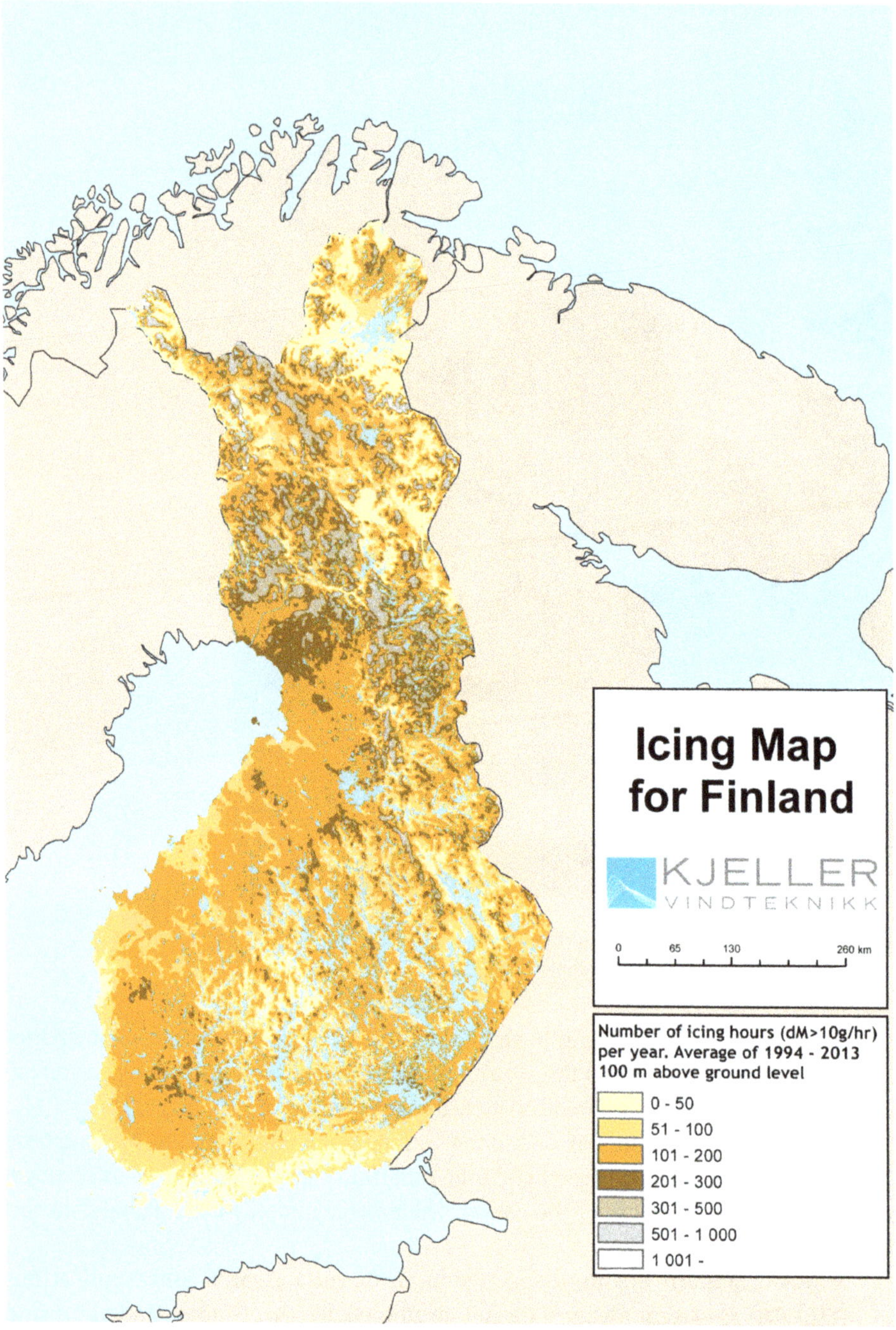

Figure 2.9: An example of icing map for Finland. The colors show number of hours annually with active icing.

- ERA5 is a new data set replacing the ERA-Interim data set from the European Centre for Medium-Range Weather Forecast (ECMWF). The data set is available at a resolution of 31 km globally with one hour temporal resolution. ERA5 data is available from 1950.

In addition, there is a wide range of down-scaled data sets available where one of the global data sets above have been processed in a meso-scale weather model to obtain a data-set with higher resolution than for instance MERRA or ERA5 for a region or a country. The resolution of the meso-scale data sets can be 1–5 km.

The length of reference data should preferably be in the order of 20 years. A shorter period will not cover all the relevant periodic variations that can be found. A longer period can cover data from periods not relevant for the future.

In practice it can be difficult to document which data set is most accurate for a specific project. A good practice is therefore to use more than one data set. The result from the different long-term corrections can then be averaged to the final result.

There are a number of techniques available for doing the long-term correction. A high quality EYA report should include a paragraph with the background for the choice of long-term correction method.

2.5.4 Wind Flow Models

It is not common to install wind measurement equipment at every turbine position. It will therefore be necessary to use some kind of model to extrapolate the wind from the measurement locations and out to the turbine positions. If the measurements are not available at hub height, extrapolation of the measurements vertically is also necessary. Three different models are commonly used in the wind industry:
- Linear models (WAsP)
- CFD models (WindSim, Meteodyn)
- Meso-scale meteorological models (WRF)

Many more are available, but the models in parentheses are the most commonly used in the wind industry. It is necessary for a commercial wind farm project that the model being used is verified by independent studies done in similar terrain.

The advantage of the linear models is the fast calculation and the ability to use a very high spatial resolution. The WAsP model in particular is tested and verified in a large number of projects all around the world, giving access to a large number of verification test. Its disadvantage is the accuracy in steep terrain, where flow separation might occur. Since the WAsP model has a small degree of freedom in the parameter settings, the risk for human errors is limited.

The advantage of the CFD models is the accuracy in complex and steep terrain. For the most commonly used CFD models, there are also a large number of verification tests available, making them well suited to commercial projects. A disadvantage of a CFD model is the complexity in use. There are usually a number of parameters and options in how to run the models, increasing the risk of human error. The latest versions of the model and modern computers make it possible to run CFD models with relatively high resolution.

In contradiction to the linear models and the CFD models, the meso-scale model simulates the wind in the time domain, which means that it calculates the wind speed every hour or more often. A meso-scale model calculates the entire set of weather parameters such as temperature, humidity, precipitation, clouds and more. The lowest practical resolution of a meso-scale model is approximately 0.3 km x 0.3 km and complex terrain features can therefore not be accounted for. However, if the features of the terrain can be accounted for, the accuracy of a meso-scale model can be very high. The simulation time also limits the use of meso-scale models in commercial wind farms.

2.5.5 Energy Losses in a Wind Farm

An assessment of the energy production of a wind farm must include all probable and possible losses in the production. Some of the production losses can relatively easily be quantified and other losses are more difficult to quantify. If the losses are difficult to quantify in a scientific manner, the best estimate of the loss must be included instead of omitting it.

Wake Losses

Since a wind turbine extracts energy from the wind, the wind speed behind a wind turbine will be reduced compared to the free, undisturbed wind. The production of the turbines downstream will therefore be reduced compared to the turbine facing the undisturbed wind. The reduction in the production is called the wake loss.

Especially in large wind farms, the wake losses usually account for the largest production loss; for offshore wind farms, more than 20% of the energy production can be lost due to the wake effect. For an onshore wind farm, the wake losses are lower due to the increased background turbulence intensity generated from the interaction between the wind and the ground surface. In addition, onshore wind farms are usually smaller than offshore wind farms. The wake loss increases with the size of the wind farm and decreases with the distance between turbines. The industry standard wake models are typically developed for wind farms with an internal spacing between the turbines that is larger than 3 times the rotor diameter of the turbines.

Wake losses should be calculated for the planned wind farm as well as losses caused by nearby wind farms. Plans for future wind farms in the vicinity should also be considered.

New wind farms increase in size and have relatively short turbine spacing. The experience with very large onshore wind farms is limited, and extra care must therefore be taken when calculating the wake losses.

In addition to the wake effects, there is new research indicating that a wind farm also introduces blockage effects [11]. The turbines in the first row in a wind farm will experience lower wind speed than they would if the first row was the only row of turbines in the wind farm. These kinds of blockage effects are normally not included in commercial Energy Yield Assessments. The findings underline the need for more research on wake effects and other turbine interaction effects.

Unavailability

Modern wind turbines are very reliable, and are available to operate for the greater part of the year. Nevertheless, there will be periods where the turbines need service and there will be periods where the turbine will stop and repair is necessary. The turbine manufacturer usually gives a warranty for the availability, either as a percentage of time or a percentage of the annual energy production. A warranty will usually refer to codes in the SCADA system defining the type of fault. A thorough Energy Yield Assessment should go into detail on the availability warranty and identify whether there are possible turbine errors that are not covered by the warranty.

If a proposal for the availability warranty is not available, both the contractual and the non-contractual availability must be assumed. Assuming that the wind farm area is not too remote and that the wind farm has a well-organized service team, a total operational unavailability of 3% can be used.

Electrical Losses

An Energy Yield Assessment shall normally calculate the energy that can be sold on the high voltage side of the substation in the wind farm. The power curve received from the turbine manufacturer is normally valid for the low voltage side of the transformer in each wind turbine. There will be electrical losses in the transformer in the wind turbine, in the cables from the wind turbines to the sub-station and in the substation itself. If a design of the electrical system is available, a study of the electrical losses should be carried out in the Energy Yield Assessment. Often the Energy Yield Assessment is needed before the investment is decided upon, and a detailed design of the electrical system is then normally not available, and a total loss figure of 2% can then be used [8].

Icing Losses

Wind farms operating in cold climates can be affected by icing. Depending on the climate where the turbine is installed, the icing can be caused by a variety of factors, for example freezing rain, wet snow or in-cloud icing.

When the layer of ice becomes thicker, the power output of the turbine will be affected. Some turbine models will continue to operate with ice on the blades, but some models will shut down.

When ice is formed on the blades, there is always a risk for ice to be thrown away from the turbine and be a danger to people, animals or objects in the vicinity. It may become necessary to stop the turbine in periods with icing, therefore it is important to take requirements at the site into account when calculating the energy yield.

Some manufacturers offer turbines with heated blades. The heating can either be hot air circulating inside the blades or electrical resistors close to the surface of the blades. The blade heating systems can be divided into de-icing or anti-icing systems. The de-icing systems will stop the turbine when a certain ice thickness is accumulated and heat the blades when the turbine is standing still. The anti-icing systems intend to keep the turbine running through an icing event.

If icing is very severe, the production loss can reach 20%, but a production loss of about 2–8% is more common at developed sites. A blade heating system will not be able to recover all the lost energy, but a recovery of 40–70% can be expected. If the production loss is 2% or lower it is usually not profitable to install a blade heating system, but if the expected production loss is 8% or higher it will probably be profitable. For production losses between 2% and 8% a detailed assessment of the profitability of installing blade heating system is recommended.

Some countries have icing maps available in the public domain and these are a good place to start to get an overview of the icing climate. If the icing loss is expected to be significant, a more detailed study is recommended. An example of a publicly available map is shown in Figure 2.9.

Curtailment

A wind turbine is curtailed when the power output is actively reduced to mitigate a problem on the site. Typical issues to be aware of is: turbine loads due to turbulence, wind shear or other wind parameters, noise on nearby houses, the risk for ice throw, shadow flicker on nearby houses or issues related to birds or bats. When doing the Energy Yield Assessment it is necessary to have a full overview over possible issues that can lead to a need for curtailment.

In practice the curtailment can take the form of reduced rotational speed, full stop in periods or reduced cut-out wind speed.

It is recommended that an independent party calculates the yield consequences of the curtailments.

Wind Turbine Performance

Wind turbine manufacturers document the performance of their wind turbine with a power curve. The power curve is derived at a test site or another well suited site with open and flat terrain using a met mast with an anemometer at hub height and equipment to measure the produced power. The anemometer is supposed to represent the wind speed that would have been present at the turbine location at hub height. The most common standard to follow when measuring power curves is IEC 61400-12-1. One of the requirements in the standard is that the anemometer should be located 2–4 times the rotor diameter in front of the wind turbine, with 2.5 diameters as the recommended distance. There are indications that 2.5 diameters are too close to avoid blockage effects [9]. A blockage of the measured wind will result in a too optimistic power curve.

At a real wind turbine site the wind conditions will in many cases not be as ideal as the test site. Turbulence intensity, wind shear, wind veer, and wind direction variability are factors that might cause performance losses.

Preferably, a wind farm in complex terrain should have a site specific power curve. Wind turbine manufacturers usually don't provide that. To account for the lack of site specific power curves, an Energy Yield Assessment should include a section with an evaluation of the wind turbine performance in the actual terrain.

Other Losses

In addition to the losses above, the Energy Yield Assessment must also include a discussion on whether any other losses may occur. Examples of other losses are:

- Wake losses from neighboring wind farms, already built or possible in the future.
- Low or high temperature down time.
- Cut-out hysteresis at high wind speed.
- Blade and turbine degradation.

2.5.6 Uncertainties

One of the most important parts of an Energy Yield Assessment (EYA) is the calculation of the uncertainty. It is a mandatory part of an EYA report and transforms the result to a form that can be used in the decision process.

There are some key terms commonly used in EYA reports. Below is a list of some of the most important ones, followed by a simplified explanation:

- Uncertainty (σ): This expression usually refers to one standard deviation in a normal distribution. If the uncertainty is normal distributed there is 68% probability that the real production is within +/- one standard deviation from the estimated value.
- P50: The expected production. It means that the probability for the real value to be higher than the given value is equal to the probability for the real value to be lower than the given value. Both probabilities are 50%.
- P90: The production that will be exceeded with 90% probability.

The uncertainty and confidence levels is illustrated in figure x. A project with large uncertainty will have a wide distribution and a project with low uncertainty will have a high and narrow distribution.

The total uncertainty in the net production should be calculated by dividing the task into sub-tasks. The uncertainty in each sub-task should be calculated using known variables or by drawing on experience in the wind energy community.

Each individual sub-task, or sub-uncertainty must be added together. Before adding the sub-uncertainties, it must be determined whether the uncertainties are dependent or independent. Most of the uncertainties in an EYA are independent. The total uncertainty can then be calculated using the formula below:

$$\sigma_{total} = \sqrt{\sigma_1^2 + \sigma_2^2 + \ \dots \ \sigma_n^2}$$

Where:
σ_{total} = Total uncertainty
σ_1 = The uncertainty of part 1
σ_2 = The uncertainty of part 2
σ_n = The uncertainty of part n

One very important result of the equation above is that the large uncertainties contributes more to the total uncertainty than the ratio between the large and the small uncertainty. When considering measures to reduce the total uncertainty it is therefore important to put most effort into the large uncertainties.

Uncertainty Elements

In each wind farm, there are a number of factors that must be considered. In addition, it is important that each project is investigated individually to ensure that all uncertainties are taken into account.

In the list below, the typical uncertainties in an on-shore wind project is given:

- **Wind measurements:** Uncertainty considering wind measurements is normally one of the more important ones. If the measurements originate from one or more masts, the following issues should be considered: documentation, instrument calibration, sensor characteristics, mounting effects and icing on the sensors.
- **Long-term correction:** Uncertainty regarding long-term corrections is normally significant. The following issues should be considered: consistency of the reference data, method for long-term correction, length of the reference period and inter-annual variability in the wind speed.
- **Horizontal extrapolation:** For large wind farms in complex terrain this is typically one of the greatest uncertainties. Multiple measurement locations will reduce the uncertainty and also make it possible to quantify this uncertainty.

- **Vertical extrapolation:** If the wind measurements are collected at hub height, the uncertainty in the vertical extrapolation will be zero. In many cases however the met masts are lower than the turbine hub height. It is recommended to have a measurement height exceeding 2/3 of the hub height in order not to introduce a very large uncertainty due to the vertical extrapolation.
- **Turbine performance:** It is normally difficult to quantify the production loss due to reduced turbine performance in complex terrain compared to the performance at the test site. A significant uncertainty in the turbine performance loss must therefore be accounted for. It means that if the turbine performance loss is estimated to 2%, the uncertainty can typically be 1%. Or half the performance loss.
- **Wake losses:** In modern wind farms, the turbines are in some cases put very closely together compared to earlier wind farms. Short interspacing, in addition to the large sizes of modern wind farms, results in high wake losses. The lack of experience with large and dense wind farms must be taken into consideration in the uncertainty assessment.
- **Icing losses:** For sites with heavy icing this uncertainty can be very important. Both the meteorological conditions at the site and the performance of the specific turbine during icing conditions must be taken into account when assessing this uncertainty.
- **Other losses:** Any other factors that may influence the uncertainty must also be considered and included in the uncertainty assessment, such as electrical losses, unavailability, curtailment and more.

2.5.7 Post-Construction Energy Yield Assessment

With an increasing number of wind farms in operation, there is a growing need for post construction Energy Yield Assessments. Post construction assessments can be needed if ownership of the wind farm changes, or for refinancing purposes. It is also important for all wind farm owners to have realistic figures for the expected energy production in a normal year, both for communication purposes and for budget purposes.

The main challenge in doing assessments of the production after the wind farm has been in operation for a period of time is the variability of the wind. One standard deviation from the annual production for some wind farms can be more than 10% of the normal production. It means that the production will be lower than 90% of the normal production once every 6 years and lower than 80% of the normal production every 40 years. If the wind farm is affected by icing, the variability can be even larger. It is therefore necessary to correct the observed production with the wind conditions in the period compared to normal to be able to present an updated normal year production based on the real production data.

In addition to the variability in the wind and icing, it can be variations in the losses that have to be accounted for.

There are a number of methods available for yearlong-term correcting observed production in a wind farm. The methods can principally be divided in two different classes:

- Index-based methods.
- Methods based on historical power curves.

Index-Based Methods

Index-based methods can be very simplified or more detailed. A recommended version is to use monthly observed production and monthly wind indexes for the site. A wind index for the region can be used but local variation of the wind index can introduce uncertainties.

The monthly production and the wind index should be plotted as shown in Figure 2.11. The long-term corrected production is the production at 100% wind index. The wind index must be defined as the average wind speed in the month divided by the long-term corrected annual wind speed.

The most convenient Index method is to use all the production data as the observed production without any filtering. All losses are then assumed to be identical in a normal year as it was in the period of observation. Months with very exceptional incidents or very low data availability can be removed.

Methods Based on Historical Power Curves

The methods based on historical power curves are far more detailed than the index methods. The basis of the historical power curve methods is to create a link between a long wind speed time series and the power of each wind turbine. When creating the link, it is important to only use data when the turbine is in full operation. The long time series of the wind speed is normally based on a weather model. The link between the power output and the time series of wind speed is a power curve where the wake effect from the other turbines in the wind farm is included.

Instead of creating the link directly between the power of the wind turbine and the long time series, the anemometer on the nacelle can be used in between. In that case it is important to use a period where no changes to the anemometer or the calibration of the anemometer have been done.

When the link to the long time series of wind is established, a long time-series of production can be produced. The average of the long time-series of production is the long term average of gross production minus the wake losses. The expected losses in a normal year must then be deducted. An advantage of the methods of historical power curves is that all the losses can be long-term corrected and analysed separate from the production when the turbines are in full operation.

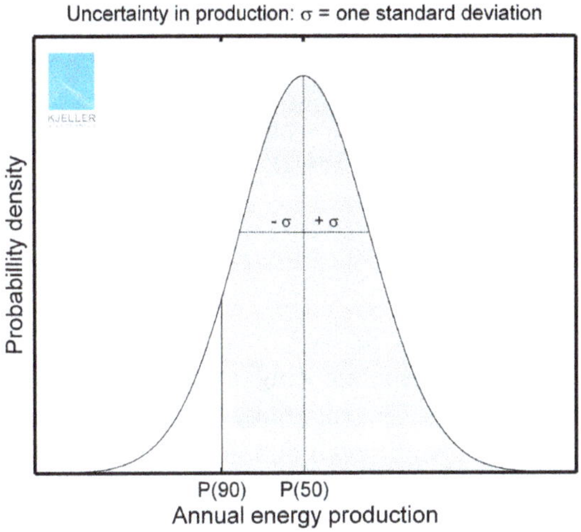

Figure 2.10: Calculating the long-term corrected energy production using the Index Method (own representation).

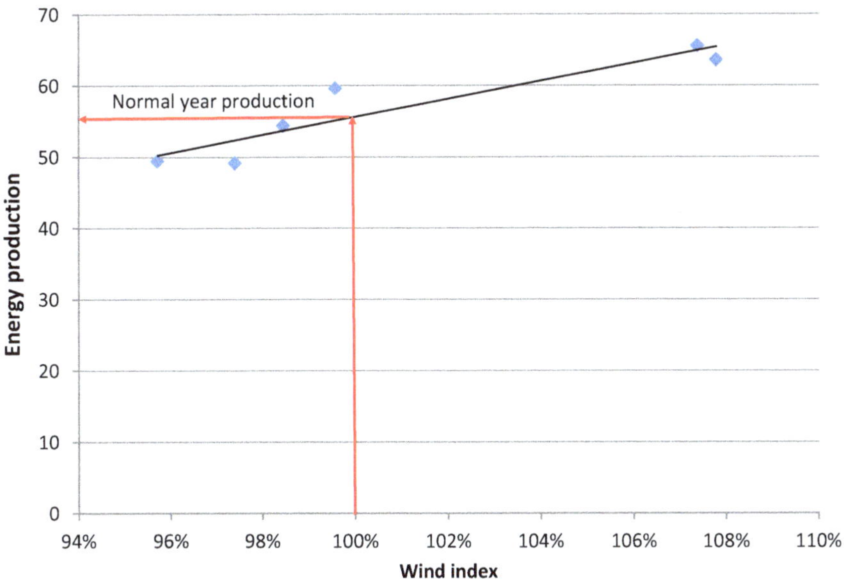

Figure 2.11: Illustration of uncertainty (σ) and the confidence levels P50 and P90 (own representation).

A summary of the methods based on historical power curves:

1. Filter operational data; identify episodes when WTGs are not running in full performance.
2. Assess the experienced losses during these non-full performance episodes.

3. Long-term correct the actual full-performance production with long-term reference dataset. Gross value to be reduced since operational data already includes wake losses.
4. Apply experienced operational losses (2.) to the gross value (3.), long-term correct the experienced losses if necessary. The result is P50.
5. Assess the uncertainty.

Selection of Method and Uncertainties

The most suitable method for long-term correcting observed production will be site dependent. If the site is highly affected by atmospheric icing, one of the methods using historical power curve will the best option. The variability of the icing is usually not correlated with the variability of the wind speed and in such cases it will therefore be important to long-term correct the ice free production and the icing separately. In cases where significant start-up challenges have been experienced, an historical power curve method will usually be the best option. If the icing is not significant and the wind farm has been in steady operation in the observation period, the wind index method may be the better option.

Compared to the pre-construction energy assessment, many of the uncertainties can be omitted:

- Horizontal extrapolation of the wind speed.
- Vertical extrapolation of the wind speed.
- Wake losses.
- Electrical losses.
- Power performance.

The most important uncertainties in a post-construction energy assessment are then:

- Long-term correction.
- Energy losses (availability, icing).

Using two years of operational data, the uncertainty in the normal production can be expected to be around half the value of the corresponding uncertainty in the pre-construction assessment.

References

[1] Van der Hoven, Isaac. "Power Spectrum of Horizontal Wind Speed in the Frequency Range From 0.0007 to 900 Cycles per Hour." *Journal of Meteorolgy* 14 (1956?), pp. 160–64.

[2] Lileo, Sónia et al. "Long-term correction of wind measurements – state-of-the-art, guidelines and future work." ELFORSK report 13:18. Stockholm, 2013.

[3] https://rmets.onlinelibrary.wiley.com/doi/full/10.1002/joc.5182

[4] Betz, Albert. *Introduction to the Theory of Flow Machines*. Translated by D.G. Randall. Oxford, 1966. [Originally published as: *Windenergie und ihre Ausnutzung durch Windmühlen*, 1926.]
[5] Fördergesellschaft Windenergie und andere Erneuerbare Energien (ed.). *Technical Guidelines for Wind Turbines*. Part 6: *Determination of Wind Potential and Energy Yield*, Revision 9. Dated April 23, 2015. Berlin, 2015.
[6] IEC 61400-12
[7] MEASNET, ed. *Evaluation of Site-Specific Wind Conditions*, Version 2. April 2016.
[8] Spengemann P., and V. Borget. "Review and analysis of wind farm operational data Validation of the predicted energy yield of wind farms based on real energy production data." DEWI GmbH, 2008.
[9] Tindal, Andrew, Clint Johnson, Marc LeBlanc, Keir Harman, Elisabeth Rareshide, and Anne Marie Graves. "Site-Specific Adjustments to Wind Turbine Power Curves." Poster presentation at the AWEA WINDPOWER Conference, Houston, Garrad Hassan America, Inc., 2008.
[10] Bleeg, James, et al. "Wind Farm Blockage and the Consequences of Neglecting Its Impact on Energy Production." *Energies* 11, no. 6 (2018), p. 1609.

3 Support Scheme for Onshore Wind Farms in France

Sibylle Weiler, Ann-Claire Beauté

3.1 General Background

France has the second largest wind power potential in Europe and the French onshore wind market is one of the most active and attractive markets in Europe. During 2016, €1.07 billion of funding was obtained for new onshore wind farm projects in France.[1] This amount slightly dropped to €1 billion[2] in 2017, mainly due to changes in the support scheme (as described below) and regulatory uncertainty. 2018 has shown stable investment volumes.

The French market is expected to remain very dynamic and competitive not only because of the decrease of project costs, cost competitiveness and the continuing increase of turbine capacity, but also because of ambitious French wind energy targets and the setting-up of a new support mechanism.

3.2 Ambitious Wind Energy Targets

Despite a long and strong history with nuclear power, France has steadily increased its renewable energy targets, in particular wind energy targets.

While the European Union Climate and Energy Package in 2008 aimed for a 20% share of renewable energy out of total EU energy consumption by 2020, France committed to a 23% national objective by 2020, which was implemented in the 2009 Grenelle I law and the 2010 Grenelle II law.

3.2.1 Previous Energy Targets

Current Situation

At the end of 2017, France had an installed onshore wind capacity of 13.5 GW. In November 2018, France was on track to meet the aforementioned target of 15 Gigawatt of installed wind power capacity (onshore) by the end of the year (see Table 3.1).

1 https://www.windeurope.org./about-wind/reports/financing-and-investment-trends2018/#data.

2 Source: WindEurope.

https://doi.org/10.1515/9783110607888-026

Table 3.1: Energy Targets for Onshore Wind in France (own representation).

Date	Renewable Energy Program	Targets	Deadline
1996	"Eole 2005"	250 to 500 MW	2005
2003	PPI 2003 (Multi-annual investment program 2003 / *Programmation pluriannuelle des Investissements* 2003)	2 to 6 GW (0,5 to 1,5 GW offshore)	01/01/2007
2006	PPI 2006	13,5 GW (1 GWoffshore)	2010
		17 GW (4 GW offshore)	2015
2009	PPI 2009	11,5 GW (1 GW offshore)	31/12/2012
		25 GW (6 GW offshore)	31/12/2020
2016	PPE 2016 (Multi-annual energy program 2016 / *Programmation pluriannuelle de l'énergie 2016*)	15,5 GW (0,5 GW offshore)	31/12/2018
		21,8 to 26 GW (3 GW offshore)	2023

3.2.2 New Energy Targets

Currently the new objectives presented in the national energy planning (PPE) aim for 40% of renewable energy between 2032 and 2034, subject to the scenario finally chosen. Such energy targets should lead to an increase in renewable energy project financing, in particular onshore wind farms.

Financing institutions played a key role in supporting French wind energy projects through non-recourse finance and more recently, refinancing. This trend is not expected to change in the upcoming years. However, the aforementioned financing structures require regulatory and macroeconomic stability as well as clear view on support mechanisms.

Despite several changes in the French regulatory framework and a support mechanism continuously challenged by French wind energy opponents, the French Government has always granted full support for onshore wind farms, mainly by setting up feed-in tariff from 2001.

Initial Support Scheme: The Feed-In Tariff ("FiT")

In France, generation of electricity from wind energy has been initially promoted through a legal "Feed-in Tariff" (FiT) mechanism. According to this mechanism, EDF has the obligation to buy the electricity produced by wind farms at a fixed price and for a duration determined by law. For a long time, it has been considered the most effective policy instrument for achieving national energy targets.

This scheme, as further described below, lowers investment risk since it gives producers and funders long-term certainty around revenues. Such price certainty helps to ensure that financial covenants will be met, and that developers will see a return on their investment, provided that the project is generating electricity.

Legal Framework

The FiT scheme was first introduced in France by Law No. 2000–108 dated February 10, 2000 on modernization and development of electricity public service ("Loi relative à la modernisation et au développement du service public de l'électricité") ("Law 2000"). The Law 2000 was adopted in order to transpose the Directive 96/92/EC and open the electricity market up to competition.

In addition to the introduction of the FiT scheme, the Law 2000 created Electricity Transmission Network (RTE) as French grid operator (to replace EDF), and a French independent energy regulator (Commission de Régulation de l'Energie – "CRE").

Over the past decade, eligibility requirements for the FiT scheme were modified in order to adapt the development of wind farms to French town planning rules or wind power policies.

Initially, the power purchase obligation under which EDF had to buy the electricity produced by wind generators at a preferential tariff applied only to wind farms located on a site with a maximum installed capacity of 12 MW with a neighboring wind farm controlled directly or indirectly by the same company, at a distance between generators of less than 1500 m.

Such conditions are no longer required for new wind farms according to the Law dated July 13, 2005 fixing new guidelines on energy policy ("Loi de programme fixant les orientations de la politique énergétique" – Loi POPE); therefore, bigger wind farms were entitled to benefit from the power purchase obligation. However, they had to be built within so-called Wind Development Zones ("Zone de Développement de l'Éolien" – ZDE) created by the relevant "*Préfet*" (representative of the French Government in each department) in order to benefit from such obligation and the FiT.

In 2010 and 2011, the Grenelle II law and its implementing decrees introduced the "500-meter rule" (minimum distance to housings) and the "5-tower rule" (which required wind farms to be composed of a minimum of 5 wind turbines).

Such rules hindered the development of wind power. In 2013, the Brottes law[3] abrogated them and removed the Wind Development Zones.

At the same time as the aforementioned modifications, the FiT has been revised in 2006, 2008 and 2014 in accordance with the Law 2000 (as amended by the so-called "Grenelle II-Act" of July 12, 2010) and its implementing decrees.

3 Loi 2013–312 of April 15, 2013 ("Loi Brottes").

The FiT scheme was initially financed through the public contribution to the electricity service ("Contribution au service public de l'électricité" – CSPE), a tax added to the electricity bill of each French electricity consumer.

The Main Characteristics of the FiT Scheme

Under the FiT scheme, the operator of onshore wind farm sells all its production to EDF for a single price fixed on the date of filing of a complete feed-in tariff request ("demande complète de contrat d'achat") and determined by the applicable tariff order ("arrêté tarifaire"). Such mechanism allows them to secure the tariff in advance and to develop reliable financial forecast.

In order to receive payment, at the applicable price, for the energy produced by the wind farm, each operator must enter into a 15-year power purchase agreement (PPA) ("contrat d'achat") with the French electricity supplier, EDF (or in some cases, with a local supplier). Except for the characteristics of the wind farm, the rest of such contract is standard and not negotiable. Standard contracts have made the financing process and wind farm operation easier compared to direct marketing contracts under the Feed-in Premium scheme, the provisions of which are freely negotiable.

The FiT granted under tariff orders dated 2008 and 2014 was quite similar and amounts to:
- Year 0–10: a fixed tariff of 8.2 c€/kWh
- Year 11–15: a tariff between 2.8 and 8.2 c€/kWh depending on the average amount of electricity generated (2.8 c€/kWh for 3,600 hours and more; 8.2 c €/kWh for 2,400 hours and less).

During the entire duration of the PPA, the tariff is adjusted every year on the basis of indexing formula as provided in the relevant tariff order. Since 2009, the FiT scheme has faced some changes, leading to a reshaped public support mechanism.

3.2.3 Challenging of the FiT Scheme

The 2008 tariff order was subject of a legal challenge by wind farm opponents before the French administrative Supreme Court (*Conseil d'Etat*), on the ground that the FiT scheme as State Aid should have been notified to the European Commission. On May 28, 2014, given the preliminary ruling of CJEU, the *Conseil d'Etat* canceled the 2008 tariff order for non-compliance with European State aid rules.

The French Government decided to anticipate this ruling and reported the FiT scheme to the EU Commission. On March 27, 2014,[4] EU Commission approved it for a 10-year period, provided that nothing in the regulatory framework of the FiT scheme

4 http://ec.europa.eu/competition/state_aid/cases/252225/252225_1579530_37_1.pdf.

be modified within this time period. Accordingly, French Government issued immediately a new tariff order on June 17, 2014, granting tariff similar to 2008 tariff.

The EU Guidelines on State Aid for environmental protection and energy[5] entered into force on July 1, 2014. According to these guidelines, renewable energy shall be progressively exposed to competition of EU electricity market. In order to promote better integration in such market, they provide for gradual introduction of market-based mechanisms, which means gradual replacement of the FiT scheme by a feed-in premium scheme and the introduction of a bidding process. As a result, producers of renewable energy who benefit from a public support scheme, must sell the electricity directly to the market, be subject to market obligations and, as from January 1, 2017, with respect to wind farms with a capacity of more than 6 MW or 6 turbines, participate in a competitive tender process.

In order to implement the aforementioned guidelines, the French Government has adopted law No. 2015–992[6] on energy transition dated August 17, 2015 (the "Energy Transition Act") and its subsequent Decrees No. 2016–682 dated May 27, 2016, and No. 2016–691 dated May 28, 2016. These regulations provide for a gradual switch to a new support mechanism, the feed-in premium scheme.[7] In addition, as part of a more flexible electricity market in France, the Energy Transition Act[8] also provides that renewable energy producers are entitled to entrust the management of their PPA to authorized operators other than EDF or local distribution companies.[9]

With such regulations, onshore wind farms were supposed to benefit from the FiT scheme, as approved by EU Commission in 2014, up to the end of 2018. However, in 2015, the financing rules of the FiT scheme were modified (CSPE replaced by TICFE (domestic tax on final electricity consumption)).[10] As a consequence, in 2016, the FiT scheme was challenged by the European Commission. According to the EU Commission, such a scheme was not compatible with the aforementioned EU Guidelines due to such modification. At the same time, opponents to wind projects challenged the Decree No. 2016–691 dated May 28, 2016 which allows onshore wind farms to benefit from the FiT scheme.

To avoid any uncertainty with respect to the applicable support mechanism and validity of PPAs under the 2014 tariff order, French Government decided to actively negotiate with EU Commission. As a result, French State switched much earlier than expected to the new support scheme, the feed-in premium scheme, to comply with the European Guidelines.

---

5 EU Guidelines No. 2014/C200/01, published on June 28, 2014.

6 "Loi relative à la transition énergétique pour la croissance verte."

7 Comparable to the English Contract for Difference or the German "geförderte Direktvermarktung."

8 Art. L314-6-1 of the French Energy Code (initial version).

9 The first authorization delivered to an independent supplier in October 2016, was limited to 75 PPAs for a maximum installed capacity of 100 MW.

10 Introduced by the "Loi de finances rectificative No. 2015–1786" dated December 29, 2015.

3.2.4 The Current Support Scheme: The Feed-in Premium ("FIP") ("complément de rémunération")

The legal framework of the FIP scheme is defined under articles L314-18 to L314-27 of the French Energy Code, as created by article 104 of Energy Transition Act. In order to implement the FIP scheme, the French Government has issued additional regulations:

- as a first step, ministerial order dated December 13, 2016 (the "FIP 2016"), as approved by EU Commission, to ensure a transition between the FiT scheme and the FIP scheme;
- as a second step, Decree 2017–676 dated April 28, 2017 according to which onshore wind farms are no longer entitled to the FiT scheme and only "small" wind farms can benefit from FIP in the context of "open window" mechanism;
- as a third step, a tariff order dated May 6, 2017 (the "FIP 2017") and specifications for the call for tender dated May 5, 2017, to clarify rules applicable in the context respectively of the "open window" mechanism and tender process.

Overview of the FIP Scheme: A Dual and Market-Based Structure

Under this mechanism, EDF is no longer obliged to purchase electricity produced by onshore wind farms. To benefit from the FIP, the producer must enter into a contract with EDF (additional remuneration contract) according to which the latter commits to paying an additional remuneration if the market price does not reach a "reference tariff."

Therefore, the onshore wind farms will no longer benefit from FiT for the whole energy produced, as referred to in a standard PPA concluded with EDF (or a local supplier), but receive revenues from two different sources:

- a market-based price in consideration of:
  - the electricity sold directly on EPEX SPOT (which is not common practice) or to an aggregator[11] through a direct marketing contract; and
  - the capacity certificates exchanged by auctions on EPEX SPOT or on OTC (Over the Counter) market,[12] either by the producer or by an aggregator;

11 "Aggregator" as defined under article R314-1 of the French Energy Code, means a person in charge of the sale on electricity markets of the electricity produced by the plant on behalf of the producer. Electricity (and capacity certificates) can be sold on "EPEX Spot" or in OTC (Over the Counter) transactions. Aggregator is rather an "intermediary" than a "purchaser proxy." It generally handles a portfolio of different electricity production plants and is authorized to trade electricity on the EPEX SPOT market.

12 Capacity mechanism has been introduced by the Law No. 2010–1488 dated December 7, 2010 (the Nome Law) in order to satisfy peak demand (in particular, during winter) and secure national electric power supply. Initially, under the FIT scheme, only EDF as purchaser of electricity was involved in the capacity mechanism. In the framework of the FIP scheme, power plant operators must now take

- an additional remuneration,[13] which is paid by EDF and corresponds to:
  - the difference between energy premium (i.e., the difference between a so-called "reference tariff"[14] as fixed by French Government, and average market-based value of the energy produced (MO) as published by the French energy regulator (CRE)) and the revenues from the sale of capacity certificates[15]; and
  - management premium to cover the balancing costs and costs incurred by the producer (in most cases, the aggregator) to sell electricity production and capacity certificates.

The aggregator usually grants the monthly average tariff for electricity transactions (MO) and the reference market price of the capacity certificates ($P_{ref\ capa}$). EDF pays an amount equal to the difference between the "reference tariff" and such MO. Therefore, despite fluctuations of the EPEX spot market, the FIP scheme should ensure to reach the so-called "reference tariff" and then, a reasonable return on investment.

In the event of negative energy prices for the day ahead trading on EPEX spot for a period exceeding 20 hours (consecutive or not) during a calendar year, the producer will receive compensation in accordance with the applicable order (or specifications in a tendering procedure) from the 20th hour of negative EPEX spot prices, provided that the plant has not injected any power into the public grid during the negative price period.

---

part in such mechanism. They will receive capacity certificates issued by the national Transmission Grid Operator (RTE) in consideration of their availability commitment during peak periods for one given delivery year. As for energy suppliers, they must hold sufficient amount of capacity guarantees for the same period in order to guarantee power supply to their portfolio during peak consumption periods; otherwise, they must reduce the consumption within their portfolio. The first auction occurred on EPEX SPOT at the end of 2016 for the delivery year 2017 and EPEX SPOT plans to hold between one and six auctions per year, depending on the capacity guarantees available as well as the liquidity of the market (6 auctions for 2019). One capacity guarantee corresponds to 0.1 MW of certified capacity. Trading volume and prices of the guarantees can be checked on the website of EPEX SPOT: https://www.epexspot.com/en/market-data/capacitymarket/capacity-table/2018-04-26/FR.

13 The amount of additional remuneration is calculated on the basis of various criteria set forth in article L 314.20 of the French Energy Code. Such criteria will be subject to periodic reviews to take into account market fluctuations and avoid excessive return of investment.

14 The reference tariff is subject to a double indexation (coefficients "K" and "L"). The adjustment based on the coefficient K is made initially depending on the date of filing of a complete feed-in tariff/feed-in premium request. The adjustment on the basis of the coefficient "L" is made annually on November 1. Both coefficients take into account the index of hourly labor costs and the index of industrial production costs.

15 Calculated by multiplying number of capacity certificates by reference market price (as published by the CRE) which corresponds to the average price observed during auctions the calendar year preceding the given delivery year ($p_{ref\ capa}$).

If the producer is not able to sell electricity directly or indirectly on the market (e.g., due to a failure of the aggregator), a purchaser of last resort ("acheteur en dernier recours") appointed by French Government is obliged to sign a power purchase agreement for a maximum duration of 3 months; the power purchase price cannot exceed 80% of the "reference tariff." However, to date, this purchaser has not been appointed.[16]

As a result of this new mechanism, it is necessary for all stakeholders to adapt quickly and for financing banks to reshape their lending schemes and financial models.

To demonstrate the bankability of wind farm project, focus will be made on the choice of the aggregator and the content of the direct marketing contract.

With respect to the aggregator, producers and then the banks will assess mainly its technical skills, its experience to trade energy (and capacity certificates – as explained above) and its financial standing.

With respect to the content of the direct marketing contract, they will carefully analyze the remuneration of the producer, the fees to be paid by the producer, the strategy of the aggregator to control costs, additional services eventually provided by the aggregator (such as system services, reporting of electricity market transactions, or production forecast).

In addition, it is crucial that the directing marketing contract is correlated with the content of the other maintenance and operation related contracts, such as the maintenance contract or the technical and commercial management contracts. Whereas in the past there was one standard PPA with EDF to comply with, producer must now comply with direct marketing contracts with various content and ensure appropriate coordination between the different actors. In most cases, such coordination tasks will be carried out by the technical and commercial manager, in order to avoid financial liabilities of the producer, in particular due to production forecast variations and scheduled or unscheduled maintenance.

2016: Transition Year

The ministerial order dated December 13, 2016 (the "FIP 2016") sets out a transitional scheme:

- it specifies which plants will continue benefitting from the FiT scheme;
- it sets forth criteria in order to determine the plants eligible for the new support scheme (FIP);
- it has been tailored in order to target remuneration broadly similar to the FiT as fixed in the tariff order dated 2014.

Plants eligible for the FiT scheme

16 Article L 314–26 of the French Energy Code.

According to the FIP 2016, the following plants are entitled to benefit from the FiT scheme and electricity purchase obligations set out in tariff order dated June 17, 2014:
- plants with a PPA signed at the latest on December 14, 2016;
- plants for which the producer applied for a PPA before January 1, 2016 or obtained a power purchase certificate (*CODOA*) before such date.

However, in order to be eligible for the FiT scheme, such plants must be completed[17] within 3 years following the application for a PPA, or no later than November 30, 2017.[18] This deadline can be extended if the commissioning of a wind farm is delayed by grid connection works, legal challenge against administrative authorization to build the wind farm or force majeure event.[19]

If the deadline cannot be met, producers are entitled to benefit from the FIP as further explained below.

The FIP 2016 has replaced the aforementioned tariff order. As a result, EDF and the producers are no longer entitled to enter into new PPA.

Plants eligible for the FIP under the FIP 2016

Under the FIP 2016, onshore wind projects can benefit from the FIP subject to the following conditions:
1. The producer filed a complete PPA application (*Demande compléte de contrat d'achat* (*DCCA*)) after January 1, 2016 and the execution of the PPA occurred at the latest, on December 15, 2016; or
2. The producer filed a complete PPA application between January 1, 2016 and December 31, 2016 but no PPA was signed as of December 31, 2016; or
3. The producer filed before December 31, 2016 a complete application to enter into an additional remuneration contract (*Demande complète de complément de rémunération* (*DCCR*)) for a new wind farm.[20]

Under (1.) and (2.), the producer had the opportunity to withdraw the complete PPA application in order to replace it with a complete application to enter into an additional remuneration contract.

In any case, in order to be eligible for the FIP scheme, the onshore wind project must be completed[21] within 3 years following the application for a power purchase

---

17 Completion of a wind farm is evidenced by a certificate issued by a certified body as set forth in art. R314-7 of the French Energy Code.

18 Art. 6 III of Decree No. 2016–691 dated May 28, 2016.

19 Art. 6 of Decree No. 2016–1726 dated December 16, 2016.

20 A plant is "new" if the complete application to enter into an additional remuneration contract was filed before the beginning of the construction works or any binding commitment making the investment irreversible.

21 Completion of a wind farm is evidenced by a certificate issued by a certified body as set forth in art. R314-7 of the French Energy Code.

agreement/a contract for difference. In the event of any delay for a reason other than grid connection works, legal challenge against administrative authorization to build the wind farm or force majeure event,[22] the duration of the additional remuneration contract will be reduced accordingly.

The FIP 2016 was withdrawn on July 30, 2017.[23] Accordingly, producers as referred to in the above-mentioned (i) and (ii) were entitled to file a complete application to enter into an additional remuneration contract, governed by the FIP 2016, until July 29, 2017. Bitte Absatz einfügen

Main characteristics of the FIP under the FIP 2016 Bitte Absatz einfügen

The duration of the additional remuneration contract entered into with EDF is 15 years. The additional remuneration is paid each month and calculated on the basis of the following formula:

$$CR = \sum_{i=1}^{12} E_i \times (\alpha T_e - MO_i + P_{Gestion}) - (Nb_{capa} \times P_{ref\ capa})$$

Where:
- i = month; $\sum$ = sum for 12 months
- E_i = for the month i, electricity volume produced by the power plant during spot price period, to be delivered on the Day-ahead market in France
- T_e = reference tariff – 82 €/MWh (before L and K indexations) for the first 10 years, between 28 and 82 €/MWh for the last five years depending on the average amount of electricity generated
- $\alpha = 1$
- MO_i = reference market price for month i
- $P_{gestion}$ = management premium amounting to 2.8 €
- /MWh
- Nb_{capa} = number of capacity certificates for a calendar year (in MW)
- $P_{ref\ capa}$ = average price observed during auctions the calendar year preceding the given delivery year (in €/MWh)

Under the FIP 2016, the reference tariff is similar to the FiT granted under tariff order dated June 17, 2014. French government wanted to ensure that an onshore wind project received a remuneration equivalent to the FiT of 2014.

The publication of the tariff order dated May 6, 2017 (the "FIP 2017") and the specifications for the call for tender dated May 5, 2017 have put an end to the transitional regime as set forth in the FIP 2016.

Outlook: As mentioned, the FIP 2016 was meant to be a transitional regime, enabling a smooth switch from the former FiT system to a direct marketing regime with

22 Art. 6 of Decree No. 2016–1726 dated December 16, 2016.

23 In accordance with the Decree No.2017–676 dated April 28, 2017.

a Feed-in Premium (FIP). When France notified the European Commission at the end of 2016 that it would be switching to a FIP scheme, a pre-determined volume of 1.5GW per year was indicated. This corresponded to the average yearly installation volume of new wind farms in France. However, the FIP 2016 contained no requirements with respect to authorizations already obtained for a project. Therefore, a large number of developers applied for this FIP 2016, although the respective projects were often in a very early development phase. In addition, projects that had secured the previous FiT 2014, but which were considered unlikely to achieve commissioning by November 2017, switched to the FIP 2016. As a consequence, the FIP 2016 was largely over-subscribed, which raised the question, in August 2019, as to whether granting a FIP for a volume above the 1.5GW notified initially would be illegal with respect to European State Aid Law. As a result, projects in an earlier development stage switched to the FIP 2017, assuming that they met the requirements, or to a tender procedure.

In addition, projects which have already signed binding investment contracts might not be able to apply for FIP 2017 or participate in a tender procedure, as they do not meet the criteria of "new installation."

While awaiting clarification from the French authorities, banks engaged in project finance are exploring alternative remuneration schemes, such as the Corporate Power Purchase Agreement (Corporate PPA) in France.[24] Corporate buyers have become increasingly interested in such alternative energy procurement schemes, including both on- and off-site Corporate PPAs. Besides state-organized tender procedures, corporate tender procedures driven by industrial off-takers are becoming more and more common. There is also an increasing demand for local guarantees of origin ("GOs"). Under the previous FiT and FIP regimes, such guarantees were not attributed to projects benefitting from a state support scheme. However, such guarantees have since been attributed to the French State with the recent launch of the first auction rounds in France. The prices obtained for such guarantees differed significantly from the geographical origin of the renewable energy.

Financing banks will have to review and adapt to the requirements with respect to revenues generated by projects under a Corporate PPA, taking into account both the risk of termination and counter-party risk.

3.2.5 Since 2017: A New Support Scheme for Smaller Projects

According to European State Aid Guidelines dated 2014, the French Government is entitled from January 1, 2017, to grant any State Aid provided that such aid be granted "*in a competitive bidding process on the basis of clear, transparent and non-discriminatory*

24 See also section 9 (General Part).

criteria." However, the EU Commission accepted to exclude such process for wind farms with up to 6 wind turbines (WTG) and a maximum installed power capacity of 3 MW per WTG. Accordingly, the support scheme for onshore wind farms, as approved by EU Commission,[25] sets out two different procedures depending on the size of the plant: the "open-window" mechanism and the tendering procedure.

The "open window" ("Guichet ouvert") for "small-scale" onshore wind farms

The right to benefit from the FIP 2017 has been strictly limited:

- only wind farms[26] with 6 turbines or less and a maximum output of 3 MW per turbine are eligible for the "open window" mechanism; and
- the environmental authorization has to/have been obtained;
- on the date of application for an additional remuneration contract under the FIP 2017, the wind farm must be located more than 1500 m from another existing wind farm or a wind farm for which the application for an additional remuneration contract has been filed within the last 2 years, unless the producer can duly justify that the special purpose vehicles of the wind farms are completely "independent" of each other.[27] This avoids artificial splitting of a sole project in two projects in order to benefit from the FIP 2017.

Both FIP 2016 and FIP 2017 set out similar rules with respect to calculation formula, payment of the FIP on a monthly basis, amount of the management premium, compensation in the event of negative prices, 3-year deadline to complete the projects,[28] purchase of last resort. However, there are noteworthy differences.

The additional remuneration contract concluded with EDF under the FIP 2017 will be concluded for 20 years, instead of 15 years for the additional remuneration contract under the FIP 2016.

Reference tariff is now calculated depending on rotor diameter and annual production cap (calculated itself depending on number of turbines and rotor diameter) in order to limit producers' revenues and avoid "over-supporting" wind farms with good wind conditions:

- Below such cap, reference tariff (before indexation) is between 74 €/MWh (for rotor diameter of 80 m or less) and 72 €/MWh (for rotor diameter of 100 m or more)[29];

25 Decision dated May 5, 2017.

26 Art. 2 of the ministerial order dated May 6, 2017 refers to "new" installations (as defined in art. 4) for which complete application for an additional remuneration contract under FIP 2017 has been filed from January 1, 2017 and installations for which complete application for an additional remuneration contract was initially filed under the FIP 2016.

27 Art. 3 of the FIP 2017.

28 Extension of the 3-year deadline in the event of grid connection delay is much more complicated to obtain under the FIP 2017.

29 Tariffs in between are calculated by "linear interpolation."

- Beyond this cap, reference tariff amounts to 40 €/MWh whatever the rotor diameter.
- Outlook: The open wind mechanism was initially granted for a volume of 1.5GW over a 10 year period. However, the current FIP 2017 will be, by 2020–21, further restricted, able to grant this tariff only to very small projects.

3.2.6 The Tendering Procedure ("Appel d'offres")

Eligibility for the Tendering Procedure

On May 5, 2017, the CRE published the specifications with respect to the tendering process. According to article 1.2.1 of the specifications, "new"[30] installations as described below can take part in such tendering process:

- Installations of at least 7 wind generators, or
- Installations of at least 1 wind generator with a nominal output over 3 MW, or
- Installations for which EDF refused to sign an additional remuneration contract under the FIP 2016 or FIP 2017.

Organization of the Call for Tenders

The call for tenders is organized by the French energy regulator (CRE) which puts in place online application website and automated ranking system.

Online application must be submitted by candidates with all the requested documents in French.[31] To guarantee equal treatment between the candidates, questions and answers are posted on the CRE website. The candidates are not entitled to amend their bid between the application deadline and the award decision of the Energy Minister.

Six tender periods are planned between November 2017 and June 2020, each of 500 MW.

Selection of the bids

Each complete application (not dismissed) is awarded a score out of 100. The sole selection criterion is the price offered by the bidder, which must be between a maximum tariff (T_{max}) and a minimum tariff (T_{min}) as defined for each bidding period (see Table 3.2).

The score is calculated according to this formula:

$$NP = NP_0 \times [(T_{max} - T)/(T_{max} - T_{min})]$$

30 As defined in art. 2.4 of the specifications.

31 Identity of the bidder, application form, environmental authorization (not requested for the 1st and 3rd bidding periods.), delegation of signature (if necessary), a commitment to crowd funding (if proposed by the bidder), a copy of EDF refusal of the additional remuneration contract.

Table 3.2: Tariff borders for Bidding Periods.

Bidding period	T_{max}	T_{min}
1st (November 1, 2017 – December 1, 2017)	74,8 €/MWh	0 €/MWh
2nd (May 1, 2018 – June 1, 2018)	74,8 €/MWh	0 €/MWh
3rd (March 1, 2019 – April 1, 2019)	71,0 €/MWh	0 €/MWh
4th (July 1, 2019 – August 1, 2019)	71,0 €/MWh	0 €/MWh
5th (May 1, 2020 – June 1, 2020)	70,0 €/MWh	0 €/MWh

Where:
- **T** = "reference tariff" in €/MWh, as proposed by the candidate.
- $\mathbf{T_{max}}$ / $\mathbf{T_{min}}$ as defined hereabove.
- $\mathbf{NP_0}$ = the maximal score.

The instruction period is 6 weeks. Once the instruction closed, the CRE submits to the Ministry of Energy:
- the list of proposed successful bids and rejected bids, with the grounds for rejection (not public);
- the rating of the bids;
- the file of each bid;
- a summary note of the call for tenders.

The Energy Minister appoints the selected candidate(s). If the choice contemplated by the Minister differs from the ranking drawn up by the CRE, the Minister shall beforehand obtain the opinion of the CRE with respect to such choice. The Minister announces at the same time the successful and the unsuccessful candidates.

Procedure Following the Award Decision

The successful candidates must complete the installations in accordance with their bid. However, they are entitled to request modification of the bid subject to restrictions pursuant to article 5.4 of the specifications[32] and/or prior authorization of the "Préfet."[33]

32 Art. 5.4 of the specifications refers to restrictions such as: no modification of the reference tariff proposed by the bidder; no change of producer before the completion of the plant; no change in the capital structure before the setting-up of the financial guarantee to be provided; change of project location within the neighboring towns; modification of the installed capacity within ± 10% compared to the capacity mentioned in the bid (except for downwards modifications as a result of the environmental authorization or a court decision with respect to such authorization)

33 The Préfet must decide on the request within 1-month period. In the absence of decision, the request is deemed refused. The decision of the Préfet can be subject of an appeal.

Obligations of the successful candidates

The successful candidates must fulfill the following obligations:

- apply for a grid connection agreement within two months following the award decision (following the date of environmental authorization, for the 1st and 3rd bidding periods);
- provide a financial guarantee to secure the completion of the plant, within two months following the award decision;
  - such guarantee is either a letter of credit issued by a bank or an insurance company to the benefit of the French Government, or an escrow with the "*Caisse des Dépôts et Consignations*" (French sovereign fund);
  - the duration of the guarantee must be at least 51 months depending on the bidding period[34];
  - it amounts to 30,000 EUR per installed MW.
  - the guarantee will be returned 15 days after completion of the wind farm.
- complete the installation in accordance with (i) the eligibility requirements pursuant to article 2 of the specifications and (ii) the bid (as may be modified), within 36 months following the award decision,[35] evidenced by a certificate of compliance sent to EDF[36]; and
- additional obligations as listed in article 6.8 of the specifications, which consist mainly in transferring (making available) to the Distribution System Operator (ENEDIS), EDF or the CRE, data or information regarding the wind farm.[37]

The installation will be subject to inspections at the time of commissioning and then, on a periodic basis, pursuant to article L 311-13-5 of the French Energy Code.

Remuneration of the successful candidates

As for the FIP 2017, the successful candidates have to:

- sell electricity on the wholesale market, mainly through a direct marketing contract with an aggregator;
- enter into an additional remuneration contract with EDF to receive the FIP.

34 At least 57 months for the 1st and 3rd bidding periods.

35 This deadline can be extended if the commissioning of the wind farm is delayed due to grid connection works as set forth in art. 6.4 of the specifications, legal challenge against environmental authorization (for the 1st, 3rd and 4th bidding periods) or unforeseeable event (subject to the discretion of the Energy Minister). In any case, deadline extension is subject to extension of the validity period of the financial guarantee.

36 Standard form to be completed by approved organization as referred to in art. L 311-13-5 of the French Energy Code.

37 Such as production data, detailed costs and revenues, documents to evidence such data (to be forwarded within 1-month period upon request of the CRE), business plan in accordance with the standard form available on the CRE website.

The duration of the additional remuneration contract is 20 years from the expiration date of the above-mentioned 36-month period (as may be extended from time to time), subject to the delivery of the compliance certificate to EDF. If this deadline is not met, the duration of the additional remuneration contract will be reduced accordingly.

The additional remuneration contract refers in particular to the provisions of the specifications and the details of the bid.

The FIP will be paid to the producer on a monthly basis. The amount of the FIP corresponds to the difference between the reference tariff as proposed by the bidder (T)[38] and the average monthly EPEX Spot price (MO_i).[39] The reference tariff will increase if the bidder commits to crowdfunding: the increase will depend on the part of crowdfunding in the project financing[40]; conversely, the reference tariff will be reduced equally.[41] In addition, as under the FIP 2017, the producer is entitled to benefit from compensation in the event of negative prices, and the purchaser of last resort mechanism. However there is no management premium.

Results of the First Four Tender Periods

The first tender period for which award decision was published on February 28, 2018 was successful. Bids totaling around 900MW were submitted. Twenty two bids totaling 500 MW were selected by the Energy Ministry upon proposal of the CRE. The average winning price amounts to 65,4 €/MWh, lower than the current tariff for small-scale onshore wind projects (€72 MWh) under the FIP 2017 and the €82 MWh under the FiT scheme. A third of the successful bids (7/22) have obtained a premium due to their crowdfunding commitment.

With only 300 MW of projects that took part in the second call for tenders,[42] such call for tenders did not meet the target of 500 MW. Only five projects with a capacity of 118 MW were selected on September 6, 2018. The weighted average price of the tender has not yet been published. One of the winner is a repowering project.

Such low participation rate may be explained by the fact that obtaining environmental authorization was now required in order to be entitled to submit a bid and there was an uncertainty with respect to the validity of the procedure for obtaining such authorization, following rulings of the *Conseil d'Etat* dated December 6 and 28, 2017.

---

38 As under the FIP 2017, the reference tariff is indexed annually on the basis of the coefficient "L" (as explained above).

39 As a result of the following calculation formula: $CR = \sum 12i{=}1\ E_i \times (T - MO_i)$.

40 1st bidding period: increase between 2 and 3 €/MWh; other bidding period: 3 €/MWh for equity crowdfunding and 1 €/MWh for debt crowdfunding.

41 1st bidding period: reduction of 3 €/MWh; other bidding period: 3 €/MWh for equity crowdfunding and 1 €/MWh for debt crowdfunding.

42 According to a survey carried out by France Energie Eolienne. And only nine projects with a capacity of 216 MW fulfilled the eligibility requirements.

As a result, the CRE published on August 28, 2018 and March 4, 2019 amended specifications for onshore wind projects. The application deadline for the third and fourth tendering periods has been postponed until April 1, 2019 and August 1, 2019 respectively; the maximum "reference tariff" (Tmax) has been fixed at 71 €/MWh for the third and fourth tendering periods and 70 €/MWh for the fifth and sixth tendering periods; obtaining the environmental authorization is no longer a requirement to bid in the third bidding period; target volumes for the fifth and sixth bidding periods are 630 and 752 MW, respectively (instead of 500 MW each).

The third tender period attributed a weighted average tariff of 63 €/MWh for 21 projects for a volume of 516 MW and the fourth tender period granted a weighted average tariff of 66.5 €/MWh for 20 projects for a volume of 576 MW.

Financing banks and investors need long-term market stability and profitability for both existing and future onshore wind projects. This means stability and visibility on support mechanism. With the new support mechanism as describedabove, the French onshore wind market is expected to remain attractive in order to meet French energy targets. However, besides state-driven support mechanisms, Corporate PPAs will be increasingly used in the French market, which is to be seen as a challenge and as an opportunity for all involved parties. Financing banks will have to adapt to this rapidly changing environment.

4 Supportive System: The Example of India

Prashant Agrawal

4.1 Introduction of Power Sector in India

India is the third largest producer and third largest consumer of electricity in the world, with the installed power capacity reaching 356.10 GW as of April 2019. The country also has the fifth largest installed capacity in the world.

India's total installed electricity generation capacity stands at 344,002 MW which is dominated by coal-fired power plants, accounting for 88% of thermal installed capacity and 57.31% of total installed capacity. Other renewable energy (RE) sources, which include wind, solar, biomass and small hydro, are at a distant second, accounting for just 20% of the total.

Power failures are a common occurrence in India due to the inability of existing plants to meet peak demand. In fact, all regions of the country except Eastern region failed to meet peak demand based on February 2018 data. By 2022, the power ministry expects demand to hit 239 GW based on an annual GDP growth forecast of 8%. Estimates show that electricity demand growth is 0.9% of GDP growth. Since India is heavily dependent on energy imports to fulfill its requirements, its import bill will continue to rise unless significant steps are taken. Approximately 80% of oil, 28% of liquid natural gas, 22% of thermal coal and 70% of methanol, for instance, come from imported sources. In recent years, the government has been aggressive in trying to cut coal imports by ramping up production and improving the efficiency of coal-fired plants.

Meanwhile, access to electricity is also an issue. IEA estimates that up to 237 million people or 19% of the population in India does not have access to electricity. In particular, connectivity rates in rural areas are much lower compared to urban areas.

In response to this, in recent years the government launched the "Deen Dayal Upadhyaya Gram Jyoti Yojana (DDUGJY)" scheme for rural electrification, which is currently being implemented by the Rural Electrification Corporation. Under this program, the Ministry of Power sanctioned 921 projects to electrify 121,225 villages, improve the electrification of 592,979 partially electrified villages and provide free electricity connections to some 40 million households below the poverty line.

Ever since the power sector has been thrown open for investments, the distribution segment has been one eternal problem that has concerned investors. The sector faces a plethora of issues, including political interference, low cost recovery, huge electric losses, poor operational performance, weak regulatory compliance, etc. Over the years, these issues have translated into major operational and financial inefficiencies in Distribution Companies (DISCOMs).

https://doi.org/10.1515/9783110607888-027

A number of attempts have been made in the past to manage these issues, but the situation has only worsened with time. These developments have jolted investor concerns in the power sector. The Government has made a strong attempt to rectify the problem through its carefully crafted scheme called the UDAY (Ujwal DISCOM Assurance Yojana) Scheme. The scheme is introduced in FY 2015–16 in order to reduce the debt burden of DISCOMs, and helping them to improve their balance sheets temporarily. UDAY Scheme also included many measures to reduce AT&C losses, through improvement of the distribution infrastructure.

UDAY scheme is expected to drive the adoption of new technologies and solutions in Transmission and Distribution segment enabling to reduce the AT&C losses. To illustrate this, if a DISCOM buys say 100 units of electricity at USD 0.06/kWh, average tariff is 0.08/kWh and AT&C loss is 30%, then the DISCOM is able to sell only 70 units of electricity and thereby its revenue is only USD 5.60 whereas its cost of supply is USD 6.00. Due to this, the DISCOM incurs a loss of USD 0.40. Now, if the AT&C loss of DISCOM reduces to 15%, its revenue will be USD 6.80 and it will start earning a profit without even increasing any tariff. That is power of improving operational efficiencies and the UDAY policy advocates the same.

4.2 Evolution of Wind Energy in India

Renewable sources account for 80,047 MW of installed capacity as on 31.05.2019. Renewable sources collectively enjoy the fastest growth rate in terms of installed capacity, averaging 25% per annum over the past decade. From the current 80,047 MW, government targets are set at 175,000 MW of installed capacity by 2022, powered to a large extent by solar and wind. The Ministry of New and Renewable Energy (MNRE) has formulated targets for each RE technology and region up to the year 2022, which are shown in Figure 4.1 below.

With government's ambitious green energy targets, the sector has become quite attractive for both foreign and domestic investors. Renewable energy received FDI inflow of US$ 7.48 billion between April 2000 and December 2018. By 2028, India can see renewable energy investments worth US$ 500 billion.

The country ranks fourth in the world in terms of total installed wind power capacity. As of May 2019, Government of India has installed 36 GW of wind power capacity against the target of 60 GW by 2022. Wind power capacity addition is expected to reach 3 GW in FY19–20. In wind power, most states are still offering the Feed-in Tariff (FiT) system. The FiT for most states where the plant load factor (PLF) is more than 23% is below USD 0.07/kWh (excluding Generation Based Incentives). Maharashtra and Rajasthan are the only ones above USD 0.07/kWh now. In Madhya Pradesh, the wind tariff has decreased from USD 0.09/kWh to USD 0.07/kWh for the period of April 2016 to March 2019 mainly due to higher plant load factor and lower specific cost of turbine being considered as compared to last determined tariff.

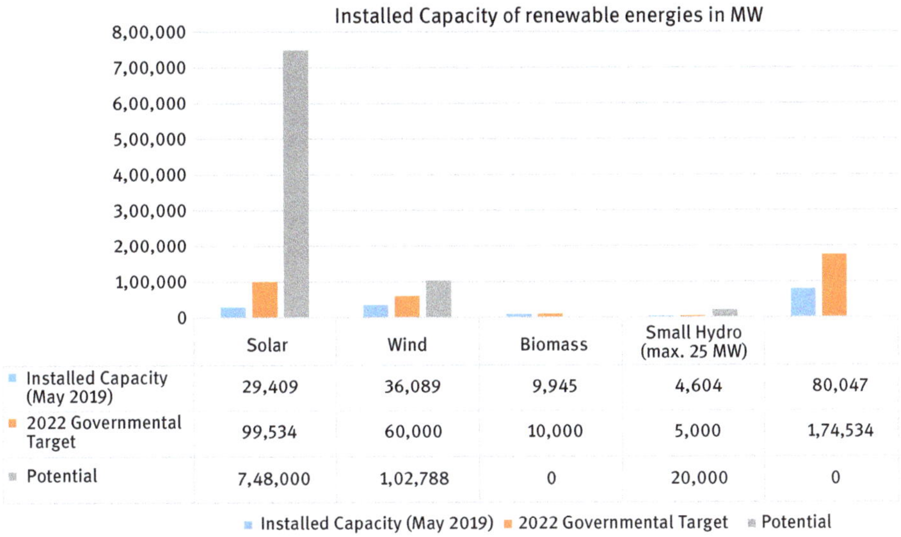

	Solar	Wind	Biomass	Small Hydro (max. 25 MW)	
Installed Capacity (May 2019)	29,409	36,089	9,945	4,604	80,047
2022 Governmental Target	99,534	60,000	10,000	5,000	1,74,534
Potential	7,48,000	1,02,788	0	20,000	0

Figure 4.1: Installed capacity of renewable energies in India in MW (own representation).

Introduced in 2017, competitive bidding for wind power projects has yielded several positives. The bidding mechanism has created a more transparent and competitive industry, as tariffs are determined based on developers' analysis of location, counterparty risks, wind conditions and other project specific factors as well as company's ability to do financial engineering. Project sizes have become much larger, thereby providing better economies of scale.

India's first ever wind power auction has resulted in a record low wind power tariff of USD 0.05/kWh. In December 2017, SECI floated India's largest wind energy tender and announced the results of the competitive auction in February 2018. Against the offered capacity of 2 GW, prospective developers placed bids to set up 2.75 GW of capacity. All successful bidders placed bids of USD 0.038/kWh, which matches the lowest-ever solar power bid in India.

Since the first auction, the lowest wind energy tariff has declined by a whopping 29.4%. The tariffs have declined so much and so rapidly due to the seismic changes in the government policies. The federal as well as state governments have now moved from a feed-in tariff regime to auctions policy for wind energy projects. Projects can now only be installed through auctions. This has made developers desperate for projects which can be seen in the steep fall in tariff bids.

As a result, making wind energy a preferred source of power for discoms, which were earlier reluctant to purchase this power due to its higher price. These tariffs may propel non – wind generating states to procure wind power from windy states by installing transmission lines, which will overall, increase the offtake from wind projects.

Notably, the winners under all auctions so far have been large entities, mostly backed by international financiers and global strategic players in the power space. it has brought the margins of both developers and original equipment manufacturers (OEMs) under tremendous pressure. The auctions could have been enabling provisions to allow small investors to participate in the bidding process as this would facilitate investments from domestic investments with long-term commitments. Currently, the small companies' difficulty in raising cash is keeping them away from government-led power project auctions, restricting their growth and crippling their ability to refinance loans.

Even as the Centre has ramped up the renewable energy target for the country, nearly 18% of the existing wind capacity is due for repowering. Repowering refers to the practice of installing more powerful wind turbines in existing sites to generate more power and drive higher efficiencies. The Govt. promotes optimum utilization of wind energy resources by creating facilitative framework for repowering. Apart from extending all fiscal and financial benefits offered to new wind power projects, an additional interest rebate of 0.25% will be provided.

4.3 Challenges Faced by the Wind Sector in the Country and the Way Forward

It is now established that the biggest issue facing the wind industry is evacuation of power from sites where developers have decided to install wind farms. The problem magnifies especially in the case of large wind farms requiring connectivity to the interstate transmission system. The issue came to light in the recent auctions, a huge bid capacity (about 2.6 GW) came up in Gujarat due to the high wind sites in the region. However, the evacuation infrastructure was insufficient to cater to such high capacities.

Other issue that wind power developers want resolved relates to the honoring of PPAs as any violation has an adverse impact on developers, investors and financial institutions. There have been attempts in the past by discoms to renegotiate PPAs, but their proposals have so far been rejected by the courts. Another issue pertains to declining margins. According to India Ratings' estimate, the bidders that won in the first auction would be able to earn an equity internal rate of return (IRR) of just about 9% against IRRs of 18–20% achieved with feed-in tariffs (FiTs). However, the returns rise to 12–14% with a slightly higher plant load factor (PLF), which can be achieved through more efficient equipment, and a reduction in the cost of finance. While the bidding mechanism is likely to lead to pressures on the revenue side, one would expect these to be balanced by the cost benefits accruing from technological improvements, increasing PLFs, execution efficiencies and enforceable payment security mechanisms.

To conclude, the wind power segment is surely undergoing a transition. Competitive bidding has definitely brought along issues, especially pertaining to transmission and uneven state-wise growth, but it may prove beneficial in the long run. It has brought the power utilities, nodal agencies and developers on a common platform to resolve offtake challenges, and once this issue is sorted, the segment will move to better utilization of evacuation capacity. It will also address the issue of skewed growth across states. The introduction of solar-wind hybrids and battery storage will further add up to higher utilization. Low tariffs, meanwhile, will ensure better efficiencies and optimum utilization of resources by developers. New sub-segments such solar-wind hybrids and offshore will also create greater opportunities for developers and OEMs. As far as the 60 GW target is concerned, 2022 seems too early to achieve it as there are several short and medium term issues that need to be resolved. Till these are addressed, it will not be feasible to achieve the target on time.

Solar Energy: Photovoltaics

1 Technology of PV-Modules: Current Status and Economic Assessment

Jörg Böttcher

1.1 Photovoltaic Projects

We will mainly describe in this section how solar irradiation is converted directly into electricity. Photovoltaic (PV) is the conversion of light into electricity, which uses the photovoltaic effect.

Photovoltaic (PV) makes out about 1.2% of energy production worldwide, whereas the national quota is sometimes significantly higher.[1] The main driver of the PV-industry has been the adoption of feed-in tariff regimes in several countries (see 1.6). The decrease of feed-in tariffs has led to a sharp decrease of overall PV project's costs as well as the Levelized Costs of Energy (see 1.10), which makes this form of energy production quite attractive for a number of countries.

We will describe in the following sections the technology as well as a number of economic effects which may describe the chances and the risks in PV-projects within the next few years.

1.2 Energy-Economic Importance

The solar irradiance at the Earth's surface would be more than sufficient to cover the global need of energy. Therefore, the solar energy offers enormous potential. Although PV-applications only reach 1,000 full load hours in Germany, the direct use of solar energy still requires subsidies in those countries. The requirement for state-support vanishes with higher energy yield and lower module costs.

One major advantage of PV-technology is the fact, that also scattered radiation can be used for the production of electricity. Figure 1.1 shows that scattered radiation has some importance in temperate zones.

The main advantages of photovoltaics are:

- Low complexity of technology,
- Low maintenance of technology,
- Low volatility of irradiation,
- High scalability,

1 In Germany, currently 7% of electricity demand is covered by PV. On a global scale, Photovoltaics is now – after hydro and wind power – the third most important energy source in terms of globally installed capacity.

https://doi.org/10.1515/9783110607888-028

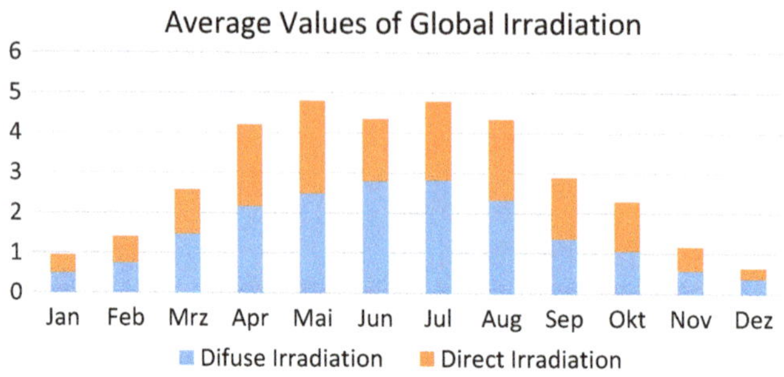

Figure 1.1: Average values of global irradiation.

However, the following disadvantages have to be considered:

- Low efficiency of the PV-cells,
- Use of scarcely resources (rare earth)
- Energy-intensive process of production

From a lender's perspective, PV-projects offer a low risk profile, which makes them attractive for project financings.

There are further technologies which can be used within the context of solar energy – especially the different forms of solar thermal collectors and CSP (concentrated solar power).[2]

1.3 Technical Solutions

The photo-electric effect was discovered in the year 1887 by Heinrich Hertz and Wilhelm Hallwachs. The photo-electric effect is the emission of electrons – called photo electrons – when light falls on a material. This effect is used in PV-cells for electricity production. PV-cells consist of a lattice pattern semiconductor-material, in most cases of solar grade silicon. Radiation, which penetrates this material, can remove electrons out of the structure. In order to direct the free electrons into one direction, which generates an electric current, an electric field has to be present. This requires that during their manufacture, the semiconductor material of the solar cells is deliberately contaminated with impurities. Within a semiconductor-structure consisting of silicon-cells a small part of the silicon-atoms is exchanged on the upper side with arsenic atoms and on the bottom side with indium atoms. The upper side is then the n-type semiconductor, and the bottom side is the p-type semiconductor. Metallic conductors are placed on the front side and on the back

2 See the chapter by Andreas Wiese [see section 1] and Jörg Böttcher (2011).

side, which collect the electricity. Whereas the rear electrode covers the whole cell, the semiconductor on the front has to allow the entry of light into the semiconductor. The following Figure 1.2 shows the schematic structure of silicon-cell.

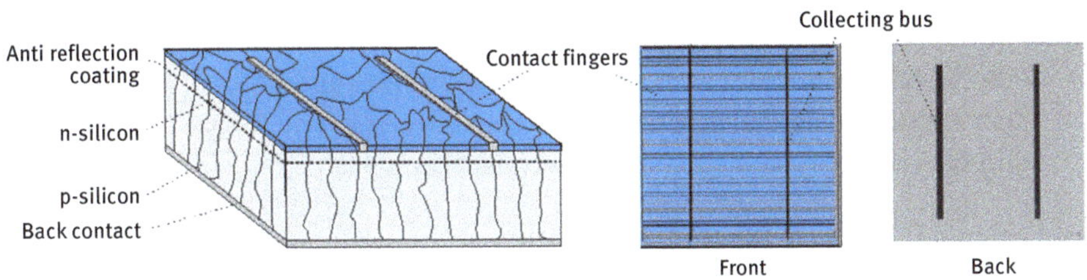

Figure 1.2: Crystalline Silicon Solar cells (SOLPEG AG).

The operating behavior of a solar cell is described by its current voltage-characteristic (I-U-characteristic). U is the voltage, and I is the current rating, measured in Amperes. Two points of this characteristic describe the case of short circuit ($U = 0$, $I = I_{SC}$) and the idling-case ($U = U_{OC}$). The power output P is the product of voltage and current rating ($P = I * U$).

The characteristics of PV-cells depend on the spectral distribution and the intensity of the solar radiation. Whereas the voltage only varies little with the intensity of radiation, the radiation has an high impact on shortcircuit current. The output P of a PV-cell rises on a linear basis with radiation, see Figure 2.5. According to Figure 2.5 the voltage of the PV-cell is lower than 1 Volt. To achieve higher voltages, several PV-cells must be connected in series to a PV string. The combined voltage of n PV-cells in series is:

$$U_{total} = U_1 + U_2 + \ldots + U_N$$

Since all combined PV-cells show the same current I, the combined voltage are prone to failure. The reduction of the power of one cell reduces the power of the whole PV-string accordingly. And a total failure of one PV-cell the whole string provides no current. This means, that it is not advisable to combine all PV-cells in a series connection, but to connect several PV-strings in parallel. A parallel connection of PV-moduls leads to a uniform voltage U for all modules, whereas the total current I Total and therefore the total power is the total of the individual values:

$$I_{Total} = I_1 + I_2 + I_N \text{ as well as } P_{Total} = P_1 + P_2 + P_N$$

A parallel connection can provide current, even when a whole PV-string is in failure.

The name plate capacity of PV-systems [kWp] is related to standard test conditions (STC): irradiation of 1000 W/m^2, airmass AM 1, and cell temperature of 25 C.

In typical operation mode, solar cells will show a higher temperature leading to a lower efficiency. This is especially the case in summer months. PV-simulation programs will usually take care of this effect as well as the ongoing degradation of PV cells.

Solar cells are available in different technical concepts. The most common ones are:
- Polycrystalline modules with efficiencies between 13 and 15%,
- monocrystalline modules with efficiencies between 14 and 20%,
- thin-film modules with efficiencies between 5 and 9%,

The efficiencies rates seem to be low. For practical questions, the costs have to be taken into account.

PV-systems generate direct current. Inverters are required to convert the direct current to alternating current and thereby make the electricity usable. For the feeding into the public European net a voltage of 230 Volt and a frequency of 50 Hertz are required. There are three inverter types available:
- Solar micro-inverters: Those micro-inverters are offered for solar module output up to 1,4 kWp. An isolation transformer is a safety measure.
- String inverters are several PV-modules which are connected in series. They provide high voltages and have some problems amid partial shadow.
- Central inverters are inexpensive inverters with a high efficiency. Their main disadvantage is, that a failure within a string leads to a failure of the whole system.

The process of transfer from the direct current to changing current leads to losses of 3% up to 7%. N most countries, new PV-installations must be fully controlled from remote by the grid operator.

1.4 Planning of PV-Projects

Typically, PV-projects are planned via ED-programs.

The expected annual global radiation plays an important role. There are many experts available who are in a position to calculate the annual energy yield with a high degree of certainty.

Irradiation and Temperature Data

For the assessment of the irradiation data sources, experts often consider the following criteria (see Table 1.1).

As a first step, different data sources are available:

Table 1.1: Meteorological data sources (own representation).

Item	Solar GIS	PVGIS	Satel-Light (SL)
Covered Region	Europe, Africa, Asia, Brazil, West Australia	Europe, Africa, parts of South-West Asia	Europe
Satellites	Depending on the region (satellite data coverage)	Depending on the region (satellite data coverage)	Based on the meterological satellite METEOSAT
Temporal Coverage	1994–2019	Monthly Global Irradiation Data	1996–2017
Space Resolution	Meteosat, < 3 km	Europe: 566 stations, interpolation: 1×1 km^2	about 5×7 km^2
Time Resolution	Hourly	Long-term monthly averages	30 minute intervals

PVGIS (Photovoltaic Geographical Information system) is a research, demonstration and policy-support instrument for solar energy resource, part of the SOLAREC action at the JRC Renewable Energies unit of the European Communities (Ispra). PVGIS provides a large and accurate solar radiation free database for Europe, Africa Mediterranean Basin and South West Asia. It is used as tool to estimate the solar electricity production of photovoltaic (PV) system. PVGIS delivers the annual output power of solar photovoltaic panels. The model algorithm estimates beam, diffuse and reflected components of the clear sky and real-sky global irradiance/ irradiation on horizontal or inclined surfaces.

Satel-light results from a European Project Team, which has used data from the METEOSAT Geostationary satellites, and provides detailed irradiance time series in half-hourly values for five complete years (1996 to 2000) and for any pixel of about 5x7 km^2 in Europe. These data are prepared, involving complex treatment of multiple satellite photographies in several wavelengths.

SolarGis is an industry standard and a well recognized source for solar historical, recent and forecast data. It offers solar data calculated fom Meteosat MSG and MFG satellite data and from atmospheric data by Solargis method. The datasets include hourly time series for GHI, DHI, air temperature and wind speed. State-of-art solar irradiance models as Solargis make use of modern input data (satellite and atmospheric), which are systematically quality-controlled and validated. Models and input data are integrated and regionally adapted to perform reliably at a wide range of geographical conditions. Today SolarGis is considered one of the most reliable sources for the modeling of irradiation data.

The following Figure 1.3 shows the different irradiation sources for a typical German location:

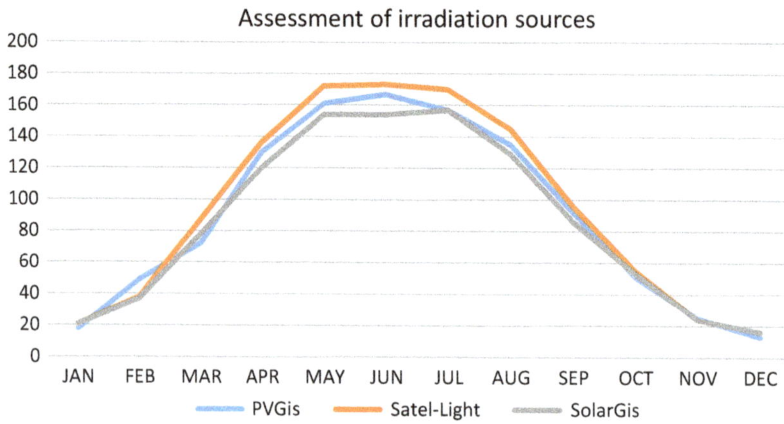

Figure 1.3: Comparison among pre-selected irradiation sources (own representation).

1.5 System Losses between PV Module and Feed-In Point

Typically, a solar expert will make a site visit and analyze the following items (see Table 1.2):

Table 1.2: Outcome of a site inspection (own representation).

Evaluation of the shading situation	
Natural Obstacles	No natural obstacles were identified within the buildable area. The terrain is yet to be fenced.
Tilts and Slopes on the Ground	The terrain is mostly flat. According to the values logged during site assessment, the terrain has an average altitude of 300 m. The surface affected by constraints (HVTL, public roads, and service areas) within the buildable area is about abc 16,000 m^2.
Horizon Analysis	The limiting effect on the radiation due to horizon shading is marginal.
Near Shading	The PV site is located next to the highway. There are two high voltage transmission line towers within the project site. These high elements (average height: app. 36 m) will project a shadow on top of the modules throughout the year.

Table 1.2 (continued)

Topographic Survey	
Surface Boundaries	Typically, here the boundary coordinates are stated. Waypoints are marked to evaluate altitude, slope and position of the boundary lines, service areas and natural constraints.
Natural Water Drainage / streams	The climate characteristics of the region result in rainfall throughout the year, with cool summers and cool winters.
Ground Preparation for the Execution Phase	During the erection phase, the use of neighboring areas for logistic purposes and temporary storage is (not) allowed.
Final net PV surface as a result of the above mentioned points	The GPS coordinates taken at site and the constraints due to legal, public and utility issues the final net buildable area is 100,000 m^2.
Risks	
Water drainage channels	Water drainage tunnels should be built to avoid damage to the PV plant. Erosion of the mounting structure pillars might be an issue.
Additional PV Surface Area	No additional surface area will be required for the plant. The integral design will include temporal storage areas for activities during construction phase.
Tree Stumps	The vegetation of any project is an essential aspect. The aim is to ensure that the associated impacts of the project development will be minimized to guarantee that the immediate and near environment will not be endangered. A social and environmental assessment has been carried out accordingly.
Social Impact Assessment	This aspect refers to the acceptability of the project by the neighborhood or host communities. An exhaustive stakeholder consultation should be executed to ensure that all interested parties have the opportunity to provide input into the project planning process.
Soiling	Based on the site conditions, cleaning with fresh water may become an expensive solution for soiling problems. Accurate soiling measurements are suggested to assess optimal cleaning procedures (if required).

Apart from the global radiation on-site the horizontal and vertical inclination of the PV-modules play an important role. Usually, their inclination is constant. However, PV-tracking systems are available in many forms. Our experience is that the advantage of an increase in yield of up to 30% (2-axes) is often fully compromised by the higher investment and operating costs.

It seems obvious, that shadowing plays an important role in the assessment of the solar field and also the changes which might or will occur within the next 20 years. Therefore, a site visit of the solar expert is highly recommended.

Rooftops are in many jurisdictions a special asset class which show several advantages, like space-saving and direct use nearby the customer. However, the following aspects have to be considered:

- Statics and the substance of the building,
- Fire protection,
- Insurance issues,
- Legal issues, when the owner of the building and the owner of the rooftop-installation are different persons,
- A roof renovation has to be planned in order to minimize costs for dismantling and refitting.

These hints are hints only. The following subsection shows some examples of the economic world.

1.6 Markets for PV-Installations

The potential solar energy that can be used differs with factors like geography, time variation, cloud cover and air pollution. Areas that are closer to equator have a greater amount of solar radiation (see Table 1.3):

Table 1.3: Examples of irradiation in different countries (own representation).

	Netherlands	Bavaria (Germany)	Italy (center)	Aquitaine (France)	South Spain	Egypt
Usable Irradiation	963	1050	1387	1430	1834	2400

Since 2004, the installed capacity of PV-installations has experienced an enormous rise. In the beginning, the vast majority of installed capacity was concentrated in Germany, followed by Spain in 2004. Further countries followed quickly, showing a development which is similar to the development in the onshore wind markets.

The dynamic of the PV-markets is astounding: Whereas Germany and Spain dominated the market up to 2010, the US and especially China are nowadays the countries with the highest amount of installed PV-capacity (see Figure 1.4).[3]

3 The installed capacity in China was 131.1 GW by the end of 2017.

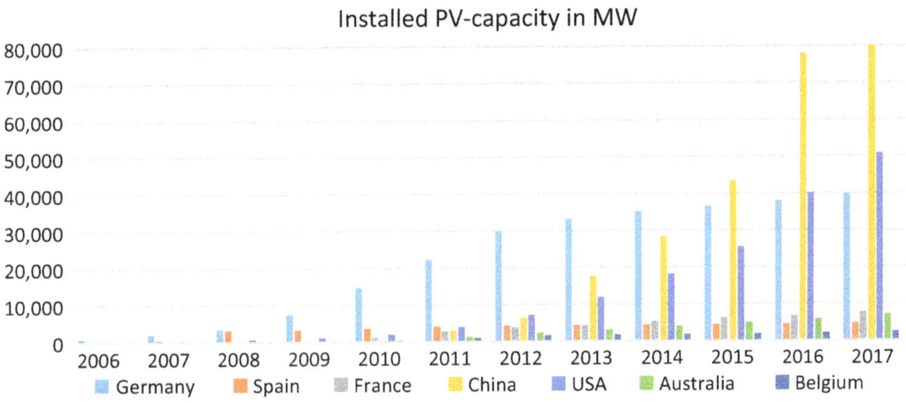

Figure 1.4: Development of installed PV-capacity (own representation).

Initially, the growth of the PV-market was driven by fixed feed-in tariff systems, which can be seen in the following Figure 1.5. There we have shown the market in Germany with its feed-in tariff-system starting in 2003: Germany started its deployment of ground-based PV-systems with an initial tariff of 45.7 Cent/kWh, which lead to the realization of a number of PV-projects, especially in the Eastern part of Germany and Bavaria.

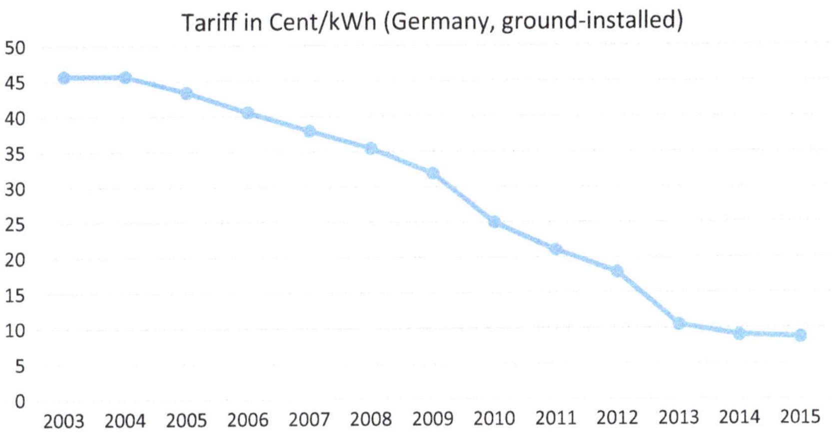

Figure 1.5: Development of Feed-in tariff in Germany (ground-installed) (own representation).

The first PV-farms were erected in the 2003 and large-scale ground-installed projects followed in the next few years.[4] In a time span of 12 years, the German legislator has decreased the tariffs to 8.7 cents/kWh in 2015. Afterwards, the legislator changed the regulatory system to a tender process.

1.7 Photovoltaics and Specific Energy Yield

Quite interesting is the development of the **Specific Energy Yield** ("SEY") – that is the quota of energy yield and installed capacity. This figure may give some information about the progress in technology. We have derived the figures from numerous ground-installed projects in Germany, Spain, Italy and France (see Table 1.4).[5]

The first graph (1. SEY) of Figure 1.6 shows how much energy can be produced at a given site with 1 MW of installed PV-capacity. The ratio is between 0.95 and 2.1. The quota basically reflects the usable solar irradiation on-site, so this figure needs to be adjusted in the second step. Therefore, the SEY is further divided by the usable irradiation on-site. Basically, we can see that the revised quota is close to 1.0 with almost no changes occurring during the 14 years under review. This is at least an indication that the technical progress has been limited in the period under review.

However, some efficiency improvements have occurred in the recent years, but those are related to higher efficiency of a project, so that less space is needed for the same capacity. Especially the temperature coefficient has been improved, whereas no progress under weak lighting conditions has occurred. Many designs of nowadays PV projects accept higher shading losses to allow for more capacity on-site. This approach has become quite familiar due to the fact that the module prices have dropped significantly while the costs for the land have risen slightly.

1.8 Photovoltaics and the Development of Total Investment Costs

Another quite interesting aspect is the **development of the total investment cost** in the period under review. Again, we have analyzed a number of real project

4 A number of special FIT were available for different types of installations and sizes. We are referring to ground-mounted PV-projects with a capacity of typically more than 10 MW.

5 We eliminated any project with a tracking system to allow a comparison of stationary ground-installed PV-projects only. According to our experience, a tracking system will effectively increase the performance: A two-way-tracing may lead to an increase of up to 40%, whereas a single-tracking system may lead to an increase of up to 20%. However, the PV-projects we have seen so far have not shown an economic benefit for the capital providers, since the total investment costs have been respectively higher.

Table 1.4: Specific Energy Yield of different PV-Projects (own representation).

	2003	2004	2007	2008	2009	2010	2011	2012	2014	2015	2016	2017
1. SEY: Specific Energy Yield (GWh/MW)	0,950	1,395	1,100	2,055	2,067	1,917	1,946	0,957	1,218	1,732	1,358	1,423
2. SEY/Usable Irradiation	0,905	1,127	0,998	1,001	1,181	1,045	1,014	0,964	0,966	1,000	0,979	0,995

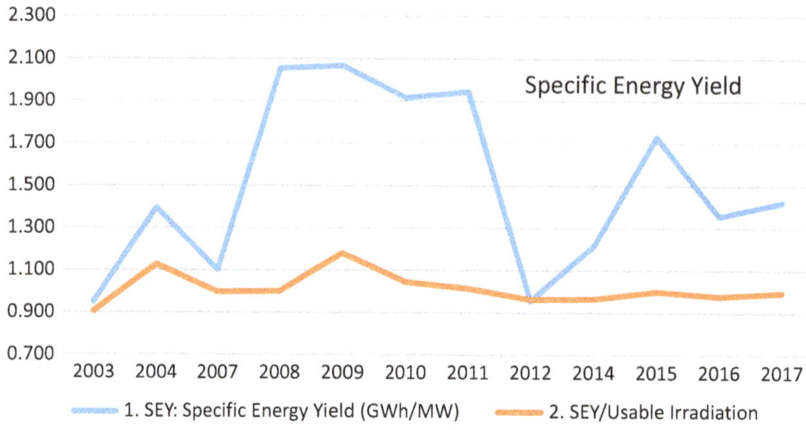

Figure 1.6: Specific Energy Yield of PV-Projects (own representation).

financings in PV. In order to make the different projects comparable we have adjusted them to a hypothetical 20 MW capacity. The basic results are shown in the following Table 1.5.[6]

Especially the relation "Specific Investment Cost" (row 6) and "Specific investment cost/irradiation/" (row 7) give some interesting insight into the mechanics of the PV-market. The basic results are shown in the following Figure 1.7.

Although now several European countries are included, the overall development of tariffs is quite similar: Up to the year 2010, we have seen Feed-In Tariffs around 40 cents/kWh, which have decreased gradually to a value below 10 cents/kWh in 2017. This is basically in line with the development we have already shown in Figure 1.5.

1.9 Relationship of Total Investment Costs and Applicable Tariff

The interesting point is the development of the **relation between total investment costs and applicable tariff (SIQ)**: The quota is shown in Figure 1.7 above (No. 6). The graph shows clearly that the development of the total investment costs is a linear function to the applicable tariff. This means that a drop in the tariff of 10% has led to a drop in total investment costs of also 10%.

This relationship also explains why in some cases PV-projects were realized in only very few countries: With the introduction of the "Regimen Special" in Spain in 2004, the Spanish investors were in a position to pay almost the double amount for the

6 Now projects from different countries are included: G (Germany), E (Spain), I (Italy) and F (France).

Table 1.5: Development of Total Investment Costs (own representation).

	G	G	E	E	I	I	F	G	F	F	G	G
	2003	**2004**	**2007**	**2008**	**2009**	**2010**	**2011**	**2012**	**2013**	**2014**	**2015**	**2017**
1. Energy Yield in GWh	19,008	21,994	41,103	38,913	34,633	27,150	28,454	19,132	30,537	24,353	19,940	20,125
2. Usable PV–irradiation	1050	1102	2054	1918	1731	1387	1430,3	992	1570	1260	964	988
3. Tariff in cents/kWh	43,4	45,7	44,04	44,04	43,28	42	32,98	22,07	11,4	10,51	8,73	6,35
4. Total Investment Costs in M€	86,835	97,908	182,356	163,436	123,810	100,000	71,983	43,477	32,918	25,699	20,500	22,645
5. OPEX-quota	12,29%	14,39%	17,72%	11,97%	11,12%	19,25%	11,94%	15,25%	21,79%	21,57%	13,61%	26,80%
6. Total Investment costs/Tariff/ Installed capacity ("Specific Investment Cost")	0,905	0,998	1,001	1,014	1,000	0,979	0,995	0,964	0,973	0,966	1,034	1,018
7. 6./Usable PV-irradiation	0,953	0,972	1,008	0,967	0,826	0,858	0,763	0,993	0,920	0,970	1,218	1,805

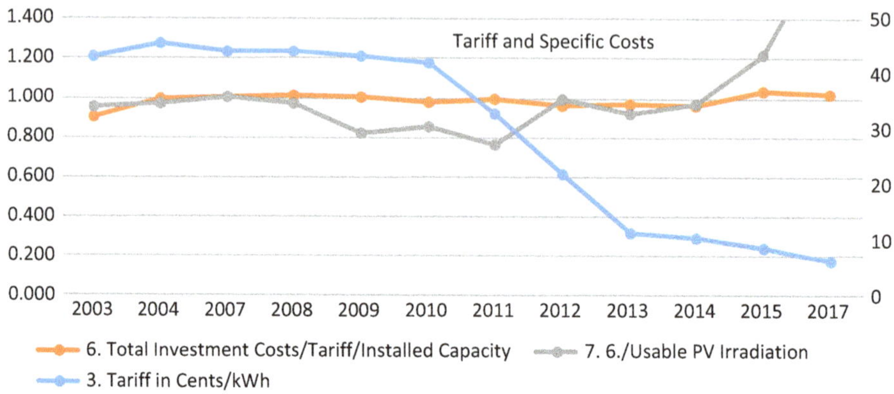

Figure 1.7: Development of Tariffs and Specific Costs (own representation).

same capacity compared to Germany: The tariffs were quite similar – 43.4 cents/kWh in Germany compared to 44.04 cents/kWh in Spain – and a quite different value of usable irradiation – roughly 1.000 kWh/kWp in Germany compared to 1,900 kWh/kWp in Spain. Not surprisingly, also the total investment costs in Spain were roughly 90% higher compared to Germany. Thus, the regulatory regime introduced a strong incentive to invest in Spain and consequently, the German market for large ground-based PV-projects was no longer existing for several years.

Another insight can be derived from the relation "**SIQ/PV-irradiation**" (graph 7): Here we can see that the ratio decreases slightly after the year 2008, before it comes back at the old level after four years. My suggestion for this development is that in the wake of the financial crisis banks were more reluctant to finance long-term project financings, so that the financing needs to show a better relation between investment costs and tariff, thus resulting in a higher robustness. This requirement was no longer existing as the financial market recovered. The increase in this quota in the year 2015 stems from some German projects: As this point in time, the market participants knew that a change in the regulatory framework in Germany would occur. Yet, the impact on the market and the side conditions were still unknown. Therefore, the lenders accepted less favorable terms – as measured in the quota of total investment cost and tariff – given that they felt still comfortable with this asset class.

The **development of the OPEX-quota** (Figure 1.8, OPEX/income, left column) shows a higher volatility compared to the development of the quota of "total investment costs/tariff." Still, the influence of the tariff development on the opex-quota is existing: In the period under review, a decrease in tariff has led to a decrease in operating expenses. Given the sample of projects – all with an installed capacity of more than 5 MW – the quota of opex has not been influenced by the size of the projects.

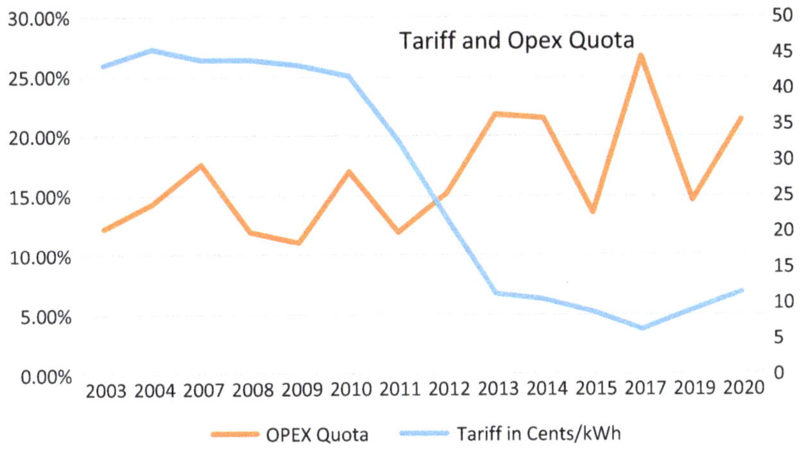

Figure 1.8: Tariff Development and Opex-Quota (own representation).

1.10 Solar Energy and LCOE

The **Levelized Costs of Energy** (LCOE) is the net present value of the electricity costs over the lifetime of a generating asset. It includes a number of costs over its lifetime – especially the initial investment and all operating costs as numerator and the total electricity output of the asset as denominator. All of these values are calculated on a net present value basis, which adequately reflects the cost of capital. The LCOE is often taken as a proxy for the average price that the generating asset must receive in a market to break even over its lifetime. The LCOE metric is widely used, since it offers a simple method to calculate the cost per unit of electricity for a given asset. And it seems fit and adequate for a calculation of these costs as long as it takes into consideration also the integration costs and the system costs of the energy under review.

The development of the LCOE in this sample shows the following characteristic according to Figure 1.9 (costs are nominated in cents/kWh).

According to the project contracts within the different project financings, we see an overall significant decrease of LCOE in PV-projects.[7] This mainly reflects the decrease both of total investment costs and operating expenses, which is – as stated above – directly linked to the overall decrease in tariff. The sample of the last five years consists of projects in Germany and the Netherlands, which means that the costs of ground-based PV-projects in those countries is close to 7.5 cents/kWh and further decreasing.

7 The peak in 2010 results from some Italian projects which have shown an opex-quota which is 50% higher than comparable European projects. The main driver here are local and national taxes.

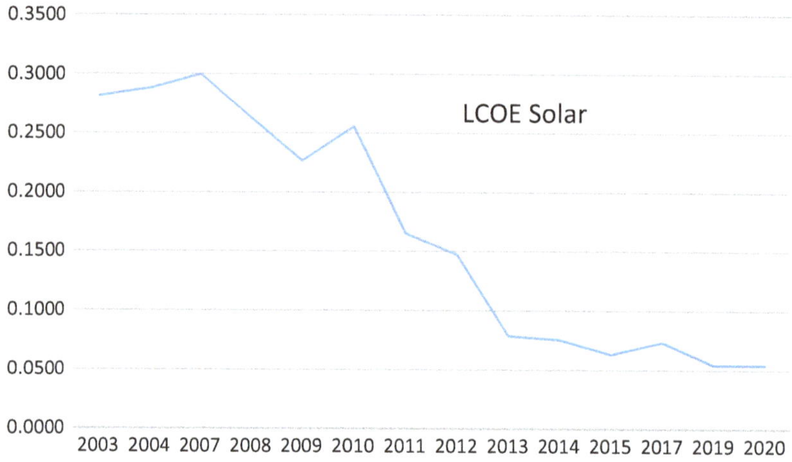

Figure 1.9: LCOE in PV-projects (own representation).

The decrease of the total investment costs has led to another trend in financing of PV projects: Whereas in the beginning only larger banks were willing to finance larger PV-projects, the decrease of total investment costs as well as the emergence of a track record of existing PV-projects has led to the emergence of smaller banks which are now also financing PV-projects. However, given that the project volume has decreased considerably, the scope of the due diligence process has also been reduced considerably since the costs cannot be borne by smaller projects. Since a full due diligence process has always been a requirement of the financing process of the larger banks, a number of these banks were no longer able to finance PV-projects.

Additionally, a comparison of the LCOE with the applicable tariff give some additional insight (see Figure 1.10).

Since 2012, LCOE Solar and applicable tariff show a high degree of matching, both in terms of development as well as in the absolute amount. This shows that – at least from 2012 – a WACC of 4% seems to be a commonly used rate.[8] Potentially an information, which should be kept in mind when assessing a regulatory regime.

The onshore wind market in Germany shows a slightly different picture: Up to the year 2017, WACC has been slightly higher than 4% for projects. Afterwards, the regulatory system has been amended which has led to a decrease in the WACC.[9]

---

8 However, up to the year 2012, the tariff is significantly higher than 4%. This means that the WACC was considerable higher than 4%.

9 The German EEG 2017 has two important features in this respect: First, the support regime changed from a Feed-In Tariff System to a Tender Process, which has led to a decrease in investment and operating costs. Additionally, for Onshore-wind projects a Cashflow-stabilizing mechanism has been implemented by an adjustment of the project specific tariff every five years. This

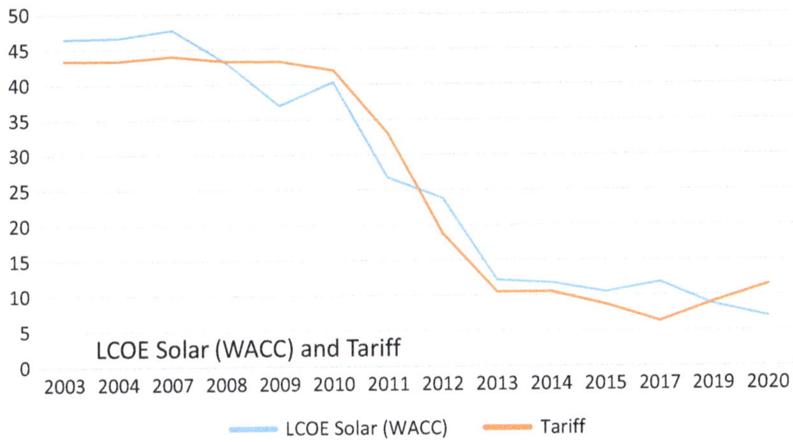

Figure 1.10: Comparison of LCOE Solar and Applicable Tariff (own representation).

In contrast, we have compared the development of the LCOE of the PV-market with the figures of the onshore-wind market in Germany. The results are shown in the following Figure 1.11:

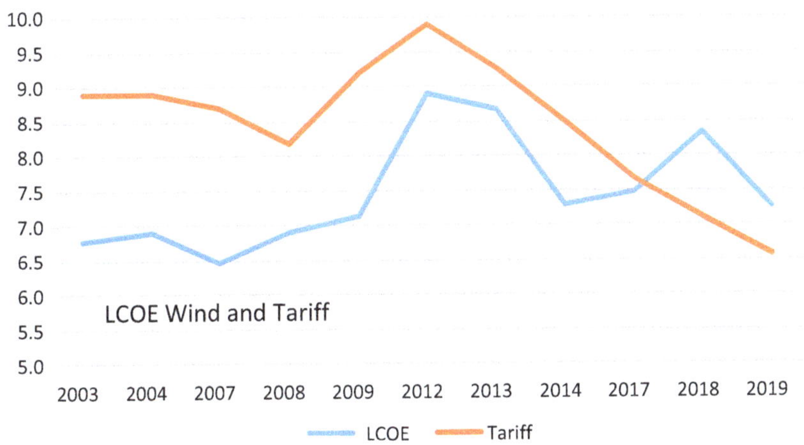

Figure 1.11: LCOE for PV- and Onshore Wind Projects (own representation).

Whereas the LCOE-values for the PV-markets have fallen considerably to a current level of 7.5 cents/kWh, the LCOE-values for onshore wind projects have remained

means that competition as well as the awareness of a more or less stable income have reduced the requirements regarding the WACC.

almost stable at a level of Ø 7.0 cents/kWh over 18 years. This means that onshore wind energy and photovoltaics have in the meantime reached a tipping point, since their LCOE is already close or below those of conventional energy.

This development seems to remain stable for the forthcoming years, as can be seen by the following Figure 1.12:

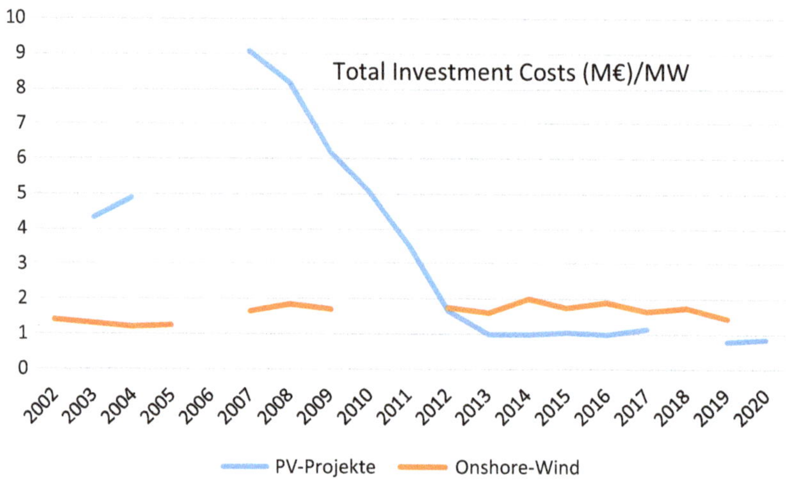

Figure 1.12: Development of Total Investment Costs/MW (own representation).

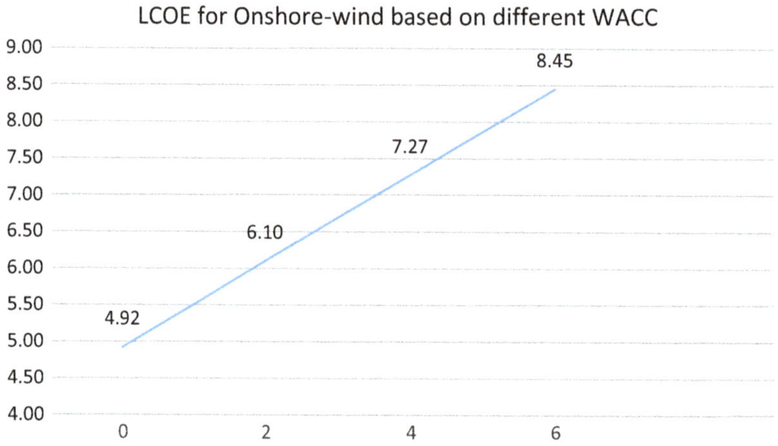

Figure 1.13: LCOE for Onshore-Wind (own representation).

Whereas the total investment costs for onshore wind energy are within a range of 1.2 M€/MW and 2.0 M€/MW, this ratio has fallen for PV-projects considerably from 9.0 M€/MW in the boom years in Spain to 1 M€/MW in the last few years. Again, this development is triggered by the development of the applicable tariff.

Obviously, the level of assumed WACC has an enormous impact on the LCOE, as can be seen in the following Figure 1.13.

The Figure 1.13 shows the LCOE (cents/kWh) for onshore-wind projects with different levels of WACC. For example, an expected WACC of 6% p.a. results in LCOE of 7.87 cents/kWh. This means that a regulator has to keep in mind that the current level of WACC is adequately reflected in the tariff to allow investment in this asset class. If a WACC of 4% should work as an adequate proxy for the WACC, nowadays a typical onshore wind farm in Germany should receive a remuneration of at least 6.96 cents/kWh.

2 Energy Yield Assessment for Photovoltaic Systems

André Schumann

2.1 Introduction

2.1.1 General Methods and Resources for PV Yield Assessments

This article is a more detailed and current version of prior publications by the author (Schumann 2015) (Schumann 2016 "State"). It discusses the various parameters, models and external data sources that need to be considered and processed for a reliable energy yield assessment of a photovoltaic (PV) system. In most cases simulation software is used for the calculation of the expected energy production. But simulation software is just a tool that gives a broad spectrum of possible results depending on the input by the user. It hence needs expertise, experience, independence and transparency to achieve a reliable outcome. In order to ensure transparency the whole process has to be described in a way that another experienced person can fully understand how the result has been obtained. In addition the key factors should also be understandable for laymen. This description is called yield analysis report. There are several other expressions with the same meaning such as yield report, yield study, yield assessment or energy (sales) forecast report. This text will mainly use the expression yield report and will just focus on grid-connected PV systems.

As any documentation a yield report should be clearly structured. The first sections should describe the task and the given situation, hence dealing with the location, the technical system and the most important components. Then the report should continue with the selected methods and data to fulfill the task, mainly the meteorological input data as well as the selected models and simulation approaches. The presentation of the results and uncertainties should be the final part of the document. It is best practice to combine the description of the methods with the corresponding partial results of each step on the way to the final result. Nevertheless the report should have a separate section in which all results are summarized.

2.1.2 Motivation and Use of Independent Expertise

As a yield report is a written opinion about the expected energy yield, it is important to obtain this magnitude from well experienced and independent parties because it represents the income of the project. If the other fixed and running costs are known the energy yield determines the return on investment and payback time. This goes hand in hand with the financial risk of a project and the financing conditions.

https://doi.org/10.1515/9783110607888-029

The determination of the energy yield is needed at several stages of project phases. A first assessment is often demanded already in the early project development phase. The calculation should be updated with any change of the system concept and specifications, ending with a review as built. If a project is sold after several years of operation a new issued yield analysis allows the integration of the monitored system behavior as well as possibly changed environmental conditions or even new meteorological data and simulation methods.

The following section describes the recommended structure of a yield report pointing out the options and particularities of each topic in detail.

2.2 Yield Assessment Process

2.2.1 Characterization of the Site Influences

The local conditions at the project site and its surroundings can influence the energy production of a PV system. Thus, besides a general description of the location, the site has to be specified as exact as possible regarding the following yield relevant aspects. The character of the surrounding terrain, vegetation and buildings as well as the kind of installation of the PV system may influence the wind conditions inside the PV field and the ventilation conditions of the PV modules. The efficiency of the modules is depending on the operating temperature which is influenced by the exposure to airflow. The mentioned surroundings may not just cause wind but also sunlight shadings. Also the terrain inside the PV field is important because it can lead to different self-shading conditions of the module tables. The location should also be analyzed concerning influences that could lead to module surface soiling. E.g., there might be nearby emissions of dust and pollution, flight of pollens and leaves, erosion of dusty soil or population of birds that could cause droppings on the modules. Also special influences of the local atmosphere on module degradation should be documented like salty, acid, alkaline or humid air.

The reflectivity of the ground and surroundings which is characterized by the Albedo factor influences the irradiation in module plane and the rear side irradiation of bifacial PV modules. The most exact and independent evaluation of the location is obtained if the yield assessor visits the place.

Specialized equipment can be used to document the surrounding 360° far shading situation. An example is given in Figure 2.1. The red lines represent the sun paths over the year. The green line indicates the horizon shading line.

Laser measurement devices help to meter dimensions and distances of near shading objects. In addition the roof or terrain tilt can be checked independently. If a site visit by the assessor is not feasible a lot of information can also be gathered from geographic information tools. In addition pictures and topographic maps should be provided by the project development to obtain the best possible impression of the site.

Figure 2.1: Horizon profile recorded with special equipment (own representation).

2.2.2 Relevant Technical Aspects of the PV System

After the description of the place where the PV system is planned to be built its relevant technical properties should be characterized. It is common to give this information in tables. The main properties of a PV plant are its DC and AC power that result from the number and wattages of PV modules and grid inverters. The AC power may also refer to the final power at the grid connection point that might also be limited. The exact product types as well as series and parallel connection of the modules to the inverters should be listed. In this context it should be checked if the design complies with the maximal allowed system voltage (e.g., 1000 V) also at the lowest expected operating temperatures. Regarding the grid-connection voltage level, frequency, type and amounts of transformers are important information. The major electrical properties and all specifications that can be integrated in the simulation models of PV modules, inverters and transformers should be listed in separate tables. Besides the electrical components also the mechanical side of the system is of interest. The module orientation, mainly tilt and azimuth angle(s) or if applicable tracking angles, is relevant for the solar irradiance in module plane. The properties of the module installation like module alignment per table, row distances or roof mounting are essential regarding the self-shading and ventilation conditions.

If available further relevant system specifications like bifaciality, cable dimensioning, flashed module power, module cleaning concept, own consumption, or reactive power feeding should be listed.

The description of the photovoltaic system should also show figures of the module layout in top and possibly also side view.

2.2.3 Meteorological Resource Assessment

The solar irradiance is the fuel PV modules work with. Other meteorological parameters have a secondary influence on the yield. The verification of the used meteorological data set for the simulation is hence a major aspect in yield reports. The report should describe all considered data sources and meteorological parameters as well as the method to select the data for the yield simulation in a comprehensive and transparent way.

PV projects are often built at places where no long-term high quality ground measurements of the solar irradiation are available. In such situations irradiation data can be obtained by interpolation from surrounding ground stations or derived from geostationary satellite imagery of could coverage. There are diverse data providers for these kinds of services and it is not the intention of this work to give a general recommendation for a certain product. Benchmarking e.g., of satellite derived products is available from other authors, amongst others (Ineichen 2014). But findings of such studies should not be imprudently transferred to other places because selected stations for benchmarking are also often used as reference calibration points by the data providers. Thus it is always recommendable to research validation of a certain data product at the region under study. The data products also often offer different spatial resolution and averaging periods. Products with long and up-to-date averaging period as well as high spatial resolution should be preferred. Nevertheless it is often not possible to identify one data source as best suited if no reference measurements at the site are available. In such cases the statistical confidence can be increased if multiple data sources are weighted and averaged on monthly level. The weights of the single products should respect their averaging period, spatial resolution and general level of confidence (validation).

Figure 2.2 shows an exemplified graphical comparison of the kind, level and period of different irradiation data sources analyzed for a single location.

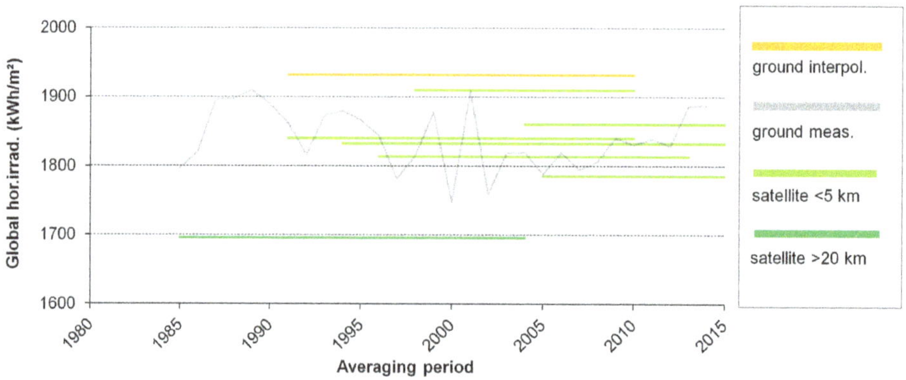

Figure 2.2: Graphical comparison of different irradiation data sources (own representation).

Also for reasons of transparency multiple data sources should be presented in the yield report. The use of just one data source is only accepted if it can clearly be proven as best choice, e.g., by comparison with high quality ground measurements.

In order to judge the quality of ground measurements it is not enough to know that the measurements are done with secondary standard equipment of low uncertainty. A proper and shading free installation as well as adequate maintenance and recalibration concept are of same importance. The judgment of ground measurements hence demands a detailed documentation of the station and its upkeep. If onsite or nearby ground measurements can be judged to be high quality often the interannual variability of the meteorological conditions combined with a too short measuring period bars the direct use of the measured data. But the measurements can be used to verify or calibrate other data products that provide data of the same period as well as long-term data. Calibration methods for satellite derived irradiation data have been published e.g., by (Mieslinger et al. 2014).

Regarding the solar energy the horizontal global and diffuse irradiation are mostly used as input data for the yield simulation. In case of tracking systems also direct normal irradiation is often used.

Irradiation data sets in spectral resolution and its computation in commercial yield simulation software are not common yet. But corresponding scientific work is available by (Müller et al. 2012), (Gracia et al. 2014) or (Huld and Gracia 2015) and results have implemented in version 5 of the Photovoltaic Geographical Information System by the Joint Research Center of the European Commission. A model by (Lee and Panchula 2016) that derives spectral response influences of different cell technologies considering air mass and secondary meteorological parameters like precipitable water or relative humidity has been recently implemented in commercial simulation software.

Other meteorological parameters that have a secondary influence on the yield of a PV system should also be described and discussed. For instance wind velocity and ambient temperature influence the solar cell's temperature which reduces the energy production when it rises. Concerning precipitation rain can clean the PV modules and reduce soiling losses whereas snow cover can stop the energy production.

Since a yield report aims to estimate the future production of a PV system also possible trends in the meteorological data should be respected and documented. Nevertheless the whole analysis can only be based on foretime data. This fact should be explicitly mentioned.

The yield report is supposed to present the analyzed and used meteorological data in monthly values. Regarding the accuracy of the yield simulation the original data is preferably available in higher temporal resolution.

2.2.4 Data Processing

After the meteorological input data is selected the simulation work starts. The requirement of at least hourly calculation steps demands programmed solutions. The simulation should hence be done with accepted and approved software tools. Again it is not the intension of this article to highlight one specific product. But it is important that the software is able to compute all important losses described in the following sections. Of course the yield assessor must be an expert in the use of the selected software. Its possibilities and limits should be well understood. It is also advantageous to know about the physical models the software is based on. Approved and accepted software products document the used methods and models for the different calculation steps. Typically these are no proprietary calculations and have been published in scientific papers. Theoretically the yield assessor could also use own programmed software. The advantage to use a commercial product is that the underlying principles are documented publicly and that a simple reference to the software is sufficient. In case of own programmed software a detailed documentation about the used methods has to be provided together with the yield report in order to ensure transparency. Commercial software with many users has also the advantage of quality control and reduced risks of software bugs.

The first task of the simulation software is the processing of the meteorological data. If the input data is only available in monthly values a (sub-)hourly dataset has to be synthesized (e.g., (Aguiar and Collares-Pereira 1992)). The (sub-)hourly horizontal diffuse and direct irradiation data is then transferred to the irradiation module plane. For this calculation several methods have been published (e.g., (Perez et al. 1990), (Hay and Davies 1978), (Gueymard 1987)). Also benchmarking of different methods exists (e.g., (Ineichen 2011)). The results of the models also depend on the meteorology. Some models perform better at clear sky, others better at cloudy conditions. In order to increase the statistical confidence the calculation should be done at least with two different methods and the results should be averaged. Only if a certain model is clearly validated as best choice for the specific climatic conditions at the project site it should be used exclusively. The level of irradiation in module plane is also strongly influenced by the ratio between direct and diffuse light since mainly the direct light is augmented. Hence, not only the selected transposition model but also the selected meteorological data source influences the results. In addition to atmospheric sunlight a tilted module plane also receives reflected sunlight. The reflectivity of the environment is described with the Albedo factor that should be documented in the report. For large-scale PV systems in row construction method the additional Albedo irradiation is majorly compensated by corresponding additional shading losses. But the Albedo factor is important for the calculation of the rear side illumination in case of bifacial PV systems. Besides ground reflected irradiation bifacial solar modules also receive sky diffuse and at some sun positions even direct sunlight (not in case of tracking systems) on the rear side.

The irradiation in module plane as well as the corresponding transposition factors (ratio between in plane and horizontal irradiation) should be presented in monthly values in the yield report.

All further simulation steps on the way to the final result should follow logically the way of the sunlight and the electrical current through the system. The first kinds of losses in this order are shading losses.

2.2.5 Determination of Irradiation Losses

Shading Analysis

Important and common losses in PV systems are often caused by shadings. Typically far shadings by the horizon and near shadings by close objects and neighboring PV module tables should be distinguished.

A horizon shading object is that big and far that typically the entire PV field is shaded from direct sunlight when the sun is behind the object (e.g., mountain). The horizon line due to surrounding elevation can be obtained from several software and online tools based on digital elevation models. A more exact approach is the above mentioned recording of the horizon line with special equipment that also allows the integration e.g., of actual woods or skylines. The computation of horizon losses is an easy task for the simulation software. It has just to decide if the defined horizon line is higher or lower than the sun position at a certain calculation step.

Concerning near shading the computation is usually complex and based on three dimensional modeling. Only in case of module table self shading on even terrain with homogenous table distances a simple two dimensional geometrical calculation can be done. In case of inhomogeneous self shading due to terrain and/or shadings by close objects like trees or buildings the situation has to be modeled in 3D as illustrated in Figure 2.3. Due to the series connection of solar cells and modules the electrically effected area is usually larger than the visible shadow. The simulation hence needs to be set in a way that the electrical and geometric connection of the module strings is respected and also the working point behavior of the connected maximum

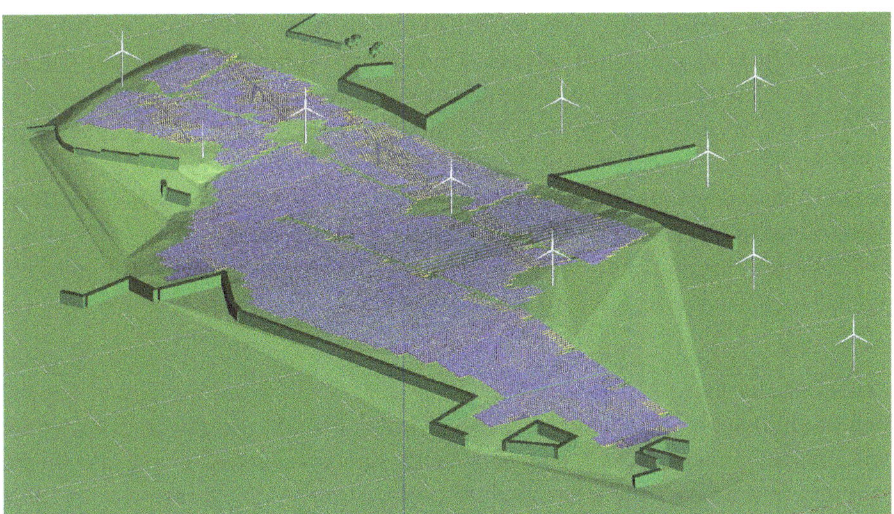

Figure 2.3: 3D model created to determine the self and near shading in a complex terrain (own representation).

power point tracker (MPPT, see inverter) is considered. In some systems even a module level MPPT needs to be considered in case of use of so called optimizers.

The report should describe the whole shading situation and the method to determine its effect on the yield in detail.

Soiling and Snow Losses

The influence of soiling depends on several factors. Besides the module inclination and meteorological effects (rain, wind) the conditions on and nearby the site are important to estimate the factor of soiling. In addition to natural rain manual cleaning should be considered if this is planned. Common simulation software usually just allows the subtraction of fixed monthly soiling losses defined by the user. These losses need to be assessed externally and the report should justify the settings. A method to assess soiling losses based on rainfall or cleaning events has e.g., been published by (Kimber et al. 2006) for different environments.

Despite the progress in researching soiling losses their exact prediction can still be a difficult task due to site-specific particularities. Thus it is highly recommended to monitor soiling losses at sites where soiling is expected to play a role e.g., due to aridness and dust. This monitoring can be realized by comparing the output of regularly cleaned and not cleaned reference modules or strings. Whenever the determined soiling rate exceeds the accepted tolerance manual cleaning can be indicated. In such a case the accepted soiling loss should be assumed as loss factor in the yield report.

Also snow cover losses can be treated as soiling losses in the simulation because common software does not offer automatic calculation of this factor as well. If snowfall data is not available periods of snow can be assessed based on (sub-)hourly temperature and precipitation data. Information like snow cover days can also be requested from local weather services. Usually snow drops off the module surface after some time even if the snow in the environment still does not melt. Depending on the amount of dropped snow and the distance to the ground snow may also pile up in front of the module tables. A model for snow loss assessment respecting this ground interference and the geometry of the module installation as well as divers meteorological parameters is available by (Townsend et al. 2011).

The used assumptions and methods for the snow loss assessment should be described transparently in the yield report.

Reflection Losses

Reflection losses at perpendicular incident irradiation are already included in the rated module power. But the part of reflected sunlight reflected is increasing with the incidence angle. Only a few module manufacturers publish this so called IAM (incidence angle modifier) behavior in their specifications. If such information is available the simulation software should be fed with the specific reflection profile. Otherwise a default behavior can be used and described in the report. Figure 2.4

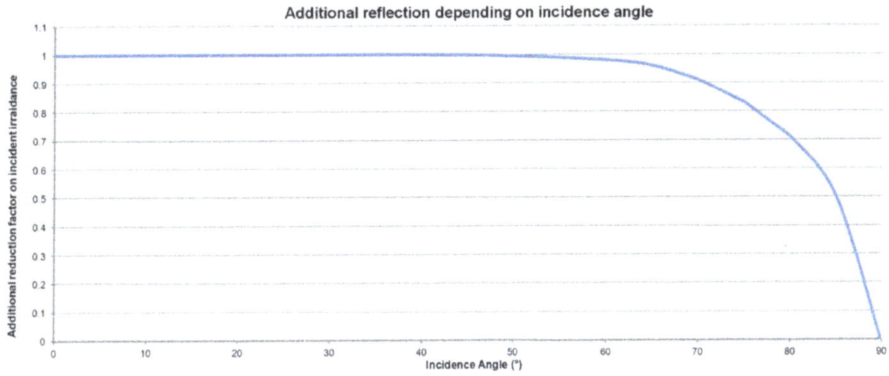

Figure 2.4: Typical reflection profile of a standard PV module (own representation).

illustrates a typical incidence angle depending reflection behavior averaged from divers independent laboratory tests of different standard PV modules.

2.2.6 Module Level Losses

Module Model

The simulation software should be able to model the behavior of the PV modules at various irradiance and temperature conditions. In order to receive reliable results the model should be set by the yield assessor. Only if detailed module specifications are available at various conditions this task can be fulfilled accurately. Common data sheets usually contain information at three different irradiance and two different temperature levels. In addition temperature coefficients of the electrical parameters are typically given. This information is generally sufficient for acceptable accurate models of crystalline silicon modules. If other module technology is used more detailed specifications are required. The report should prove the match of the simulation model with the specifications as exemplified in Figure 2.5 that shows representative measurements of the part load behavior.

Irradiation Level and Spectral losses

The module efficiency depends on the level of irradiation in module plane. Depending on the specified behavior of the module model and the simulated level of irradiance in module plane losses or gains with respect to the rated efficiency result on annual level. The report should document the losses or gains.

Additional losses or gains may result from the deviation of the real varying solar spectrum from the test spectrum AM 1.5. E.g., crystalline modules show higher efficiencies under clear sky with low sun heights. But under cloudy conditions the

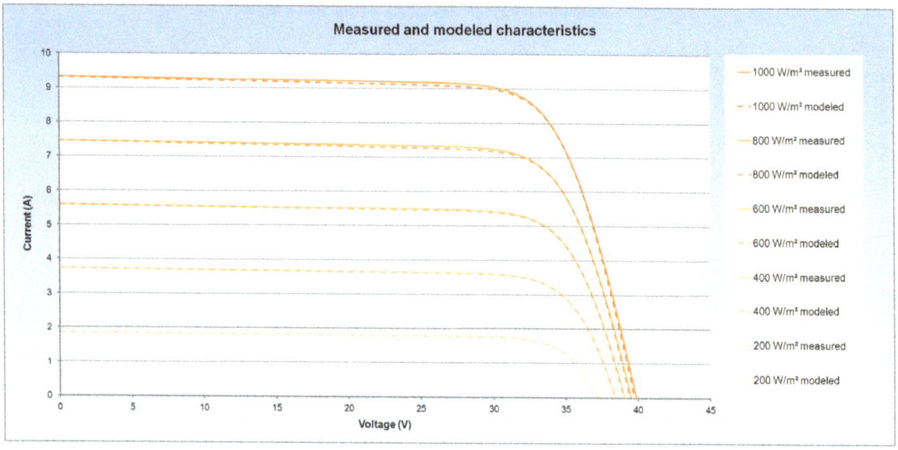

Figure 2.5: Measured and modeled characteristics of a standard PV module (own representation).

blueshift of the spectrum may cause efficiency reductions. Over the year positive and negative spectral effects often lead to no significant annual average loss for crystalline cell technology. For the majority of sites and orientations the effect is even slightly positive. For thin film technology spectral effects usually play a more important role. Tools and methods for the assessment of spectral effects have already been mentioned above in the section about meteorological resource assessment.

The yield report should discuss the spectral influence and possible effects on the result respecting the considered module technology.

Temperature Losses

With increasing cell temperature solar cells show a decrease in power (usually in the range of -0.4% per °C for crystalline silicon modules). Modules are rated at 25°C cell temperature. At normal operating conditions cell temperatures above 45°C are common because the part of the absorbed solar energy that cannot be converted to electricity is lost as heat. The temperature depending behavior is defined by the simulation model of the module (see above). In order to determine temperature depending losses the simulation software has to calculate the solar cell temperature on basis of the meteorological input data (irradiance, ambient temperature, wind velocity). Typically an equation that represents an energetic equilibrium of heating and cooling based on the thermal transmittance of a PV module is used. The thermal transmittance also depends on the ventilation of the module. Typically the transmittance to the front side is free because this surface has to collect the sunlight. The transmittance to the backside is depending on the installation conditions, a fact that has to be respected and documented in the yield assessment. If reliable wind data is available for the project side the cooling effect of the wind should be

respected in the calculation. Eventually the wind velocity needs to be transferred from a free measurement at a certain height above ground to the conditions around the modules inside a PV field. (Schumann et al. 2012) provides an approach for this calculation. In most cases reliable site specific wind data is not available. In such cases a conservative approach based on a low average wind velocity should be selected and documented.

The report should explain the approach to calculate the temperature losses. Besides the annual average temperature loss it is sometimes also demanded to present the monthly average and maximal module temperatures.

Module Quality and Degradation

The power of PV modules is typically given with a certain tolerance. These days only positive power tolerances are common. Assuming the nominal module power for the simulation is hence a conservative approach but could be compensated by low mismatch losses (see next section). If flasher protocols of the used modules are available the real average power of the modules can be determined (within the measurement tolerances). If this exceeds the nominal power a corresponding yield gain can be respected as module quality factor.

Different effects usually lead to a loss in module power of the installed modules compared to their condition in which they left the factory. These effects should be discussed and respected as initial degradation in the yield report. On cell level the so called light induced degradation is typical. In the first days crystalline modules (with p-cells) are exposed to sunlight the efficiency falls usually by approx. 1%. In addition shipping and mounting effects will always lead to a slight reduction in power (e.g., micro cracks) even if the modules are handled carefully.

In the history of photovoltaic several special degradation effects have been discovered and solved. Such effects are hardly predictable and hence have to be excluded in the yield report. Degradation phenomena that are already known since years but still current are PID (Potential Induced Degradation) and LeTID (Light and elevated Temperature Induced Degradation for solar cells with PERC technology). Guaranteed PID free and LeTID free modules are available.

After the light induced degradation the solar cell power usually stays stable. Only for solar cells affected by micro cracks a further reduction in power can be expected due to growth of the fractures under thermal and mechanical (wind and snow loads) stress. Other parts of the modules and system components may suffer long-term degradation e.g., due to corrosion of conducting elements, module glass and cell encapsulant (EVA browning). Such processes depend on the environmental conditions already mentioned above in the description of the location. As a contrary effect an inverter replacement in several years may result in a better efficiency of the new inverter (technical progress).

the DC wiring concept of the simulated system and the corresponding losses at nominal conditions and on annual average.

Inverter Losses

The inverters' main tasks are the so called MPP-tracking and the conversion of the direct current (DC) provided by the PV modules to grid-conform alternating current (AC). MPP tracking means that a working point (voltage level) at the DC side is regulated and continuously adjusted at which the maximum power is obtained from the PV generator (maximum power point, MPP). The inverter only offers a limited voltage range in which this task can be fulfilled. The yield report should document the typical operating voltage range of the connected modules and the offered MPP tracking voltage range by the inverter. Possible related losses have to be respected. Modern inverters usually find the MPP accurately and quickly within the specified voltage range. Losses due to MPP tracking accuracy are hence often negligible. The main inverter losses result from the DC-AC conversion efficiency which usually varies with the power and voltage level as illustrated in Figure 2.7. The simulation model of the considered inverter should reflect this behavior and the report should prove the match of the simulation model with the specifications including possible different properties of single inverter inputs.

Often electrical inverter specifications are given at different ambient respectively cooling air temperatures. If the simulation software is not able to reproduce this behavior the inverter model has to be defined for the expected average temperature conditions at the site.

Additional inverter losses occur if the PV modules deliver more power than the inverter is able to convert. These so called power limitation or clipping losses may occur in times of high irradiation and low module temperature depending on the ratio between maximum inverter power and module power. The report should mention this so called AC-DC ratio.

Power limitation losses cannot be determined in hourly simulation steps with sufficient accuracy. Especially during periods with changing irradiation conditions and cloud-enhancement effects hourly mean values do not display the reality. Additional power limitation losses should be respected manually and justified in the report as a consequence. (Schumann 2014) indicates power limitation losses at real conditions.

Depending on the local electricity grid it may be demanded that the PV system feeds-in at a certain phase angle. The reactive power portion to realize a certain power factor is assigned by the grid and only the active power portion represents the PV energy. Under consideration of the maximal apparent power of the inverter this mechanism has to be understood in the assessment of power limitation losses.

In some cases a maximum offered power by the PV system is contracted at the grid connection point. The compliance is usually realized by monitoring the PV

respected in the calculation. Eventually the wind velocity needs to be transferred from a free measurement at a certain height above ground to the conditions around the modules inside a PV field. (Schumann et al. 2012) provides an approach for this calculation. In most cases reliable site specific wind data is not available. In such cases a conservative approach based on a low average wind velocity should be selected and documented.

The report should explain the approach to calculate the temperature losses. Besides the annual average temperature loss it is sometimes also demanded to present the monthly average and maximal module temperatures.

Module Quality and Degradation

The power of PV modules is typically given with a certain tolerance. These days only positive power tolerances are common. Assuming the nominal module power for the simulation is hence a conservative approach but could be compensated by low mismatch losses (see next section). If flasher protocols of the used modules are available the real average power of the modules can be determined (within the measurement tolerances). If this exceeds the nominal power a corresponding yield gain can be respected as module quality factor.

Different effects usually lead to a loss in module power of the installed modules compared to their condition in which they left the factory. These effects should be discussed and respected as initial degradation in the yield report. On cell level the so called light induced degradation is typical. In the first days crystalline modules (with p-cells) are exposed to sunlight the efficiency falls usually by approx. 1%. In addition shipping and mounting effects will always lead to a slight reduction in power (e.g., micro cracks) even if the modules are handled carefully.

In the history of photovoltaic several special degradation effects have been discovered and solved. Such effects are hardly predictable and hence have to be excluded in the yield report. Degradation phenomena that are already known since years but still current are PID (Potential Induced Degradation) and LeTID (Light and elevated Temperature Induced Degradation for solar cells with PERC technology). Guaranteed PID free and LeTID free modules are available.

After the light induced degradation the solar cell power usually stays stable. Only for solar cells affected by micro cracks a further reduction in power can be expected due to growth of the fractures under thermal and mechanical (wind and snow loads) stress. Other parts of the modules and system components may suffer long-term degradation e.g., due to corrosion of conducting elements, module glass and cell encapsulant (EVA browning). Such processes depend on the environmental conditions already mentioned above in the description of the location. As a contrary effect an inverter replacement in several years may result in a better efficiency of the new inverter (technical progress).

the DC wiring concept of the simulated system and the corresponding losses at nominal conditions and on annual average.

Inverter Losses

The inverters' main tasks are the so called MPP-tracking and the conversion of the direct current (DC) provided by the PV modules to grid-conform alternating current (AC). MPP tracking means that a working point (voltage level) at the DC side is regulated and continuously adjusted at which the maximum power is obtained from the PV generator (maximum power point, MPP). The inverter only offers a limited voltage range in which this task can be fulfilled. The yield report should document the typical operating voltage range of the connected modules and the offered MPP tracking voltage range by the inverter. Possible related losses have to be respected. Modern inverters usually find the MPP accurately and quickly within the specified voltage range. Losses due to MPP tracking accuracy are hence often negligible. The main inverter losses result from the DC-AC conversion efficiency which usually varies with the power and voltage level as illustrated in Figure 2.7. The simulation model of the considered inverter should reflect this behavior and the report should prove the match of the simulation model with the specifications including possible different properties of single inverter inputs.

Often electrical inverter specifications are given at different ambient respectively cooling air temperatures. If the simulation software is not able to reproduce this behavior the inverter model has to be defined for the expected average temperature conditions at the site.

Additional inverter losses occur if the PV modules deliver more power than the inverter is able to convert. These so called power limitation or clipping losses may occur in times of high irradiation and low module temperature depending on the ratio between maximum inverter power and module power. The report should mention this so called AC-DC ratio.

Power limitation losses cannot be determined in hourly simulation steps with sufficient accuracy. Especially during periods with changing irradiation conditions and cloud-enhancement effects hourly mean values do not display the reality. Additional power limitation losses should be respected manually and justified in the report as a consequence. (Schumann 2014) indicates power limitation losses at real conditions.

Depending on the local electricity grid it may be demanded that the PV system feeds-in at a certain phase angle. The reactive power portion to realize a certain power factor is assigned by the grid and only the active power portion represents the PV energy. Under consideration of the maximal apparent power of the inverter this mechanism has to be understood in the assessment of power limitation losses.

In some cases a maximum offered power by the PV system is contracted at the grid connection point. The compliance is usually realized by monitoring the PV

respected in the calculation. Eventually the wind velocity needs to be transferred from a free measurement at a certain height above ground to the conditions around the modules inside a PV field. (Schumann et al. 2012) provides an approach for this calculation. In most cases reliable site specific wind data is not available. In such cases a conservative approach based on a low average wind velocity should be selected and documented.

The report should explain the approach to calculate the temperature losses. Besides the annual average temperature loss it is sometimes also demanded to present the monthly average and maximal module temperatures.

Module Quality and Degradation

The power of PV modules is typically given with a certain tolerance. These days only positive power tolerances are common. Assuming the nominal module power for the simulation is hence a conservative approach but could be compensated by low mismatch losses (see next section). If flasher protocols of the used modules are available the real average power of the modules can be determined (within the measurement tolerances). If this exceeds the nominal power a corresponding yield gain can be respected as module quality factor.

Different effects usually lead to a loss in module power of the installed modules compared to their condition in which they left the factory. These effects should be discussed and respected as initial degradation in the yield report. On cell level the so called light induced degradation is typical. In the first days crystalline modules (with p-cells) are exposed to sunlight the efficiency falls usually by approx. 1%. In addition shipping and mounting effects will always lead to a slight reduction in power (e.g., micro cracks) even if the modules are handled carefully.

In the history of photovoltaic several special degradation effects have been discovered and solved. Such effects are hardly predictable and hence have to be excluded in the yield report. Degradation phenomena that are already known since years but still current are PID (Potential Induced Degradation) and LeTID (Light and elevated Temperature Induced Degradation for solar cells with PERC technology). Guaranteed PID free and LeTID free modules are available.

After the light induced degradation the solar cell power usually stays stable. Only for solar cells affected by micro cracks a further reduction in power can be expected due to growth of the fractures under thermal and mechanical (wind and snow loads) stress. Other parts of the modules and system components may suffer long-term degradation e.g., due to corrosion of conducting elements, module glass and cell encapsulant (EVA browning). Such processes depend on the environmental conditions already mentioned above in the description of the location. As a contrary effect an inverter replacement in several years may result in a better efficiency of the new inverter (technical progress).

Some studies state only minor long-term degradation for several installations in central Europe (e.g., (Kiefer et al. 2011)). An annual degradation of 0% can hence not be considered as impossible but is clearly the best case. The worst case on the other hand is the guaranteed minimal module power by the manufacturer. A lot of manufacturers these days grant a maximum linear annual reduction in power for 25 years (e.g., 0.7% p.a.). As a likely scenario for the yield report it can be comprehensibly reasoned to respect an annual degradation which results from the average of best and worst case (e.g., 0.35%). But of course also other factors can be used if they are justifiable. In experienced markets with moderate climate conditions like Germany or the United Kingdom also smaller degradation factors of e.g., 0.25% p.a. are usually accepted by all involved parties.

2.2.7 Balance of System Losses

So called balance of system (BOS) losses include all the losses in the components that are used to make the electricity of the entity of the single PV modules serviceable. In common grid connected systems this describes the energy transfer from the PV modules to the public electricity grid.

Mismatch Losses

It can be argued if mismatch losses are better classified as module losses or as BOS losses. But they clearly result from the interconnection of the modules. Because this interconnection is necessary for the further energy transfer this article considers mismatch as BOS losses. Mismatch losses occur if modules with (slightly) different electrical properties are connected in series or in parallel as exemplified in Figure 2.6. Each module in the system has small tolerances in its power but also in the electrical factors that lead to the power compared to nominal values. Even two modules with an identical measured maximum power may have different pairs of voltage and current. Nevertheless the inverter can adjust only one voltage which is an optimal compromise for all modules connected to it. Within a module string the module with the lowest current limits the whole string current. The difference of the summation of all module powers with each single module at its optimal working point and the actual power tapped by the inverter is described with mismatch losses.

Major mismatch losses occur in the series connection of modules. If the measured electrical properties of the modules in the PV system are known (flash protocols) or assumed as typical, the mismatch losses and their uncertainties can be assessed by statistics of random module combinations that might also respect a certain presorting of the modules. Nowadays the electrical differences between the PV modules are usually small and result in mismatch losses significantly smaller than 1%.

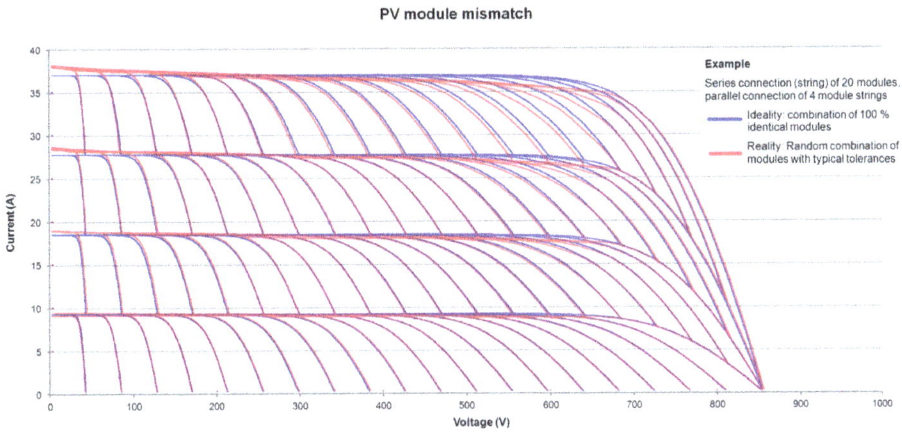

Figure 2.6: Explaining graph for mismatch losses (own representation).

There might also be other sources of mismatch than the module tolerances as discussed in (Schumann 2016, "Retrofitting"). For example modules installed at the bottom of a module table always receive less diffuse light than modules at upper table positions. If the module strings are not connected horizontally but modules on top of each other are connected to the same string, this will cause mismatch. Also terrain influences on the table orientation can cause mismatch if a string is connected over two neighboring tables. Parallel mismatch, e.g., due to heterogeneous voltage drops on the different strings cables is usually insignificantly small.

In case of use of optimizers each module is working in its MPP without mismatch but the operational losses of the optimizers needs to be considered in the yield simulation.

The mismatch loss is usually set by the user in the simulation software and not directly computed. It should therefore be carefully analyzed and explained in the yield report.

DC Wiring Loss

The connection of the PV modules to the inverters is done by electrical wires that behave like Ohmic resistances. The level of resistance depends on the cables' lengths and cross-sections. Depending on the inverter concept groups of DC (direct current) cables may also be combined in junction boxes. The considered Ohmic resistance on the DC side should therefore include junction and protection devices. Also temperature depending resistances should be considered. The Ohmic power loss can be calculated by multiplying the resistance with the squared DC current. Since the current depends on the irradiance level the percentage cable loss varies with the irradiance for each simulated situation. The yield report should describe

the DC wiring concept of the simulated system and the corresponding losses at nominal conditions and on annual average.

Inverter Losses

The inverters' main tasks are the so called MPP-tracking and the conversion of the direct current (DC) provided by the PV modules to grid-conform alternating current (AC). MPP tracking means that a working point (voltage level) at the DC side is regulated and continuously adjusted at which the maximum power is obtained from the PV generator (maximum power point, MPP). The inverter only offers a limited voltage range in which this task can be fulfilled. The yield report should document the typical operating voltage range of the connected modules and the offered MPP tracking voltage range by the inverter. Possible related losses have to be respected. Modern inverters usually find the MPP accurately and quickly within the specified voltage range. Losses due to MPP tracking accuracy are hence often negligible. The main inverter losses result from the DC-AC conversion efficiency which usually varies with the power and voltage level as illustrated in Figure 2.7. The simulation model of the considered inverter should reflect this behavior and the report should prove the match of the simulation model with the specifications including possible different properties of single inverter inputs.

Often electrical inverter specifications are given at different ambient respectively cooling air temperatures. If the simulation software is not able to reproduce this behavior the inverter model has to be defined for the expected average temperature conditions at the site.

Additional inverter losses occur if the PV modules deliver more power than the inverter is able to convert. These so called power limitation or clipping losses may occur in times of high irradiation and low module temperature depending on the ratio between maximum inverter power and module power. The report should mention this so called AC-DC ratio.

Power limitation losses cannot be determined in hourly simulation steps with sufficient accuracy. Especially during periods with changing irradiation conditions and cloud-enhancement effects hourly mean values do not display the reality. Additional power limitation losses should be respected manually and justified in the report as a consequence. (Schumann 2014) indicates power limitation losses at real conditions.

Depending on the local electricity grid it may be demanded that the PV system feeds-in at a certain phase angle. The reactive power portion to realize a certain power factor is assigned by the grid and only the active power portion represents the PV energy. Under consideration of the maximal apparent power of the inverter this mechanism has to be understood in the assessment of power limitation losses.

In some cases a maximum offered power by the PV system is contracted at the grid connection point. The compliance is usually realized by monitoring the PV

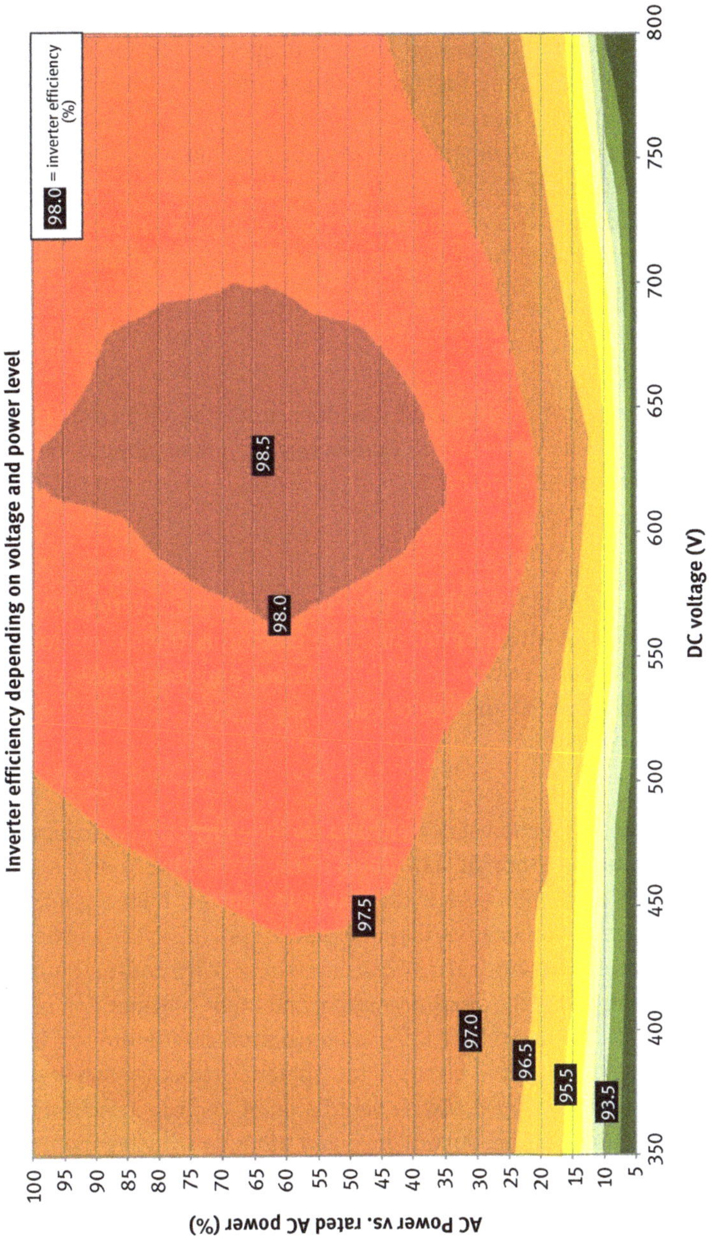

Figure 2.7: Example of typical inverter conversion efficiency (own representation).

power supplied to the grid and possible control commands to actively reduce the inverter output power. This behavior can be simulated by reducing the maximal power of the inverter model respecting the system losses after the inverter and the maximal allowed power at the grid connection.

Also the installation and local temperature conditions should be considered to evaluate possible inverter derating due to excess temperature.

The yield report should provide a comprehensive description of the relevant inverter behavior and the corresponding modeling approaches. All different kinds of inverter losses should be given.

AC Wiring Losses

Analogous to the DC side the AC cables and junctions until the grid connection point principally act as Ohmic resistances. Corresponding losses should be respected and discussed in the yield report at all voltage levels.

Transformer Losses

Transformers are used to convert the voltage level offered by the inverters to the voltage level of the relevant electricity grid. In some cases this transformation is done in multiple steps. For each voltage level the constant and load losses of the transformers should be documented and respected.

Own Consumption

A yield report can be a pure production statement and exclude any own consumption of the system. This makes sense if not all consumers in the system are known at the time the report is created or if the operational power is sourced from a separate power supply with own meter at other costs than the production. It is clearly better to have a pure production statement than a partly consideration of own consumption. If own consumption is excluded also the auxiliary supply and night consumption of inverters and transformers should be excluded. If own consumption is subtracted from the production as a loss factor it should be made transparent that all consumers are respected. Consumers in a PV system could be ventilation or cooling devices of inverter and transformer stations, lights, surveillance and other security components, monitoring system, motors and controls of tracking systems as well as the already mentioned night consumption of inverters and transformers as well as their auxiliary supply. If own consumption is excluded this should be clearly mentioned so that the related costs can be respected in economical calculations.

Often only night consumption is excluded and day consumption is included since the night consumption can usually be metered separately without extra meter and because the electricity price at night usually differs from the feed-in tariff.

Availability and Failures

Often yield reports present their results assuming a failure-free system and grid. But it should clearly be mentioned that availability losses are excluded in this case.

In reality a PV system will likely suffer from break downs of single system components. The magnitude of yield loss when a component fails is strongly depending on the kind of component. E.g., a broken fuse might only affect a single module string whereas a defect AC switchgear can stop the production of the entire system. The annual yield loss depends on when the failure happens and how long the interruption lasts. The latter is a matter of the availability of technical staff and spare parts. The chance that also minor defects are detected depends on how well the plant is monitored. If a likely average availability of the system should be predicted the whole operation and maintenance (O&M) concept has to be evaluated. Sometimes O&M contracts also agree a guaranteed minimum availability that could be considered in the yield report. Concerning grid availability losses performance reports of the local utility should be taken into account (e.g., historic System Average Interruption Duration Index (SAIDI)).

The global availability losses respected in the final results should be well discussed and explained in the yield report.

2.2.8 Post Processing and Presentation of Results

At latest after all losses and gains in the PV system have been explained and discussed the Performance Ratio (PR) should be introduced. The PR is the relation between the real energy the system feeds into the grid and the theoretical production that is obtained when the nominal module efficiency is multiplied with the solar irradiation sum in the module plane. If the PV modules would always work with their nominal efficiency under all conditions and their energy could be injected into the grid without any losses a PR of 100% would be reached.

Due to known limits of simulation software the hourly calculation results may be post-processed to increase the accuracy (e.g., averaging of runs with different physical models or inclusion of additional haircuts for inverter power limitation). A post-process also allows for presenting the results clearly arranged in more detail than offered by the simulation software.

The yield report should summarize the yield assessment by presenting a table that documents line by line all losses and gains that happen in the system starting with the ideal reference energy for a PR of 100%. An example for such a table is given in Figure 2.8. After step-by-step accounting of all losses and gains the final electrical yield and PR should be presented in the last line. In order to allow an easier comparison with other PV systems the table should list the specific energy production with reference to the installed module power in kWh/kWp. The total production of the system in MWh should be given as additional text information. In case the

Irradiation					
Step				Annual yield (kWh/m²)	Uncertainty (% (±))
Global horizontal irradiation				1142	3.5
Irradiation in module plane				1302	2.0
Electricity					
Step	Gross loss (%) *reference: PR 100 %*	Net loss (%) *reference: previous step*	PR (%)	Annual yield (kWh/kWp)	Uncertainty (% (±))
Available solar energy	-	-	-	8256	-
Nominal module efficiency	-	-	100.0	1302	-
Horizon shading	0.6	0.6	99.4	1294	0.5
Self and near shading	4.3	4.3	95.1	1239	1.0
Soiling and snow losses	1.7	1.8	93.4	1216	1.0
Reflection losses	2.5	2.7	90.9	1183	0.7
Bifacial gain	-6.0	-6.6	96.9	1262	2.0
Module quality (flash reports)	-0.9	-0.9	97.8	1273	1.0
Initial degradation	1.5	1.5	96.3	1254	1.0
Irradiation level losses	1.6	1.7	94.7	1232	0.5
Temperature losses	2.4	2.5	92.3	1202	1.0
Mismatch losses	0.4	0.4	91.9	1197	0.2
DC wiring loss	0.5	0.5	91.5	1191	0.1
Inverter losses (incl. clipping)	2.4	2.6	89.1	1160	0.7
AC wiring losses (low voltage)	0.6	0.7	88.5	1152	0.1
Medium voltage transformer losses	0.7	0.8	87.8	1143	0.1
AC wiring losses (medium voltage)	0.2	0.2	87.6	1140	0.1
Own consumption	0.2	0.2	87.4	1138	0.1
Availability (system + grid)	1.3	1.5	86.1	1121	1.0
Result			86.1	1121	5.3

Figure 2.8: Example for overview result table (own representation).

total PV system consists of several different subsystems (e.g., roof) individual results for each subsystem might be presented. The described overview table should present average values in the first year of operation. Additional tables may indicate the long-term production (e.g., over 20 or 25 years) based on the discussed annual degradation as well as the monthly variation of electricity production and PR. Depending on the variation of prices at which the electricity can be sold or if a certain load should be served even hourly production profiles might be of interest.

The yield report should also discuss the uncertainty of the presented results. Uncertainties lie in the irradiation and PR calculation methods as well as in assumptions. It is in the expert's discretion to judge the uncertainties of the input data and the single calculation steps. The global uncertainty is usually given as standard deviation following rules of error propagation. It is a good idea to present the uncertainties in the overview table together with the electrical yield and PR in each line.

For the risk analysis of PV projects the presentation of so called probabilities of exceedance or banking cases are common. This consideration is based on a normal distribution of the expected yields. The p90 value for example means the yield exceeded with a probability of 90% (analogous: p75 with 75%, etc.). The predicted yield represents the p50 value. Individual banking cases result mathematically directly from the p50 value, the standard deviation and the considered probability (e.g., 90% = p90).

Since there are often different conceptions what banking cases should include the report should clearly state which uncertainties are considered in the standard deviation the calculation is based on. E.g., often the probability yields are only given for average meteorological conditions and thus exclude the risk that the first year(s) of production might offer less irradiation than an average year. If this risk is wished to be included the standard deviation of the variability of the solar resource has to be analyzed based on a site-specific time series and combined with the general uncertainty for an average meteorological year.

If long-term average yields are considered, it can make sense to include the risk that the real degradation might be higher than the assumed one. This risk can be evaluated based on the differences between assumed degradation and maximal degradation based on the power guarantee of the module manufacturer.

2.2.9 Additional Content of the Yield Report

The document should follow typical standards concerning the layout of technical reports like project-specific title and cover, list of contents as well as signatures and creation date. Due to possible changes in the system concept a version number and document history might be included. A separate section may give some general and project specific advises for system optimization. Finally the report should also include a disclaimer that documents the purpose, addressees and validity of the document as well as copyright issues.

In order to transparently document the way the yield has been predicted the report should include an appendix that shows all considered external input data as well intermediate results used to determine the final yield figures. As a consequence data sheets and other used specifications of all relevant components like PV modules, inverters and transformers are usually presented followed by documents of the considered meteorological data sources and simulation reports of the used simulation software. Hourly simulation results and analyzes may be provided as digital appendix.

2.3 Quality Guidelines

Summarizing the discussed yield report requirements the quality demand can be expressed with the following four key factors that are also illustrated in Figure 2.9.

1. Done by independent experts
   Due to the high level of essential specialized knowledge and the dependency of simulation software results on the user input, PV yield assessments have to be conducted by dedicated solar energy resource assessors. At least three years of professional experience in this domain are recommended. The prediction of the energy yield by an independent third party ensures transparent and credible input data for the financial aspects of the project.

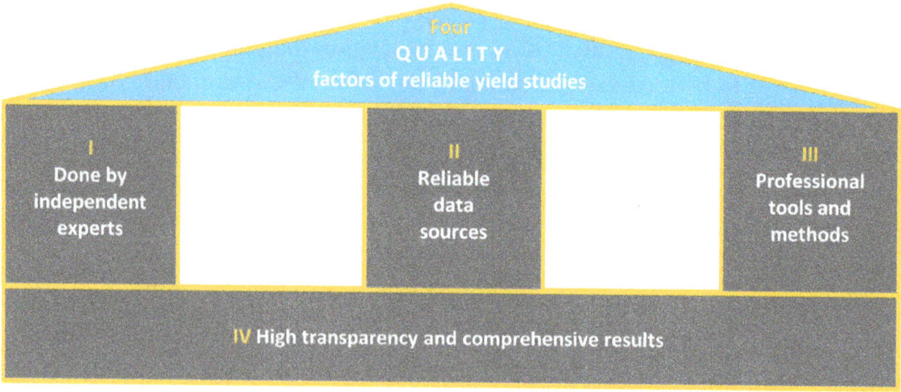

Figure 2.9: The four quality key factors of yield studies (own representation).

2. Reliable data sources
   The yield assessment should be based on the verified use of multiple meteorological data sources as well as valid and detailed technical specifications of the used components.
3. Professional tools and methods
   The simulations have to be done at least in hourly steps with accepted and approved yield simulation tools. All settings and used models have to be verified and adapted to the specific project and components. The presented results in the yield report should refer to the simulation results. Necessary corrections of the simulation results (e.g., inverter clipping) need to be documented transparently in the report.
4. High transparency and comprehensive results
   The simulated system design has to be described in all relevant details. All used methods, procedures and data have to be transparent and comprehensible with reference to the system under study. If certain information is not available the report has to mention this explicitly and describe the used assumptions. The uncertainties of the results have to be documented.

2.4 Critical Assumptions, Limits, and Uncertainties

A yield report is much more than its result section. Only if the whole documentation is read carefully the assumptions under which the results are valid can be understood. For the risk analysis of a PV project this information has the same importance as the results.

Yield reports are often issued in a very early project phase. The technical system design might change until the plant is built and not all information might be available so that some important calculation steps are based on assumptions. The transparency of the assumptions goes hand in hand with the careful reading the report. E.g., exemplary figures might have been used for system and grid-availability, own consumption or degradation. Or these aspects might have been excluded explicitly from the consideration. A Technical due diligence and inspection of the built plant should investigate the validity of the assumptions made in the yield report.

Furthermore it is important to understand that yield reports present system yields at average meteorological conditions. Single years and especially short test periods will give less or more yield depending on the variability of the solar resource. A variability statement should be included in every yield report. Depending on the ordered scope the yield report may also offer a detailed variability analysis.

The yield of PV projects in established markets with moderate climate and installation conditions can usually be predicted with an uncertainty in the range of 5% if standard technology is used and all assumptions are valid.

Higher uncertainties should be considered at different situations as already indicated at some stages above. In the following sections some aspects are more deeply revisited that might importantly influence the reliability of a yield assessment.

2.4.1 Meteorological Data

This article has discussed the particularities of meteorological data in detail. An ideal meteorological dataset should provide the following parameters in high temporal resolution (e.g., minutes) precisely for the site under study: global horizontal irradiation, diffuse horizontal irradiation, spectral composition of irradiation, ambient temperature, ground-level wind velocity, rainfall and snowfall. Of course the reality differs from ideality. A yield prediction of a PV system can never be more precise than the prediction of the relevant meteorological parameters that drive the yield. In situations where different data sources provide highly different results and reliable validation or ground measurements are not available a corresponding high uncertainty has to be respected.

Any prediction is based on meteorological foretime data even if future scenarios are considered. There is always a risk of unforeseeable future effects like major volcano eruptions that might strongly influence the meteorological resource.

2.4.2 Irradiance for Tracking Systems

Mounting systems that follow the sun often show high innovation potential. Individual tracking control demands on sub-hourly basis are hardly possible to simulate with the typical hourly simulation steps. Strategies to avoid self shading of neighboring module tables by back-tracking are also highly product-specific and often not exactly reproducible with common software. Although experienced yield assessors should be able to approximate corresponding yields higher uncertainties need to be respected.

2.4.3 Soiling

If a project site does not offer regular rain soling can get a significant and hardly predictable loss. On the other hand the author also knows about self cleaning effects in desert climates based on wind and dew so that only moderate soling losses occurred at a no rain site. Also the adhesiveness of soil is highly specific (e.g., (Kaldellis and Kapsali 2011)) with the consequence that a dusty and arid site might show more or less soiling losses depending on the kind of soil. But soiling can not only be a problem in arid climates if local sources of pollution are affecting the PV installation. Rain often fails to wash away greasy or solidified layers of soiling. Combined with a low tilt angle such problems have often been reported for installations on barns. In a polluted atmosphere rain can even be a source of soiling itself.

The effect of soiling has also been found to depend on incidence angle and spectral composition of the sunlight (e.g., (Qasem et al. 2011)).

If a PV project is planned at a site that shows any of the mentioned particularities it is highly recommended to monitor soiling losses and to provide a financial buffer that would allow regular manual cleanings. If the corresponding finical risk should be determined prior to the realization of the project and a delay is accepted a small pilot installation could be built and analyzed.

2.4.4 Snow

Like soiling snow can be a site specific problem. In moderate climates even worst case considerations that count no PV production for any day with snow cover only lead to relatively small annual losses. At sites at which sunny times meet thick and durable layers of snow such a simplification will lead to unacceptable high losses. In reality snow often melts off the PV module surfaces. The mechanisms in the background are complex and highly depending on the kind of snow as well as the meteorological conditions after the snowfall as well as on the geometry of the module installation.

Even the established snow loss model by (Townsend et al. 2011) has only been developed on basis of measurements at one reference site in a climate with temperatures constantly below the freezing point in winter. It is therefore uncertain how well the results can be transferred to climates with shorter freezing periods. If no experiences with reference systems exist in the considered region again a pilot installation makes sense if a financial buffer for manual snow removal is considered as too risky. Theoretically snow could also be melted by warming the modules with help of reverse currents. Such technical solutions need the agreement of the module manufacturer in order to not peril warranty claims.

2.4.5 Module Technology

Simulation models for standard crystalline silicon modules are established and validated. Even if the temperature and irradiance level characteristics for a specific product are not known the yield can be simulated based on average standard behavior with acceptable accuracy. If other technology is used a reliable yield simulation is only possible if the module's electrical behavior is defined at a variety of environmental conditions including spectral response.

Alternative solar cell technologies might also show individual effects (e.g., thermal annealing, light soaking) that could only be factored if they are understood and specified by the manufacturer. This accounts also for special technology that might be available for other parts of a PV module than the solar cell, e.g., anti-glare or soiling layers applied to the module glass.

Also degradation can be a hardly predictable mechanism. Even if there is experience with the degradation behavior of a certain module technology in a certain climate a feasibility analysis based on the power guarantee of the module should always be considered.

2.4.6 Temperature Losses Considering Wind Effects

The dependency of the solar cell temperature on irradiation and ambient temperature is well understood. But the cooling influence of wind has often to be neglected in a yield simulation due to the unavailability of precise ground-level wind velocity data. For hot and sunny as well as windy sites simulated temperature losses should therefore be regarded with a higher uncertainty.

2.5 Outlook and Conclusion

Figure 2.10 summarizes the discussed process of the energy yield assessment of a PV system. Obviously this is a complex and interdisciplinary task that should only be done by qualified and independent parties.

Yield reports have to be fully transparent and understandable. It should be reproducible for another qualified third party how the results have been obtained. But the report has also to be written in a way it is understandable by readers without special

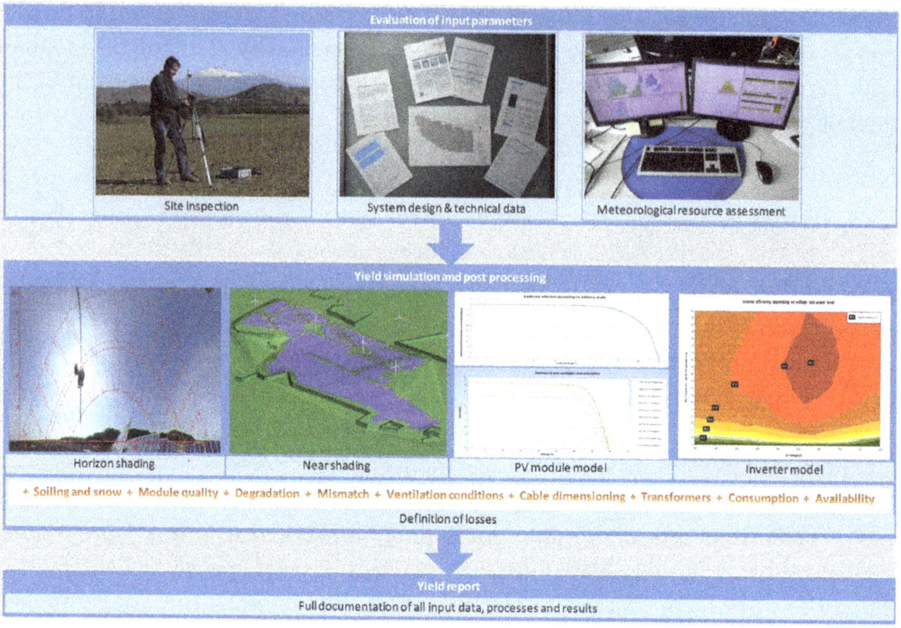

Figure 2.10: Energy yield assessment process chart (own representation).

technical background. The author of the yield report should always have in mind that the major purpose of the predicted electrical yield is the determination of the financial risk. Investors and financiers have to carefully read the whole report in order to understand under which assumptions the results are valid. Only if the whole report is read and understood its quality can be judged. This article has discussed relevant quality criteria as well as state of the art methods. It should therefore help rating different yield reports. If multiple yield reports are ordered for one PV project their results should not simply be averaged. Possible different qualities and assumptions of the yield reports should be considered. This paper might also help to identify unclear assumptions like e.g., the grid availability for which additional studies are needed.

The energy yield of a PV system can be assessed with good accuracy if all aspects in this article are considered carefully. As research is ongoing also the discussed limits and uncertainties are expected to decline continuously.

References

Aguiar, Ricardo, and Manuel Collares-Pereira. 1992. "TAG: A Time-dependent, Autoregressive, Gaussian Model for Generating Synthetic Hourly Radiation." *Solar Energy Volume* 49, no. 3: 167–74.

Gracia Amillo, Ana María, Thomas Huld, and Richard Werner Müller. 2014. “A new database of global and direct solar radiation using the eastern meteosat satellite, models and validation.” *Remote Sensing* 6, no. 9: 8165–89.

Gueymard, Christian A. 1987. “An Anisotropic Solar Irradiance Model for Tilted Surfaces and its Comparison with Selected Engineering Algorithms.” *Solar Energy* 38: 367–86.

Hay, John E., and J. A. Davies. 1978. “Calculation of the Solar Radiation Incident on an Inclined Surface.” Proceedings of the First Canadian Solar Radiation Data Workshop, Toronto: 59–72.

Huld, Thomas, and Ana María Gracia Amillo. 2015. “Estimating PV Module Performance over Large Geographical Regions: The Role of Irradiance, Air Temperature, Wind Speed and Solar Spectrum.” *Energies* 8: 5159–81.

Ineichen, Pierre. 2011. “Long Global Irradiance on Tilted and Oriented Planes: Model Validations.” Archive ouverte UNIGE. http://archive-ouverte.unige.ch/unige:23519.

Ineichen, Pierre. 2014. “Long Term Satellite Global, Beam and Diffuse Irradiance Validation.” *Energy Procedia* 48: 1586–96.

Kaldellis, John K., and Marina Kapsali. 2011. “Simulating the Dust Effect on the Energy Performance of Photovoltaic Generators Based on Experimental Measurements.” *Energy Volume* 36, no. 8: 5154–61.

Kiefer, Klaus, Daniela Dirnberger, and Björn Müller. 2011. “Langzeiterfahrungen mit verschiedenen PV-Technologien in kommerziellen Kraftwerken.” 26. Symposium Photovoltaische Solarenergie: 581–86.

Kimber, Adrianne, L. Mitchell, S. Nogradi, and H. Wenger. 2006. “The Effect of Soiling on Large Grid-connected Photovoltaic Systems in California and the Southwest Region of the United States.” Conference Record of the 2006 IEEE 4th World Conference on Photovoltaic Energy Conversion, vol. 2: 2391–95.

Lee, Mitchell, and Alex Panchula. 2016. “Spectral Correction for Photovoltaic Module Performance Based on Air Mass and Precipitable Water.” IEEE Photovoltaic Specialists Conference.

Mieslinger, Theresa, Felix Ament, Kauschal Chhatbar, and Richard W. Meyer. 2014. “A New Method for Fusion of Measured and Model-derived Solar Radiation Time-series.” *Energy Procedia* 48: 1617–26.

Müller, Richard, Tanja Behrendt, Annette Hammer, and Axel Kemper. 2012. “A new algorithm for the satellite-based retrieval of solar surface irradiance in spectral bands.” *Remote Sensing* 4: 622–47.

Perez, Richard, Pierre Ineichen, Robert Seals, Joseph Michalsky, and Ronald Stewart. 1990. “Modeling Daylight Availability and Irradiance Component from Direct and Global Irradiance.” *Solar Energy* 44, no. 5: 271–89.

Qasem, Hassan, Thomas R. Betts, Harald Müllejans, H. AlBusairi, and Ralph Gottschalg. 2011. “Dust Effect on PV Modules.” Proceedings of the 7th Photovoltaic Science Application and Technology Conference and Exihibition (PVSAT-7). https://dspace.lboro.ac.uk/2134/8459.

Schumann, André, Julia Dittberner, and Timon Kampschulte. 2012. “Ermittlung der mittleren Windverhältnisse in Photovoltaik-Freiflächenanlagen und die resultierende Ermittlung der Modultemperaturen.” 27. Symposium Photovoltaische Solarenergie: 528–33.

Schumann, André, Fabian Knust, and Timon Kampschulte. 2014. “Tatsächliche Leistungsbegrenzungsverluste von Wechselrichtern in aktuellen, wirtschaftlich optimierten PV-Großkraftwerken.” 29. Symposium Photovoltaische Solarenergie: 200–201.

Schumann, André. 2015. “Quality Standard for Energy Yield Studies.” Proceedings of the 31st European PV Solar Energy Conference and Exhibition: 2282.

Schumann, André. 2016. “State of the art in PV yield assessments.” *PV TECH POWER Magazine* 7: 52–57.

Schumann, André. 2016. "Retrofitting von PV-Großanlagen durch den Einsatz von Leistungsoptimierern: Kosten-Nutzen-Analysen anhand präziser Simulationen bestehender PV-Anlagen." 31. Symposium Photovoltaische Solarenergie: Online-Tagungsband.

Townsend, Tim, and Loren Powers. 2011. "Photovoltaics and snow: An update from two winters of measurements in the SIERRA." 37th IEEE Photo-voltaic Specialist Conference (PVSC): 19–24.

3 Key Policies behind the Development of Solar Energy in Chile

Miguel Saldivia, Matías Guiloff

3.1 Introduction

Chile is looking to become a world power in solar energy. This ambitious objective was reflected in the Energy Agenda launched in 2013, which proposed actions to strengthen renewable energies and incentives for investment in the sector.[1] And these efforts are already being recognized internationally: A former US energy minister has said that Chile is an example of an emerging economy capable of developing its natural resources, such as the sun, at competitive prices and without subsidies.[2] Some media have called Chile as the "solar Saudi Arabia"[3] while Al Gore said in his latest documentary that "Chile is inspiring the world."[4]

According to technical studies, the potential of solar energy in Chile is 1,300 GW.[5] If a portion of only 5% of the Atacama Desert were occupied, 30% of the demand in South America could be supplied.[6] In relation to the current electricity generation, in January 2019, renewable energies represented 20.7% of the energy matrix.[7] On the other hand, photovoltaic solar energy was the 10% of the total electricity in Chile, that is, almost half of the renewable energy. In addition, there are 136 renewable energy projects under environmental evaluation, of which 91 are solar photovoltaic.[8]

---

1 Pilar Moraga and Miguel Saldivia, "Evaluación de Impacto Ambiental de proyectos de energía solar: propuestas para una tramitación ambiental mejorada," *Revista de Derecho Administrativo Económico* 19 (2014), 199.

2 Ernest Moniz, "Chile, un ejemplo mundial," in *Revolución Energética en Chile*, ed. Máximo Pacheco (Santiago: Ediciones UDP, 2018), 12.

3 New York Times, "Chile's Energy Transformation Is Powered by Wind, Sun and Volcanoes," August 12, 2017, https://www.nytimes.com/2017/08/12/world/americas/chile-green-energy-geothermal.html.

4 Al Gore, "An Inconvenient Sequel: Truth to Power" (2017).

5 Paula Estévez, "El nuevo lugar de Chile en el mapa energético internacional," in *Revolución Energética en Chile*, ed. Máximo Pacheco (Santiago: Ediciones UDP, 2018), 236.

6 Paula Estévez, "El nuevo lugar de Chile en el mapa energético internacional," in *Revolución Energética en Chile*, ed. Máximo Pacheco (Santiago: Ediciones UDP, 2018), 236.

7 Comisión Nacional de Energía (CNE), *Reporte Mensual ERNC*, vol. 30 (February 2019), 6,https://www.cne.cl/nuestros-servicios/reportes/informacion-y-estadisticas/.

8 Ibid., 7.

https://doi.org/10.1515/9783110607888-030

Chile is a particularly interesting case study because the renewable energy industry has been developed without direct subsidies like Feed-In Tariffs.[9] The most important supportive system for clean energies is the quota regime established by Law No. 20,257, which set a 10% target that was to be accomplished by 2025. Some years later a much more ambitious 20% target was established by Law No. 20,698.[10] This statute establishes that the quota at issue is applicable to those electricity generators that effectuate withdrawals to commercialize electricity with distribution companies or end users.[11] Nonetheless, during the last years, some public policies have been issued with a main focus on solar energy.

The overall purpose of this paper is to examine the main policies for supporting the development of solar energy projects in Chile. Particularly, it focuses on two regulatory instruments which have had a relevant role for this industry in the last years. First section explores the design and implementation of a new system of public auctions for electricity supply which has helped the entry of solar projects in the Chilean energy matrix. Second Section describes the policy of public land concessions for the development of renewable energy projects. Finally, Third Section refers to the pending challenges for the photovoltaic industry in the country. As our main target of this article is to address these policies and challenges, this paper will not deal with are all the permits required for the construction or operation of a renewable energy project in Chile.[12]

3.2 Bespoke Auctions for Solar Energy Projects

This section examines the design and implementation of Law No. 20,805, of 2015, which established a new system of auctions for electricity supply in Chile. This represented a landmark policy in order to incorporate renewable energy sources to the energy matrix. Law No. 20,805 has been considered a successful public policy case, since it substantially reduced energy prices, increased competition and diversification in the electricity sector, but at the same time considered the citizen demand for greater participation.[13]

---

9 In Chile there are only some specific subsidies for farmers, small industries, indigenous communities or householders who want to install solar panels in a small scale, thus they do not include medium or big electricity companies.

10 Matias Guiloff and Miguel Saldivia, "Law of Renewables: Chapter Chile," in *Rechtliche Rahmenbedingungen von EE- Projekten*, vol. 2, ed. Jörg Böttcher (Berlin: BWV, 2017), 157.

11 Article 150 bis, LGSE.

12 For further information on the legal framework of the renewable energies in Chile and the corresponding permits, see Matías Guillof and Miguel Saldivia "Law of Renewables. Chapter Chile," in Rechtliche Rahmenbedingungen von EE- Projekten, vol. 2, ed. Jörg Böttcher (Berlin: BWV, 2017).

13 Chilean Ministry of Energy, "Nueva Ley Chilena de Licitación de Suministro Eléctrico para Clientes Regulados: un caso de éxito" (2017), 4.

Law No. 20,805, which improves the Electricity Supply Auction System for Customers Subject to Price Regulations, entered into force on January 29, 2015 through its publication in the Chilean Official Gazette. This regulation, which was proposed as part of the 2050 Energy Agenda, changed the prevailing paradigm in the electricity sector in Chile for more than 30 years since the enactment of the General Electric Services Act ("LGSE") in 1982. This paradigm was relying solely on the market for the development of the electric sector.[14] This section refers first to the scenario prior to the legal reform of 2015, and then to the modifications established by the Law No. 20,805.

3.2.1 Scenario before the Legal Reform

Before the amendments introduced by Law No. 20,805, each electricity distributor company tendered the supply of its regulated customers to a "supplier," which corresponded to an electricity generating company.[15] Regarding the price of this supply, the law established that the price of energy transferred to the customers was the price determined semi-annually by the authority, through the issuance of a decree (*Decreto de Precio de Nudo de Corto Plazo*).[16] The price should reflect an average over time of marginal costs at the generation-transport level. As a result, these prices were permanently subject to fluctuations related to conjunctural situations, such as variations in hydrology, demand, fuel prices, among other factors.[17]

In 2005, Law No. 20,018 (called "Ley Corta II"), gave the distribution companies the responsibility of preparing the auction regulations, defining the volume of energy to be tendered, evaluating the bids and awarding them.[18] In turn, the National Commission of Energy ("CNE" by its acronym in Spanish) only had the power to approve the auction regulations and authorize their modifications.[19] This law was enacted as a way to advance through a market mechanism in the need to promote investment in electricity generation, after the Argentine gas crisis.[20] But in 2012 and 2013, the system did not obtain auspicious results and the last tenders attracted little interest and prices reached 130 dollars per Megawatt hour ("USD/MWh").[21]

14 Chilean Ministry of Energy, "Agenda de Energía: Un Desafío País, Progreso para Todos" (2013), 16.
15 Chilean Ministry of Energy (no. 537), 30.
16 Ibid.
17 Ibid.
18 Andrés Romero and Gonzalo Tapia, "La Agenda de Energía de 2014," in *Revolución Energética en Chile*, ed. Máximo Pacheco (Santiago: Ediciones UDP, 2018), 73.
19 Ibid.
20 Ibid.
21 Chilean Ministry of Energy (no. 537), 38.

The Ley Corta II established that the contracts between generators and distributors signed after an auction for electricity supply should be established for periods of up to 15 years.[22] Likewise, the prices were those of the bid awarded in the auction, remaining fixed throughout the term of the contract. As part of the tenders, a maximum public price was established, set semi-annually by the CNE, together with the short-term node price, value that could not be exceeded by the bids submitted by the generators in the auctions. The purpose of this ceiling price was to protect regulated customers from excessive prices.[23]

In the 2006 auction, the award prices were close to the current node price, with bids below 55 USD/MWh. However, in 2008 the prices offered suffered a drastic increase, surpassing 100 USD/MWh in the average price of adjudication, which in a way reflected the high international oil prices. The most critical cases were the bids of 2012 and 2013, where the average prices offered varied between 128 and 139 USD/MWh.[24] With these prices, by 2013 electricity prices in Chile were one of the highest in Latin America,[25] and above the average price of the OECD countries for both the industrial segment and households.[26]

Finally, in the auctions under the regime of the Ley Corta II, there was no entry of new actors. Of the total energy awarded in that period, 92% corresponds to the largest three electricity companies in the country.[27]

3.2.2 Relevant Amendments to the New Regulation

Law No. 20,805 was proposed as part of the 2050 Energy Agenda, which has among its objectives to promote the participation of renewable energies in the Chilean energy matrix. In particular, Law No. 20,805 introduced a series of legal modifications to the LGSE to improve the current auctions system through several provisions described below.

Active Role of the State

In consistence with the purposes of the 2050 Energy Agenda, the State must have a more active role "in the long-term planning of the energy sector, reconciling economic, environmental and social objectives, for the common good of

22 Ibid.

23 Ibid.

24 Ibid.

25 Chilean Ministry of Energy (no. 538), 12–13.

26 Samuel Argüello, "Comparación de Precios de Electricidad en Chile y países de la OCDE y América Latina," Informe Final para la Comisión Permanente de Recursos Naturales, Bienes Nacionales y Medio Ambiente de la Cámara de Diputados (Congreso Nacional de Chile, 2012), 3.

27 Ibid., 40.

all Chileans."[28] Thus, Law No. 20,805 and, in particular, Article 131 bis of the LGSE establishes that the CNE "shall design, coordinate and direct the execution of such auction processes, whose purpose shall be that the distribution companies have long-term supply contracts to satisfy the consumption of customers subject to price regulation."[29] Likewise, the process is ruled by basic principles, such as non-discrimination, transparency and strict adherence to the auction regulations.[30]

Early Anticipation of Auction process

The legal reform also establishes that the auction processes for long-term supply contracts must be carried out at least five years before the supply start date.[31] This term is very relevant for generating companies because it is related to the risk associated with the development of an energy project and, therefore, with the possibility of accessing to project finance.[32] Additionally, the CNE is also vested with the power to call short-term auctions, with a shorter notice period established in the tender conditions.[33]

Long-Term Contracts

Law No. 20,805 modified the term of supply contracts from 15 to 20 years. This increase gives greater stability to the income of a company, which is the key for project finance. Therefore, this change promotes the entry of new competitors to the market. This competition also has an impact on the decrease in prices.[34] The law specifically regulates 20-year-long term contracts, but also gives faculties to the CNE in order to design auctions for shorter terms that are not expressly determined in the law, just in case of urgent problems or unforeseen variations on the projected consumption.[35]

Unpublished Maximum Price

According to Article 135 of the LGSE, the maximum price of the offer is determined by the CNE and remains unknown until the opening of bids. Along with this, and to avoid the discretion of the authority, the statute establishes that this maximum

28 Chilean Ministry of Energy (no. 538), 16.
29 Article 131, LGSE.
30 Article 131 bis, LGSE.
31 Article 131, LGSE.
32 Chilean Ministry of Energy (no. 537), 56.
33 Chilean Ministry of Energy (no. 537), 110.
34 Chilean Ministry of Energy (no. 537), 56.
35 Chilean Ministry of Energy (no. 537), 111.

price should be based on an efficient supply, quantitative criteria.[36] As a result, the prices offered in the last tenders have been well below the ceiling price, reaching, for example, 47.59 USD/MWh when the ceiling price was fixed at 94 USD/MWh.[37]

Review Mechanisms for Regulatory Changes

The legal reform also established that supply contracts could consider price revision mechanisms for "causes not attributable to the supplier," such as substantial and non-transitory changes to the sectoral electricity regulations that cause an excessive economic imbalance of the contract's profits. In any case, those regulatory changes applicable with general scope to all sectors of economic activities are expressly excluded.[38]

Flexibility in the Award Criteria

Under the regime of the Ley Corta II, the auction was awarded to the bidder that offered the lowest price of energy, independent of any other factor included in its proposal. Currently, Article 134 of the LGSE establishes that the tender will be awarded to those more economical offers, however the assessment of such offers must ensure compliance with all the objectives of the law.[39] These objectives are economic efficiency, competition, security and diversification.[40] Under this criteria of flexibility,[41] it is possible to carry out exclusive tenders for new projects, leaving for other processes the projects already installed, as a way to encourage the entry of new players in the market. In any case, differentiated auctions by technology are not allowed due to the principle of technological neutrality.[42,43]

Incorporation of "Time Blocks"

Although the amendment did not include the possibility of carrying out exclusive auctions for projects of certain technologies – for instance, only for solar energy projects – the CNE has the power to design the bidding rules for the accomplishment of other objectives beyond the economic criterion, namely, competition, security and diversification. As a result, since 2013, the authority has included the so-called "time

36 Article 135, LGSE.
37 Ibid., 60.
38 Article 134, LGSE.
39 Article 134, LGSE.
40 Article 131 bis, LGSE.
41 Hugh Rudnick and Andrés Romero, "Hacia un modelo en competencia: Licitaciones de suministro eléctrico," in *Revolución Energética en Chile*, ed. Máximo Pacheco (Santiago: Ediciones UDP, 2018), 434.
42 Ibid., 64.
43 The principle of technological neutrality refers to not discriminating in favor of a certain type of energy source during a tender process.

blocks" during the day, with the aim of promoting the entry of technologies that they can only generate during day time hours. That is precisely the case of the energies obtained through solar radiation and wind energy.[44] Prior to this measure, renewable generators had to offer a complete block (24 hours), which obliged them to buy to conventional generators energy at highly volatile prices at the spot market because they were not able to generate or procure long-term contracts.[45]

Successful Implementation

Since the entry into force of the amendments introduced by Law No. 20,805, five tender processes have been carried out. In the 2015/02 tender, awarded in October 2015, 30 bidders submitted valid bids. The average adjudication price for this tender was of 79.3 USD/MWh. This represents a 40% price decrease in comparison to the adjudication price of the last tender process held before these amendments.

Moreover, the USD 47.6 adjudication price for the 2015/01 auction of August 2016 was the lowest so far.[46] It must be underscored that this price was obtained in the largest electricity supply tender process for regulated customers in the history of Chile, where a total of 12,430 GWh/year, equivalent to approximately one third of consumption of regulated customers, was auctioned.[47] In this, the second tender under the new legal regime, 84 offers from 64 different generators were received.[48] Moreover, in an unprecedented event for this type of tender, 50% of the awarded energy was from non-conventional renewable energies, with 2/3 of them coming from wind and solar power plants.[49]

In the first two tenders, consumption was implemented in three time-blocks: (i) Block A: from 00:00 hrs to 07:59 hrs, and from 23:00 hrs. to 23:59 hrs.; (ii) Block B: from 08:00 hrs. to 17:59 hrs.; and (iii) Block C: from 18:00 hrs. to 22:59 hrs.[50] This allowed the photovoltaic projects to offer a convenient price for the hours of higher generation of solar energy. Additionally, and concerning the entrance of new competitors, the results of these auctions were satisfactory also, as for the two processes following the reform of Law No. 20,805 the number of bidders significantly increased.

In the case of the 2017/01 auction, the results were even more impressive. The process was qualified as a milestone in the energy sector, due to the "historical" level of prices obtained. The adjudication price was USD 32.5/MWh, the lowest price since

44 Ibid., 65.
45 Aldo González and Isidora Palma, 14 and 15.
46 Chilean Ministry of Energy (no. 537), 8.
47 Ibid.
48 Ibid., 80.
49 Chilean Ministry of Energy Report, 8.
50 Ibid., 80.

the tendering system for regulated customers was established. The bidding resulted in 100% of the energy being awarded to new renewable energy projects.[51]

Thus, as a result of the regulatory changes, the main objectives have been met in the auctions carried out in Chile during the last years. These objects are reducing the prices of electricity, increasing competition in the electricity sector, incorporating new actors in the generation segment and diversifying energy sources.[52]

3.2.3 Availability of Public Lands

This section aims to explore the main provisions related to a public policy consisting of the facilitation of public lands in Chile for the development of solar and wind energy projects. This policy has been implemented by the Ministry of National Lands (*Ministerio de Bienes Nacionales*), which is the public agency in charge of the administration and use of the public lands.[53]

Since 2008, after the enactment of Law No. 20,257 which established specific targets of energy generated from renewable sources, this Ministry became a key actor for this industry. Chile has a considerable amount of public lands that can be used for various productive activities, including energy projects. Indeed, the country has more than 75 million hectares in total, of which more than 51% are under the management of this Ministry.[54] Naturally, since these lands are very useful for the placement of renewable energy projects, the Public Lands Ministry has signed several cooperation agreements with the Ministry of Energy.[55]

Provisions from the Ministerial Order

The public policy regarding the availability of public lands for energy projects is contained in the Ministerial Order No. 1/2017 of the Ministry of National Lands, which was published on the Chilean Official Gazette on May 11, 2017. The Order

51 ACERA, "Resultados del proceso de Licitación 2017/01," 2017."

52 Hugh Rudnick and Andrés Romero, "Hacia un modelo en competencia: Licitaciones de suministro eléctrico," in *Revolución Energética en Chile*, ed. Máximo Pacheco (Ediciones UDP, 2018), 425.

53 Article 3, Law Decree No. 1,939 of 1977. Unlike the common law tradition, under the civil law tradition public property is not a monolithic category. The latter tradition draws a distinction between public property (*bienes nacionales de uso público*) and State property (*bienes fiscales*). The Public Lands Ministry is entrusted with the management of the latter property. The main difference between both categories concerns who can use these properties. While the public in general is entitled to use public property, the use of State property is, prima facie, reserved for the state. This is prima facie in that the State can nevertheless authorize private parties to use this property through granting concessions or can even sell this property.

54 Ibid., 6.

55 Ministry of Energy, "Documentación Política Publica de Disponibilización de Bienes Nacionales para ERNC," 2017, 7.

No. 1/2017 provides the terms and conditions applicable to onerous land concessions ("CUOs" by its acronym in Spanish) granted over State-owned land for the development of renewable energy projects.[56] The Ministerial Order aims to facilitate the existing conditions and support the development of energy projects over State-owned lands by providing flexible mechanisms to promote the study of energy sources and develop new power plants.[57]

Application for a Concession

In accordance with the Ministerial Order No. 1/2017, as a general rule, the concession for energy projects is to be awarded through a public bidding process and, exceptionally, through direct assignment for due reasons, which the Ministry of National Lands must analyze and determine. The administrative procedure for a direct onerous use concession starts with a request from an interested party, which must contain, at least, the specific activity that is proposed to be developed in the public area; the term in which the project will be executed; the works that will be executed in the property and the proposed rent in accordance with the provisions of clauses 1 and 2 of Article 58 of Law Decree No. 1,939, of 1977. The administrative procedure of the public tender may also be initiate ex officio by the Ministry of Public Lands in specific cases, such as those lands with special energy potential.[58]

Steps of the Tender Process

The steps for granting a concession are the following: (i) The interested party must submit a request to the respective Regional Office of the Ministry of Public Lands indicating the area of interest (polygon), its location and surface. (ii) The Regional Office then analyzes if the property corresponds to an available public land and if the proposed area is consistent with basic criteria of efficiency and reasonableness in the administration of such lands. (iii) The Regional Office may deny the request or propose modifications to it within 30 days after the request's submission. (iv) Once the polygon has been approved by the Regional Office to initiate the bidding process, the interested party is notified and must deliver a guarantee bond within 30 days. (v) This guarantee bond warrants the participation of the interested party in the bidding process and the submission of an offer that complies with the minimum requirements established in the respective Bidding Terms. (vi) The Regional Office sends the necessary information to the Special Commission of Disposal of Public Lands to determine the commercial value of the land and propose the amount of the concession rent. (vii) Once the Bidding Terms have been approved

56 The Ministerial Order No. 1/2017 modified some aspects of the Ministerial Order No. 6/2013, which was applicable for previous applications of concessions.

57 Ministerial Order No. 1/2017 of the Ministry of National Lands.

58 Ibid.

by the Regional Office of the Ministry of National Lands, this authority makes the call for the public bidding.[59]

Term of the Concession

The term concession can be granted for a term up to 35 years, that starts once the concession contract is signed. Nevertheless, the concessionaire to put an early end to it during the Study Period and during the Period of Operation. During the term of the concession, the following three periods are considered: (a) Study Period; (b) Construction Period; and (c) Period of Operation. The term for the Study Period and Construction Period as a whole may not exceed 10 years, with no possibility of extension.[60]

Minimum Generation Requirement

The concessionaire must develop in the granted land a renewable energy generation project that meets a minimum requirement of electricity generation according to the type of energy. In the case of photovoltaic solar technology projects, the concessionaire must develop at least 1 MW for every 7 hectares of public land. As for wind technology projects and concentrated solar thermal, the concessionaire must develop at least 1 MW for every 12 hectares of granted fiscal land.[61]

Concessional Rent

The minimum concessional rent is fixed by the ministry, after a proposal from the Special Commission of Lands Disposal, according to the procedure established in Article 61 of Law Decree No. 1,939, of 1977. The concession contract establishes the two following rents: (a) the income concession for the Study Period, and; (b) the concessional income for the Construction and Operation periods.[62]

Awarding Criteria

The factors that the Public Lands Ministry must consider for the awarding of the concession are: (a) the amount that the concessionaire will pay to the Ministry of Public Lands in the Study and Construction Periods, which has to be equal to or greater than the minimum income established in the Tender Conditions, and (b) the income offered by the concessionaire in the economic offer for the Construction and

59 Ibid.
60 Ibid.
61 Ibid.
62 Ibid.

Operation periods. This rent must be equal or greater than the minimum income established in the Tender Conditions.[63]

Reserved Area

The Ministerial Order No. 1/2017 establishes that certain fiscal properties with special energy potential must be reserved. The tender of this so-called "reserved areas" can only be proposed by the authority.[64]

Permits for Prospecting and Monitoring

The execution of studies of prospection or monitoring of renewable energy resources must be requested through an "Occupation Permit for Prospecting and Monitoring Studies." This permit is requested before the Regional Office of the Ministry of Public Lands and can be granted for a maximum area of one hectare, though such authority can grant it for a larger area in special cases. This permit does not require the payment of rent and is granted for a period of 12 months.[65]

Outcomes of Policy of Concessions

Up to now, the public policy of availability of public lands has been highly useful for the development of renewable energies, in particular, for photovoltaic projects. According to a report from the Ministry of Energy, by the end of 2016, 313 applications of electric companies were registered for the granting of an onerous concession for energy generation purposes, of which 224 were approved. These concessions correspond to 124 different projects in public lands.[66]

Considering these 124 projects with granted concessions, the lands correspond to 42,529 hectares in public lands that can generate energy from renewable energy sources, of which 10,543 hectares are currently used by projects in operation. Of this surface of public lands, 6,264 hectares correspond to solar projects.[67]

3.3 Pending Challenges and Final Remarks

There is no doubt that Chile is proving to be a world power in renewable energy. That success is extremely related with the aforementioned public policies. On one hand, the design and implementation of a new system of public auctions for

63 Ibid.
64 Ibid.
65 Ibid.
66 Ministry of Energy (no. 579), 15.
67 Ibid., 16.

electricity supply has helped the entry of solar projects in the Chilean energy matrix. Therefore, the Chilean experiences with renewables can be helpful in conveying an important message for other countries that face the tough choices required to increase the participation of non-renewable sources in their energy generation matrix. Such a message is that the quest for competition and lower prices might help these sources when it is able to identify and eliminate those entry barriers that hinder their entrance to the generation market.

In addition, this significant reduction in the price of energy represents an important contribution to the social aspects of sustainable development, as it directly benefits local communities. On the other hand, the policy of disposal of public land through the concessions for the development of renewable energy projects has been helpful, as well, in that it reduces the costs that generators would otherwise incur to develop these projects.

Notwithstanding the above, the development of solar energy projects has still some pending issues as follows.

Environmental Impact Assessment

Until now, solar energy projects must enter the Environmental Impact Assessment System only when they refer to power generation plants greater than 3 MW, or when they are located in protected areas. In addition, during this process, citizen participation is only possible in those cases when requested by a group of at least 10 people or by two organizations. In practice, this has resulted in that most solar projects have never been consulted with the communities.[68] On the other hand, in the Chilean environmental legislation, there is no express mention of solar energy. This contrasts with the case of several other legislations that, for example, establish different evaluation standards considering the size of the project.

Barriers to Connection

Photovoltaic projects are located in remote areas, such as the desert in the north of Chile. Hence, their connection to transmission systems is not easy. So far there are no clear policies to promote the connection of these projects. Obviously, this results in a barrier to their development. In addition, the implementation of the connection to the local generation system (net metering regulation) has been deficient and unsuccessful.

In order to improve the incentives to solar energy generation, these policies must be constantly reviewed and updated.

68 Pilar Moraga and Miguel Saldivia (no. 525), 203.

4 Supportive System: The Example of Indonesia

Dr. Yolanda Tobing

4.1 Background

Indonesia is the largest archipelago nation in the world, consisting of 34 provinces encompassing 17,000 islands spanning 5,000 km. Its economic development has flourished over the past 20 years and this has not only contributed to poverty reduction, but has also uplifted the country status to the 10th largest economy in the world (World Bank, 2018). With an expected 6.8% annual growth of electricity demand in coming years and some 30 million out of 269 million population still without basic access to electricity, Indonesia faces an immense electricity challenge (UNDP, 2018). Large investments are needed to supply reliable power for households and industries across the country.

During the 2010–2018 period, the electrification ratio increased from 67.2 in 2010 to 84% in 2014, then 98.05% in 2018. Government of Indonesia (GoI) commits to carry out their best efforts, to increase the electrification ratio to 99.9% in 2019 through infrastructure development and local energy resources optimization.

Although the country targets 23% of electricity be generated from renewable energy (**RE**) sources by 2025 as stipulated in the National Energy Plan (RUPTL) 2019, the main energy source of electricity generation since 2007 is still coal power (58.64%), and other fossil fuel based energy such as gas (22.48%), and oil fuel (6.18%). RE is the smallest portion namely 12.71% (see Figure 4.1). This is an important improvement from 2017, when a couple years ago, the percentage of RE only accounted for 8% of primary energy mix while the other 92% fulfilled by fossil fuels, but there is still a need to increase efforts to meet GoI's goals.

As a result, Indonesia is the world's tenth largest greenhouse gas (GHG) emitter, not only because of the above mentioned fossil fuel based electricity sources, but also due to emissions which resulted from land use change, specifically the clearing and burning of millions hectares of tropical forests and peatlands to develop palm oil monoculture plantations. While Indonesia currently comprises the third largest tropical forest area in the world and functioned as the "Lungs of the Earth," the clearing of forest and peatland has deleterious effects on Indonesia's ecology.

Considering its important role in reducing GHG, at the COP Paris 2016 Indonesia pledged to reduce its GHG emissions by 26% against the business-as-usual scenario by 2020 and 41% if international support is granted. Part of its Nationally Determined Contribution (NDC) also includes a commitment to increase RE to become 23% of its primary energy mix by 2025, and 31% by 2050. Within the 23% of RE in the energy mix, the projections of Solar Power Plants are 5000 Mega Watt peak (MWp) in 2019

https://doi.org/10.1515/9783110607888-031

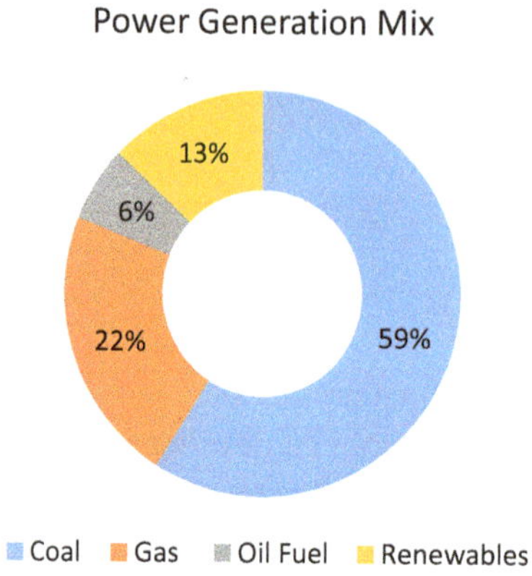

Figure 4.1: Indonesia electricity power generation mix (Source: Ministry of energy and mineral resources, 2019).

and 6400 MWp in 2025. This goal is part of Indonesia's plan to reduce greenhouse gas emissions in line with the 2016 Paris Agreement on Climate Change. This target is cohesive with the Association of Southeast Asian Nations (ASEAN) Plan of Action for Energy Cooperation's regional targets. To reach its targets, by 2025 Indonesia should supply 45 GW of its electricity from RE sources viz.:

- Approximately 92.2 Million ton of oil equivalent (Mtoe) of Total Primary Energy Supply (TPES);
- 23% RE share of TPES and 31% RE share of TPES 2050;
- 69.2 Mtoe (equivalent to 45.2 GW) electricity;
- 23Mtoe for non-electricity
  (ACE & CREEI, 2018)

Furthermore, according to the State Electricity Company (PT Perusahaan Listrik Negara/**PLN**)'s most recent data, the potential of RE in Indonesia reaches around 443 gigawatts (GW) which consists of solar power (60,65 MW), among other RE sources of hydro (94,48 MW), bioenergy (32,65 MW), geothermal (29,55 MW), and sea (17,99 MW). Despite an ambitious target and abundant potentials, RE seems to have not become a priority yet, thus necessary incentives have not been put in place. Nevertheless, to increase electrification ratio of nearly 1.1 million households who have no access to the national electricity grid (e.g., those who have been living at the outlying areas, smaller islands of the archipelagic country, and the eastern part of Indonesia), solar energy policy has to consider the affordability aspect of electricity production cost.

4.2 General Nature of the Support Regime for Solar PV Development in Indonesia

RE sources in Indonesia are still heavily reliant on large-scale hydro and geothermal power generation. Solar PV has not yet become a significant RE source. The development and the utilization of solar PV in Indonesia is still in its early stage. Its huge potential may reach 207.8 GWp due to the fact that Indonesia is geographically located along the equator, where the sun shines most of the year with the average daily radiation approximately 4.5 to 4.8 per square meter (MEMR BPPT, 2018). Moreover, the less-developed eastern region of Indonesia has a higher intensity of sunlight radiation compared to the more-developed western region. Nonetheless the installed solar PV capacity was still less than 100 MW in 2017 (0.018% of the potential) and currently is only 0.09 GWp (Source: IESR; GIZ in Antara News, Nov 2018).

The initiative to increase deployment of solar PV is led by the Ministry of Energy and Mineral Resources (MEMR) c/o the Directorate General of New, Renewable Energy, and Energy Conservation (DGNREEC) through a general policy on energy in 1998. A long term National Energy Policy specifically included the target to install 6.6 GWp solar energy sources by 2025 to comprise of:

- a large-scale solar power generation system
- solar home system (SHS)
- solar PV rooftop.

The policies support from government for solar PV development in Indonesia is implemented through a Feed-in Tariff (**FiT**), then a tender or quota-based system, and then a ceiling price setting based on the local and national PLN generation cost of electricity (see Figure 4.2).

In 2002, MEMR established a guiding principle that small-scale renewable generators could sell excess production to the national grid. Then in 2003 a national energy policy was formulated. Next, in 2004 MEMR stipulated subnational RE subsidies. In the following year, a Blueprint for National Energy Implementation 2005–2025 was established and the sectoral roadmap to reach the target for 17% RE of the primary energy by 2025 was stipulated. Next, MEMR Regulation No. 2 Year of 2006 on Medium-Scale RE Power Generation set an increased RE target to 23% to the total energy mix by 2025. This was legally confirmed by Law No. 30 Year of 2009 Chapter V Paragraph 2 on prioritization for RE in the National Energy Policy. Subsequently, in the same year, the MEMR Regulation No. 31 obliged the State Electricity Company (*PLN*) to buy power from IPPs which have capacities under 10 MW.

In order to further engage the private sector, the Minister of Finance (MoF) Regulation No. 77 substituted by MoF Regulation No. 139 of the same year of 2011 created an incentive in a form of a guarantee to pay for PLN financial obligation in its Power Purchase Agreements (PPA) with private electricity developers. When a private electricity developer has signed a loan agreement and has obtained

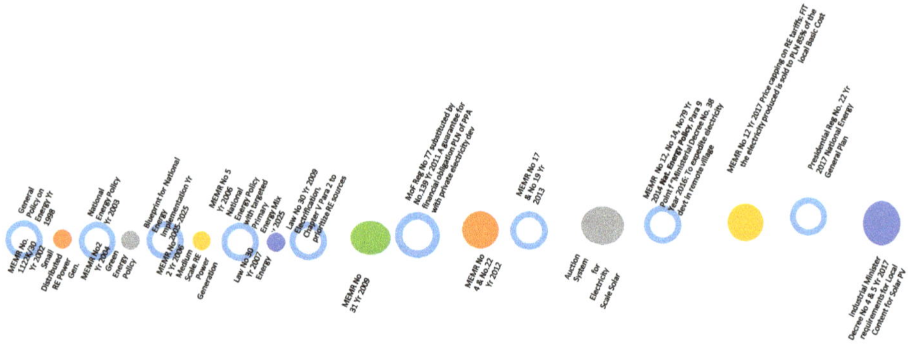

Figure 4.2: Transformation of RE policies in Indonesia, 1998 – 2018 (summarized by Author).

draw-down of bank's financing facilities to develop a power plant, the private electricity developer will receive a financial close from PLN. However, this scheme has not been able to increase the investment "appetite" of independent power producers (**IPPs**). Furthermore in 2013, MEMR defined an auction program to award FiTs to utility-scale solar projects. Subsequently in 2014 in the National Energy Policy, the government reaffirmed their target for 23% of RE in primary energy by 2025.

During the last five years (2015 through 2019) Indonesia has experienced dynamic regulation changes which led to low deployment of RE (Antara News 2018). The slowing development of RE in Indonesia has been caused by several factors such as regulatory uncertainties, higher perceived risk to investor, financing barriers, market barriers, and an undeveloped local renewables industry. These have caused investors to wait and see until the next regulations on RE provide an better investment climate and more certainty.

In all, despite the abundant solar energy potential in Indonesia due to its geographical location along the equatorial line, Indonesia's solar policy framework has failed to deliver cost-effective renewables for neither commercial, nor residential utilization. The government continues to institute policies which have hindered the adoption of solar PV. As a result, it is hard for investors to see the financial benefits, for example in the case of installing rooftop solar systems. The new Ministerial Regulation No. 49 which was launched last November 2018 is intended to enable owners of residential, commercial and industrial rooftop PV systems to "sell" their excess energy production to the national grid. In the current landscape, it is simply too difficult to realize financial benefits from installing rooftop solar systems. A more detail chronology of FiT implementation in Indonesia will be discussed as the following.

4.3 When Is the Feed-In Tariff Secured?

Feed-in tariffs (FiT) are fixed electricity prices that are paid to RE producers for each unit of energy produced and injected into the electricity grid.[1] The payment of the FiT is guaranteed for a certain period of time that is often related to the economic lifetime of the respective RE project. FiT are usually paid by electricity grid, system or market operators, often in the context of Power purchasing agreements (PPA). Indonesia applied FiT for hydropower since 2003, and geothermal power since 2008. FiT was initially seen as an effective scheme to create a market as it helped RE generation costs to be competitive with fossil fuel based power generation such as coal. FiT is also commonly implemented in several other ASEAN Member States included Philippines, Thailand and Vietnam (ACE and CREEI, 2018). Overall, FiT evolvements were implemented as shown in Table 4.1:

Table 4.1: FiT evolvements in Indonesia.

2003	**Electricity purchase from hydropower**
2008	Electricity purchase from small and medium scale RE excess power Electricity purchase from geothermal power plant
2012	Additional FiT for biomass, biogas, and waste Adjustment of Geothermal FiT FiT is based on region
2013	Electricity purchase from Municipal Solid Waste (MSW) Adjustment of MSW FiT Electricity purchase from **Solar PV**
2014	Electricity purchase from hydropower, biomass and biogas Adjustment of FiT for hydropower, biomass and biogas
2015	Adjustment of FiT for MSW, hydropower
2016	Adjustment of FiT for Solar PV, biomass and biogas
2017	FiT with new incentive scheme
2018	Withdrawn and Simplification of Various Minister Regulations

In 2012, Indonesia established FiT for several other technologies such as biomass, biogas, and waste, and then in 2013 it included solar PV. Afterwards, FiT has been

1 See for an overview of the different support regimes Goldner/Torwegge (chapter 5).

adjusted several times to reflect the technological advancement and cost reduction of RE technology. Although FiT has been enacted in Indonesia, the country still experiences a slow growth of installed solar PV capacity. In the period of 2012 to 2016, average annual growth of installed solar PV capacity is 3 MW as compared with other RE sources such as hydropower (309 MW) and geothermal (75 MW).

During the first two years of President Jokowi's administration (2014–2016), FiT was continuously implemented, particularly for geothermal and, micro/mini-hydro, and biomass and was later expanded for solar PV and wind energy. MEMR envisioned establishing an Energy Security (Revolving) Fund to accelerate RE deployment. During the last two years of President Jokow's administration (2017–2019), the national government's intention to support RE industry is not as strong as the earlier phase, as shown by uncertainties in the provision of FiT system

The MEMR Regulation No. 10 Year of 2017 specifically excludes several power plant types of its PPAs namely intermittent renewable energy, hydropower plants below 10 MW, biogas power plants, and municipal waste power plants. Then, the MEMR Regulation No. 12 Year of 2017 Article 5 paragraph 2 specifically stated that solar PV energy which will be purchased by PLN shall be implemented through a tender. The tender is to be determined by a capacity quota stipulated in the PLN Ten Year Business Plan for Electricity Supply (*RUPTL*) which published annually by the Directorate General of Electricity (DGE) of MEMR.

Recently, Indonesia replaced FiT mechanism by a new incentive scheme namely a ceiling price setting. It is based on the local and national production cost of electricity (**NPCE**). Through the MEMR regulation No. 50 Year 2017, it introduced a Build-Own-Operate-Transfer (BOOT) scheme for IPPs which signed contracts with State Electricity Company. All IPPs are expected to transfer solar PV projects back to PLN after the PPA expires. This restricts the economic life of solar projects to 20 years. It also sets the maximum price of electricity produced from RE sources to the State Electricity Company's network at 85% of the local reference price: the Local Production Cost of Electricity (**LPCE**) of *local BPP*. LPCE was determined differently in regions in Indonesia cf. the Ministerial Decree No. 1404 Year of 2017 and amended by the Ministerial Decree No. 1772 Year of 2018.

Table 4.2: Ceiling price setting mechanisms in Indonesia (Source: MEMR regulation no. 50 year 2017).

Energy	Mechanism	Condition	Tariff
Solar PV and wind	Direct selection based on quota	LPCE > NPCE	Maximum 85% of LPCE
	Build-Own-Operate-Transfer (BOOT)	LPCE ≤ NPCE	Agreement of parties

Table 4.2 (continued)

Energy	Mechanism	Condition	Tariff
Hydropower	Direct selection	LPCE > NPCE	Local Production Cost of Electricity
	BOOT	LPCE ≤ NPCE	Agreement of parties
Biomass, Biogas, Tidal	Direct selection	LPCE > NPCE	Maximum 85% of LPCE
	BOOT	LPCE ≤ NPCE	Agreement of parties
Waste, Geothermal	Refer to applied regulations	LPCE > NPCE	Local Production Cost of Electricity
	BOOT for geothermal	LPCE ≤ NPCE	Agreement of parties

This new incentive aimed to decrease the cost of electricity whilst lighten the financial burden of PLN as the State Electricity Company to pay the PPA. The policy was supposed to encourage RE investment in the eastern region of Indonesia as the LPCE in these areas were higher than the NPCE. Yet these drastic changing policies created uncertainties which increased risk profiles of RE projects and created bankability challenges for some developers. As a result, financial institutions became more risk averse, which resulted in limited funding sources for RE projects. Therefore, despite its intention, the BOOT reduced the likelihood of attractive refinancing opportunities, severely damaged exit opportunities for investors and discouraged long-term solar investments. From the point of view of the State Electricity Company, the absence of financing instruments such as surcharge and coal levies further discourages PLN to purchase renewables as the utility sees RE as burden to its budget when the electricity tariffs remain flat and the electricity subsidies have been reduced.

In the same year, the Indonesian Ministry of Industry (MoI) published regulations related to solar PV projects' local content requirement. MoI Regulation No. 4 Year of 2017 directed how various components of solar PV has to contain certain percentage of the local content, including the solar panels. Even though silica sand natural source is abundant in Indonesia and should be utilized, the requirement for local solar manufacturers to use certain percentage of "local content" of solar panels particularly has resulted in a significantly more expensive solar panels of lesser quality than imported products, whilst at the same time it suffers from lack of economies of scale. To achieve economies of scale, manufacturers need solid market prospects that will support investment. Unfortunately, solar energy policy roadblocks have stifled the market and projects have largely been limited to less economically attractive size of 5–15 MW range.

On one hand, solar PV producers are forced to match the price of base load coal-powered units which up to now are still heavily subsidized. In 2017 the total amount of subsidy for energy sector reached approximately US$ 5.57 million. PLN is heavily sustained by this energy subsidy (ACE & CREEI, 2018). At the same time, solar energy stakeholders do not receive any incentives, even implementation of FiT is not in favor of solar PV development.

4.4 Some Indication about the FiT Ceiling Price

FiT's price cap in Indonesia has evolved since 2013 and its funding source is secured by the State Revenue and Expenditure Budget (*APBN*). FiT implementation shows continued struggle derived as policymakers face a steep learning curve. Notably, characteristics of the DGNREEC policy roadmap were a lack of consistency and a number of course corrections. These uncertainties increased risk profiles of projects and created investment challenges for investors/financiers and project developers. Clearly, the inconsistencies of solar PV indicative prices and their associated procurement methods are shown in Table 4.3:

Table 4.3: Development of FiT price cap and procurement methods of solar energy in Indonesia. Source: Institute for energy economics & financial analysis, february 2019.

	MEMR Regulation No. 17 Year 2013	**MEMR Regulation No. 19 Year 2016**	**MEMR Regulation No. 12 Year 2017 amended by Regulation No. 50 Year 2017**	**MEMR Regulation No. 49 Year 2018 (Solar Rooftop)**
FiT Price Cap	US$ 0.25/kWh (if use solar PV modules with <40% local content). For the first ten years, and US$ 0.13/kWh for the second ten year period. US$ 0.30/kWh (if use solar PV modules with >40% local content).	Range between US$ 0. 145–0.25/kWh depending on project location.	Tariff should be lower than National supply cost of electricity (National BPP) or no more than 85% of local electricity supply cost (regional BPP) which ranges from US$ 0. 048–0.144/kWh depending on the location	Net metering scheme. Exported electricity will be offset with imported electricity from PLN. Exported electricity is valued at 65% for compensation. If export is higher, the balance can be accumulated for up to 3 months before it expires

Table 4.3 (continued)

	MEMR Regulation No. 17 Year 2013	MEMR Regulation No. 19 Year 2016	MEMR Regulation No. 12 Year 2017 amended by Regulation No. 50 Year 2017	MEMR Regulation No. 49 Year 2018 (Solar Rooftop)
Procurement method	Auction based on quota per annum. Direct appointment allowed if only 1 company bids.	Auction based on quota for certain pre-determined regions. Project size per developer is subject to a limit based on the available quota in the region.	Direct selection based on quota capacity.	Self-procurement.

Revenue of PLN mainly relies on consumer tariffs that are still under the power generation cost recovery rate and government subsidy. Consequently, the tariff as formulated in the PPA will have a reference to a tariff below the power generation cost of PLN. The changes in recent regulations and the issuance of tender system are both positive signals, and may indicate the willingness of industry to consider solar PV as a solution especially since the State Electricity Company is mandated by the government to purchase generated electricity from RE sources. According to the current regulations, the tender for RE power generation including solar PV project will have a ceiling tariff of 85% of the Local Production Cost of Electricity/ LPCE (Local BPP) if the local production cost is higher than the National Production Cost of Electricity/NPCE (National BPP). Figure 4.3 shows the FiT price cap range in twenty seven regions from the western to the eastern part of the country.

The ceiling price range varies from US$ 0.0668/kWh (the lowest, see Table 4.4) up to US$ 0.17/kWh (the highest). LPCE (*Local BPP*) in some developed areas where the grid is already over-supplied, such as in Java and Bali Island, are under the NPCE (*National BPP*). Whereas LPCE in other provinces are higher than the National BPP, particularly in Bangka Belitung islands, the eastern part of Indonesia i.e., Sulawesi, Nusa Tenggara, Maluku and Papua and in the Special District Aceh. The following table is a sample of detailed FiT ceiling price and its quota capacity:

The current pricing structure which caps the RE prices at 85% of Local Production Cost of Electricity is deemed as the main market barrier to obtain funding for new projects. In 2019 onward, the investment opportunities in RE projects in Indonesia will be heavily depend on successful implementation of 35 projects which signed PPA in 2017 which were eligible for bank loans (IESR, 2019).

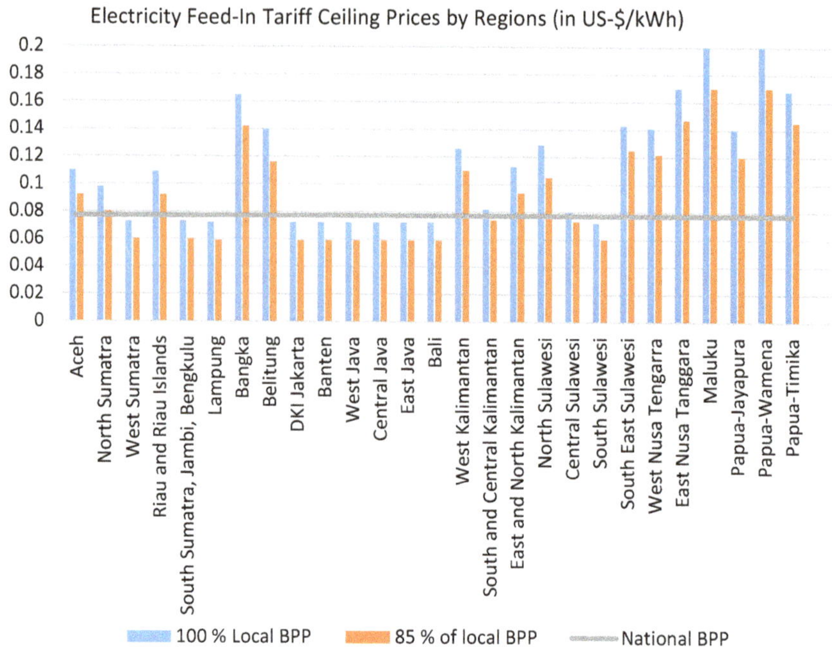

Figure 4.3: Electricity Feed-In Tariff ceiling prices by regions in US $/kWh (Source: Institute for energy economics & financial analysis, February 2019).

Table 4.4: FiT ceiling price in Sumatra Island.

PLN Regional Business Unit	Capacity Quota MWp	Generation Costs US$/kWh	Ceiling Price US$/kWh
Aceh	20	0.1039	0.0883
North Sumatra	35	0.0928	0.0789
Riau, Riau Islands, Bangka Belitung	38.68	0.1014	0.0862
West Sumatra	16	0.0807	0.0686
South Sumatra, Jambi, Bengkulu	33	0.0786	0.0668
Lampung	24.90	0.0777	0.0660

4.5 Grid Connection and Grid Management Practices of PLN

MEMR's purported role is to oversee the State Electricity Company, but in reality it is PLN that holds immense power when it comes to all aspects of grid connection and grid management in Indonesia.

In general, Indonesia has not yet established a special institution to function as a Transmission Service Operator (TSO) or Distribution Service Operator (DSO). In global best practice, IPPs will request the grid connection and pay for the connection charges to those entities in order to integrate their excess power to the national grid. While there are three type of connection charges available: connecting cost, parallel operating cost, and energy charge, they have not yet become a practice in Indonesia.

The grid connection policies of the Directorate General Electrification (DGE) MEMR stated that an electricity installation must satisfy safety and equipment standards determined by the MEMR by securing a SLO from an institution accredited by the DGE before it can connect to the transmission grid. The power generation facilities which connected to the transmission grid are subject to a power purchase agreement (PPA) or a grid lease agreement in accordance with an electricity supply business plan of the TSO (2019). Formally, a PPA should include a grid connection charge, however, this practice has never been the case due to the fact that the RE connection has always been demanded by PLN, as the sole state electricity company in the country.

PLN, the single buyer as well as the single seller of electricity in Indonesia, typically has the authority to decide which projects are approved and prioritized. It has ultimate control of the transmission and distribution systems meaning it gets to choose where and when new parts of the grid should be built. The increasing demand from multinational companies to use RE based electricity in Indonesia has to compete with PLN's interest to keep the national grid under its sole control.

The disregard of subsidies, price interventions, and externalities of coal creates an uneven playing field for solar PV development and, the enabling environment policies for renewables in Indonesia have not yet been in place. Some specific recommendation for Solar PV development should include:

- maintain policy consistency,
- remove regulatory barriers and streamline processes for licence/permits;
- ensure off-grid electrification projects of the outlying areas, smaller islands and the eastern part of the country
- use the declining costs of solar PV;
- support the development of appropriate sites where large-scale solar PV projects are likely to produce electricity price below the LPCE (*local BPP*) prices and develop these sites through RE auctions, and most importantly
- level the playing field for RE by phasing out burdensome subsidies to fossil fuels including coal.

References

2019

Adiatma Julius Christian, and Deon Arinaldo. 2019. "Indonesian Clean Energy Status Report 2018." http://iesr.or.id/wp-content/uploads/2018/12/Indonesia-Clean-Energy-Outlook-2019-new.pdf.

Brown, Melissa. 2019. "Indonesia at the Tipping Point: Will it be Coal Lock-in or a Clean Future?" Article published by the Institute for Energy Economics and Financial Analysis (IEEFA). http://ieefa.org/wp-content/uploads/2019/04/Indonesia-at-the-Tipping-Point_April-2019.pdf.

Hamdi, Elrika. 2019. "Indonesia's Solar Policies: Designed to Fail." Report published by the Institute for Energy Economics and Financial Analysis (IEEFA). http://ieefa.org/wp-content/uploads/2019/02/Indonesias-Solar-Policies_February-2019.pdf.

IESR. 2019. "Infographic on Status and Development of Energy Transition in Indonesia." http://iesr.or.id/wp-content/uploads/2019/04/IESR_Infographic_Status-dan-Perkembangan-Transisi-Energi-di-Indonesia.pdf.

Indonesia Population. 2019. https://www.worldometers.info/world-population/indonesia-population/.

Liputan 6 News. 2019. "State Electricity Company Provides Special Electricity Services of Renewable Source." https://www.liputan6.com/bisnis/read/3972521/pln-berikan-layanan-khusus-listrik-dari-energi-terbarukan.

Norton Rose Fulbright. 2019. "Renewable Energy Snapshot: Indonesia." https://www.nortonrosefulbright.com/en/knowledge/publications/0552a1f0/renewable-energy-snapshot-indonesia.

Sulaiman, Stefanno Reinard. 2019. "Is Indonesia Losing Favourable Clean Energy Policies?" *Jakarta Post*. https://www.thejakartapost.com/news/2019/03/04/explainer-is-indonesia-losing-favorable-clean-energy-policies.html.

Tumiwa, Fabby. 2019. "Reflection on RE Development in Indonesia 2015–2018 and Prospect for 2019" IESR website. http://iesr.or.id/refleksi-perkembangan-energi-terbarukan-indonesia-di-2015-2018-dan-prospeknya-di-2019/.

2018

ACE & CREEI. 2018. "ASEAN Feed-in-Tariff (FiT) Mechanism Report." Published by the ASEAN Centre for Energy (ACE), in collaboration with the China Renewable Energy Engineering Institute (CREEI).

AKSET. 2018. "Electricity Regulation: Indonesia." November 2018. https://gettingthedealthrough.com/area/12/jurisdiction/42/electricity-regulation-2019-indonesia/.

Antara News. 2018. "Indonesia and Germany commemorate 25 years cooperation in RE." November 22. https://en.antaranews.com/news/120697/indonesia-germany-commemorate-25-years-cooperation-in-renewable-energy.

Bridle, Richard, Philip Gass, Aidy Halimajaya, Lucky Lontoh, Neil McCulloch, Erica Petrofsky, and Lourdes Sanchez. 2018. "Missing the 23 Per Cent Target: Roadblocks to the development of renewable energy in Indonesia." Report published by the International Institute for Sustainable Development and the Global Subsidy Initiative. February 2018. https://www.iisd.org/sites/default/files/publications/roadblocks-indonesia-renewable-energy.pdf.

CLUA (Climate and Land Use Alliance). 2018. "Indonesia Initiative 2018–2022." http://www.climateandlandusealliance.org/initiatives/indonesia/.

Donker, Jasper, and Xander van Tilburg. 2018. "Grid Integration in Indonesia: Contribution of Variable Renewable Power Sources to Energy and Climate Targets." Report of the Ambition to Action project, part of the International Climate Initiative (IKI). The Federal Ministry for the Environment, Nature Conservation and Nuclear Safety (BMU) supports this initiative on the basis of a decision adopted by the German Bundestag. http://ambitiontoaction.net/wp-content/uploads/2019/04/A2A-2018-Grid-Integration-Indonesia.pdf.

IESR. 2018. "Igniting A Rapid Deployment of Renewable Energy in Indonesia: Lessons Learned from Three Countries," online access: http://iesr.or.id/wp-content/uploads/2019/05/IESR_Research_Igniting-a-Rapid-Deployment-of-RE-in-Indonesia.pdf.

MEMR & BPPT. 2018. "Indonesian Solar PV Rooftop Program: Facilitating Implementation and Readiness for Mitigation Project." NAMA Proposal prepared by Ministry of Energy and Mineral Resources in collaboration with the Agency for the Assessment and Application of Technology (BPPT), the UNEP DTU Partnership and the Danish International Development Agency (DANIDA) of the Ministry of Foreign Affairs of Denmark.

2017 and prior

Victor Pamela. 2017. "An overview of solar energy in Indonesia." October 24. https://theaseanpost.com/article/overview-solar-energy-indonesia.

Deloitte. 2016. "35,000 MW A Light for the Nation," a report by Deloitte Consultant Firm. https://www2.deloitte.com/content/dam/Deloitte/id/Documents/finance/id-fas-35000mw-a-light-for-the-nation-noexp.pdf.

Yuliani, Dewi. 2016. "Is Feed-In-Tariff Policy Effective for Increasing Deployment of Renewable Energy in Indonesia?" Helsinki: UNU-WIDER. https://www.wider.unu.edu/sites/default/files/wp2016-59.pdf.

ASEAN Centre for Energy. 2015. "ASEAN Plan of Action on Energy Cooperation." http://www.aseanenergy.org/wp-content/uploads/2015/12/HighRes-APAEC-online-version-final.pdf.

MCAI. 2014. "Guidelines for Electricity General Construction Renewable Energy to PLN Distribution System." http://www.mca-indonesia.go.id/assets/uploads/media/pdf/Pedoman-Penyambungan-PLT-EBT-ke-JARDIS.pdf.

Veldhuisa, A. J., and Angelina H.M.E. Reinders. 2013. "Reviewing the Potential and Cost-effectiveness of Grid-connected Solar PV in Indonesia on a Provincial Level." *Renewable and Sustainable Energy Reviews* 27 (November): 315–24, published by Elsevier. https://doi.org/10.1016/j.rser.2013.06.010.

Main Websites

Official website of the State Electricity Company / PT Perusahaan Listrik Negara (PLN). https://www.pln.co.id/.

Official Website of the Ministry of Energy and Mineral Resources (MEMR), Directorate General of New and Renewable Energy. http://www.ebtke.esdm.go.id/.

Minister of Energy and Mineral Resources (MEMR) no. 12 (2018) an amendment to MEMR no. 39 (2017) on Implementation of Physical Activities for the Utilization of New Energy, Renewable Energy and Energy Conservation. February 23, 2018.

MEMR Regulation no. 9 (2018) Revocation of MEMR Regulation on New, Renewable and Energy Conservation Business Activities. February 8, 2018.
MEMR Regulation no. 5 (2018) an amendment to the MEMR Regulation no. 33 (2017) concerning Procedures for Provision of Energy-Saving Solar Power Lights for Communities that Have Not Gained Access to Electricity." February 2, 2018.
Presidential Regulation no. 47 (2017) on "Provision of Energy-Saving Solar Power Lights for Communities that Have Not Gained Access to Electricity." April 13, 2017.
MEMR Regulation no. 17 (2013) on "The Purchase of Electricity by PT Perusahaan Listrik Negara (Persero) from Solar PV Power Plant."
Ministry of Finance Regulation no. 136 (2011) on "Procedures of Business Feasibility for the State Electricity Company / PT Perusahaan Listrik negara (Persero) to develop Power Plants of Renewable Energy, Coal, and Gas in Cooperation with Private Developers." http://fiskal.depkeu.go.id/pkppim/id/site/index/energi-baru-dan-terbarukan.
MEMR. "Solar PV plants along the the state border outermost regions, outlying and remote islands." November 17, 2018. https://www.esdm.go.id/id/media-center/arsip-berita/plts-akan-terangi-pos-jaga-perbatasan-tni-al-di-sulawesi-tengah.
MEMR Regulation on Rooftop Regulation. https://www.esdm.go.id/id/media-center/arsip-berita/regulasi-plts-roof-top-segera-diterbitkan. July 19, 2018. MEMR To Prepare a Rooftop Regulation. July 16, 2018.
Agency for the Assessment and Implementation of Technology (BPPT). "Recommended Solar Energy as an Electricity Source." September 5, 2018. https://www.bppt.go.id/kebijakan-teknologi/3269-bppt-rekomendasikan-energi-surya-sebagai-sumber-daya-kelistrikan.
Renewable Energy Colored the Asian Games 2018 in Palembang. July 2, 2018. http://ebtke.esdm.go.id/post/2018/07/02/1974/energi.terbarukan.warnai.asian.games.2018.dengan.hadirnya.plts.jakabaring.?lang=en.
"Renewable Energy Sources in South Sulawesi Province." May 9, 2018. https://www.esdm.go.id/id/berita-unit/direktorat-jenderal-ebtke/hadirnya-pembangkit-energi-terbarukan-di-sulsel-hasil-nyata-untuk-masyarakat.
"Do and Don't on Solar Power Plant-Off Grid." August 31, 2018. http://ebtke.esdm.go.id/post/2018/08/31/2007/buku.panduan.instalasi. pembangkit.listrk.tenaga.surya.
"Rooftop Net-metering of State Electricity Company's Customers will start January 1, 2019." November 28, 2018. http://ebtke.esdm.go.id/post/2018/11/28/2062/ekspor.impor.listrik.pelanggan.plts.atap.mulai.berlaku.1.januari.2019.
MEMR. 2016. Minister of Energy and Mining Resources regulation No. 19 Year of 2016: Purchase of Electricity Power from Solar Photovoltaic Power Plant by State Electricity Company.
MEMR. 2017. Minister of Energy and Mining Resources decision No. 1404 Year of 2017 on Power Generation Costs.
2017. Presidential Regulation No. 47 Year of 2017 Energy Saving Solar Lights Provision for Communities without Access to Electricity.
MEMR. 2018. Minister of Energy and Mining Resources regulation No. 49 Year 2018 Utilisation of Consumer Rooftop Solar Power Plant System by State Electricity Company.
MEMR. 2018. Minister of Energy and Mining Resources regulation No. 53 Year 2018, an amendment of regulation no. 49 Year of 2018 on Utilization of Renewable Energy Sources to Supply Electricity https://jdih.esdm.go.id/peraturan/Permen%20ESDM%20Nomor%2053%20Tahun%202018.pdf.

5 Supportive System: The Example of Thailand

Supawan Saelim

5.1 Introduction

Back to the past decade in 2007, renewable energy development is still nascent in developing countries including Thailand. At that time, the government needed to provide subsidies and supporting policies to provide incentives for investment in renewable energy markets.

Thailand is one of the earliest countries in South East Asia implementing supporting systems for solar power development since 2007 through its first supporting system, the Adder program, which offered a high fixed premium rate on top of wholesale electricity rates for solar power producers. Following the Adder program, a number of feed-in tariff (FiT) programs and a solar rooftop for self-consumption pilot scheme have been implemented in Thailand during the past decade. These supporting systems for solar photovoltaic (PV) have spurred significant investment in solar power market in Thailand. Consequently, Thailand is the leading country for solar power development in South East Asia in terms of installed capacity. The year 2017 marked a significant milestone reaching a 3 GW of solar installed capacity which accounts for about half of its solar target set under the Alternative Energy Development Plan (AEDP) for the years 2015–2036.

From the year 2007, when the first solar PV policy was announced through the introduction of the Adder program, the target for solar PV was increased from 500 MW in 2007 to 2000 MW in 2010, then further increased to 3,000 MW in 2013 with the introduction of FiT programs and to 3,800 MW in 2015 with the launch of the FiT Agro-solar program. Adding the target of 100 MW from solar rooftop for self-consumption pilot project, the target for solar PV in Thailand totaled to 3,900 MW in 2016, comprising of 3,600 MW for solar farms and 300 MW for solar rooftop.

As of 2017, Thailand has a cumulative solar PV installed capacity of about 3,211 MW, achieving about 82% of solar target under implemented supporting systems. Figure 5.1 illustrates key milestones of Thailand's implementation of supporting systems for solar PV development, including solar farms and solar rooftop systems. The installed capacity of solar PV under each supporting system are provided in Table 5.1.

Comparing solar PV installed capacity as a result of each supporting systems, Figure 5.2 shows that the Adder program and FiT for solar farm are the main drivers of solar installed capacity in Thailand. Meanwhile, the development of solar rooftop systems are emerging even without any supporting schemes due to rapid declining cost of solar PV in the past few years which incentivizes the installation of solar rooftop systems. The government expects to officially announce schemes for promoting solar rooftop installations soon in early 2019.

https://doi.org/10.1515/9783110607888-032

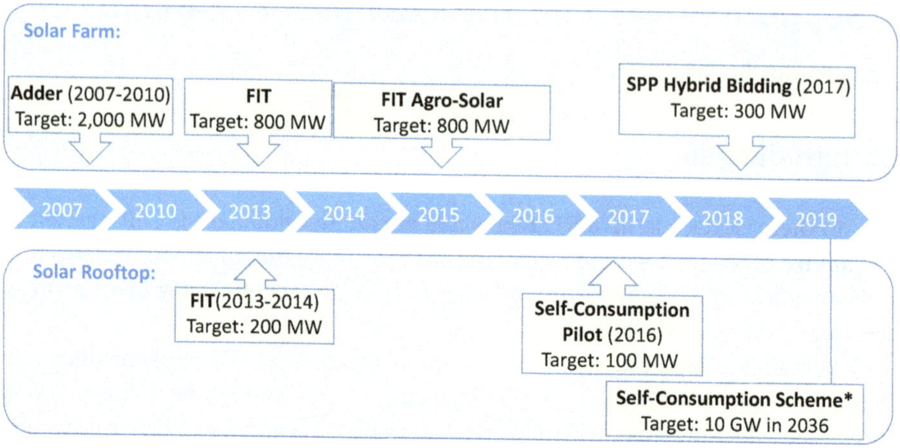

Figure 5.1: Key milestones for Thailand's solar PV supporting systems (own representation).

Table 5.1: Thailand's current solar PV installed capacity (own representation).

Project with power generation licenses as of May 2018	Target (MW)	Installed Capacity (MWp)
Solar farm	3,600	3,013
Adder	2,000	1,570
FiT (2014)	800	969
FiT Agro-Solar (2015–2017)	800	474
Solar rooftop	300	137
FiT (2013)	200	131
Self-consumption pilot (2016)	100	6
Solar PV from supporting schemes	3,900	3,150
Solar PV for self-consumption*		111
Solar PV for retail (private PPA)*		32
Total Solar PV		3,293

Source: Author's compilation from DEDE (2018) and ERC (2018)
**Without any supporting schemes, these solar projects are driven by private sector (no export of electricity to the grid is allowed) for the purpose of self-consumption and private power purchase agreement (PPA) among consumers and developers. The government expects to officially announce the self-consumption scheme in 2019 with the target of 10 GW by 2036*

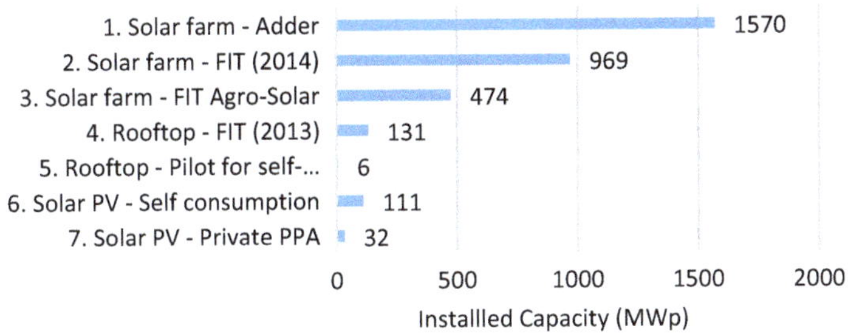

Figure 5.2: Key milestones for Thailand's solar PV supporting systems (own representation).

Section 5.2 and 5.3 provide the details of each supporting schemes for solar farms and solar rooftop, respectively, and Section 5.4 summarizes challenges and future opportunities for solar PV in Thailand.

5.2 Supporting Schemes for Ground-Mounted Solar PV or Solar Farms

Adder Program (2007–2010)

Thailand implemented its first supporting scheme for renewable energy in 2007 through the "Adder Program"' to incentivize renewable energy investment including solar PV. The solar PV target for the Adder Program was set at 500 MW in 2007 and increased to 2,000 MW in 2010.

Adder, or feed-in premium, is a premium rate paid on top of wholesale electricity rate for power generated from renewable energy resources. The government announced a fixed adder rate for solar PV at 8 Baht/kWh (or 0.23 USD/kWh) in 2007 and then reduced the adder to 6.5 Baht/kWh (or 0.19 USD/kWh) in 2010. Adder for solar was applicable for the very small power producers (VSPPs, up to 10 MW) and small power producers (SPPs, 10–90 MW) for the period of 10 years. The application for the Adder program was accepted until June 2010.

As a result of the Adder Program, there were huge applications leading to 300 solar projects commissioning with total installed capacity of 1,584 MW. The Adder program has later stimulated exponential growth of solar power market in Thailand during 2011–2013 with investment surged from backlog of applications coupled with rapidly declining cost of solar PV (Tongsopit, Chaitusaney, Limmanee, Kittner, & Hoontrakul 2015).

Despite the growth of solar market emerged from the Adder program, solar supporting schemes faced policy uncertainty with frequent changes and non-transparency in regulatory framework during 2007–2010 and the discontinuity of policy supports for solar power during 2010–13 before the new supportive scheme through feed-in tariffs (FiTs) was reopened for solar power development in 2013.

Feed-In Tariffs for Solar Farms (2013–2014)

After the Adder Program ended in June 2010, there was no supporting policy for solar power since 2013 when the first FiT policy was introduced in Thailand. The National Energy Policy Commission (NEPC) approved the feed-in tariff (FiT) rates for community ground mounted solar and solar rooftop in 2013. The combined solar PV quota under this FiT scheme was 1,000 MW, 800 MW for community ground-mounted solar and 200 MW for solar rooftop. This added up to solar PV target of 2,800 MW for solar farms and 200 MW for solar rooftop.

FiT program provides a fixed guaranteed purchasing price at FiT rates per kWh for the period of 25 years in Thailand. The FiT program for community ground-mounted solar (1 district, 1 MW) offered the electricity purchasing price at fixed degression rates, at 9.75 Baht/kWh for the first three year, then 6.50 Baht/kWh for Year 4–10 and 4.50 Baht/kWh for Year 11–25. All projects with the quota of 800 MW must be installed by December 2014 and administered by Thailand's Village Fund. However, due to lack of support from financial institutions to guarantee loans for the 1-MW system, the incentives for this community solar projects have stalled. As of May 2014, the government has transformed this 800-MW quota for community solar projects into a new program (see more detail in FiT for Agro-Solar program) for solar projects sited on the properties of the government and agricultural co-operatives through public private partnerships with a new set of rules and regulations released in 2015.

In addition, the government announced in August and October 2014 to procure solar power under FiT scheme at the FiT rate of 5.66 Baht/kWh for 25 years for solar projects to fill up total quota of 2,800 MW. This opportunity was offered to 178 solar projects earlier proposed under Adder program but not yet accepted with total capacity of 1,013 MW and be commissioned within December 2015. Financial guarantee was 200 Baht/kWp of installed capacity and capacity factor was 16%. As a result, 165 solar projects with total installed capacity of 969 MW have been commissioned under this FiT program in Thailand.

Feed-In Tariffs for Agro-Solar Program (2015–2017)

As mentioned in the previous section, the quota of 800 MW for community solar projects announced in 2013 was transferred to a new program called "Governmental agency and Agricultural cooperative (Agro-Solar) program" to procure power from solar free-field installations located on land owned by two groups, governmental agencies or agricultural cooperatives,[1] with the quota of 400 MW each.

1 Governmental agencies include universities regulated by the government, governmental organizations (excluding public organizations and state enterprises) and local administration unit. Agricultural cooperatives include land settlement cooperatives, fishing cooperatives.

In 2015, the government announced the details and regulations for this program applicable for VSPP's solar farms with the capacity up to 5 MW in the form of public-private partnerships (PPP). The program was split into two phases: In Phase 1, solar projects which had submitted their applications in November 2015 were entitled to receive a FiT rate of 5.66 Baht/kWh for 25 years whereas Phase 2 application which opened in May 2017 with a quota of 219 MW (100 MW for Government and 119 MW for agricultural cooperative) and received a FiT rate of 4.12 Baht/kWh for the same duration (see Table 5.2). The FiT rates are applicable for power purchase not exceeding a capacity factor of 16% (GIZ 2017).

Table 5.2: Feed-in tariffs under Agro solar program (own representation).

Characteristics	Phase I	Phase II
FiT	5.66 Baht/kWh	4.12 Baht/kWh
PPA duration	25 years	25 years
Application period	November 2015	May 2017
Commercial Operation Date (COD)	December 31, 2016	December 31, 2018

Application under this program is eligible for only either a government agency or agricultural cooperative as the project owner or PPA holder, which can form a public-private partnership with a project supporter. Each project supporter must be a company registered in Thailand and can support more than one project up to 50 MW in total.

As a result of the program, there were about 59 projects with total installed capacity of 255 MW commissioned under Phase I. There was huge oversubscription under Phase II with total proposed capacity of about 3,510 MW from 720 applicants[2] compared to the target of only 219 MW. The criteria for selection was based on first-come first-served basis and considered feeder capacity. The ERC closed Phase II with announcement of 35 applicants eligible for PPA contracts with total installed capacity of 154.52 MW in Phase II. The selected applicants included 11 governmental agencies (52.52 MW) and 24 agricultural cooperatives (102 MW). These projects must be commissioned by December 2016 under Phase I and December 2018 under Phase II as well as signing the PPA with distribution utilities (MEA and PEA) within 120 days after announcement of the results. Solar projects commissioned under Agro solar program account for about 14% of solar PV in Thailand.

2 Applicants include 3 universities (15 MW), 37 governmental agencies (195 MW), 40 agricultural cooperatives (200 MW) and 680 industrial estate and fishing cooperatives (3,310 MW).

5.3 Supporting Schemes for Solar Rooftops

Feed-In Tariffs for Solar Rooftop Program (2013–2015)

The Thai government announced the first FiT policy to support solar rooftop PV in the country in 2013 with a total target of 200 MW, a 100 MW for commercial (10–250 kW) and industrial (250–1000 kW) rooftop system size, and a 100 MW for residential rooftop (up to 10 kW) systems. The government announced "Solar rooftop Phase II" in 2015 to reopened the program only for residential rooftop systems to fulfill the remaining quota.

Different FiT rates are applied for three rooftop PV systems classified by system size as specified in Table 1.1. FiT rates for solar rooftop PV are in the range of 6.16 to 6.96 Baht/kW for projects applied during Phase I in 2013 (commercially operated by the end of 2014) and 6.85 Baht/kW for residential rooftop system applied during Phase II in 2015 (commercially operated by the end of June 2016), see Table 5.3.

Table 5.3: FiT rates for solar rooftop installations (Baht/kWh), own representation.

Type by capacity	Phase I (2013)	Phase II (2015)
Residential (up to 10 kW)	6.96	6.85
Commercial (10–250 kW)	6.55	Not applicable
Industrial (250–1000 kW)	6.16	Not applicable

As a result of the FiT program for solar rooftop PV, while the quota of 100 MW for commercial and industrial rooftop systems was fully subscribed, there were only approximately 21 MW achieved out of the 100-MW target for residential rooftop system in Phase I. Later in 2015, the remaining quota of 78.63 MW was fully allocated to fulfill the 100-MW target for residential solar rooftop systems in Phase II. While the incentives for solar rooftop investment at commercial and industrial scale were realized by private sector resulting in an oversubscription to the FiT program in the first round, the market for solar rooftop at residential scale was still developing and new to households at residential scale. Due to the complicated permitting process and licensing, many of systems could not be commercially operated by the original deadline, hence; the deadlines for commercial operations of solar rooftop systems in both two phases were postponed several times by the regulator.

Solar Rooftop Self-Consumption Pilot Scheme (2016)

The National Energy Regulatory Commission proposed in 2015 the policy "Solar Quick Win Project" aiming to promote solar rooftop installations for self-consumption which is connected to the grid. The policy has the long-term target of 10,000 MW for rooftop solar. According, the Energy Regulatory Commission (ERC) officially announced the Solar PV Rooftop Self-Consumption Pilot scheme in August 2016 to allow government agencies to first monitor and evaluate data under the scheme in order to plan for appropriate future scheme to support solar rooftop. The pilot scheme targeted a 100 MW quota of solar rooftop installations for self-consumption.

Under the pilot scheme, a 100 MW quota is allocated equally between two distribution utilities with a 10 MW each for residential rooftop (up to 10 kWp) and 40 MW each for commercial rooftop (up to 1 MWp). Electricity generated from solar rooftop PV systems must be produced for self-consumption and there is no compensation for any excess electricity fed to the grid. The application for the pilot project was opened for submission from August 22, 2016 to October 7, 2016 and the rooftop systems must be installed by January 31, 2017.

As a result of the pilot scheme, there were about 358 projects with 32.75 MW capacity applied. However, only 6 MW out of 100 MW quota was commercially in operation as of August 2017. This low uptake of solar rooftop under the pilot scheme was partly due to consumers' lack of awareness, complicated permitting process and short submission period.

Self-Consumption Installations without Supporting System

Despite low uptake of solar rooftop systems under the pilot scheme, rooftop solar systems outside the pilot scheme have been emerged in Thailand due to the economic incentives from rapid declining cost of solar PV for both self-consumption purpose to reduce electricity bills and retail sale of electricity by private sector under private PPA model, especially for commercial and industrial consumers. As of May 2018, there were about 342 solar power generating licenses with total 92 MWp registered for self-consumption and about 17 solar power producers for private PPA. Since the solar rooftop pilot scheme in 2016, the government has not yet announced any supporting scheme putting in place to support solar rooftop installations.

5.4 Challenges and Potential Future Supporting Systems for Solar PV

Notwithstanding the fact that Thailand is the first mover in the region implementing supporting systems for solar PV, there have been a lot of past and future uncertainties about government policies to support solar power development. During its past 10 years of implementing the solar supporting systems, Thailand has faced several transformation of policy support: transitioning from the Adder to the FiT, replacing the FiT program for a community solar projects by FiT Agro-solar program, and from lucky draw selection criteria to competitive bidding process. In addition, discontinuity of policy support and uncertainties around future supporting systems could potentially deteriorate the growth of solar PV development in Thailand.

Future supporting systems for solar farm in Thailand is transitioning from FiT towards competitive bidding. Thailand implemented its SPP-hybrid firm auction in 2017 which allows, for the first time in the country, solar projects and the combination of solar and energy storage projects to deliver firm power to compete in the bidding. However, after SPP-hybrid firm auction, next schedules and quota for procurement of solar power through competitive bidding are still unknown as of December 2018.

For solar rooftop installations, the government announced in public hearings of the country's power development plan (PDP) 2018 that a 10 GW quota will be added for solar rooftop generated from private sector for self-consumption by 2036. The detailed regulations have not yet been set for fulfilling the quota. In October 2017, the government proposed net billing scheme for self-consumption of solar rooftop systems which offer the compensation for the export of excess electricity to the grid at the rate lower than wholesale tariff. However, the net billing scheme has not yet been approved. The trends towards electricity trading and the roles of blockchain have recently become the focus of the government. The introduction of future supporting systems for solar rooftop installations is promising in Thailand.

6 Supportive System: The Example of the Philippinest

Claire Marie Yvonne C. Lee

6.1 Introduction

Solar Energy remains to be one of the most viable renewable sources of energy in the Philippines. The Philippine National Renewable Energy Program (NREP) aims to increase the utilization of renewable energy in the energy mix. As of 2015, the renewable energy Share in the power industry is at 33.9% and most of the capacity comes from combined solar, wind and biomass. According to the Philippine Department of Energy (DOE), the total installed capacity of utility solar in 2017 is at 900.17 MW with a potential capacity of 5,181.67 MW (see Table 6.1). Only 526.0 MW of this capacity was able to avail of the Feed-in Tariff (FiT). After two rounds of the FiT, it was discontinued and succeeding installations must fall under the auction scheme, Power Supply Agreements (PSA), merchant solar market and other policy mechanisms under the renewable energy Act.

The archipelagic nature of the Philippines combined with the high average daily insolation of 5 kWh/m^2 make solar installations the most obvious and practical solution for electrification among all the renewable energy technologies. Microgrids and hybrids that make use of PV technology increase energy resilience and grid reliability in the country's numerous islands.

The history of solar PV usage in the country can be traced back to the 80s, when small PV systems were being utilized for the country's rural electrification program. Many islands in the Philippines are not connected to the major electric grids. In 1989, the Philippine German Solar Energy Project introduced solar technology in Burias Island, Masbate through a 280 Wp solar powered medical refrigerator, a 72 Wp PV system to power a local telegraph and radio station, and several Solar Home Systems. During that time, a training center called the UP Solar Laboratory was established in the University of the Philippines to train local installers.

The first utility scale solar power plant was built in Indahag, Cagayan de Oro in 2003 by the local electric cooperative Cagayan Electric Power & Light Co Inc. (CEPALCO).The 1.1 MW solar power plant was built in partnership with Sumitomo Corp. and provides energy to about 900 residential customers of CEPALCO.

In 2008, the Renewable Energy Act was signed into law, promoting the use of renewable energy and providing incentives to investors and developers.

In 2012, the first tranche of the Feed-in Tariff (FiT) was issued with the solar allotment capped at 50 MW. In that year, the first solar carport was installed in Laguna by Trans Uyeno Solar Company. Around the same time, the Asian Development Bank launched its 571 kWp rooftop solar on its headquarter office in Ortigas, Pasig City.

https://doi.org/10.1515/9783110607888-033

The following year saw the Energy Regulatory Commission's (ERC) adoption of the Implementing Rules and Regulations of Section 10 of the renewable energy Act to enable the Net Metering Program. In 2016, the ERC registered 2.95 MW of solar rooftops nationwide from twelve distribution utilities.

In 2014, DOE and ERC expanded the solar FiT cap from 50 MW to 500 MW. Under DC2013-05-0009, the guidelines for the Certificate of Endorsement for FiT eligibility was outlined. DOE affirmed the date for the deadline of start of commercial operation for FiT eligibility on March 15, 2016. Twenty projects totalling 526.0 MW were listed under the FiT scheme under a "first come first served" policy.

Upon the announcement of the DoE in May 2017 that the FiT will no longer be extended, the industry has shifted its focus to PSAs, micro-grids and rooftop installations. Other policy mechanisms under the renewable energy Act has been recommended by the NREB for adoption to create a new market for solar. These will be discussed in the following paragraphs.

6.2 Background on the Philippine Energy Sector

6.2.1 Electric Power Industry Reform Act (EPIRA)

Prior to 2001, the Philippine power sector was vertically integrated under the National Power Corporation (NPC). Under the Presidential Decree No. 40 issued in 1972, NPC had jurisdiction on both transmission and generation of electricity nationwide. A decade later, the NPC had accumulated billions in debt and could not operate its mandate efficiently. NPC was not able to respond to the increasing power demand, through maintaining and developing its generation portfolio.

In 1987, Executive Order No. 215 was passed to encourage privte sector participation in the power sector. The Build Operate Transfer (BOT) Law was enacted three years later to permit private contractors to construct and operate power generation facilities. Despite these two legal frameworks, power generation was still not proportionate to the increasing energy demand of the country. Investors were still negotiating power contracts with the NPC which slowed the process and discouraged private sector participation in the power sector. At this point NPC power plants were only operating at 50–70% of their capacities.

In 1994, a World Bank study recommended radical reforms to the Philippine power sector. This drove the improvements made on the existing laws to encourage private sector participation and eventually the implementation of the Electric Power Industry Reform Act of 2001 (EPIRA).

The EPIRA was meant to reorganize the entire power industry and to unbundle transmission and generation responsibilities from the NPC.

Key highlights of the EPIRA are as follows:
1. The deregulation of the energy sector,
2. Creation of new government-owned transmission company and the eventual privatization of the operation of the transmission system,
3. Unbundling of supply activities from the regulated distribution sector,
4. Elimination of cross subsidies within and among various grids, and among various classes of consumers,
5. Creation of an independent regulatory body and a Joint Congressional Power Commission to oversee implementation of the law,
6. Privatization and sale of NPC assets and contracts with Independent Power Producers (IPPs) which would give government the cashflows needed to pay off NPC's debts and create a fair competitive atmosphere among generators and encourage private entity participations.
7. Creation of a Wholesale Electricity Spot Market (WESM) for energy trading.
8. Implementation of retail competition and open access.

6.2.2 The Renewable Energy Law

The development of renewable energy sources is central to the country's sustainable energy agenda. In 2008, the Renewable Energy Act was executed to show the full commitment of the Philippine government to develop the country's renewable energy resources. It recognized the potential of renewables in addressing energy security, climate change and access to energy by providing incentives to the private sector investors, equipment manufacturers, suppliers and developers. It was aimed at encouraging the utilization of renewable energy sources to achieve energy self-reliance and decrease dependence on fossil fuel imports, minimize exposure to fuel price inflations, mitigate climate change, and promote socio-economic development in rural regions.

6.2.3 Incentives under the Renewable Energy Act

Fiscal Incentives

The high upfront cost of the development of solar PV systems was identified as one of the challenges during the implementation of the renewable energy Law. Thus, the Law provided numerous fiscal incentives to encourage the utilization and lower investment costs of renewable energy in general.

The following fiscal incentives were applied to developers and some may also apply to local renewable energy suppliers.

- Seven Year Income Tax Holiday (ITH)
- Reduced Government Share

- Duty-free Importation of Equipment
- Special Realty Tax equal to 1.5%
- Net Operating Loss Carry-over
- 10% Corporate Rate after ITH
- Accelerated Depreciation
- 0% VAT on renewable energy Sales and Purchases
- Cash Incentive of 50% of Universal Charge for Missionary Electrification
- Tax Credit on Domestic Capital Equipment and Services
- Tax Exemption on Carbon Credits

However, in reality, these incentives were only availed by utility scale solar projects. Smaller solar installations such as rooftop solar, fall under the other non-fiscal incentives such as Net Metering. Government technical working groups both in Congress and the Senate still debate on the employing these incentives on smaller solar system projects.

Another issue is that, ten years after the passing of the Law, these incentives may become invalid. Under the present administration's Tax Reform for Acceleration and Inclusion or TRAIN Act, the incentives promoting renewable energy in the country will be reduced or completely stopped. Some of the proposed reforms under the TRAIN include: removal of the VAT incentives and special realty taxes, repeal of the Net Operating Loss Carry-over, accelerated depreciation, tax exemption on carbon credits, tax credit on domestic capital equipment and cash incentives for Missionary Electrification. The ITH has also been amended to being applicable only to the first five years and for a period not exceeding three years. These are only to name a few. The renewable energy industry feel that with only two incentives fully implemented under the renewable energy Law (FiT and Net Metering), the full benefits of these incentives have not been fully realized. Arguments and counter propositions are being discussed to continue the incentives or at least provide alternatives for investing in renewable energy projects.

Non-Fiscal Incentives

Feed-In Tariff

The biggest driver for the development of the solar in the Philippines was the implementation of the Feed in Tariff (FiT) in 2012. As of June 2017, NREB lists a total of 900.2 MW installed on-grid solar power plants – including those that were not subscribed under the 2-phase FiT program.

The FiT refers to a renewable energy policy that offers guaranteed payments on a fixed rate per kWh for emerging renewable energy sources, excluding any generation for own use, or to rate itself.

Under the FiT Rules, eligible renewable energy Projects are entitled priority connection to the grid, priority purchase and transmission of and payment for by grid system operators, and a fixed tariff for 20 years.

In 2012, the ERC announced the approved FiT rate of Php 9.68/kWh or USD 0.24/kWh. The cap for the first round was set at 50 MW and was quickly met. The first round of the FiT program closed at 108 MW distributed across six solar projects. Resolution No. 6, Series of 2015 revised the original rate to Php 8.69/kWh or USD 0.18/kWh and increased the cap to another 450 MW. The policy was on a "first come, first serve" basis and interconnection to the grid to avail of the FiT rate was set on March 15, 2016.

The policy lead to oversubscribed contracts and stranded projects. The Philippine Government is looking at an auction scheme to address the issue, as well as provide a framework for future solar installations and usage in the country.

FiT-All

The FiT Rules also envision the establishment of the FiT-All. It is the uniform charge imposed on electricity consumers who get their electricity through the distribution or transmission network. This is to ensure that there is equitable sharing in the cost of the FiT. The FiT-All is set by the ERC on an annual basis upon petition by the National Transmission Corporation (TransCo), which is tasked with the settlement of the FiTs of all eligible RE plants.

On December 16, 2013, the ERC issued Resolution No. 24, series of 2013, which laid down guidelines in determining the FiT-All, the disbursements of the FiT-All Fund, the roles of stakeholders, the collection of the FiT-All and administration of the FiT-All Fund.

TransCo, as FiT Administrator, must ensure that the FiT-All fund is sufficient to pay all RE producers regularly. As such, TransCo must include an adequate allowance for the working capital requirements in case some customers default in their obligations. TransCo is therefore authorized to enter into an RE Payment Agreement (REPA) with eligible RE plants.

Net Metering

On July 24, 2013, the rules on Net Metering took effect after its approval from the Energy Regulatory Commission. The rules enable on-grid customers to export excess energy from their installed renewable energy systems in their premises for their own use. The law limits the nameplate capacity of the renewable energy system to under 100 kWp. The reason for the capacity limit being that under the renewable energy Law, Net Metering is only applicable to small generation entities supplying directly to the distribution grid – the definition of small generation providing for the cap. This has always been an area of contention which will be discussed more in the succeeding paragraphs.

Once a residential or commercial facility owner decides to install a renewable energy facility in his premises there are three major permits that need to be applied for. The small installations covered under the Net Metering scheme may be of any renewable energy technology – biogas, biomass energy, mini hydro, wind and solar. Although majority of the applications for net metering are from solar rooftops due to its modularity, scalability and fast installation time.

On-grid customers or consumers with good credit standing under the Distribution Utility franchise are referred to as Qualified End-users (QEs). These QEs must first apply for Net Metering service application from their distribution utility. There are 144 distribution utilities and electric cooperatives nationwide and each has its own requirements for application. Unfortunately, lack of knowledge and proper training on the rules and interconnections often cause blocks in the implementation of Net Metering in the country.

One of the biggest DUs in the Philippines, MERALCO, has the largest number of Net Metering applications. As of end of 2018, they have received about 12 MW applications from its franchise area. During the first couple of years, the DU has been criticized for its vague fees and requirements, as well as delays in providing a bi-directional meter to its applicants. Through numerous dialogues with the solar industry in the Philippines, MERALCO has improved its Net Metering procedures.

Local Government Units (LGUs) must be consulted as well if one installs a small renewable energy system, even a PV rooftop system. The Office of the LGU Engineer usually issues an electrical permit and conducts an ocular inspection during the commissioning test of the system. However, due to the lack of uniform and streamlined requirements, each LGU may have a different set of permitting system.

The final permit that needs to be complied with is from the Energy Regulatory Commission. It is a registration for a renewable energy system either for own-use or under the Net Metering scheme. Once the final commissioning test has been finalized and all other permits secured, an application fee of Php 5,000 is paid to the ERC office and the system is registered once a Certificate of Compliance (CoC) is issued or thirty days have passed.

Renewable Portfolio Standards (RPS) for On-Grid

The RPS for On-grid Rules is a market-based policy that requires electric power industry participants to source an agreed upon portion of their supply from eligible renewable energy resources. The following entities are mandated to comply:

1. Distribution Utilities
2. Licensed Retail Electricity Suppliers
3. Any supplier of last resort
4. Generation Companies
5. Entities that operate within the economic zones
6. Other entities recommended by NREB and approved by the DOE

It was proposed with the goal of increasing the renewable energy contribution in the country's energy mix to 35%. The minimum annual target per grid is based on the net electricity sales of the 1% annual increment and percentage share of FiT plant generation. It is calculated as equal to the sum of the minimum target of all mandated participants in the grid calculated with the formula, all expressed in MWh:

$$RPS_{(n)} = ES_{(n-1)} * \sum_{m=0}^{n} K_m$$

The RPS for On-grid areas is applicable to the grids in the three archipelagos – Luzon, Visayas and Mindanao. The eligible facilities and renewable energy Generators are those who have started the Commercial Operation Date (COD) after the effectivity of the renewable energy Act. Their compliance will be measured based on RECs generated by the participants with 1 MWh = 1 renewable energy Certificate. The trading, monitoring and registration of these RECs will be governed by the RE Market and the RE Registrar which are yet to be established. A bidding or the Competitive Selection Process (CSP) will observed when sourcing for the RE generators.

Currently, the Department of Energy is conducting information campaign programs to familiarize mandated participants on the procedures for the RPS for On-grid. Conversely, data have been gathered from the participants for the determination of the RPS requirements.

6.2.4 Green Energy Option

The Green Energy Option Program is a voluntary and non-regulated activity that empowers the end-users to choose renewable energy sources in meeting their energy requirements. It was promulgated through Department Circular No. DC2018-07-0019 which was published in August 2018. The document indicates the general rules and procedures to properly guide the end-users, renewable energy suppliers, network providers, to facilitate the decision of the end-users to choose renewable energy sources. It also considers the various options for the consumers to utilize renewable energy sources in an inexpensive and sustainable manner. The rules will also make transparency possible in all transactions through full disclosure. The rates and charges to the end-users will be itemized and unbundled.

Only a draft of the GEOP has been completed and is set for the issuance of an operating permit. DOE is set to conduct public consultations on the matter.

6.2.5 Renewable Portfolio Standard (RPS) for Off-Grid

The RPS for both On-Grid and Off-Grid are part of the renewable energy Law mechanisms to promote the use of renewables. The RPS envisions the creation of a renewable energy Market. Currently, the rules governing the establishment of the RPS for Off-Grid areas are under review.

The RPS Off-Grid Rules mandates that the NPC-SPUG and its partners, successors, and QTP parties must source a minimum portion of its annual generation from qualified renewable energy resources in its missionary electrification activities.

The policy dictates that an optimal supply mix must be indicated as part of the Missionary Electrification Development Plan (MEDP). A minimum percentage of renewable energy share in the portfolio must be maintained by all mandated participants consistent with the optimum supply mix. The baseline annual requirement is still being finalized. Annual incremental renewable energy requirement for succeeding years shall also be determined and shall not be lower than 1.0% of the previous year renewable energy generation.

The following mechanisms may be used by the mandated participants to fulfill the requirements under the RPS Off-Grid Rules:

1. Contracted eligible renewable energy facilities covered by PSAs from NPD-SPUG's own generation facilities
2. Generation supplied by NPPs or QTPs covered by PSAs with DUs
3. Embedded generation facilities within the franchise areas of the DUs
4. renewable energy Certificates (REC) purchased in the renewable energy Market

6.3 Solar Off-Grid Development in the Philippines

Being an archipelago, the Philippines has many areas that are regarded as unviable for provision of electrical services due to its disconnection to the three main power grids of the country. As of 2016, there are about 2,123,110 households that have no electricity, resulting to only 90.65% nationwide electrification level.

Rule 13 of the EPIRA Law of 2001, prescribes the general rules and procedures to encourage the private sector to participate in electrifying the off-grid areas determined by the National Power Corporation or what is called the NPC-SPUG areas. Therefore, there are several Department Circulars that advise on the involvement of the private sector in missionary electrification. These rules are applicable to both traditional and renewable sources of energy.

According to the DOE Department Circular 2004-001-01, unviable areas refer to the "geographical area within a Franchise Area of a Distribution Utility where extension of a distribution line is not feasible." These areas are determined by the NPC-SPUG. Aside from accelerating the total electrification of the country, it is the hope of the government to reduce the obligation on the Universal Charge on Missionary Electrification or the UC-ME, by allowing private parties to take part of the responsibility of electrifying theses unviable areas.

Private sector participants are referred to as New Private Participants (NPP) or Qualified Third Party (QTP). To distinguish between the two classifications, NPPs are private entities that are deemed capable to serve or take over an NPC-SPUG Area, while a QTP is an alternative service provider that meets standards under DOE Department Circular 2005-12-011, to serve unviable areas. Both must undergo a competitive selection process (CSP) which is conducted either by the Department of Energy, the Distribution Utility or the NPC-SPUG. Both NPPs and QTPs shall undergo a qualification process before being able to participate in the (CSP) and once chosen, their contracts or PSAs are regulated by the ERC.

6.4 Other Relevant Policy Frameworks

6.4.1 Distributed Energy Resources (DERs)

The draft Licensing Rules for Distributed Energy Resources under the ERC is an important issuance for on-grid distributed generation. Prior to this rule, PPAs were vague as it was legally impossible to execute under the EPIRA which exclusively grants franchise areas to DUs and ECs. The DER Rules allow for the commercial arrangements to take place within franchise areas of DUs. It also clarifies the different certificates issued by ERC per category. The DER Licensing is an addendum to the 2014 rules on CoC Issuance.

The DER Licensing Rules differentiates between the following Certificates of Compliance (CoC)

1. Net Metering CoC
2. Self Generation CoC
3. Independent Power Producer (IPP) CoC
4. DER CoC

A CoC is a requirement for all entities to operate generation facilities. The Net Metering CoC refers to renewable energy facilities that are connected to the grid 100 kW and below, and exports excess production to the DU/EC under which the facility is registered. Self Generation CoC refers to energy facilities that do not export to the grid and whose owner consumes all power generated for its own operations. IPP CoC refers to the sale made by IPPs under RA 9136. The CoC DER addresses the gray area where microgrids and distributed power technologies are grid connected and have commercial operations within a DU franchise. Usually the DERs that fall under this category is greater than 100 kW, with the maximum capacity depending on the Distribution Impact Study (DIS) or System Impact Study (SIS), but the rule limits the maximum capacity at point of connection to 10 MW for DERs located in Luzon and 5 MW for DERs located in Visayas and Mindanao.

The draft Licensing Rules also state that a RES is not required if a DER serves the requirements of a single contestable customer under a commercial agreement. Once it involves multiple contestable customers, then a RES will be required.

6.4.2 Senate Bill 1719: Solar Rooftop Adoption Act of 2017

On June 3, 2018, a bill was filed in the 17th Congress of the Philippine Senate. The draft law was authored by Senator Grace Poe, with inputs from the solar private sector players. The bill incorporates lessons learned from the past ten years and amends the portion of the renewable energy Law on Net Metering.

There are five proposed amendments under the Senate Bill 1719.

1. Removal of the 100 kWp cap on distributed generation to allow large electricity consumers on commercial and industrial buildings to avail of the Net Metering program under RA 9513
2. Insertion of an explicit provision that the same reference price should be applied to both electricity imported from and exported to the grid by end-users.
3. Requiring the Department of Energy, Energy Regulatory Commission, National Renewable Energy Board, Department of Interior and Local Government to standardize permits and licenses needed to install rooftop panels (harmonization).
4. Institutionalization of the rooftop solar loan program of the PAG-IBIG Housing Fund
5. Mandatory installation of rooftop solar panels on government buildings, which shall increase by 5% every five years.

As of July 2019, the bill is set to be refiled in the 18th Congress of the Philippine Senate. The Philippine solar industry, Solar and Storage Energy Alliance (PSSEA) PSSEA, continues to support and monitor the bill.

6.4.3 Moving Forward

The country's renewable energy roadmap aims to reach at least 20,000 MW installed capacity for all renewables by 2040. To achieve the target, the government plans to finalize the remaining RE policy mechanisms and incentives to develop the market for solar and other RE technologies. These include implementing the RPS and the Renewable Energy Market, the Green Energy Option, as well as review other RE policy mechanisms. The government also plans to conduct RE resource assessments, determine real RE potential in the country and maintain a resource database. The government will also focus on creating greater access to energy in the off-grid areas and intensify rural development.

Recently the DOE has been improving the business atmosphere for RE projects by streamlining the administrative procedures for the different permitting and registration processes. More importantly, DOE aims to harmonize of local and national related initiatives. This will avoid the confusion in the current practice where each LGU and electric cooperative has different requirements. DOE has also made the EVOSS, a computer platform, online to make application for service contracts easier.

DOE will also continue to provide technical assistance and incentives to local technology producers.

The RE roadmap also includes strengthening technology infrastructure which includes improving the transmission grid system to accommodate the increasing RE injection onto the grid. This also includes carrying out research on the efficiency of RE technologies on the smart grid system. There are also plans to develop geographical installation targets. In-country technical capacity building also remains a priority in achieving the target MW installation by 2040.

Table 6.1: Utility Scale Solar Installations in the Philippines as of June 2017.

Installed Utility Solar Capacity in the Philippines, as of June 2017					
	Proponent		**Grid**	**Size (MW)**	**Approved FiT**
	Solar Installations Under the FiT				
1	San Carlos Solar Energy Inc. (SACASOL)	SACASOL 1A & 1B Solar Power Plant	Visayas	22.00	Yes
2	Majestics Energy Corp.	Solar Power Plant	Luzon	41.30	Yes
3	RASLAG Corp.	Solar Power Plant	Luzon	10.00	Yes
4	San Carlos Solar Energy Inc. (SACASOL)	SACASOL 1 C & 1D Solar Power Plant	Visayas	23.00	Yes
5	Solar Philippines	SM North EDSA	Luzon	1.50	Yes
6	RASLAG Corp.	Pampanga Solar Power Project Phase II	Luzon	13.14	Yes
7	Petrosolar Corp. (PSC)	Tarlac Solar Power Plant	Luzon	50.07	Yes
8	Mirae Asia Energy Corp. (MAEC)	Curimao Solar Power Plant	Luzon	20.00	Yes
9	YH Green Energy Inc. (YHGEI)	Solar Power Plant	Luzon	14.51	Yes
10	Monte Solar Energy Inc. (MONTESOL)	MONTESOL Solar Power Plant	Visayas	18.00	Yes
11	Helios Solar Energy Corp.	Cadiz Solar Power Plant	Visayas	132.50	Yes
12	Solar Philippines	Calatagan Solar Philippines	Luzon	63.30	Yes
13	Valenzuela Solar (VALSOL)	Valenzuela Solar Plant (embedded to MERALCO)	Luzon	8.50	Yes

Table 6.1 (continued)

Installed Utility Solar Capacity in the Philippines, as of June 2017					
	Proponent		**Grid**	**Size (MW)**	**Approved FiT**
14	Enfinity Philippines Renewable Resources, Inc.	Clark Solar Power Project (embedded with CEDC)	Luzon	22.33	Yes
15	Asia Greenergy Corp.	Kibawe Solar Power Project	Mindanao	10.49	Yes
16	SPARC	Palauig Solar Plant (embedded to ZAMECO I)	Luzon	5.02	Yes
17	Energy Development Corp.	Burgos Solar – Phase 1	Luzon	4.10	Yes
18	Energy Development Corp.	Burgos Solar – Phase 2	Luzon	2.66	Yes
19	CleanTech Global Renewable	Bulacan Solar Power Plant	Luzon	15.00	Yes
20	NV Vogt Philippines	Centrala Solar Power Project	Mindanao	6.23	Yes
21	First Cabanatuan Renewable Ventures	Cabanatuan Solar Power Project	Luzon	10.26	Yes
22	Absolut Distillers, Inc.	Lian Solar Power Project	Luzon	2.04	Yes
23	First Soleq Energy Corp.	Ormoc Solar Power Project	Visayas	30.00	Yes
			SubTotal	**525.95**	
	Filed for Reconsideration to be Included Under the FiT				
24	Negros Island Solar Power Inc. (ISLASOL)	ISLASOL II Solar Power Plant	Visayas	32.00	No
25	Negros Island Solar Power Inc. (ISLASOL)	ISLASOL III Solar Power Plant	Visayas	48.00	No
26	Megawatt Clean Energy Inc. (MCEI)	Silay Solar Power Plant	Visayas	25.01	No
27	Next Generation Power Generation Corp. (NGPT)	Mariveles Solar Power Project	Luzon	18.00	No
28	Enfinity Philippines Renewable Resources, Inc. Fourth	Digos Solar Power Project	Mindanao	28.59	No

Table 6.1 (continued)

	Installed Utility Solar Capacity in the Philippines, as of June 2017				
	Proponent		**Grid**	**Size (MW)**	**Approved FiT**
29	SPARC	Morong Solar Plant (embedded to PENELCO)	Luzon	5.00	No
30	SunAsia Energy Corporation	Toledo Solar Power Plant	Visayas	60.00	No
31	Sulu Electric Power and Light	Palo Solar Power Project	Visayas	49.81	No
32	Pure Energy Holdings Corp./ Solar Powered Agri-Rural Communities Corp.	San Rafael Solar Farm	Luzon	3.82	No
33	NV Vogt Philippines	Armenia, Tarlac	Luzon	8.84	No
34	NV Vogt Philippines	Dalayap Victoria Tarlac	Luzon	7.48	No
			Subtotal	**286.55**	
	Operating Under Other Mechanisms Such as PSA or Merchant Solar				
36	Sun Carlos Sun Power Inc.	San Carlos Solar Power Plant	Visayas	58.98	No
37	Cosmo Solar Energy, Inc.	Miag-ao Iloilo	Visayas	5.67	No
38	Jobim-Sqm Inc	Sta.Rita Solar Power Project	Luzon	7.14	No
39	Bosung Solartec, Inc.	Sarrat Solar Power Project	Luzon	1.00	No
40	CW Marketing and Development Corporation	CW Home Depot	Luzon	1.68	No
41	Kirahon Solar Energy Corporation	Kirahon Solar Power Project	Mindanao	12.50	No
42	Solar Philippines Commercial Rooftop Projects inc.	Central Mall Binan Solar Power Project	Luzon	0.70	No
			Subtotal	**87.67**	
			TOTAL	**900.17**	

Solar Energy: Concentrated Solar Power

1 Technology of Solar Thermal Projects: Current Status and Developments

Andreas Wiese

1.1 Basic Considerations

The term "solar thermal power generation" is described as an energy conversion process wherein the solar radiation from the sun is converted into heat, which is channeled into mechanical energy through a thermodynamic cyclic process and results in electrical power being supplied. Since the radiation is concentrated, these systems are usually defined as Concentrated Solar Power (CSP).

CSP is distinctively different from CPV (Concentrated Photovoltaics) technology. Although CPV also concentrates solar radiation, it is using the photovoltaic effect to generate electricity out of solar light and not via the energy conversion chain of heat and rotational (mechanical) energy as it is the case in a CSP plant. CPV technology will not be addressed further in this section.

Since solar radiation is diverted, directed and concentrated in solar thermal power generation, only the direct radiation portion can be used because the diffuse radiation cannot be concentrated. Such power plants are therefore applicable in regions where the direct radiation percentage is correspondingly high – for example the Earth's equatorial sun belt region.

1.1.1 Usable Solar Radiation for CSP Power Plants

Direct Solar Radiation

The radiation conditions on the earth's surface are important for the utilization of solar energy in CSP power plants. Solar radiation represents a key input for the CSP plants and thus has a significant influence primarily on the economic parameters of the plant.

The division of the total radiation into a direct radiation component and an indirect, diffuse radiation component is important for the implementation of CSP technology. The scattering mechanism within the atmosphere causes direct and diffuse radiation to hit the earth's surface. Under the term direct radiation, we thus understand, radiation which originates directly from the sun and without any scattering hitting a particular point on earth. The radiation is characterized by uniform direction. On the other hand, diffuse radiation is the radiation that arises due to scattering in the atmosphere and indirectly reaches a certain receiving point. This scattering arises essentially due to reflection of the radiation on clouds and/or aerosols (water droplets, subpar-particles). Smaller proportions of the diffuse radiation

https://doi.org/10.1515/9783110607888-034

also result from the atmospheric counter radiation and the radiation reflected by the earth's environment.

The direct radiation that takes place at a flat area oriented at 90 degrees to the direction of irradiation is also known as the direction normal irradiation. The direct irradiation which occurs on a horizontally aligned surface is referred to as direct horizontal radiation (DHI = Direct Horizontal Irradiation). The sum of DHI and diffuse radiation on the horizontal receiving surface is called the Global Horizontal Irradiance (GHI).

For solar thermal power generation, an intense concentration of radiation must take place in order to achieve sufficiently high temperatures. This is done by directing the direct radiation onto a receiving surface with the use of optical devices such as mirrors or lenses. Such optical devices can only focus the direct radiation at a defined point. Due to this, the direct radiation is the relevant radiation component in solar thermal power generation technology.

The global irradiation varies during the course of the day and year and its annual sum of global irradiation is strongly dependent on the position. In addition to this, the share of direct radiation at the total global irradiation varies substantially daily and seasonally, depending on the location. All in all, this results that the annual sums of direct radiation on earth are subject to much greater differences than the annual sum of global irradiation. This is a major reason why CSP power plants cannot be built in almost any region as it is the case with photovoltaic power plants.

Since the average radiation outside the earth's atmosphere is known as 1.367 W/m^2 (the solar constant), the radiation on earth's surface can be calculated using the cloudiness, monitored and documented by satellite images. However, this method does not always lead to precise results. One reason is because the influence of aerosols cannot always be adequately captured by satellites. Satellite data for DNI are therefore only suitable for initial assessments. Before using this assessment for further planning, it is recommended that the values are compared with ground measurement and to be corrected as necessary.

For an accurate estimation of radiation on a particular location, measurements taken ideally over a long term period (several years) are appropriate. Depending on the quantity and quality of the available long term measurements taken at surrounding locations, long term forecasts can be derived from the results of a one year measurement, correlated with the long-term data, with notable accuracy.

Radiation Concentration

As mentioned above, the direct radiation is concentrated in order to achieve a higher energy density. This concentration can be on a line or on a point. In the first case it is addressed as line concentration (typical application: parabolic trough power plants), in the second case point concentration (typical application: solar power tower power plants). An important factor in this context is the concentration factor. This is defined as the ratio of the aperture area to the absorber area. Assuming ideal concentration, the concentration factor can also be calculated as the radiation density on the absorber surface to the radiation density on the aperture surface. In the case of line focusing, the theoretically maximum possible concentration factor is 213, with a point focusing a maximum of 46,050.

Real concentration factors are smaller because:

- the reflective surfaces are not ideally flat, but are real bodies with manufacturing tolerances.
- the placement and alignment of the overall systems are not ideal.

1.1.2 Basic Energy Chain and Classification of Technologies and Systems

The typical steps of energy conversion in solar thermal power plants can be summarized by the following:

1. Capturing of solar irradiation with the help of a mirror system.
2. Concentrating the radiation on the solar receiver.
3. Conversion of radiation energy to heat in the solar receiver.
4. Transfer of thermal energy to the energy converter unit.
5. Converting thermal energy into mechanical energy with the help of a heat-power machine (e.g: steam turbine, sterling engine).
6. Converting mechanical energy into electrical energy using a generator.

Figure 1.1 shows the basic energy conversion chain of solar thermal power generation.

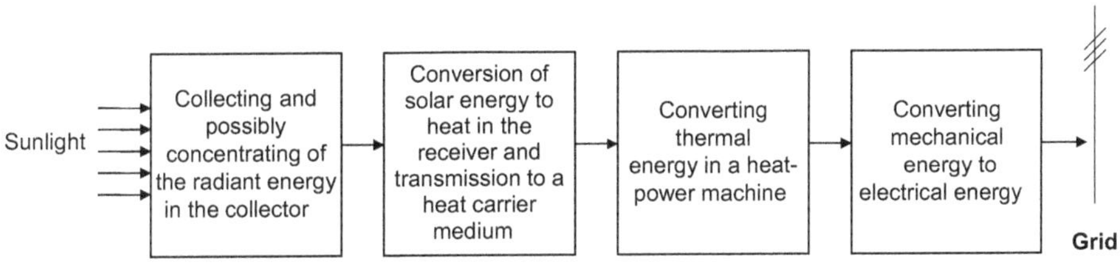

Figure 1.1: Energy conversion chain in solar thermal power generation [2].

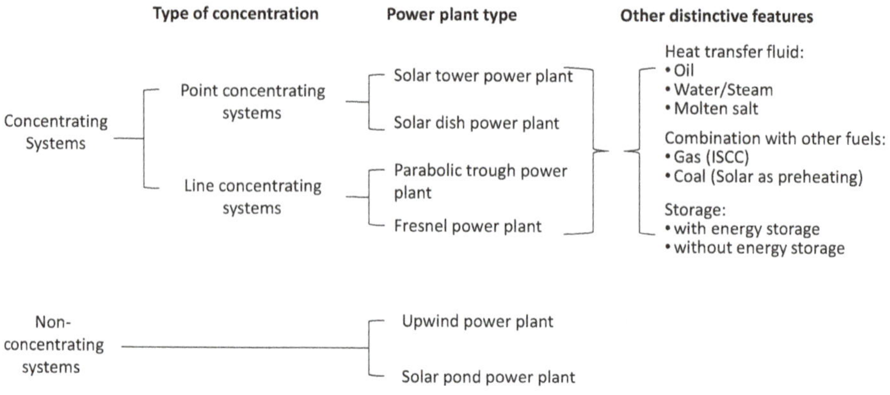

Figure 1.2: Classification of various solar thermal power plant technologies [2].

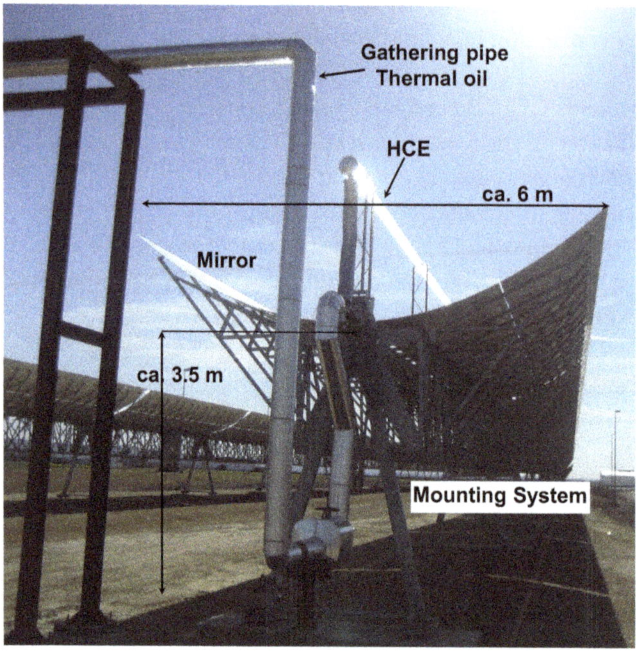

Figure 1.3: Components and typical geometries of the collector [2].

1.1.3 Classification of Technologies

Solar thermal plants can be classified into concentrated and non-concentrated systems (Figure 1.2). Among the latter are solar updraft power towers. This technology is not discussed further in the section. The concentrated power plants are further subdivided into point and line-focus solar concentrating systems. These are subsequently divided into various criteria's: (i) depending on the type or principle of radiation receiver used (parabolic trough, linear fresnel reflectors, heliostat), (ii) in accordance to the type of heat transfer medium (thermal oil, water vapor, less irrelevant so far: salt or gas), (iii) with regards to the combination with other fuels (oil, gas or coal) and with other types of power plants (Integrated Solar Combined Cycle (ISCC)) or (iv) whether storage is included or not.

1.2 Parabolic Trough Power Plants

Parabolic trough power plants belong to the line-focusing solar thermal power generation plants. In this solar thermal power generation technology, the reflective surface of a parabolic mirror focuses the sun's energy onto a receiver pipe located along the focal line of a parabola. The direct sunlight is reflected so that the receiver pipe located in the center is irradiated and heated. The concentration ratio C is between 70 and 90. The heat transfer fluid (HTF) located in the receiver pipe is heated by the concentrated solar radiation and flows through the pipe into a steam generator where the thermal energy is transferred to the steam of the steam turbine process and with a downstream generator is converted into electrical energy.

A parabolic trough power plant consists of two main areas, the solar field and the power plant. The essential components of a solar field are (i) parabolic reflectors, (ii) receiver tube, (iii) the support frames for the absorber tubes, mirrors and the tracking system, (iv) the heat transfer medium (v) the pipelines through which the heat transfer medium is pumped, (vi) the control devices and (vii) the heat exchange between the solar field and the power plant unit. The power plant block includes a (i) steam generator together with solar preheating and solar superheating, (ii) steam turbine, (iii) generator, (iv) condenser and usually (v) a boiler with additional fossil fuel heating to provide steam.

1.2.1 Components

Parabolic Mirror

The mirrors are assembled segmentally. Each segment contains a significant curvature which forms a parabolic shape after assembly. The mirror segments have to be very precise and have a high form of degree which is the reason why they are quite complex in terms of manufacturing. In addition to dimensional stability, features such as good reflection properties, high resistance to environmental influences and certain breakage stability are required.

In the currently operational power plants, the mirrors are usually made of white glass with very low iron content. The glass is mirrored with a silver layer on the back and protected against the weather conditions with an epoxy paint coating. The alternatives to this are polished surfaces, foils, thin metal foils, thin glass and plastic. Until now no alternative material have been used commercially on a larger scale.

Receiver Pipe

After the reflection of the radiation on the focus line the radiation is absorbed by the receiver pipe and converted into heat. The receiver is formed by a coated tube that is surrounded by a glass tube. The space between the coated tube and the glass tube is evacuated. This prevents heat conduction and minimizes thermal losses. The glass itself reflects back a substantial portion of the long wavelength radiation which is emitted from the tube. This system comprising of a coated pipe and glass tube is referred to as the Heat Collecting Element (HCE). The HCE must:

- have a high transparency at its outer surface (glass tube), so that the radiation can impinge on the receiver tube;
- have high absorption levels for the radiation of the entire solar spectrum at the surface of receiver tube;
- secure the vacuum in the intermediate space and compensate the different expansions with temperature fluctuations of metal and glass body.

Collector

Mirror systems and receiver tubes are applied to carrier systems. These three components form the collector. A collector consists of a series of segments. The lengths of each segment is approximately 12 m. Up to 12 segments are assembled into a single collector. The length and aperture are important indicators to the estimated size of a collector. The geometric concentration of sunlight (aperture area to absorber cross-sectional area ratio) is generally between 50 and 90. For a Euro-trough collector the value would be approximately 82. A Euro-trough collector has an aperture width of 5.76 m and a length of 99 m (EURO Trough I Collector) and 144 m (EUROTROUGH II collector).

These types of collectors are mounted on the floor with several columns. The collector can follow the sun around its axis of rotation during the day, which is why it is known as a uniaxial tracking system. The large aperture width of over 5 m means that the collector must be mounted with some distance above the ground so that there is no contact between the collector and the grounds when it is turning. The collectors are correspondingly high. The distance between the axis of rotation and the ground is approximately 3.5 m (Figure 1.3).

The collector itself includes mechanical devices for tracking, such as motors and hydraulics along with solar control technology, which is attached to the collector.

Collector Field

Multiple collectors are connected together to form collector loops. Generally, a loop has a length of about 600 m, containing a cold end and a warm end which is directly connected to the system. Inside the collector fields, the axis of the collectors are orientated in the north-south direction.

With regard to the design of the collector fields, the distance between the collector rows is an important criterion to take into consideration. The selected space has an impact on the shadowing in the morning and the evening causing a loss in collected solar energy and therefore lesser energy available for conversion and power generation in the overall system. In other words, in order to achieve the highest levels of efficiency, the space should be large so that minor shading effects are minimized. On the other hand if the land area increases this would lead to an increase in land costs as well as the piping costs.

Shading effects are dependent on the latitude. The optimal distance must be recalculated for each location. As a rule of thumb, the distance between collector rows (from HCE to HCE) is three times the aperture width. Collector fields are erected on horizontally oriented surfaces. Only very small inclinations are tolerable, inclined surfaces are either avoided or terraced. In addition to the collectors and their foundations the components of the collectors include the complete piping in which the heat transfer medium is circulated, pumps and valves and the infrastructure required along the required for construction and operation. For example, paths or roads between collector fields and access roads.

Heat Transfer Medium

The purpose of the heat transfer medium is to remove the solar energy concentrated on the absorber tube and convert it into thermal energy. Synthetic oil is commonly used in almost all commercial applications. The temperature of the synthetic oil is limited to about 400 degrees due to chemical stability.

At higher temperatures, the oil is decomposed and must be replaced. The synthetic oils used are generally expensive and are needed in large quantities. For a solar farm with an electrical output of 50 MW, about 900 tons of thermal oil at a price of 5,000–10,000 euros per ton are required. As a result – and also because of the temperature limit – alternatives to thermal oil are sought. One possibility is to generate steam directly in the collector pipes without an intermediate heat transfer medium. This means that water respectively steam circulates in the HCEs. In such a concept other aspects have also to be taken into account. Such as:

- The pipe systems must be resistant to higher pressures at the same temperature and as a result they are heavier.
- Since a partial phase change from liquid to vapor will occur as it passes through the HCE, 2-phase currents and a sudden phase transition is expected. In this case, jerkily loads occur, which take effect on the connecting elements at the ends of the channels and can lead to the breakage of pipes.

Another technology that has also been tested is allowing the HCEs to flow through with liquid salt. The salts used are stable for temperatures well above the thermal oil-induced temperature limit of 400 degree. However, molten salts have downwards critical temperature limits. Crystallization is expected at temperatures below 250 degrees. This leads to the formation of solid salt crystal in the elements or the transport pipes which can be removed only with a large degree of effort. In order to avoid the crystallization process to take place, the receiver pipes must be heated.

Direct evaporation and molten salt are currently seldom used in the field of transport fluids in connection with large commercial parabolic power plants. The following descriptions therefore assume thermal oil as the heat carrier.

Heat Exchanger

The heat transfer medium of the solar field is pumped through the heat exchanger where the heat is transferred to the water steam cycle of the power plant process. The structure of the heat exchanger is similar to that of a classic steam generator.

Steam Cycle

In the steam cycle, warm water is initially pre-heated by thermal oil, after which it is evaporated and finally overheated. Depending on the design of the system, the steam, which has to be overheated solely with thermal oil, is further overheated by heat from the combustion of natural gas or oil or through other heat sources. Subsequently this overheated steam is directed to a steam turbine and expanded between the turbine blades. A part of the thermal energy is converted into mechanical rotational energy of the turbine. The expanded steam is condensed to water in the condenser and is subsequently brought back to the appropriate pressure with a feed water pump, so that the cycle can repeat itself (Figure 1.4).

The total efficiency of the steam cycle (between the energy transferred from the steam cycle in the heat exchanger and the energy delivered to the steam turbine) is approximately 20–30% in case the power plants is operating at rated power. The degree of utilization which is the average efficiency over the year, is usually between 12 to 15%.

Steam Turbine

The basic output range of steam turbines for parabolic trough power plants is from 1 MW up to several hundred megawatts of power. Nowadays trough power plants are usually built in the range of 50 MW, going as far as 100 MW. The steam turbines which are commercially available for CSP power plants are mostly those which are cut down by higher possible outputs and undergo necessary adjustments for special operation in CSP power plants in order to work in the desired output range. Companies that manufacture steam turbines include Siemens, GE and Alstom. The

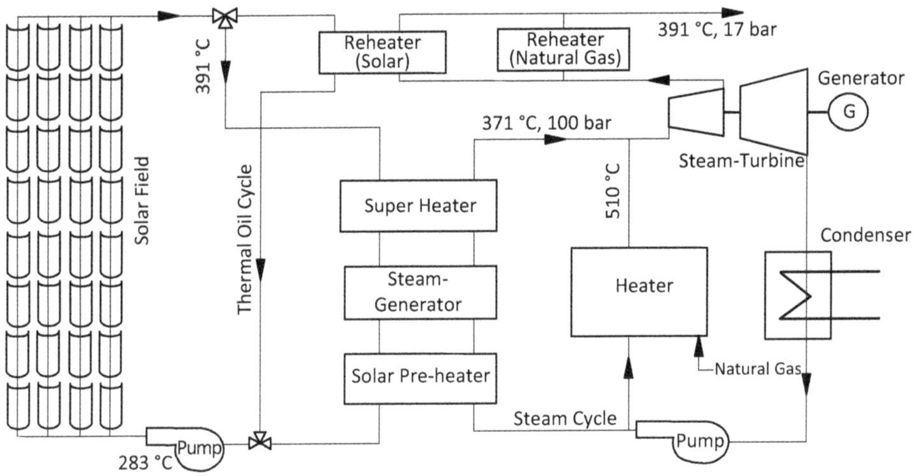

Figure 1.4: Steam cycle of a parabolic trough power plant [2].

efficiency in the rated operation (known as the quotient between (i) the mechanical energy at the steam turbine shaft and (ii) the energy difference between ingoing and outgoing steam of the turbine) of such steam turbines is around 80–85%.

Electric Generator

Electric generators used in parabolic trough plants are taken over from conventional commercial thermal power plants. Efficiency and utilization ratio are well above 95%.

Cooling

The power plant process not only establishes the supply of heat, which is provided by the solar collector fields but also a method of heat dissipation. The "cold" side of the power plant process is a critical factor in order to achieve a high level of efficiency. Cooling at a higher temperature level leads to a higher condensation temperature which results in a higher condensation pressure behind the turbine. A higher pressure behind the turbine would lead to a constant pressure inside the turbine lowering the pressure difference and thus a lower efficiency.

The aim of this process is the dissipation of heat at the lowest possible temperature. Regions which receive a large amount of direct radiation are often the regions with the highest annual average temperatures. These temperature values can serve in the first approach as an order of magnitude for the local water temperatures. Often these regions are known to for being very dry regions, where there is an insufficient quantity of cold water available.

There are three types of power plant cooling systems available: (i) wet cooling, (ii) dry cooling and (iii) hybrid cooling.

Wet cooling is the most effective way of cooling. However it requires a large quantity of water. For a 50 MW project in the south of Spain, a cold water demand of more than 600.000 m^3/a was observed. The costs that are incurred per m^3 of water play a significant role in determining the cost-effectiveness of a CSP plant.

Dry cooling works without the use of water. Only the water, which is lost through leaks in the system, is replaced. Large bundles of tubes are surrounded by ambient air and allow the cooling and condensation of the steam. Large bundles of tubes are surrounded by ambient air and allow the cooling and condensation of the steam. The air is forced through the tube bundles with the help of large fans. A significant amount of electrical energy is used to drive the fans. The increasing condensation temperature decreases the efficiency of the process. The two factors which are important here are (a) decreasing efficiency and (b) increased self-consumption of electrical energy. However in some locations this technique is the only solution available because water is scarce and costly.

Hybrid cooling combines the wet and dry cooling techniques. The processed steam is used for condensation in closed tube bundles and cooled through the use of fans. Nevertheless, in addition, the tube bundle surface can be wetted with water and the evaporative cooling be exploited. In some cases, this technique can hold an advantage because lower condensation temperatures are achieved in comparison to the condensation temperatures in the dry cooling process.

1.2.2 Power Plant System

Plant Concepts, Flow of Energy, and Technical Data

Figure 1.5 shows a simplified schematic of a parabolic trough power plant. Figure 1.6 shows the energy flow chain from the incoming solar radiation to the power output at the output of the power plant and the respective average losses in the main power plant components. A plant with an installed capacity of 100 MW in North Africa may receive an annual average of 1,200 GWh of solar radiant energy on the solar field surface. This ultimately produces 160 GWh of electrical energy. The largest losses take place during the energy conversion process (from thermal to electrical energy) and in the solar field.

Table 1.1 provides with some general key data of typical CSP power plants of parabolic trough technology.

Based on the energy flow diagram and Table 1.1, certain numerical values can be derived:

- area specific yield of electrical energy: 100–110 kWh/m^2 and
- area specific installed capacity: 25–30 W/m^2,

whereby the area is in this case defined as the entire power plant area.

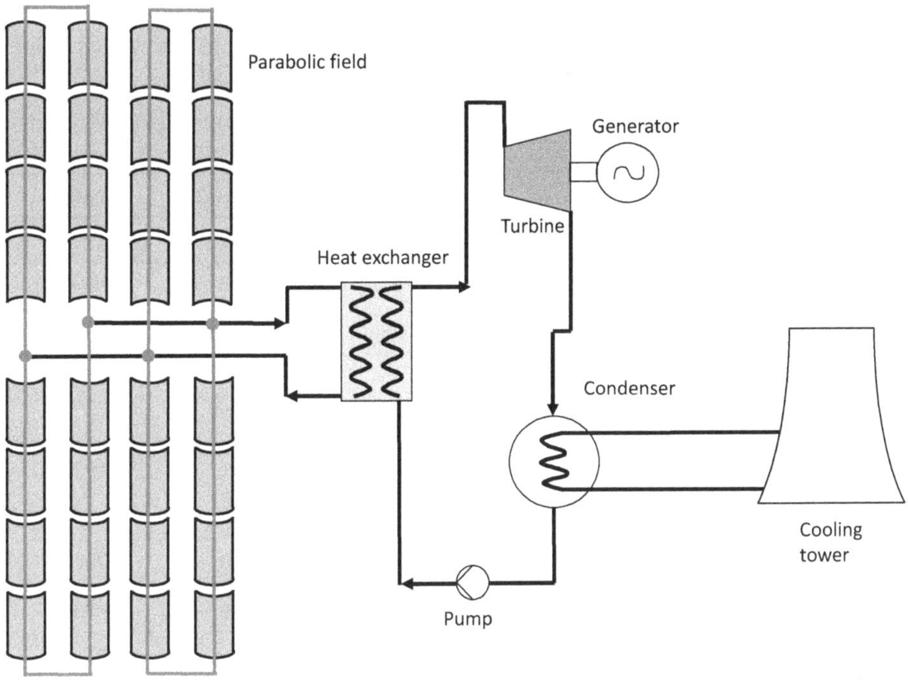

Figure 1.5: Simplified schematic of a parabolic trough power plant [2].

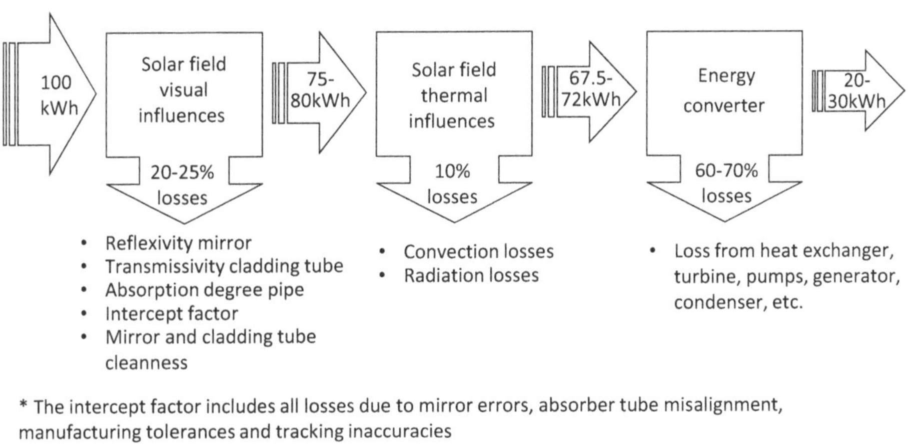

Figure 1.6: Energy flow chain for parabolic trough technology [2].

Combination with Other Technologies

The combination with storage systems is discussed in section 1.5. Beside this, other typical system combinations are:

The Booster Burner is located inside the turbine just before the steam enters and its function is to raise the steam parameters of the steam to the typical values

Table 1.1: Important figures for parabolic trough power plants with storage.

Technical specification		Type 1	Type 2	Type 3
Installed capacity	MW	50	100	200
Location (region)		North Africa	North Africa	North Africa
Base Direct Normal Irradiation DNI	kWh/(m^2/a)	2500	2500	2500
Storage duration	H	6	6	6
Own power consumption	MW	5,5	11	22
Mirror area	1000 m^2	491	961	1870
Area of solar field	Ha	128	250	486
Area of power plant	Ha	180	350	720
Length of receiver tube	Km	85	166	486
Type of cooling		Dry	Dry	Dry
Total water demand	m^3/a	42500	83100	157200
Annual energy output	GWh/a	185	374	727
Efficiency at nominal output	%	26%	27%	27%
Average annual efficiency	%	15,0%	16,0%	16,0%
Technical lifetime	Y	25	25	25

*Expected value

of conventional power plant processes. As a result, a significant increase in the efficiency with the usage of fossil fuels is achieved.

Integrated Solar Combined Cycle (ISCC) describes the integration of a solar field in a gas and steam turbine power plant. (CCGT): In a combined cycle, a conventional energy source such as natural gas or fuel oil is burned. The gas turbine is powered with the use of smoke gases. After the gas turbine has passed through, the heat that is still a part of the exhaust gas is transferred to a steam cycle which results in the steam turbine to be powered. The turbines drive the generator(s). A typical process design generates approximately about twice the electrical power for the gas turbine than for the steam turbine.

If in such an ISCC a solar field is integrated, it will deliver its heat to the steam turbine section in addition to the waste heat of the gas turbine. Therefore, the steam turbine is designed larger than usual.

The advantage of this integration of solar energy in conventional energy provision is its constant availability during the day and night and the resulting high full load hours per year. Even at night when there is no sunlight available and the solar power plant does not have capacity to produce any energy, the ISCC power plant operates and provides electricity. The disadvantage of this system is that the proportion of solar energy in the operation of such a power plant can only be a small part of the total energy input, due to the fact that for e.g., 50% of the supply of heat from the exhaust from gas turbines belongs at least 25% supply of steam turbine through heat from the waste gas. Only the remaining 25% of the steam turbine will be provided by the solar field. Thus even in the regions which receive a large bulk of solar irradiation only up to 25% of the year of the annual solar energy can be used under with full load (i.e., on average over 6 hours per day). As a result, solar contributions already at 6% of the annual operation of the power plant can be regarded as high.

1.3 Fresnel Power Plants

Fresnel power plants belong to the category of linear CSP power plants, but instead are equipped with an altered mirror field compared to a parabolic trough power plant. The mirrors consist of relatively narrow, flat strips that are arranged on a horizontal plane. They follow the sun radiation and reflect it in a focus line on a common receiver tube. The different mirror segments form an arranged parabolic trough. Fresnel reflectors are identically also parabolic arrangements, apart from the fact that they consist of a series of many individual mirrors arranged on a single plane (Figure 1.7).

1.3.1 Components

Similarly to a parabolic trough power plant, a Fresnel power plant comprises of a solar fields and a power plant block. In the power plant block no major differences to parabolic trough power plant in principle exist with regard to the components and the arrangement of a power plant unit (see section "Parabolic Trough Power Plants," Section "Components"). With reference to the solar farm, the fundamental difference is in the mirror arrangement.

The fundamental components of the solar field are (i) the fresnel mirrors, (ii) the absorber tube, (iii) the support frames for the absorber tubes and mirrors and their tracking device, (iv) the heat transfer medium, (v) the pipes, through which the heat transfer medium is being pumped, (vi) the control level-sensing devices and (vii) the interface to the power plant block with the entry or exit area of the steam into the

Figure 1.7: View of fresnel collector [2].

water-steam cycle of the power plant unit. The power plant block includes (i) a steam turbine, (ii) a generator, (iii) a compensator and optionally a boiler with a fossil auxiliary heater to provide steam which is used e.g., to start the operation.

Mirror, Receiver, and Fresnel Collector

The dimensions of the individual mirrors are usually in the range of 75 centimeters width and 6 meters in length. In most cases, 16 individual mirrors are arranged next to one another and together they concentrate the solar radiation from the plane on to the receiver tube. In nowadays state-of-art design of the fresnel systems, the receiver tube has a length of 36 m, which means that 6 mirrors are arranged one behind the other, all of which focus on the same receiver tube.

The same materials which are used in parabolic collectors are also used in mirrors and receiver tubes of Fresnel power plants.

The main advantages of this arrangement are:

1. The receiver tube is firmly mounted in one place and does not move simultaneously with the mirrors, unlike the arrangement on the parabolic trough. Therefore, a more stable assembly can be installed and by this means the impacts of abrupt, sudden evaporating fluids in two phase flows on the overall structure can be better handled.

2. The production of the mirror is considerably simplified because the individual segments now require almost none or very small curvature. In addition, the mirrors are considerably thinner.
3. The plane arrangement offers considerable advantages both during the process of installation as well as during maintenance due to the fact that the mirror field is easily accessible.
4. Arrangements of secondary concentrators that reflect the radiant energy over the HCE and reflect to the HCE again, become more facile.
5. Due to the floor arrangement of the mirrors, the wind pressure decreases.
6. Large mirror surfaces per unit length HCE become possible and thus the HCE can be shortened while the power remains constant.

The disadvantages are the following:
1. A large number of elements have to be tracked individually compared to a parabolic trough power plant, due to this, the overall technical and operational effort for the tracking is higher.
2. Associated with this are lower concentration factors, as long as secondary reflectors are not provided (C = 60 to 120).
3. The efficiency of a fresnel collector is slightly lower than those of a parabolic trough collector since the optical losses are slightly higher.

Collector Field

The collector fields are similar to parabolic trough power plants in terms of their orientation. Due to the different mirror classifications, different ratios mirror surface area to distance between the Fresnel lines, because the plane arrangement of the mirrors near the ground does not results in shadowing.

The spacing is however necessary, for example in order to ensure the accessibility of the fresnel collectors during cleaning. With a row spacing of approximately 4 m between Fresnel collectors and a width of 16 m, a total floor area of the solar power plant of approximately 64 ha and a mirror surface of 320,000 m^2 results in a 50 MW Fresnel power plant.

While the cleaning of a parabolic trough mirrors and heliostats is still widely carried out manually due to the geometrical structure or the individual freestanding arrangement, robotic vacuums can much easier be used to clean the mirror surfaces of the flat mirrors of a Fresnel system. Figure 1.8 displays such robots in regular operation.

Heat Transfer Medium

In principle, the fresnel systems can have the same heat transfer medium as the parabolic trough technologies. However, due to its modified design, it is easier to generate higher temperatures inside the receiver tube with Fresnel collectors in comparison to

Figure 1.8: Robotic vacuums cleaning the mirrors of a fresnel system [2].

the parabolic trough collectors despite having a relatively low or similar concentration factor. The reason being that (i) the energy on a receiver tube can be concentrated from a larger area and (ii) the receiver tube can normally be longer. For that reason it is a primary goal to achieve temperatures of about 450 °C in a fresnel collector system, in contrast to the < 400 °C temperatures reached in a parabolic trough system. Amongst others, this results in the fact that fresnel collectors are suitable for direct steam generation in the receiver tube (today at approximately 270 °C and 55 bar). Also because of this, the heat transfer medium is usually not thermal oil (because of its decreasing stability at high temperatures), but rather water or steam or molten salt.

As of to date, 2018, the largest fresnel based solar power plant in operation is located in Spain with a capacity of 30 MW. Additionally, some few larger plants are currently being constructed, such as the Lanyhou Dacheng Dunhuang 50 MW Molten Salt Fresnel CSP Demonstration Project in China.

1.3.2 The Power Plant System

Overall Plant Concept, Energy Flow, and Key Technical Data

Figure 1.9 displays the block diagram of a fresnel power plant in this case with direct steam evaporation in the HCEs. The primary difference in comparison to the block diagram of the parabolic trough power plant (see Figure 1.10) is with regard to the direct evaporation in the absorber tubes. This eliminates the heat exchanger between the solar farm and the power plant block. The steam generated in the receiver pipes is routed directly to the steam turbine.

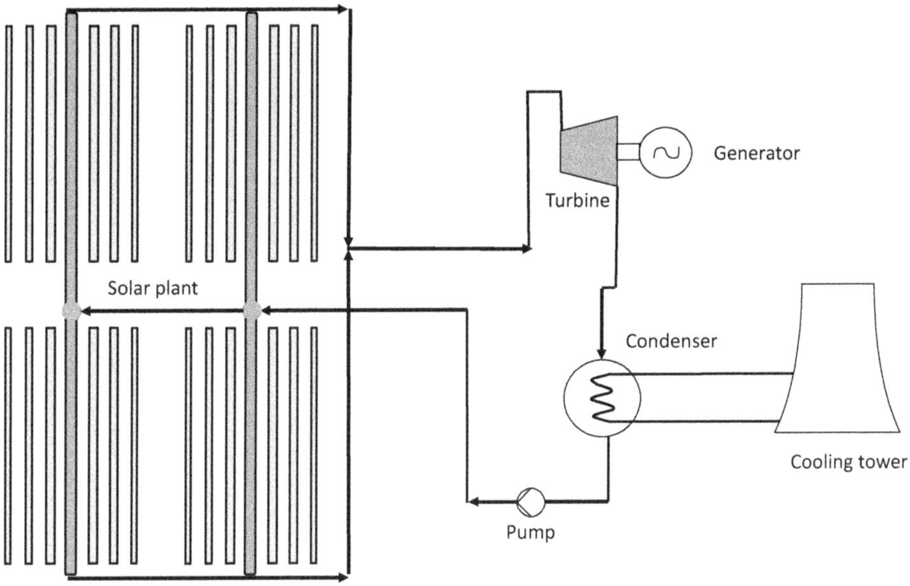

Figure 1.9: Simplified illustration of a fresnel power plant [2].

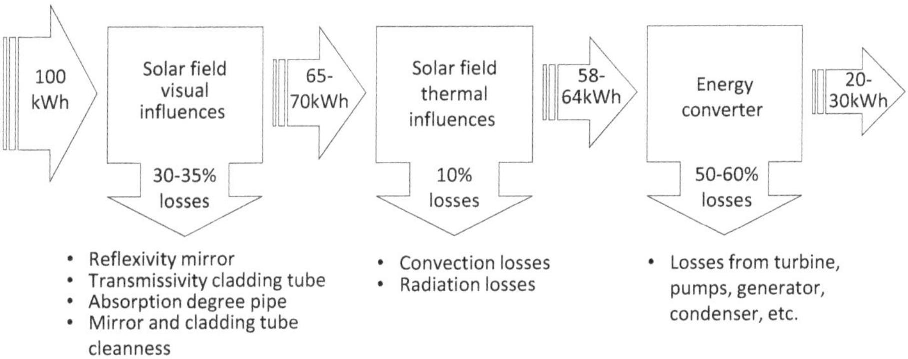

Figure 1.10: Energy flow chain for fresnel technology with direct steam generation [2].

Fresnel Power plants are nowadays only offered by few contractor companies, as the technology has difficulties to succeed against competing other solar thermal power plant technologies. This is also the reason why so far there are only very few reference systems installed and with only limited operational. Compared to the parabolic trough, the basis for a reliable technical specification is limited to a narrow performance range.

Table 1.2 provides with some general key data of typical CSP power plants with fresnel technology.

Table 1.2: Key technical data of a typical fresnel power plant.

Technical specifications	Unit	Type 1	Type 2	Type 3
Installed capacity	MW	30	50	100
Location (region)		North Africa	North Africa	North Africa
Base Direct Normal Irradiation DNI	$kWh/(m^2/a)$	2500	2500	2500
Storage duration	H	0,5	0,5	0,5
Power consumption	MW	3	5	10
Mirror area	$1000\ m^2$	300	500	1000
Area of power plant	Ha	48	75	150
Length of receiver tube	Km	24	40	80
Type of cooling		Dry	Dry	Dry
Total water demand	m^3/a	7500	12500	25000
Annual energy output	GWh/a	60	115	225
Efficiency at installed capacity	%	15%	16%	17%
Average annual efficiency	%	8,0%	8,5%	9,0%
Technical lifetime	y	25	25	25

*Expected value

Based on the energy flow diagram (Figure 1.10) and the key data of Table 1.2, some important figures can be derived:
- area-specific yield of electrical energy: app. 150 kWh/m^2 and
- area-specific installed capacity: app. 40–50 W/m^2,

whereby the area is in this case defined as the entire power plant area.

Combination with Other Technologies

With regard to the combination with other technologies, the fresnel solar thermal power plant technologies are fundamentally similar to those of the parabolic trough systems (see section 1.2). However, it must be taken into consideration that in the fresnel system there is usually direct steam generation in the HCEs. As a result, the combination with other technologies is to be analyzed differently in terms of its advantages and disadvantages.

1.4 Solar Tower Power Plants

In solar-thermal tower power plants, two-axis sun mirrors (known as heliostats) follow the course of the sun and reflect direct solar radiation onto a radiation receiver mounted centrally on a tower (Figure 1.11). This is also known as a point focusing system. In the radiation receiver, the radiant energy is converted into heat and transferred to a heat transfer fluid (e.g., air, liquid salt, water/steam). This heat is used to drive a turbine and thus a generator via a conventional steam process.

Figure 1.11: Solar plant at Seville, Spain [2].

The concentration factor of the tower power plants depends heavily on the accuracy of its heliostats and its tracking. It reaches values between 500 and 1.000 [1].

1.4.1 Components

Similar to parabolic trough power plants and also Fresnel power stations, solar tower power plants consist of the following two areas: the solar field and the power plant block. However, in difference to the other mentioned systems, the solar field contains only the heliostat, no liquid or gaseous heat transfer medium is circulated in the solar field.

The receiver is integrated into the actual solar tower along with the power plant block. The primary components of the solar field are therefore (i) the heliostats combined together with the mirror, mirror support frame, foundation and biaxial tracking and (ii) the associated ground infrastructure (access and wiring for the tracking). The solar tower with power plant block includes the (i) solar tower building itself, (ii) the receiver, (iii) the heat transfer medium, (iv) the steam generator (unless steam is used directly as a heat carrier in the receiver), (v) the steam turbine, (vi) the generator, (vii) the condenser and (viii) the control and regulation devices. The most important components are discussed below.

Heliostat

A heliostat has a very large mirror surface made up of numerous segments. Some types of heliostats have a total area of approximately 120 m^2 and consist of 28 individual mirrors. The individual mirrors are assembled on a common support element. Each mirror can be individually aligned for basic settings. Each support element is installed as an individual element in the solar field. Between the foot of the element, having the function to fix the element on the ground, and the actual support element, two motors organize the biaxial movement of the element. The entire mirror can follow the course of the sun during the day and the year in both dimensions. This allows each heliostat to reflect the radiation into focus at the top of the tower.

The mirror can follow the course of the sun during the day and throughout the year in both dimensions. This allows each heliostat to reflect the radiation onto a focal point at the top of the tower.

With regards to the materials, a distinction can be made between faceted glass metal and membrane heliostats as the primary types. Faceted glass-metal heliostats usually consist of support tube mounted on a framework structure where a variety of rectangular single mirrors ranging from 2 to 3 m^2, known as facets, are located. The tracking unit consists of a steel pipe bolted to foundation with an elevation gearbox mounted on it to which the carrier pipe is fixed. In this case we refer to T-type heliostats. Typical widths of such heliostats are approximately 13m with single facet sizes ranging from 3 m to 1.1 m. The total weight without the footing is around 5 tons.

The individual facets are spherically curved according to the focal length. The radius of the curvature is twice the focal length. The facets are aligned so that the individual images overlap to form a common focal point of the heliostat. This process of facet alignment is termed as "canting."

Membrane heliostats are stretch membranes that are used to avoid the production and assembly costs associated with single facets and at the same time achieve a high optical quality. The concentrator is made up of one or more "drums" which consist of a metallic pressure vessel and stretched membranes on the front-side and back side. Plastic foils or metal membranes are used as material. In the case of using metal membranes that have a much higher durability, the pre-side membranes are coated with thin glass mirrors to achieve the desired high reflectivity. Inside the concentrator a low pressure (a few mbar) is adjusted by a cooling fan or a vacuum pump. As a result, the membrane deforms, and the plane mirror becomes a concentrator. In other constructions, a centrally mounted mechanical or hydraulic punch serves to deform the membrane.

The optical quality achieved with large metal membrane heliostats is significantly higher than those that are reached at reasonable costs in glass-to-metal heliostats which are of comparable size. Another advantage is that the pressure in the concentrator and the focal length can be easily varied. Thus, unlike the conventional glass-to-metal heliostats, different facets do not have to be built for heliostats that are distant from the receiver. In metal diaphragm heliostats it is sufficient to set a lower pressure set point or the desired curvature accordingly. As a result canting is completely omitted in heliostats with a single membrane concentrator. The disadvantage is the energy requirement for maintaining the low pressure in the concentrator.

Heliostat Field

The individual heliostats are arranged around the solar tower in mainly two different ways: On one hand, the tower can be placed on the edge of the field (Figure 1.12). Then the heliostat field is oriented towards the northern direction in the northern hemisphere and the south in the southern hemisphere. On the other hand, the heliostat field can also be arranged around the tower, at a 360° orientation. This arrangement makes sense in locations that are located around the equator.

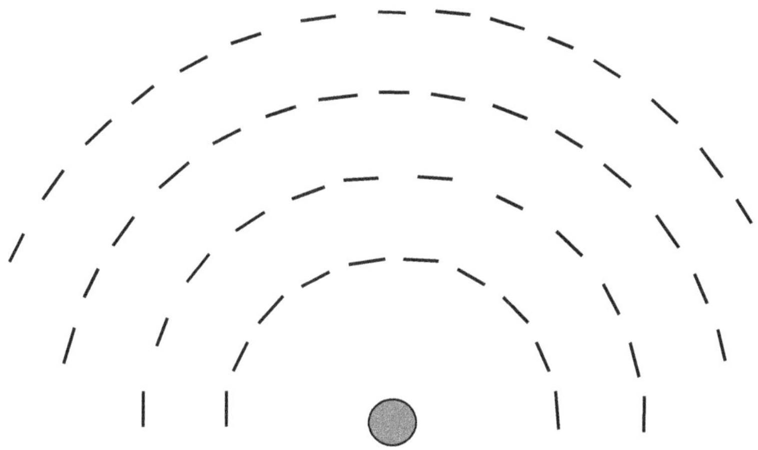

Figure 1.12: Arrangements of the heliostats [2].

The optimal distances of the heliostats are dependent on the location and for this case the latitude. In addition, the size of the individual heliostats, the ratio of tower height to tower spacing and the local conditions of the terrain play a significant role. The purpose is to achieve an optimization between the shading of the heliostats with each other, the cost for the additional tower increase, as well as other induced costs and the total plant area. For example the total area of 50 MW solar tower power plant constructed in Spain would be around 240 ha for the solar field and around 330 ha for a solar tower power plant.

For the cleaning of heliostats, the similar process that takes place during the cleaning parabolic troughs can be followed. Occasionally brush systems are also used for cleaning in heliostats (Figure 1.13). The brush is installed on the truck. It moves in front of the heliostat after which then changes in a vertical position for cleaning purposes. Subsequently, the rotating brush is steered along the mirror system.

Figure 1.13: Cleaning of heliostats with brushes [2].

The control and regulation of heliostats takes place centrally or through several distributed computers. The heliostats are controlled in such a way in which they do not all point at the same point on the receiver. In order to achieve the desired radiation intensity distribution on the absorber surface of the receiver, it is necessary to divide the heliostat field into groups which are each directed to their own, relatively offset, target point.

Receiver

The receiver construction varies in different ways. If the tower is irradiated from all sides (360° arrangement), the receiver must also be able to collect focused radiation. In contrast to such "360° receivers," the tube bundle can also be surrounded by a solid, non-transparent structure. This structure has transparent access on one side, over which the radiation meets the tube bundle. The advantage of this arrangement is that all the complete radiation is absorbed in a cave-like arrangement.

With regard to the different construction methods of the receivers, the heat transfer fluid (see the next section), receiver geometry or the associated receiver structure can be used to distinguish the different available receiver concepts. Using the receiver geometry or the receiver structure a distinction is made between shapes: flat, hollow, cylindrical or conical all round receivers.

Nowadays water/steam receivers are used. These so-called solar tube receivers are made up of tube bundles and primarily function as recuperators in conventional power plants. The radiation is converted into heat on the outer layer of the tubes and transported away through a heat transfer medium – in this case water/steam.

Intense research is currently being done on open volumetric air receivers, where the solar radiation gets in contact with an absorber material, which consists of steel wire mesh or porous ceramic. The concentrated solar radiation penetrates into the structure and is converted into heat on the outside of the absorber material. A fan vacuums the surrounding air from outside through the irradiated absorber material. The air absorbs the heat. Such receivers operate at ambient pressure. The air is heated to over 700 °C after which it is transferred to a steam cycle. Further research and development work would lead to the operation of such systems as a combined cycle process such that the steam turbine and gas turbine are also integrated into the system.

In contrast, closed pressurized air receivers generally operate under low pressure. The aperture of such receivers is closed by a quartz glass window. For example, the air heated at pressures above ambient pressure can be injected directly into the combustion chamber of a gas turbine. The air outlet temperatures at the receiver are above 800 °C.

Heat Transfer Medium

Either air, water/steam, salt or liquid metal are used as heat transfer fluids. At present commercially under construction or operational power plants, salt and air are most commonly used. Water/steam as a heat transfer fluid has the advantage that a heat exchanger for the water/steam cycle of the downstream power plant process is unnecessary. Air in turn has an advantage due to the significantly higher temperatures that can be achieved at the outlet of the absorber. For example, pressured receivers can go approximately up to 800 °C.

When salt acts as the heat transfer medium, molten salts of sodium and potassium nitrate (NaNO3, KNO3) can be applied. Due to its high specific heat capacity, in constrast to air, molten salts can additionaly be used as a heat storage medium. This avoids the heat exchange between the heat transfer medium and heat storage medium. Similar to air receivers, and unlike the water-steam systems, the heat transfer medium is in the liquid phase throughout the temperature range encountered during regular operation. The solar heat is coupled into a steam process via a salt-water steam heat exchanger. In this process there is no two-phase flow that occurs. The solar heat is then coupled into a stream process via a slat-water/steam heat exchange.

Power Plant Unit

In the plants which are built nowadays, saturated steam is generated, which undergoes a similar steam cycle power-heating process to other CSP plants. The aim is to achieve higher temperatures using this or other mediums and to ultimatley provide super heated steam at the turbine inlet. Therefore, intensive work is currently being done with other heat transfer mediums presented above, the use of which also has a significant influence on the technology in the power plant unit. In the case of air as the heat transfer medium, the air can be supplied directly to a gas turbine, for example in the open volumetric receiver, which is eased into low pressure. This simplifies the structure considerably, though up till now this method has not yet been implemented. In pressure air receivers, the air can be fed directly into the combustion chamber of a gas turbine. Subsequently, the waste heat of the gas turbine process can be used in another steam cycle to run a steam turbine. Such systems are still not available for commercial use.

1.4.2 The Power Plant System

Overall Plant Concept, Energy Flow, and Key Technical Data

Figure 1.14 shows the block diagram of a solar tower power plant. The figure illustrates an example with water/steam as a heat transfer and a downstream turbine. Figure 1.15 shows the energy flow in the power plant.

Table 1.3 provides with some general key data of typical CSP power plants of tower technology.

Table 1.3 presents important specific figures:

- area-specific yield of electrical energy : ca. 130 kWh/m^2 and
- area-specific installed capacity: ca. 15 W/m^2,

whereby the area is in this case defined as the entire power plant area.

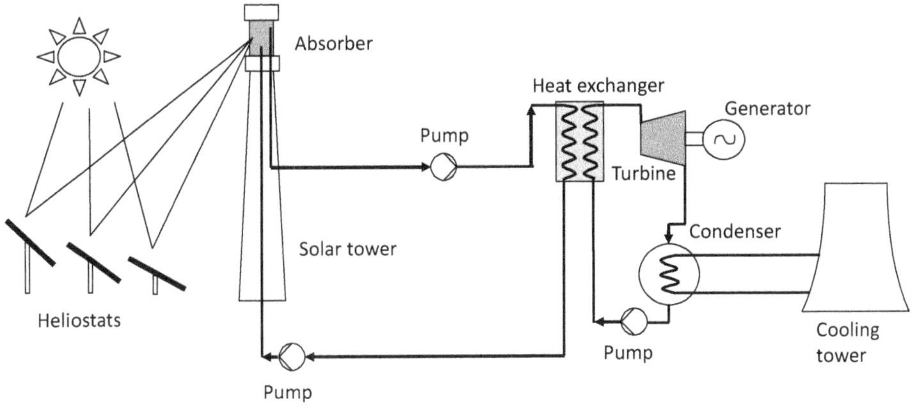

Figure 1.14: Simplified illustration of a solar tower power plant [2].

Combination with Other Technologies

With regard to the combination with other technologies, we can refer hereunder to section 1.2. However, in difference to parabolic trough, such kind of combinations, e.g., with CCGTs are actually not commercially applied with tower technologies.

1.5 Energy Storage Technologies and CSP

The function of the thermal storage systems is to ensure the continuous supply of thermal energy to the turbine even after sunset, sometimes until sunrise next day. Simultaneously, the thermal storage systems harmonize the temporal fluctuations of solar radiation during the day which can result for example due to passing cloud fields. A steady operation due to the thermal storage technology is particularly beneficial as it allows to shift power production of the plant to peak times, which are out of the sunshine hours. This has several economic advantages: Most important are the ability to sell power at higher prices (during peak times) and the ability to provide firm power with a high availability guarantee during the operation hours of the plant.

1.5.1 Aspects of the Integration of Storage Systems

The actual electrical output of CSP systems without storage depends on the actual meteorological conditions during the course of the day. Beside the short-term and unpredictable changes in the intensity of solar irradiance between sunrise and sunset, as well as the seasonal changes in sunrise and sunset, CSP power plants do not receive any radiant energy between the periods of sunset to sunrise. In many countries

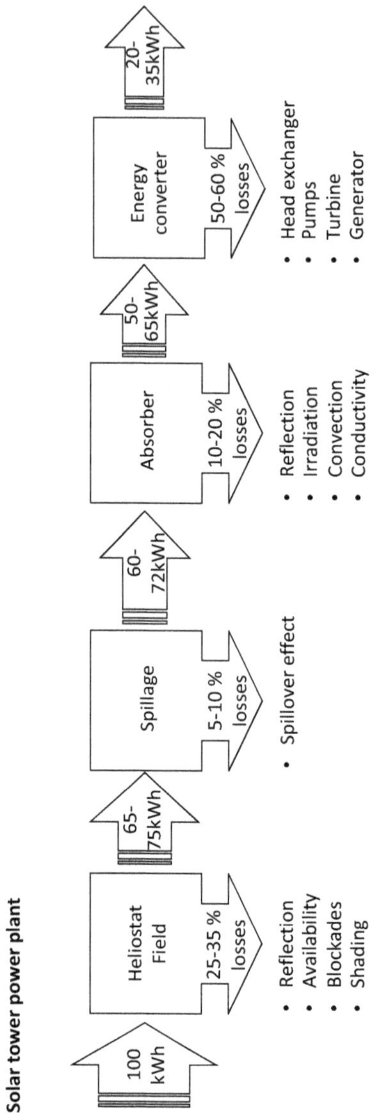

* The spillover effect describes losses due to inaccurate irradiation from the heliostats on the receiver

Figure 1.15: Energy flow chain of the solar tower plant operating at nominal power range [2].

Table 1.3: Key technical data of a typical solar power tower plants.

Technical specifications		**Type 1**	**Type 2**	**Type 3**
Installed capacity	MW	50	100	200
Location (region)		North Africa	North Africa	North Africa
Base Direct Normal Irradiation DNI	kWh/(m^2/a)	2500	2500	2500
Storage duration	H	15	15	15
Power consumption	MW	5	10	20
Mirror area	1000 m^2	757	1453	2846
Area of power plant	Ha	420	798	1562
Tower height	M	220	220	220
Receiver area	m^2	740	1480	2960
Type of cooling		Dry	Dry	Dry
Total water demand (rain, etc)	m^3/a	60000	120000	240000
Annual energy output	GWh/a	313	639	1290
Efficiency at nominal output	%	44%	44%	44%
Average annual efficiency	%	17%	17%	17%
Technical lifetime	Y	25	25	25

(in particular countries which show great potential for CSP plants), the peak of the electrical energy demand is caused by active cooling systems and thus is time-wise parallel to the sunshine hours. However, even after sunset the power demand for cooling increases or remains at a high level in many countries for some hours since many air conditioners are still in operation.

For that reason energy providers find it useful if the energy supply is dispatchable. Since CSP techniques convert sunlight through the conversion of thermal energy into electrical energy, they offer the possibility of storing the energy in the form of thermal energy in order to convert it into electrical energy during periods of low solar energy availability. Storage tanks allow solar energy to be converted into electricity in the evening and at night. In this way the operating time of the steam cycle is increased significantly. In general, the following storage options in connection with CSP power plants are currently being discussed extensively:

- Steam accumulator;
- Thermal oil storage;
- Concrete storage;
- Salt storage.

1.5.2 Different Types of Storage Systems for CSP

Steam accumulators store thermal energy directly before entering the turbine. The pressure and temperature of the stored steam correspond to the parameters at the turbine inlet. This form of storage is a well-known and common technique used in many conventional power plants. It is quite expensive because of the required pressure resistance and has a considerable volume of construction. It is therefore used exclusively as short-term storage for buffering operational fluctuations at the turbine inlet.

The storage system is usually installed in parallel to the heat exchanger, so that still a direct transfer of heat from the solar field into the steam cycle occurs.

In the case of ***thermal oil storage***, a considerable amount of thermal oil is heated and stored at a high temperature (of almost 400 °C) in a tank. In case electricity is needed when no sunshine is available (e.g., at night), the oil is pumped through the heat exchanger which is delivering heat to the steam cycle and releases the heat accumulated during the day during the process of conversion to electrical energy. The disadvantage of this approach is that thermal oil is expensive and the requirements for environmental protection are high.

Another concept (***concrete storage***) includes a large thermal storage out of concrete mass, which is run through and heated with hot fluid. In order to discharge the storage, the cold thermal oil flows through the concrete storage tank and heats up. It releases the heat to the steam circuit and powers the turbine. The storage volumes for thermal energy storage are sizeable. The costs of heating the entire block with short paths of heat conduction lead to many tube bundles. However the loading and unloading processes are quite slow. The thermal energy storage facilities are currently in the development and testing phase and are not yet operational and up to date, particularly with regard to the cutback caused by the change in temperature.

The most common concept nowadays applied in new CSP plants are tank systems with liquid salts (***molten salt storage***). This arrangement is usually implemented with the usage of two tanks, one "cold" and one "warm." The temperature of the "cold" tank should not fall under 250 °C, otherwise there is a risk that the salt will change from the liquid to the solid state and to "defrost" again becomes almost impossible. The temperature of the "warm" tank reaches almost 400 °C and is restricted since the thermal oil cannot be heated to a higher temperature. In the case of an increase in the heat supply, the warm tank is loaded. For this purpose, cold, liquid salt from the cold tank is loaded in a heat exchanger through the heat from the solar field and stored in the warm tank. During the night, warm salt is abstracted from the tank after which the heat is transferred to the thermal oil in the heat exchanger. From this, the heat is transferred in a wider heat exchanger to the steam circuit in order to power the turbine.

The larger the storage system is, the more the collector field has to be increased in order to convert more radiation into heat than the turbine requires only during operation during sunshine hours.

1.6 Environmental Impact

CSP technology provides electricity without direct emissions during operation. The main positive environmental impact of this is climate change mitigation. However, as with all other technologies, not only this, but also all other possible influences and effects on the environment through the usage of CSP power plants have to be considered when analyzing this technology and comparing it with other means of electricity provision. In Tables 1.4–1.5 we have therefore provided some key figures for an exemplary CSP plant.

Table 1.4: Energy and emission balances of parabolic trough and solar tower power plants of different sizes, with and without storage.

Reference plant	Unit	1	2	3	4	5	6	7
Technology		parabolic trough						tower
Installed Capacity	in MW	50	50	100	100	200	200	50
Storage		yes	no	yes	no	yes	no	no
Energy	in GJ_{prim}/GWH^a	340	360	333	347	342	352	241
SO_2	in kg/GWh	99	115	97	111	99	113	34.5
NO_X	in kg/GWh	176	206	169	200	178	197	41.5
CO_2 equivalent	in t/GWh	20.9	22.5	20.4	21.6	21-0	22.3	16.2
SO2 equivalent	in kg/GWh	228	263	223	255	229	261	66

Table 1.5: Water consumption, land usage and material consumption of parabolic trough power plant in comparison with conventional power plant technologies.

	Parabolic trough power plant	Natural gas power plant	Lignite power plant
	50 MW, Spain	**400 MW, Germany**	**800 MW, Germany**
Water consumption	ca. 0,20–0,25 l/kWh*	ca. 1,0l/kWh**	ca. 2,5 l/kWh**
Land usage	ca. 100–110 m^2/MWh	0,008–0,01 m^2/MWh	0,02–0,04 m^2/MWh
Material consumption	Medium	Low	Low

*dry cooling
*wet cooling

Table 1.6: Investment and O&M cost for different type of CSP technologies (status 2018, only for parabolic trough and solar tower technology).

		Parabolic Trough				Solar Tower	
		100 MW		200 MW		100 MW	200 MW
		without storage	with storage	without storage	with storage	with storage	with storage
Investment							
solar farm	Mio €	149	221	252	387	208	360
power block (and storage system)	Mio €	182	270	308	473	312	540
Total	**Mio €**	**330**	**490**	**560**	**860**	**520**	**900**
Specific Investment cost	Mio €/MW	3,3	4,9	2,8	4,3	5,2	4,5
O&M Cost		10000					
Total	**Mio €/a**	**9,5**	**14,5**	**18**	**27**	**18**	**30**
Specific O&M cost	Mio € /a/MW	0,10	0,15	0,09	0,14	0,18	0,15

Some environmental aspects presented in the tables are discussed in the following:

Climate change mitigation: CO_2 equivalents of CSP plants derive almost exclusively from the materials used, the components production and transportation to the site and the construction of the power plant itself and the CO_2 emitted due to all such processes. The emissions during operation is zero or almost zero. The CO_2 equivalents for parabolic trough technologies are in the range of around 20–22 t/GWh electricity produced. This is not much different to other CSP technologies, somehow only 10–20% lower at solar towers (around 16 t/GWh, see the table) or fresnel power plants, due to their higher efficiency and better use of solar radiation per m^2 surface, mainly. However, important is the difference of this figure compared with conventional fossil fuel fired power plants: a modern lignite power plant has CO_2 equivalent emissions in the range of 800–900 t/GWh and a modern gas combined heat and power plant in the range of 350 and 400. This relation shows one of the key advantages of CSP technologies: savings in CO_2 emissions.

Water consumption: Another environmental impact which has to be carefully considered in CSP plants is the water consumption. Especially the parabolic trough technology with the largest market share in the CSP power plants has a water consumption per MWh electricity produced in the case of wet cooling, which is significantly higher than the consumption of a fossil fuel power station. However, for dry cooling, which would be the usual application at sites suitable for CSP, this goes down considerably below wet cooling for conventional power plants. In addition to the water demand for cooling, for cleaning the mirrors, the wash intervals must run depending on the dust load of the surrounding air. This leads to a further load on the water balance of the power plant at locations which have favorable direct radiation (for example in desert areas). As a result, if dry cooling techniques can be applied, the total water consumption for a parabolic trough power plant can be in the range of 0,2–0,25l/kWh and thus substantially lower than for a natural gas or a lignite power plant (Table 1.4).

Hazardous thermal oil leakages. Since most parabolic trough plants work with thermal oil in the solar field circuit, certain measures and devices are provided to prevent leaks. For ecological relevance, the risk and safety rates of thermal oil must also be taken into account, in particular, the reference to the harmful effect on aquatic organisms and possible long-term harmful effects in waters. In addition, separate operating procedures as well as training of the personal on the procedure in case of fire are to be implemented, since thermal oil can form explosive mist atmospheres, when escaping under pressure with atmospheric oxygen.

Land use and visual impact. Land utilization is substantial for CSP plants compared to other technologies. As can be seen for parabolic trough technologies in Table 1.5, this is in the range between 100–110 m^2/kWh. The lower range is for parabolic trough CSP plants without storage, the higher end for parabolic trough CSP plants with storage. However, beside the pure amount of land consumption, the visual impact is low for CSP plants compared to various other technologies. On one hand, this is due to the low height of the plants (an exception is the tower in solar tower power plants) and also the usual locations of such plants such as in deserts or stepped areas with a tendency of being sparsely populated.

Other environmental issues. One aspect in the context of solar tower power plants, which may initially prove problematic, is reflections from the heliostat or tower receiver beyond the contact surface. However, analysis have shown that this concern is marginal during regular power plant operation.

After the end of the economic life cycle of power plants, an orderly demolition must be carried out. While nuclear power plants, in particular, bring extreme problems due the long term radioactive exposure of the entire power plant components, there is nothing like this hindering a direct dismantling of CSP plants.

Remaining quantities of thermal oil in the pipelines may need to be washed out before they are removed before they are removed by suitable measures. Although there are none or only very limited experiences in the demolition of CSP plants, a complete reprocessing of the plant surface, i.e., a 100% dismantling, can be assumed.

1.7 Cost and Economics

In the following some indications are provided about the actual status of CSP cost and an exemplary economic calculation, showing the levelized electricity generation cost, is provided. The cost indications and economic calculations always refer to the typical power plants according to the specifications as given in Table 1.6.

1.7.1 Cost of Components and Systems

Regarding the overall cost for CSP power plants, we have to differ between investment (before the start of commercial operation) and the annual cost, which we usually summarize as O&M cost. The estimation of these cost is more difficult than for several other renewable energy technologies, since (i) still there are only few suppliers of CSP key components, (ii) the market is still quite small, (iii) the future market volume is difficult to predict and therefore (iv) the real cost learning curves are difficult to predict as well. The latter is – beside the market volume and several other items – dependent on the policy and the legal framework in the respective countries – now and in future.

Nevertheless, with some uncertainties, estimations can be provided and are given exemplary in Table 1.5. In this table, we focus on the most common technologies parabolic trough and solar tower; no figures are given for fresnel technology. The costs reflect basically a cost estimation for the respective plants as specified in previous tables. Investment include all key and non-key components and in addition cost for planning, advisory, installation and unforeseen. Costs are differed between the solar field and the power block.

We can conclude three main results from Table 1.5:

1. As can be seen, for both technologies and independently whether it is with storage or without, the power block cost take the larger part. This part is even higher in solar towers, as in solar towers also the tower itself and the receiver are counted to the power block.
2. Overall investment cost increase, if for the same rated power plant a storage system is added, which is very common in project nowadays. The reason is not only the additional cost for the storage system, but also the additional cost for the solar farm, which is needed to collect the solar radiation to fill the storage system. So that it can provide heat for electricity after sunset.
3. It can also be seen that the overall investment and specific investment cost, if same size of technologies are compared, are nowadays higher for towers plants as for parabolic trough plants. However, this difference was much higher some years ago. So tower cost reduced stronger in recent years as parabolic trough cost.

1.7.2 Example Economic Calculation

On the basis of the investment and O&M cost, and the technical specifications from the other previous tables (particularly electricity yield, and technical lifetime) and assumptions on financial parameters, the levelized cost of electricity generation (LCOE) can be calculated. This has been done for the systems of Table1.5, assuming

- An equity to credit ratio of 30/70;
- An average interest rate for loan of 2%, as still in most of the CSP power plants most of the loans are concessional loans with very low interest rate);
- An average profit expectation for the equity of 10%.

The result is shown in figure Figure 1.16. As can be seen, LCOEs are in the range between 7 and 15 €cents/kWh, whereby the highest cost are for parabolic trough without storage.

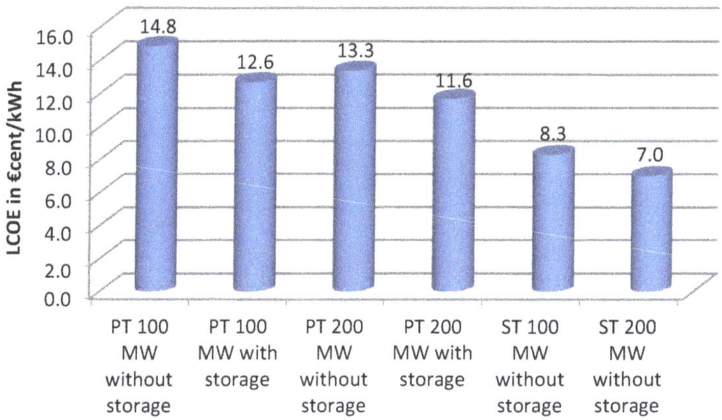

Figure 1.16: Levelized cost of electricity generation (LCOE) for different type of technologies and cost status 2018 (PT = parabolic trough, ST = solar tower).

Such LCOEs provide useful information if we compare then with other, competing forms of electricity generation. Figure 1.17 shows this comparison for other renewable energy technologies and some conventional power plant technologies.

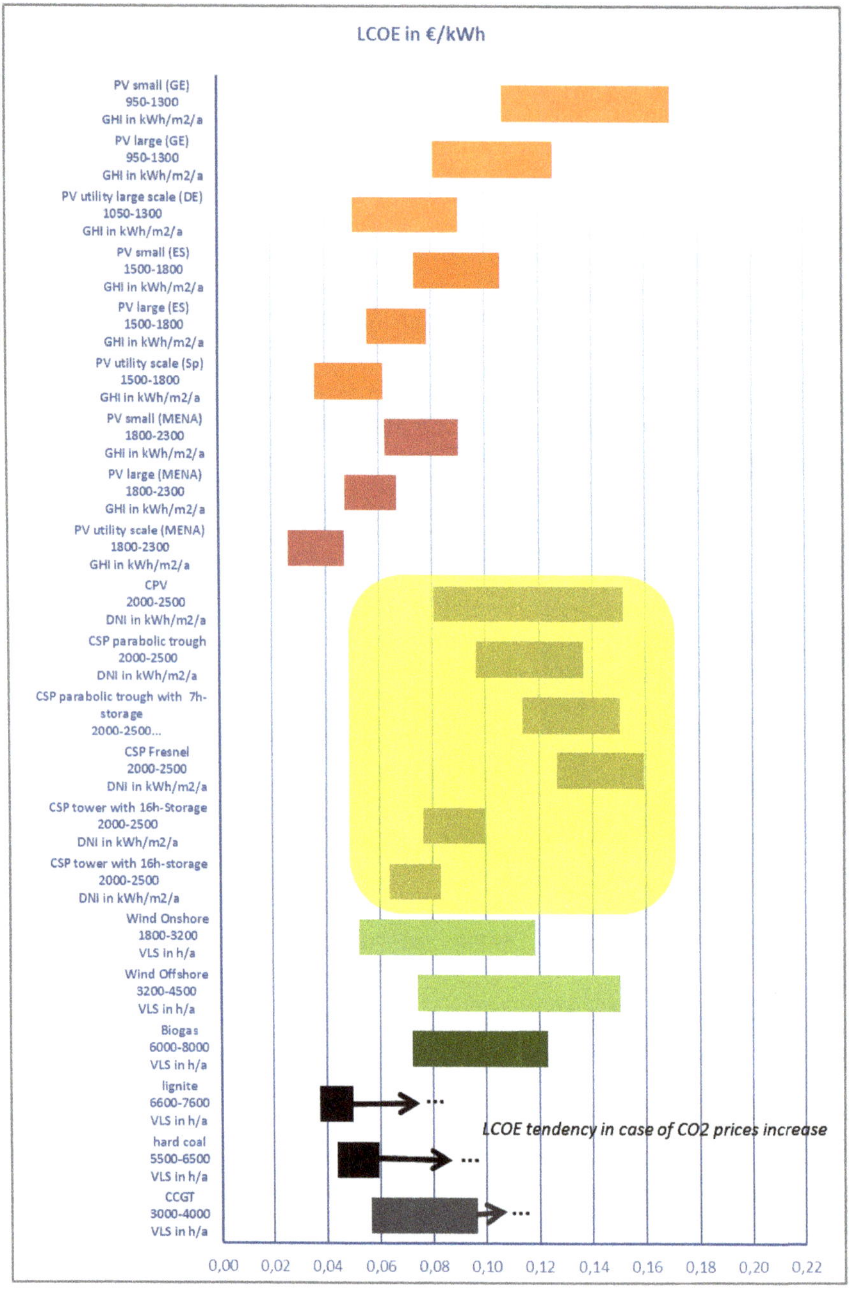

Figure 1.17: Comparison of LCOES of different technologies, all calculated with the same methodology; CSP technologies in the yellow area; cost basis 2018.

1.8 Market Status, Potentials, and Perspectives

1.8.1 Market Status

By the end of 2018, over 5 GW of cumulative power has been installed in CSP plants worldwide generated using parabolic troughs (83%, solar towers (13%)), linear fresnel reflectors (3–4%) and single dish engines (0.02%). With a majority of them still situated in Spain. In addition, about 2 GW of solar thermal power plant capacity are currently under construction, e.g., in Morocco, in Dubai and Saudi Arabia. China plans to produce solar electricity out of 10 GW by 2020. The largest CSP operational power plant is Ivanpah Solar Power Facility in the United States, which has an electrical capacity of 392 MW.

1.8.2 Technical and Economic Potentials

The vast technical potential for solar thermal power plants lies in the sun belt regions of the earth such as Southern Europe, North and Central Africa, the Middle East, parts of India and China, Mexico, southern part of the United States, as well as in individual countries in South America, e.g., Chile. In short, regions which receive a vast quantity of direct solar radiation.

From the standpoint of the technical potential in these regions, the majority of the electrical energy demand can be covered by CSP power plants. However, this would only exhaust a small percentage of the solar potential of these regions. In addition to the self-sufficiency of these sun-blessed regions, remote power shipments to neighboring demand centres could export excess production – ideally even to regions beyond the sunbelt.

The economic and the exploitable potential of solar thermal electricity generation is therefore mainly driven by the cost competitiveness of this technology compared to competing technologies. Solar thermal capacity generation can be very competitive in suitable locations compared to conventional and other renewable power generation technologies. In 2017, contracts were awarded for power plants with specific electricity costs of $ 0.073/kWh.

However, pure electricity cost is only one side of the coin. Other services of power plants are valuable as well and can lead to additional income streams. This is particular the case for CSP which can particular – if combined with storage – easily stabilize power grids. This could open up new market opportunities for CSP as a system service provider – the advantage of improved predictability can outweighs at least partly the current cost disadvantage in terms of cents/kWh in many locations/regions. For these reasons, the economic potential of CSP is already very high in many places today.

1.8.3 Future Technical and Economic Developments

The prerequisite to achieve the great economic and exploitable potential of CSP, however, is that the technology will be further developed, leading to efficiency increases and overall cost reductions. Some of these are:

- Increasing efficiencies, for example: through higher temperatures of the heat transfer medium and/or use of salt not only as a storage, but also as a heat transfer medium (thus less heat exchange necessary and no temperature gradient in the heat transfer);
- Optimization of the production of individual components;
- Further optimization of the overall system;
- Operational optimization.

Which individual technology (parabolic trough, tower or fresnel technology) would prevail on the market is not yet foreseeable. According to current developments, all the mentioned technologies may occupy certain areas of the market. Currently, a significant increase in the market share of solar tower power plants can be recognized. In particular, solar tower and parabolic trough power plants may establish themselves for power generation, whereby the respective site conditions strongly influence the selection of the technology. Fresnel technology could eventually play a more important role in heat production.

References

[1] Kaltschmitt, Martin, Wolfgang Streicher, and Andreas Wiese, eds. 2013. Erneuerbare Energien: Systemtechnik, Wirtschaftlichkeit, Umweltaspekt, 5th ed. Berlin: Springer.

[2] Böttcher, Jörg, ed. 2011. *Solarvorhaben: Wirtschaftliche, technische und rechtliche Aspekte.* Section 3.2: "Technische Aspekte Solarthermieprojekte" by Andreas Wiese and Kuno Schallenberg. Munich: Oldenbourg Verlag.

List of Authors

Agrawal, Prashant

Prashant Agrawal, MBA in Finance and a qualified Company Secretary, has experience of more than 8 years of working in Project Finance division of Banks. As a Credit Analyst, he has worked on numerous transactions related to financing of solar and wind power projects. He is a certified Green Finance Specialist from RENAC, Germany and trains the industry professionals who are working in the field of Renewable Energy and Energy Efficiency.

Barth, Volker

Dr. Volker Barth studied physics with a major in atmospheric physics in Marburg and Heidelberg. After his doctorate at the Max Planck Institute for Meteorology/University of Hamburg and many years of research related to renewable energy at the University of Oldenburg, he joined DEWI GmbH in 2010, which became UL in 2012. His main fields of work are resource and site assessments of offshore wind farms and related model simulations.

Boensch, Alexander

Alexander Boensch (M.A., Dipl.-Kfm. (FH)) trained as a financial economist and held postgraduate Project and Structured Finance positions at Commerzbank. In 2003, he switched sides to industry and since then has been working as freelance consultant at Director's level for different German and international renewable energy project developers and IPPs, being in charge of structured and corporate finance, risk and treasury management, procurement of capital, bank marketing and M&A activities. Alexander is also a lecturer for corporate finance, valuation and capital markets classes at Berlin School of Economics and Law and Academic Project Director of Renewables Academy (RENAC)'s Green Banking Programme.

Böttcher, Jörg

Jörg Böttcher, a graduate in economics and a qualified bank management assistant, has been working with Hamburg Commercial Bank AG (formerly: HSH Nordbank AG) since 1995. As a risk adviser at this bank he is responsible for arranging and structuring wind and solar power projects. After joining Landesbank Schleswig-Holstein, one of the present bank's two predecessors, in 1995, he was initially involved in corporate client business for two years, followed by international project finance; since 1999, he has been specializing in renewable energies projects. Jörg Böttcher has produced a series of publications on project finance and renewable energies since 2004. He completed his doctorate at Justus-Liebig University in Giessen in 2011 with a thesis entitled "Possibilities for Financing CSP Projects."

Cañadillas, Beatriz

Dr. Beatriz Cañadillas studied physics with a focus on astrophysics in Tenerife, Spain. From 2001 to 2006 she worked for the wind turbine manufacturer Gamesa as a project manager for micrositing and power curve verification. In 2009, she received her doctorate in atmospheric turbulence from the University of Hannover. Since 2006 she has been employed at DEWI GmbH – German Wind Energy Institute in the Research and Studies Department, which became UL in 2012. Her areas of expertise in the wind industry include wind measurement with meteorological mast and remote sensing, wind simulation, offshore meteorology and atmospheric turbulence.

https://doi.org/10.1515/9783110607888-035

Chaves-Schwinteck, Patricia
Dr. Patricia Chaves-Schwinteck studied industrial engineering with focus on power systems in Rio de Janeiro, Brazil. After a few years of experience with a German Independent Power Producer (IPP), she engaged in renewable energy through a post-graduate program hosted at the University of Oldenburg, followed by her doctorate in Business Administration from the same university. She joined DEWI GmbH in 2007 (now UL) and currently works with due diligence and project certification of offshore wind farms.

Egli, Florian
Florian Egli is a PhD candidate in the Energy Politics Group at ETH Zurich, Switzerland. His research focuses on public policies for the low-carbon transition with a particular focus on renewable energy finance. Prior to joining ETH Zurich, he was a Mercator Fellow on International Affairs. He has worked for think tanks, governments (Switzerland and Senegal), the OECD, a Silicon Valley start-up and a foundation – all in the area of finance, climate change and access to energy. He is the vice president of foraus – the Swiss Foreign Policy Think Tank and studied Economics (M.Sc.) at the Graduate Institute (IHEID) in Geneva, the University of Bern and the Toulouse School of Economics (TSE).

Engelbert, Jan
Jan Engelbert started his professional career at Deutsche Bank in 1992. From 1995 to 1999 he studied Business Law in Lüneburg, Germany, and Edinburg, Texas, USA. Between 1999 and 2004, Jan worked in the advisory business of pwc and EY with a focus on energy companies and subsidized projects. In 2004, Jan joined HSH Nordbank where he held various positions with a focus on structuring and execution of renewable energy project finance transactions. From 2008, Jan was involved in some of the first project-financed offshore wind farms in Germany. In 2015, Jan joined the market leader in offshore wind, Ørsted (formerly DONG Energy). He served as a member of the leadership teams for the construction of all German offshore wind assets. In 2018, Jan took over the role as Head of Portfolio Germany. In 2019, he took over Commercial and Asset Management responsibility for the region Continental Europe.

Frohboese, Peter
Peter Frohböse is a structural engineer by education. In 2004, he joined DNV GL (at that time known as Germanischer Lloyd) as a professional engineer, working as in the turbine certification unit. He soon was appointed to lead the onshore certification team. In 2009, he was offered the opportunity to join the advisory unit as team lead & expert. Within the advisory unit he became responsible for the offshore wind team in Germany. Since 2015 Peter is focused on offshore wind energy as a principal engineer within the project engineering team.

In more than a decade working in renewable energy, Peter gained an in-depth understanding of turbine technology, offshore logistics, project development, consenting, contracting, project operation & maintenance and risks management in numerous projects as an owner's engineer as well as independent expert.

Peter is appointed Member of the Scientific Advisory Board to the German Offshore Wind Energy Foundation. Details see here: http://www.offshore-stiftung.de. Starting 2010 he became responsible for organizing the Hamburg Offshore Wind Conference (aka HOW Conference) that is hosted by DNV GL and takes place on a yearly basis. For past events and information: www.hamburgoffshorewind.com. Since late 2017 Peter has been invited by the DNV GL's Executive Leadership Team (ELT) to join the Global Excellence Team for offshore wind. The team is serving the ELT as the expert group to the offshore wind market.

Geddes, Anna
Anna is an Energy Policy Consultant with IISD and has been a PhD Energy Researcher at ETH Zurich since 2014. Her research explores the energy system transition with a focus on the role public finance and state investment banks in crowding-in finance for low-carbon energy projects and the interaction of finance and innovation. Prior to entering research she was a Senior Environmental Consultant at Environmental Resources Management (ERM) in London, analysing the impacts of energy, climate change and environmental policy for energy and mining clients in West Africa, USA, Canada and South East Asia. Anna started her career as a Chemical Engineer and Risk Consultant in the energy and mining sectors, for clients including Rio Tinto, BHP Billiton and Glencore Xstrata, spending 9 years working in various countries including Australia, Indonesia and South Korea.

Goldner, Thies
Thies Goldner is a corporate lawyer based in the Hamburg office of Osborne Clarke. He has a focus on the Energy & Utilities Sector and advises banks, institutional and private-equity investors as well as developers and construction firms primarily in the areas of renewable energy generation, particularly on- and offshore wind and photovoltaics. Since 2007 he has worked for two other international law firms before he joined Osborne Clarke in 2016. He has a doctor's degree from the Georg-August University in Göttingen. During his professional practice, he has published several publications mostly in respect of banking and reals estate aspects of renewable energy projects.

Göbel, Jens
Jens Göbel started his professional career at Enron Capital & Trading at the Continental European Power desk in London in 1998. Eventually Jens held positions in Origination, Trading and Principal Investments at Enron's offices in London, Houston and Frankfurt. In 2002, he joined Statkraft Markets in Germany as Head of Structuring and eventually assumed more commercial responsibility as Head of Origination for Western Europe, managing director of Statkraft's Hungarian affiliate and "Prokurist" for Statkraft Markets GmbH.

In 2008, he joined the Leadership Team of Shell Energy Trading where he was responsible for Power Trading Development. After the merger with Shell Energy Europe Jens became Head of Structured Trading Power at the merged entity Shell Energy Europe. He also served on the Board of the Shell UK Pension trust company and served on its Investment Committee.

Since July 2013 Jens has been with Eni Trading & Shipping in London and currently serves as Head of Power and Emissions Trading. Since June 2015 Jens has also been a Deputy Chairman on the EEX Exchange Council.

Guiloff, Matias
Mr. Matías Guiloff is a Chilean attorney and Law Professor. He holds an LL.M. from Columbia University and a SJ.D. from the University of Arizona. His research deals with the intersection of governmental regulation and individual economic rights. He has authored several publications concerning Environmental and Natural Resources Regulation, Property Rights and Administrative Law. He also works as of counsel at Quintanilla & Busel Niedmann law firm where his practice focuses on Administrative Law.

Härig, Michael
Dr. Michael Härig is general manager of VMD-PRINAS GmbH Versicherungsmakler, one of the leading insurance brokers for technical risks in Germany. Since joining the insurance branch in 2001 he advised the major companies of the conventional and renewable energy branch. Prior to this role, he served as program manager for reliability and safety analysis in the explosives

industry. Graduation in Physics, Max-Planck-Institute, Stuttgart. Diploma in Physics, University Karlsruhe. Michael Härig has a teaching assignment at University of Applied Sciences Biberach.

Hampl, Nina

Nina Hampl is a full professor for Sustainable Energy Management and is head of the Institute for Operations, Energy, and Environmental Management at the University of Klagenfurt. She is also affiliated with the Institute for Strategic Management at WU Vienna University of Economics and Business where she is head of the Energy & Strategy Think Tank and deputy head of the Institute for Strategic Management. She holds a PhD in management from the University of St. Gallen, Switzerland, where she also worked as a research associate at the Good Energies Chair for Management of Renewable Energies. Her PhD thesis on energy investment decision-making under uncertainty received the Student Award 2013 from the Swiss Association for Energy Economics. In fall 2015, she was a visiting scholar at Stanford University. Before joining academia, she worked for several years as a management consultant in the energy industry practice of an international consulting firm. Her research projects received funding from e.g., the Austrian Climate Research Program, Austrian Research Promotion Agency (FFG), the International Energy Agency and the Swiss National Science Foundation. She has published her work in journals such as Energy Policy, Strategic Entrepreneurship Journal, Business Strategy and the Environment and Energy Research & Social Science. Her main field of research is social acceptance of renewable energy technologies with a specific focus on consumer acceptance of electric mobility and local acceptance of large-scale renewable energy projects.

Herbold, Thoralf

Thoralf Herbold is an Attorney and Partner in the Cologne and Hamburg office of GÖRG Partnerschaft von Rechtsanwälten mbB. He is specialized in the area of energy law, in particular renewable energies. Thoralf advises national and international investors, project developers and power plant constructors in the project development and M&A-transactions in the energy sector (onshore and offshore wind farms, solar plants, energy storages).

He is also an expert on the field of energy regulatory law, energy trading and the development of decentralized energy concepts. Thoralf is further specialized in the area of public commercial law (permits, grid connection). Prior to joining GÖRG, Thoralf had an engagement with Hengeler Mueller in Düsseldorf from 2007 through 2009. He joined GÖRG in 2009 and was announced Partner in 2016.

Hilgedieck, Jerrit

Jerrit Hilgedieck studied Energy and Environmental Engineering as well as Renewable Energy at the Hamburg University of Technology (TUHH). He has been doing his PhD in renewable energy system technology since 2016 with a focus on the integration of renewable energies in the electricity system at the Hamburg University of Technology.

Hirschmann, Matthias

Matthias Hirschmann heads the German Energy and Natural Resources practice group of Hogan Lovells. Through his years of focusing on the energy sector, he has gained substantial knowledge of the energy industry and focuses on advising on various legal challenges and issues in the energy sector.

Matthias concentrates on all relevant aspects in the energy sector, particularly in relation to national or international M&A transactions, acquisitions, joint ventures, general energy law and regulatory advice. He has vast experience in advising on all regulatory matters relevant to the energy sector. For years, Matthias has been recognized as a leading lawyer for M&A transactions, corporate law and energy sector-related advice by JUVE, Chambers, Legal 500 and Best Lawyers. Matthias Hirschmann was named the Best Lawyers™ 2019 Energy Lawyer of the Year in Germany.

Hoff, Julian
Julian Hoff is partner of the German lawfirm Hoffmann Liebs. He is a member of Hoffmann Liebs' Corporate and M&A practice group. He advises domestic and foreign clients in corporate law matters and M&A-transactions, in the last years in particular with regard to renewable energy projects. He therefore has particular expertise in advising clients in acquisitions of renewable energy projects. He furthermore advises clients in the operating stage of such projects.

Julian Hoff has been working for Hoffmann Liebs since 2012. He became partner of the lawfirm in 2017.

Jaensch, Volker
Volker Jaensch joined Renewables Academy (RENAC) in August 2010. As Head of Division he is responsible for the areas of Bioenergy and RE & EE Finance. Mr Jaensch has more than ten years professional experience in project development, due diligence, financing and implementation of renewable energy projects with a focus on biomass and wind-energy (at daughter companies of Veolia Environment and Gamesa Energia). He also gained experience in the political arena of renewable energy at the German Energy Agency (dena). Before joining RENAC Mr Jaensch was active for four years in the development and implementation of sustainable Carbon Credit generating projects (according to the Kyoto Protocol and the Gold Standard) in developing countries. Mr Jaensch holds degrees in Environmental Engineering and Master of Business Administration (MBA).

Kaltschmitt, Martin
Martin Kaltschmitt did his PhD as well as his Habilitation in the field of renewable energies at Stuttgart University/Germany. After a research stay at King's College in London and at the University of California at Berkeley he became the managing director of the Leipzig Institute for Energy non-profit research company. In 2006, he has been promoted to a full professor at Hamburg University of Technology where he is heading the Institute of Environmental Technology and Energy Economics. Between 2008 and 2010 he was in parallel the scientific managing director of the German Biomass Research Centre (DBFZ).

Kirch, Thorsten
Thorsten Kirch is an Attorney and Associated Partner in the Cologne office of GÖRG Partnerschaft von Rechtsanwälten. Thorsten is specialized in the area of renewable energy law. He advises national and international investors, project developers and power plant constructors in the project development and M&A-transactions in the energy sector (onshore and offshore wind farms, solar plants, energy storages).

He is also an expert on the field of energy regulatory law, energy trading and the development of decentralized energy concepts. Before he joined GÖRG, Thorsten was an advisor at the German Federal Ministry of Education and Research.

Lange, Jelto
Jelto Lange studied General Engineering Science (B. Sc.) and Energy Engineering (M. Sc.) at Hamburg University of Technology (TUHH). In December 2017, he started his work as a research assistant and PhD student (Dr.-Ing.) at the institute of environmental technology and energy economics at TUHH. His research is focused on the improved integration of fluctuating renewable energies into electricity systems by means of sector coupling.

Lee, Claire Marie Yvonne C.

Ms. Lee started her career in renewable energy in 2009. Her early exposure to renewable energy technologies involved business development and project management for biogas power plants and rural electrification using solar home systems. She was the former President of the Philippine Solar and Storage Energy Alliance, under which she served as an officer for 10 years. She is also a current Director at the Renewable Energy Association of the Philippines. She was also appointed as a Board Director for Women in Renewables, an international NGO based in Shanghai. She headed the Renewable Energy Division of ORIX Metro Leasing and Finance, Corp (OMLF), a JV between ORIX of Japan and Metrobank of the Philippines. She provided financing and integrated solar rooftop system services to prime clients of OMLF. She is also a certified Green Finance Specialist under the Green Finance program of RENAC. Ms. Lee has also spoken in several local and international forums in the fields of renewable energy and women empowerment.

Marhewka, Daniel

Daniel Marhewka is a partner in the Munich office of Fieldfisher and advises on corporate and energy law. He is the head of the renewable energy group at Fieldfisher. His particular expertise is advising his clients on energy and infrastructure transactions. Furthermore, he deals with M&A, private equity, venture capital and real estate transactions regularly. Predominantly, he is working on international and cross border transactions. Daniel advises in all aspects of corporate and energy law, with a specific focus on the renewable energy sector, where he already has been involved in 3,600 MW of solar and wind projects in Europe and internationally. Amongst his clients are domestic and international investors, financial institutions, companies and private clients. Before joining Fieldfisher, Daniel war a corporate and energy lawyer at an international law firm for seven years and worked for three years for an US law firm in Munich and New York. Daniel studied law in Heidelberg (Germany) and London. He advises his clients in German and English.

Moslener, Ulf

Ulf Moslener is professor for sustainable energy finance at the faculty of Frankfurt School of Finance and Management and Head of Research of the FS-UNEP Collaborating Centre for Climate and Sustainable Energy Finance. His broader research interests are the economics of climate change, financing sustainable energy systems and climate finance.

In addition to his research he combines the results from academic work related to international climate policy, carbon regulation, carbon emissions trading, and promotion of renewable energy with practical experience from working with KfW Development Bank, dealing with financing renewable energy and energy efficiency in developing countries, notably Asia.

He applies his know-how within numerous projects for Ministries, the European Commission or national and international financial institutions. He was representing Germany in the UN Standing Committee on Climate Finance and currently serves as Vice Chair of the Advisory Group to the Clean Investment Funds (CIFs) at World Bank and as Vice Chair of the Green and Sustainable Finance Cluster Germany (GSFCG).

Neumeuer, Björn

Dr. Björn Neumeuer is partner of the German law firm Hoffmann Liebs. He is a member of Hoffmann Liebs' Corporate and M&A practice group. He has particular expertise in advising on transactions and infrastructure projects, both domestic and international. The scope of advice contains small and mid-sized mergers and acquisitions as well as transactions and projects (including joint ventures) involving globally operating companies. He also provides ongoing advice on the implementation of projects. In the past years, he has been advising utilities, financial investors and developers on all sorts of renewable energy projects during various phases (planning, construction, operation).

Prior to joining Hoffmann Liebs in 2003, Björn Neumeuer practiced law at a major UK and major German law firm. Prior to his University studies he attended a two year banking training with Deutsche Bank and worked during his studies with Deutsche Bank inter alia in London. He is recommended by JUVE and by Chambers.

Reichert-Facilides, Daniel
Dr. Daniel Reichert-Facilides is a partner at Freshfields Bruckhaus Deringer LLP, where he leads the German project finance team. His renewable energy experience covers photovoltaic, onshore and offshore wind projects across a wide range of jurisdictions including Germany, Spain, Italy, Greece, Turkey, Vietnam, Canada, the United States of America, Uruguay and South Africa. Daniel is one of the lead authors of the TWI IRENA Open Solar Contracts, a standard documentation for the implementation of photovoltaic power projects in emerging and frontier markets, and a member of the German council of the International Project Finance Association.

Ritschel, Uwe
Since 2014 Uwe Ritschel works as Professor for Wind Energy Technology at the University of Rostock in Germany. His research interests focus on the mechanical aspects of wind turbines, offshore wind energy, and the coupling of electricity generated from wind to other energy sectors.

Uwe Ritschel studied physics at the TU Darmstadt and received his doctoral degree from the University of Oldenburg in 1989. After research positions at various universities and research institutes he moved to wind industry in 2000, where he worked for the wind turbine manufacturer Nordex SE and later started his own engineering consulting company Windrad Engineering.

Saelim, Supawan
Dr. Supawan Saelim is currently a Renewable Energy Policy Specialist for USAID Clean Power Asia program, which encourages power sector investments in environmentally-friendly, grid-connected renewable energy sources. Dr. Saelim has focused primarily on activities to provide technical assistance to Lao PDR, Thailand, Vietnam, and the Philippines related to renewable energy auctions and the impact of distributed PV policies on key stakeholders. Prior to joining USAID Clean Power Asia, she gained research experience with international organizations on energy and climate mitigation policies, and has several years of experience at PwC Thailand assisting the public and private sector on feasibility studies, valuation, and high-level market analysis. Dr. Saelim holds a Ph.D. in Economics from the National Institute of Development Administration, Thailand and an M.Sc. in Project Analysis, Finance and Investment from the University of York, United Kingdom.

Saldivia, Miguel
Mr. Miguel Saldivia is PhD candidate at the University of Cambridge. His research is focused on the law and policy of renewables in developing countries. He is also a Chilean lawyer and journalist graduated from the Universidad de Chile and holds a Master of Laws (LLM) in Environmental Law from the University College London (UCL). His practice has been focused in project development, due diligences and environmental impact assessment. He worked as associate attorney at Carey law firm, in Chile, while also working as Professor of Right to Information and as Teaching Assistant of Environmental Law at the Universidad de Chile. Additionally, he is a member of the Centre for International Sustainable Development Law (CISDL) and Researcher at the Solar Energy Research Centre and at the Andean Geothermal Centre of Excellence (CEGA).

Schaffarczyk, Alois
Since 1992, Alois Peter Schaffarczyk (APS) works as Professor for Mathematics and Engineering Mechanics at the Kiel University of Applied Sciences (KUAS) in Germany. His research interests focus on the fluid dynamics aspects of wind turbines and wind turbine blades. He helped establishing an International MSc program in Wind Engineering and was one of the heads of CEwind, a research association focusing on all aspects of wind energy. After merging CEwind into eek.sh, Schleswig-Holstein's center for Renewable Energies and Climate Protection, he is one of the spokes-persons there.

APS studied physics at the University of Goettingen where he also received his doctoral degree in 1986. Then he moved to industry until he joined KUAS.

Schmidt, Tobias S.
Professor Tobias S. Schmidt is the head of ETH Zurich's Energy Politics Group. He holds a Bachelor of Science and Dipl. Ing. (MSc equivalent) in electrical engineering (energy focus) from the Technical University Munich and a PhD from ETH Zurich in management, technology, and economics. During his postdoc, he spent time as a visiting scholar at Stanford University's Precourt Energy Efficiency Center (PEEC) and acted as consultant to the United Nations Development Programme (UNDP) working on UNDP's De-risking Renewable Energy Investment (DREI) project. In his research, which is published in leading scientific journals, he analyzes the interaction of energy policy and its underlying politics with technological change in the energy sector. His research covers both developed and developing countries.

Schumann, André
André Schumann passed with distinction as best graduate 2005 from the University of Applied Sciences (HAW) Hamburg as engineer in environmental engineering (title Dipl.-Ing.(FH)). Already in summer 2004 he joined SunTechnics GmbH (member of the Conergy group) as a trainee and also wrote his diploma thesis "simulation and yield analysis of a grid-connected PV system with high efficient solar cells" there. He stayed with the company until 2008 and worked as project engineer in the department Global Engineering PV. He has been responsible for the global development, implementation, training and maintenance of yield simulation, meteorological resource and economic calculation software. Furthermore Mr. Schumann was often consulted in order to contribute own yield estimates and to judge external reports for big PV projects around the world. In the year 2008, Mr. Schumann co-founded SolPEG GmbH and is since then member of the board. He is mainly managing and actively working in the business fields yield analysis, plant inspection and training. In 10 years, SolPEG GmbH has contributed to over 1800 PV projects with over 12 GWp accumulated power worldwide.

Sposato, Robert Gennaro
Robert Sposato holds a master's degree in Psychology from the University of Vienna and was awarded a President's scholarship with the School of Psychology, Cardiff University, where he obtained his PhD focusing on public perceptions of climate change adaptation and mitigation. Robert Sposato has previously been employed as a research fellow at the Medical University of Vienna working on sustainable mobility choices and has further held a research assistant post with the Understanding Risk Group working on a study of public engagement with climate change. Mr. Sposato now works as a Postdoc researcher in the Sustainable Energy Management Unit at the Institute for Operations, Energy, and Environmental Management at the University of Klagenfurt. He has published work in journals such as Energy Research and Social Science, Climatic Change, and Transportation Research Part F: Traffic Psychology and Behaviour. His research focuses on

social acceptance of renewable energy technologies, electric mobility and local acceptance of large-scale renewable energy projects in particular, but also more generally, on public perceptions of climate change and climate change adaptation.

Steffen, Bjarne
Bjarne Steffen is a senior researcher and lecturer with the Energy Politics Group at ETH Zurich, Switzerland. His research addresses low-carbon innovation and finance in the energy sector, building on ten years of experience with renewable energy and infrastructure finance. From 2008 until 2016 he was part of the Boston Consulting Group's energy practice, and also served as a project manager for the Strategic Infrastructure Initiative at the World Economic Forum. Since joining ETH Zurich, he works at the intersection of economics, political science, and innovation studies. He studied economics at University of Mannheim and holds a PhD in energy economics from University of Duisburg-Essen. In 2019, he was a visiting Scholar at the Center for Energy and Environmental Policy Research at the Massachusetts Institute of Technology.

Tallhaug, Lars
Lars Tallhaug holds a Master of Science in Mechanical Engineering from the University of Trondheim. After a short period in a utility, he started his carrier in wind energy in 1990 at the Institute of Energy Technology with both development of wind turbine technology and wind measurements and wind analysis. In 1998, he took the initiative to start up Kjeller Vindteknikk AS, first with 2 employees and growing to 32 employees in 2018. He has been the Managing Director for Kjeller Vindteknikk from the start and been important for the development of the company. During the last 20 years he has been involved in calculating and analyzing the energy production of more than 100 wind farms. The wind farms have been installed in different terrain and climate involving mountainous terrain, forest and icing climate.

Tarragó, Rosa
Ms. Rosa Tarragó is Director Structured Finance at VIRIDI RE GmbH, originally a spin-off Würth Solar GmbH. For the last six years she has been financing her own developed projects and, in total, she has worked for almost twenty years in the renewable energy field. From 2007 to 2013, she worked in the banking sector, serving for almost five years as Vice President at KfW IPEX-Bank, where she was responsible for the origination and structuring of project financing for renewable energy transactions, focusing on Abu Dhabi, Germany, France, Canada, Italy, and South Africa, and prior to that as Relationship Manager, Renewable Energy at Commerzbank. Before, she worked for an engineering consulting company, contributing, among others, to the structuring of the first bond financing in Europe: a portfolio of about 40 wind farms. Prior to that she worked as a Business Development Manager at a daughter of E.ON Energie AG.

She received a Masters Degree in Financial Engineering and Insurance Mathematics from the University of Karlsruhe (TH) in 1999. She also has received a postgraduate diploma in Environmental Studies from Abat Oliba University (Barcelona), Spain (1997), holds a Master Degree in Economics and Business Administration from the Copenhagen Business School, Denmark, and a Bachelor in Economics and Business Administration from the University of Barcelona, Catalonia. Since 2014 she is guest lecturer at the Technical University Hamburg-Harburg (TUHH) in Germany.

Tobing, Yolanda
Yolanda started her professional career at Indonesian Architects Associations, two UNDP and UN Habitat projects and fourteen years at a state-owned bank, the top four largest in Indonesia. After her PhD study on "Corporate Sustainability of Private Finance Institutions in the transition to a Low Carbon Economy: cases in Australia and Indonesia" at UNSW Sydney under an Australian

Leadership Awards, since 2015 she worked as a Senior Advisor for Renewable Energy Support Program for ASEAN (ASEAN RESP) jointly implemented by GIZ and the ASEAN Centre for Energy. Since October 2017 up to now she is working as an Economic Specialist of US-ASEAN Connect, U.S. Mission to ASEAN where energy is one of her portfolios. In her spare time, she campaigned for community awareness on the climate change together with other climate leaders member of the Climate Reality Project Indonesia, volunteered in a humanitarian organization to combat housing poverty: Habitat for Humanity Indonesia, and trained as a trainer of Green Finance Specialist, a project of Green Banking funded by the German International Climate Initiative (IKI) qq the German Federal Ministry for the Environment, Nature Conservation and Nuclear Safety (BMU) implemented by Renewables Academy (RENAC) Berlin. She got her master degree of DPU Faculty of Economics and Political Sciences at UCL London under the Chevening scholarship, and her Bachelor Engineering was from Faculty of Technology at University of Indonesia.

Torwegge, Christoph
Christoph Torwegge is corporate and M&A partner and focuses his advice on matters of M & A transactions and selected areas of national and international commercial law in the Energy & Utilities and Infrastructure Sectors.

His clients are benefitting from his long-term experience gained in numerous international M & A transaction work and as General Counsel of an international group. Being focused on Energy & Utilities and Infrastructure Christoph advises regularly investors, banks, project developers and operators in planning, construction, financing and on transactions of renewable energy and infrastructure projects. Besides his experience in drafting and negotiating supply, maintenance and service agreements as well as engineering, procurement and construction agreements he has achieved numerous successful closings of transactions driven by his special expertise on transaction work in projects.

Christoph studied in Bielefeld, Bristol, and Leipzig. He worked for an international law firm and as head of legal before becoming a partner in Osborne Clarke in 2012. He is a member various associations and author of numerous publications.

Urbanke, Claus
Claus Urbanke has been working in the European power and energy trading industry for 18 years. He spent most of this time with Norway's largest power producer Statkraft where he held different managing positions. Among other things, Claus Urbanke was responsible for Statkraft's trading business in Central and South Eastern Europe and for the Origination activities in Germany, Austria and Switzerland. Currently, he mainly works with the expansion of Statkraft's power trading and solar power activities in India as Manager Strategy & Business Development. Claus Urbanke holds an Economics degree from Universität zu Köln and a Master's degree in Economics (USA).

Veestraeten, Dieter
Dieter Veestraeten (LL.M. Universität Konstanz) is a partner since April 2014 at the Belgian law firm Astrea (based in Antwerp and Brussels) and heads the banking & finance department. Before he joined Astrea, he worked 13 years at an international law firm. He has extensive experience in project finance and asset finance and regularly acts for sponsors, borrowers and lenders in the renewable energy sector. He has been involved in a number of larger (international) asset finance and project finance transactions.

Vermeire, Nino
Nino Vermeire (University of Antwerp) is a lawyer since 2014 and joined the Belgian law firm Astrea (based in Antwerp and Brussels) as associate attorney in 2017. Nino is part of the environment

department and specializes in urban planning, environment and energy law. He works for major international clients in the petrochemical and energy sector and publishes regularly in professional literature about his field of expertise.

Weiler, Sibylle
Business lawyer in France and Germany: Sibylle Weiler is an experienced renewable energy specialist who works across corporate, financing, project-related and investment matters. Partner at Bird & Bird in Paris, she advises on all deal aspects related to the energy sector, with a core focus on Project Financing, M&A transactions and Project Development. She assists with energy and energy-efficiency projects from their inception, taking into consideration the legal aspects as well as the strategic, fiscal and economic issues.

A regular speaker and author on related topics, Sibylle has been a Member of the Steering Committee (comité de pilotage) of the French Office for Energy Transition (OFATE, L'Office franco-allemand pour la transition énergétique) and lectured at Paris II Panthéon-Assas University (Paris), the Institut de Droit Comparé (Paris) and Humboldt University (Berlin).

Wiese, Andreas
Prof. Dr. Andreas Wiese is working since more than 25 years in the international renewable energy consultancy business and has successfully led or participated in a large number of well recognized renewable energy studies and implemented major wind and solar power projects around the globe. He studied mechanical engineering at TU Darmstadt and performed his thesis in wind and solar integration in traditional power systems at University Stuttgart. After 18 years in Lahmeyer International, he is since 2014 Managing Director of Gopa-intec, a company which provides technical consultancy services in the area of power generation, transmission and distribution, with a strong focus on renewable energy consultancy services in developing and emerging countries in Middle East, Africa and Asia. He is lecturer at the Technical University Hamburg Harburg since 2010 and has been granted the title of Honouree Professor in 2018.

Zhuang, Menglu
Menglu Zhuang is a sustainable finance expert at the Frankfurt School – UNEP Centre and a researcher at the Frankfurt School faculty. Her role at the FS-UNEP Centre is to manage the content development of educational programs on the topic of sustainable finance. As a researcher, Menglu Zhuang works closely with professors at the Frankfurt School to further the understanding of the role of the financial market in transitioning to a low-carbon economy and in sustainable development.

Besides research, Ms. Zhuang has many years of experiences in international projects. Amongst others, she was a key member in the projects Developing Sustainable Energy Investment Metrics for the Financial Sector (SEI Metrics) funded by the European Commission and Results-based Climate Finance Initiative mapping, Outlining and Assessment supported by the World Bank.

Ms. Zhuang has a background in mathematics and holds a M.Sc. Finance degree from Frankfurt School of Finance & Management. She is writing a PHD level dissertation in an interdisciplinary area that connects finance with energy economics. She is working on identifying financial market imperfections and investor behaviors in sustainable finance to find out if there is necessity for policy interventions so that the policymakers can better understand the measures and instruments needed to facilitate transitioning to a sustainable economy.

Index

https://doi.org/10.1515/9783110607888-036

www.ingramcontent.com/pod-product-compliance
Lightning Source LLC
Chambersburg PA
CBHW080936240926
51849CB00004BA/471